Jack

The Struggles of John F. Kennedy

Also by Herbert S. Parmet

AARON BURR: Portrait of an Ambitious Man
  (with Marie B. Hecht)
NEVER AGAIN: A President Runs for a Third Term
  (with Marie B. Hecht)
EISENHOWER AND THE AMERICAN CRUSADES
THE DEMOCRATS: The Years After FDR

Jack

The Struggles
of John F. Kennedy

HERBERT S. PARMET

 THE DIAL PRESS   NEW YORK

Published by
The Dial Press
1 Dag Hammarskjold Plaza
New York, New York 10017

Every effort has been made to locate the proprietor of
the following material:
  Photos numbered 3, 11, 33, 39, 40.
If the proprietor will write to the publisher, formal
arrangements will be made.
Unless otherwise noted, photographs are courtesy of
the John F. Kennedy Library.

Manufactured in the United States of America

First printing

Design by Jean Callan King/Visuality

Library of Congress Cataloging in Publication Data

Parmet, Herbert S.
  Jack: the struggles of John F. Kennedy.

  Includes bibliographical references.
  1. Kennedy, John Fitzgerald, Pres. U.S., 1917–1963.
2. United States—Politics and government—1945–.
3. Presidents—United States—Biography.   I. Title.
E842.P33   973.922'092'4 [B]   80–10506
ISBN: 0-8037-4452-8

For Marie B. Hecht
Friend and colleague

Contents

Photographs follow pages 44 and 396

Illustrations

Unless otherwise noted, photographs were supplied by the John F. Kennedy Library.

FOLLOWING PAGE 44

1. Rose Fitzgerald Kennedy as a young mother with her first three children.
2. Jack Kennedy as a Dexter Academy student.
3. A freckled Rosemary, the Kennedys' third child. September 1931.
4. Rosemary with her grandfather "Honey Fitz" (Courtesy of *Boston Herald American*).
5. Big brother Joseph Kennedy, Jr., star collegiate athlete.
6. Jack with LeMoyne Billings during their 1937 European trip.
7. Ambassador Joseph P. Kennedy hosts a party at the London Embassy, June 5, 1939 (Courtesy of Magnum Photo).
8. On the '39 tour of Europe.
9. Joe Junior vacationing at St. Moritz.
10. Joe Junior holding out against FDR's third nomination as a delegate to the Democrats' 1940 presidential convention.
11. At the controls of his bomber.
12. Inga Arvad in 1936 (Courtesy of UPI).
13. Inga Arvad in 1941 (Courtesy of UPI).
14. Lt. Kennedy and two of his wartime friends, Paul "Red" Fay and Lenny Thom.
15. Kathleen "Kick" Kennedy roughhousing with brother Jack.
16. Rosemary, Teddy, Rose, Bobby, Eunice, and Jack.
17. Kick wearing her Red Cross uniform in wartime London.
18. Joe escorting Kathleen to the Chelsea Register Office in London (Courtesy of AP).
19. Billy and Kathleen moments after their wedding (Courtesy of Portman Press Bureau).
20. Jack in early September of 1944 (Courtesy of *The Boston Globe*).
21. Jack Kennedy leading the St. Patrick's Day parade through South Boston in March 1946.

Prologue:

"Within the Sanctuary"

We worship our kings. We give them our brains, our souls, our bodies, whatever they assume is rightfully theirs and whatever we assume is naturally theirs. As in the sacred grove and sanctuary of Diana of the Wood, the king "retained office till he was himself slain by a stronger or a craftier rival." And then, once dead, the fallen are memorialized. One distinguished American historian concluded a massive volume by quoting from lyrics that he thought were appropriate to characterize a life and presidency as the "one brief shining moment that was known as Camelot."

Once dead, the king can also be damned. Within two decades, the image of Camelot became discredited. One critic wrote that the "record of the Kennedy Presidency should serve as a warning to those who still believe that major changes in American society can be instituted if only the right liberal makes it to the White House."[1] Others saw him as a "cold warrior," one driven by diplomatic machismo headlong toward "brinksmanship." And, once the king is dead, having venerated and wept, we can denounce the "imperial presidency" and lament the clay feet of "the best and the brightest."[2]

In a gentle and intelligently affectionate portrait, written in the aftermath of Kennedy's death, Tom Wicker was able to view John F. Kennedy "without tears" and predict that, whatever the biographers and political analysts might have to say, he would be "certain to take his place in American lore as one of those sure-sell heroes out of whose face or words or monuments a souvenir dealer can turn a steady buck."[3] Of all the commentaries, Wicker's proved the most enduring. However the historians describe him, Kennedy's personal imprint is irrefutable.

No one understood better than Kennedy himself the mysteries of communications and the vagaries of perceptions. During one White House conference, he declared that "there is no history" because history is often in the eye of the historian. With their need to be insightful, analytical, and fresh, their tendency is to develop something significant from what is really quite routine. Whatever the commentators may write, then, they cannot dismiss Wicker's essential insight: call him a schemer, a hawk masquerading as a man of peace, a conservative who adopted liberal rhetoric, an idealist hampered by his father's "robber baron" mentality, an elegant, sophisticated gentleman of principle who couldn't wait to tumble the first available skirt—he became a legend and symbol for the masses all over the world. In the homes of the poor, in America and elsewhere, his picture hangs on walls along with those of Jesus Christ, Martin Luther King, and Franklin D. Roosevelt.

And not only the unlettered venerated him. Laura Berquist, a veteran White House correspondent somewhat disillusioned by Kennedy conservatism and a victim of his displeasure when her professional work stamped her as less than loyal to his efforts to manage the press, found the news from Dallas more traumatic than the death of her own father.[4] Henry Brandon, the Washington correspondent of *The Times* of London, who was in Moscow several months after the shooting, observed that, "It was absolutely fantastic the impact that this assassination had made in the Soviet Union, the loss of Kennedy." He told an interviewer in 1967 that in "a curious way he had in a very short time been able to give them the feeling that he was the man who understood the problems between the United States and the Soviet Union and that he was the man to introduce a new relationship. . . . The sudden loss of the man in whom they had all these hopes hit them extraordinarily hard. . . ." Virtually the first Russian Brandon talked to wanted to know whether he thought Lyndon Johnson had organized the assassination.[5] Nikita Khrushchev himself, in his own memoirs, recalled that Kennedy "showed great flexibility" and how, together, they "avoided disaster. When he was assassinated, I felt sincere regret. I went straight to the (U.S.) embassy and expressed my condolences."[6]

Even before November 22, Fidel Castro told Jean Daniel, a French journalist, how he valued Kennedy's sincerity, realism, and "good ideas." He suggested that he might become a greater leader than Lincoln.[7] The American Ambassador to the Republic of the Ivory Coast, James Wine, in that African country when the assassination occurred, heard the news together with President Felix Houphouet-Boigny. The African president, broken up, left a social engagement immediately, then declared a two-day national holiday and held a state mass at the same hour as the funeral in Washington. He told Wine he thought Kennedy was the "greatest personality that he had known."[8] And in their home in Sussex, England, Frank O'Ferrall, who had known the Kennedy family since they were in London in 1938, was just sitting down to dinner with his wife when the TV announced what had just happened. "We couldn't believe it," O'Ferrall remembered, "and we didn't have any dinner."[9]

In America, it became a weekend of shock, emotion, and discovery of how viewing a tragedy could unite a nation. Richard Nixon, arriving back home in Manhattan after a flight from Dallas, was met by a doorman who had tears streaming down his cheeks. "Oh, Mr. Nixon, have you heard, sir?" he asked. "It's just terrible. They've killed President Kennedy."[10] Richard Russell of Georgia was on the Senate floor when he heard the news. He left, pale and stunned and, with his administrative assistant, turned to a portable TV set, and then walked out alone.[11] Kay Halle, the Washington writer and socialite who had known Jack Kennedy since 1932, was in her Georgetown home having lunch when Alice Roosevelt Longworth telephoned. Referring to the prophecy that Jeane Dixon, the professional medium, had made since June that the President would be murdered in Dallas, Mrs. Longworth said, "What you were told, has happened."

Kay Halle went out to the garden, where, in November, there were three roses in bloom.

"So we brought them in," she remembered, "and I had a picture Jack gave me which I brought down here and I put the roses in front of it. You know that those roses lasted for three solid weeks. Couldn't believe it. Roses don't last long. It was the weirdest thing I'd ever known. It was the strange, strangest, phenomenon."[12]

The next few weeks brought stories, some almost bizarre, of how the murder inspired ordinary people all over the world, even remote tribal villagers. Fletcher Knebel was driving through the jungle of Liberia with a member of the Peace Corps in 1965 when they came to a little town way off the main road. Along unpaved and muddy trails, they moved at perhaps three or four miles an hour. "All of a sudden, to the right was a clearing," Knebel recalled, "maybe as big as fifty yards by a hundred, just cut out of the dense jungle. And in the middle of it, cut down with machetes, was some kind of natural altar, some pile. It was a memorial to Jack Kennedy."[13]

Why? Why did his death and why does his life, even after nearly two decades, stir such emotions? One so cool, methodical, pragmatic, dispassionate, has provoked the intense reactions he himself tried to avoid. The absence of deep feelings, suspected as failures of commitment, encouraged opposition. During the 1960 presidential campaign, Arthur Schlesinger, Jr., was persuaded to write a little book in response to Eric Sevareid's contention that Kennedy was just a Democratic Nixon. James MacGregor Burns, who had known Kennedy since the early 1950's and authored a biography timed to coincide with the presidential campaign, has recalled in a private memoir his feeling "that there was little emotional sentiment in him. He as much as said this to me," Burns wrote. "He seemed almost to be reacting against the over-sentimentality of his grandfather Fitz. I doubt that he was easily moved to tears, and I think he would have been ashamed to show tears."[14] Still, he could and did shed tears.

Passionless leaders inspire indifference. Martyrdom failed to create deep feelings for Garfield and McKinley, and even the deep national mourning provoked by the premature death of Warren Harding did not outlast subsequent revelations about the tenor of his presidency.

Clues to Kennedy's mystique may be found elsewhere: his youth, the power of the Kennedy family. By themselves, however, they seem inadequate, mere substitutes for explanations. Jack Kennedy, the first American president born in the twentieth century, may, alas, have appeared in the messianic role that fulfilled profound needs within both the industrialized and relatively primitive parts of the world. Some connections must have been made. Yet, without emotion, passion, or the qualities of leadership, his physical attraction and sophistication alone could hardly have turned hearts. There are and have been others equally pragmatic, equally dashing and fresh, more credible as mature statesmen.

There is always, of course, the father, the "founding father," as Richard Whalen's book calls him. Still, however significant, his patrimony cannot explain everything. Cast in his father's image, Jack could hardly have been worthy of the endless inquiries into what gave Joe Kennedy's second son such universal appeal.

And he wasn't even the "golden boy." That was Joe Junior, the oldest. Joe had health, charm, and brains. He was the one bound for political success. Much closer to his father, perceived as a leader in every way, there is no reason to doubt the accounts of how he was groomed. Compared to Joe, Jack was a poor second: sick much of the time, an indifferent student, an inferior athlete, bookish rather than gregarious. All the Kennedy offspring were disciplined by the father, but Joe Junior was Joseph P. Kennedy's creation.

Remarkable for an Irish Catholic family, they—including Jack—were infatuated with British government and society, most of all, the obligations of the gentry to provide leadership for those less well endowed. Other men were naturally born into farming, or coal-mining, or business; Jack Kennedy was born to public service and could hardly have sought anything other than a position of influence in the world. All the careers he contemplated at all seriously—law, a university presidency, politics —involved that sense of duty to mold others, a matter of noblesse oblige.

But there was nothing docile about Jack Kennedy, not even as his father's son. The paternal ties were there; the theme has been replayed countless times. It tells little about his lifelong struggle for freedom from domination of any kind. A striking aspect was his long struggle to regain control over his own body, to counter physical ailments with self-possessed athletic poise, to forge from the bedridden young man the presidential candidate who, while campaigning, would agilely climb from one car to another.[15]

Nor can the mystique be explained by growth, as has been attempted. That Kennedy's education developed was self-evident. That not all leaders learn, that a Johnson and Nixon were driven inward, to self-justification, is also true. Mere growth is neither unique nor necessarily productive. Truman grew but ran into disastrous times, with heavy losses to both his country and to himself. Adlai Stevenson grew; his loyalists worked to bring him along, away from his Lake Forest milieu, until he became the exemplar of 1950's liberalism. Somehow he failed public expectations, and his associates, as well as the general public, fell away. John Kennedy's qualities, however, were distinctive, more subtle than generally perceived, and not hitherto understood.

One cannot help but compare the tenor of the devotion of Eisenhower's friends with the loyalty of Kennedy's personal worshipers. Interviewing Ike's associates invariably evokes laudatory comments: praise

for his geniality, kindness, humanity, temperance. But the common denominator centered on his love for the country and value to America,
his sense of duty, and his ability to bind the wounds of the early 1950's
just as he had handled delicate wartime alliances. Eisenhower, in short,
was what America needed. A reincarnation of George Washington, he
was the father of his postwar country. Kennedy intimates, equally loyal,
sometimes feverishly so, guard his memory in a "cult of the individual"
fashion. Emphasizing his brilliance, charm, wit, sophistication, he—
rather than the country—becomes the center of value. Eisenhower presided over an institution; Kennedy, in his very brief reign, *was* the
institution.

The contrast was the dilemma of a democratic society—or, more
precisely, a society that thought of itself as democratic. Eisenhower
appealed to benign concepts of security, providing a leadership regarded
as sober, fair, and true to the national character, together with all the
happenstance and mediocrity inherent in egalitarianism. Kennedy,
meanwhile, rising through the Eisenhower decade, gradually offered an
alternative appeal: the desire that masses have demonstrated throughout
history, to be led by wise, gifted superiors, congenitally prepared to show
the way. Just as Lyndon Johnson suffered from self-conscious comparisons with his predecessor, so did the Nixon White House nurse an
obsession with all things Kennedy.[16]

Democracy, it is clear from his youth, was something Kennedy put up
with. It imposed the rules of the game. Neither efficient nor malleable,
popular rule lacked the advantages of societies that could be more easily
mobilized. His early European travels and work on a Harvard honors
paper had revealed disturbing limitations; the view was shared by others
in his family, such as his mother, whose visit to the Soviet Union left her
with admiration for the way society could be managed. But fulfilling the
destiny of a new American gentry meant abiding by the rules, suffering
its banalities and popular ignorance (he grinned with wry amusement
when his Bay of Pigs disaster earned him his highest level of popularity),
inhibiting cynicism lest it become counterproductive, and, above all,
manipulating the process. He would become the great legislator, but only
in ways in which the democratic society would find acceptable—for a
world without an arms race, for an efficient international economy, for
rational domestic behavior.

The public might have to be cajoled. They might be ignorant about
their own self-interests. But of one thing the Kennedys were certain: even
self-proclaimed democratic societies wanted to be led by the gifted, an

understanding made clear by Niccolò Machiavelli himself, whose *The Prince* contains the following observation:

The prince must . . . avoid those things which will make him hated or despised; and whenever he succeeds in this, he will have done his part, and will find no danger in other vices. . . . He is rendered despicable by being thought changeable, frivolous, effeminate, timid, and irresolute; which a prince must guard against as a rock of danger, and so contrive that his actions show grandeur, spirit, gravity, and fortitude. . . .

When emphasizing the limitations of "the best and the brightest," the historians have not responded to the real imperatives: the ambivalence within American government and society to a leadership that knowingly risks mistakes by granting their desires and playing by their rules. John Kennedy's early career, his rise toward the presidential nomination, demonstrated how the new gentry had to adhere to that paradigm, even by converting their Irish Roman Catholicism into a WASPish reflection of the society. Both the citizenry and Kennedy began to see the public and private merging into one—into Jack Kennedy.

Jack

The Struggles of John F. Kennedy

"It was not until the second or third generation that Irish intelligence, quickness of apprehension and wit asserted themselves, and the children and grandchildren of the poor famine immigrants became successful and powerful in the countries of their adoption."
—Cecil Woodham-Smith, *The Great Hunger*

1

"A Happy Family"

Jack Kennedy's political career began with an explosion high over the English coast. On August 12, 1944, while Allied troops were still battling to liberate France and the Low Countries, a PB$_4$Y bomber packed with over twenty thousand pounds of high explosives was guided by its two-man crew toward the Channel and the opposite shore. At its controls were Lieutenant Bud Willy and Lieutenant Joseph P. Kennedy, Jr.

The twenty-nine-year-old Kennedy, eldest son of former Ambassador Joseph P. Kennedy, had volunteered for the suicidal exploit after having already completed fifty airborne missions. Cynics of a later, more "sophisticated" day would suspect that he had been motivated by more than patriotism. Perhaps the achievement would make him a genuine war hero. That would have happy implications for his civilian political career. Always, behind such speculation, was the suspicion that a son of Joe Kennedy had no other choice.

Still, the mission was genuinely heroic. Nazi rockets, fired at Britain from the occupied French coast, had given Hitler a powerful weapon, both strategically and psychologically. They could only be stopped by destroying launching sites. Their thick protective bunkers, however, were immune to conventional attack and could withstand anything short of a devastatingly powerful direct attack, which could best be accomplished by crashing into the site with an airplane loaded with explosives. Flying a converted bomber that could not possibly return for a landing, its crew had to remain in place until the plane became a drone, a radio-controlled missile that would be electronically directed head-on toward the target. At that point the crew would bail out, hopefully still over England. Several attempts had already failed and lives had been lost. Lieutenant Kennedy's mission was no more successful. The PB$_4$Y manned by Kennedy and Willy vanished within the fiery ball of what may have been the greatest nonnuclear explosion of all time.

With his brother Joe's death, John F. Kennedy followed the logical path previously trod by the good Whigs, the English gentry who devoted their careers to public service. Left unresolved, however, was the intensity of internal family compulsion upon Jack to take his brother's place, to abandon a contemplated career in either journalism, law, teaching, or business. After all, Joe Junior had been very pointed about his own presidential ambitions, and so had their father. That Joe Junior had the sponsorship of his family was clear. Journalist Bob Considine reported that after Jack Kennedy reached the White House he said, "I was drafted. My father wanted his eldest son in politics. 'Wanted' isn't the right word. He demanded it. You know my father."[1] Earlier, the senior Kennedy told an interviewer quite bluntly, "I got Jack into politics, I was the one. I told him Joe was dead and that it was therefore his responsibility to run for Congress. He didn't want it. He felt he didn't have the ability and he still feels that way. But I told him he had to."[2] Arthur Krock, the Washington correspondent and close family friend, also remembered that the Ambassador did not believe Jack was particularly qualified for politics until Joe's death made him the oldest son. "After that I believe his father decided that Jack did have a great aptitude for politics."[3] An old Navy friend, Paul "Red" Fay, remembered that during those months after Joe's death, Jack told him, "I can feel Pappy's eyes on the back of my neck."[4]

Others recalled things differently. Charles Bartlett, the syndicated columnist with whom Jack Kennedy formed a lasting friendship, never thought there was a clear connection between the father's desires and a political career. "I gather that it was a fulsome, full-blown wish on his part," Bartlett told an interviewer.[5] With the passage of time and the institutionalization of the "Camelot" legend, the Bartlett view seemed to confirm the portrait of an assertive, determined young man with all the assets and drive for future success. More than that, his dedication to political leadership merely utilized his father's assistance, among his many other advantages.

The man who married Jack's sister Eunice, R. Sargent Shriver, Jr., recalled no evidence of compulsion by the older Kennedy, no conflict between father and son. Admittedly, young Joe's death traumatized the father. Family accounts confirmed the stories about a period of seclusion when the father saw nobody and did nothing, an extended time of paternal mourning. But the family that Shriver joined reminded him of the opening lines of Tolstoy's *Anna Karenina.* "Happy families are all alike; every unhappy family is unhappy in its own way." Reports that Jack complained about having been drafted for his political career simply contradicted the realities of the family relationship. "Jack was a very dutiful, loving son," said Shriver. "You know, I just think that family, that Kennedy family, is a superb family. So therefore, this is a happy family. They're all happy, therefore, in the same way all families are happy, and this business of trying to psychoanalyze them as if they were an unhappy family, like it was *The Brothers Karamazov,* or something like that—that's not the Brothers Kennedy, see. It just isn't that way." While there was mutual love, there was also independence. And Shriver added, "Jack Kennedy was, as a human being, the kind of a person who would resist having something imposed upon him, by his father or by anybody else. He was not that kind of a person." If his father's ideas differed from his own, he would laugh and talk about it and say, "Dad would do it this way, Dad would do it that way, but that's not my way."[6]

Others equally close to Jack Kennedy offered a less idyllic view. Brother-in-law Steve Smith said that the "old man" was tough and kept pushing his children. His expectations were high. Jack, less forthcoming and gregarious than his older brother, could not be made into a duplicate of the lost son.[7] Journalist Joseph Alsop made distinctions between the early Jack Kennedy and the later Jack Kennedy, between the period when the young man had reasons to doubt he would live beyond his early forties and afterward, when the physicians decided he could enjoy normal longevity. At that point, Kennedy "found ambition"; but until then, said Alsop, "he did what his father wanted him to do without paying much attention."[8]

Joseph P. Kennedy was a peculiarly American product. In common with other families transplanted to this side of the Atlantic, the descendants of his father, Patrick Kennedy, acquired the assumptions and aspirations conditioned by the new environment—fulfilling, it may be argued, the expectations that had prompted immigrants to find a place in the new world. Devastatingly obnoxious to some, charming to others, Joseph Kennedy materialized as an Irish Sammy Glick. Driven by nothing beyond personal gratification, which included his immediate family as an extension of himself, he can never be said to have been especially enchanted by ideological convictions. Virtually inheriting the Columbia Trust Company and his father's managerial talents, he determined to find riches quickly. Everywhere he operated, whether in America or at the Court of St. James's, he quickly displayed a pronounced flair for self-interest. He did what was best for Joe Kennedy and his possessions.

Joe had the third-generation advantage of birth under relatively opulent circumstances. In 1888 the family moved to an elegant address on East Boston's Webster Street. That year, in the four-story house overlooking the harbor from that community's most prestigious location, Joseph P. Kennedy was born on September 6.

Joe's father, Patrick Joseph, was born in America some ten years after the arrival of Patrick Kennedy, who began life in a two-room cottage in County Wexford, Ireland, in the southeastern corner of the country. Patrick had left Ireland sometime between 1848 and 1850. One writer pinpointed the date as October of 1848, the year 150,000 others sailed from that impoverished land.[9] Others contend that he began the trip by walking the six miles to New Ross. From that embarkation point, a steady flow of immigrants sailed on the packet boats to America.

Since the start of the decade, the landing point in the Boston area was at Noddle's Island. Not shown on present maps, and sometimes incorrectly spelled as Noodle's Island, the strip of land was located in Boston harbor just east of Charlestown and accessible to the mainland only by ferry service. During the middle of the nineteenth century, it began to be called East Boston; for a period, both names were used interchangeably. Later, one of the landfill projects that enlarged Boston connected it with Revere and the mainland to the north. Today, East Boston forms an isthmus providing the only direct land link with Logan International Airport. When Patrick Kennedy came, Noddle's Island was not only a genuine island but one gaining in importance as a place that also offered expanding job opportunities for the displaced, untrained Irish agricultural workers who did not have the means to venture any further into the American interior. Its entire economy was virtually tied to the sea; most laborers worked as longshoremen, dockhands, and in the new shipyards that had recently been constructed. With a population of more than nine thousand in 1849, rapid expansion was inevitable. It would ultimately become a prime base for Kennedy political power.

Perhaps what characterized Patrick Kennedy were the traits that applied to others who undertook and survived the rigorous transition from Ireland to America: toughness and determination, plus a sizable amount of courage. For Pat Kennedy, in the decade of life available to him in his new country, hard work meant mere subsistence without any further material benefits. He found employment as a cooper, or barrel-maker, and located a cheap place to live in a dockside boardinghouse. He married a lovely colleen named Bridget Murphy, who was two years older than he. They had three daughters and one son. The boy arrived on January 8, 1858, and was named Patrick Joseph Kennedy, who later became known as P.J. Less than a year after his son's birth, Patrick Kennedy died from cholera. He was only thirty-five. His widow then supported the family by working at odd jobs and later became a hair-dresser at the Jordan Marsh store in downtown Boston.

Having been raised largely by his older sisters, Patrick J. Kennedy obtained a limited education. He attended a school run by the Sisters of Notre Dame and then a public school in East Boston. Maturing into a healthy young man, he went to work as a dockhand. From his meager wages, the austere P.J. managed to save enough money to buy a tavern in East Boston's Haymarket Square. Not only did that become the basis for his further commercial success, it enabled him to parlay the prominence of that function in local society into a political career, a route followed by other Boston Irish politicos. As Martin Lomasney, one of the chief deans of the city's Democratic ward politics, had taught, P.J. catered to the needs of the poor in his district, actually operating what one writer has termed "a midget welfare state," which helped attract a crop of supporters.[10] With the support of the machine, he won election to the state house of representatives in 1886. The following year, Patrick J. Kennedy married Mary Hickey, a union that represented an upward climb.

Patrick advanced via the twin opportunities offered by business and politics. From his single saloon, he invested his profits with sufficient skill to become a wholesale liquor distributor as well as a partner in two other saloons. As his family grew and he became the father of three children, he was elected to the state senate in 1892 and again the following year. After that second one-year term, however, he never again ran for public office. Much of his attention went to developing business interests, which included getting together with other prosperous Irish businessmen and founding an independent bank in East Boston, the Columbia Trust Company. Politically, P.J. wielded behind-the-scenes power. He belonged to the triumvirate that ruled the machine's inner circle, even earning the distinction of being described as the "Nestor of the board" and, by a contemporary newspaper, as "unquestionably one of the shrewdest men in Boston politics."[11]

Young Joe's early patterns markedly resembled his father's entrepreneurial skills. Most of his education was in Protestant schools instead of the usual institutions favored by Boston's Irish, a fact that foreshadowed the family's persistent efforts to enter the WASP establishment. Within those Yankee surroundings, Joe used athletic proficiency as a lever for attention. So, too, was he skilled at making money. His instincts were sufficiently aggressive and keen to fully exploit every opportunity that his good connections offered.

He attended parochial school through the lower grades. While there, he earned extra money by selling newspapers. At the age of eight he organized a military "regiment" to march in a Memorial Day parade. He also put together a baseball team and became its business manager. They bought uniforms and charged admission. Like most things he touched, that, too, became profitable. Joe also found a way to get some additional income by working as a ticket-taker on an excursion boat. Then, in preparation for Harvard, Pat and Mary Kennedy sent him to Boston Latin.

He quickly became a school leader, not through academic distinctions, but by energetic extracurricular and athletic activities. He won the Mayor's Cup, which went to the leading hitter among the city's high school players. None other than the mayor himself, John F. Fitzgerald, presented the award to young Joe.

Harvard was an unusual place for an Irish Catholic student. Considered as the stronghold of the Brahmins, it was the enemy camp to Joe Kennedy's East Boston neighbors. Nevertheless, the youth plunged into the college and its society as another obstacle to be overcome. Academic concerns seem to have been secondary to acceptance and making additional money.

Most of all, he worked at social climbing. Although admitted to some of the more elite campus clubs, Kennedy's pride suffered from rejection by the most prestigious groups. To Joe, Brahmin exclusion evoked prejudice, pure and simple, a perception that certainly cannot be argued away very easily. At the same time, his own denial of the clubs' values, as implied by an aggressiveness more consistent with ambitious lower classes, undoubtedly stiffened their opposition: a vicious cycle, in effect

—one that Joe Kennedy never got over. It deprived him of the recognition he most prized. Possibly, as has been suggested, his close association with so many Yankees made him more vulnerable to their hostility. He was more sensitive than most other Irish Catholic Bostonians about how the "proper people" viewed one with his background.[12]

After Harvard the determined Kennedy rose quickly. By the fall of 1913 he had manipulated a takeover of the Columbia Trust Company, winning undisputed recognition as the nation's youngest bank president. Having declared his desire to become a millionaire by the age of thirty-five, the young man of twenty-five was well on his way.

On October 7, 1914, in the Back Bay chapel of His Eminence William Cardinal O'Connell, Archbishop of Boston, Joseph P. Kennedy married the daughter of Mayor Fitzgerald. "Fitzie," as many called him, or "Little Nap," because of his stature, later came to be better known as "Honey Fitz," a nickname obviously inspired by his skill at blarney. They all helped to enhance his reputation as somewhat of a buffoon, although sympathetic observers preferred to view him as a fascinating personality, one well versed in the art of self-publicity. To Bostonians, both proper and improper, he was as familiar as the Bunker Hill Monument. Honey Fitz could be found everywhere, and sometimes, so it seemed, at different places at about the same time. During his first two years as mayor, for example, in 1906 and 1907, he was said to have attended twelve hundred dinners, fifteen hundred dances, two hundred picnics, and a thousand meetings. He went along at the rate of two dinners, six speeches, and three dances a night.

His later reputation became inseparable from the song "Sweet Adeline." After rendering it publicly during his 1909 mayoralty campaign against Good Government candidate James Jackson Storrow, his Yankee Republican opponent, Fitzgerald thereafter repeated it too loudly and too often.

Honey Fitz may be remembered as a buffoon, but he was no fool. As a young man, John F. Fitzgerald readily made the most of his situation by utilizing to the hilt the instincts of the effective street politician: shrewdness, wit, a friendly and gregarious manner. As one of the first Irishmen admitted to the Boston Latin School, if not *the* first, Honey Fitz's athletic ability helped him overcome social liabilities as well as the physical handicaps presented by his five-feet two-inch height and a lisp. Excelling in track and swimming, he also played right field on the school's baseball team and led the football team for two years as its captain. Shortly after graduation, he formed and became the first president of the Interscholastic Athletic Association. So remarkable was his ability to penetrate Protestant society that he even became the captain of a polo team that competed in New York as well as New England. He then enrolled at Harvard Medical School. Despite the uncertain standards of contemporary medical education, that was a considerable achievement for a first-generation Irish Catholic. But his father's death in 1881 compelled him to drop out. Honey Fitz, by his account, assumed the burdens of providing for his family's needs, although he was not the oldest son.

Much like his Tammanyite contemporary in New York, George Washington Plunkitt, Honey Fitz also could have said, "I seen my opportunities and I took 'em." Like P.J., Honey Fitz learned his ward politics from Martin Lomasney. Fitzgerald understood the quid pro quo relationship between the political clubs and the poor. Following the traditional route toward City Hall, Honey Fitz worked his way upward, first serving in both city and state legislative bodies. Then, before becoming Boston's first mayor who had descended directly from immigrant stock, he spent three terms in the United States Congress.

His greatest political coup came from winning the mayoralty in 1905. In that triumph he defied his former mentor, Lomasney, who later characterized the episode as having brought him to "the lowest position in my career."[13] Indeed, Fitzgerald's achievement was considerable, in effect a double victory over the most potent Boston politicians. The sudden death of Mayor Patrick Collins provided the opportunity. Fitzgerald announced his desire to vie for the Democratic nomination to succeed Collins. He had the support of the powerful ruler of Ward Eight, Lomasney, the so-called "Mahatma" of Boston politics. The prospect of that powerful combination actually winning displeased the inner circle of power brokers that had, in effect, been dominating the party's decision-making apparatus. Lomasney, who exerted political power through control over the Hendricks Club, his personal vote-getting machine, could negate their authority by winning with Fitzgerald. The inner circle's power came from ability to dominate the awarding of patronage, nominations, and lucrative city contracts. Initially having evolved as an unofficial advisory group, Lomasney had labeled them the "Strategy Board." For some years Democratic Party politics in the city had become a clash between the board and Lomasney. Fitzgerald himself, although ostensibly on the board, was excluded from its center of three leaders who held the real power, probably for the sort of individualism that made him somewhat of a prima donna.

In effect the board chose to maintain their favorable position in the balance of political power. Separating Fitzgerald from Lomasney became the immediate goal. To do that, they supported City Clerk Edward J. Donovan, a candidate whose entry would test the Mahatma's personal power and loyalty. Donovan, in addition to having been Lomasney's protégé, was also the president of the Hendricks Club. As expected, then, the Mahatma dropped Honey Fitz in favor of Donovan.

Opposed by both the board and Lomasney, Fitzgerald nevertheless came out on top. With the support of many of the other ward leaders, he won the party's nomination. Lomasney, seeing Donovan beaten by a 3,743-vote margin, decided to stop both Fitzgerald and the board in the general election by backing the Republican candidate. But the Mahatma's only real demonstration of power came by converting the eighth ward's normally one-sided Democratic electorate into Republican majority. Fitzgerald carried the city, the final triumph in a sequence of events that gave the Mahatma his most humiliating defeat.

By the time Mayor Fitzgerald neared the completion of his four-year term that had begun in 1910, the first four-year term served by any Boston mayor, new alliances and new rivalries were being formed. Most significant for the history of the Kennedy family in Massachusetts politics was the opposition to his renomination that came from James Michael Curley, as astute, articulate, and commanding an Irish political figure who ever came out of ward politics, the future prototype for Edwin O'Connor's fictitious Frank Skeffington in *The Last Hurrah*. Curley's all-out assault proved devastating. Chagrined that Fitzgerald had abandoned his earlier promise to vacate the mayoralty, the contender used every means of attacking the incumbent, including threats to expose scandalous revelations about a rumored Honey Fitz affair with a blond cigarette girl named "Toodles" Ryan. Prudently, Fitzgerald withdrew. With the nomination in hand, Curley went on to defeat the Republican candidate.

Honey Fitz remained active in Boston politics for a long time. After the end of his final year as mayor, he became an unsuccessful candidate for the United States Senate in 1916 and in 1918 he was elected to a congressional seat. After actually serving from March to October of 1919, his election was invalidated because of irregularities. He then ran for the governorship in 1922 without success and four times served as a presidential elector. Although a member of the Port of Boston Authority from 1934 until 1948, he lost a final attempt at a congressional seat in 1942. But before he died in 1950, Honey Fitz had the satisfaction of seeing his grandson, the child of his daughter Rose and Joe Kennedy, installed on Capitol Hill.

Of course, marrying Rose Fitzgerald gave Joe Kennedy's ambitions another lift. She became a proper Victorian wife and mother, creating for herself, as in her memoirs, an idyllic world of familial love, purity of religious devotion, and sacrifices to serve society and those less fortunate. Her personal values emphasized proper behavior together with refined dress and comeliness of figure. Exceptionally pretty at her marriage, she worked to retain the sort of appearance that led a gracious gentleman, upon meeting the mother of nine children, to say that he could now believe in the stork. A New York makeup specialist, commenting on her regal manner, said that "she stands very straight, and she moves with great sureness; her whole personality is in line with her beauty. Everybody today seems to slouch, but there's something, somehow, *regal* about Rose Kennedy."[14] There was, at the same time, the private person who coveted solitude and insulated herself from life's rougher swirls. Honey Fitz had worked hard to remove his daughter from any possible identification with the shanty Irish, through clothes, culture, travel, and a European education. At the Convent of the Sacred Heart in Blumenthal, Prussia, she mingled with the European aristocracy. That was better than anything that P.J. could give to Joe.

Resistant as Honey Fitz was to their marriage, however, he helped Joe get another source of leverage. Through Charles Schwab, the Bethlehem Steel magnate whom the politician had known from his Washington days in the 1890's, he got Kennedy a valuable job when World War I came. Having heard from the Bethlehem firm's Boston attorney about young Kennedy's financial acumen, Schwab became naturally amenable when Honey Fitz added his own endorsement. That led to Joe's appointment as the assistant general manager of the company's large Fore River shipyards at Quincy, Massachusetts. Second in charge, supervising twenty-two hundred employees, Kennedy received an annual salary of twenty thousand dollars, a remarkable amount for 1917. He was not quite thirty. In 1919, with the war over, he left Fore River to manage the Boston branch of the brokerage house of Hayden, Stone and Company.

Kennedy's association with Hayden, Stone turned out to be especially useful. It enabled him to learn about the intricacies of stock market manipulations and how to maneuver his way through corporate holdings to compile a vast personal fortune. He quickly succeeded in starting his accumulations. He bought control of a chain of thirty-one New England movie theaters and soon afterward acquired the regional franchise for

Universal Pictures. He became a major investor in Todd Shipyards, one of Fore River's competitors. During a seven-week period of concentrated manipulating, he engineered a halt to the downturn of Yellow Cab stock, as a result of which, as Kennedy himself put it, "Several of us emerged wealthy men."[15]

Entering the still adolescent motion picture industry, he quickly became a producer of highly commercial Hollywood potboilers. Taking control of one company, called Film Booking Offices, he turned out almost one picture a week. Artistic considerations counted for nothing; westerns, melodramas—whatever could make money received Kennedy's attention. With his associates he took over the Keith-Albee-Orpheum theater chain. Then came a series of mergers and the establishment of a holding company, all of which was designed to enrich the investors at the expense of corporate interests. According to a later estimate made by *Fortune* magazine, Kennedy made five million dollars in stock transactions pertaining to Film Booking Offices and Keith-Albee-Orpheum alone.[16] He also received weekly salaries in the two- to three-thousand-dollar range. By the time he withdrew from Hollywood in 1930, he and his associates were said to have had fifteen million dollars still in Pathé films. Pathé, in turn, had large amounts of its stock bought up by another company, RKO, and a merger followed.

Other than his extraordinary profiteering, Kennedy's Hollywood ventures are best remembered for his involvement with Gloria Swanson, the glamorous actress. As a producer of many of her films, Kennedy's close association with her encouraged rumors of a lively romance. Kennedy made no effort to dispel the gossip. Swanson told an interviewer that she was once delighted by Joe Kennedy's gift of a Rolls-Royce only to later discover that he had charged it to their joint bank account.[17] Joe did not keep her away from his home and family, which led to inevitable reports that the relationship created tension in his marriage. One well-known Hollywood columnist even informed her readers that an indignant Honey Fitz had ordered his son-in-law out of Hollywood, an unlikely role for a veteran of "Toodles" Ryan.[18] In her memoirs Rose Kennedy subsequently made no effort to ignore Swanson; she implies a very professional, detached relationship.

Instead of suffering from the great stock market collapse of 1929, Kennedy turned disaster into personal profit. Before the actual crash, he retained substantial shares of Pathé, but little of anything else. He had made a timely withdrawal. Thereafter, Kennedy engaged in considerable short-selling.

Joe supported FDR's presidential aspirations. No ideological inclination had determined Kennedy's support. He, along with so many others, had little confidence in the governor's ability. Right after the convention, he determined to keep a careful watch over the nominee. As one newspaper publisher explained that summer, "Kennedy expects to fly to whatever port Roosevelt is in for the night, to be present at the evening conferences, because he knew that if he were not present, the other men —notably Louis Howe and Jim Farley—would 'unmake' Roosevelt's mind on some of the points Kennedy had made it up for Roosevelt."[19] Kennedy could not accept that. His entire support for FDR was based on the fact that he felt he had found a winner and would profit from being in the winner's circle.

Kennedy's association with Roosevelt gave him an advantageous position when Prohibition was repealed. The benefits actually did not come directly from the President but through FDR's son Jimmy. It had been Joe Kennedy who had been the most instrumental in helping the younger Roosevelt's insurance business in Boston, especially in getting Jimmy workmen's compensation policies for the Ford Motor Company. With Prohibition coming to an end, Kennedy scurried after attractive liquor-importation franchises, and Jimmy Roosevelt accompanied him to England. There, supported by the presence of the President's son, Kennedy obtained the most impressive, and persuasive, introduction to the appropriate parties. As a result, Joe Kennedy's company, Somerset Importers, became the sole American importers of such lucrative brands as Gordon's gin, Dewar's Scotch, Ron Rico rum, and Haig and Haig.[20]

By the 1930's, when most Americans were coping with the Depression, Kennedy's fortunes had reached astounding proportions. In 1929 he had established a trust fund for his children. He added to it on two different occasions. By the provisions drawn up in 1949, each of the Kennedy children were to receive over ten million dollars.[21] Holdings passed on to his children included shares in oil and natural gas companies.[22] Subsequent investments in real estate, an enterprise that captured his serious interest in the 1940's, had helped amass a fortune that was estimated in 1957 as worth somewhere between $200 and $400 million, although Kennedy himself insisted that the lower figure was more accurate.

Having made his financial conquests, Joe Kennedy had not, however, exhausted his goals. He looked to his sons to fulfill the political objectives of a family which assumed obligations to govern.

2

The Kennedy Children and Their World

The growth of the Kennedy family paralleled Joe's financial fortunes. While Joe and Rose lived in a comfortable but modest home on Beals Street in Brookline, they had four children within five years; two boys, Joe Junior and Jack, followed by Rosemary and Kathleen. During the next eight years, Rose gave birth to three more children, Eunice, Patricia, and Robert. Jean and Edward Moore ("Ted") followed later.

If her husband served as the family's chairman of the board, absenting himself much of the time to compile his fortune, Rose acted as the household's president. Blessed with the luxury of domestic help, she nevertheless established a firm pattern of tending to daily responsibilities for each child. "I remember that I would make no engagements after five in the evening," she recalled, "so that I could be with the children to help them with their schoolwork, to doctor their colds, or to find out activities they had been interested in during the day."[1] She supervised their schedules, selected their books, read aloud their favorite stories, and, above all, guided their religious and moral upbringing. "When you hold your baby in your arms the first time and you think of all the things you can do and say to influence him," her tape-recorded voice tells visitors in the Brookline home, "it's a tremendous responsibility. What you did with him and for him can influence not only him but everyone he meets; not for a day, a month or a year, but for time and eternity." A Harvard classmate of Jack Kennedy recalled that "Mrs. Kennedy is the one that kept the family together—an absolutely marvelous woman." During those early years, he added, "she was able to knock off the edges of these various boys and girls, and somehow she made the home possible with the father; although without her, the home wouldn't have lasted. The father was very difficult."[2] Rose's biographer quotes one of her close friends as saying that "Joe provided the fire in the family, but Rose provided the steel, and she still does." In short, she was, as Gail Cameron has noted, "the glue that has always held the family together."[3] That function was even more demanding than her own memoirs acknowledge.

The oldest girl, Rosemary, was born with a severe handicap—mental retardation. Insofar as possible, however, the family attempted to treat her in public as a normal child. Distant observers viewed her as just another happy, attractive addition to a contented family. Years later when they all joined their father for presentation at the Court of St. James's, Rosemary was included. Pictures of that occasion show a pleasant, smiling teen-ager. Nevertheless, her condition became more acute with age. She could do less and less for herself. Finally, desperation led to extreme solutions. After conferring with several doctors, an operation was performed to make her more tractable and thereby relieve brain damage that probably stemmed from a forceps delivery. Sister Paulus, the nun in charge of Rosemary, has been quoted to confirm an assertion that the neurosurgery was a prefrontal lobotomy, while Rose Kennedy simply states that "a certain form of neurosurgery" was done.[4] Steve Smith, acknowledging the operation, never heard anything about a prefrontal lobotomy. "In any discussion of the matter," he said, "never have I heard that choice of words to describe the operation. It is my impression that, very definitely, that was not the nature of it."[5] All agree, however, that the surgery left Rosemary permanently incapacitated. Few choices were left.

For the Kennedys, the tragedy was a blemish, marring the perfection of what was increasingly portrayed as a remarkable family: a beautiful and devoted mother; a powerful father, one who excelled at the most manly of all American arts, money-making; and a brood of attractive, intelligent children with strong familial ties. Further, it happened when mental disability was regarded as shameful. Many private decisions to institutionalize such children were for the benefit of other siblings and to ensure proper care. They also relieved the need for daily confrontation of unpleasant realities.

The Kennedys made a similar decision in the case of Rosemary. They sent her to Wisconsin. Early accounts of the family could only accept their official explanation, that Rosemary had different aspirations from the other youngsters. She was quieter, they said. She was less ambitious for herself, wanting only to work among the less privileged and the handicapped. That fiction found its way into all family discussions published before Jack won the presidential nomination. Even the generally perceptive, well-balanced biography by James MacGregor Burns repeats the tale that at St. Coletta's, "a Catholic school near Milwaukee, Rosemary helped care for mentally retarded children."[6] Not until after Burns's book appeared did the family publicly acknowledge Rosemary's actual condition. Imperfection, they had to admit, had indeed touched the household. All was not one happy, gifted family.

Jack and the other children were raised largely by their mother and hired help. For weeks, even months, especially when on the West Coast during his movie-producing, Joe Kennedy was away from home. The nurse, Katherine Conboy, who spoke in a thick Irish brogue and cost Joe Kennedy twelve dollars a week, took care of the children, especially the younger ones. For five dollars less, Kennedy also hired a live-in maid, actually a sort of jack-of-all-trades. All in all, after Rosemary, Jack required more attention than any of the others.

The psychological facts will never be known, only presumed by those who are ready to interpret physical distress as a manifestation of inner protest. The portrait of Jack that emerges is that of a sick child, one who seemed to suffer not only most diseases common to youngsters, but some extraordinary ones as well. As brother Bobby wrote in a book that later memorialized his life, "At least one half of the days that he spent on this earth were days of intense physical pain. He had scarlet fever when he was very young, and serious back trouble when he was older. In between he had almost every other conceivable ailment. . . . But during all this time, I never heard him complain. I never heard him say anything that would indicate that he felt God had dealt with him unjustly."[7]

Always, in his public life, Jack Kennedy would epitomize masculine fitness. Debilities were hidden from public view. An affected image of health and strength, of ability to withstand physical rigors and temperature extremes, attempted to deny his medical history. Jack's frail condition contrasted with the household emphasis on physical fitness and stamina. Almost obsessive athletic competitions usually involved all members of the family. William O. Douglas, who knew the Kennedys during the 1930's, remembers that "the father particularly laid it on hard trying to make the boys, and the girls, excellent in something, whether it was touch football, or tennis, or boating, or something else."[8] That also meant pain and discomfort were to be accepted without complaint. Dave Hackett, one of Bobby's closest friends, contributed an animated description of life with the family, calling it "Rules for Visiting the Kennedys." Warning those about to join them in touch football, he advised, "To become really popular, you must show raw guts." And then, with only slight hyperbole, he added: "To show raw guts, fall on your face now and then. Smash into the house once in a while going after a pass. Laugh off twisted ankles or a big hole torn in your best suit. They like this. It shows you take the game as seriously as they do."[9] One visitor recalled a chilly and foggy evening at the seashore. A Kennedy child, obviously having just received a minor injury while playing, rushed to complain to his mother. Looking for sympathy, he fell to the floor and began to whine. "On your feet!" she ordered. He promptly rose and practically stood at attention. "Now you know how to behave," she added. "Go out there and behave as you know you should."[10]

Jack lived by the same code. Often he drove himself needlessly. To Jack as well as to the rest of the family, his poor health was virtually an aberration. It could not, of course, compare with Rosemary's problem, but, at the same time, it was hard to reconcile with Kennedy pride. While the other children were often battered from play, his disabilities had natural causes. Bobby later recalled their standing joke. "When we were growing up together we used to laugh about the great risk a mosquito took in biting Jack Kennedy—with some of his blood the mosquito was almost sure to die."[11] Even at an early age, Jack suffered from backaches, foreshadowing a condition that would later become excruciatingly painful and debilitating. Dr. Gilbert Haggart of Boston's Lahey Clinic later found that Jack was born with a weak back.[12] And, on February 20, 1920, shortly after Kathleen's arrival and three months before his own third birthday, he succumbed to his most serious childhood illness, scarlet fever. A frequently fatal disease at the time, his survival was in doubt when he was rushed to Boston City Hospital. "Jack was a very, very sick little boy," Rose later wrote in her memoirs. "Joe was in church praying for him, and in his prayers he promised that if Jack were spared he would give half of all his money to charity."[13] As Rose has also acknowledged elsewhere, the scarlet fever may have left its mark on the child's general physical condition, exposing him to more than his share of diseases.

Rose Kennedy kept an index-card file with notations of her children's medical histories, their illnesses, inoculations, etc., a record reminiscent of how her father followed the special needs and favors he had performed for his North Boston constituents. The only card that has been revealed, which shows notations pertaining to Jack through 1933, indicates that he had whooping cough, measles, chicken pox, and attacks of bronchitis. He also developed asthma, a condition his mother believed came from an allergic reaction to dog hair. The index card reveals that on March 21, 1931, a Dr. John Wheeler had prescribed reading glasses for the boy. Sometime before that date, Jack had written to her from the Canterbury School that he was having trouble with his vision. "Doctor Hume said he was going to write to you about my right eye. I see things blury [sic] even at a distance of ten feet. I can't see much color through that eye either."[14] Later, during the final autumn at Choate, his preparatory school, his eyes became more troublesome. An occulist said Jack had a low degree of nearsightedness in his right eye and a little farsighted astigmatism in the left, in addition to granular conjunctivitis. No treatment was required for the conjunctivitis, as it did not bother Jack. But new glasses were needed, as they would be throughout his life. As could be expected from one so concerned with covering up signs of weakness, his sensitivity about using his glasses was great and photographs showing Jack wearing reading glasses are rare.

Rose Kennedy read aloud to her children at bedtime. Jack, of all her children, was easily the most receptive. Books became a vital part of his life; Rose called him a "natural reader." When Nathan Pusey, the Harvard University president, asked her why Jack read so much, she explained that as "a child and many times thereafter he had to spend long periods in bed, often on weekends when the others were out playing; and as a consequence he learned to love to read, and always did read much more than any of the others."[15] He enjoyed *Billy Whiskers,* a story about a goat which his Grandmother Fitzgerald brought from a department store. He also went through books like *The Arabian Nights,* and John Bunyan's *Pilgrim's Progress.* But his childhood favorite was *King Arthur and His Knights.*

Gradually, his reading turned almost entirely toward nonfiction. Ideas became important for their relevance to current problems; fantasies began to lose their charm. History and biography, and particularly those that described outstanding leadership, dominated his reading. He advised his youngest brother to read all ten volumes of David Brewer's *World's Greatest Orators.*[16] He especially praised David Cecil's life of Lord Melbourne and recommended it to friends.[17]

Acquaintances frequently were bewildered not only at the quantity of his reading but by the quality and speed. Kay Halle, introduced to him the first time when, at age fifteen, he was confined to Massachusetts General Hospital, found that while he was lying in bed "very pale, which highlighted the freckles across his nose," she could hardly see him because he was so surrounded by books. "I was very impressed because at that point this very young child was reading *The World Crisis,* by Sir Winston Churchill." Jack later told her he had read everything Churchill ever wrote, even in *Hansard,* Britain's *Congressional Record.*[18] Aide Priscilla Johnson recalled visiting his hospital room after one of his back operations and finding three tall piles of books stacked up at the head of his bed.[19] Later in life associates were usually surprised that he could manage to "steal" reading time during the midst of the most demanding campaign. And when he met authors, he enjoyed playing a private joke by referring to their more obscure work.

The maturing Kennedy would evolve into the aggressive campaigner and activist, concerned almost entirely with considerations of gaining and keeping power; and, once having achieved that, with going on to more prominence. For Jack Kennedy, though, there was the intellectual appetite far less common to that breed. Jacob Potofsky, the leader of the Amalgamated Clothing Workers of America, found Kennedy far more comfortable with intellectuals than with ordinary people, enjoying the company of those who had educated minds to be picked.[20] One of the ironies of Kennedy's later career involved his competition with Adlai Stevenson for the support of the nation's intellectuals. Each man could both charm and exasperate; but of the two, Kennedy was the voracious reader. Stevenson much preferred personal companionship to being alone with a book.[21] But for Kennedy the conflicts between the attractions of scholarship and the competing drive for attaining positions of influential leadership created a lifelong ambivalence. Ultimately, the marriage of the two impulses afforded an intellectual dimension that gave his personality a quality so many found attractive.

Jack was not a typical Kennedy. Sister Jean called him their most intellectual member.[22] Eunice said he was "brighter than the rest of us," and then, noting a quality confirmed by Rose Kennedy, she added, "Whenever we discussed things, he was always the one who looked things up."[23] One of Jack's friends remembered that, unlike some of the others in the family, Jack was "neither pushy nor calculating," certainly much less so than either Bobby or Ted.[24] Another simply said that he was "the least competitive" of the Kennedys.[25] Ted Sorensen, contrasting Jack with brother Bobby, wrote that Jack "could be smoother, more soothing, less intense, less explosive, more given to understatement, less quick to reveal his likes and dislikes."[26] Compared with Joe Junior, Supreme Court Justice William O. Douglas found him quieter, "a little more subtle" and more like his mother, while the older boy was an extrovert.[27] Expanding on the differences between Jack and the other Kennedy males, William V. Shannon described him as "a loner, a self-contained person. It may be that in the intensely competitive family situation he withdrew somewhat into himself, learned to keep his own counsel, and put a layer of insulation between himself and other people."[28]

Unquestionably, the introspective second son was the one who resembled his father least of all.

Jack enjoyed summers at Cohasset, and being driven out by the family chauffeur in their father's Rolls-Royce. There, in the early 1920's, amid the rocks of the New England shoreline, Jack and the other children became fine swimmers. When his health permitted, Jack's participation in the family's outdoor activities was as zestful as anyone else's, at times even more enthusiastic.

Brother Joe clearly provided most of the direct competition. As in traditional Irish Catholic families, the oldest son had a special responsibility. In a continuation of the ancient practice of primogeniture, he was the natural heir, the bearer of the family's aspirations. His rank carried an unchallenged title. Moreover, Joe Junior was taller, stronger, far more outgoing than Jack.[29] When their father was not around—which was often in those years—Joe took charge and all the younger children looked up to him.

The relationship between Joseph P. Kennedy and his first son was clearly one of warmth and mutual affection. The father saw Junior as an extension of himself. "To a great extent he epitomized the traits, both positive and otherwise, that became the hallmark of his three younger brothers and perhaps of the decade they dominated."[30] A Navy chaplain who later knew Joe Junior explained that the "great idol in his life was his father. I imagine that he argued with his father . . . as he had with me, but there was a fine filial loyalty to everything his father had done or said."[31]

That intimacy was clearest at the dinner table. More than just meals, especially when Joe was home, dinners were intense seminars, with Mr. Kennedy presiding over whatever topics he thought would spark interest and conversation, money being the only taboo subject. The exchange of viewpoints was a privilege reserved for members of the family. Guests who were invited to participate could properly interpret the gesture as a high compliment and a sign of acceptance. As was discovered later by Jack Kennedy's visitors in the Oval Office, one had to be prepared for challenges amidst the Kennedys, to display an eclectic knowledge of the latest in the press, books, and newsmagazines. Walking into their lair was often embarrassing for those who had neglected their homework.

One guest found two weeks at the family's Palm Beach house among the most demanding days of his life. Mornings began with swimming, tennis, and then came baseball and sailing. Since, during that particular time, the Kennedys were devoted to scrutinizing *The Federalist Papers*, the visitor and each of the boys, including young Teddy, had to take the parts of Madison, Jay, or Hamilton and argue the points of each author.[32]

During those early years, dinner-table exchanges were largely reserved for the father and Joe Junior. Only as they matured were the other boys included, each taking his turn entering the exclusive male circle. The girls were expected to observe respectfully while Mr. Kennedy enjoyed such repartee with his sons, although one close friend, LeMoyne Billings, said that Kathleen, who was "bright and on the ball" and more "like Jack in many ways," "got into the table conversation a lot right at the beginning."[33]

"You know," Joe Junior told a family friend, "I'm the oldest of my family and I've got to be the example for a lot of brothers and sisters."[34] The older children were guardians of the younger. For Jack, Joe Junior was both brother and surrogate father and one who possessed all the traits revered by every family member. Then, too, there was a special affinity between Joe Junior and Dad, a relationship from which Jack was largely excluded. That distance was exacerbated by Joe Junior's age and authority, together with his dynamism and lack of diffidence that so many found in Jack. "They were very close," recalled William O. Douglas, "but were quite different people."[35] Jack himself later said that Joe "had a more pugnacious personality," which caused problems in his boyhood.[36] Despite their greater age difference, Joe Junior—not Jack— was young Bobby's idol.

"My brother Joe took the greatest interest in us," Bobby said. "He taught us to sail, to swim, to play football and baseball." Not until his brother's death did Jack fill that role.[37]

"I don't believe he feared Joe," Arthur Krock, head of *The New York Times* Washington Bureau, reminisced about Jack. "I don't think Joe in any way wished to bully him; they loved each other dearly, but Jack was a slight, a very slight, young man and Joe was strong and sturdy, and Joe, as I say, was an extrovert and Jack had his doubts about many things that Joe did not seem to feel, and so I think there was a challenge there, and as often with brothers, especially so close in age, one word led to another. The fighting was not more intense than usual, but it was very intense when it went on. I don't think fear was involved at all. Jack did not fear his brother; he loved his brother and his brother loved him."[38] Their mother has also recalled that the brotherly relationship developed into what she termed "affection and understanding." Even she, however, had to describe their childhood rivalry as a case of "friendly enmity."[39] When a sympathetic biographer later showed Jack Kennedy the manuscript of his work, the author subsequently revised a passage by deleting the reference to Joe having been "rather a bully," not because of its inaccuracy but "in deference to your feelings about your family."

At the age of fourteen Jack informed his father with considerable glee that his bully brother was really a cream puff. "When Joe came home he was telling me how strong he was and how tough," Jack wrote from Choate on December 9, 1931. "The first thing he did to show me how tough he was, was to get sick so that he could not have any Thanksgiving dinner. He was then going to show me how to Indian wrestle. I then threw him over on his neck. Did the sixth formers lick him. Oh man, he was all blisters, they almost paddled the life out of him. He was roughhousing in the hall a sixth former caught him he led him in and all the sixth formers had a swat or two [sic]. What I wouldn't have given to be a sixth former. They have some pretty strong fellows up there if blisters have anything to do with it."[40]

Once, while they were still living in Brookline, the two boys decided to have a bicycle race, with each going around the block in the opposite direction. On Abbottsford Road, around the corner from their home, they approached head-on. Stubbornly, each refused to give way. Joe was unhurt, but the collision cost Jack twenty-eight stitches.[41]

Throughout their young-adult lives, Jack had to contend with the formidable presence of Joe. While at Harvard, Jack expressed astonishment about his brother's "clout" with their father.[42] As late as the winter of 1940, a visitor to Joseph P. Kennedy's Palm Beach, Florida, home found that "Joe was then the figure, with Jack a charming, attractive son, but . . . very much in the shadow."[43] Liabilities of age and physique were not easily overcome by Jack. Books were an important means of establishing his own identity, an escape from the furiously driven little world of the Kennedy family. Often his father would express surprise at his progress. Nevertheless, Jack was proud of his dad's accomplishments, followed newspaper accounts of his latest deals, and respected his authority.[44]

In much the same way, he looked up to brother Joe. Only periodically did the furies surface and not necessarily at the moment of challenge when, for example, the football Joe Junior tossed to Jack would be a little swifter, a little more challenging, a little more intimidating, than Junior would hurl toward anyone else. Joe, however, was the big brother who taught him about sailing, how to be a good crewman, shift ballast in a jibe, and how to compete on the water. From the older boy, Jack acquired (with the additional aid of a hired sailing instructor) ability as an exceptionally adept sailor, winning races at the Wianno and Hyannis Port yacht clubs. He became good enough to win the Nantucket Sound championship in 1936, going on from there to compete in the Atlantic Coast championships, where he won four races but failed to win the title.[45] The family itself owned a succession of boats, including a cruiser, *Davilis,* which they turned over to the Coast Guard when the war started. Mastering them helped certify Jack's credentials as a Kennedy male.

Yet some of his most important emotional needs were supplied by two female members of the family. For warmth, attention, and satisfaction, he turned to his mother, by all accounts a strong woman who gave great attention to the details of routine family needs. From her, Jack received more kinship than he ever got from his often absent father.[46] And then there was Kathleen—"Kick." Pugnacious, vivacious, with the slender figure and elegance that Rose tried to instill in all her daughters, Kathleen shared with the unfortunate Rosemary the distinction of being the prettiest of the girls. Three years younger than Jack, the ebullient and outgoing Kathleen was the compatible kid sister. She, rather than Joe Junior, offered a special relationship. But the oldest son set the pace.

For the Kennedys, after all, lived in a male-oriented world. The men accomplished things, and respect and pride came from their ability to make things work and their single-mindedness about reaching goals. Jack had great charm. But Joe Junior was the doer, the gregarious charmer who, backed by enormous money and a powerful father, was guaranteed to turn his attributes toward the leadership of others.

They shared the kind of disciplined determination that struck others as excessively egocentric. Neither was a gracious loser, nor tolerated much criticism from outsiders.[47] Descendants of an underclass—poor Irish immigrants—they were ready for a new role, not unlike the English gentry. "First-generation millionaires tend to give us libraries," Garry Wills once wrote about the Rockefellers. "The second and third generation think they should give us themselves."[48]

In a WASP world Joseph P. Kennedy, in particular, was ready to extract the fundamentals of survival and achievement inherited from his grandfather and P.J. and the insights of accommodation taught by Honey Fitz. While Rose preserved the spiritual ballast, tending especially to the proper social upbringing of the girls, Joe's sons could go beyond the grubbiness that had established the family's power.

3

Period of Adjustment

In 1926, Joseph P. Kennedy, Sr., gave up summering at Cohasset, forever afterward recalling how anti-Catholicism had made that South Shore vacation home untenable, especially for the children. Looking for a more congenial environment, he rented a house at Hyannis Port on Cape Cod. Far from ostentatious, nothing like the Newport mansions of the very rich, the white clapboard cottage with green shutters came with two and a half acres of lawn, the property fronting on a private beach and Nantucket Sound. He remained a renter for just two years before buying the place and hiring the architect who had built the house in 1903 to double its original size. The Kennedys also left their home in Brookline, Massachusetts, and the Boston area for a new permanent residence. All the Kennedys were transported in a railroad car chartered for their exclusive use.

They relocated in Riverdale, an enclave of the borough of The Bronx in New York City. A wooded and rugged sector within the city's northwestern limits, its sloping terrain rises above the Hudson River directly opposite the Jersey Palisades. The immediate neighborhood of the Kennedy home at Independence Avenue and 252nd Street was suburban in character, far removed from the rest of the borough. Elegant, with many mansions, that part of Riverdale crested then dropped down toward the nearby Hudson. Just above the water's edge stood the Wave's Hill estate, once lived in by Mark Twain and Theodore Roosevelt. From the third-floor bedroom of their stucco, slate-roofed house, Joe Junior and Jack could see Wave's Hill and the river just beyond.

Ideal for commuters, the site was thoroughly desirable for Kennedy. From the convenient local station, New York Central's Harlem Division transported passengers to mid-Manhattan within a half hour. Kennedy was ready to operate in the big city, and Riverdale was an ideal base. Joe Kennedy began to pull away from Hollywood toward Wall Street.

Those who knew him tended to cite business requirements to explain his move. Rose Kennedy has also implied as much. However, one explanation that was advanced at various points of his career to explain Kennedy moves was the promotion of the family's social aspirations rather than pecuniary considerations. According to Arthur Krock, Joe feared that his daughters would not be received by proper Boston society because of the anti-Irish pressures.[1] John Corry, in his account of two aristocratic Irish-American families, makes much the same point. "The successful Boston Irish," he writes, "considered themselves successful only by the standards that the Protestants set for them. . . . Beacon Hill never did accept the Irish, although it tolerated men like William Cardinal O'Connell, who walked so easily among the bankers and merchants and made their ways his ways, but O'Connell, after all, had a red hat. Rose Kennedy had no red hat, but she had respectability and she had all those children. The sons among them would prosper and be famous. They would have to; they would be Rose Kennedy's revenge."[2]

Many years after the move to New York, when Jack was a Harvard student, Blair Clark, the son of a socially prominent family, was being driven back to Boston in the Kennedy limousine. Rose Kennedy sat in the front seat. Suddenly, she turned to Clark and asked, "When do you think the nice people of Boston will accept us socially?"[3]

It was particularly significant that Kennedy should have offered his daughters' social problems to explain the move. Just as he had designs for his sons, he had plans for the girls, only they were quite different—to function as devout, socially prominent, and responsible wives and mothers, emulating the ways of the finest Yankee aristocracy. Accordingly, their educational training was distinctive from that of Joe and Jack, following in the footsteps of Mother rather than Father. The girls were sent to elite Catholic institutions, and their credits came from such places as Manhattanville College, the Sacred Heart Academy at Noroton, Connecticut, and the Portsmouth Priory in Rhode Island. Portsmouth, led by Father J. H. Diman, who had converted after having been an Episcopalian schoolmaster, attempted to give its students an aristocratic classical education. The Kennedys, along with the socially prominent Hoguet banking family, were among its chief benefactors.[4] Still, there was flexibility even within this pattern. Eunice, for example, majored in sociology at Stanford. But there was far more concern about a proper Catholic education for the girls.

Jack had followed his older brother to the Dexter School, when the family lived in Massachusetts. It was a private academy associated with an older one founded in 1866 by an overseer of Harvard. Hardly the average neighborhood grade school, it provided early preparation for those born to positions of leadership and influence, its sixty boys comprising a social register of the area. Among their classmates were James Jackson Storrow, Jr., the grandson of the reform Yankee politician who lost the mayoralty to Honey Fitz in 1910 and the future publisher of *The Nation;* Edmund P. Richardson, a brother of Attorney General Elliott Richardson; and Frederick Josiah Bradlee, whose brother Ben became *Newsweek*'s managing editor and *The Washington Post*'s executive editor during the Watergate exposures. Another Dexter boy, two years younger than Jack, was McGeorge Bundy.[5] The Kennedy contribution to the school consisted largely of Mr. Kennedy's service on its board of trustees and Jack's scrappy efforts to play with the grade-school football team. Before leaving, Jack would become the squad's quarterback.

The Riverdale move interrupted his early education. Enrolled in the Riverdale Country Day School, Jack went through grades four through six. He finished "reasonably well," compiling about a B minus average.[6]

But the Riverdale home was temporary, one that Joe had rented. Joe Kennedy would always demand a better return for his money than rent receipts. So in 1929 he moved his family to Bronxville, a wealthy Westchester County suburb of New York City. That home was a Georgian mansion at 294 Pondfield Road that had been built for Anheuser-Busch and was surrounded by a half-dozen acres of lawns and carefully tended gardens. The purchase price was a quarter of a million dollars, a considerable sum, especially by 1929 standards, and in remarkable contrast with the six thousand dollars Kennedy had paid for their Beals Street home in Brookline, Massachusetts. By then he was also established in a white stucco Spanish-style winter home on North Ocean Boulevard in Palm Beach, Florida.

Two classes ahead of his brother, Joe went on to Choate, a prep school in Wallingford, Connecticut. For the first time the two boys were separated. At the age of thirteen, in the fall of 1930, Jack entered the Canterbury School in New Milford, also in Connecticut. Unlike Episcopalian Choate, Canterbury was a Catholic school, a unique experience in Jack's education that was short-lived. An emergency appendectomy in May of the following year forced him into a period of convalescence, terminating his enrollment.

The decision to send Jack to Canterbury, and afterward to Choate, illustrated the family differences over the prescribed education for the two oldest boys. No serious conflict occurred over having Joe enter Choate. That decision clearly corresponded with the senior Kennedy's desire to expose his oldest son to an upper-class Protestant environment. No doubt he would have preferred that route for Jack also but Rose's memoirs report that both parents were "advised that he [Jack] should have first a year away, at some other boarding school, so he could mature and become accustomed to boarding-school life. As I have said, I wanted each of them to have at least a while in a Catholic school, so it was decided he would go to the Canterbury school."[7] But if acclimating the younger, frailer boy to an experience away from home was indeed the main problem, Choate should have been more logical as a first choice.

Joe Junior was already there. The family presence had been established. But Rose's victory in a family conflict, which she chose to ignore in her memoirs, may have dictated that Jack first attend Canterbury. She also omits her husband's reason for selecting Choate over any of the several other comparable New England schools. That decision was strongly influenced by the presence on the staff of Choate of Mr. Kennedy's former Harvard classmate, Russell Ayres.[8]

There are few glimpses of Jack during his brief Canterbury stay. One fellow student was Robert Sargent Shriver, Jr. Shriver knew Jack in those days as a "very wiry, energetic, peppy youngster, who played football quite well, and despite the fact that he wasn't very heavy or physically large, did extremely well playing on the lightweight football team." Shriver then offered a common observation of young Kennedy during those years. "I can remember vividly," he said, "both seeing him myself and hearing others talk about how agile and quick and spunky and energetic he was, on the football field. And many people talked about it."[9]

Inwardly, however, Jack was less serene and less imbued with the vitality that he seemed to exude, not only to Shriver's eyes, but to virtually all who knew him. Was there an inverse relationship between his private feelings and the need to drive that much harder before the outer world? He had the normal concerns of the adolescent. He complained to his mother about being unable to gain weight. Despite his efforts, he had actually lost a pound. Nor had he grown at all. "I guess the only thing wrong with me," he wrote, "is that I am pretty tired." He added with some resignation, "I have also been doing a little worrying about my studies because what he [Dad] said about me starting of [sic] great and then going down sunk in. I will admit I did not work anymore than usual and I got pretty good marks. I am not doing as well in Latin having a [sic] average of about 60 so far and I don't want to flop. My marks may not be so high . . ."[10] He later also wrote to his father that during mass he "began to get sick dizzy [sic] and weak. I just about fainted and everything began to get black so I went out and then I fell and Mr. Hume caught me. I am O.K. now. Joe fainted twice in church so I guess I will live. The Latin has gone up about twelve points. My marks are approximately now as far as I can tell:

Math	93	
English	95	Average 78.50
History	80	
Science	78	These marks may be higher or lower
Latin	68	

"We are now reading Ivanhoe in English and though I may not be able to remember material things such as tickets, gloves and so on I can remember things like Ivanhoe and the last time we had an exam on it I got a ninety-eight.

"There goes the bell and that is not just a form of finish [sic] because it really did ring."[11]

From his own little insulated world at Canterbury, one year after Wall Street's notorious "Black Thursday," Jack wrote home requesting "the Litary [sic] Digest because I did not know about the Market Slump until a long time after, or a paper. Please send some golf balls."[12]

Even before Jack's arrival at Choate, Rose Kennedy tactfully advised the headmaster, Dr. George St. John, that the two boys were not at all alike. While carefully pointing out that Jack did have a personality regarded by many as "very attractive," she added that he was "quite different from Joe for whom we feel you have done so much."[13] Her advice was clear: Jack needed watching.

But first he had to pass the qualifying examinations. After being tutored during his recuperation, Jack took the three tests. He got by two of them, with grades of 75 and 83 in English III and Math IIIB, respectively, but failed his Latin I test by eight points.[14] So, along with the need to regain his health, Jack's summer had to include preparing for a makeup in the subject that plagued him. In Hyannis Port, Jack was aided by a local tutor, Bruce W. Belmore. Using a standard Latin textbook and with intensive drilling, Jack passed the qualifying exam on his second attempt.

Finally he arrived at Choate in the fall of 1931. Located just north of New Haven, in the Quinnipiac River village of Wallingford, a small and pleasant New England community, Choate had admitted only boys since its start in 1896. It appealed to those desiring their sons to have a classical education modeled after Eton. Overwhelmingly Protestant, it had already graduated two students who would later figure prominently in Jack's political career. Chester Bowles and, even more significantly, Adlai Stevenson. Like Kennedy, Stevenson was a marginal student, one who needed special tutoring in French. Unlike Kennedy, however, Stevenson had World War I to keep him from graduating from Choate before going on to Princeton, a college Jack would also sample. Choate had made immense gains since Stevenson's days, largely under the personal control of Dr. St. John.

Eager to bring to America the best of British public school education and convinced that Eton was the standard for the proper training of young lads, St. John had taken over in 1908 after the retirement of the original headmaster. Together with his wife, the former Clara Seymour —the strong, severe-looking sister of Yale's Wilsonian scholar, Charles Seymour—St. John secured personal financial and administrative control over the institution. The combination of a strong authoritarian personality and paternalism toward both students and faculty gave him almost feudal authority over the campus.[15]

The St. Johns acted as lord and mistress, with everybody very much under their personal domination. The human privileges enjoyed by the St. Johns were not easily granted to the staff. Since each teacher, or master, also had dormitory responsibilities as housemasters, they were expected to live with the boys. For seven days a week, with classes also on Saturdays, they were involved as teachers, housemasters, and coaches. That existence precluded the exercise of such personal liberties as marriage, a step that required St. John's personal approval. Two of Jack's masters were forced to wage a difficult battle to win the headmaster's consent to have wives. St. John, who lived in a house fronting on North Elm Street, just down the slope from the white-columned red-bricked complex known as Hill House, had not only a private residence but a family that included four children. His two sons were also very much a part of the Choate community. (The older, George Junior, known as Jim, taught Jack's senior-year history class; the other, Reverend Seymour St. John, succeeded his father as headmaster in 1947. A cousin, Wardell St. John, was assistant headmaster under George during Jack's years.) It was a rigidly run fiefdom that, even during those post–Great Crash years of national rebellion against the "money changers," offered a cloistered, highly conservative atmosphere. Both students and faculty were relatively untouched by what was happening in the rest of the world. Each boy had to attend chapel once a day, the few Catholics remaining silent at the recitation of the Psalms. On Sunday two services had to be attended. Jack and his brother went to mass in the local Catholic church "downtown."

Admitting Roman Catholics was about the outer extreme of Choate's liberalism. The yearbook, called *The Brief,* listed school favorites in various categories and included one for the "most conservative" without allowing for any other ideological possibility. Young Jack Kennedy was about as remote as possible from the New Deal idealism of most Americans. When Joseph Kennedy published a book called *I'm for Roosevelt* before the '36 election, St. John bluntly wrote to tell him that "there are large numbers here who feel the opposite way."[16] The 1929 application completed by Rose Kennedy included the question: "Is the boy any part Hebraic?"

Jack moved into the dormitory known as Choate House for his first year. Its master was Earl G. "Cappy" Leinbach, who later taught Jack algebra, coached the crew squad, and long remained a personal favorite. For that freshman stay, called the third form, his roommate was a boy named Godfrey Kauffmann, whose mother, as Mrs. St. John pointed out reassuringly in a letter to Rose, decorated the room with curtains to make it cozy. For his fourth form, he had a room for himself in East Cottage under the supervision of Eugene F. Musser, and experienced a relationship that was far less compatible than the one he managed with Cappy Leinbach.

Joe Junior's presence at Choate compounded Jack's adolescent problems. Jack's sensitivity and intelligence and awareness of how Joe Junior excelled at those very skills that brought parental approval, made the problem of sibling rivalry acute. It was a significant dilemma of Jack's adolescence, a period marked by youthful rebelliousness and aggravated by Joe Junior setting the pace and during those first two years at Choate, being his constant supervisor.

Joe's undoubted success and popularity were tough models. Far healthier and more physical, far less introspective, Joe was important on the prep school campus. He seemed to have everything. Not that he was an exceptional student; he was merely better than most. Still, St. John's comment to their father that "Joe is a growing source of strength in our school" was not hyperbole but a truth confirmed by those who remember him.[17] Forty-seven years later, Seymour St. John still considered him "the all-around combination. . . . one of the strong people in the school."[18] He was the "charmer," the "natural leader," the boy who won respect both in classes and on playing fields. A Choate contemporary remembered Joe as "a very humane, amiable fellow, and quite attractive, more an attractive personality than Jack had while in school."[19] He became editor of *The Brief* and excelled at all sports. But it was on the football field that a Choate boy could most easily gain distinction, and Joe did just that. In his final year he was awarded the Harvard Trophy, a small bronze trophy that contained the name of each sixth-former who best combined scholarship and sportsmanship. It was presented on behalf of the Harvard football team in 1931 in appreciation of their traditional overnight stay at Choate before the big game with Yale.

About the only distinction shared by the brothers was being called "Rat Face," a reference seemingly more appropriate to describe Jack's features than Joe's. Among the Choate boys, the term was somewhat affectionate and Jack himself habitually bestowed such labels as gestures of friendship.

At no point was Jack a good student. He had taken an Otis Intelligence Test at Hyannis Port in the spring of 1930 and had scored 119,[20] indicating an above-average but far from spectacular intelligence. Even granting its accuracy, Jack demonstrated little motivation to perform at that level. His teachers recalled his willingness to settle for the minimum passing grade.[21] His mother noted that the "more pressure that was put on Jack, the more he seemed to find ways to frustrate and annoy those in charge."[22] His scholastic record was not much more successful than had been foreshadowed by his initial difficulties.

Foreign languages remained a severe obstacle. Perhaps because of an unfortunate relationship with his Latin teacher at Canterbury, he never did master the subject. His record shows a mere 62 for his first year of

Latin; the next year, one devoted to Caesar's *Commentaries* under the instruction of Owen Morgan, resulted in just a seven-point improvement. Fortunately for Jack, that ended his struggle with the language. But he went on to take French during each of his four years, ending up with a cumulative average of just under 67. The remainder of his scholastic record was not much better. Not even in English, supposedly one of his better subjects, did he excel. In mathematics he averaged only 69.67. In physics he earned 77. During the 1933–1934 school year, he received instruction in ancient history by his father's former classmate, Russell R. Ayres, and ended up with 75. During his sixth form, the final one at Choate, he took English history under Jim St. John and managed a 74. His final scholastic rank, contrary to published accounts, placed him sixty-fifth in a class of 110.[23]

Such records can be deceptive, however, showing the adolescent's inadequate motivations rather than his intellect. Harold L. Tinker, Jack's fifth-form English teacher, gave him a low mark for that year; nevertheless, Tinker thought enough of his essays to suggest that he had a "very definite flair for writing" and advised a literary career.[24] His Latin teacher remembered Jack's relentless inquiry into the structure of a series of sentences placed on the blackboard; he repeatedly made the same inquiries of each one until finally satisfying himself that he had the answer.[25] LeMoyne Billings, Jack's roommate during his last two years, remembers that Jack was the only "kid who subscribed to *The New York Times* at fourteen, fifteen, and read it every morning."[26] He went through the paper "from cover to cover."[27] Accounts of political and international affairs caught his special attention and at one point they swayed him toward considering a diplomatic career. He thought carefully about each article, analyzing them and then producing a clear mental picture of what he had learned. The self-imposed discipline became instrumental toward developing what became a keen ability to digest the printed word. Schoolmates aware of his mediocre academic standing were surprised by his ability to recall information about a wide range of items, from sports to the opera. When listening to *Information Please,* a popular radio program that purported to measure encyclopedic knowledge, Jack could supply the correct responses to most of the questions. One of the masters who knew Jack best insisted that his academic work was below his true ability. Most of all, as even Headmaster St. John so readily confirmed, Jack was clever and gifted with the ability for satirizing mundane situations and exploiting them for laughs.

Jack's activities included the school's yearbook. During his final form, he became its business manager, not letting his usual sloppiness keep him from doing a decent job with its accounts. Most of all, however, he drove himself at sports, expending the energy that all the concerned adults thought should also have been applied to academic excellence. He was especially eager to prove himself in football, the area of his brother's greatest fame. "The most burning thing I can remember about Jack was that he was a fighter," his coach later recalled. "You take Joe, he was a real athlete. But Jack made up for what he lacked in athletic ability with his fight."[28] It was not so much that he lacked natural athletic abilities, for, in some ways, he showed a fine sense of coordination. The first time he picked up a golf club, for example, he showed an easy grace and form. His problem, especially for a sport like football, was his physique and health. Nevertheless, he fought; teammates thought him a "tiger" on the line. During intramural football in 1932, Jack played end, which he preferred to the backfield. His best, though, was only good enough for the junior squad. Cappy Leinbach reported that as a tackle on the junior first team in 1933, he was "aggressive, alert and interested. Jack was a tower of strength on the line," compensating for his lack of brawn with determination.[29] He also went out for intramural baseball and basketball, as well as crew and golf. Unfortunately, Choate, unlike Canterbury, did not have a pool, and so Jack's transfer cost him an opportunity to excel where his ability was greatest.

Jack's outstanding talent, and the area of his greatest success at Choate, was in making friends. "With Jack," said Seymour St. John, "nobody really admired what he did nor respected what he did, but they liked his personality. When he flashed his smile, he could charm a bird off a tree."[30] Billings, whom he met while working on *The Brief,* was a doctor's son from Pittsburgh. Tall and personable and always ready to join in Jack's zest for fun, Billings became one of his closest friends, their relationship surviving the White House years. Lem also became a familiar figure around the Kennedy homes at Hyannis Port and Palm Beach. "I think our sense of humors must have jibed," Billings told an interviewer. "We had a hell of a good time together and I think that's what makes two people like each other."[31] Possibly also helping to seal their relationship was Billings's similar position as a second son. Like Jack, his brother had also gone to Choate; and Frederic Billings, Jr., known as Josh, also had been a luminary on campus. Having moved on to Princeton, he had left behind a difficult record for Lem to match: editor-in-chief of *The Brief,* class president, letters in football and crew.[32]

Ralph Horton, "Rip," was another close pal. Horton's family was important in New York City's dairy industry: they owned one of the major firms, Sheffield Farms. Like Billings, Rip qualified as one of Jack's intimates by being out for a good time. Their encouragement helped young Kennedy achieve his outstanding "success" at the school, "leadership in jokes."[33]

After Joe Junior graduated, Jack was on his own. With his friends he began to disrupt the staid campus, testing their ability to break as many rules as possible: curfews, orderly rooms, attendance at chapel, respect for campus authorities. The more Choate tried to enforce its regulations, the more unruly Jack, Rip, and Lem became.

Jack's circumstances made him a special problem. Even at the elite prep school, his position was unique. Not only had his father achieved an important rank in Washington as director of the Securities and Exchange Commission, but he was already known for his wealth and power. Whenever he could, and sometimes when he could not, Jack signed out to go elsewhere, to New York City, to date a local girl named Olive Cawley or just to have some night life in the big city with Rip and Lem; or to the Cape, Boston, or Miami. There were times when his parents contributed to absences by making special requests to have him elsewhere. Before they left for Europe in the company of James Roosevelt for the 1933 trip (on which Joseph Kennedy secured key liquor importation franchises), Rose called to excuse Jack for the first five weeks of the new term. That would enable him to accompany them as they met the "important people of Europe," including Mussolini. As impressed as the school authorities may have been, they were not convinced Jack should leave. Their remonstrance was tactful, avoiding any temptation to apply direct persuasion, but they gently pointed out how harmful it would be for Jack to miss the first weeks of two new subjects, geometry and ancient history. By remaining in school he might even have "some prospects in football, if he continues to add weight." Choate finally won and Jack's schooling was not interrupted.

By 1934 Jack's defiance had acquired the character of an open rebellion. His departure for Palm Beach to spend the Christmas vacation of 1934 was under strict disciplinary supervision imposed by Headmaster St. John, who notified Mr. Kennedy that "I know how thoroughly you agree with me that Jack just ought not to be allowed any leeway whatever."[34] With his friends, principally Rip and Lem, he had formed what they called the "Muckers Club." St. John had used that name often, both when speaking to the faculty and when addressing the students during chapel sermons, to deride those whose behavior disgraced Choate's honorable traditions by scoffing at the rules and acting independently. "It was more of an anti-establishment thing," Horton later said. "Rough-housing. Sneaking out at night to get a milkshake. Maybe we didn't like to be structured."[35] Undoubtedly, the boys had fun with the word *muckers* itself, pricking St. John's stuffiness and mimicking him by its similarity to an Anglo-Saxon word the headmaster would hardly have tolerated. To enhance their comraderie each Mucker obtained a special badge of membership, a small gold charm shaped like a shovel with its owner's initials inscribed together with the letters CMC, for Choate Muckers Club. With Kennedy the ringleader, the West Wing room he shared with Lem became their meeting place. There they were, a coterie of dissidents, defying, mocking, scorning regulations, for no better reason than that they were meant to be obeyed.

In chapel St. John lectured the student body about their sins. As Rip Horton later recalled, the headmaster "let loose at the Muckers Club, the thirteen of us. He named the members, he named the club. We were the bad apples. We were corrupting the morals and integrity of the other students in the school. He made us feel very important."[36]

That blowup came during the winter of Jack's senior year, only a few months before graduation. St. John had clearly become exasperated at the latest outrage and proceeded to suspend the boys and summon their parents. Mrs. Billings, a widow, dutifully traveled from Pittsburgh to Wallingford. When she arrived and listened to the headmaster's description of the wayward boys' crimes, she understandably concluded that it had been "much ado about very little."[37] Jack's father was also summoned to the scene of the "uprising," directly from Washington and the headquarters of the SEC. He, too, like the other family heads responsible for the delinquent juveniles, rushed to the shores of the Quinnipiac.[38]

St. John's concern of course lay with the institution's responsibility for turning out proper youngsters for the Ivy League colleges. Also he reacted to the Muckers Club after a series of deliberate "provocations."[39]

In the case of Jack's father, George St. John was dealing with a parent who had more than the usual power and standing. Joseph Kennedy, Sr., was also more closely involved with what was gong on than were most "busy" fathers. Two of his sons had been connected with the school, and no institution ever touched by a Kennedy could escape the dual forces of their assistance and involvement. And that went beyond giving money and keeping in touch with events.

Years earlier St. John had written to Kennedy about the breakdown of the school's fifteen-year-old Powers Cameograph #6 film projector. It had failed during a Saturday movie, disappointing the boys terribly. Once it had to be replaced, the headmaster suggested the school should consider buying equipment to show sound films. "I suppose," he wrote, "it is about time we became more modern anyhow."[40] Kennedy, the film magnate with a chain of New England theaters then operating mainly out of the offices of Pathé Exchange, Inc., proved the ideal man to turn to. Kennedy arranged for St. John to finance half of the cost through him. He paid the rest, and Choate got its sound picture equipment: two DeForest Simplex projectors, speakers, a screen, and the necessary wiring, were installed in the speech room under the chapel. The gala premier was the movie version of Rudolf Friml's *The Vagabond King*. "If you could have been here to sense the enthusiasm last night," St. John wrote Kennedy, "it would have been some return for your great generosity to these five hundred boys. The picture and sound were both perfect."

But as far as Jack was concerned, his father's real interest involved constant pressure to raise his academic standing. Long before being summoned to the school during the Muckers Club episode, Kennedy had intervened. Much agitated by Jack's grades, he pressured St. John for a closer evaluation of the boy from each of the masters, including, in particular, the house master responsible for Jack during his junior year, John J. Maher, who was strict with Jack and not his favorite. After showing the reports to Jack, St. John sent the following appraisal to Joseph Kennedy:

. . . The fact of the matter is that I cannot feel seriously uneasy or worried about Jack. The longer I live and work with him and the more I talk with him, the more confidence I have in him. I would be willing to bet anything that within two years you will be as proud of Jack as you are of Joe.

Jack has a clever, individualist mind. It is a harder mind to put in harness than Joe's—harder for Jack himself to put in harness. When he learns the right place for humor and learns to use his individual way of looking at things as an asset instead of a handicap, his natural gift of an individual outlook and witty expression are going to help him. A more conventional mind and a more plodding and mature point of view would help him a lot more right now; but we have to allow, my dear Mr. Kennedy, with boys like Jack, for a period of adjustment. All that natural cleverness Jack has to learn how to use in his life work, even how to cover it up at times, how to subordinate it and all the rest. I never yet saw a clever, witty boy who at some stage in his early development

was not considered fresh. It is only because he hasn't learned how to use
his natural gift. We must allow for a period of adjustment and growing
up; and the final product is often more interesting and more effective
than the boy with a more conventional mind who has been to us parents
and teachers much less trouble.[41]

In reacting to the Muckers Club affair, St. John abandoned the pose
of the tolerant, sympathetic paternal educator. Confronted with what he
regarded as a challenge to his authority, he later reported having told
himself: "Well, I have two things to do, one to run the school, another
to run Jack Kennedy and his friends."[42] That led to their "three-cornered
talk," which took place in St. John's study in February of 1935. Both
adults enumerated all the manifestations of his misconduct, most of
which, as the headmaster later admitted, "were just peccadillos." The
older Kennedy nevertheless confronted Jack with strictures about self-
reform. "Jack's father didn't hold back," wrote St. John. "In fact, he
spoke very, very strongly, and also with some Irish wit. You know, in
dealing with Jack, you need a little wit as well as a little seriousness. Jack
didn't like to be too serious; he had a delightful sense of humor, always.
His smile was, I think, as a young boy, when he first came to the school
— Well, in any school he would have got away with some things, just
on his smile. He was a very likeable person, very lovable."[43] Inevitably,
that conference must have included many a sermon about the disgraceful
condition of his room. Apparently, too, it marked the only visit to the
school by either of Jack's parents.

Jack had wanted to return to Cappy Leinbach's house although the
headmaster's normal policy mandated changing houses and masters each
year, regardless of their compatibility. Having spent his junior year at
West Wing under John Maher, the boy was due for a move. But Mr.
Kennedy again intervened, insisting that Jack remain right where he
was, with Maher. Maher, also the head football coach, could be expected
to provide the strong discipline that Joseph Kennedy felt his son needed.
He was also an Irish Catholic. St. John capitulated, and Jack remained.
But not even Maher, tough as he was, had an easy time of it. Jack
frustrated him, using ingenuity and cleverness to defy the master's authority. "Once in a while he'd get him a little way along," remembered
Seymour St. John. "He'd feel he was succeeding. And then it would fall
apart again."[44] In early December, having been admonished by his father
for his poor performance, Jack replied that he and LeMoyne had discussed the situation and had "definitely decided to stop any fooling
around. I really do realize how important it is that I get a good job done

this year if I want to go to England."[45] Therefore, the Muckers Club affair took place not only despite the paternally imposed continued residence in West Wing, which had been designed to keep the boy in line, but almost at the very time Jack had resolved to reform himself.

Jack's reference to England showed his eagerness to follow his brother. After graduating, Joe Junior enrolled in the London School of Economics, largely at the suggestion of Felix Frankfurter. The future Supreme Court justice, then still with the Harvard Law School, was a good friend of Professor Harold Laski. A Marxist of Jewish birth, Laski had returned to London after being compelled to give up a Harvard instructorship because he had defied the hysteria of the day and supported the Boston police strike of 1919. Frankfurter had the highest praise for Laski. He advised Joseph Kennedy to give his sons the opportunity to study under the man he considered the "greatest teacher in the world; the most stimulating teacher in the world."[46]

The idea of placing Joe and Jack under the influence of a socialist scholar contradicted all of their father's values. Few had exploited capitalistic opportunities as successfully; few were as single-minded about the accumulation of still more money. Roosevelt had placed Kennedy at the head of the newly established Securities and Exchange Commission to assuage the bitter Wall Street rebellion that helped lead to the formation of the American Liberty League. Laski's view of the world and its economic relationships embodied the very concepts most abhorrent to Kennedy. Perhaps for that very reason, perhaps through a shrewd appraisal of the sort of exposure his sons would need to advance in the modern world, Joe Kennedy agreed with Frankfurter. His reasoning recalled his insistence that they not be raised in Catholic schools. So Joe went off to London before entering Harvard.

Jack's liberation after his brother left Choate was tempered by poor health. Strenuous activities were out. In evaluating Jack for his Harvard application, St. John noted the following:

"Part of Jack's lack of intellectual drive is doubtless due to a severe illness suffered in the winter of his Fifth Form year. Though he has recovered, his vitality has been below par, he has not been allowed to enter into any vigorous athletics, and has not, probably, been able to work under full pressure. There is no reason to suppose, however, that Jack will not come up to par soon."[47]

Jack's health was a serious liability during his Choate years. From his very first year, there were frequent visits to the infirmary, both for medication and for overnight stays. Colds in particular plagued him his first winter. Clara St. John informed Rose Kennedy that "Jack is in a body building class." Having so notified Mrs. Kennedy, Mrs. St. John promptly sent an interoffice directive advising that "if Jack Kennedy is not in the body building class will you see he is put there right away. His mother is troubled about him."[48] When he was confined in January, Clara St. John informed Rose Kennedy about Jack's disposition and added that the headmaster would be pleased to discover that he had gone there with all his schoolbooks. She marveled at how "picturesque" he looked in his lavender bathrobe and green and lavender pajamas.[49] Rose replied that she had consulted with her own nurse about Jack and recalled that he had had a similar condition about three years earlier. "He had had mumps and the doctor thought it was a cold which settled there."[50] His latest stay in the infirmary lasted nearly a week. He returned in April for five more days, again suffering "noninfectious parotitis," an inflammation of the salivary gland.

That following winter, Jack had knee trouble. The discomfort was considerable. The Choate infirmary dispatched him to nearby New Haven, where he was seen by Dr. Winthrop Phelps, an orthopedic surgeon who cared for Yale athletes. Dr. Phelps attributed the condition to weak muscles and especially severe growing problems. His solution: a prescribed regimen of daily exercises in the Choate infirmary. But Rose knew better. Continuing to monitor the situation from afar, she informed George St. John that Jack "has always been troubled with his arches." The condition seemed to run in the family.[51] Rebuilt shoes with supports alleviated the distress.

During the second half of his fifth form he returned from his usual Christmas holiday vacation at Palm Beach looking pale. Thin and frail as he was, the pallor of his skin added to the portrait of a physically distressed sixteen-year-old. By Sunday, February 4, 1934, Jack's body was covered with hives and he was removed to the New Haven Hospital, where he was visited by a family representative, Mr. Kennedy's secretary, Edward Moore. His father's emissary told the boy how pleased the doctors were to have the trouble come to the surface instead of staying inside. Jack replied, "Gee! The doctors must be having a happy day today!" Another visitor was Mrs. St. John. Jack told her that "if this had happened fifty years ago, they would just say, 'Well, the boy has had a case of hives, but now he's all over it,' and that would be all there was to it; but now, they've got to take my blood count every little while, and keep me here until that corresponds to what the doctors think it ought to be."[52] At the end of February, with the hives cleared up but with the boy still weak and obviously ill, he was discharged from the hospital to join his parents in Florida. Meanwhile, his masters were notified not to expect him back for the rest of the term. His schooling would be in the care of tutors.

A careful monitoring of his blood count followed. During the early part of the summer, with a diagnosis yet to be made, Jack went to the Mayo Clinic in Rochester, Minnesota, the first of many such trips. But even a month at that well-known facility failed to shed much light.[53] The next fall he returned to Choate for his sixth form, carefully supervised, prohibited from rigorous athletics, and with his blood count still scrutinized through periodic trips back to New Haven Hospital. The readings were normal.

Despite poor health and disciplinary difficulties, Choate served him well. Never before had he experienced the freedom of those last two years, the conviviality of friends in an atmosphere that was embroidered with such a tone of cultivation. Most of all he learned the art of exploiting adversity, of turning disadvantages into advantages. He also learned that he could charm as well as exasperate and, both for his personal qualities and family standing, could attract loyalty from others. Not only had he made such lifelong friends as Billings, but he had used his personal appeal to good advantage. Many were confounded that his mediocre academic and athletic limitations, certainly in comparison with his brother, had nonetheless not kept the class of '35 from honoring him as "most likely to succeed."

He had indeed earned it. As a final joke he had helped to manipulate the election so that an adroit trade-off of votes gave him that distinction.[54] Checking later, Seymour St. John found strong circumstantial evidence that the vote had been rigged. Making a study of thirty class yearbooks, with his knowledge of the students and classes involved, St. John determined that vote totals for "Most To Be Admired" were, year after year, almost identical with those for "Most Likely to Succeed." In Kennedy's year, he was the only one listed as "Most Likely to Succeed" who got no votes in the other category.[55]

Not least of all, Jack Kennedy had learned the art of making friends, attracting loyal followers, and of using them for his purposes. "I can remember the problem child he was at Choate," Joseph P. Kennedy reminded George St. John after learning about Jack's South Pacific adventures, "and it just goes to prove that just so long as a boy is basically right, no matter how many pranks he is identified with, he'll deliver, and that's what Jack did."[56]

4

A Harvard Man

When Jack Kennedy arrived at Cape Cod to spend the summer after graduation he had yet to decide what college to go to. He wanted to follow Joe Junior to the London School of Economics so that he, too, could study under Professor Laski. Nevertheless, he also applied to Princeton. He inclined toward Harvard, however, completing the preliminary examinations. George St. John had sent his principal's report at the end of April, followed a few days later by Jack's own application with references that listed New Deal administrator Harry Hopkins, and publisher and journalist Herbert Bayard Swope. Jack's College Board entrance tests of June 1933 and his Scholastic Aptitude Tests had each averaged a mediocre 69. Nor did any other achievements embellish his academic record.

At the end of August Jack asked to have the college defer his admission until the following year, explaining that his "father has decided that a year abroad, studying at the London School of Economics, a branch of the University of London would be beneficial to me and to my college career."[1]

At the same time, while all such preparations were being made, the monitoring of his blood count continued. Relapses were constant. Sometime during the early part of that summer, Jack again succumbed to what George St. John called "that rotten bug."[2] As always, his struggle against ill health was marked by a determination to avoid self-pity and an effort to counter reality with self-denigrating humor.

Despite his illness, Jack traveled to Europe in late September, along with his parents and fifteen-year-old sister Kathleen, to begin the year of study with Laski. Much was later made of exposure to the famous teacher, which enhanced the impression of Jack's distinguished academic credentials. What he got from Laski during that stay, however, was very little, if anything—again his health interfering. The recurrent blood condition, described as "jaundice," forced an abrupt withdrawal only a month after registering. He returned to America in November.

Back from London, the Kennedys again used their personal resources to help Jack. Despite his physical condition and prior application and acceptance at Harvard, he decided to enter Princeton. Later, when explaining that decision to Harvard, he attributed the move "to the proximity [of Princeton] to New York where the doctors who were treating my illness could be located."[3] Jack also chose Princeton to avoid further competition with brother Joe as he said later when contemplating a law school.[4] But more importantly he wanted to be with old friends, for both Lem and Rip had already started at Princeton.

Bending to Jack's desire, his father used a contact to overcome the barriers to late admission. Lacking personal leverage with Princeton, Joe Kennedy turned to one with influence, Herbert Bayard Swope. The newspaperman talked Princeton's Dean Christian Gauss into some "enlightened" flexibility. In mid-October, Jack's father received Swope's wire that Gauss had waived the rule prohibiting such late admissions "in response to picture I painted young Galahad [sic] . . . Hurrah new tiger."[5] Jack rejoined Lem Billings and Rip Horton in South Reunion, an inelegant old dormitory with a basement toilet, more suitable for Lem's modest pocketbook. While there, his blood problems continued. Joe Kennedy consulted with doctors and followed suggestions offered by Dr. William P. Murphy, who was connected with the Peter Bent Brigham Hospital in Boston. Attempting to avoid the loss of the college year, Jack's stay at Princeton became somewhat of a trial. "A year is important," Joe Kennedy wrote to his son, "but it isn't so important if it's going to leave a mark for the rest of your life."[6]

Somehow, Jack did manage to take the second uniform examinations. Under far from optimum circumstances, he passed four but failed the fifth, trigonometry. By early December, however, his health simply did

not permit continuing. Once having lost the year and fallen out of step
with his friends, that college had no further appeal.[7]

Under Dr. Murphy's care, he entered the hospital in Boston. Instead
of being able to salvage what remained of the collegiate year, Jack was
confined for more than two months. Curiously, Rose Kennedy's memoir
sidesteps Jack's hospitalization, gliding over it, in fact, as though it never
happened. Her account simply states that "Jack left Princeton a few
weeks after Thanksgiving," and then reports his going out West to
recuperate. "Most of the rest of that school year of 1935–1936," it adds,
"he spent in Arizona, since the sunny and dry climate there was said to
be good for health and especially good for asthma, because he had that
also."[8] Jack and his father exchanged letters while he was at Peter Bent
Brigham Hospital. Their correspondence does not mention treatment or
diagnosis, if one was made. Two months later Jack left for Arizona.[9]

A logical remedy for allergies and relief for asthma, Jack's southwestern sojourn most likely had no connection with professional medical
advice. Arthur Krock appears to have suggested the salutary benefits of
some good outdoor physical work as a rancher at a place owned by one
of his acquaintances. Located southeast of Tucson, not far from the
Mexican border, it kept Jack busy with outdoor labor and provided a
rugged experience.[10]

Jack returned East by July and immediately renewed efforts to enter
Harvard. A checkup by Dr. Murphy cleared the way. Already one year
behind, his request for admission contained some desperation.[11] Joe
Kennedy supported his son's appeal with an attempt to volunteer that
his son was prepared to accelerate his work. "Jack has a very brilliant
mind for the things in which he is interested. This is, of course, a bad
fault. However, he is quite ambitious to try and do the work in three
years," wrote the father.[12]

Jack Kennedy arrived at Harvard in the fall of 1936, a lank, bony,
six-foot-tall youth who looked even lighter than his 149 pounds.[13] His
presence on campus became notable mainly for his relationship to Joe
Junior. The older brother had already become a star of the class of '38,
succeeding in all the usual facets of campus prominence: academics,
athletics, student government. At the end of his sophomore year, just
before Jack came, he had been chosen for membership on the council. By
contrast, Jack's impact was meager. Having failed to qualify for the runoff
elections among twenty-nine candidates vying for the freshman class
presidency, he withdrew from campus politics.[14] Nor did he involve

himself with such groups as the Harvard Liberal Union or the Young Democrats. Thus he remained aloof—at least in those early days—from the local ferment about the ominous overseas events of the mid-1930's. He did, however, join the St. Paul's Catholic Club and was a regular member. Socially, he failed to make the most elite of the clubs, the Porcellian. Finally, in somewhat of a coup for a Roman Catholic at Harvard, he was admitted to the Hasty Pudding Institute of 1776, a "waiting" club, before advancing in the social hierarchy by being "punched" for the Spee Club, an upper-echelon "final" fraternity that ranked among the campus's more esteemed, highly stratified eating clubs.

Most of all, again forced into a competitive relationship with Joe Junior, Jack created his own identity and operated in his own little world. Of course, Joe was two years ahead and enjoying his own life. But they kept respectable brotherly rapport and maintained mutual admiration and loyalty, even while Joe continued his paternal attitude toward the younger man.[15] Having drawn Room 32 in Weldon Hall for his freshman year, as a sophomore Jack chose to move to Winthrop House, the residence of not only Joe Junior but the leading campus athletes. Payson Wild, who was master of Winthrop in the fall of 1937, remembered Jack sitting on a sofa in his office, his hair tousled, and saying, "Dr. Wild, I want you to know I'm not bright like my brother Joe." He was very much under the older Kennedy's spell.[16]

Not unfairly, Jack's first two Harvard years have been described as a virtual replay of his Choate career.[17] And again, comparisons with the older brother were inevitable. The brawnier, athletic Joe Junior distinguished himself and, of the two, was the better bet for future success. Jack remained more introspective, giving the aura of a philosopher, dreamer, and idealist, not as one prepared for worldly enterprises. One friend found Jack "attractive, witty, and unpurposeful," while Joe was better "pointed to where he was going."[18] Jack's goals were more personal, less concerned with outdoing others, which helped make him less combative and mellowed his charm. "Joe had a sense of humor," recalled a contemporary, "but it was a biting sense of humor, whereas Jack had . . . a very real sense of humor. I always felt in Joe's presence that he was very competitive in a bitter way, always with a bit of a chip on his shoulder, whereas Jack was competitive but in a pleasant way."[19] A note appended to his sophomore-year housing application stated that Jack Kennedy was "one of the most popular men in his class."[20] A later roommate reported never seeing him "standing still. I never saw him studying. I know he got good marks, but I don't know where he studied. It sure wasn't in our place."[21] To his contemporaries, he did not seem

1. Rose Fitzgerald Kennedy as a young mother with her first three children: Baby Rosemary, Jack, and Joe Junior.

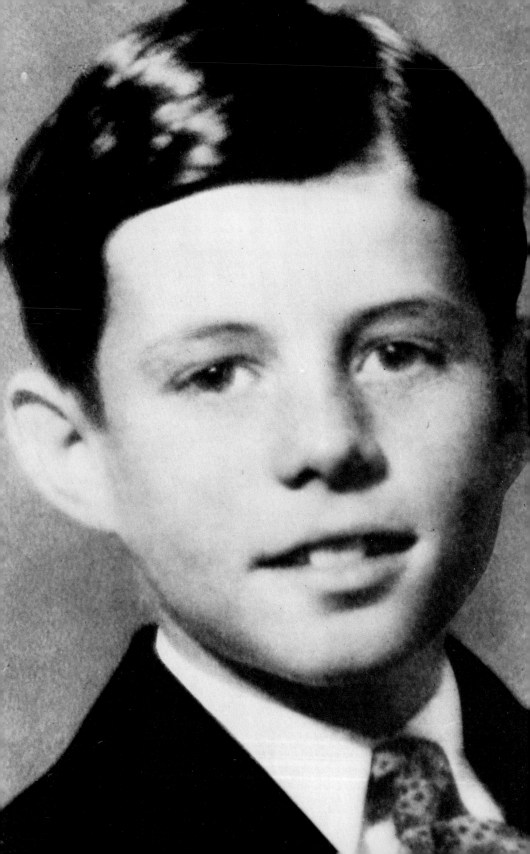

2. *Facing page:* Jack Kennedy as a Dexter Academy student, before the family's move to Riverdale, New York, in 1926.

3, 4. *Left and below:* A freckled Rosemary, the Kennedys' third child, September 1931, and again with her grandfather "Honey Fitz" on the occasion of his sixty-ninth birthday.

5. *Right:* Big brother Joseph Kennedy, Jr., star collegiate athlete.

6. *Below:* Jack with LeMoyne Billings during their 1937 European trip. In Rome, Jack wrote in his diary: "Very beautiful girls, although our not speaking Italian was a temporary damper. Billings knew some Italian parlor tricks that were worth remembering and we went to bed tired but happy!"

7. *Facing page:* Ambassador Joseph P. Kennedy hosts a party at the London Embassy, June 5, 1939. Jack, to his left, is about to embark on a grand tour of the continent in the midst of Europe's preparations for war.

8. On the '39 tour of Europe.

9. *Above:* Joe Junior vacationing at St. Moritz in neutral Switzerland a few months after the outbreak of World War II.

10. *Right:* Joe Junior holding out against FDR's third nomination as a delegate to the Democrats' 1940 presidential convention, even after his state had closed ranks behind the President.

11. *Below:* At the controls of his bomber. Joe had completed fifty missions when he volunteered for the fateful attempt to destroy Nazi rocket-launching sites.

12, 13. *Facing page:* Lovely Inga Arvad, an enterprising Danish stringer who landed a newspaper job with her exclusive interview of Hermann Goering, whose wedding she also later attended and whose best man—Adolf Hitler—invited her to the 1936 Olympic games as his personal guest. Five years later in Charleston, South Carolina, FBI surveillance recorded her romantic encounters at the Fort Sumter Hotel with a young naval intelligence officer, Ensign John F. Kennedy. Later she would marry cowboy film star Tim McCoy, thirty years her senior. March 1936 *(top)*, and 1941 *(bottom)*.

14. Lt. Kennedy and two of his wartime friends, Paul "Red" Fay *(l)* and Lenny Thom *(r)*, a member of Jack's *PT 109* crew.

15. *Facing page:* Kathleen "Kick"
Kennedy roughhousing with brother Jack,
her favorite sibling. Both resisted the
family's marital and other ambitions,
unlike the other children.

16. *Above (left to right):* Rosemary,
Teddy (about seven years of age), Rose,
Bobby *(standing)*, Eunice, and Jack.

17. *Right:* Kick wearing her Red Cross
uniform in wartime London. "She was
the best thing the Americans ever sent,"
said one nobleman about the enormously
popular Kathleen.

18. *Facing page:* Joe escorting Kathleen to the Chelsea Register Office in London just prior to his sister's wedding, May 6, 1944.

19. *Below:* Billy and Kathleen moments after their wedding, flanked by the Duchess of Devonshire and Joe. The groom, the Marquess of Hartington, is in the uniform of the Coldstream Guards. His bride's brother wears the uniform of an Army Air Force lieutenant. He will die in four months' time over the English Channel, and Billy Hartington will be killed in action less than a month later.

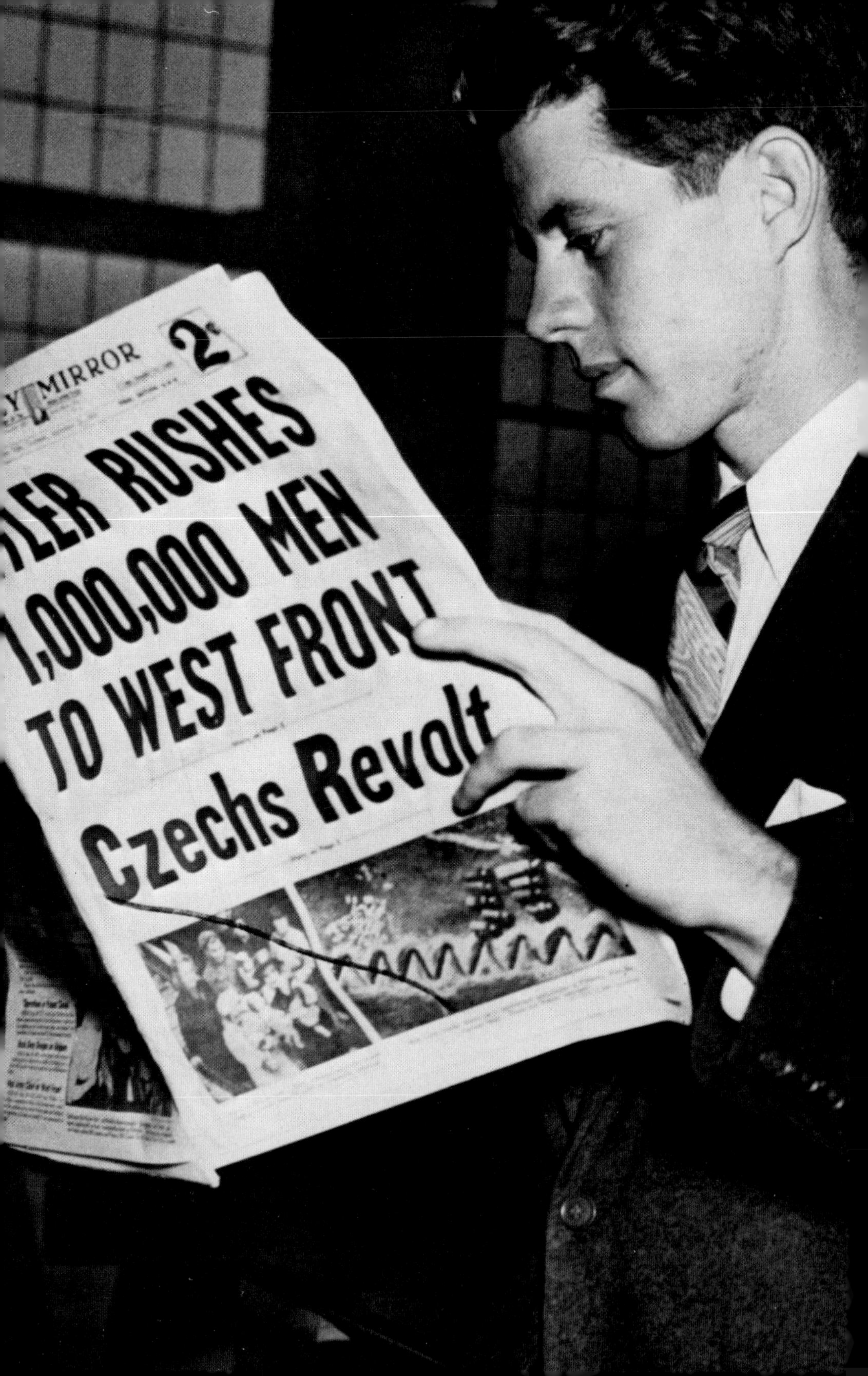
MIRROR
2¢
RUSHES
1,000,000 MEN
TO WEST FRONT
Czechs Revolt

20. *Facing page:* Jack in early September of 1944 following back surgery to correct the wartime injury he had sustained in the South Pacific. The second son is now the oldest male child. At a family gathering in the fall of the following year his grandfather Honey Fitz would toast Jack with all seriousness as "a future President of the United States."

21. *Right:* Jack Kennedy leading the St. Patrick's Day parade through South Boston in March 1946, a few weeks before declaring his candidacy for the congressional seat vacated by James Curley.

22. *Below:* Jack, accompanied by Grandmother and Grandfather Fitzgerald, voting in the 1946 Massachusetts primary, which gave him the Democratic nomination for a seat in the House of Representatives.

23. The Kennedy clan gathers at Hyannis Port in 1946. *Left to right:* Jack, Jean, Rose, Joe, Pat, Bobby, Eunice, and Teddy *(kneeling).*

destined to fulfill a specific role and led some to regard him as a mere "playboy."[22] As at Choate, establishing his own coterie and being eager to excel on the football field were the main drives of this young man battling his natural liabilities.

At Harvard also, Jack's football reputation rested on spunk. He worked to gain weight, feasting on a prescribed diet that included red meat and red wine, together with potatoes, ice cream, and milk.[23] The special diet also involved raw cream. Fortunately, the Spee Club, where he spent much of his time, bought a machine to make ice cream because, as one of his friends remembers, he ate it "like it was going out of style."[24] But all the stuffing helped little. Only perseverance could minimize his problems. "It was a matter of determination," recalled Torbert Macdonald. "After practice was over, he'd have me throw the ball for him and he'd practice snagging passes for an hour at a time, hundreds of passes. . . . Once he makes up his mind to do something, he does it, and nothing is going to stand in his way."[25] Coach Henry Lamar agreed that Jack "played for keeps," that he did "nothing half way." Harvard's *Freshman Red Book* listed Jack as the most adept pass receiver. Lacking prominence in Harvard's freshman football that season, in which the team won none and managed only a tie against Worcester Academy, Jack nevertheless was awarded a major letter *H.* Still, even with his ability as a receiver and for all his fight, he failed to make the first team. Too light for the line and not speedy enough for the backfield, he had to settle for the junior varsity.

The most significant event of his collegiate football career resulted from his JV work that sophomore year, when he had a football injury with long-range consequences. An early biographer of the Kennedy family, journalist Joe McCarthy, was very explicit. According to his version, Jack scrimmaged in practice against the much heavier varsity squad and was thrown to the ground. Landing at a bad angle, he ruptured a spinal disc. Much more recently, Rose Kennedy, whose account otherwise minimizes or even ignores Jack's more desperate moments, essentially duplicated the McCarthy version, which came from family sources.[26] Rose noted that the injury ended his football career. Much more significant was the damage to his general physical condition that later involved additional complications.*

While his back became a permanent memento of Harvard days, so did

*The interview comments of Torbert Macdonald about the nature of Kennedy's back injury, as quoted by Joan and Clay Blair, Jr., in *The Search for JFK,* p. 50, unwittingly repeat deliberate distortions given to the researchers by Kennedy's friend. Cf., Eleanore Carney to Author, Feb. 15, 1978.

Jack's relationship with Torbert Macdonald. A handsome, natural athlete from Malden, Massachusetts, Macdonald came from a family of schoolteachers. Equally adept at studies as on the gridiron, track, baseball diamond, or hockey rink, Macdonald's modest background did not keep him from the educational opportunities offered by Andover Academy. Too proud to accept scholarships, the family sent him to the prep school and later to Harvard with the assistance of his grandparents, who sold a parcel of property to make it all possible.

In some ways, Torby was Harvard's counterpart of Lem Billings. Just eight days younger than Jack, he, too, was a second son. But, more relevant for Jack, Torby was also the junior sibling in an Irish Catholic family, which, like the Kennedys, venerated the first-born male and looked toward him for leadership. Jack Macdonald, Jr., just like Joe Junior, was the "star" of the family. The older Macdonald boy, however, died at the age of fourteen; and not until then did Torby become, as his daughter now puts it, "himself." Having had to fight to win recognition from his family, and endowed with intelligence as well as the physical strength that eluded Jack, Torby Macdonald had little trouble understanding his friend's personal battle.[27]

Other qualities drew them together. They shared a passion for independence and were equally irreverent about pretense and pomposity. Torby had Jack Kennedy's free spirit without the pressures of a preordained destiny. Together, they could privately burlesque the formalities and inanities of life. Their mutual laughter often involved matching wits while subjecting acquaintances to rollicking Rabelaisian dissections, a style of humor in which they meshed perfectly and which was to continue throughout their lives together. "Torby Macdonald was his foil," remembers one of their classmates, "because Torby was a very brilliant person, and Torby and he would have a dialogue with a laugh a second for four or five minutes at a time, and the rest of us would just sit there and enjoy it."[28]

Torby was a campus star when he and Kennedy met, he was "the big man on campus" and the luminary of Winthrop House, where the two young men shared a room.

Macdonald would be permanently honored in Harvard's Football Hall of Fame, best remembered as the team captain whose fourth-quarter runs of sixty and twenty yards provided the two touchdowns and the only score against Yale in 1936. He had also done everything possible to help Jack make the team. One summer, before studying law, he played professional baseball with the Amsterdam, New York, farm team of the

New York Yankees. He had turned down a Rhodes Scholarship in his brief effort to make the big leagues. Jack Kennedy always worshiped athletes, and Torby became one of his first heroes. When he proposed Macdonald for membership in the Spee Club, however, the application was rejected through reluctance to let "in more of the Irish," but neither friend contested the decision very hard because Torby had sufficient campus adulation to weather that particular snub.[29]

Nevertheless, teaming up with Macdonald was undoubtedly of social value for the physically weaker and modest Jack Kennedy. In that sense, the campus luminary was "protective" of his frail friend. But intellectually they were also compatible, sharing an interest in books. Torby, in fact, helped direct Jack's attention toward history.[30] Not until Macdonald saw a copy of Joe Kennedy's 1936 book promoting Roosevelt's reelection did he realize the status of his friend's background.[31]

Without Torby's help, Jack's participation in the important intercollegiate swimming meet against Yale would have been improbable. Jack's determination compensated for inadequate strength and he became a backstroke artist, winning six minor numerals for freshman swimming and helping to lead his side to victory in the three-hundred-yard relay against Dartmouth. Such achievements helped Coach Harold Ulen recall him as "a fine kid, frail and not too strong, but always giving it everything he had."[32] But in the spring of 1937, just before the Yale meet, illness again intervened. Confinement to the campus Stillman Infirmary threatened to keep Jack from qualifying. Torby Macdonald came to the rescue, aiding the attempt to boost Jack's weight by sneaking steaks and malteds into Stillman. He also helped him out the back door of the infirmary and drove his friend to the indoor pool, where he watched Jack struggle to overcome his weakness and practice his backstroke. Each outing was followed by a return to the infirmary, a routine repeated several times during Jack's month-long confinement.[33] His best effort fell short, however, as Richard Tregaskis, later of World War II reportorial fame as the author of *Guadalcanal Diary,* won the preliminaries for the Yale competition.

But it was Torby's pride and independence that complemented Jack more than any other quality. They developed a similar view of life and mutual trust that survived one later disappointment on Macdonald's part and was sustained by their special personal rapport. (Not until after Jack's death did Bobby Kennedy shed his jealousy over his brother's closeness with Torby.[34]) When Jack wanted to travel abroad, Joe

Kennedy, conscious of his son's precarious health, always made certain he did not have to go alone. At one point he begged Macdonald to become his traveling companion and made it possible by paying the bills for both.[35] Still, Jack's friend took care to avoid being gobbled up by Kennedy power. Despite his own background, he remained zealous about preserving personal freedom. One day at Harvard, when he saw Joe Junior bully Jack, he intervened on his friend's side. Jack, however, later admonished him for getting involved in a Kennedy family affair. Torby was one of the few people bold enough to tell Joseph P. Kennedy, Sr., to "shove it up your ass," and, in a New York nightclub just before the war, criticized the "founding father" for "riding" Jack.[36] He was also one of those who fell in love with Kathleen Kennedy.

While still at Harvard, he kept her picture on his desk. When Ted Kennedy delivered a eulogy at the funeral services for Macdonald in 1976, he recalled how, when his own family was in England during his father's ambassadorship, the long-distance telephone bills were so high because "Torby was burning up the wires with calls to my sister, Kathleen. Torby was the most expensive telephone Romeo my sisters ever had." Finally, Macdonald became engaged to marry Jack's favorite sister. Their plans fell through, however, when Torby realized how much becoming the husband of one of Joe Kennedy's daughters would automatically compromise his own much-valued independence. Macdonald's son recalls that his father did not want to become a "corporate son-in-law." Yet he never overcame his affections toward Kathleen, which he revealed when commending his own daughters.[37] Only his uncompromising self-sufficiency kept him from becoming an official member of the Kennedy family.

Jack's overall academic record during his first two years remained mediocre. Willing to settle for "gentlemanly" C's, he got just that. Only in economics, listed for a Professor Burbank but mostly taught by a young instructor named Russ Nixon, did the freshman student rise above a C, receiving a B minus. Nor did his avowed interest in history and government help him in Professor William Langer's two history courses on "Continental Europe," for which he only earned D and C. He did, however, manage in his sophomore year to get a B in Professor Bruce Hopper's Government 30 course, entitled "New Factors in International Relations: Asia," but had to settle for a C in the "Modern Government" class taught jointly by professors Arthur Holcombe and William Y. Elliott. Finally, he received a straight C for French, reflecting his continuing difficulties with foreign languages.

Jack's Freshman Adviser's Report noted that government was his first choice, with history and literature secondary. The summary added that the student was "planning to do work in Government" and explained that his "father is in that work."[38] The unsigned Tutorial Record for 1937–1938, following his sophomore year, offered the view that "though his mind is still undisciplined, and will probably never be very original, he has the ability, I think, and gives promise of development."[39]

As guided by his tutors, Jack's reading shows a heavy concentration in politics, history, and economics. The record lists such works as Guy Stanton Ford's *Dictatorship in the Modern World,* Calvin Hoover's *Germany Enters the Third Reich,* Mussolini's autobiography, Gilbert Seldes's *Sawdust Caesar,* Herman Finer's *Mussolini's Italy,* the *Communist Manifesto* by Marx and Engels, Lenin's *State and Revolution,* and Charles Beard's *Economic Basis of Politics.*[40]

The grades and bibliographies, however, tell only part of the story. Payson Wild, one of his tutors, who also taught Jack's "Elements of International Law" course, remembered Kennedy as one who "really did have ability to think deeply and in theoretical terms." He probed, read, and asked questions. He was particularly fascinated with what he considered the fundamental political problem: "Why do people obey?" Jack and Wild had many discussions over that concept, especially after the instructor had claimed the essence of political theory was that "given a few people at the top and masses below, why do the masses obey?" Together, Jack and Wild went through Plato and Aristotle and the Aristotelian theory of the state and then the Platonic, which Jack could discuss thoroughly and with understanding. They also went on to Hobbes, Locke, and Rousseau and the contract theory of the state. Wild stressed both in class discussions and privately, that the physical frontier was closed and that, as the professor later recalled his words, the "new frontiers are the political and social ones." The point was drawn from historian Frederick Jackson Turner's famous thesis and had been an intrinsic part of FDR's Commonwealth Club address of 1932. Wild was "convinced that he [Jack] had basically the deep interest, that there was in him a basis for all the pragmatic interests and concerns that he showed later on, which he had to show." The head of the Winthrop dining room, who was as a mother to many of the men in the house, compared him with Joe Junior when she said that Jack was "really the diamond in the rough" and the one who was the "deep thinker."[41]

In Holcombe's government class, Jack wrote a paper on a little-known Republican congressman from upstate New York, Bertram Snell. A strange selection, indeed: Snell had only local influence, came from remote Potsdam, New York, supported the restrictive Immigration Act of 1924 with its imposition of national quotas, and was the sole owner of the Snell Power Plant at Higley Falls, New York. Though elected to five congresses, his career was unmemorable, except for his diligent support of the electric power interests in his area. But the topic was not Jack's choice. Holcombe, a conservative, figured that his student would "learn more if he studied a Republican" and so made the assignment.

Jack became engrossed. He probed into the elements that limited Snell's influence. "He did a very superior job of investigating, and his final report on his congressman was a masterpiece," Holcombe later wrote. "He got so much interested that when Christmas vacation came, he goes down to Washington, meets some of his father's friends, gets a further line on his congressman and on Congress. Well, that was the method of the course. And Jack was interested in it, did a superb job."[42]

One night a popular female entertainer, Gertrude Niesen, four years older than Jack Kennedy and later a wartime musical-comedy singer, was brought to Cambridge. Kennedy, as chairman of the committee that arranged the events for the annual spring smoker, met Niesen at the airport and, with a classmate, brought the attractive singer to massive University Hall for the performance. During the rehearsal, with the auditorium darkened and only a spotlight on the performer, Kennedy began directing wisecracks toward her. Niesen, known for her suggestive style, responded in kind. "It was not uncommon for one or two of us to have a bottle in those days," remembers a fellow member of Jack's committee, "so we were able to liven the proceedings up a little bit. . . . She was giving it back and Kennedy was giving it to her in humor, and it was a very, very funny two hours, and it was a tremendous night. . . . It was one of the high points of his college life even though it was fairly early on. It was because he had this sense of humor. He didn't take Gertrude Niesen seriously and she didn't take him seriously. It just worked very well. . . . And by eight or nine o'clock when the performance went on, I think we were all pretty well along in the evening, and Gertrude Niesen was just enjoying the hell out of it, and Jack Kennedy was joking with her the whole time."[43]

When Jack went to Europe at the end of his freshman year, in the summer of 1937, his inquiries into events on the Continent offered a sharp contrast with the way many then perceived him. As his guide to current European political affairs he relied on John Gunther's *Inside*

Europe, which had recently been revised after first appearing in 1936. For Jack, accompanied by Lem Billings, the trip was an opportunity limited to a privileged few and an experience that helped teach him something about the discrepancies between first-hand information and gossip.

Leaving New York on the first of July aboard the S.S. *Washington,* Jack also took along a 1936 four-door Ford convertible. The voyage was both smooth and dull, with Jack's main diversion the young female passengers. "Looked pretty dull the first couple of days," he wrote in his diary, "but investigation disclosed some girls—chiefly Ann Reed. Had cock-tails with the Captain who knew Sir Thomas Lipton and thus grand-pa [Fitzgerald]. The chief source of interest was General Hill and his rather mysterious daughter. He was a congressman;"—John Boynton Philip Clayton Hill of Maryland—"she might have been anything."

Once in France, Jack and Lem made the rounds of cathedrals at Rouen and at Rheims. "My French improving a bit & Billings breath getting French," he noted later. "Went to bed early. General feeling seems to be that there will not be another war."[44]

Other entries showed that all was not play. "The general impression seems to be that while they all like Roosevelt, his type of government would not succeed in a country like France which seems to lack the ability of seeing a problem as a whole. They don't like Blum as he takes away their money and gives it to someone else. That to a French man is *très mauvais.* The general impression also seems to be that there will *not* be a war in the near future and that France is much too well prepared for Germany. The permanence of the alliance of Germany and Italy is also questionable."

Partly out of consideration for Lem's more limited means, Jack monitored their expenses carefully. The search for a *pension* normally lasted until both young men could find lodgings at the right price. As Jack interpreted matters, the French would take them for all they had. "Have now acquired the habit of leaving the car around the block to keep the price from going up," he wrote in Paris. "Had the lights fixed and got another screwing. These French will try & rob at every turn."

In Paris, Jack looked up Ann Reed, the girl he had met on the *Washington,* and they went out together several times, usually taking in a movie. The films he saw were American, including *The Good Earth* and *The Plainsman,* with Gary Cooper. He was especially amused at hearing Cooper and the Indians speaking French, which alone "is worth the price of admission."

In St. Jean-de-Luz, he went with a French girl, discovering in the process that local customs required a chaperone. Later, upon reaching Rome, Jack and Billings dated some Italian women. "Very beautiful girls," Kennedy wrote, "although our not speaking Italian was a temporary damper. Billings knew some Italian parlor tricks that were worth remembering and we went to bed tired but happy!"

Early one morning while in Paris, Jack and Lem went to Notre Dame to hear Cardinal Pacelli, whom they found very formidable, although Billings, a Protestant, "had to wait in the body of the Church." Leaving the French capital, they drove to the château country at Blois and Amboise. Kennedy swam in the Loire and was surprised at the river's strong current. From St. Jean-de-Luz, in extreme southwestern France near the Pyrenees and on the Bay of Biscay, they crossed the Spanish border to the town of Irún, where Jack saw his first bullfight. "Very interesting," he wrote in his diary, "but very cruel, especially when the bull gored the horse. Believe all the atrocity stories now as these southerners, such as the French and Spanish, are happiest at scenes of cruelty. They thought funniest sight was when horse ran out of the ring with his guts trailing."

The political situation especially fascinated him. Most intriguing were both the Spanish Civil War and Italy's corporate fascist state under Mussolini, about which he had done much reading at Harvard. Along with many American Catholics, young Kennedy favored Generalissimo Franco's Falangists, believing that the Loyalists would make Spain vulnerable to communism.[45] He had also approached the scene with simple assumptions about the inevitability of Franco's victory, notions that had undoubtedly dominated his own political upbringing. Once near the scene, mainly from a vantage point in southern France, where he encountered refugees and gathered first-hand information about the bitterness of the opposition, he began to realize that all was not so simple. "Shows that you can be easily influenced by people around you if you know nothing and how easy it is for you to believe what you want to believe."[46] To his father, he wrote about "the almost complete ignorance 95% of the people in the U. S. have about situations as a whole here. For example, most people in the U. S. are for Franco, and while I felt that perhaps it would be far better for Spain if Franco should win—as he would strengthen and unite Spain—yet at the beginning the government was in the right morally speaking as its program was similar to the New Deal."[47] Viewing the Spanish situation as an international battleground instead of the more parochial concern about the viability of the Church as opposed to communism, he concluded that the crux of the situation lay in the extent to which the intervening powers—Germany, Italy, and Russia—would go "in trying to secure victory for themselves."

In Italy, Jack found much to admire. The streets were livelier, the atmosphere more prosperous. What he had seen in France could not compare. "Fascism seems to treat them well," he noted. By the time he reached Milan and had completed reading Gunther, he became convinced, in fact, that "Fascism is the thing for Germany and Italy, Communism for Russia and democracy for America and England." Reacting to Gunther's liberal outlook, Kennedy agreed that the book was very interesting but "more than partial to socialism and communism and a bitter enemy of Fascism." At that point, Jack also asked himself, "What are the evils of Fascism as opposed to communism?"[48] An interesting meeting with Arnaldo Cortesi, *The New York Times*'s Italian correspondent in Rome, assured him that war seemed unlikely because there had already been enough excuses to fight if anyone really wanted it. Cortesi also explained that fascism was not unfair to workers, who had, he argued, realized many advantages under the system, and he also lauded the corporate state. Fascism, the correspondent explained to Jack, was "out and out socialism." All such notions and personal observations prompted Kennedy to ponder the following questions that struck him about European conditions:

1 Is Mussolini more popular now than before the Abyssinian question?
2 If the belligerent foreign troops were withdrawn, how much chance would Franco have [?] England's attitude.
3 If Franco wins, what will be the extent of Mussolini's control? Hitler's? Is there any chance of conflict of those 2 countries?
4 Isn't the chance of war less as Britain gets stronger—or is a country like Italy liable to go to war when economic discontent is rife [?]
5 Wouldn't Mussolini [illegible] if there was a war—as in all likelihood Italy would be defeated in a major war [?]
6 Would Fascism be possible in a country with the economic distribution of wealth in the U. S. [?]
7 Could there be any permanence in the alliance of Germany and Italy or are their interests too much in conflict . . . [?]
8 France's position? Russia's position?
9 Gunther says Fascism momentarily powerful. May be the convulsive last agonies of the capitalist order, in which case Facism [sic] will have been merely the prelude to communism. Is that true [?]

At the American Express office in Rome, Jack received a wire from his father advising that his mother and Joe Junior were en route to Europe with Kathleen. Jack, meanwhile, met three nieces of Bishop Spellman and then had a private audience with Cardinal Pacelli, who asked about his mother and father. Driving out to the country, he reached the Pope's summer place. "Afterwards had an audience with the Pope with nearly 1,000 in the room, which was packed. He looked very sick but made a long speech. . . . We then returned to Rome—and had dinner at Galiazzi's. He gave me quite a talk about the verities of Facism [sic] and it really seemed to have its points especially the corporative system which seems an interesting step forward."

Kennedy then reached London on August 26 and spent some time with Kathleen and Joe, who were leaving by train for Southampton. The next day, Jack overindulged in chocolates and became "damn sick" and had a "very tough night." Lem got a doctor, but the physician seemed interested in knowing whether Jack had mixed his chocolates and tomato juice in a big glass. He convinced him he had not, and promptly got another doctor. Jack was troubled with hives; but, by the next day, he had both fewer hives and a new physician. And then the summer was over.

In December, Joseph P. Kennedy, after campaigning for the appointment, became the recipient of the nation's most prestigious diplomatic post: Franklin D. Roosevelt announced the appointment of Kennedy as the American ambassador to England. A third-generation Irish Catholic had become the envoy to the Court of St. James's, undoubtedly a most curious choice. Not surprisingly, the President had personal misgivings about the move. There is also some evidence that he contemplated backing off but that Joe Kennedy seized the opening and insisted that it be granted.

Kennedy's relationship to Roosevelt had been relatively close, particularly since that 1932 convention, when he gave fifteen thousand dollars to the Democratic campaign fund and loaned the party fifty thousand dollars, plus turning over anonymous contributions with his personal checks.[49] Kennedy was not one driven by any kind of liberal zeal. He was one of the few Roosevelt advisers unmoved by political motivations. Undoubtedly, aside from his open checkbook, it appeared that the financial operator had two additional attractions for the President. For one, he was a link with the business community. Through that connection he had been most helpful after the establishment of the Securities and

Exchange Commission. To Jim Farley, Roosevelt said that he could not give Kennedy the post as treasury secretary "because Joe would want to run the Treasury in his own way, contrary to my purpose and views."[50] Unquestionably the second function served by Kennedy, as far as the shrewd politician in the White House was concerned, was his relationship to the substantial Irish-American powers within the Democratic Party. Such Catholics as Father Coughlin, the "radio priest" of Royal Oak, were able to use Kennedy as a link to the President.[51]

After Kennedy's service as the chairman of the SEC, Roosevelt named him to head the Maritime Commission. Although never a real New Dealer, nor, in particular, a vocal FDR loyalist, Kennedy was quoted as saying, "I wanted him in the White House for my own security and for the security of my kids, and I was ready to do anything to help him."[52] Indeed, in 1936, before that year's election, Kennedy published his little book called *I'm for Roosevelt,* largely written by newsman Arthur Krock.[53] Again, that was an attempt to influence the business community in behalf of a second term for the Democratic administration.

At the Economics Club in New York, Jack's father spoke extemporaneously about the New Deal. He explained, "I looked to Washington as a great enthusiast of the New Deal. I still am an enthusiast of the New Deal," he declared in that 1937 talk. "It isn't going to do you any good to bellyache or to say Roosevelt is no good or that everybody in Washington is crazy. Whether you like it or not he is going to be there three more years."[54]

Meanwhile, Jack's attitude toward Roosevelt, as remembered by a friend named Charles Spalding, was devoid of idolization of the President but contained "a great enthusiasm . . . for Roosevelt's point of view about the people who he felt were getting the short end of the stick in America. And he picked that up and he espoused that thoroughly." But there just was not anything about FDR that stirred Jack Kennedy emotionally. His greatest sympathy was for the New Deal's basic mission, "what the New Deal was trying to accomplish and that that was what government should do where it could."[55]

The impending announcement of Joe Kennedy's ambassadorship became known in December of 1937. As usual, Kennedy got especially good treatment from the Boston papers. *The Boston Globe* grandly announced that the "wise men in the State Department, who appreciate the situation in Great Britain and on the Continent, are frankly gratified that the United States is to be represented in London by a man of the Kennedy type."[56] Three days later, the same paper, while reporting that

Kennedy was preparing to leave for London, added the comment that he was, in effect, the chief friend of business in the New Deal.

Roosevelt was hardly euphoric. Under very few illusions, he said to Henry Morgenthau, "I have made arrangments to have Joe Kennedy watched hourly, and the first time he opens his mouth and criticizes me, I will fire him." The President also told Dorothy Schiff that sending Kennedy to London was "the greatest joke in the world."[57] Two or three times, he told Morgenthau, "Kennedy is too dangerous to have around here."[58]

In early 1938, Joseph and Rose Kennedy, with their younger children, went to London, where they resided at the American embassy at 14 Princess Gate, a six-story house opposite Hyde Park. From that point on, for the next few years, Jack virtually shuttled back and forth across the Atlantic between Harvard and London. Joe Kennedy's friend, Felix Frankfurter, sent the advice that both John Adams and Charles Francis Adams had established a precedent by having had their sons on the embassy staffs in London, and that encouraged Kennedy to take Joe Junior to the embassy; and so, both older sons served on the staff at various times while on leave from Harvard. Jack took off from school during the last half of his junior year.

Sir John Wheeler-Bennett, a guest at an informal dinner party in London, heard the Ambassador indulge in one of his characteristic bits of gasconading. "I'll tell you about these boys," he said, pointing to Joe, Jack, and Bobby, sitting on the other side of the table, "there's young Joe—he is going to be President of the United States; and there's Jack —he's going to be a University President; and there's Bobby [tapping his nose in a cunning manner]—he's the lawyer."[59] Little did he suspect that he would become a permanent liability to their careers.

From the outset it quickly became obvious that Ambassador Kennedy had become close to the "Cliveden set," the band of British aristocrats who met at the Astor country residence and plotted to keep England out of the war. That was the group later recalled as the British "appeasers" of the 1930's. Kennedy, passionate about keeping the United States out of a future European conflict, and conscious of the potential harm to his own children, viewed English neutrality as vital for maintaining his own country's peace. Never very shy about offering his opinions, the diplomat failed to be discreet before his English servants and his attitudes soon became well known. Josiah Wedgwood, a member of Parliament considered liberal and opposed to Prime Minister Neville Chamberlain's foreign policy, complained about Roosevelt's choice for the ambassadorship. Instead of having sent the best possible diplomat to Britain at that crucial time, said Wedgwood, "We have a rich man, untrained in diplomacy, unlearned in history and politics, who is a great publicity seeker and who is apparently ambitious to be the first Catholic President of the United States." Secretary of the Interior Harold Ickes soon noted in his diary that Kennedy "appears to have been taken in hand by Lady Astor and the Cliveden set."[60] Later, the *New York Post* reported that the Ambassador was being identified with the "Germanophile clique," and that Claud Cockburn, a British writer, had noted that "Kennedy goes so far as to insinuate that the democratic policy of the United States is a Jewish production."[61] Of considerable embarrassment to the Roosevelt White House was the Ambassador's designation as the "Man of the Week" by Father Coughlin's pro-Nazi, anti-Semitic *Social Justice,* which devoted its February 1939 cover to a full-page picture of the Kennedy family.[62]

In supporting the Chamberlain government, Kennedy's inclination was to avoid war by letting Germany and Russia fight and destroy each other. Very early in his diplomatic career, he developed close contact with the German ambassador in London. The British monitored German dispatches based on conversations with Kennedy and learned that he had told about Chamberlain's anxiety for a settlement with Hitler.[63] As Kennedy saw it, only constant Washington pressure made England and France regard the Polish situation as worth going to war. Chamberlain was maintaining that America and the world's Jews had forced England into the war. When Roosevelt told Kennedy by phone in the summer of 1939 to put some "iron up Chamberlain's backside," as James Forrestal described the conversation, Kennedy responded that even that would be futile unless the British had iron with which to fight.[64]

Not surprisingly, the Roosevelt administration began to show increasing irritation with Kennedy. To Morgenthau, his treasury secretary, the President complained that the Ambassador had always been an appeaser.[65] Kennedy's closest friends in London were those most opposed to Winston Churchill, who was warning about the threat from Hitler. Churchill denounced Kennedy, charging the diplomat with giving the impression that he, Churchill, was anti-American and anti-Roosevelt. Back in Washington Kennedy's blatantly pro-Chamberlain position was the butt of a joke at a White House stag dinner. Ickes told the President that Chamberlain had decided to increase his cabinet so that he could include Joe Kennedy.[66]

The war began later that month. Once England became a belligerent

Kennedy's position grew even more untenable. At a farewell dinner before his children left to return to the United States, he toasted the Germans with the statement that they "would badly thrash the British." The British Foreign Office, hearing about that incident from a witness, began a file labeled "Kennediana."[67] Roosevelt, exasperated but politically limited from overt actions against Kennedy because of the growing restlessness among Irish Catholic Democrats, tried to circumvent his emissary by the covert use of William J. Donovan as a special agent to the British. When he learned about that move, Kennedy was naturally infuriated but unable to do much beyond attempting to interfere with Donovan's English contacts.

The suspicion about the American ambassador current in London was that he had not lost sight of his personal business interests, that he feared the detrimental impact upon his own commercial exports in the event of the outbreak of war, a hunch Roosevelt shared.[68] In addition, Kennedy encouraged talk of a possible presidential candidacy for himself in 1940.[69] His concern also included the conviction that a war with Germany would simply result in a Bolshevik victory, and that would plunder all that he, a self-made man, had achieved.[70] Churchill denounced Kennedy. Unknown to the Ambassador, his cables to Roosevelt's administration were received very skeptically as the work of an appeaser. As Cordell Hull noted in his memoirs, neither he as secretary of state nor the President "could see eye to eye with him in his extreme pessimism over Britain's future."[71] Others within the State Department were contemptuous of Kennedy's passion for serving his personal interests.[72]

The Ambassador's relationship with Germany also revealed his anti-Semitism. Despite his wish that the Nazis become more discreet about their persecutions, if only to lessen American antagonism, Kennedy conveyed his own forbearance. On June 15, 1938, the German ambassador telegraphed his version of Kennedy's views on the subject of the Jews. Germany was hurting her own cause, Kennedy had explained, "Not so much because we wanted to get rid of the Jews but rather by the way we set out to accomplish this purpose with such a lot of noise. At home in Boston, for instance, Kennedy said there were clubs to which no Jews were admitted in fifty years. . . . People simply avoided making a fuss about it. He himself understood our policy on Jews."[73]

Some may rationalize Kennedy's view as that of a man who was attempting to meet the Germans on their own terms, to show them that he was sympathetic and, as a diplomat, understood their point of view.

Yet an English friend, Hugh Fraser, has recalled that Kennedy was "anti-Semitic in a rather willful, old-fashioned sense. I remember traveling . . . up to Palm Beach with Jack and the Ambassador, and the Ambassador saying pointing to some golf club, 'They're none of them in there.' And I said, 'What do you mean?' And he said, 'Jews, don't be stupid.' "[74] Once, in a moment of rage, he warned his sons to "never do business with Jews," a stricture he himself failed to heed.[75]

5

The First Book

A father who was Ambassador to the Court of St. James's was no minor advantage. It immediately enabled Jack to acquaint himself with the elite of British society, the governmental leadership, and the opposition. Joining his father after his academic year, Jack was present when the American embassy threw a huge dinner in honor of the Duke and Duchess of Kent. The magnificence of the affair matched the splendor of the embassy itself. Likened to a luxury hotel, it contained twenty-three house servants, three chauffeurs, and, for such functions, a reserve force of twenty part-time employees. At that particular dinner, with Winston S. Churchill in attendance and a representative from the Roosevelt administration, Interior Secretary Ickes, Kennedy worried out loud that "hell might break loose at any time over Czechoslovakia." He also denounced what he called "the career boys" in the State Department and lambasted their ignorance of European affairs.[1]

That same month Joe Junior graduated from Harvard, with a *cum laude* for a thesis on a history of the Hands Off Spain Committee. Joe himself was involved with the group, which feared American interference with the Falangist drive to overthrow the Spanish Republic. The thesis argued against risking neutrality in trying to help a dying, Communist-permeated government against a Catholic-led overthrow.[2]

His father, however, failed to attend the graduation, citing Jack's current illness, an explanation that appears contrived. More likely, Kennedy's animus against Harvard had become complete by then, despite the award of *cum laude* for Junior's thesis. First, football coach Dick Harlow had drawn his anger by keeping young Joe on the bench during the closing minutes of the Yale game, thereby depriving him of a football team letter. Not long after that the Ambassador's exalted position failed to win him election to the Harvard Board of Overseers, a defeat which severely affronted his pride. He attributed his rejection to Harvard's anti-Catholic bias.

Harvard notwithstanding, he was determined to expand his sons' education in other ways, ways that would be useful for their future careers. Once Jack and Joe Junior were in Europe, Mr. Kennedy accompanied them to Paris, where they spent a week in Ambassador William C. Bullitt's house on the Avenue d'Iéna. Studying French, they remained from late June through the better part of the summer, until the Munich crisis. They failed to absorb much French, but managed to have a good time. Foreign Service Officer Carmel Offie recalled that Joe and Jack got invited "to various parties in the diplomatic corps where they could meet young ladies and it was there they formed some friendships which lasted as long as they lived. No one took them very seriously but just by being around the Embassy for a time each day they sat in with various officers of the Embassy and thereby learned a lot of what was going on. I remember Jack sitting in my office and listening to telegrams being read or even reading various things which actually were none of his business but since he was who he was we didn't throw him out."[3]

After Jack returned to Harvard for his junior year, he demonstrated a greater sense of purpose than ever before. Without Joe Junior, Jack exhibited more self-assurance and confidence, an improvement noticed by instructors.[4] That fall, despite his heaviest course load, he received his best grades, sufficiently high to warrant a place on the Dean's List.[5] There were three government courses, one dealing with the national government of the United States, another with state governments, and the third covered recent European international developments. He also studied Russian history, had a semester of economics devoted to "The Corporation and its Regulation," and a course on English composition.

He went on leave in the spring, having filed an application right after his father's ambassadorial appointment. But by the time he sailed back to England aboard the *Queen Mary* in early February, he had gathered thoughts and information for a senior honors thesis on Great Britain's lack of preparation for war. Both that project and a list of books had been laid out for him by his tutor, Bruce Hopper, who, together with Payson Wild, supervised the project. Wild later said that Jack "would write it during the week, and we would talk about it. I don't know anybody else he knew around there who could do it or who had the background to write what he wrote."[6]

That was the period after the collapse of the Munich agreement when, in March, Hitler helped himself to the rest of Czechoslovakia, the sensational news of the Russo-German nonaggression treaty that followed in August, and before the German and Russian invasion of Poland in September. Amid such portentous developments, Jack traveled along an itinerary greatly facilitated by his father. As always, whenever he needed something done, Joe Kennedy had only to make the right calls. First working through Herbert Feis at the State Department, he obtained from Secretary Cordell Hull a formal letter of introduction. Hull also forwarded to the Ambassador his personal notes.[7]

Altogether, that seven-month European stay was Jack's most significant educational experience abroad. After spending more time with Bullitt in Paris, he went on to Poland, Latvia, Russia, Turkey, Palestine, and the Balkans. Later in the summer Torby Macdonald arrived as a member of the Harvard track team. Jack joined him and they went off together to Berlin, Danzig, and Italy. From each point Jack sent his father detailed reports of his observations. His letters showed some remarkably astute views of the situation, displaying the talents of a perceptive, detached observer. His valuable contacts helped in the gathering of information that, together with his reading, made substantial contributions to his thesis.

From Poland he sent his father a long letter analyzing the prospects of war and peace. "Probably the strongest impression I have gotten is that rightly or wrongly the Poles *will fight over* the Question of Danzig."[8] When he arrived in Russia, Kennedy was assisted by Foreign Service Officer Charles "Chip" Bohlen in the Moscow embassy. He covered a great deal of that territory by airplane and obtained what became a lifelong impression of a "crude, backward, hopelessly bureaucratic country." He visited Leningrad, Moscow, and the Crimean Peninsula before moving on from Russia into Turkey by ship. A steamer brought him to Istanbul. From there he went on to Palestine.

From Jerusalem he sent his father a long analysis of the situation in the Holy Land. The first part summarized the historical background of the Palestinian question. Going back to Palestine's Turkish domination and explaining the background of the Zionist movement, Kennedy pointed out the difficulty and seriousness of the situation, particularly the growth of the refugee problem. He cited the coming of the Jewish immigrants and their wealth, which was pouring into Palestine. "This capital," he wrote, "while economically a poor investment as it only brought in a fraction of a percent on the original, nevertheless enabled the Jews to acquire about 15% of the land which included the most fertile. The Arabs naturally objected to the Jewish encroachment. They felt that the Jews, if permitted, would dominate in their country numerically as well as economically." He discussed the partition plan of 1936, which advocated dividing Palestine into two independent states. He then pointed out the results of the 1939 conference in London when differences between Jews and Arabs led to the issuance of a White Paper. Representing the current policy of the British government, the White Paper was viewed by the Jews as a setback to Zionism by diluting the Balfour Declaration of 1917, holding that it "could not have intended that Palestine should be converted into a Jewish State against the will of the Arab population of the country." It also cautioned against further unlimited Jewish immigration to Palestine—in effect, shutting off a haven at a desperate time for refugees.[9]

But the White Paper also offended the Arabs, Kennedy pointed out. They disliked the undefined period during which the British would have control, and believed the formation of an independent state depended upon Jewish cooperation, which they regarded as impossible. They also objected to the lack of a provision for an elected assembly under their own leadership. Furthermore, while the White Paper sought to limit immigration, the Arabs insisted on an absolute complete cessation. The Arabs, according to Kennedy, did not feel that the Jews were their problem; while there were 450,000 Jews in Palestine, only 250,000 had become citizens. Therefore, the Arabs wanted to know why the Jews were entitled to become members of the state.[10]

Jack wrote that "on the Jewish side there is the desire for complete domination, with Jerusalem as the capital of their new land of milk and honey, with the right to colonize in Trans-Jordan. They feel that given sufficient opportunity they can cultivate the land and develop it as they have done in the Western portion. The Arab answer to this is, incidentally, that the Jews have had the benefit of capital, which had the Arabs possessed, equal miracles could have been performed by them. Though this is partly true, the economic setup of Arab agricultural progress with its absentee landlords and primitive methods of cultivation, cannot under any circumstances probably have competed with the Jews. However," added Kennedy, "this very fact lies in the background of the Arabic objection to the Jews. They realize their superiority and fear it."

Jack's view of the substance of the Palestinian situation embodied sound analysis, especially for one so relatively inexperienced, and had the journalistic strength of resisting propaganda from either side. Then Jack received an especially intimate view of the conflict on his last evening in Jerusalem as thirteen bombs were set off in the Jewish quarter. All, he told his father, were detonated by the Jews themselves. "The ironical part," he wrote, "is that the Jewish terrorists bomb their own telephone lines and electric connections and the next day frantically phone the British to come and fix them up." Watching the British in action made Jack even more pro-British than during his earlier visits to England. Their on-the-spot performance was impressive.

And yet, recognizing the Palestinian situation, Jack said to his father that "the important thing and the necessary thing is not a situation just and fair but a solution that will work. . . . It seems to me that the only thing to do would be to break the country up into two autonomous districts giving them both self-government to the extent that they do not interfere with each other and that the British interest is safeguarded. Jerusalem, having the background that it has, should be an independent unit." Recognizing the difficulty of that solution, Jack added that it was the only one that would have a possibility of working. Selecting the means of resolving the conflict from among the options seemed to him more urgent than placating all interests.

Most people he met seemed to sympathize with the Arabs and attributed that bias to the presence among some Jewish leaders of "an unfortunately arrogant, uncompromising attitude," and [to] the Moslem argument that their country has been Arabic for several centuries. Rather than expressing criticism of the Jews as Jews, Kennedy agreed that the obstructionists were the "strongly orthodox Jewish group, unwilling to make any compromise, who wish to have a government expressing this attitude. . . ." Mostly the Zionist problem stemmed from their own divisions, with a liberal young element fearing the zealots, whom Kennedy called "reactionaries," and wanting "to establish a very liberal, almost communistic form of government." While there were those amenable to a compromise, there were even further subdivisions of differences cutting across these groups. At the moment, Jack reported, they were managing to present a united front; but, "if and when they get their claims, then the break-up will start." Conditioned by aversion toward uncompromising extremes, the youthful observer denigrated any solution that omitted the Arabs.[11]

From Palestine, Jack went on to Bucharest, Rumania. After his trip through the Balkans, he concluded the first part of his travels by returning to London. There, on June 22, he attended a coming-out party for his sister Eunice as well as a reception, five days later, at 10 Downing Street. He then teamed up with Torby Macdonald, who had competed at White City Stadium in London against a joint track team that had been formed by Oxford and Cambridge. Then off went Jack with his friend, back to the Continent.

From Western Europe, they moved toward Germany, which they reached in August. In Munich, Jack renewed his acquaintance with Byron "Whizzer" White, an American from Colorado he had met in London. With White, Kennedy and Macdonald toured the city in a borrowed car. There, too, they became involved in a tense incident. They encountered a group of storm-trooper types engaged in a patriotic Nazi demonstration. Spotting the car with its English license plates, the Nazi youths began to pelt it with bricks. Only some swift acceleration got them out of it and they continued on their trip. After visiting Vienna, Jack and Torby split up temporarily, with Macdonald going on to Hungary and Kennedy determined to visit Czechoslovakia.

With the Prague government under Nazi control, such visits were forbidden. Having only recently been overrun by the Nazis, the city was in turmoil. The advancing German troops hastened the fleeing of Czech inhabitants of the Sudenten area, and the American embassy in Prague was braced for the arrival of thousands of refugees. The great concern of the Americans there, at that time, with a staff of just six to eight persons, was how to provide the necessary food and shelter. "Yet in the midst of this confusion," recalled George F. Kennan, then a Foreign Service officer, "we received a telegram from the embassy in London, the sense of which was that our ambassador there . . . had chosen this time to send one of his young sons on a fact-finding tour around Europe, and it was up to us to find means of getting him across the border and through the German lines so that he could include in his itinerary a visit to Prague." The embassy staff, angered at having to contend with young Kennedy at that moment, disposed of the "upstart" and "ignoramus" as expeditiously as possible.[12]

Within the month following his return to London, World War II began. Two days after the Nazis began their invasion of Poland, England and France went to war against Hitler's Germany. At the same time an incident gave Jack his first opportunity to see precisely the impact a war has on individuals. Ambassador Kennedy, at his country home outside London, was awakened and told that a British liner, the *Athenia,* was sinking in the North Atlantic, torpedoed by a German submarine. Its more than fourteen hundred passengers included about three hundred Americans. Unarmed, the 13,500-ton vessel was going under the waters west of the Hebrides. Kennedy immediately cabled the President to inform him that those who had not been killed by the immediate explosion had been rescued. He then contacted the American consulates in Belfast, Dublin, and Liverpool and ordered that the names of the passengers be sent to London at once. Quickly the Ambassador awakened Jack and dispatched his son on an assignment. With Kennedy's secretary, Eddie Moore, Jack hurried to Glasgow, Scotland.

Since twelve Americans were missing and perhaps killed, Jack faced an immediate clamor for the protection of American passengers on the high seas. Accordingly, Jack phoned his father and was told that there could be no convoy. President Roosevelt had acted only a few days earlier to safeguard neutrality by banning the use of Navy convoys for refugee ships in European waters. So Jack's mission was to placate the passengers with assurances that the U.S. *Orizaba,* an American liner, would convey them to New York. Harried as he was, Jack handled it competently, delaying his return to the U.S. for the start of his senior year at Harvard. "As I am now working in charge of the Committee for the Evacuation of the 'Athenia' survivors, and due to the lack of transportation, it appears now that I shall not be able to return to America before the 29th of September. . . . I hope that this will not endanger my standing, and I shall endeavor to get back as quickly as I can," he wrote to the registrar's office.[13]

He returned to America on a Pan American clipper, the *Dixie,* arriving at Port Washington, Long Island.

Jack Kennedy's European adventures reinforced his intellectual processes as well as added to his maturity. So, undoubtedly, did the gravity of the international situation. "We all were either restless or more serious after war broke out in Europe," a classmate recalled, "but Jack seemed to mature faster than the rest of us."[14] An indication of the change was his eagerness to join the *Crimson*'s editorial board, something he should have attempted earlier, when candidates normally applied for that position. Despite assistance from Blair Clark, the current editor, Jack had to settle for a place on the business board.[15]

The Harvard campus in the spring of 1940 was considerably agitated over European developments. Inevitably, pro- and anti-interventionist divisions materialized. The leading campus voice against breaching neutrality was the *Crimson* and its editorials by Clark. Others, such as Harvard President James P. Conant, advocated American military preparation and peacetime conscription of young men. Joe Junior, even as a Democratic delegate from Massachusetts to the party's presidential nominating convention that summer, was much closer to his father's sentiments. Despite a great deal of pressure to get into line behind a third-term nomination for Roosevelt, young Joe supported Jim Farley. Even phoning Ambassador Kennedy in London, urging him to get his son behind the President, failed to keep him from leading a minority within the Massachusetts delegation that cast eleven and two thirds votes for Farley, who was really leading an intraparty revolt against both the New Deal and another term for FDR. Junior, it was clear, was doing what the Ambassador could, at that point, not do openly.

Jack's views evolved independently. He did not engage in the overt campus demonstrations of the period, which were vehemently against interventionism. Nor did his thesis, which was written during that academic year, seem to contradict his father's position, principally because of its ostensible defense of Chamberlain. Originally conceived as "England's Foreign Policy Since 1731," it evolved into a paper called "Appeasement at Munich." Superficially, at least, it attempted to explain Chamberlain's position at Munich as one that was predetermined by considerations more complex than willfully selling out Czechoslovakia to the Nazis, an analysis that seemed consistent with his father's well-known position. Still, Jack's dissent differed significantly, with some embarrassment, from Joe Kennedy's attitude.[16]

Jack became closely involved with trying to change the course of the *Crimson*'s editorial policy. The strongly noninterventionist paper devoted several editorials against the pro-Allied policy of President Conant, who, along with such faculty members as Bruce C. Hopper, William Yandell Elliott, and Carl Friedrich, were among the nucleus of the Massachusetts branch of the Committee to Defend America by Aiding the Allies. After Dr. Conant's radio address of May 29, under the committee's auspices, urging immediate aid, the *Crimson* replied that the United States was, in effect, already at war and castigated the Harvard president for fearing that a German victory "will menace us directly.

Such fears should hardly be made the basis of our national policy."[17] A few days later, the paper declared that "America's battle against Fascism is in America, not Europe; Fascism in this country will not be caused by insidious international plotters, but by sincere though short-sighted one-hundred per cent Americans; and we must deal with internal Fascism not in the future, but right now."[18] As to conscription, a leading bête noire of noninterventionists, that was "unnecessary for America's best interests and dangerous as one step nearer to involvement in the present war."[19] But Jack began to join the editorial staff's nocturnal sessions and through his visits and discussions tried to influence their analyses, arguing his points articulately and forcefully.[20] The combination of his reading, travels in Europe, discussions with well-placed observers, and work researching and writing his honors paper had brought him to a conclusion quite contrary to what seemed like the family line. Young Kennedy's most visible disclaimer was contained in a letter carried by the *Crimson*'s issue of June 9.

In defense of Conant's speech, and protesting the paper's reasoning that "there is no surer way to war, and a terribly destructive one, than to arm as we are doing," Kennedy argued that recent English experience had been overlooked. Nowhere else did people believe more strongly "that armaments are the prime cause of war," he wrote, and cited the equivalent American position as expressed by Senator William Borah's opposition to the Naval Appropriations Bill of 1938. Britain's failure to build up armaments, Kennedy reasoned, had not spared her from war, "and may cost her one. Are we in America to let that lesson go unlearned?"[21]

Before the appearance of his *Crimson* letter, Jack had submitted "Appeasement at Munich." The writing of his honors paper evolved through experiences on the Continent and access to key individuals and British government records, and then received guidance and encouragement at Harvard from Payson Wild and, principally, Bruce Hopper, the thesis adviser. Professor Elliott also made the later claim that Jack's idea came from studying the British Commonwealth during the prewar period in his Government 10A course.[22] How many conversations Jack had with Harold Laski during his subsequent visits to England, especially in the fall of 1939, is not quite clear, but James Landis later said that the paper was written in large measure under that professor's stimulus, if not his tutelage.[23] The intellectual momentum also profited from Kennedy's own observations of the state of Britain's unpreparedness for war.[24] Finally, with Joe Junior having graduated with a *cum laude* honors paper, Jack could do no less.

Caught up by his convictions, driven by his thesis, he had worked hard that fall and winter to compile his information. At Harvard's Widener Library, he combed through speeches and government documents and articles, which, as he later admitted to Liddell Hart, "don't always give the true story."[25] With the aid of hired secretarial help, typists, and stenographers, he managed to get the paper in under the deadline. To further expedite the work, the bulk of the thesis was dictated, a method that caused him trouble with Harvard authorities.

The problem stemmed from his violating the regulation against having women in men's rooms, a prohibition he and Torby had ignored on previous occasions under somewhat different circumstances. Jack enlisted stenographers by contacting employment agencies and the Darling Secretarial School. Unable to get satisfaction through those sources, he decided to place an ad in the *Boston Herald*. Since he had to leave for the weekend to attend a wedding in Chicago, Jack let Torby handle the affair until his return. "I took care of it all right," Macdonald recalled, "except for one thing. I forgot to give the paper a cutoff date, and the ad ran for ten days."[26]

Jack returned to a minor scandal. Torby's ad had playfully specified that the stenographer be "young," and the response created chaos around Winthrop Hall. "On the day I'd set for interviewing applicants," said Macdonald, "I spent an uncomfortable half-hour in the office of one of the college administrators trying to explain the presence of 60 clamoring females outside our dormitory at 9:30 A.M."

"You always were a ladies' man, Torby," Jack told him, "but this time I think you carried things a bit too far."[27]

Skirting the rules had not impeded Jack and had in fact expedited the work. Finding himself "called on the carpet" was inconsequential—all that mattered was the final product, and that was completed and dated right on the deadline.

Subtitled "The Inevitable Result of the Slowness of Conversion of the British Democracy from a Disarmament to a Rearmament Policy," the paper was awarded a *magna cum laude*, the second highest possible grade. Professor Carl J. Friedrich, a distinguished historian, thought Jack's title inappropriate. It should have been called "British Armament Policy." Friedrich wrote in his report on the thesis that not only was the paper much too long but that its fundamental thesis was never analyzed. Repetitious and wordy, it nevertheless showed a "reasonable amount of work, though labor and conversation would have helped."[28] Another professor evaluated the paper as having been badly written, but a "laborious, interesting and intelligent discussion of an interesting question."[29]

Professor Friedrich's retrospective comment is that "While Daddy Slept" would have been a more appropriate title.

The thesis did seem to rationalize Joe Kennedy's pro-Chamberlain position. Actually, it defended Chamberlain, explaining why he had to accommodate Hitler in order to delay any possible war. The Prime Minister, Kennedy argued, had no choice. Unlike Hitler, he was the leader of a democracy unwilling to make necessary sacrifices despite obvious international power rivalries.

Kennedy's manuscript contained anxieties about the limitations of democracy for national security. How England reacted was noted when discussing that nation's disillusionment with the League of Nations after Hitler's march into the Rhineland. The Versailles Treaty had been defied, the Locarno Agreements of 1925 repudiated. Still, the Conservative English government under Prime Minister Stanley Baldwin could not respond. Kennedy, in an especially Whiggish analysis of the dissembling of democracy under stress, wrote:

> Now a shattering in the ideal that was the League and the dawning realization of Germany's great productive capacity had made the country ready for rearmament. But it was still a democracy which was leisurely and confidently turning to rearmaments, not a frightened and desperate nation. It was not a nation with a single purpose with all its energies directed in a single direction; this was not to come until after Munich. No, it was still a democracy and the fear for their national self-preservation had not become strong enough for them to give up their personal interests, for the greater purpose. In other words, every group wanted rearmament but no group felt that there was any need for it to sacrifice its privileged position. This feeling in 1936 was to have a fatal influence in 1938. [30]

Kennedy's analysis foreshadowed later conflicts about formulating responses to totalitarian philosophies while upholding civil liberties and democratic government. He saw that different powers could more easily mobilize resources to defeat democracies, while the latter impotently tried to reconcile competing internal interests. "Thus the efforts of democracies are disjointed," he wrote. "They don't have the intensity or the long-range view that the dictators do." Their leadership must "gloss over facts and hope that they will not be 'called.'" To ensure its own existence, a democracy cannot afford the luxury of permitting particular interests to "run counter to the idea of national organization." His skepticism questioned the self-deceptive attitudes of assuming that popular government had made America so strong. He wrote, "In this calm acceptance of the theory that the democratic way is the best way, it seems to me, lies the danger. Why, exactly, is the democratic system the better? It may be answered that it is better because it allows for the full development of man as an individual. But it seems to be that this only indicates that democracy is a 'pleasanter' form of government—not that it is the best form of government for meeting the present world problem." His most cogent apprehensions about the efficacy of liberal democracies appeared in the concluding section:

It may be a great system of government to live in internally but it's [sic] weaknesses are great. We wish to preserve it here. If we are to do so, we must look at situations much more realistically than we do now. Our foreign policy must take advantages. We must keep from being placed on an equal keel with the dictators because then we will lose. We can't afford to misjudge situations as we misjudged Munich. We must use every effort to form accurate judgements—and even then our task is going to be a difficult one.

Written while Jack's father was viewed as a close associate of the Chamberlain government, the paper was submitted almost exactly two months before Churchill took over. An essential element in the background was the Ambassador's increasingly great alienation from Churchill. What has drawn surprisingly little recognition is that Kennedy's thesis, while trying to blunt the personal criticism of Chamberlain, separated itself from the older Kennedy. It viewed Churchill as an accurate prophet and it urged the importance of American readiness to respond to a similar situation. About Churchill, Kennedy wrote, "In the light of the present day war, we are able to wonder at the blindness of Britain's leaders and the country as a whole that could fail to see the correctness of Churchill's arguments."[31] It was perhaps this kind of point that Torbert Macdonald recognized when he asked Jack whether the paper might not embarrass his father.[32]

A recent work on John F. Kennedy's relations with Great Britain, by David Nunnerly, pointed out that Jack was "utterly opposed to the position taken by his father," that he rarely accepted the soundness of his political judgments and, as the years went by, became "increasingly conscious that his father had played a hard role in Anglo-American relations during the War."[33] D. W. Brogan, the British historian, writing about this in *The New Leader* during Kennedy's presidency, remarked that "one of the most interesting things . . . is that Kennedy seems to have been very little affected by his father's views of his father's friends, notably Neville Chamberlain."[34]

"Finished my thesis," wrote Jack to his father. "It was only going to run about the average length, 70 pages, but finally ran to 150. Am sending you a copy. It is the third carbon, as the other two had to be handed in. . . . I'll be interested to see what you think of it, as it represents more work than I've ever done in my life."[35]

The Ambassador wasted very little time in helping Jack's paper become more than a mere contribution to the Widener Library of Harvard University. Joe Kennedy's friend, newsman Arthur Krock, had been visiting the embassy in London at about the time the war was beginning and was very much involved in the situation concerning Britain's lack of preparedness. The Ambassador saw Krock as the man who should look at his son's thesis. He then suggested to Jack that he send it to Krock, who immediately judged it amateurish in many respects. But Krock was always ready to help the Kennedys. He told Jack he thought it very timely and made the offer, if Jack and his father would go along, to try getting a publisher through his own agent. Krock urged Jack to join him in his Georgetown library, where they could edit the manuscript for publication. Krock later minimized his own editorial role, saying he did nothing more "than polish it and amend it here and there, because it was very, very definitely his own product." But he did suggest the book's title should be inspired by Churchill's *While England Slept.*[36]

While Krock arranged for his literary agent, Gertrude Algase, to handle it, Joe Kennedy moved into action. Believing that a foreword by publisher Henry Luce would give the book additional stature, the Ambassador attempted several overseas phone calls and finally succeeded. Luce was impressed with the work because it showed, in his mind, that the Conservative government was not alone in being responsible for what had happened, but, as he said, "there was certainly just as much lack of foresight on the part of Labourites."[37]

Meanwhile, the senior Kennedy continued to help promote Jack's book for publication. He consulted with as many Englishmen as possible. The timing coincided with the end of the "phony war," the invasion by the Nazis of Denmark, Norway, and the Low Countries, the obvious proof that Hitler's Germany could not be pacified by negotiations or conciliation. So the events of the spring of 1940, coinciding with the efforts to market the manuscript, strengthened the authority of the thesis, immediately underlining the fallacies of European isolationism and, in particular, the policies of the Cliveden set and the Chamberlain government. On May 20 the Ambassador sent Jack a rather remarkable letter, one that appeared to disassociate itself from the Ambassador's own role.

Joe Kennedy wrote Jack that he had shown the manuscript to many people in London and that he had gotten many fine compliments for the work. Some, however, felt that it had gone too far in absolving the leadership of Stanley Baldwin and the National Government, including Chamberlain, from responsibility for the situation that England found herself in at the time of Munich. Others pointed out that the National Government had been in absolute control from 1931 to 1935; when it had been returned to office in November of 1935 it was with a huge majority, a sufficient margin to give them a mandate to have moved at that point to have made the country strong. "If the country supported such a policy well and good," wrote Ambassador Kennedy; "if not, then the National leaders should have thrown caution out of the window and attempted to arouse their countrymen to the dangers with which Britain obviously was confronted." Baldwin was being let off too easily.[38]

It was rather remarkable, given his own closeness to the Chamberlain government, for the Ambassador to advise his son not to "give the appearance of trying to do a complete whitewash of the leaders." He carefully reconciled his own position with the changed situation and the desire to help his son. "Why not say that the British national policy was the result of British national sentiment and then everyone, leaders and people alike, must assume some share of the responsibility for what happened," he suggested. "It is not fair to hang it all onto the leaders; it is equally unfair to absolve them of all responsibility. For some reason, Britain slept. That means pretty much all Britain, leaders and people alike." And then he made the following points in words that Jack subsequently copied almost verbatim for the final part of the published version: "To say that democracy has been awakened now by the horrible events of the past few weeks does not prove anything; any system of government would awaken at a time like this. Any person would wake up when the house is burning down. What we want is the kind of government that will wake up when the fire first starts or, better yet, one that will not permit a fire to start at all."

Gertrude Algase quickly got a publisher, who sensed both its timeliness and the significance of its authorship. Wilfred Funk, Inc., of New York, moved rapidly. By late July, the first copies were off the press and ready for shipping. The Ambassador also arranged to supply individuals and periodicals with review copies, sending forty-six names to the publisher and devoting himself to ensuring a favorable reception.[39] That plus the enthusiasm of Funk prompted the mailing out of some 250 copies instead of the normal hundred. "The publisher is so enthusiastic that he is putting on a really big campaign . . . and when you come to town next week, we will probably have worked out some plans for publicity . . . and you can be sure it will be dignified," the agency wrote to Jack.[40]

Both with and without the aid of his father, Jack quickly became the proud owner of significant notices for his book. Reviewed late that summer and fall by all the important popular publications, commentators readily noted the timeliness of the message. Generally, reviewers found many positive things to say about the scholarship, insights, and skill with which the young author had constructed his work. They especially agreed with the tone. *The New York Times Book Review* praised it for displaying "mature understanding and fair-mindedness" and cited the "young man from Boston" for his "clear-headed, realistic, unhysterical" message.[41] That paper's daily reviewer noted that Kennedy's approach was "unemotional" and lauded his "careful analysis of the data."[42] In the pages of *The Christian Science Monitor,* Jack was cited for his "dispassionate eye" and absence of partisanship.[43] Under a banner headline that announced JOHN F. KENNEDY WARNS AMERICA, the *Boston Herald* equated the act of reading the book with "an act of national preparedness" and called it "remarkable for its calm, its grasp of complex problems, its courageous frankness, its good manners, and its sound advice."[44] *The Washington Post,* dissenting from the general laudatory comments, faulted Jack for having been too harsh on the British Labour Party, charging that the author had been superficial about England's internal politics. "It is quite natural that Labour should refuse to deliver itself bound hand and foot into the hands of the Tories by voting the National Government the dictatorial power which alone would permit an effective armament," the reviewer pointed out, and then added that it would be just as glib to blame France's unpreparedness on the Popular Front government.[45]

For the Ambassador, the existence of the book outweighed any other consideration, including inferential criticisms of his own past position. He had always advised that a book would help his son's standing with the "right people." Writing to Rose from London, he showed obvious delight. "I read Jack's book through and I think it is a swell job," he told her. "There is no question that regardless of whether he makes any money out of it or not, he will have built himself a foundation for his reputation that will be of lasting value to him. Tell him I am taking the book today to Laski and I'm going to have Laski give me some suggestions as to what people here might be helpful to get letters from for Jack, and I'm also looking up who will be likely to do the best job publishing it [in England].'"[46] The next day, he promptly dispatched a copy to the man whose opposition was already beginning to force him out of the Court of St. James's, the new Prime Minister, Winston Churchill.[47]

It was Laski's response, however, that was brutal.

The easy thing for me to do would be to repeat the eulogies that Krock and Harry Luce have showered on your boy's work. In fact, I choose the more difficult way of regretting deeply that you let him publish it. For while it is the book of a lad with brains, it is very immature, it has no structure, and dwells almost wholly on the surface of things. In a good university, half a hundred seniors do books like this as part of their normal work in their final year. But they don't publish them for the good reason that their importance lies solely in what they get out of doing them and not out of what they have to say. I don't honestly think any publisher would have looked at that book of Jack's if he had not been your son, and if you had not been ambassador. And those are not the right grounds for publication. I care a lot about your boys. I don't want them to be spoilt as rich men's sons are so easily spoilt. Thinking is a hard business, and you have to pay the price for admission to it. Do believe that these hard sayings from me represent much more real friendship than the easy price of "yes men" like Arthur Krock. [48]

Freda Laski recalled that her husband was not willing to write any blurb for the book. He felt that, in twenty years time, the author would be very sorry that he had written it.[49]

A comparison between the thesis and the book shows some startling stylistic differences. The published version is far more professional than the sparse, inelegant original. *Why England Slept* has far more journalistic verve. Although the book was submitted in the spring of 1940, it was off the presses in July, so there is reason to doubt the publishers could have spent very much time reworking the manuscript. However, Arthur Krock's literary talents undoubtedly refined the prose.

But probably the most significant single difference relates to the problem of the international crisis and democracy. The thesis emphasized Kennedy's long-standing deliberations over the limitations of democracy vis-à-vis totalitarianism, doubts that had been especially reflected in his thinking while touring the Continent, when he had been impressed with the efficiency and order of fascism and speculated that democracy might be an unaffordable luxury. The finished book has a far different tone. It includes lyrical endorsements of democracy and views its preservation as the reason for rearming, rather than seeing it as an impediment to national security. Omitted, also, is the critique of the assumptions linking democracy to the high standards of living in America, while the final paragraph pronounces faith in its ultimate efficacy: "We should profit by the lesson of England and make our democracy work. We must make it work right now. Any system of government will work when everything is going well. It's the system that functions in the pinches that survives."[50]

The changes in emphasis between the two versions could not have occurred because of overnight transformations of beliefs that had become fundamental to Jack Kennedy's view of society and government. Yet he recognized that modifications were necessary before breaking into print. As democracies themselves were becoming more imperiled, and as the United States was beginning to fear the real possibility of involvement in the war, the climate changed between the writing of the thesis and its publication. It was more important to defend democracy as an ideology, and so Kennedy's eventual political career was spared the need to explain insufficient faith in popular government.

The two versions were also symptomatic of the differences between Jack Kennedy's incipient political outlook—not always consistent, somewhat inchoate, but leaning toward assumptions of gentry wisdom —and recognition of how to get his message across. At the same time, his intellectual powers were becoming better defined, his independence of thought sharper within the appreciation that he was, above all, a Kennedy.

The book also considerably sharpened the applicability of the thesis to the increasing American consciousness over defense needs. So the introduction in the published version differs from the preface; it stresses the similarity between English and American reluctance to arm, making the intended lesson clear. And it contains modifications that reflected his father's advice not to try to exonerate English leadership. "That is not my view," wrote Jack Kennedy. "This is not merely a pro-Baldwin or anti-Baldwin, a pro-Chamberlain or anti-Chamberlain discussion. I believe it is one of democracy's failings that it seeks to make scapegoats for its own weaknesses."[51]

The young author became an instant celebrity. By mid-July, even before the book reached the stores, reports were encouraging. A thousand copies were quickly sold and the outlook for a large audience was good. Requests to write articles, and offers from lecture agencies poured in.[52]

William L. Batt, Jr., later an assistant to the Secretary of Labor under Truman and Kennedy's Area Rehabilitation Administration director, wrote for the Advisory Commission to the Council of National Defense, requesting that Jack take advantage of his newfound fame as an author by writing an article supporting conscription. Batt advised, "It would be more effective for you to ask to appear before one of the committees for hearings on either the Burke-Wadsworth or other bills which may be put up. That, of course, might be bolloxed by your Dad's position, but some device to get the view of the majority of our generation before public notice ought to be used."[53]

By late August, Jack's agent reported that the book was already in its fourth printing, totaling eighty-five hundred copies, and the expectations were that, beyond a doubt, it would go beyond ten thousand.[54] By September, *Publishers Weekly* was listing it as a candidate for the national best-seller's list and it appeared on the lists carried by the *Herald Tribune, The New York Times,* and the *New York World-Telegram.*[55] Word also came from England that Ambassador Kennedy had approved the sale to a British publisher, Hutchinson, for eight hundred dollars and that English publication was set for October 11.[56]

At the same time, Jack's new fame spurred an interest in his brother Joe. Joe had gotten some publicity for his role at the Democratic convention, but Jack had now begun to have, as Gertrude Algase wrote to him, "stolen quite innocently to be sure . . . the thunder."[57] The agency continued to press to find out whether Joe Junior also had plans for a book.

But Jack, having graduated from Harvard *cum laude,* had already become a celebrity and successful author. Sales responded to the widespread reviews and moved along at seven hundred a week that September, then leveled off to three hundred by late the following month, reaching a total of ten thousand in February.[58] By the spring of 1941, they numbered eighty thousand, good for forty thousand dollars in royalties, not bad for a young man of twenty-three. He turned his British earnings over to assist the bombed-out city of Coventry while the American dollars went for a new automobile. Visiting Hyannis Port during the late summer of 1940, his friend Charles Spalding remembered the scene vividly.

"We walked in, and Jack was downstairs with a whole pile of these books of his, *Why England Slept.* It was just a wonderful disarray of papers, letters from prime ministers and congressmen and people you've heard about, some under wet bathing suits and some under the bed. . . . He was seeing that the books were handed out and he was really moving the books. He was getting the books out. It was just a sort of amusing pragmatism that he hadn't just written the book and then he was going to disappear. He was going to see that it got sold. He was just laughing at his own success. . . . He was doing everything he could to promote it. And he was good at that. . . . the interviews, radio programs, answering letters, autographing copies, sending them out, checking bookstores, tie-ups . . ."[59]

Young Jack was finding the limelight to his liking.

6

The War

Unlike Jack, Joe opposed conscription, actively and vigorously. While at Harvard Law School, he formed a Cambridge prototype of Stuart's America First Committee, joining with classmates Quentin Roosevelt and Robert Taft, Jr. They argued that American assistance to Great Britain, especially convoying ships through the North Atlantic, would inevitably mean full American participation. Quite contrary to the position taken by Jack the preceding spring, Joe Junior's group was called the Harvard Committee Against Military Intervention and was recognized locally as a vigorous and emotional proponent of isolationism.

William G. Carleton, a distinguished professor of political science and occasional speechwriter for Joseph P. Kennedy, remembered both brothers as he saw them at Palm Beach. "And although I believe it was spring vacation, Easter," the professor recalled, "and Joe Junior and Kathleen were all dressed up and eager to meet their dates, we had to wait two hours while we had a question for discussion over a kind of round table." Among the Ambassador's sons, Jack's historical and political mind surpassed that of his brother and even the father. "Jack seemed to be, in appearance and manner, an old English Yankee Brahmin and a typical

Ivy Leaguer, whereas Joe had none of that."[1] Carleton was a noninterventionist influence, a believer in the inevitability of Communist expansion in Europe after the defeat of the Nazis and Fascists that would only force America to police the Continent indefinitely after the war. He thought that Jack, and not Joe Junior, was sensitive to such nuances; and Jack, like Carleton, may have been trying to influence Stuart and his America First Committee in that direction.

The activities of both Kennedy brothers were significant in view of the controversies that surrounded Ambassador Kennedy at the Court of St. James's. The big change in London came in the spring of 1940 when Winston Churchill replaced the discredited Chamberlain. Suddenly, an ambassador who had been considered by many, including President Roosevelt, as even more pro-British than Walter Hines Page in Woodrow Wilson's day, was virtually ignored at 10 Downing Street. The enlarging "Kennediana" file in the British Foreign Office documented the attitude toward Kennedy, which was epitomized by the following entry: "Mr. Kennedy is a very foul specimen of double crosser and defeatist. He thinks of nothing but his own pocket. I hope that this war will at least see the elimination of this type."[2]

In a personal meeting between Kennedy and Churchill, Churchill's distrust was confirmed. Kennedy's own version of their talk betrayed his defeatism to Roosevelt as he expressed opposition to the kind of American assistance that would "leave the United States holding the bag for a war in which the Allies expected to be beaten."[3] Less than two weeks later, Kennedy cabled Roosevelt that only "a miracle can save the BEF from being wiped out, or, as I said yesterday, surrender . . . Churchill, Attlee, and others will want to fight to the death but there will be other members who will realize that physical destruction of men and property in England will not be a proper offset to a loss of pride."[4] Mary Welsh Hemingway found Kennedy's pessimism deepened by the fall of France. He thought it madness to hold out against the Nazis. "They haven't got a hope," he told her.[5]

With the British government thoroughly exasperated, the Prime Minister desired the Ambassador's ouster. Churchill certainly had no further appetite for dealing with him, preferring to work directly with Roosevelt or through the President's unofficial emissary, "Wild Bill" Donovan. Facing a difficult third-term reelection attempt, Roosevelt feared having Kennedy return in the weeks before Election Day. Undoubtedly, FDR worried that a flamboyant gesture by his disgruntled ambassador, who had been enjoying some modest support for his own candidacy, could shake loose from the Roosevelt column countless Irish Catholic votes, which had already shown dangerous signs of defection.[6] Substantial local pols such as Congressman John McCormack thought Joe Kennedy might be the right man to replace the mighty FDR. Kennedy himself was enchanted with the idea. The possibility, however, never went beyond a latent party rebellion against the President. In the reelection of Roosevelt, British and American interests were similar, with Churchill preferring to rely on Roosevelt rather than any potential successor. As Lord Beaverbrook said, it was vital to help keep the right man in the White House, especially since "Kennedy claims he can put 25 million Catholic votes behind Wendell Willkie to throw Roosevelt out."[7] Foreign Minister Lord Halifax also reported that Kennedy had talked about arranging the widespread publication of an article by himself in the United States five days before the election. He warned that it would indict the administration. News of such Kennedy activities were relayed to the President. Finally, Roosevelt, having been notified of the several threats by his ambassador, cabled Kennedy to return to Washington. He chided him by wiring that the liquor trade in Boston was now "challenging" and that the girls in Hollywood were "more fascinating."[8]

In London, Kennedy had been making the rounds for some time, expressing very clearly his anxiety to return. His activities were accompanied by considerable comment, which was circulating even before the President's cable.[9] On October 23, he returned to the United States, ready for an all-out attack on the President.

His arrival at the airport was awaited by Rose Kennedy, who told him: "The President sent you, a Roman Catholic, as Ambassador to London, which probably no other President would have done. He sent you as a representative to the Pope's coronation. You might write yourself down an ingrate in the view of many people if you resign now."[10]

Kennedy was invited for dinner in the White House. When he emerged that evening, "instead of throwing the bombs he had prepared he was quietly putting them back into his pocket."[11] Two days later, Kennedy gave his radio endorsement of the President. "Franklin D. Roosevelt should be reelected President." At a subsequent press conference, he denied having made anti-British statements or having been responsible for defeatist talk. Perhaps flattery and his wife's advice prevailed. Or perhaps Roosevelt's possession of a sufficient pile of evidence demonstrating his disloyalty may have provided the necessary leverage. In any event, on November 5, Roosevelt was reelected. Five days later, with the third term assured, Kennedy sat down in his Boston hotel room at the

Ritz-Carlton and gave an interview, which had been arranged by Honey Fitz, to two reporters, Leonard M. Lyons of *The Boston Globe* and Ralph Coghlan of the *St. Louis Post-Dispatch*. Kennedy's free-wheeling observations, in what he claimed was an off-the-record session, created an instant sensation, particularly rocking the British, whose view of the American ambassador was suddenly completely confirmed. When asked about Eleanor Roosevelt, Kennedy complained "that she bothered us more on our jobs in Washington to take care of the poor little nobodies who haven't any influence, than all of the rest of the people down there together. She's always sending me notes to have some Susie Glotz to tea at the embassy." Mrs. Roosevelt's subsequent hostility toward Jack could never be disassociated from such remarks.

Kennedy reiterated his determination to keep the United States out of the war, vowing that he was willing to spend all he had to prevent that possibility.

The practical wisdom, Kennedy told his interviewers, was to support England as a way of self-preservation, as a way of insurance, to give the United States more time. "As long as she is in there, we have time to prepare. It isn't that she's fighting for democracy. That's the bunk. She's fighting for self-preservation, just as we will if it comes to us. . . . It is a practical question of judgment, how much to send. It is a question of how long England can hold out. If she collapses soon, then stop."[12]

In London, the American military attaché, General Raymond E. Lee, observed that in all the British papers that he had seen "there is not one which does not have an indignant fling at Mr. Kennedy for his interview. He is, without question, going to be *persona non grata* in this country for the rest of his life."[13]

Until his death in 1969, the "founding father" could never overcome the memory of association with defeatism, anti-Semitism, and an inclination to tolerate a Nazi victory. The latter view again reached the public, only a few months after the Ambassador's recall, when his oldest son addressed a meeting at the Ford Hall in Boston. In a clear expression of the isolationist sentiment of the day, as well as a faithful rendition of his father's views, Joe Junior declared that the United States would be better off accepting Nazi domination of the Continent rather than plunging into the war on the British side. That would mean, he warned, total war, a war that could last six or seven years. It could tax the American economy beyond its ability. It would be better, he suggested, to do business with the Nazi conquerors under a barter system than to tolerate what seemed to him the inevitable result of sending "an air force to

Britain with pilots and battleships to convoy supplies. . . ."[14] At the same time, President Roosevelt castigated such appeasement notions.

"This includes our late Ambassador and also his son," wrote General Lee in London; "a smart aleck of a boy who has apparently given an interview in the American press suggesting that we accede to the idea of barter with Germany. This could not be more, both in idea and expression, than a quotation from Hitler's speeches. The youngster will not help his father's standing in the United States."[15]

Clearly identified with the isolationists—or noninterventionists, as they preferred to be known—Kennedy retired from public life to concentrate on his greatest strength, making more money. In early 1941 he sold his sumptuous Bronxville home. Unlike the state of New York, Florida had neither an income nor an inheritance tax, so Palm Beach became his legal residence. On business trips to New York, he could always stay at the Waldorf Towers.

Jack was at Stanford. Joe Junior was carrying on antiwar activities at Harvard Law School. Thanks to the ever-useful Krock, Kathleen had found a job with the *Washington Times-Herald,* which, for a time, involved writing a gossip column. The young Kennedy children were away at various schools. Brain-injured Rosemary, meanwhile, was becoming more difficult to manage and her parents feared sexual maturity could compound matters.

Jack's decision to attend the West Coast university at Palo Alto, near San Francisco, had marked a significant change from earlier plans to enter Yale Law School. His enrollment at the Stanford School of Business Administration was, in part, the result of the influence of his brother's roommate, Tom Killefer. Killefer, the son of "Reindeer" Bill Killefer, a longtime major-league catcher and minor-league baseball manager, had a home at Hermosa Beach, California, which Joe Junior visited in the summer of 1940. Through Joe, Killefer helped convince Jack about the virtues of California: Palo Alto's salubrious climate, favorable for his back problems, one of his current health concerns. Intestinal difficulties had necessitated a visit to Dr. Sara Jordan that summer at the Lahey Clinic in Boston. A gastroenterologist, she had treated Jack since he was eleven. Her prescription indicated the existence of a severe gastrointestinal disorder. Jack's father further explained, in a letter to James Landis, that while Jack had intended to go to Yale, "principally because he felt it would be better not to be constantly in direct competition with his brother," that stomach problems had led to medical advice to take a year off. "I hate to see him lose a year in these crucial times, but, after all, his health is more important."[16]

Why the change to business, however, is not clear. An article in the *Stanford Daily* explained that he intended to spend a year at Palo Alto and would then return East to attend Yale, a plan Jack seemed to confirm by requesting Harvard to send his records to the registrar at Stanford because he was taking prelaw work in California.[17] The assistant dean in charge of records at Harvard explained to the Stanford registrar that Kennedy had asked for his transcript, since he was applying for admission to the Stanford Law School.[18] Under a "permit to attend," enabling him to audit classes without credit, he took two courses, one in political science and the other in government.[19]

Off-campus life was much more active. His attractions to young women, personal charm, fame as an author and heir to the Ambassador's fortunes, fondness for good times—including speeding around the Bay area in his convertible and making the rounds of the local night spots —made him a popular and exciting addition to the university community. All this was in spite of his ill health. Pleasant and bright, but gaunt looking, he often chose his clothes at random and they hung on his sparse frame and gave him an unkempt appearance, while his tousled hair preserved an adolescent look. Such characteristics, however, were hardly liabilities with his female friends. A glamorous figure, he got involved with several women who may have had illusions of marriage.

Just before setting out for Stanford, his most serious relationship had ended unhappily. While still at Harvard, he had gone out with Frances Ann Cannon, who attended Sarah Lawrence, a women's college near his Bronxville home. Frances Ann was a beautiful, bright girl, from a fine family known as wealthy, prominent, and powerful in Charlotte, North Carolina. Jack and Torby often drove down from Cambridge to doubledate with Frances Ann and her friends. Writing to her father in September of 1939, when the Kennedy-Frances Ann friendship reached its height, Kathleen had included the gossip that "Jack is taking out Frances Ann this weekend so we can all hardly wait."[20] Marriage possibilities were rumored, but that was never really likely. Frances Ann's Protestantism was unacceptable to the Kennedy family, as, indeed, his Catholicism was to hers. To break up the romance, her mother shipped her off on a round-the-world cruise on the *Kungsholm.* They probably need not have worried so much, actually, because Jack Kennedy's desire for marriage at that stage of his career seems doubtful. It was also inevitable that she would soon find someone more eligible, less controversial, and ready for such a step. And that she soon did, with a young journalist named

John Hersey. On April 29, 1940, one month after Jack had deposited his thesis at Harvard, Frances Ann became the first wife of the soon-to-become-prominent writer. To this day, she refuses to discuss her relationship with Jack Kennedy. Yet those who knew Frances Ann believe she was the woman he almost married.[21]

At Stanford, he developed close attachments to two other young women, Harriet Price and Nancy Burkett. Harriet, nicknamed "Flip," dated Jack quite seriously and fell in love with him. She also assumed reciprocity. As with Frances Ann, he talked of marriage but, one suspects, rather deviously. He and Harriet made the rounds of the Palo Alto and San Francisco night spots. So, too, with Nancy. From an old, conservative, socially proper San Francisco family, she herself was one of the best-looking girls on the campus, and also one of the most prim. With Jack, Nancy went to such night spots as the Mark Hopkins Hotel and student hangouts in Palo Alto.

Jack, Nancy recalls, was a celebrity as the Ambassador's son, running around in his casual Ivy League clothes, polo shirts, and sneakers, and his big Buick convertible with red leather seats. Harriet, like so many others, remembers how swiftly he drove and how his car was a common landmark parked outside L'Omellette, a campus favorite meeting place on El Camino Real.[22]

It was while at Stanford, on October 16, that Jack joined seventeen million other Americans between the ages of twenty-one and thirty-five in registering for the draft. Thirteen days later Secretary of War Henry L. Stimson, blindfolded, reached into the ten-gallon "fishbowl" and began drawing numbers for the draft lottery. On the eighteenth draw he pulled out number 2748, Jack's.[23] But, as a college student, he was entitled to a deferment until at least July of 1941. An AP wirephoto circulated a picture of young Kennedy spotting his draft number in a newspaper.

California was partly a lark. There seems to have been no higher goal or seriousness of purpose or continuity involved with his work at Stanford. Jack was still unclear about his future course, a condition possibly exacerbated by the probability of forthcoming military service. He was still contemplating law as a field, at least sporadically, as indicated by a letter he wrote to Harvard as late as March, 1941, requesting that a transcript copy be sent to Yale.[24] Yet there is no evidence that Jack actually filed an application to enter the law school. According to Rose Kennedy, Joe Junior's preparation for law may have finally discouraged Jack from that career.[25]

Health remained a serious concern. Jack returned to the Lahey Clinic in Boston for treatment by Dr. Sarah Jordan. He entered the clinic, located at the New England Baptist Hospital, and spent part of January in confinement. On the first Sunday afternoon of the new year, 1941, Joe Satz, a representative of Jack's literary agency, went to the Bronxville home and found nobody there. Attempting to reach him, the agency wanted to convey a request from King Features, a subsidiary of the Hearst Syndicate, to capitalize on his fame by writing an article on the subject "Is Ireland Sleeping?" They hoped for a piece that would contain his impressions of the current controversies in Ireland, controversies that centered on Great Britain's demand for military bases despite that country's neutrality. They were willing to pay a hundred dollars for twelve hundred to fifteen hundred words strictly for the value of Jack's name on its by-line.

Unable to reach Jack, a telegram relaying the request was then sent to him at the New England Baptist Hospital.[26] Somehow during that month, Jack turned out an article about the debate. It was published in Hearst papers; on February 2, the *New York Journal-American* ran the story under the headline IRISH BASES ARE VITAL TO BRITAIN.

That spring, Jack went on an aimless trip to Latin America. His mother and Eunice had gone by cruise ship to the Caribbean and to Rio de Janeiro, where Jack joined them after a Pan American clipper flight from Miami. From there, he went on to Argentina and then to Chile.

By the time he returned to the States, President Roosevelt had declared a "state of national emergency." Joe Junior had also signed up with the Naval Aviation Cadet Program and had been sworn in as a seaman second class in the U.S. Naval Reserve.[27] In mid-July, Joe reported to the Squantum Naval Air Station, just outside Boston.

Joe's enlistment became Jack's challenge, immediately ending his ennui. Jack volunteered for the Army Officers Candidate School. After having failed the physical, he tried the Navy, which also came to the same conclusion. So he devoted the rest of the summer to back-strengthening radial exercises. Applying once more to the Navy, he was accepted to the Navy officers training course and, in early winter, received his commission.

Through his father, Jack had some additional assistance, not only in getting into the Navy but in obtaining a military occupational preference. The helpful individual was Captain Alan Goodrich Kirk. Kirk had been the American naval attaché in London when the senior Kennedy was there as the ambassador and was now director of the Office of Naval Intelligence.

On August 4, Ambassador Kennedy had written to Captain Kirk: "I am having Jack see a medical friend of yours in Boston tomorrow for physical examination and then I hope he'll become associated with you in Naval Intelligence."[28] Four days later Jack applied for a naval commission, and at the same time Kirk assured Ambassador Kennedy that he would see to it that Jack was given an interesting job.[29]

On September 25 he was sworn in and received his commission as an ensign. As Clay and Joan Blair have aptly noted, "Thus, a young man who could certainly not have qualified for the Sea Scouts on his physical condition, entered the U.S. Navy."[30]

That brought Jack to Washington in the Office of Naval Intelligence. Starting in October, he worked under Captain Samuel A. Dulany Hunter. In that office, the Navy's chief intelligence arm, he helped in the preparation of bulletins, both daily and weekly, which distilled information from various foreign sources. He worked in a sparsely furnished room that held four metal desks, and spent the day mainly writing, condensing, and editing. One of his co-workers remembered him as exhibiting high intelligence and quick wit.[31]

Jack's stay in Washington coincided with Kathleen's career in the national capital. Having graduated from the two-year course at Finch Junior College, she had moved on to a job with the *Washington Times-Herald,* a vehemently anti-interventionist, anti-Roosevelt paper. There, as wherever she went, personal radiance ensured her popularity. To a much greater degree than Jack, Kick's relations with people were relaxed and congenial. She displayed little of her brother's reserve and was also probably the most assertively independent Kennedy child.

She dated a number of men. One was her *Times-Herald* colleague, John B. White. But ever since her days in London, several Englishmen maintained contact with her from overseas, including Hugh Fraser, who finally married author Antonia Fraser. Kathleen's eye, however, was on a young nobleman she had met in 1938, Billy Hartington. His parents were the Duke and Duchess of Devonshire, and their landed holdings were enormous, making them among Great Britain's wealthiest dynasties. Billy was the heir to their titles as well as to their estates, which included Chatsworth House, Hardwick Hall, Bolton Abbey, Compton Place, and Lismore Castle in Ireland, as well as Carlton Gardens, a large town house in London that had been blitzed by the Germans in 1940. The family lands totaled some 180,000 acres.

But the impending marriage carried one major liability, especially for Rose. Billy's parents, among the most conservative of Britain's ruling class, were also pillars of the Church of England. The Duke even headed the Freemasons, the traditional opponent of the Roman Catholic Church. Billy, the Marquess of Hartington, was descended from Sir William Cavendish, who had received a large share of the Church lands when Henry VIII broke up the monasteries while establishing the Church of England. More than a century later, during the reign of King Charles II, the first Duke of Devonshire withdrew from the Privy Council in protest against Roman Catholic influence. But the young woman, fully conscious of the probable impact upon her parents of a Hartington, was nevertheless not dissuaded by that prospect.

With Kathleen probably exerting the stronger force, she and Jack shared a personal sentiment: skepticism about their religious faith. The managing editor of the *Times-Herald,* who knew them, as well as their parents, recalls that "there was no sense of piety as an internal characteristic of either one of them." They had little feeling for religion other than what "was the conventional proper thing to do." John White thought that, for a time, Kathleen toyed with the idea of actually leaving the Church.[32] Jack told Kay Halle that he wished "we could start a new religion that would bring all people together." To another friend he expressed skepticism about the Church and the clergy.[33] Later, as a senator, he confided to a colleague that "religiously, I'm a Catholic."[34] Cardinal Cushing, reaffirming Jack Kennedy's faith, acknowledged that "he never liked the idea of being in the public eye when he was at prayer" and said that "his religion was between himself and God, and that's what religion is." When dropping into the archbishop's house in Boston, "he never kissed my ring nor did he ever genuflect when greeting me."[35] Except when it became a factor in his political career, Jack was too much of a rationalist to take it very seriously. What feelings he did have were hereditary and instinctive, devout in a personal way but not intellectualized. As in many other matters, Jack and Kathleen were compatible souls in questions of faith. Together during those Washington days just before and immediately after Pearl Harbor, they led hectic social lives, usually traveling in the same circle, frequently giving the appearance of constituting a team.[36] They seemed to know all the right people. Quite naturally, too, it was Kathleen who led Jack to Inga.

One of Kick's *Times-Herald* friends, Inga Arvad was a former Miss Denmark and about four years older than Jack. She wrote three profile columns per week for the paper in a style that embodied an innocent artlessness, while her own life-style was far less so. On November 27, at just about the time when the Office of Naval Intelligence was placed on a full alert due to the deterioration of Japanese-American relations, the *Times-Herald* carried a profile about Jack under Inga Arvad's by-line, lauding the young man as a twenty-four-year-old with a future. Readers were told about his Harvard accomplishments and reminded about *Why England Slept,* carefully recalling Arthur Krock's role in its publication. "Jack hates only one subject—himself," said the article. "He is the best listener I have come across between Haparanda and Yokohama. Elder men like to hear his views, which are sound and astonishingly objective for so young a man."[37]

Inga was a fascinating woman. After her marriage to an Egyptian preparing to enter his country's foreign service, and finding life intolerable in that alien land and society, Inga Arvad obtained a divorce and returned to Denmark. Then in the 1930's she went to Germany. Well connected, she finagled an interview with Hermann Goering on the pretext of being a journalist. The interview involved Goering's forthcoming marriage. Inga's piece did find its way into a Copenhagen paper, which subsequently rewarded her with a job as its Berlin correspondent. Following that success, she landed an invitation to the Nazi Field Marshal's wedding. Appropriately enough, the best man at the affair was Adolf Hitler himself. Inga managed exclusive interviews with not only Propaganda Minister Joseph Paul Goebbels, but also two with Der Fuehrer. Very much taken with Inga, Hitler had her accompany him at the Berlin Olympic games in 1936. Much was subsequently made of the Nazi dictator's statement that Frau Arvad was a "perfect example of Nordic beauty." At least according to one account (a source with an interest in rehabilitating her reputation) Foreign Minister Joachim von Ribbentrop later proposed that she spy for the German government in Paris. She was to mingle in French cafe society, attend the proper parties, and relay the scuttlebutt back to Germany. Allegedly offended by the suggestion, she decided to leave Berlin. She returned to Copenhagen, made a movie, and was married to a Hungarian World War I air ace named Paul Fejos.[38]

Life with Fejos, however, proved somewhat too much for Inga, who found herself taken on an expedition to the Dutch East Indies. Fejos was interested not only in making movies but in capturing wild animals and in archaeological digs. Her marriage petered out, without having been officially terminated. She then became the mistress of a Swedish journalist, a shadowy figure named Axel Winner-gren, who was described in *Time* magazine of January 26, 1942, as "a mysterious globe-trotter, one of the last of the international capitalists," who was also blacklisted by the American State Department because of his Nazi connections.[39] Apparently the State Department's reaction stemmed from Winner-gren's own association with Goering, who, at one point, asked him to play a role in negotiating a peace in 1940 between Russia and Finland. The industrialist never did participate but told a correspondent that he regarded Goering as the best hope for bringing Germany into the negotiations.

On the strength of the reporting that she had done during her Berlin days, and given her fluency in French, German, English, and Dutch, Inga was admitted to the Columbia School of Journalism, where she became involved with Arthur Krock, then editor of *The New York Times.* She joined the *Washington Times-Herald,* which was still under the control of Cissy Patterson, and worked with Kathleen Kennedy at the paper. Inga began her column, called, "Did You Happen to See?" Two ingredients thus joined to create a sensitive situation: the newspaper's staunch isolationist, anti-interventionist position; and the presence in that camp, already anathema to the Roosevelt administration, of a woman with such distinguished Nazi connections.

By the time the bombs dropped on Pearl Harbor, Miss Arvad had become intimate with Ensign Kennedy. He called her Inga-Binga and for a time they lived together in an apartment where John White, her *Times-Herald* colleague would pick them up when he and Kathleen double-dated with Jack and Inga. Inga's relationship with Jack seemed intense,[40] a passionate sexual involvement.

Once the war came, however, Inga was too hot for the *Times-Herald* to handle. One young lady denounced her to Frank C. Waldrop, the paper's editor, as a German agent. In the hysterical atmosphere five days after Pearl Harbor, as American cities were bracing for anticipated air attacks, Waldrop personally turned Inga in to the FBI field office, handing her over along with her accuser.[41]

In Palm Beach that winter there was a confrontation between Ambassador Kennedy and his son over the Danish woman. Jack talked about the possibility of marrying her. "Damn it, Jack," the Ambassador said, "she's already married." But Jack said he did not care.[42] As recounted later by Inga's son, Joe Kennedy was a tough individual, someone who could be very charming when she and Jack were with him. But if she left the room, he would excoriate him about her; if Jack left, "he'd try to hop in the sack with her. He did that one weekend at the Cape, she said. She thought it was a totally amoral situation, that there was something incestuous about the whole family."[43] John White's sister, Patsy, was close to Kathleen and Rose Kennedy, sharing with the family the days of grief that followed and as familiar with them as any of Jack and his sister's mutual friends. Asked about the printed speculation that the Ambassador contemplated making a lavish donation to the Church to buy an annulment for Inga so she could be free to become Jack's wife, she had a simple response. "No, I don't like that story. It just doesn't ring true. Joe would not have countenanced that kind of marriage no matter what. After all," explained Patsy White Carter, "he married old Honey Fitz's daughter. He wasn't going to have his son marry beneath him."⁴⁴

Meanwhile, of course, Jack's intelligence work and Inga Arvad were incompatible. Even before Waldrop did his patriotic duty, the FBI was watching her. Their files reveal that she first came to their attention in November of 1940, when a classmate at the Columbia School of Journalism advised that she may have been sent by the Germans to influence American morale. Her friendship with Hitler was reported by the FBI's New York office on June 7, 1941. The *Times-Herald* reporter, presumably the young lady who denounced her to Waldrop, had advised the bureau as early as November 14, 1941, that Mrs. Inga Fejos might be a spy. In mid-January, the Office of Naval Intelligence informed the FBI that "Ensign Jack" had been "playing around" with her, and a "confidential informant" confirmed he had "apparently been spending the night with Mrs. Fejos."⁴⁵ Suddenly, Jack was reassigned to the 6th Naval District Headquarters in Charleston, South Carolina, an assignment more dignified for the Ambassador's son than discharging him from the Navy under a cloud, which was the desire of Captain Howard Kingman, the assistant director of the Office of Naval Intelligence. Captain Samuel Hunter argued against cashiering the young man, arguing that he had not had access to information that could be anything more than mildly embarrassing. Then came the assignment to South Carolina.⁴⁶

The new job was tedious. Jack's function involved instructing defense-plant workers on how to defend both themselves and their plants against enemy bombing. In Charleston he roomed at 48 Murray Boulevard, the home of Mrs. George Abbott Middleton. But when Inga visited, as she did two weekends in February, they stayed in a room taken in her name at the Fort Sumter Hotel. By now Attorney General Francis Biddle had authorized the tapping of her telephone, and President Roosevelt himself sent a memo to J. Edgar Hoover that Inga Arvad should be "specially watched." While she and Jack were in Charleston, the FBI's technical "surveillance coverage disclosed that they engaged in sexual intercourse on a number of occasions in the hotel room" and that he "disclosed to Mrs. Fejos in general terms his tentative official assignment plans and the fact Presidential Adviser Harry Hopkins had gone to the hospital and was expected to leave same." A titillated J. Edgar Hoover was delighted at hearing Jack's voice with Inga's. Additional periodic contacts between the two were monitored, the last in June of 1942. That summer she divorced Paul Fejos, resigned her *Times-Herald* job, and moved to New York City under her maiden name.[47]

The transfer to South Carolina had been the Navy's reaction to the FBI's monitoring of his relationship with Inga. Getting him out of South Carolina, on the other hand, was clearly his father's way of preventing further relations. One family friend, while driving to Florida with Joe Timilty, the former Boston police commissioner and Kennedy sidekick from Honey Fitz days, heard about Joe Kennedy's agitation that a girl was on the verge of causing a real problem for Jack.[48] Extricating his son from his Inga-Binga was clearly done in the style of an Ambassador Kennedy who stopped at very little to achieve his goals.

On March 23 Jack was at Palm Beach with his father. As soon as he returned to Charleston—the very next day—he requested a ten-day leave from the Navy so he could consult with Dr. Sara Jordan at the Lahey Clinic. The request was granted, and on April 9 he put in for six-months inactive duty, stating that he needed an operation and would require the time for convalescence. The operation would be performed by the family surgeon at a private hospital to take care of a condition that had predated his entry into the Navy. Six months of inactive duty was approved. On April 11, 1942, Jack was formally transferred from the 6th Naval District to the Charleston Naval Hospital. From there he was sent closer to home for further treatment—the Naval Hospital at Chelsea.[49]

Investigations of this period show no evidence of any major illness requiring surgery. While confined in Boston, Jack suddenly qualified for sea duty. Later, he told Inga, he had not wanted to go to the war zone; he didn't like the war, was not at all interested in going out to the South Pacific. He saw her in Washington and complained that some "son of a bitch had transferred me to sea duty and I'm going to find out who it was." He later explained that his father had pulled the strings. Joe Kennedy had gotten on the wire to the undersecretary of the Navy. Very conveniently, that was James Forrestal, with whom Joe Kennedy had been friendly on Wall Street. Kennedy had asked that his son be transferred to sea duty in the Pacific. "Apparently he was really pissed off at the old man," Inga's son, Ronald, claimed his mother told him. Jack asked her to wait for his return.*

Such recollections, however, seem fanciful, resting on romantic reconstructions. While there is no need to doubt that the Ambassador wanted to separate Jack from Inga, the desire to experience military action during those early post-Pearl Harbor months was hardly exceptional among young American men. Given the patriotic fervor of the time, a Kennedy could not have done less. To duck the challenge of war, to avoid combat, to hold, instead, an innocuous desk job, simply denied their concept of mission. Even if, somehow, Jack's more reflective and introspective side had resisted that momentum and he had not flattered Inga's ego by assuring her he really did not want to leave, Joe Junior's entry into the Navy Air Force pretty much limited his own options.

And so, on July 27, 1942, Jack Kennedy joined the thousands of other "ninety-day wonders" who prepared for sea duty by reporting to the U.S. Naval Reserve Midshipmen's School at Northwestern University in Evanston, Illinois. There, at Abbott Hall, overlooking Lake Michigan, he attended classes and learned the rudiments of seamanship. At the same time Joe Kennedy's purpose was satisfied, as Jack's relationship with Inga trailed off into sporadic contacts. Letters were exchanged and Jack did manage to see her several times afterward. There was even a story, totally unverifiable, that cast doubt about the paternity of Inga's son.

In 1947 she married a western film star, Tim McCoy, who was some thirty years her senior. Six months later, Ronald was born.[50] The Blairs then speculated that "had the story of the Inga Arvad affair surfaced along Jack's political climb, we feel sure he would never have been seriously considered as a presidential candidate."

The idea of marrying Inga, as with Francis Ann earlier, was again inconsistent with Jack's own inclinations. Could Jack have been ready to make any kind of commitment to family life at twenty-five, which he reached in May of 1942? Much more characteristic was his desire to relish good times with many different women and avoid permanent entanglements with a single person. Kathleen's frequent Washington escort, John White, noted that Jack's temperament was of a rather unpolished pursuer of women. He tended to come on without much

---

*Joan and Clay Blair, Jr., in their close reconstruction of Kennedy's movements, found to their complete satisfaction that Joe Kennedy had used Forrestal to get Jack out to sea and away from Inga. Blairs, *Search,* pp. 151–52.

subtlety. "He was completely driven to dominate them," recalled White. "Once he got them, he lost interest and moved on to the next."[51] Yet his continued preoccupation with Inga seemed an exception to this general tendency and inspired the gossip that she enchanted him because he had been a virgin until he met her, which was most unlikely.[52]

Sexual conquest, or perhaps simple lust, certainly had enhanced her attractions for him. But there were other enticements. Inga, older than he, had seen even more of the world than Jack, had experienced places and people he must have found exotic. She had far more to offer than the coeds he had met at Stanford or the society belles he took nightclubbing, while, at the same time, also providing the company of feminine beauty, always important for his happiness. Throughout his life, Jack Kennedy was most satisfied when surrounded by lovely women, and Inga Arvad doubtless helped meet that need. But one also senses the affair as having been another of his little rebellions, exasperating his father and satisfying his own free spirits. The affair never had much of a chance of going anywhere, and with its conclusion Jack returned to where his father thought he belonged.

Once on active duty, Jack seemed preoccupied with his new pursuits, enjoying the companionship of his buddies and thriving equally well in that masculine world. One of his Navy friends who crossed the Pacific with him on the long voyage aboard the *Rochambeau* did not remember Jack as having been particularly interested in being a "swordsman" with women during that period, giving little evidence in their conversations of preoccupation with sex.[53] To such acquaintances Jack was a serious young man, deeply interested in politics and looking forward to a postwar career of some kind of government service.

Still, he had little reason to deny his older brother's inherent right to a political career. Joe Junior was the obvious beneficiary of whatever the family could do, financially and in other ways, to support his political ambition. Asked whether Jack felt Joe was standing in his way, Patsy White Carter responded that he tended to accept the circumstance for what it was. He could do nothing about it. "This is a great tribe, you know," she said, "with all the strength of the tribe and with all the detriments of the tribe. You took your turn, and everybody pushed you. Then, when you got there, everyone pushed the next one." Such was the Kennedys' tribal custom.[54]

7

A Hero in the South Pacific

Service on PT boats offered Jack the opportunity to see military action. The Northwestern installation was visited by two naval officers, John Harllee and John D. Bulkeley, whose early PT exploits had been celebrated in a best-selling book called *They Were Expendable,* a very popular work early in the war which served to glorify the PT-boat service. Bulkeley had won the Congressional Medal of Honor for commanding the boat that had rescued General MacArthur, his wife, and young son from the Philippines in early 1942. Having already demonstrated their effectiveness in the waters around the vast chain of islands surrounding the Philippines, their usefulness in Southwest Pacific operations then became obvious.

Extremely light, the nocturnal boats were also very maneuverable. Most of the time they were designed to move along at better than forty knots, the equivalent of forty-five miles per hour on land. But speed alone was not as significant as the deviousness with which they were able to operate. They could move in on targets silently with muffled engines, launch torpedoes, and then skim away smoothly, outmaneuvering pursuers. Their speed enabled them to start out at dusk and venture deep into enemy waters and still return by sunrise.[1]

Lieutenant Bulkeley, having returned from his exploits with MacArthur, reported back the general's desire to have the PTs form a special arm of the service because of their value within coastal defenses, straits, narrows, and potential blockades. By the time the war finally ended, there were 212 PT boats, eleven tenders, and a string of PT bases that were in operation throughout the Southwest Pacific area.

At Northwestern, Kennedy was in the right spot for the recruitment visit by Bulkeley and Harllee. Harllee had been named the executive officer of a new PT school that the Navy established at Melville, Rhode Island, just north of Newport. He and Bulkeley visited the training centers at colleges and universities to find the reserve officers to man the vessels. Jack Kennedy was an interested and highly eligible applicant. He struck the two officers as very boyish in appearance, but his Harvard background in athletics, knowledge of sailing, and eagerness to get into combat, made him an excellent prospect.[2]

The PT service quickly became an elite, virtually aristocratic branch, perhaps more than any other within the American military services. It tapped a corps of young men, disproportionately Ivy League, whose families owned cabin cruisers or power boats. Marinas and yacht clubs had been indigenous to their upbringing, and the Navy considered them not only especially capable of handling small boats but, as Harllee recalled, "they had good educations and mental qualifications as well as physical qualifications."[3] Jack was, therefore, thrown in with a contingent that would later contribute to his future personal and political associations: Paul Pennoyer, Jr., a grandson of J. P. Morgan; Anthony Akers, of a socially prominent New York family; Paul B. "Red" Fay, Jr., of San Francisco, whose father owned a construction company.[4]

Completely sold on the Melville school by Bulkeley, Jack arrived at his new installation on September 27, his officer's training at Northwestern completed.[5] Accordingly, then, with a full year of active duty to his credit, and with his training at Northwestern, he was promoted from ensign to lieutenant junior grade, which gave him an advantage in rank over most of his fellow officers who were just out of universities.[6] The courses Jack took in seamanship, gunnery, navigation, engineering, and the handling of torpedoes were in themselves rigorous, but the regimen at Melville was toughened by the addition of calisthenics, athletics, and long daily periods of training. Ironically, his excellent record kept him from seeing action sooner, because Harllee felt he would be more valuable as an instructor. Angered, Jack argued with his superior; he wanted to get out to the war zone and get into the fighting and saw no reason for being kept within the United States.[7] Nevertheless, he drew an assignment to MTB Squadron 4 at Melville and was made skipper of *PT 101,* a training boat. He shared his Quonset hut with Lieutenant John Iles of Baton Rouge, Louisiana, and his old friend from Harvard, Lieutenant Junior Grade Torbert Macdonald. Torby's presence was no coincidence. Ambassador Kennedy had intervened to rescue him from a desk job in Boston so he could join Jack at Melville.

With Torby, Jack had a companion for weekend dating trips to New York and Boston. Torby went out with a young woman named Polly Cotter of Boston, while Jack became involved with Angela Greene. Born in Dublin in 1921, she came to America when very young, went to Catholic schools and then Bayside High School in New York before becoming a secretary and then working for the Powers Model Agency. Angela later recalled those weekend meetings. With Torby and his date and Jack, they would make the rounds of such New York night spots as Sardi's and El Morocco. At the Stork Club she met Joe Junior and little brother Bobby. As others who also knew Jack during that period, Angela Greene saw no evidence that he was especially inclined to be what she called a "sex maniac." She found him "the most simple, wonderful, beautiful man," one who had very little to drink except for an occasional daiquiri and one whose bad back kept him off the dance floor. She also noted Jack's serious involvement with ideas and felt that he would have loved, basically, to have been a professor.[8]

In addition to having Torby with him at Melville, Jack met someone else who was to become a lifelong friend, Red Fay. Fay remembered a skinny kid wearing a sweater turned inside out, with an *H* sewed on the inside, playing touch football. That skinny kid turned out to be John F. Kennedy, the most aggressive participant in the game.

At Melville, Jack acquired the nickname of "Shafty." The complaint "I was shafted" was very common during those days, a gripe about having been dealt out of some kind of entitled position. According to Robert Donovan, it was first applied to Jack by Ensign Joe G. Atkinson of Lebanon, Tennessee, who overheard Kennedy telling Torby "I've been shafted," referring to having been denied his request for overseas duty. It was Torby, however, who claimed the credit for having the nickname stick. The explanation for its derivation was similar to that reported by Donovan. Macdonald related it to Jack's having been "shafted" somewhere "along the line with this Navy business."[9]

Later, during the winter, Jack's boat was ordered to proceed with others to Panama. His *PT 101* was transferred to the newly formed Squadron 4 to be commissioned in Jacksonville, Florida, en route to its new assignment. But Jack never made it to Central America. Fearing being stuck in Panama, he finally managed to pull the right string to get himself a war zone assignment through the assistance of Massachusetts Senator David I. Walsh, then chairman of the Naval Affairs Committee.[10] Relieved from Squadron 4, Jack was ordered to the Solomon Islands in the South Pacific, while Torby and Red went off to different squads. Such movements were not made without awareness of the wartime progress of Joe Junior. As their mother later wrote about her second son's overseas assignment, "In their long brotherly, friendly rivalry, I expect this was the first time Jack had won such an 'advantage' by such a clear margin. And I daresay it cheered Jack and must have rankled Joe Jr."[11]

Jack's voyage to the South Pacific began with his departure from San Francisco in the late afternoon of March 6, 1943. The ten-year-old vessel had originally been known as the *Marshal Joffre* and then converted into a transport called the *Rochambeau,* making regular runs from San Francisco via San Diego. On Jack's sailing it stopped to take on fifteen hundred personnel at the southern California port.

An interview with Kenneth P. O'Donnell, who attended Harvard with Bobby Kennedy and later worked closely with both brothers, offered an additional insight into Jack's highly celebrated, much publicized stint in the South Pacific, which led to the incident that made him a war hero. O'Donnell, a die-hard Kennedy loyalist, placed a great deal of importance on that entire episode of Jack's life. The experience, he suggested, was invaluable for giving him an opportunity to learn about the problems of ordinary people. At the same time he sharpened his knack for giving people the impression that he liked them.[12] Patsy White Carter's recollection was corroborative, but she added an inevitable comparison, saying that Jack lacked "Kathleen's heart and he didn't have her real love for people, because Kathleen did, and she cared about people. But Jack never really cared." Asked about what did concern Jack, she replied, "His own ambition. He was a very, very ambitious boy. And Kathleen, she was just darling and warm and sweet, with all the best qualities of the Irish and a great deal of strength, which Jack had, too."[13]

The South Pacific experience inevitably did improve Kennedy's insights into others and his personal relationships. This was his first real experience as a leader. Most of his comrades represented a different world, a world of simple notions and even simpler desires that he was just now coming to know and appreciate.

In a long letter from the Solomons straightening out his parents (especially his father) about some misconceptions they had heard both about the war and the latest military heroes, he noted a disinterest in politics among his fellows. Their only concern—a concern expressed morning, noon, and night—was just to get home. There was no sense of idealism, no indication of any greater purpose. And despite what apparently had been the Ambassador's high regard for General Douglas MacArthur, that feeling was not at all shared by the men. Jack bluntly informed his father that among the men in that war zone he was "in fact, very, very unpopular. His nick-name is 'Dug-out-Doug,' which seems to date back to the first invasion of Guadalcanal. The Army was supposed to come in and relieve the Marines after the beach-head has [sic] been established. In ninety-three days no Army. Rightly or wrongly (probably wrongly) MacArthur was blamed. He is said to have refused to have sent the Army in—'He sat down in his dug-out in Australia', (I am quoting all Navy and Marine personnel) and let the Marines take it." Furthermore, Jack added, he had no doubt that, whatever the Ambassador may have indicated about a postwar political career for the general, as soon as the men returned from the South Pacific, they would spread word about "Dug-out-Doug" and that would be enough to kill him off. Besides which, added Jack with disdain, "they wouldn't give a damn whether they could vote or not and would probably vote for Roosevelt just because they knew his name."

Evidently, a question had also been raised about Joe Junior joining the South Pacific Theater, a matter that Jack discouraged quite directly, warning that he would be no different from anybody else and would want to return home the day after his arrival. "As regards Bobby," Jack added, "he ought to do what he wants. You can't estimate risks, some cooks are in more danger out here than a lot of flyers." Then, very considerately, he added a postscript to his mother, assuring her that he did get to church on Easter Sunday. "They had it in a native hut and aside from having a condition red Enemy Aircraft in the Vicinity it went on as well as St. Pat's."[14]

A few days earlier he had written to his parents about encounters with the Japanese and, in the face of combat, the fierce resistance of their officers as contrasted with enlisted men, who were not as likely to go down fighting. He told them about Paul Pennoyer and his relationship to J. P. Morgan. Specifically addressing himself to his mother, he suggested that she read *Blind Date with Mars* by Alice-Leone Moats because the "part about Russia will interest her extremely."[15] Mrs. Kennedy had traveled to the Soviet Union, following a trip taken by Joe Junior with Professor and Mrs. Laski, and had been impressed that "the masses really were better off in a good many ways than they had been under the czarist system." She could also better understand why many of the regime's aims, "if not many of the methods, were worthy of respect and discussion and study in some of our Western societies."[16] Jack Kennedy, reading the Moats book while in the South Pacific, found an intimate journalistic account of Soviet life just before and immediately after the Nazi invasion that portrayed a regimented, drab society surprisingly resigned to permanent imprisonment. Only the churches, persisting despite the regime, offered any solace.[17] Moats's melancholy view of Russia was, Jack evidently thought, a necessary corrective for his mother's superficial impressions.

Jack's South Pacific adventures inevitably made him a legendary war hero. Efforts to question his responsibility for having enabled a Japanese destroyer to cut across the bow of the craft under his command, *PT 109*, brought vehement protests from the surviving crew members, who remained passionately devoted to their skipper. The incident that took place on the night of August 2, 1943, and the harrowing week that followed became perhaps the most widely described episode of his early life.

On April 23, 1943, Lieutenant John F. Kennedy took command of *PT 109*, which was already battle-worn from eight months of war, its three Packard engines sluggish and its hull patched in three places. Built by the Elco Naval Division of the Electric Boat Company in Bayonne, New Jersey, the Navy received it in July of 1942, and it was fitted out in the New York Naval Shipyard. Then it joined Motor Torpedo Boat Squadron 2 as part of the Panama defense force, about which there was a great deal of insecurity. But after Japanese troops stormed ashore at Guadalcanal and the neighboring islands of Tulagi and Florida that August, the squadron was alerted for shipment to a combat area. A newly formed Motor Torpedo Boat Squadron 3 that took boats from the parent Squadron 2 was first ordered to the Solomons, which afforded bases for such operations. On October 14, 1942, the first four-boat division reached Tulagi, later joined by a second division of four boats, which completed the squadron.

The command of Squadron 2 was taken over by Lieutenant Rollins E.

Westholm, who made *PT 109* his flagship. The boat arrived at Tulagi at the end of November, and on December 15 Motor Torpedo Boat Flotilla 1, under Commander Allen P. Calvert, was activated with headquarters at Sesapi, Tulagi Island, an event that brought all PT boats in the Solomons under a single command.

Kennedy was stationed at Tulagi in the old Chinese trading village of Sesapi when informed that he would take over *PT 109.* His first job was to familiarize himself with the boat. He had to rehabilitate the craft and select a new crew and to combine both the boat and the men into an efficient fighting unit in time for the offensive that would come during the summertime.

The essential problem centered on the reinforcement of the Japanese base of Vila on Kolombangara Island. Supplies were delivered during the night by a flotilla of Japanese warships known as the "Tokyo Express," which would head down the "slot," the broad passage of water between New Georgia and Santa Isabel Island. The mission of the PT boats was to prevent the provisioning of the Japanese base at Vila. On the night of January 2–3, 1943, the PTs met head-on with the Tokyo Express. Two bombs from an enemy plane exploded off the port beam of *109* as an enemy destroyer opened fire off her port quarter. During night patrol on January 15, *PT 109* dodged three aerial bombs, then searched the shores of Cape Esperance for opportunities to attack enemy troops and stores.

During the next three months the Japanese troops that had been ousted from Guadalcanal devoted themselves to strengthening the garrisons in the Upper Solomons, and so the activity in the so-called "slot" (really New Georgia Sound) slowed down except for occasional raids, a respite that was sorely needed by *109* and her sister boats of the flotilla. By that point there were barely enough men to run the PTs. The crews were exhausted and easy prey to malaria, dengue fever, and other tropical diseases.

Both the crew and the craft needed refurbishing. Extra crewmen came aboard also and most of the spring was spent repairing the hull and overhauling the engines at Sesapi. After several test runs and firings of the guns, the motorboat patrolled from Cape Esperance to Savo Island, not far from Tulagi. Again, however, it had to berth at Sesapi for additional repairs to the engines, requiring subsequent test runs. Patrols were routine and dull. Two "suspicious" sightings were logged: a white light seen from the center of Savo Island, and a red light on the water's surface some four miles from Tulagi. They were *109*'s most significant findings. Through July security patrols continued as the motorboat shifted her base to Rendova Harbor on Lombari Island. During this period the fleet of PTs, along with *109*, suffered no serious damage or losses.[18] More time was spent battling cockroaches and insects. "Our life here isn't too bad," Jack informed his parents. "We live in tents—no hot water or anything, but the food is better than I ever had in Chicago, though there is still no sign of all those steaks that 'the boys in the service' are getting."[19]

The confrontation with the Tokyo Express came when four enemy destroyers were scheduled to run from Bougainville Island to Blackett Strait on the west side of Kolombangara. From there, they had to head to Vila, on the southern tip of the island.[20]

On the night of August 1, fourteen boats were ordered into Blackett Strait from the Rendova PT base. Four patrol sections were formed. The first, under Lieutenant G. E. Cookman, was stationed in Ferguson Passage. Led by a Lieutenant W. Rome, the second patrol was deployed east of Makuti Island. The third, under Lieutenant A. H. Berndston, was stationed between Makuti Island and Kolombangara. The fourth, of which *PT 109* was a part, was under Lieutenant Henry Joseph Brantingham, and positioned five miles west of the third section. Brantingham's boats were further subdivided into two sections. *PT 159* was radar equipped, operating with *PT 157*, while *PT 162*, under the command of Lieutenant Junior Grade J. R. Lowery, was the lead boat of the second section, with *PT 109* following. *PTs 159* and *162* both carried TBY radios for interboat communications.

Lieutenant Kennedy, captaining *PT 109*, received instructions to follow *PT 162* closely, which would keep in touch with the radar-equipped *159* by TBY. The boats departed from Rendova at 6:30 P.M., and they reached their patrol station around 8:30, without incident until gunfire and a searchlight was seen in the direction of the southern shore of Kolombangara Island. No radio or other warning of enemy activity in the area had been received. It was impossible to determine whether the searchlight came from the shore or from a ship close to shore. Presumably, it was not a ship, as *PT 162* retired on a westerly course toward Gizo Strait. Kennedy followed and inquired about the source of the firing. *PT 162* replied that it was believed to be from a shore battery. But *PT 109* intercepted a terse radio message that said, "I am being chased through Ferguson Passage. Have fired fish." While that was all, it was enough to inform the group that significant action with the enemy was in progress. At this time *PT 169* came alongside to inquire about the firing in Blackett Strait and to report that one of her engines was out of order. *PT 169* lay waiting with *PTs 109* and *162*.

Meanwhile, all contact with *159* had been lost. Instructions from the base were requested and orders were received to resume normal patrol stations. *PT 162,* being uncertain as to its position, requested *109* to lead the way back to the patrol station, which it proceeded to do. When Kennedy thought he had reached the original station, he started to patrol at idling speed, thereby reducing the size of the wake that could be spotted by Japanese planes, a common cruising practice in those dangerous waters.[21]

At about 2:30 in the morning, August 2, Ross was on the bow at lookout with Kennedy at the wheel. Suddenly, at a distance of some two hundred to three hundred yards, a dark shape loomed up over *109*'s starboard bow. The first thought was that it was the other PTs. But it was soon realized that it was the Japanese destroyer *Amigari* bearing down at high speed. The *109* started to turn to starboard, rapidly, preparatory to firing torpedoes. But when *PT 109* had scarcely turned thirty degrees, the *Amigari* rammed the boat, striking just ahead of the forward starboard tube and shearing off the starboard side of the boat, including the starboard engine. The destroyer, traveling at an estimated speed of forty knots, neither slowed nor fired as she split the PT. In all, scarcely ten seconds had elapsed between the sighting and the crash.

Immediately, a fire ignited; fortunately, it was gasoline burning on the water's surface at least twenty yards away from the remains of the still-floating PT hull. It appeared that the wake of the destroyer carried off the floating gasoline, thereby saving *PT 109* from fire. Clinging desperately to *109*'s hull were Kennedy, Maguire, Ross, Thom, Mauer, and Albert. When it appeared that the fire would spread to the hull, Kennedy ordered all hands to abandon the ship. When the danger had passed, they all scrambled back aboard, then quickly realized that Harris, McMahon, and Starkey were in the water a hundred yards to the southwest, while Zinser and Johnston were an equal distance to the southeast. Kennedy swam toward the group of three, and Thom and Ross struck out for the other two. McMahon, helpless because of serious burns on his face and hands, was towed back to the boat by Kennedy, who worked against the strong current and needed about an hour to get him back aboard the hull. Kennedy then returned for the other two men, one of whom was suffering from minor burns. He gave his life belt to Harris, who was uninjured, in return for Harris's water-logged kapok life jacket, which was impeding his swimming. Together, they towed Starkey to the PT.

Meanwhile, Ensigns Thom and Ross had reached Zinser and Johnston, who had both been made helpless by the gas fumes. Thom towed Johnston, and Ross took Zinser. By the time the boat was reached, both regained consciousness. Within three hours after the crash, all survivors who could be located were brought abroad *PT 109*. Marney and Kirksey were never seen again.

PT 109 did not fire its signal pistols for fear of giving away its position to the enemy; instead it blinked its light until dawn. Despite the fact that all watertight doors were closed down at the time of the crash, *109* was slowly taking on water. The eleven survivors were still aboard by the time daylight arrived on the second of August. It was obvious that *PT 109* would sink, and it was decided to abandon it in time to arrive before dark on one of the tiny islands east of Gizo. A small island three and a half to four miles to the southeast was chosen.

At 2:00 P.M. on August 2, Kennedy took the badly burned McMahon in tow. Using the breaststroke, he clenched the wounded man's kapok in his teeth, converting the garment into a towline. He faced down into the water while McMahon floated along above him, the kapok connecting the two men via Kennedy's teeth; he and the burned man literally floated back to back, pausing only for periodic rests. Ensign Thom led the second group, with Barney Ross and the others following. Johnston and Mauer could not swim and were tied to a float rigged to a two by eight, which was part of the 37 mm gun mount. Harris and Maguire were fair swimmers, but Zinser, Starkey, and Albert were much weaker. The stronger swimmers pushed or towed the float to which the nonswimmers were tied.

With McMahon, Kennedy arrived at tiny Plum Pudding Island at about 6:00 P.M. Plum Pudding was about one hundred yards long and, at the most, seventy yards wide, with six coconut trees and some brush. To their relief, there were no Japanese. Located in Blackett Strait, unfortunately, it was south of Ferguson Passage, the only place where there was much hope of meeting other PT boats.

The gamble was for Kennedy to make a foray toward the passage to probe for rescuing vessels. Kennedy left on a long, solitary swim, guided by the barrier reef, to reach the confluence of Ferguson Passage and Blackett Strait. He had a .38 to be fired into the air as a signal to any passing PTs.

But nothing was in sight. His only choice was to turn back along the reefs and resume swimming. He moved on through darkness and, with the help of the current through Ferguson Passage, found himself being carried sideways into Blackett Strait and finally, in a great swirl of the current, back into Ferguson Passage. At Plum Pudding Island his men awaited his return and word of rescue.

Early in the morning of the third, two natives in a dugout canoe paddled down Blackett Strait. Those on shore feared that Kennedy had drowned fighting the currents. Actually he had stopped to rest on a small island. At dawn, having slept, he swam the half mile to rejoin the others. His bare feet were cut and bleeding from the coral and he was vomiting when his mates greeted him.[22]

On the night of the third, Ensign Ross, following Kennedy's route, entered the passage by himself in another effort to intercept PT patrols on the way to Rendova. Ross moved past the reefs along the west side of the passage and had no better luck, but he did avoid the kind of current that had diverted Kennedy. Thwarted, they changed islands, moving to what they called Olasana Island, a mile and three quarters southwest of Plum Pudding. Their hope was to get closer to Ferguson Passage. McMahon was again towed with his kapok between Kennedy's teeth to Olasana, where the eleven survivors gathered amid the trees that flanked the beach at the southeastern tip. From there they looked across the half mile of water to Cross Island, from which they could get to Ferguson. The question, then, was whether they should remain and explore Olasana, which was much larger than Plum Pudding, or push on for Cross.

The days were hot, the nights cool. On Thursday, Kennedy and Ross decided to swim to Cross Island, which immediately faced the passage and, therefore, offered the best chance of rescue.[23] They would really be no better off except they were that much closer to Ferguson Passage; but still there was no sighting, and aside from becoming more desperate and exhausted from their long ordeal, on this their fourth day out, they were running a greater risk of being spotted by the Japanese.

As they approached Cross, they had an ominous sign of the presence of Japanese. Three New Zealand P-40's flew over the island and one of them made a strafing run. Nevertheless, when they arrived, Kennedy and Ross ducked into the bush and saw nothing. But they did find a small box with Japanese writing on one side, which turned out to be a container with thirty or forty small bags of crackers and candy. They also found a barrel of water, a native lean-to, and a one-man canoe. The canoe contained two natives.

Kennedy and Ross took the canoe that night and again went into Ferguson Passage and waited there until close to 2100 hours, but again no PTs. Kennedy returned, with Ross deciding to swim back the following morning. When Jack arrived at the base, at about 2330 hours, he found that two natives had circled around and landed on Olasana, where the rest of the group was. When the natives were finally convinced that the men were not Japanese, they were helpful and performed every possible service.

On Friday the sixth, Kennedy and the natives returned to Cross. They also intercepted Barney Ross, who was swimming back to the group. After finding no Japanese on the island, the natives showed the PT survivors where a two-man native crew was hidden. That pair of Melanesians was dispatched with messages for the coast-watcher, an Australian named Arthur Evans. One had a penciled note written the day before by Ensign Thom. Thom reported that the eleven men lost since Sunday were still alive. He added that the natives were aware of their position and would bring the boat back to Olasana.

The second message was the one that became famous. Kennedy, using a sheath knife, quartered a coconut and on the polished interior side inscribed a message to the PT commander:

NAURO
NATIVE KNOWS POSIT
HE CAN PILOT 11 ALIVE NEED
SMALL BOAT
KENNEDY[24]

Remaining low in their boat to conceal themselves from any passing Japanese observers, the natives carried the messages to Rendova Harbor, thirty-eight miles away. Finally, Lieutenant Evans, the coast-watcher, sent seven of his scouts to Olasana Island, where they met the survivors. Kennedy was amused when handed a communication that began with the words *On His Majesty's Service* by a black man naked except for a cloth around his waist. Kennedy himself hardly resembled an officer in dress uniform: he was half-naked, had a six-day growth of beard, and was blotched by festering coral wounds. On finding himself addressed as though he were still in the embassy in London, he said to Ross, "You've got to hand it to the British."[25]

Under cover, hidden from the Japanese, they were removed by the United States Navy and taken to Rendova, the ordeal finally over. The survivors had made it through a combination of courage, ingenuity, and luck—luck that neither sharks nor Japanese nor storms had destroyed whatever chance they had. Their fortitude had just one notable exception: Raymond Albert, the young seaman first class from Cleveland, who, judging from Kennedy's disclosure in a letter to John Hersey, had displayed qualities that added to the burdens of the others. Of Kennedy himself, the best judges were those whose lives were entrusted to his leadership—not only McMahon, whose life was saved through remarkable stamina and determination, but the others who also profited from the example set by their commanding officer. Not a word of criticism about how their leader conducted himself after the ramming has ever come from them. Kennedy subsequently talked little about his own role; his spoken words and letters reveal the regrets about Albert's failure to cope with the situation, which he tried to suppress to spare the young man's family, but also his increased respect for the others. "Previously," he wrote to his parents in September, "I had become somewhat cynical about the American as a fighting man. I had seen too much bellyaching and laying off. But with the chips down—all that faded away. I can now believe—which I never would have before—the stories of Bataan and Wake," thereby revealing much about his own assumptions of human imperfections.[26]

Among the first letters Jack received after returning to the base came from Headmaster St. John. "God bless you," the older man wrote. "I have just been reading the account of your rescue—and of the resourcefulness you used in making the rescue possible. I wish I could be with you and the other Choate men these days. To be in the sixties . . . is almost a humiliation."[27] Jack's warm response reassured the educator of the importance of his own job. "What you and others are doing at Choate and schools like it constitutes an essential ingredient to any worth while peace—which is what we are all hoping and working for."[28]

The PT incident illustrated the remarkable stoicism of Joe Kennedy. Rose herself had been oblivious of the collision and subsequent events. Official reports that Jack and his men were missing in action had not been issued. Not enough time had elapsed. But from the very early hours following the disaster, possibly shortly after the news reached officials in Washington at the Navy Department, the Ambassador learned about it on a confidential basis. With numerous contacts, especially Forrestal, it was not surprising that he had been told to prepare for the worst.

So, for several days, he lived with the real possibility that his son had been lost in action. Yet he did not change his routines. At the Cape during those days, he combined relaxation with business. Early sources report that the news of Jack's rescue reached him while he was at his riding stables.[29] More recent information suggests he found out about the survival while returning from a drive to nearby Osterville, when the bulletin over the car radio hit with such impact that he was forced off the road.[30]

With two sons in the war, one in the Pacific and the other in Europe, the chances of disaster were great. He had feared war, had advised against it, had provoked suspicions and enemies that would last throughout his life and haunt his sons. While, as his unpublished memoirs confirm, financial considerations were very much on his mind, he had also been acutely aware that it would inevitably involve his family. That was the essential fear, the one expressed over and over again. Now the reality had struck. This time it had worked out. Jack was safe. He was not only an author but a war hero.

8

Joe

Along with the rest of the crew, Jack Kennedy checked into the hospital at Tulagi with several aftereffects, fortunately all minor—sores from coral cuts, some infected; fungus, or, as it was more popularly known, jungle rot; and, not uncommon, ear infections from the water. For Jack, especially, his back was the greatest concern. The collision and subsequent strains had intensified the condition.

Hospitalized only briefly, he was declared fit for duty and assumed a new command. By October 1, Jack took over *PT 59* and supervised its conversion from a torpedo launcher into what the men then called "Gunboat #1," with the mission of intercepting and breaking up the barges used by the Japanese to provision the various installations throughout the adjacent islands.

Meanwhile, in the States, the details of the events surrounding the *PT 109* affair were being unraveled. The news made the front page of *The New York Times* and, quite naturally, the Boston papers. Several influences determined the prominent media handling of the rescue, with Kennedy's involvement easily the most important. Other survivors, such as the Executive Officer Lenny Thom, certainly deserved more attention than they got, but it was Jack's presence that put it on the front page.

The most recent account of the affair, by Joan and Clay Blair, Jr., states that Jack exploited his heroics to promote his career.[1] Certainly the adventure became a symbol of courage, and *PT 109* tie clips were worn long afterward as badges of loyalty. His transformation into a military hero is an undeniable fact. As Jack's political career began to develop, the original news stories were magnified by an account written by John Hersey and published in *The New Yorker,* then given much wider distribution when abridged in the *Reader's Digest.* A television version followed. Later, when Jack moved toward the presidential nomination, *U.S. News & World Report* again reprinted the Hersey article. Washington correspondent Robert J. Donovan further popularized the episode by writing a best-selling book, *PT 109: John Kennedy in World War II.* Finally, with Kennedy's personal assistance and advice in designating an actor for the lead, the story became a popular Hollywood motion picture. (Originally, Kennedy wanted Warren Beatty for the role. But when that choice got to Warner Brothers and producer Brian Foy, they found that Beatty would take the part only if he could portray Kennedy as a pacifist who managed to avoid combat.) With Kennedy's approval, Cliff Robertson became the leading man.[2]

And Jack has also been charged with having been "inordinately" proud of his war record. To support this statement, *Washington Post* editor Ben Bradlee is used to cite a telephone conversation in which Kennedy asked whether the newspaper was planning to look into Nelson Rockefeller's war record. "Where was old Nels when you and I were dodging bullets in the Solomon Islands?"[3]

But such accusations are less than fair. Hardly unique in American political campaigning, real or fabricated records of military heroism have always been a staple of the quest for votes. To accept the spirit of the Blairs' contention, moreover, misunderstands Jack Kennedy. In fact, the Blairs ignore their own evidence. At one point, they cite an article by Inga Arvad that was based on an interview with Jack in early 1944, after their romance had dissipated. Referring to the South Pacific, she quoted Kennedy as having said, "None of that hero stuff about me. The real heroes are not the men who return, but those who stay out there, like plenty of them do, two of my men included." Cynics may, of course, ascribe that statement to false, politic modesty, but neither did he at any point claim that he had actually been able to fire a torpedo at the onrushing Japanese ship; and even after Inga, trying to squeeze out the last bit of drama from the story, said, "Then you are a hero," she recorded that he looked at her "reproachfully" and explained that, after all, it was the job of PT officers to return their men safely.[4] Quoting Jack's later interview with John Hersey, the Blairs noted that the journalist found nothing self-serving about his recollection. In fact, Hersey said, "There was a real kind of officer modesty about it. He said all along that some of his crew members were the ones who really ran the boat, although I don't think that was true. He had a kind of diffidence about himself that seemed to be genuine at that time."[5] Although Hersey can be considered a friend, and a possibly biased source, especially at the time he wrote the account of the incident, his recollection of Kennedy's attitude was given more than thirty years later, long after he had become far more critical. Paul Pennoyer, Jr., also remembered an incident during Kennedy's 1946 congressional campaign. Getting more uncomfortable and impatient about the embellishment of the affair, Jack turned to Pennoyer and observed with some amusement, "My story about the collision is getting better all the time. Now I've got a Jew and a Nigger in the story and with me being a Catholic, that's great."[6]

Furthermore, the Donovan book itself was suggested not by Kennedy but by the publishers, McGraw-Hill, and they, not Kennedy, chose the author, hoping to utilize the newspaperman's access. So Donovan was someone who did get in to see him; but when he did, he experienced Kennedy's skepticism over the project. "Bob," said the President, "this thing has been flogged to death. We've had myriads of reprints of the Hersey article, and that's all there is to the story." Donovan remembered arguing the point, stressing that every phase of a President's career is normally written up in some book and that that happened to be an episode worth recounting. But the President, who had only been in office about a week, remained doubtful. Finally, he turned to one of his aides and said, "Give him all the help you can with research." Then, to Donovan, he said, "If you still think you have a book after doing all this, why not come back and I'll talk to you about it."

Donovan dutifully went to the South Pacific for a firsthand view of conditions in Blackett Strait. When he returned to the White House, satisfied that the story was pretty much under control, a luncheon was set up for him in the Oval Office. The timing coincided with the Berlin Crisis of 1961. The President, having hardly gotten over the Bay of Pigs disaster, was preoccupied with the crisis. In the middle of it all, Donovan tried to get Kennedy to talk about the night the boats were out on the trip that led to the destruction of *PT 109*. The President thought about it for a minute, shook his head, and said, "That whole story was more fucked up than Cuba." Donovan, in relating the incident, regretted he could not use the story at the time, contemplating that it would have made great copy "in the *Herald Tribune* in those days." After that statement President Kennedy went on to some speculation. "How do we ever win any wars anyway?" he asked. "You know the military always screws up everything."[7]

"In other words," Donovan recalled, "he tried very hard to talk me out of doing this book. Lots of people think this was some sort of hero-worship book promoted by Joe Kennedy. Not at all. Joe Kennedy had no idea of any of this. He had nothing whatever to do with this book. With the movie, yes; but nothing to do with the book. This was the idea of Edward Kuhn, who was the editor of the trade book department of McGraw-Hill."[8]

So Jack Kennedy never felt comfortable exploiting the military record; his own actions had not been extraordinary. What else could he have done? A letter received from Jack by Joe and Rose Kennedy on September 12, little more than a month after the affair, revealed his true feelings about responding to the challenge of survival. He called the Blackett Strait affair an "otherwise completely black time," with the only saving factor having been the way "everyone stood up to it." Then he added: "When I read that we will fight the Japs for years if necessary and will sacrifice hundreds and thousands if we must—I always like to check from where he is talking—it's seldom out here. People get so used to talking about billions of dollars and millions of soldiers that if those thousands want to live as much as the ten I saw—they should measure their words with great, great care. Perhaps all of that won't be necessary —and it can all be done by bombing."[9]

He had seen death, and at first hand the desperation with which men would fight to remain alive, a struggle analogous to his own lifelong contention with illness. It left him with an intense understanding of survival, one that later puzzled those who could not understand his desire to negotiate a deal exchanging tractors for men captured at the Bay of Pigs.

The South Pacific war was a long way from being won in the fall of 1943. As soon as he could take over a new command, Jack did. That was *PT 59,* which sorely needed renovations. He informed his father that it was the first they had ever had of its type. The craft's function was to fight all the small Japanese auxiliaries, which they were now using instead of the regular boats. He had fortunately managed to gather a crew of experienced volunteers, all of whom, he explained in a somewhat hyperbolic statement, had been sunk at least once. Then, recalling his *PT 109* experience, he wrote, "It was sort of a dubious honor to be given the first, so I'll have to stick around and try to make a go of it."[10]

Meanwhile, remoteness from the South Pacific helped magnify his performance. On September 10 Kathleen wrote from London about the great excitement. *The New York Times* account left her eager to hear the whole story. She was sure that Clare Booth Luce, a convert to Catholicism, was attributing his survival to the sacred medal she had given him when he went off to war. In fact, the letter written to his parents after returning to the safety of the base contained a postscript not only thanking them for a camera and reading glasses, but irreverently saying, "At their present rate of luck production, there is no telling where it will all end."[11]

By October 7 all the refitting work on *PT 59*—the removing of the torpedoes and replacing them with guns—had been completed. And from the eighteenth of October until the eighteenth of November, Jack commanded the gunboat. During that time, the primary mission was to intercept the Japanese barges, and they made patrols from Lambu Lambu to the island of Choiseul. Their aim, in part, was to block the western and southern approaches to Choiseul Bay, an important base for Japanese barges.

They made many sorties. Jack wrote home on the first of November that he was in command of "a real good boat" and a top crew of experienced men. He also added that he had been promoted to full lieutenant and, for his mother's benefit, explained that that was the equivalent of an Army captain.[12]

Right after that letter was written on the night of November 2–3, Kennedy performed his last significant military role. He maneuvered his Gunboat #1 to rescue a group of stranded marines from an LCPR landing craft.[13] On the night of November 5–6, his gunboat patrol finally found action. In the early-morning hours, it opened fire and destroyed three Japanese barges. Only then did Jack actually fire at an enemy surface craft.[14]

Jack's achievements were among the limited satisfactions that Joseph P. Kennedy could get from the war. He did not even have the satisfaction of an assignment from the Roosevelt administration to perform any official function, an especially galling snub for one with the Ambassador's temperament. The ambitious, opinionated activist was relegated to the sidelines, tending to his own business concerns and shuttling between Palm Beach and the Cape.

At least for a while, there was relief and an opportunity to celebrate. But his children were scattered, with the three oldest sons caught up in the war by the fall of 1943. Joe Junior had reported for duty at a Coastal Command base in southern England. Bobby, who had attended the Milton School in Connecticut, enlisted in the Navy. He was only seventeen, but soon became a cadet. "The folks sent me a clipping of your taking the oath," wrote Jack to his younger brother. "The sight of you up there, just as a boy, was really moving, particularly as close examination showed that you had my checked London coat on. I'd like to know what the hell I'm doing out here while you go stroking around in my drape coat, but I suppose that what we are out here for, or so they tell us, is so that our sisters and younger brothers will be safe and secure— frankly, I don't see it quite that way—at least, if you're going to be safe and secure, that's fine with me, but not in my coat, brother, not in my coat. In that picture you look as if you are going to step outside the room, grab your gun, and knock off several of the house-boys before lunch."[15]

No less than his sons, Kathleen, in her own way, became lost to the war. Since June she had been in England. There her preoccupations were working with the American Red Cross and, second, being with Billy Hartington. Her Washington roommate thought the pursuit of young Hartington the major reason she abandoned Washington.[16] Becoming a familiar and popular figure as a Red Cross worker in London, she established a reputation as the "girl on the bicycle." She dispensed coffee and doughnuts to service men at the Hans Crescent Club in Knightsbridge and was also a frequent visitor to Joe Junior's officers' club. Brother and sister drew closer together during that period.

Joe stood by and supported her determination to marry Billy Hartington. For Rose Kennedy, especially, that impending union with the son of the Duke of Cavendish was perhaps a disaster almost the equal of the many others created by wartime conditions. But "Kathleen simply fell in love with Billy Hartington, and that was it," recalled a friend who had been close to her in Washington, "and didn't give a hoot about anything else."[17]

While Joe Junior was with Kathleen, providing her with ready support for what she wanted to do in London, there was little reason to believe that her previously close bonds with Jack had undergone any alterations or that Jack felt less supportive of his sister than did Joe Junior. Certainly Kathleen wrote quite openly to Jack about her romance. "I can't really understand why I like Englishmen so much," she told him, "as they treat one in quite an offhand manner and aren't as nice to women as are Americans, but I suppose it's just that sort of treatment that women really like. That's your technique, isn't it?"[18]

Kathleen's personal attractions were considerable. Not only in London but in Washington as well, she was never without friends.[19] Now, however, Kathleen was in another world, far removed from Torby Macdonald, Jack, and her parents. On November 17 she wrote from London to inform her family of Joe's arrival with his entire squadron, "who were feeling no pain." She and Joe shopped, dined, and then went out to join some of Joe's friends and amused themselves at the 400 Club. "Joe seems to be having a good time but no special girlfriend," Kathleen wrote about her brother. "Goodness, it makes a difference having him over. He is in wonderful spirits."[20]

The real cloud, however, was the coming marriage between Kathleen and Billy. Rose Kennedy has written that all during the winter and spring of 1944, the Kennedy family, the Duke and Duchess of Cavendish, and their children, Kick and Billy, sought some means of getting the marriage sanctioned, or at least tolerated, by both the Roman Catholic and Anglican churches. They turned to Archbishop Francis Spellman, of the New York Diocese, whom they had known from his Boston days as an auxiliary bishop. They tried Pope Pius XII, who, as Cardinal Pacelli, had been a visitor to the Kennedy home in the 1930's. But there was no way out. Marriage within the Catholic church would have required Billy's agreement that their children would be raised as Catholics, something that Hartington would not agree to. The reality of such a marriage for Rose Kennedy, would be almost as much of a disaster as Rosemary's affliction. And even Jack surprised his father by suggesting that Hartington should make some kind of a concession on the matter of faith. The Ambassador had not thought his son cared that much about religion.[21] But despite their disapproval of the marriage, the Kennedys were, as Patsy Carter remembered, "very ambivalent about Billy. They hated her being married to an Anglican, but they loved her being married to the heir of the Duke of England. You know, they never made it in Boston, but now look!"[22]

Kennedy relinquished his command when "Gunboat #1" arrived at Buloa at 1430 hours on November 18, 1943. The entry reads, "Lt. J. Kennedy left boat, as directed by Dr. at Lambu Lambu."[23] Dr. Joseph B. Wharton recalled that X-ray machines revealed an injured intervertebral disc in the lumbar region; not a fracture but, rather, a chronic disease of the lower back, undoubtedly aggravated by the pounding inflicted by the hulls of the patrol boats.[24]

Jack also had malaria. Unfortunately, however, the later sealing of his medical records encouraged speculation that malaria was simply used as a means of covering up a later diagnosis of a much more severe condition. Nevertheless, it is entirely credible to suppose that, along with so many other GIs who served in the South Pacific, Jack Kennedy also contracted malaria. Pat Lannan, who was with Jack in London in the summer of 1945, described Jack becoming very ill at Grosvenor House. "I've never seen anyone so sick in my life. He had a hell of a high temperature. It scared hell out of me. I thought he was going to die. He told me it was a recurrence of malaria. I'd never seen anyone go through the throes of the fever before. . . . I got hold of a naval officer, who was attached to Forrestal's party. Then some naval doctors came and they confirmed it was malarial fever." Torby Macdonald found him suffering from the disease in June 1944.[25]

Undoubtedly, the evidence would be strengthened if the recollections were not *ex post facto* accounts, but it is not beyond the realm of possibility—far from it—that malaria was one of Jack's problems. A more substantial account of his malaria was contained in a *Washington Times-Herald* article by Elizabeth Oldfield based on an interview with Kennedy as a freshman congressman in early 1947. It predates by some nine months his alleged fabrication of malaria to hide the presence of a more serious illness.[26] His greenish complexion, a result of Atabrine, was, moreover, common gossip among the Washington correspondents who knew him at the time.[27]

Considerably uncomfortable and in need of further medical treatment, Jack left the South Pacific after Christmas on a military leave. His condition notwithstanding, he first went to Los Angeles on January 10 and rejoined Inga.[28] He had, in September, written to her about the weary night patrols and his inability to sleep during daylight. He also wrote that "knowing you has been the brightest part of an extremely bright 26 years."[29] But their romance had cooled. Inga had been in the Hollywood swirl and she and Jack had little left in common. "She'd been through the thing about the old man's violent objections and she just didn't want to go through it again," said her son. "Her life was fine; she was having a good time. Also she could see that Jack was in no condition to make decisions about anything." She found him looking ghastly, thin and drawn. "He was just worn out. So that was the end of what had happened before."[30] Others who saw him in California at the time had substantially the same view of his health.

Instead of going directly to the East Coast, he stopped in at the Mayo Clinic. From there he went to visit his family in Palm Beach, Florida, remaining until Saturday, February 5, before the arrival of a Purple Heart medal forwarded by Lieutenant Al Cluster, with whom Jack had served on "Gunboat #1." Responding appreciatively to Cluster, the Ambassador wrote that Jack was in reasonably good shape but that the doctors did not "entirely agree" with that diagnosis. "However, Jack is insistent that he wants to get going again, so he left here on Saturday to go and see his brothers and sisters and then report for duty on the 15th."[31]

En route to the Rhode Island base, Jack stopped off in New York for a round of nightclubs and the theater. A photo taken at the Stork Club on the ninth shows a wan young man sitting at a table with Flo Pritchett. Flo, a twenty-four-year-old fashion editor with the *New York Journal-American,* later became one of his closest women friends, sufficiently intimate to be described by at least one source as his "main girl friend." She later married Earl E. T. Smith, who became best known as the last American ambassador to Cuba under the Batista regime. Kennedy also accompanied John and Frances Ann Hersey to the theater.[32]

The meeting with Hersey became the genesis for the "Survival" article that the young journalist later published in *The New Yorker.* In a New York supper club, La Martinique, where Zero Mostel was performing, Hersey received from Kennedy what he remembered was "a rapid account of the experience of the sinking of his PT boat," which was later filled in with more details. "It was quite clear that it was a good story, whether he was Kennedy or not. . . . It was the story itself that was so dramatic." They agreed that the story would be written for possible publication in *Life.* Later, when Hersey contacted him at Melville, Jack suggested that the writer should consult the *PT 109* survivors for further details, which he then did. "They were obviously attached to him, respected him, and honored him in the telling of the story," Hersey said in 1976. "So he was shrewd in putting me up to that, as a way of setting the tone for his own account."[33]

Upon his own request, Jack was transferred to a PT "shakedown" unit in Miami, Florida, a duty that made few demands on him and required spending very little time at the base itself. "In regard to conditions here," he wrote to Hersey, "may I say that I am playing it slow and deep—with no strain or pain. Once you've got your feet upon the desk in the morning the heavy work of the day is done."[34]

On May 6 Jack was still in Miami. Meanwhile, in London, after having announced their engagement just four days earlier, Kathleen Kennedy married Billy Hartington in a civil ceremony at the Chelsea Registry Office. The brief service, conducted by a British counterpart of an American justice of the peace, had few witnesses. Neither of Kick's parents were present, although the Ambassador had earlier cabled that "with your faith in God you can't make a mistake. Remember you are still and always will be tops with me."[35]

The bride, aged twenty-four, wore a frock of pink suede crepe beneath a short brown mink jacket and a small hat of blue and pink ostrich feathers. The groom, having been defeated in an attempt to win election to the House of Commons from West Derbyshire, had joined the Coldstream Guards and was in uniform, as was his best man and fellow officer, the Duke of Rutland. The small but distinguished wedding party included the Duke and Duchess of Devonshire, the Duke's sister, Lady Elizabeth Cavendish, the Marchioness of Salisbury, and Lady Astor. Standing right behind Kathleen during the ceremony—and in a photograph spread over three columns in *The New York Times*—was Lieutenant Joseph P. Kennedy, Jr., the family's sole representative. Kathleen would later memorialize Joe Junior's support during those days when she and Hartington moved toward a final decision: "Never did anyone have such a pillar of strength as I had in Joe in those difficult days before my marriage. . . . When he felt that I had made up my mind, he stood by me always." In that same little volume honoring Joe Junior, she also wrote: "But it wasn't until the year before he died that Joe and I became so very close. We were away from home in a foreign land. To each other, we symbolized the happy family we had left in America."[36]

Predictably, the entire event was traumatic for Rose Kennedy and the actual marriage undoubtedly heightened her stress. For a while, she virtually went into seclusion, having "lost" a daughter. She sent no messages to London. Officially it was explained that she had been confined to the New England Baptist Hospital for the two previous weeks "for a routine physical checkup." On May 6, which coincided with the date in London of the wedding, she left the hospital for Hot Springs, Virginia. "For a much-needed rest," said her father, Honey Fitz. Arriving by plane at New York's LaGuardia Field, en route to her vacation spot, reporters asked for a comment on her daughter's marriage. "I am not making any statements," Rose replied.[37]

Three weeks later Jack was transferred from Miami to the Chelsea Naval Hospital in Boston for further examination of his back and to determine the need for an operation. In the meantime Hersey's story had been rejected by *Life,* because it could ill afford devoting that kind of space to a feature story that would reduce its ability to cover the fast-breaking military events with appropriate pictorial spreads. Earlier, while still in Miami, Jack had commented on a draft of the manuscript. His reaction was complimentary: "Even I was wondering how it would all end."

After praising Hersey's skill and acknowledging that the story must necessarily be confined to a few central themes, Jack had two substantive suggestions. "But Thom did a splendid job—did so much to hold the group in a disciplined body that I think you might credit him more." Then he made a second request. That pertained to Raymond Albert, who after having been reassigned to *PT 163,* had been killed several weeks following the rescue while carelessly granting the request of a Japanese prisoner for a cup of water. Kennedy, responding to the allusions in Hersey's draft about Albert's lack of courage, wrote, "I realize, of course, that his fate is ironic and dramatic and that his lack of guts is an integral part of war—and one that probably is not mentioned enough. I feel, however, that our group was too small, that Albert's fate is so well-known both to men in the boats and to his family and friends, that the finger would be put too definitely on his memory—and after all he *was* in my crew. To see whether or not I was being over-sensitive on this, I asked two officers to read the story—and they both, independently of me —brought up the matter I have been just discussing."[38]

That *The New Yorker* finally accepted Hersey's article and published it in its June 17, 1944, issue was much more pleasing to the author. For Hersey it represented his first appearance in that magazine, which would later devote an entire issue to his account of Hiroshima. But to Joseph Kennedy, of course, *The New Yorker* was not *Life.* Its circulation was much more limited and the Ambassador was determined to see the article run in the enormously popular *Reader's Digest.* So Joe Kennedy approached *New Yorker* editor Harold Ross with the request that it be made available to the *Digest.* Ross hated the rival magazine. John Hersey recalled that, "There were negotiations to which I was not privy, and I have no idea what form of persuasion Joe Kennedy brought to bear, but it must have been heavy, because against the grain of the kind of stubbornness that Ross had, they did give permission for the piece to be released by the *Reader's Digest* on terms . . . which were quite unusual.

That is to say, they gave the *Reader's Digest* permission to use the piece once, and once only, and it was published there."[39]

More than three decades later, Hersey remained perplexed about how Joe Kennedy had managed that coup. However, inspection of the relevant documents shows that he followed his usual procedures, manipulating and exerting the power of his wealth and personality. There is something *déjà vu* about the origins of the relationship between Kennedy and *Reader's Digest* editor Paul Palmer. Introduced by Arthur Krock at the St. Regis Hotel in New York City during the summer of 1943, they soon arranged for a Joe Kennedy article for the *Digest* on "What Are the Facts About Peace?" in which the Ambassador recalled the punitive terms given to Germany by the Treaty of Versailles and argued for setting aside the unconditional surrender objectives of the present war. As had Professor Carleton before him, he stated that American and British statesmanship "will need after the surrender of Germany the moral force of a German peace covenant to withstand possible Russian interference in Germany quite as much as the United Nations now needs the moral factor of an offer of peace to hasten a German capitulation."[40] But nothing came of that publication plan: Palmer thought the thesis too unfocused.[41] By then, however, Joe's concern had shifted to the possibility of having the *Reader's Digest* publicize his son's exploits. That was barely one month after the collision, while Jack was still in the South Pacific, taking over "Gunboat #1." "I'm sure he'd be delighted to talk with you when he gets back," the Ambassador assured Palmer. "If the Navy would let him tell the complete story, he should have a good one then."[42]

But independent of either Joe Kennedy or Paul Palmer, Hersey met with Jack and had launched his own article the subsequent winter. Still the Ambassador was able to arrange placement of Hersey's account with his friend at the *Digest.* "I have already thanked you about the Hersey piece, and you have demonstrated very clearly to me why it is that people really want to do things for you," he wrote to Palmer in June.[43]

Meanwhile, upon Jack's insistence, an elaborate financial arrangement was set up to take care of the widow and family of one of *PT 109*'s fatalities, John Kirksey, rather than lose to taxes part of the two thousand dollars payable in reprint rights. By prior agreement with Kennedy, Hersey persuaded *The New Yorker* to grant him those rights, which he then transferred to the Navy Relief Fund. The *Digest,* in turn, bought the rights from the Relief Fund for the two thousand dollars and sent the check to the agency, with Palmer forwarding the money to the

Massachusetts branch of the fund. The head of that office had arranged that Mrs. Kirksey would get whatever portion was needed after the Red Cross had investigated the family's financial circumstances. Should they find that neither she nor the children needed the entire sum, the remainder was to be used as the Navy Relief Fund saw fit.[44]

Not even Joseph P. Kennedy could control the speed and direction of all events. As he had feared, the war had gotten matters out of hand. He had been helpless while his daughter married out of her faith. She and Joe Junior were now in London. Bobby was an ROTC naval cadet. And, as of his twenty-seventh birthday, Jack was in the Chelsea Naval Hospital, where, on June 12, a simple ceremony was held to present him with the Navy and Marine Medal for "extremely heroic conduct as Commanding Officer of Motor Torpedo Boat 109 following the collision and sinking of that vessel in the Pacific War Area on August 1–2, 1943."[45] The father's pride, however, had to be tempered by the realities of his son's condition.

As brave as the Kennedys tried to be about the situation, presenting the medal within the hospital must have been grim. Jack's back condition had deteriorated to where surgery was needed. The operation was performed not at the naval facility but by doctors connected with the Lahey Clinic. The attempt to correct the disc problem failed, badly. To a friend, the convalescent Kennedy explained, "In regard to the fascinating subject of my operation, I should naturally like to go on for several pages . . . but will confine myself to saying that I think the doc should have read just one more book before picking up the saw."[46]

A succession of visitors found him frail and very much like a man who had just been through a severe ordeal. To Torby Macdonald, who had won a Silver Star for his own heroics in the South Pacific, Jack explained that he was feeling "great considering the shape I'm in."[47] On August 1 Jack reported that he was putting in his eighth week in the hospital: "Have an advanced case of bed-sores and a slight touch of scurvy," he wrote, "due to our inability to get any limes to mix with the medical alcohol. Should be leaving here in a few days for the Old Sailors Home, where I go before a survey board—probably to be issued a rocking chair, a sunny place on the lawn—with the thanks of a grateful Republic wringing [sic] in my ears."[48] The long period of recuperation continued. Jack returned to the Chelsea Naval Hospital, followed by out-patient visits at Hyannis Port and Palm Beach.

But the many months of suffering brought no appreciable recovery.

Coping with pain would have to continue long thereafter. Gradually intensifying, it forced frequent use of crutches and therapeutic hot baths, and, for many years, cumbersome back braces. "There was a hole in his back that had never closed up after the operation he had during the war," said a friend. "You could look into it and see the metal plate that had been put into his spine."[49] Charles Spalding has given a particularly intimate description of Jack's predicament:

That wound was a savage wound, a big wound. It went maybe eight inches or so down his back. It never would heal and it was open and painful. . . . He had to fight to get the back healed and I would walk up the beach with him with the back, still open, and he'd say, "How is it now? Is it open?" or "Is any stuff running out of it? . . ." It was severe pain and severe discomfort and just, you know, real pain.[50]

On the afternoon of Sunday, August 13, on a weekend leave from the hospital, he had joined his family, including Bobby, at Hyannis Port. Together, they enjoyed a picnic-style lunch on the porch of their father's house, after which the Ambassador retired upstairs for an afternoon nap.

At about two o'clock two priests arrived. They asked to speak to Mr. Kennedy. Assuming a routine visit to solicit funds for some charity or other church matters, Rose invited them in and suggested that they join the family in the living room while the Ambassador completed his nap, but "one of the priests said no," Mrs. Kennedy later wrote, "that the reason for calling was urgent. That there was a message both Joe and I must hear. Our son was missing in action and presumed lost." Rushing to the upstairs bedroom, she awakened her husband. With his wife virtually incoherent, he heard the news directly from the priests.

The children were still on the porch. Their father walked outside and told them, reminding them to be brave and to "be particularly good to your mother."[51] "He urged them to go ahead with their plans to race that day and most of them obediently did so," Rose Kennedy remembered. "But Jack could not. Instead, for a long time he walked on the beach in front of our house."[52]

The Ambassador retreated to his own room and locked the door. "He was never the same," Gail Cameron has written. "It was left to Rose to console and hold together—as she had always done and always would do—the remaining Kennedys."[53] Arthur Krock later wrote that Joe Junior's death was "the first break in this circle of nine children" and "was one of the most severe shocks to the father that I've ever seen registered on a human being."[54] Unlike the news about Jack's collision, this report was final: Joe Junior was "presumed" to be missing in action.

Not even a stoic had any reason to hope that the report was false. *The New York Times* ran the news under the headline SON OF J.P. KENNEDY KILLED IN ACTION, complete with a picture of Joe.

For the Ambassador it meant, of course, the tragic loss of a child, a son, his oldest boy. But more than that. Joe Junior was his hope, the unquestioning bearer of the Kennedy drive to the top in arenas other than financial, to assert the family's stake in the nation's existence by overcoming the obstacles placed before an Irish Catholic family.

Jack, while still an outpatient at Chelsea, began to put together a memorial. He invited family and friends to contribute recollections and reminiscences. Serving as its editor, Jack wrote the introductory essay to the privately printed and distributed little volume that he called *As We Remember Joe*. Of his own recollections, Jack wrote:

Toward me who was nearly his own age, this responsibility consisted in setting a standard that was uniformly high. . . . I think that if the Kennedy children amount to anything now or ever amount to anything, it will be due more to Joe's behavior and his constant example than to any other factor. [55]

There are those who believe that the Ambassador could never bring himself to read this volume published in 1945. To several people, Ambassador Kennedy gave what seemed to have become a stock response, that he had never been able to read beyond the first few pages. "I never got over that boy's death."[56] Many years later, while being interviewed by newspaperman Bob Considine, he was reminded that he had omitted Joe Junior's name from a discussion about his children. "Ask Rose about that one," he said. "She can talk about him, I can't." Considine then realized that the Ambassador was crying.[57] In 1947, as a substitute speaker for Jack at the fiftieth anniversary celebration of the Knights of Columbus in Cambridge, he said, "My sons went to Harvard here in Cambridge." Then he started to talk about Joe Junior and almost broke down. "He had the most terrible time trying to control himself—the tears welled up in his eyes as he spoke of Joe and it took him about two minutes to get the grip," recalled an observer.[58]

There was much to dislike about Joe Kennedy: his grasping ambition, self-serving machinations, his anti-Semitism, and promiscuity. Nevertheless, with the loss of Joe Junior, he was a father who bled and one who at the same time exhibited those strengths that enchanted admirers. Frank C. Waldrop put it succinctly: "Joe Kennedy was a man of intelligence, passion and great devotion to the United States of America, which by extension meant that he expressed all these characteristics best in his life with his family. He was an admirable citizen, a man of his time, and I was very glad to know him. And his family. . . . The Kennedys, as a family, remain an interesting phenomenon. But I am damned if I, for one, know *what* that is."[59]

9

The Second Son Emerges

In the Ambassador's eyes, it may be said without much exaggeration, Jack became a surrogate for Joe Junior. Still, the much-discussed question of Jack Kennedy having been virtually drafted to fulfill his brother's career objectives has been oversimplified. Jack, in fact, was deeply interested in public affairs long before Joe's death, his flirtation with law school having been one aspect of that consideration. Generally overlooked, too, is that Jack, and not his brother, had made the most publicized achievements; in a popular sense, it was he rather than the older boy who had an advantage, the *PT 109* affair having added to the reputation made earlier as an author. But despite his own interests and inherent privileges, Jack's uncertainty about his capacity to become a candidate dissuaded him from rushing into anything prematurely. His physical condition was another deterrent. His earlier acceptance of Joe Junior's right to the family's backing no longer mattered. He now had few choices.

James A. Reed, one of the men Jack met en route to the South Pacific in 1943 and who became a close friend as well as a member of his presidential administration, has recalled an evening in the fall of 1945, with Jack, Ambassador Kennedy, Grandfather Fitzgerald, and a few other close friends. "We were sitting with Grandfather Fitzgerald, who proposed a toast to the future President of the United States—he looked right at Jack—to which everyone joined in. It was not really said in any degree of levity or frivolity. It was a serious toast, really, that was proposed to Jack, and I think everyone there thought that one day Jack would be President of the United States."[1]

Jack's work on the volume memorializing his brother may have been somewhat of an expiation of his ambivalence about that relationship—his jealousies, his sense of competition, his reaction to the family pecking order. Now that Joe was gone, a kind of penance was being performed. In carrying out the task, Jack was probably conscious that the loss had left him with the additional burden of replacing the "golden boy." With confused feelings, then, insecure and still in great pain from the agonizingly slow recuperative process, Jack began work on the book in September of 1944, collecting written tributes from those who had memories to share about the firstborn male. Nevertheless, in addition to such activity, he attempted something of a social life. On Labor Day he threw a weekend house party for friends, which utilized the ample facilities of the Hyannis Port home that ultimately came to be called the "big house."

Just a few days later, on the night of September 14, Jack was caught at the waterfront when one of the greatest hurricanes struck the Cape. Winds of a hundred miles an hour devastated southeastern Massachusetts. The destruction in the Hyannis Port area was extensive, especially to the summer homes in South Hyannis. The Kennedy home, however, fared relatively well. Water seeped into the house through the French doors that led to the large veranda, soaking the rug. Waterlogged books fell from their shelves and had to be spread out around the room to dry. Much of the damage affected the basement movie theater. Along the waterfront the wind cleared the sea of the boats. Jack, at the pier site, managed to secure the family's Wianno senior knockabout, the *Victura*. Then, in his Buick convertible, he drove into the village of Hyannis but found himself stranded on Chase Street as the high waters on Sea Street blocked his route. Wearing "a blue baseball cap, and open white shirt, khaki slacks and sneakers" and looking much younger than twenty-seven "despite the slightly yellow pallor remaining from his malaria," he met two sisters who didn't know who he was. "He looked ill," one of them said, "but he certainly didn't *act* it. And he had the most charming smile." After the waters had receded, he returned to the house with the young women and a reporter assigned to cover the hurricane for *Life* and then changed out of his storm clothes for an evening outing, putting on a Navy uniform that was "so rumpled and unpressed-looking it probably had just come out of a suitcase."[2]

With the debris still very much in evidence, a major disaster struck the Kennedys. Kathleen, who had returned to the Cape several days after word arrived about Joe's death, received the news from the British War Office that Lord Hartington, twenty-six years of age and a captain of the Coldstream Guards, had been killed in action in France. His actual death on September 10, had been less than one month after Joe's.

Family and friends gathered around Kathleen in New York. Widowed after her brief marriage, she returned to London to visit her husband's parents. Although she came back to America in November 1945, and her father said she would live with the family, Kick later moved back to the Smith Square apartment she had been able to share with Billy for only about a month.[3] For the rest of her life, she seemed "more a Cavendish than a Kennedy." An English nobleman was quoted as having said "We thought she was the best thing America ever sent to England."[4]

That move, however, especially since she had married an Anglican, inspired gossip in Boston that she had abandoned the Church and the Kennedys had to utilize all their significant influence with the press and subsequent biographers to reaffirm her continued devotion to Catholicism.[5]

Kick found herself attracted to another Englishman, another member of a profoundly, historically anti-Roman Catholic family. He was Peter Milton, Earl Fitzwilliam, and one of England's richest men. Billy had been young and unattached when Kathleen met him, but Fitzwilliam was in his midthirties and awaiting a divorce. As determined as her father to get what she wanted, she fell in love with Fitzwilliam and defied family censure. For his part, Joe Kennedy tried to help matters by attempting to prove that Fitzwilliam had not been baptized. "But," as a close family friend said, "if you know England at all, you know that the heir to an Earldom is baptized the minute he springs from the womb!"[6]

Meanwhile, Jack returned to the hospital at Chelsea in great pain. Despondently, he wrote to Red Fay that the doctors had abandoned hope that his back condition could be cured. "From here I'm going to go home for Christmas, then to Arizona for about a year, and try to get back in shape again," he explained.[7] On the ninth of November, he sent a telegram to Cappy Leinbach at Choate, saying, "Unable to leave Naval Hospital so must postpone visit."[8]

At Christmastime, he was with the family in Palm Beach, their first holiday since the deaths of Joe and Billy. Jack, characteristically, taking advantage of the presence of such friends as Red Fay and Ben Smith, attempted levity to distract his parents.

Two days later, Jack appeared before the Retirement Board in Washington, D.C., which resulted in his transfer to the retired list with the rank of full lieutenant "by reason of physical disability." He may have been entitled to retirement or disability pension but did not take it, keeping, however, the military's ten-thousand-dollar GI life insurance policy, the only policy he ever had.

Separated from the Navy, Jack's objective was to rebuild his health. He went to the Castle Hot Springs Hotel, located in the Bradshaw Mountains of Arizona, about thirty miles northwest of Phoenix. The former Air Force base was being converted into a semiprivate club.[9] From the Castle Hot Springs Hotel, he requested the forwarding of his subscriptions to the *Boston Post* and the *Boston Herald Traveler,* presumably to remain current with local affairs. He received a letter from Mary Richardson of the Boston Port Authority at the Custom House, which, among other things, informed him that his Grandfather Fitzgerald had been in the St. Margaret's Hospital for about a week. "He had a bad cold but his temperature is normal again but the cold settled in his knees and Dr. Foley has been treating him up there. I dropped in to see him last night and he looks great. I think the rest has done a lot of good and he is in very fine spirits. He probably will be there until the end of the week. An article in the Traveller [sic] last night said he would have his dancing shoes on next week again. Sunday, February 11th, will be his birthday. Eighty-two years old. You will probably be reminded of your return home last year."

Miss Richardson also informed Jack that he was being sent five envelopes of material which would pertain not only to the Boston Port Authority but would have all the information that could be obtained about the city's finances and real estate. Furthermore, she wrote, "There seems to be very little on the past history of the airport but I expect to have postwar plans in a day or two and will send them at that time."[10] Jack also had his father send him a batch of books on labor and labor law. Pat Lannan, who was with him in Arizona, remarked how Jack earned his respect by sitting up "to one or two in the morning reading those books until he'd finished the whole crate."[11] Before leaving Arizona, he wrote an article that he hoped would be placed with the *Reader's Digest.* The Ambassador, acting as an intermediary with Paul Palmer, explained that "Jack felt so strongly about the question of rearmament that I suggested that he put his feelings on paper. I think he has worked out a rather publishable article, which, subject to revision that news developments might call for, is about in final shape."[12]

Called "Let's Try an Experiment in Peace," the article was rather limp and colorless. That Palmer found it unsuitable was not surprising considering the mass-circulation requirements of the *Reader's Digest.* But the Ambassador didn't give up. Turned down by Palmer, he pressed Edward Weeks of *The Atlantic Monthly,* discussing with the editor the possibility of revising it for that magazine. Weeks agreed with Jack's general thesis but pointed out that the subject matter not only lacked an original argument but also that its focus was weakened by Jack's attempt to "cover too much ground in too little space, with the result that your argument does not clinch the reader as it ought."[13] Jack did submit a revised draft that spring but *The Atlantic* never did publish it.

The original draft, in particular, is very revealing for what it shows about the thoughts of the young man who had written *Why England Slept.* Jack, here, did not express faith in military power. Nor did he warn about the looming difficulties with the Soviet Union or the importance of maintaining the American military advantages that were being created by the war. Instead he pleaded for what he termed the kind of "intelligent and imaginative statesmanship" needed to prevent a postwar rearmament race. That race, not the reduction of power, he argued, would make another war "inevitable." The prerequisite for the success of any peace plan would be "an agreement for limiting rearmament to the limit of national safety requirements, militarily and economically."

In a curious reversal of his position in *Why England Slept,* Jack Kennedy cited past American experiences that followed the Washington Naval Conference of 1921–22 as having prejudiced the public against arms limitations. The folly this time, unlike the illusions of the past, was the notion that safety and peace requires overwhelming military superiority. "This," he wrote, "is a plan for superarmament!" Not a reduction of power but rearmament, he warned, "can easily prove to be a boomerang." The United States, if it attempted to maintain that kind of superiority, would not be permitted to stand alone; regardless of "our protestations of peace," large nations such as the Soviet Union will try to match our military might while weaker ones "will bind together for security against us. . . . The result will be a world rearmament race, and that can have but one ending—the explosion of war. For arms themselves are a direct cause of war," he added. Moreover, such preoccupation with a military buildup would deflect "our dwindling resources" and "the energies of the nation" from the need to secure jobs for our returning veterans to "building the unproductive machines of war." "Let us remember," he wrote, "that it was the impossibility of building and maintaining a large army under the Wiemar [sic] Republic that helped to persuade Germany to become totalitarian. And let us remember that the Nazis employed the age-old device of using religious groups as scapegoats in order to take the people's minds off the suffering they were undergoing—in order to equip the country for total war."

The need, then, would be to work in collaboration with the other great powers of the new United Nations to achieve "an agreement for limiting our post war rearmament plans." While suspicions concerning Russian intentions were justifiable, so, too, he pointed out, were Moscow's doubts about the United States. "The Russian memory is long," he added, "and many of the leaders of the present government remember the years after the last war when they fought in the Red Armies against invading troops of many nations, including Britain's and the United States'." This, of course, refers to the American intervention in the Soviet Union from 1918 until 1920.

In a remarkable acknowledgment of the inconsistency between his new position and the thesis of his prewar *Why England Slept,* he wrote: "It was not the failure to be armed sufficiently that led to World War II. That was bad enough. But the reluctance of countries that were armed to use their forces in the early 30's against the Germans invited the disaster of 1939." Evoking once more his earlier reservations about the efficacy of democracies, Jack pointed out that "if we endeavor to compete with a dictatorship like Russia in maintaining large armies for an indefinite period, our democracy would probably collapse internally. Democracy sleeps fitfully in an armed camp."

A few months later atomic bombs incinerated Hiroshima and Nagasaki. Such thoughts also foreshadowed his later concern over arms limitations.

While Jack Kennedy did a great deal of reading and writing during his southwestern sojourn, that was not the total sum of his activities. After all, he had gone there to recuperate. So at the Castle Hot Springs Hotel he enjoyed the facilities, which included hot baths, a masseur, and a good swimming pool. For a little more adventure he later moved to the nearby Camelback Inn. He even managed some daily horseback riding, obviously in spite of his back. Still, Pat Lannan, who was with him at the time, remembers that "he was having a considerable amount of trouble with his stomach—chronic indigestion—and was very uptight about his inability to digest food properly."[14]

During that stay, Jack had his first meeting with the Goldwater family of Arizona. Having been in constant telephone contact with Ambassador Kennedy, Jack received the suggestion to contact the Goldwaters in Phoenix. Barry Goldwater was still overseas with the Air Force, so Jack met his sister. On at least two different occasions, once at the Camelback and again at a Goldwater home, Jack socialized with the family.[15]

The day FDR died, Jack was still at the Camelback Inn. With his health somewhat improved, he managed to go on to Hollywood and spent some time there, sharing a room with Lannan at the Beverly Hills Hotel. Joined by Charles Spalding, Jack sampled Hollywood nightlife. He met with several prominent film industry celebrities, including Gary Cooper, Walter Huston, and Olivia De Havilland, of whom Jack became especially fond. He also visited two old girl friends, Inga Arvad and Angela Greene. From April 23 to 25, Jack was elsewhere, however—at the Mayo Clinic for another checkup.

A more than casual relationship developed during that Hollywood visit, namely with movie star Gene Tierney. Jack and Torby were together at the studio one day while she was before the cameras on the set of *Dragonwyck.* * Kennedy and the actress saw each other several times in Hollywood, New York, and on the Cape. When they first met, she was getting divorced from designer Oleg Cassini and facing the trauma of having to institutionalize a retarded child. Kennedy, understandably sympathetic about that problem, assured her that "in any large family you can always find something wrong with somebody."[16] Cassini, however, knew the Kennedys and warned Gene early on that they would never permit Jack to marry a divorced woman. Finally, after periodic meetings over the course of about two years, Kennedy abruptly told her, "You know, Gene, I can never marry you," and that ended their relationship. When she published her memoirs decades later, she said an outstanding aspect of his personality was that "he took life just as it came" but she remained mystified about the nature of his charm.[17]

Meanwhile, back East, Joe Kennedy carefully planned his son's political career by expediting the first step, getting him some exposure through newspapers as a journalist. The Ambassador used his old ties with William Randolph Hearst. On April 23 the executive editor of a Hearst paper, the *Chicago Herald American,* sent a telegram to the Mayo Clinic

*Tierney's book incorrectly identified Kennedy's companion at the time as Ken O'Donnell.

in an effort to reach Jack, which he evidently did without much trouble. Quickly, an arrangement was completed to have Jack cover the charter conference of the United Nations about to open in San Francisco. Jack Kennedy thereby became a special correspondent, or, more properly, a celebrity correspondent, serving Hearst's *New York Journal-American* as well as the Chicago paper, which paid him 750 dollars for his dispatches.[18]

Jack's articles were given special treatment. The earliest ones carried the by-line "Lt. John F. Kennedy" and a picture of Jack in his Navy dress uniform. A special synopsis with each dispatch identified him as the recently retired PT boat hero and the son of the former Ambassador, as well as the author of *Why England Slept.*

Jack's dispatches were interesting for their awareness of basic problems. He noted, for example, the strategy of the Soviets, particularly their fight over Poland. Jack held that the Russian foreign minister, Molotov, in opposing the admission to the UN of Argentina, had made a ploy to create a situation that would require a compromise whereby both Poland and Argentina could be brought into the organization together. Molotov lost that battle to keep Argentina out but gained a moral victory. He was, Jack pointed out, after all "successful in putting the United States in a very uncomfortable position of supporting a nation that its own president had called Fascist."[19]

Kennedy also informed his readers about the Russian need for peace and of the general attitude of suspicion that marked their delegation. While many were extremely suspicious of the Communists, there were those with great confidence that in "their own strange and inexplicable way they really want peace." Correspondent Kennedy added that that argument emphasized that peace was the most important consideration for the Russians. To obtain that peace, he wrote, the Russians needed security, the kind of security that would make it impossible for her to be invaded again. "The Russians have a far greater fear of the German come-back than we do. They are therefore going to make their western defenses secure. No government hostile to Russia will be permitted in the countries along her borders. . . . They feel they have earned this right to security. They need to have it, come what may."[20]

Jack roomed at the Palace Hotel while in the city and was no less engaged as a bachelor in the Bay area's nightlife than he had been anywhere else. There he deepened his friendship with the beautiful Austine "Bootsie" Cassini, who had married Igor Cassini, the Hearst gossip columnist and brother of Oleg. During the war, Bootsie had taken over her husband's column. This close friend of Jack's later divorced Cassini and became Mrs. William Randolph Hearst, Jr.

During that stay in San Francisco, Jack also met another old acquaintance, Mary Meyer. She had been Mary Pinchot when they had first met at Vassar while Jack was there for dates when still a Harvard student. A descendant of the Pennsylvania Pinchot family, which produced its two-term governor, Gifford Pinchot, she was regarded as the most beautiful girl of Vassar's class of '42. Her father was Amos Pinchot, the lawyer who helped to organize Teddy Roosevelt's Bull Moose Progressives in 1912 and later became a pacifist and American Firster. Mary was the heiress to a multimillion-dollar dry-goods business. She was also considered an unconventional free spirit.

Jack met her in San Francisco as a newlywed. She had just married Cord Meyer, Jr.[21] also from a distinguished and wealthy family, who was attending the conference as a military aide to Commander Harold Stassen. Stassen, Minnesota's former "boy governor," was then a U.S. delegate at the drafting of the charter. Meyer was regarded as a brilliant young man with every talent for a distinguished future career—in many ways a personality who showed promise similar to Jack's. Meyer, however, was more intense, more purely intellectual, less ready to appreciate a joke, or possibly the Kennedy brand of humor. That Meyer and Jack would be thrown together in the same social circles, whether in San Francisco or on the East Coast, was not surprising. But their personalities clashed rather than harmonized. In fact, Jack and Cord Meyer fought in San Francisco. The possibility that their falling-out stemmed as much from disputes over the current international situation and prospects for the United Nations is as great as the suspicion that Jack had shown excessive attention to Meyer's bride.[22] Nevertheless, the renewal of Jack's friendship with Mary Pinchot Meyer would become far more significant during Kennedy's White House days.[23] By then, Cord Meyer had died and Mary's sister had married *Newsweek* executive Ben Bradlee.

While the UN conference was closing down, Jack left the West Coast, spent a few days in the East visiting friends and family in New York and Boston, and went on to England to cover the British elections. Among the very few who foresaw the possibility that Prime Minister Churchill would actually be removed from office, Kennedy conceded that Americans would be surprised, but pointed out that "Churchill is fighting a tide that is surging through Europe washing away monarchies and conservative governments everywhere, and that tide flows powerfully in England. England is moving towards some form of socialism—if not in this election, then surely at the next."[24] Not even Churchill, whom Kennedy had worshiped above all others and who had just emerged as the great wartime leader, could counter the inevitable change.

Jack was also present in Potsdam at the time of the summit conference, arriving long after the meetings had begun. Officially there as a journalist, although he filed no dispatches, he had traveled in the company of Navy Secretary James V. Forrestal.[25]

Having completed his work, Jack returned to America in early August, coinciding with the opening of the atomic era and the end of World War II. The questions of war and peace were very much on Kennedy's mind. He had experienced too much to be oblivious of the dangers. His writings, both the unpublished and those pieces carried by the Hearst press, revealed a real sensitivity toward the postwar arms race and the potential for more slaughter, and also a perception of Soviet paranoia and security needs that rivaled the understanding of such "Yalta axiom" leaders as Henry A. Wallace. His contemporaries were, meanwhile, looking forward to an era of peace and the resumption of prosperity.

Within days after Kennedy's arrival, he heard from Forrestal. "Do you want to do any work here," Forrestal wrote from Washington, "if so why don't you come down and see what there is at hand?"[26] But Jack had other plans. By then, neither he nor his father doubted what needed to be done.

10

"A New Candidate"

Timing was essential, and Jack's could hardly have been better. If he was going to bring a new face, a new style, become a new kind of candidate, the end of the war capped the perfect set of conditions. A bright and wealthy young veteran, one of remarkable distinction for his age, already associated with selflessness, patriotism, and public service, Kennedy had all the qualifications. With veterans as the new heroes in America, he could be "present at the creation" of the postwar brand of leadership.

The America he returned to late that summer of 1945 had long since experienced wartime prosperity that had raised living standards well above the Depression decade's. Money was abundant, ready to be spent; consumer goods were at a premium, and the pent-up demand could not be satisfied overnight. Shortages of basic commodities hindered the economy and major controversies centered around the relative roles of inflation, scarcity, and the wisdom of returning to a free, unrestricted market, while demand quickly contradicted pessimists who talked about a new depression. The economy had expanded and would continue to expand at a heady rate. Labor unions, knowing the money was available, pressed to make up for overtime pay and raises sacrificed during the war, and relations with management worsened. The nation soon slid into its most damaging strike wave, with shutdowns affecting almost every major industry, thwarting industrial reconversion, and exacerbating shortages.

Those months also coincided with the uncertain leadership that marked the elevation of the poorly prepared Mr. Truman. Initially, his rise had offered hope to anti-New Deal Democrats of a postwar trend away from FDR's brand of liberalism. But the President followed a wavering course that jarred the confidence of labor and management alike. He delivered an omnibus message to Congress that suddenly re-evoked the New Deal. His bold legislative requests included full-employment legislation, expanded unemployment compensation, civil rights reforms through a permanent Fair Employment Practices Commission, increased minimum wages, comprehensive housing legislation, permanent farm price supports, and other items that accepted federal social welfare and economic responsibilities. While liberals at last felt Truman worthy of his predecessor, the conservative response came in the form of complaints such as the one from House Minority Leader Joe Martin, who declared that "not even President Roosevelt asked for so much at one sitting. It's just a plain case of out-dealing the New Deal," while Charlie Halleck, an Indiana Republican, announced, "This is the kick-off. This begins the campaign of 1946."[1]

Halleck, of course, was right. It did begin the 1946 campaign. Nationally, that vote indicated the conservative postwar course desired by most Americans, much as the stunning defeat of Churchill's Conservative government had shown the *opposite* desire among the British. Whereas the British elections in July of 1945 had produced a left-wing reaction against their own prewar Conservative Party rule, thirteen years of FDR and Truman moved Americans in the opposite direction. As the British prepared to nationalize key industries and tackle the maldistribution of wealth, the United States, in response to the clear meaning of the 1946 congressional elections, began a reaction against those who had brought the country "statism" and "creeping socialism."

In that setting, John F. Kennedy worked to improve his visibility for his undeclared campaign for an unspecified office. Jack girded himself, forcing activity undertaken only with difficulty. Scrawny, with a painful back, and suffering from periodic attacks of malaria, his yellowish and bony figure could hardly command confidence. "I am certain he never forgets he must live Joe's life as well as his own," wrote George St. John to Jack's mother that summer.[2] Mark Dalton, one of his managers, recalled that Jack did not seem "to be built for politics in the sense of being the easygoing affable person. He was extremely drawn and thin. ... Yet, deep down, he was an aggressive person, but he was always shy. He drove himself into this. ... It must have been a tremendous effort of will."[3] His speech lacked poise and confidence. "He was never a polished public speaker at that time," remembered Jim Reed, another of Jack's Navy pals. "He spoke very fast, very rapidly, and seemed to be just a trifle embarrassed on the stage."[4]

Nor did the Ambassador really have confidence in the ability of his second son. As Arthur Krock put it, "I don't believe his father thought he was particularly qualified for politics until Joe's death made him the eldest son."[5] Joseph P. Kennedy himself later said that "Joe used to talk about being President some day, and a lot of smart people thought he would make it. He was altogether different from Jack—more dynamic, more sociable and easy going. Jack in those days back there when he was getting out of college was rather shy, withdrawn and quiet. His mother and I couldn't picture him as a politician. We were sure he'd be a teacher or a writer."[6] Nevertheless, working with what he did have, the Ambassador schemed to promote Jack's political career.

Public, sometimes vociferous disclaimers of the Ambassador's role frequently argued for the independence of Jack's rise. Throughout the young man's political career, and perhaps even more so when he became a national figure, more than the perception of independence was at stake: Joe's presence could have become a distinct political liability.

The notion of Joe Kennedy being confined backstage with his bottomless checkbook, while his dashing son exploited special talents and charms to seduce the electorate, continues to be advanced and defended. A charming, highly laudatory, and romantic account by Kenneth P. O'Donnell and David F. Powers, two of the most loyal members of what came to be known as the Kennedys' "Irish mafia," depicts the Ambassador as incidental to that 1946 campaign. The co-authors carefully point out, for example, that Joe Kennedy's appearance at the first reception and tea party for Jack in Cambridge was his only public act for his son during that battle for the Democratic nomination to represent the Eleventh Congressional District. And Joe Kennedy himself modestly described his own role by saying simply, "I just called people. I got in touch with people I knew. I have a lot of contacts. I've been in Massachusetts since I was ten."[7]

For all the disclaimers, however, the Ambassador had clearly not built his own empire by leaving things to chance. He had calculated and fought single-mindedly, then, wherever possible, had moved in for the kill when the price was right. Similarly, getting his oldest surviving son started in politics bore all the signs of Joe Kennedy's business acumen. Knowing what he wanted, he was not going to let anything interfere. Thus, he passed up an investment opportunity that could have been highly profitable but, at the same time, compromised his son's political career. According to Steve Smith, Charles B. "Tex" Thornton, the electronics manufacturer, was joining with associates to form a new company. Kennedy, brought in at the outset as a major investor, was about to go ahead. But he paused when his own attorney, Bartholomew Brickley, had some second thoughts. "I wonder whether you want to be involved with it," reasoned Brickley. "It seems to me that they're going to be doing considerable business with the government. If that's the case and the boys are interested or going to become involved in politics, I wonder whether you want that sort of potential conflict." Kennedy agreed. Bart Brickley had a point. There were other ways of expanding his holdings. The gains were not worth the possible conflict-of-interest embarrassments, so Kennedy declined from becoming a charter investor in Litton Industries.[8] As Robert Kennedy wrote in a volume of tributes Teddy later compiled for their father, "The most important thing to him was the advancement of his children. . . . After the end of World War II, he decided this aim could best be accomplished by doing what, for a strong figure, is probably the most difficult thing to do—to submerge his own personality. This is what he did."[9]

Ken O'Donnell, in an interview not long before his death, became heated at suggestions that the Ambassador had played a prominent role in 1946. He scoffed at stories about Joe Kennedy's expertise and value to the campaign and pointed out that the Ambassador had been "out of touch" with Boston politics for a long time. "He no longer knew a goddamn thing about what was going on in Massachusetts," he argued.[10] O'Donnell was not one who fawned over the Ambassador.

Ethnically and politically, Joe Kennedy had never left Massachusetts. He may have sought social and economic gains elsewhere, but it was still his "old sod": his roots, his followers, and all they represented were very much in the Bay State. His natural supporters were concentrated in the land of the Kennedys and the Fitzgeralds, where coteries around strong personalities usurped party organizational loyalties, where the Church and its archbishop provided a force inseparable from temporal leadership.

Catholicism was the single unifying element of a constituency that tended to coalesce around such strong figures as, first, Lomasney and Fitzgerald, and then James Michael Curley or John McCormack. The clerical leadership of largely poor communicants tended to be conservative, even reactionary, especially under William Cardinal O'Connell, who had performed the wedding rituals for Rose and Joe Kennedy. The spiritual leader of seventy-six percent of the city's population, the cardinal was, in the words of a recent historian, "a towering figure." To the cardinal and the Church, the duty of civil government was to maintain order. Class warfare was an agent of the infidel and, with direct references to the New Deal government in Washington, he attacked "the drab uniformity of collectivism."[11] Reformers, socialists, Communists, were all dangerous enemies, distracting the poor from their god. Dangerous, too, were the Spanish Loyalists, including Americans of the Abraham Lincoln Brigade, who resisted Francisco Franco. Not surprisingly, Boston Irishmen were the most devoted followers of the anti-Roosevelt, pro-Nazi, and increasingly anti-Semitic Father Charles Coughlin of Royal Oak, Michigan.

Economic tensions exacerbated the frictions that resulted from Boston's segregated ethnic patterns. Boston's economic recovery lagged behind both New England's and the rest of the states. By 1940 its textile and shoe companies had all but vanished, while manufacturing as a whole declined. Wholesale and retail occupations picked up just part of the slack. By the end of the 1930's, the city's labor force earned only thirty-seven percent of the level reached at the time of the stock market collapse. Not even the advent of federal defense spending on the eve of World War II helped very much, because such contracts tended to move toward urban centers with a better industrial base. Competition for jobs became more heated, the ethnic enclaves more hostile. The Italo-Americans* of the North End, centering along Hanover Street, were virtually isolated from the rest of the city. Largely Italian football teams playing in South Boston became engaged in "rumbles" with "Southies." As an outlet for their own pride, Boston's Italian population admired the leadership of Benito Mussolini. The Irish poor, meanwhile, remained frustrated, unable to advance either economically or socially in a city where they had such numerical strength. Their outlets became Father Coughlin and anticommunism, which by the late 1930's was a prime issue that politicians could exploit with regularity, thus giving the poor a perpetual "Red scare" to vent their frustrations. Criticism of the Church or of

*Italo-American was the common usage in Boston.

Generalissimo Franco was associated with New Deal liberal reformers, who, in 1940, had also turned against Ambassador Joseph P. Kennedy. His recall from the Court of St. James's was met with denunciations of Roosevelt's gall and an affront to those who had praised Kennedy's anti-interventionist stand.

Only two years later, and again involving the Roosevelt administration, the Ambassador became a factor in Massachusetts politics. In 1942 John F. Fitzgerald, the Ambassador's aging father-in-law, attempted a political comeback by opposing Congressman Joseph Casey for the Democratic senatorial nomination. The Kennedy hand was largely a behind-the-scenes affair. He set up Honey Fitz mainly to block Casey, who was Roosevelt's candidate to defeat Republican Senator Henry Cabot Lodge, Jr. In his effort to indirectly lash back at the President through his father-in-law, Kennedy turned to a cousin, Joe Kane, a stereotype of the street-wise Boston Irish politico and secretary to Congressman Peter Tague. It was Kane who made the outrageous suggestion that Kennedy salvage Honey Fitz from retirement.

The enterprise, backed by Kennedy money, appealed to the old man's ego, inspiring vain fantasies of reliving earlier glories. Working very closely with kindred anti-New Dealers in New York backed by Jim Farley, the Fitzgerald campaign employed many of the same themes as its New York counterpart. It also had the support of the local Hearst paper, the *Boston Herald American,* and the Coughlinites. It was also a fiasco.

Roosevelt, for one, shrewdly nullified any open involvement on the part of his ex-ambassador with a timely telephone call requesting him to speak out publicly for the administration's candidate. A flustered Kennedy explained that he could not work openly against his own father-in-law. And Honey Fitz, a relic who still retained at least nostalgic popularity, was sadly miscast. The "Sweet Adeline" singing pol, placed in the line of fire, appeared as a ludicrous figure. At one point he rushed up to Joe Casey, his opponent, in the lobby of the Bellevue Hotel, located right across the street from the State House, and, shaking a finger, admonished the congressman. "You have maligned me," he shouted. "You have told the people of Massachusetts that I'm an octogenarian, and that's false." Casey looked at Honey Fitz and said, "Well, how old are you?" The man who had been forced to relinquish control of Boston's City Hall back in 1914 replied, "I'm seventy-nine."[12] Casey went on to win comfortably, defeating Honey Fitz by 108,000 to 80,000. Joe Kennedy had long since cut his financial losses in that affair, at least cut them from his father-in-law. But so eager was he to defeat the administration's candidate that, privately, he made a substantial contribution to enable Lodge to defeat Casey.[13] When the President ran for a fourth term in 1944, with Missouri Senator Harry S Truman as his running mate, word leaked out that Kennedy was operating behind the scenes for Tom Dewey, the Republican candidate. Further information came out of Boston about Joe Kennedy having bought twenty-five thousand dollars of radio time for a public endorsement of the New York governor. Again, as in the Honey Fitz-Casey affair, Roosevelt, knowing his man, intervened. This time he called him to Washington and flatteringly solicited his expertise to make a study of shipbuilder Henry J. Kaiser's "jobs for all" program. Facing newsmen after that White House meeting, Kennedy denied plans to boost Dewey but declined to predict the outcome.[14]

Many years later Harry Truman recalled what had happened during that campaign when he met the Ambassador in a Ritz-Carlton suite in Boston. Kennedy venomously denounced Roosevelt, claiming, among other things, that the President had caused the war. "Harry, what the hell are you doing campaigning for that crippled son of a bitch that killed my son Joe?" he demanded.

Truman, no Little Lord Fauntleroy himself, replied, "If you say another word about Roosevelt, I'm going to throw you out that window."

Bob Hannegan, the Democratic National Chairman, grabbed Truman's arm and said, "Come out here. I'm gonna get ten thousand dollars out of the old son of a bitch for the Democratic Party." Truman recalled that Kennedy, ever mindful of his self-interests, came through with the contribution.[15] Truman also liked to give some advice about Joe Kennedy. "Don't drink Scotch, drink bourbon," he told friends. "Every time you do [drink Scotch] you put money in Joe Kennedy's pocket."[16]

With his own son now primed for a political debut, the former ambassador was not about to risk another farce. He had learned some lessons. Besides, his present candidate would be a new type of Boston Irishman, more Harvard than Boston and less Irish than Yankee, a direct contrast with the era that had been personified by such politicos as Honey Fitz, Martin Lomasney, and James Michael Curley.

Of all the Boston pols, none commanded nearly as much national attention as Curley. Nor did any quite so thoroughly epitomize the unscrupulous Irishman who rose on the misfortunes of his people. And yet Curley, ethnic politician as he was, performed in essence not very differently from others in various parts of the country. Like Huey Long, his populism helped build a loyal personal following.

Between being an anti-Curley man or a pro-Curleyite, there was little ground. Nationally, of course, his name evoked the specter of corruption. Much stemmed from Curley's imprisonment early in his career for standing in for a friend's civil service examination. It cost him sixty days in the Charles Street Jail, but he always explained that incident with the following logic: "Pat couldn't spell Constantinople, but he had wonderful feet for a letter carrier."[17] Possibly his greatest piece of audacity came during the 1932 Democratic convention. Having broken with those of his fellow Bostonians who had stood staunchly behind their favorite of four years earlier, Al Smith, to support Governor Roosevelt, Curley found himself rejected in the primary in favor of a Smith backer. Curley, then, was without a forum—and worse, without his delegate's vote, which was pretty bad for the first big-city mayor to declare himself for FDR. At the convention, however, when the delegation from Puerto Rico was called upon to cast its votes, a familiar Boston-Irish voice introduced itself as "Acalde Jaimie Miguel Cureleo" and, in a Spanish accent, delivered six votes for Franklin Delano Roosevelt. Curley had simply substituted for the head of the Puerto Rican delegation, who had been called home because of illness in the family. Curley's antics had not, however, always led to success.

After powerful working-class support gave Curley the governorship in 1934, Henry Cabot Lodge, Jr., defeated him for the Senate in 1936; his former protégé, Maurice Tobin, beat him for the mayoralty in 1937; and the following year Curley lost out in a gubernatorial contest to one who was as much of a certified Yankee as Lodge, Leverett Saltonstall. Nevertheless, Curley, who had sat in Congress from 1911 to 1914, returned to Capitol Hill in 1942. His decision to relinquish the representation of the Eleventh District in favor of returning to Boston's City Hall gave Jack Kennedy the opportunity he needed.

The Eleventh was possibly the poorest in the state, a perception not easily made when scanning the district from its apex at the State Capitol atop Beacon Hill. Nor when looking westward along the south bank of the Charles River toward Brighton, a middle-class Irish and Italian community not far from Jack's birthplace at Brookline. But the district reached out like a half-shell, stretching in other directions as well, to the North End, where Ward 3 Italians lived in a highly congested tenement area around the Old North Church; across the river to Cambridge, with its impressive academic institutions of Harvard, Radcliffe, and MIT, but also with its working-class Italians to the east; to suburban Somerville, north of Cambridge, with its poor Irish and Italians living around warehouses, factories, and railroad yards; and then, to the east, to East Boston, the land of P.J.'s youth, shared by both the Irish and Italo-Americans. There was also Charlestown, the almost exclusively Irish enclave where families lived in wooden "three-deckers" and owed their survival to the adjacent Navy Yard.

"We were 'townies' and we lived in these three deckers—the Sullivans in the first and the Murphys in the second and the Daughertys at the top," Dave Powers recalled. "But what a wonderful life we had: we thought we were rich, and it was only because we were all as poor as each other and we shared in that."[18]

Almost entirely Roman Catholic, with just a scattering of Jewish voters in the West End, the district was so solidly Democratic (it was believed that not a single Republican lived in Charlestown) that victory in the primary was sufficient to guarantee election.

For the moment, however, as Jack Kennedy prepared for his own candidacy, local pols were uncertain whether he would try for Curley's vacated Eleventh District seat or would accede to Governor Maurice Tobin's desire to have the young man on his own ticket for the lieutenant governorship. It had become particularly clear to the governor that the Kennedy name would be desirable, and perhaps vital, for the statewide Democratic ticket. Not only could it tap Kennedy money, but it would attract the veterans, thereby furnishing the Massachusetts Democratic campaign with a magnet that could counter the growing postwar Republican resurgence that was as evident in the Commonwealth as it was in the rest of the country. For the Eleventh District's vacancy, Tobin preferred a political colleague, Mike Neville of Cambridge.[19]

For his own purposes, however, Tobin did everything possible to encourage Kennedy political ambitions. One month before Curley announced for the mayoralty, in April of 1945, the governor brought Joe Kennedy into the Massachusetts limelight by giving him the co-chairmanship, with Dean Donald David of the Harvard Business School, of a seven-member committee to make an "economic" survey of the Bay State to determine the feasibility of establishing its own Department of Commerce to attract capital into the area. That gave the older Kennedy the opportunity to meet with groups all over the state—local chambers of commerce, labor organizations, citizens groups, etcetera—which enabled him to scrutinize Massachusetts and establish vital contacts in preparation for his son's coming political run. Tobin also made a personal trip to Palm Beach to convince the former ambassador of the wisdom of having Jack enter public life as the governor's running mate.

Two *New York Times* journalists also figured in the buildup. Arthur Krock, who seems to have made a second career of promoting Kennedy interests, devoted his "In the Nation" column to a laudatory account of Joe Kennedy's role in Tobin's economic survey. Failing to even mention co-chairman David, Krock argued that the Ambassador was an enlightened businessman and not merely a selfish reactionary.[20] The other *Times* man was Anthony Leviero. Leviero came through with a well-timed article on October 25 based on the Navy Department's release of details about the death of Joe Junior. For the first time Joe Junior's heroism was substantiated. Readers were told about the explosive-laden drone guided by Kennedy and Bud Willy toward the V-2 launching site and the fate of the two men and their PB_4Y, a timely reminder of Kennedy courage and patriotism. The release may well have been facilitated by Navy secretary James Forrestal.

It is also reasonable to assume that Forrestal was at least helpful in securing the naming of a new destroyer after that particular war hero. Built at the Bethlehem Steel Company's shipyard in Quincy, Massachusetts, the *Joseph P. Kennedy, Jr.,* was commissioned on December 16, an event that received major headlines in the Boston papers, their accounts stressing the association of the words *hero* and *Kennedy.*[21] Jack had gone to Palm Beach and was not present for the occasion. But the ceremony was attended by brothers Bobby and Teddy, along with Honey Fitz and his wife. The ship then sailed on a shakedown cruise to Latin America and the Caribbean. Bobby went on that voyage as a seaman second class. When the destroyer returned in the spring, the Ambassador paid it a well-publicized visit, which yielded a fine display of stories and photographs in the local papers.

Throughout 1945 and into the following year, the Kennedy name was connected with patriotism, military heroism, philanthropy, and capitalistic genius. Mobilized behind such appeals were the returning World War II veterans, a new and potent bloc in a district that numbered some thirty-seven different nationalities. Their common interest in the welfare of former GIs made them a source of single-issue power—which Kennedy prepared to tap. One of them, a survivor of the fighting in the South Pacific and later commander of several veterans groups, Tom Broderick, remembered Kennedy's pitch. Putting aside his earlier misgivings about postwar armaments, he told them that with the end of the war, "we must remain strong." Broderick recalled to an interviewer that at the time he turned to his wife and said, "Well, Grace, there's two things we've got to believe in. We both believe in God and Jack Kennedy."[22] Looking backward to that period, another leader of veterans remembered Jack Kennedy as "the second coming of Christ."[23]

Instrumental in getting such messages across, in helping to place the city's newspapers in the Kennedy camp, and in arranging the heavy speaking schedule for Jack, was the John C. Dowd Advertising Agency of Boston. The Kennedy association with Dowd began with Governor Tobin's creation of the Special Study Commission. Dowd served as one of the five members, and it was he who wrote the commission's report and drew up the blueprint for the proposed new Department of Commerce. Dowd's reward from Joe Kennedy came in gaining for his agency substantial advertising revenues from Somerset Importers.[24]

Dowd publicized Joe Kennedy's activities and points of view, all of which furthered the impression of deep involvement in affairs relating to peace, veterans' welfare, religion, and charitable works. Additional publicity came that spring with Kennedy's presentation of a ten-thousand-dollar check to the Guild of Apollonia for its twenty-fifth anniversary celebration. The papers, while reporting that the money would be used by the Guild of Catholic Dentists to care for parochial school children, recalled that the Ambassador had made his first contribution to the charity many years earlier when little Jack was seriously ill with scarlet fever.[25] In June, the Navy Cross for Lieutenant Joseph P. Kennedy, Jr., was presented to Rose Kennedy by the Commandant of the 1st Naval District in Boston. In September, the Ambassador established a twelve-hundred-dollar scholarship for research study at the Lowell Textile Institute as a memorial to his son Joe.[26] That summer, too, a report from Chicago revealed that Kennedy had negotiated a contract for the purchase of the Merchandise Mart, the world's largest privately owned structure.

Nationally, the Ambassador's public reemergence was helped by the Luce publications, *Life* and *Time*. The latter, reporting that some Bostonians questioned his investment in the Merchandise Mart as a contradiction of his stated interest in the future of Massachusetts, quoted Kennedy as responding that "the condition of the real estate interest in Boston is scandalous and that of politics is worse. The only property offered to me in Boston was a building in bad condition that was 20% vacant."[27] At the same time, *Life* featured a picture story showing the Ambassador addressing a luncheon meeting in Lowell. One had him posing with Governor Tobin in the process of setting up the Joseph P.

Kennedy, Jr., scholarship fund. A second showed him talking to a woman riveter on the destroyer *Joseph P. Kennedy, Jr.* He was also posed against the background of Boston Harbor, again emphasizing that, despite investments elsewhere, his heart was in Massachusetts.[28]

Similarly, publicity had to focus on Jack's own local heritage to counter sniping that he was an "outsider," a "carpetbagger," or, as some put it, the "representative from Paris," one who had no claim to stand for a Boston constituency. In America, unlike England, one could not as easily select a constituency to represent. With or without local residency laws, voters demanded more direct ties to the community.

Most of all, perhaps, the psychological moment had come for the emergence in a leadership position of the "first Irish Brahmin." Young Jack Kennedy, from a family that had actually achieved the "American dream," provided the necessary inspirational success model. He confirmed to the less fortunate their endless possibilities. His advance was well timed also not only for his personal rise but for the presence of a war-conditioned constituency, especially returning veterans. In that immediate postwar climate of esprit de corps and euphoria, unspoiled by the advent of new and complex problems that would make both for more sophistication and cynicism, they were particularly susceptible to being wooed by a fellow veteran, especially one who could point to a heroic combat record.

All that must be understood within the context of James Michael Curley's leadership and the power of the Catholic Church as the governing element in the lives of Boston's Irish poor. In February of 1946, for instance, while Jack was still officially silent about his choice of office but while suspicions centered on the Curley seat, a *Boston Post* column by Brian Fitzhugh pointed out that a race by Jack Kennedy for that seat would be one of the more interesting political developments of the year. Noting Curley's longtime political strength in the Eleventh, especially in such strongholds as East Boston, Charlestown, and the North, West, and South Ends, it held that he could sway enough votes to decide the outcome of a close contest. Political circles were, moreover, undecided as to where his weight might be thrown.[29]

In the mid-1940's, a change took place in the lives of Boston's Irish Catholics. When William Cardinal O'Connell died in April, Bishop Richard Cushing was named by Pope Pius XII on September 28, 1944, as the third archbishop of Boston. The future cardinal rapidly became closely associated with the Kennedy family.[30] The Boston that John F.

Kennedy prepared to take on, then, had undergone a coincidence of changes that had conditioned its conservative, hard-working poor to be more receptive than usual for somebody new. It was precisely that kind of vacuum that, with all his reservations and self-doubts, Jack Kennedy determined he had to fill.

Jack's campaign for the primary was a two-pronged affair, the first before his official entry in April and the other during the weeks between April and the balloting on June 18. During the preliminary period, an essential part of his strategy was to defer the question about whether he would join Maurice Tobin on the statewide ticket or try for Curley's seat. He did everything possible during those months to make certain that his announcement would also come after he had countered sniping that he was a rich, young "carpetbagger" slumming in a poor, working-class district.

The plan encouraged speculation that he would join Tobin, a possibility that boosted his efforts to enroll followers and campaign workers who smelled political rewards that could follow from influence at the State House. Should he run for the post of lieutenant governor, declared the Milton *Tribune* on February 14, "He has a strong, compelling personality, is a gifted orator and boasts an excellent war record, all of which should stand him in good stead. . . ."

Jack, however, never entertained that option seriously. Patsy Mulkern, a Runyonesque character who knew the streets and faces of the district as well as anyone and who later became a paid worker, was momentarily caught off guard in an oral history interview. Asked about some people thinking that Jack should try for the lieutenant governorship, Patsy responded, "Oh, yeah, there were a couple of plants around trying to make—" And then he stopped.[31]

Dave Powers, too, reported the feeling that running for Congress was Jack's decision, "no matter who talked to him about the other."[32] Another associate, Hirsh Freed, remembered that Jack was "never really . . . interested in local politics in the city of Boston or in the state of Massachusetts. He was always interested in the United States as part of the world, not because he was a believer in a government of the world or a federation of nations, but his mind was away from Boston and Massachusetts." His interest lay in international politics, the topic that engaged most of his serious talk.[33]

The Eleventh District was, to Jack, nothing but a fulcrum for a political career, a constituency much as those Kennedy had come to know in

England for which the gentry contended. As Freed pointed out, "He had decided that this was the place where he would start and nothing was going to stop him, not because he was unscrupulous, but he knew—he used his father's money as a resource—he knew he had the money to run the fight. He knew he had the name, the looks, and all that, and while he wasn't contemptuous of the people who were working for him or anything, it was that really he was using them as tools for his political advancement."[34]

That strategy was, at least in part, dictated by Joe Kane. Kane was the man suggested by the Ambassador as the toughest and wisest expert on how to wage a ward-by-ward campaign in Boston's Irish political world. His philosophy of what it took to win was something that Joe Kennedy could readily understand. "The first is money and the second is money and the third is money," his cousin liked to say.[35]

Undoubtedly overestimating his son's sensitivity, Joe Kennedy doubted Jack's ability to accept Kane's tutelage. Would he wither under the older man's coarseness? Would the realities of street politics as seen by Kane destroy the spirit of his shy son? The subsequent relationship became, to the Ambassador, another test of the young man's spunk, and one that he passed with high grades.

Additional help came from a man despised by Kane, Honey Fitz. His deep roots in local politics could still produce results. In most of the district, even in the North End with its more recent Italian residents, the Fitzgerald popularity continued. Through one friend, Jack's grandfather helped to recruit some of the Italo-Americans who also lived in the East End and who had known the Kennedy side of the family for some time. It was also through his grandfather that Jack was able to induce the chairman of the Boston School Committee to arrange a speech before the Home School Association, meeting in a crowded section where halls for such engagements were scarce.[36]

It was also his grandfather's residence, the Bellevue Hotel, that became Jack's mailing address to establish his "legitimacy" within the district as required by law. Room 308 of that hotel, scarcely a block away from the State House and in the heart of the political hangouts, became the nerve center for campaign operations, the place where much of the planning and speech-writing was done. Local offices were then set up in various communities throughout the district. Five campaign offices were finally established, the main one located in downtown Boston at 18 Tremont Street.

That period of undeclared candidacy, with the question of the ultimate direction of his ambition still wide open, coincided with the Japanese surrender aboard the U.S. *Missouri* in Tokyo Bay in early September. World War II had come to an official end. John Hersey was enjoying having a dramatized version of his wartime Pulitzer prize novel, *A Bell For Adano,* on the Broadway stage in New York. Boston theaters, however, took little notice of the war: Agatha Christie's *Ten Little Indians* was still going strong, while *Life With Father* was in its last two weeks at the Colonial. The Opera House was about to get the Margaret Webster production of *The Tempest,* but the city's fervid baseball fans who packed Fenway Park had their Red Sox deep in seventh place, eleven and a half games behind first, while the National League Boston Braves were doing no better than sixth in their eight-team league.[37]

Jack, meanwhile, forced himself to make literally hundreds of speeches, not only in the district he eventually sought to represent but throughout the state, from Cape Cod as far west as Springfield. Organized with the expertise of the Dowd Agency, the quantity of such public appearances emphasized his seriousness. He faced the Guild of the Holy Name, the Men's Club of the St. Augustine Parish in Andover, the alumni of Brighton High School, a joint meeting of the service clubs sponsored by the Chamber of Commerce of Lowell, the Lions Club in Attleboro, the Kiwanis Club of Worcester, the Boston Association of Geography Teachers, the Aristos Club in Boston, and the Crosscup-Pison Post of the American Legion in the Statler Hotel, among many others. His picture appeared in local papers alongside leading organizational figures.[38]

Those early speeches, not opposing any specific candidate nor advertising his fitness for a particular office, were designed to enhance a reputation as one experienced in worldly affairs. While he wrote the basic texts, others contributed suggestions and he improvised. He borrowed heavily from experiences in England with the Labour Party victory and the emergence of British socialism. One of his earliest efforts came before the Hyannis Rotary Club on the topic of "England and Germany: Victor and Vanquished." His frail figure made him look, in the description of one Rotarian, like "a little boy dressed up in his father's clothes" and the substance of his message "more closely resembled a high-school senior chosen as Boys' State representative . . . than a young man on the threshold of his political career." The speech, both mediocre and humorless, was read from a prepared text with all the insecurity of the novice. Only when he stumbled over a word and flashed "a quick, self-deprecating grin" did he "light up the room." Most important, and what would become more important than his words, was that "an appealing waif-like quality showed through, and above all a winning sincerity impressed his audience more than did the frequently high-flown language of his speech."[39]

But his basic theme served for most early speeches. His views had not moved very far from his father's positions. Their lack of a clear ideological content, in fact, emulated the substance of the public messages being offered elsewhere by the Ambassador. Both showed great concern with the development of the social-welfare state in England. Both sounded ominous warnings about the threats to capitalism inherent in the emergence of a collectivist totalitarian government.

"He was not the ordinary type of campaigner in the sense that he was not affable and easygoing," recalled campaign aide Mark Dalton, "and certainly he was not a speaker."[40] His figure was too gaunt, even sickly. His speech was too rapid. His eyes too glued to the typescript. His demeanor betrayed embarrassment and a lack of poise. His shyness came through, whether from the rostrum or on the streets and in homes going from door to door shaking hands with the voters. He exuded self-consciousness.[41]

But, said Dave Powers, he was "aggressively shy." Knocking on Powers's door in a Charlestown three-decker only to be told that Powers had already had a commitment through friendship with one of Kennedy's rivals, John Cotter, did not discourage Kennedy. "He knew what he wanted to do," said Powers, "and he didn't leave there until he made me promise. . . . He said, 'Dave, I'm going to be speaking to a group of Gold Star Mothers at the American Legion Hall in Charlestown, and I don't even know where it is. How about coming over with me?' "[42] And so Powers, an ex-GI living on weekly government benefit payments, the so-called "52/20 Club," and a member of the local American Legion Post, became Jack Kennedy's permanent sidekick.

Powers also gave the young man his first view of Charlestown poverty. Together, they canvassed the three-decker flats from door to door, where most men lived within walking distance of their jobs at the Navy Yard. Although the "townies" did not consider themselves poor, it was Jack Kennedy's first direct contact with the struggling working classes. There is no evidence that he felt any sorrier for them than they did for themselves.[43]

Poor as they were, other young unemployed veterans in the "52/20 Club" found much appeal in the manner of the "millionaire kid" from Harvard who needed their support. He was ingratiating rather than condescending. The amateurishness of his approach heightened the impression of sincerity and contrasted with the cynical pols of the Curley era. At one gathering, for example, Jack won over the crowd by saying, "I seem to be the only person here tonight who didn't come up the hard way."[44] Even his appearance became somewhat of an asset, especially with the women. As Patsy Mulkern observed, "Him being sick at that time, crippled and everything else. I think that helped him a little bit. . . . The sympathy. . . . You can't lick sympathy; and money with it."[45] It became commonplace to say that women wanted to either mother or marry him.

The public uncertainty of his ultimate goal also helped expedite the formation of a Joseph P. Kennedy, Jr., chapter of the Veterans of Foreign Wars. One reason, of course, was to help keep alive the memory of Jack's fallen older brother and, beyond that, the further association of the candidate of *PT 109* fame with a family of heroes. The post also anchored the Kennedy association with the district and the city of Boston. For the campaign itself, it became an additional source of cadre, especially since the membership included some four to five hundred dues-paying veterans, many of them seeking to use the chapter for their own purposes. Not surprisingly, many of its young men later became prominent lawyers, politicians, and businessmen. "Sure, people said it had political overtones," recalled Edward McLaughlin in 1978, "but that was not why it was set up. No question, we hoped it would help Jack politically. You'd have to be a goddamn liar to say otherwise."[46]

The wider ramifications of the VFW chapter were evident during the arrangements to obtain the charter. Much of that spadework went through Colonel Joseph Hanken. A Curley hack who had acquired his military title through National Guard service, Hanken had gotten his reward from the governor with an appointment as state Adjutant General. A determined self-serving operator (who was arrested in 1948 for staging illegal bingo games of chance) and businessman, Hanken had to be negotiated with because, at the time the Kennedy people were trying to get their charter, he was the VFW's national junior vice-commander and convinced that the post could attract a large membership by serving a multitude of functions. Hanken, confident that he and his associates could do fine on their own, scoffed at Kennedy's ability to handle the numerous details and wanted to raise funds independently. He also went ahead with plans to organize some fifty units for Boston and the surrounding towns, all potentially useful for a statewide campaign for the lieutenant governorship.

Hanken demonstrated the importance of Kennedy's remaining vague about whether he would run for Congress or with Tobin in the gubernatorial race. While the colonel offered to help elect Jack to whatever office he would ultimately seek, he was not subtle about his real objectives. As long as there was a possibility of Kennedy becoming lieutenant governor, chances of patronage from the Commonwealth were increased. Hanken denigrated the adequacy of largesse received from Tobin and stressed that, to get himself reelected, the governor would have to offer something more attractive than promises to lure the United Nations organization to Massachusetts. If Kennedy chose to run for Congress, his value to local interests would be limited. Hanken said he could also be helpful by getting Kennedy elected as the VFW's vice-commander when the organization held its convention in Boston in late summer. His position was duly forwarded to Kennedy by Dowd and helped emphasize the need to encourage the idea that joining Tobin on the ticket was a lively possibility.[47]

The decision to fight for the congressional seat had its own peculiar implications for Jack's political training. By engaging in the primary, he became embroiled in a fight as typical of urban American elective battles as it was characteristic of the city of Boston itself. Rather than a clash of ideologies, it was a confrontation of neighborhoods, ethnic groups, and personalities. On such issues as communism and the emerging Cold War, jobs, veterans' problems, housing, and inflation, hardly any distance separated the contenders; nor were they timid about exploiting whatever anxieties the constituency had. So the votes that would be cast on June 18 ultimately had to reflect how well the various candidates had performed in their own districts in relationship to the drawing power of opponents elsewhere.

The most crucial element was the division of the vote among the many candidates. For example, when a veteran member of the Boston City Council named Joseph Russo declared his candidacy, that move had important implications for Jack's potential performance in the Italian North End as well as among the numerous Italo-Americans in the East End. The Kennedy people promptly dug up *another* Joseph Russo, one useful only for his name, and entered him to divide the councilman's vote.[48] But Jack's most serious opponents included John F. Cotter of Charlestown and Mike Neville. Cotter, the man Dave Powers had initially supported, was well known in his district. He had handled many of the local problems for its residents from Washington offices while working as an administrative assistant to Curley. Neville was equally potent, and perhaps more so, because his locality was the most populous in the district. A former mayor of Cambridge and that city's favorite son candidate, Neville's service in the state legislature had also won him the support of not only Governor Tobin but of such associates as Assemblyman Thomas P. "Tip" O'Neill. In addition, several minor candidates—ten in all—entered the field. Curley, now mayor, kept his hands off the battle despite his former association with Cotter.[49]

Through Billy Sutton, Jack made important local contacts. Sutton, recently discharged from the Army, had been brought into the campaign by Joe Kane, and he knew Charlestown very well from previous electioneering in the district. Sutton not only recommended that Kennedy visit Dave Powers, but also led the candidate around to meet others in the district who could become key workers.[50]

On Hanover Street, in the heart of the Italian-American North End, Sutton brought Kennedy together with William "Yammy" DeMarco. Yammy DeMarco took the young Irish politician to his own place, Club 28, at 317 Hanover Street, and presented him to a group of about sixty-five people. "They didn't know who the person was with me," DeMarco remembered, "but I started to clang the table for order and finally I did tell them that I had a very important person with me, a Jack Kennedy, whose mother lived around the corner, oh, many years before [on Garden Court Street]. And I told them that the grandfather was well known to us in the North End. In fact he was a Sunday parishioner of St. Stephen's Church." Once having obtained his introduction, Jack "sort of blended in with the people in the North End for the simple reason that a lot of people did remember his mother . . . and also remembered the grandfather as coming to church on Sundays at St. Stephen's and there are quite a few elderly people in the North End that remembered all these things. They sort of took a liking to this boy and they endeared him to their hearts and it just sort of went together like bread and butter. . . . He was sort of shy. But he made friends very, very easily. One thing in his favor. He had a remarkable memory. He picked up nicknames right away."[51]

At Walton's Lunch on School Street, again in the company of Billy Sutton, Jack met Patrick "Patsy" Mulkern. Patsy escorted Kennedy through other pieces of the district: Roxbury, the South End, and parts of the North End. "We took him out to taverns, we took him in hotels, we took him up to the South End, we met 'em on street corners, we took him in clubrooms. We took him every place," said Mulkern.[52] Joseph A.

deGuglielmo (a Cambridge councilman generally called "DeGug"), Mulkern, DeMarco, and Powers—the campaign managers, as finally established for the formal opening of the battle—were leaders of their particular wards, people who could get out the votes from certain neighborhoods and set up lines of communication between Kennedy and the Democratic electorate.

Through it all, he performed with remarkable stamina, displaying energy that rarely flagged, thereby taking full advantage of the fact that, among other assets, he did not have to hold down a full-time job, as did his key opponents. Billy Sutton has recalled that Jack "was probably the first of the pols around here to go into the firehouses, police stations, post offices, and saloons and poolrooms, as well as the homes, and it was probably the first time Jack ever knew that the gas stove and the toilet could be in the same room."[53]

On St. Patrick's Day, Jack joined the Bunker Hill Council of the Knights of Columbus and appeared in his first parade, pleasing the crowds in South Boston by marching in a green tie, which he had had to borrow. He'd get on the trolley car at Oak Square, walking through the double row of seated passengers, looking "like a juvenile, no hat on" and wearing a blue suit, and shake every hand while saying, "Hello, I'm Jack Kennedy." Then, inexhaustibly, he would go to the station at Park Street and repeat the process in the subway all the way until they reached Harvard Square.[54]

Those closer to Jack were in a better position to observe the physical price: his bulging eyes and jaundiced complexion. Tom Broderick saw him limping into a communion breakfast. "I knew his back was bothering him and we had to walk up three flights of stairs," he recalled. "When we came downstairs, I said, 'You don't feel good?' And he said, 'I feel great.' But he would never admit that he felt the least bit tired or anything."[55] Taking advantage of the Bellevue Hotel suite, he resorted to frequent baths, which offered some respite from the pain and an opportunity to shed the cumbersome metal braces that propped his back. The baths became essential therapy. He learned to continue working while in the tub, often consulting with associates from the water. The bathroom became what Red Fay has described as an "inner sanctum," where he could relax in the hot tub, enjoying the therapy of the soaking bath, while advisers and aides stood by perspiring. Those sessions became an essential part of his campaign routine.[56] Clem Norton, a colorful local character and political hanger-on who also found his way into Edwin O'Connor's novel (as Charlie Hennessey), remembered finding

Jack exhausted in the back room of the Bellevue and—weeping with fatigue—expressing disgust at what he had gotten himself into.[57] Withal, he drove hard, perhaps harder because of it, propelled by the need to exceed his own limitations. When left alone with aides, without the need to be on display, for all his usual good humor Jack could also become testy and demanding, behavior understandable under the circumstances.

Requirements of campaigning forced Jack to do what would have been unnecessary had he chosen to run along with Tobin. Kennedy had to become a good ward politician, something difficult for one of his disposition. His natural discomfort with strangers, his preference for withdrawing into the world of his own thoughts and surroundings, whether with books or good friends, prevailed whenever the choice was his. Hirsh Freed, while fulsome about Kennedy's brilliance, recalled that he led "a monastic life, because, at that time," said Freed, "I think his food consisted of thought and things of the mind." Tony Galluccio, a Harvard classmate who joined Jack's campaign, remembered the single-minded determination and the remoteness of the candidate from the old politicians: "He never went to the Bellevue bar to crack a few jokes with the gang," observed Galluccio. "He had his own crowd and he remained aloof. He formed a distrust for them early."[58]

The experience of Jack Kennedy's first political contest produced the first paradoxes that would become associated with his name. Freed and Galluccio were undoubtedly accurate in their recollections; others constantly testified with similar examples of Kennedy's shyness, diffidence, discomfort in social situations, preference for privacy, disdain for the old urban ward politicians. But Ken O'Donnell and Dave Powers, who knew him better than most, were able to portray their friend as having loved the Joe Kane types that surrounded him and to declare that he "was very Irish and . . . loved everything about politics, including the old pols and their stories and political jokes."[59] Tom Broderick thought he "was glad to meet everybody. . . . He felt as though he was amongst friends. . . . and he wasn't happy unless he was out meeting people, saying hello."

He loved inventing nicknames for friends. Just as George Ross of *PT 109* was called "Barney," after the well-known boxer, Broderick was the "Thin Man" and a worker named Walter Powers was called "Tyrone" by Jack, recalling the currently popular Hollywood star. He referred to Billy Sutton, who handled press relations and loved to tell jokes, as the "Firecracker." Kennedy also worked at the ways of making campaign workers feel important, flattering their contributions and turning to them for opinions, caring less for their views than for their egos. He would often forget that he had asked a particular person a question and soon afterward repeat the routine with the same individual. At one point Broderick reminded him that he had just been asked about that particular point, and Kennedy replied, "Well, I want to see if I get the same answer."[60] A former associate from *Harvard Crimson* days was amazed at running into Jack that spring at Fenway Park with a band of cigar-smoking old-type Boston politicians, "all obviously having a helluva good time," with Jack the lead man in the group.[61] Jack's own father was even surprised at seeing the ease with which his son was able to walk "up to a bunch of hard boiled guys" on the street corner, introduce himself, and ask for their vote.[62]

Such recollections were not deliberately contradictory. Jack early developed a knack for compartmentalizing all aspects of his life, an ability to respond to the needs of a particular situation as though forced by a burst of adrenaline. Different friends saw different Jack Kennedys. He learned to direct himself to the demands of each individual and each situation, skillfully giving each associate what he most wanted.

When, for example, Billy Sutton told him about Dave Powers's prominence in Charlestown and intimate knowledge of the "townies," Jack satisfied the ethnocentric pride of that veteran. He was careful to tell Powers that the place that contained the three-deckers, the docks, the Bunker Hill Monument, and *Old Ironsides* was exactly the type of district he wanted to represent.[63] To young John J. Droney of Cambridge, who had just been discharged from the service and was eager to get involved in the campaign, Jack was similarly appealing. When Droney found Kennedy surrounded by a claque of "military" types in Honey Fitz's Bellevue Hotel apartment, he started to back away, discouraged. Jack, however, followed him and began a conversation, with Droney finally explaining what bothered him: he had had enough of the military and the war. "I told him how I felt about politics and he said he had the same feeling," said Droney, "but that his brother Joe had been killed in the war, his family seemed to feel he was best fitted to carry on, and he said, 'Sometimes we all have to do things we don't like to do.' "[64] When Jack's brother Bobby enlisted his Harvard classmate and fellow footballer, Ken O'Donnell, who himself had flown many combat missions in the war, Jack impressed the young man with his own war record; but, moreover, to O'Donnell, whose father was a well-known football coach at Holy Cross, Jack explained that his political need was to attract the support of people like Cleo O'Donnell, who was a Curley man and who despised somebody like Joe Kennedy.[65]

To Hirsh Freed, one of Jack's few links with the Jewish community,

Kennedy made another pitch. He assured Freed that the fact of his Catholicism and status as a veteran did not commit him to any particular voting obligation. He could quite freely vote against items that interested the Church, such as aid to parochial schools. Even as a veteran, Kennedy told Freed, he did not feel that he had to vote for everything the ex-GIs wanted. Furthermore, as Freed recollects, "He used to tell me that he had many, not bitter, but long and strident arguments with his father; that he disagreed with his father on a lot of things."[66]

It was, then, with a touch of shrewdness, appeals to self-interest, individual prejudice, laced with a postwar new-generation spirit of idealism and simple patriotism, that Jack Kennedy made his political debut.

Meanwhile, most of America, disenchanted with prices, shortages, strikes, and the quality of leadership in Washington, edged toward a conservative reaction against liberal Democratic domination. Kennedy separated himself from the national party and campaigned by concentrating on keeping the voters aware of his personal qualities. Private polls commissioned by the Ambassador had confirmed greater interest in Jack as a *PT 109* hero than as a political candidate. The standard speech, therefore, contained generous references to the bravery of the men under his command, while the campaigner referred to himself only in the third person without taking explicit credit. But the point was made. Additionally, he pleaded for patriotic sacrifices in peace as in war. Two authors later described them as having sounded "much more like Joseph Patrick Kennedy than Franklin D. Roosevelt."[67]

The real point related to Jack's conditioning. He could no more insulate himself from his father's thinking than escape his genes. The constant political discussions within the Kennedy household, the dinner-table "seminars" conducted by the senior member, the value system that made the family operate, may not have made all the children as faithful followers as Joe Junior had been, but at the same time it hardly left them immune. Privately, *very* privately, Jack could be critical about his father. He could consider him overbearing, even oppressive. He could stage his little revolts. But he very much admired the elder Kennedy's accomplishments and pragmatism.

So his 1946 campaign positions were tailored for the situation. He endorsed the "bread and butter" needs of his working-class constituency. More than anything else, he championed the need to house returning veterans, deploring their having to spend long periods doubling up with in-laws. Minimizing direct references to President Roosevelt, he applauded New Deal measures to promote organized labor. A platform drawn up to meet a specific request included endorsement of a Fair Employment Practices Act to eliminate religious and racial discrimination in the hiring of employees, although Kennedy's public statements ignored that point.[68] Asked by a League of Women Voters questionnaire for his notion of the most important issues facing the country, Kennedy placed housing first. Then, in the following order, came four additional items: a strong military force to back our foreign policy; extension of Social Security benefits; raising minimum wages to sixty-five cents per hour; and modernization of the Congress.[69]

His views of the incipient Cold War hardly seemed consistent with the thinking of the man whose unpublished article of less than a year earlier had linked armaments with military provocation. While that 1945 piece had not yielded an essential faith in firepower, even to achieve arms control, its thrust was far different from what he now wanted his constituents to hear. Between the two statements, of course, had come the end of the war and the institutionalization of the Soviet presence in Eastern Europe. Privately he expressed misgivings about General Eisenhower's failure to keep the Russians from taking East Germany and Berlin.[70]

Still, when dealing with communism as an ideology, Jack was more moderate than some of his opponents. John Cotter made far more use of the "Red issue." In a year when the "menace" was stressed in virtually every campaign from New England to Richard Nixon's well-publicized victory over Jerry Voorhis in California, the Kennedy approach was considerably more sophisticated. Mostly the matter was placed within the context of opposing all "totalitarian" creeds, as part of an essential concern for the viability of capitalistic democracy. His platform stated that "I oppose communism, fascism, nazism, and socialism."

Essentially, the Kennedy fighting for the Democratic nomination appeared as a traditional young man committed to private enterprise and the classical liberalism of free-market economics. His friend, Jim Reed, found him "more conservative than anything else," holding views in private that contrasted with the desires of his working-class district. Sutton agreed that, like his father and friends, Jack was an "ultraconservative."[71] Blair Clark recalled arguing with Kennedy and hearing the candidate unleash an all-out attack on the Wagner Act, an "impassioned assault that contained all the conventional anti-labor points."[72] But paradoxes were present. Quietly that February, Jack Kennedy sent Elizabeth Janeway a private contribution of two hundred dollars for the National Committee to Aid Families of General Motors Strikers.[73]

In a radio address on the night of April 22, Kennedy announced his congressional candidacy, declaring that the "temper of the times imposes an obligation upon every thinking citizen to work diligently in peace as we served tirelessly in war." Immediately, hordes of additional supporters canvassed the district. The Dowd Agency supplied two hands to help with the writing and organizing: first John Galvin and, through Galvin, Mark Dalton, a young lawyer who had just opened his own office on State Street. Galvin ("Mother" Galvin, as he came to be called because of his solicitude) worked on assignment from the agency and knew that Dalton had done speech-writing before and had been involved in local politics.[74]

Jack's older acquaintances also lent a hand. Red Fay left his own business on the West Coast to be helpful at the Bellevue. Jack's old Choate roommate, Lem Billings and a Harvard friend, Charles Garabedian, were utilized for speech-writing and legal assistance. Timothy "Ted" Reardon, who had been Joe Junior's close friend at Harvard and lived in nearby Somerville, came in to help with the organizing work. Torby Macdonald, then studying for his law degree, had little extra time to spare but nevertheless volunteered his services for a brief period. There was George Taylor, Jack's old valet at Harvard, doubling as a chauffeur and cook. He drove Jack around the district but frequently found the candidate's impatience would lead him to take over the wheel. Taylor's cooking attempted to satisfy Jack's love for roast beef cooked rare, with asparagus and mashed potatoes.[75]

Then came Jack's family. Bobby, just out of the Navy, spent several weeks working in three wards of East Cambridge, hoping to reduce the anti-Kennedy vote in that Italian area from five to one to four to one. Even little brother Teddy, only fourteen, made himself handy by running errands and lending whatever help was needed. Eunice worked in the Boston office on Tremont Street. Rose Kennedy became a highly successful campaigner, whose appeals to the women in the district were extremely effective. She was on hand for one of the more valuable innovations of that campaign, later to become characteristic of subsequent Kennedy elections—teas for women voters to enable them to meet and chat with the candidate. At the first one, held in the Hotel Commander in Cambridge, attendance was assured by the simple technique of sending out formal invitations.[76]

The Ambassador was also present at that first Cambridge tea, doubtlessly pleased with how things were going. Unlike his wife, however, his public role remained much more limited. But behind the scenes, Joseph

Kennedy's involvement was incalculably great. From a suite at the Ritz-Carlton, he used two instruments for keeping in close touch with developments. One was the telephone, a device that consumed a good portion of his waking hours. He called key aides to constantly monitor what was going on. "He'd keep you on the phone for an hour and a half, two hours," Mark Dalton said. "He was very, very interested in what was going on, although he did not project himself into the picture publicly. He was a very, very able man."[77] Frank Morrissey, his aide, also served as the Ambassador's "eyes and ears." "Really, a professional tattletale," a Kennedy insider told Burton Hersh. "Because *actually* the one absolutely certain way you could always entertain Mister Kennedy, get his complete interest, was to feed him stuff about his children. . . . And I assure you Morrissey really knew how to feed the old man, help his ego along."[78]

Of greatest importance, undoubtedly, was the Ambassador's manipulation of the media and utilization of the publicity processes, an activity that supplemented the efforts of "Mother" Galvin. Outpourings ranged from the kind of puff piece that appeared in the East Boston *Times* with the statement that "Kennedy is not a political adventurer, but a political visionary," to a timely, well-illustrated *Look* article that ran in early June. Supplied with material from the Kennedy entourage, it led off with a large picture of Jack with his father and Honey Fitz; below that, there was a small picture of the war hero in naval dress uniform. He was quoted as saying, "I have an obligation as a rich man's son to people who are having a hard time of it" and noted that he was resolved to "do the job Joe would have done."[79] The Ambassador also employed the expertise of the New York *Daily News* straw-ballot crew. His resources gave Jack's campaign a virtual monopoly of subway and billboard advertising space. A typical "Kennedy for Congress" display carried a photograph of Jack with an ex-GI's father pointing at the candidate and saying, "There's our man, son." At least $1,319 went for 100,000 reprints of the *Reader's Digest* abridgement of Hersey's "Survival" article. Expedited by the Ambassador, they were mailed out in time to reach the voters on the day before the election, June 17.[80]

The final day before the election coincided with a festive event in Charlestown, the annual Bunker Hill Day parade. Jack's participation, at least officially, was as commander of the Joseph P. Kennedy, Jr., VFW Post Number 5880. In reality, of course, the occasion offered a handy platform for a last-minute appearance. Accordingly, Jack enlisted the participation of what *Look* had called his "brain trust," including Torby Macdonald. Together, they made the five-mile walk as symbolic of a "new breed" of political leaders about to displace the old.[81]

First in the line of march in the post's contingent came three men wearing slacks and white shirts and carrying the VFW banner. The candidate appeared more formal in a dark flannel suit and a hat. The hat was carried rather than worn. Not only was Jack normally uncomfortable in that kind of dress, but the sun was hot and, together with the length of the march, his clothes were inappropriate. In addition, the entire occasion was an ordeal, one that required Kennedy's total submission to the distasteful requirements of the situation, which included enduring crowds that ran up to him, grabbed his hand, and held on as long as possible.[82]

As soon as the chore ended, he found refuge in the home of State Senator Robert Lee. His exhaustion was acute—even frightening.

Lee remembers him turning yellow and blue. "He appeared to me as a man who probably had a heart attack. Later on I found out it was a condition which he picked up, probably malaria or yellow fever." Kennedy was carried up to the second floor and, said Lee, "We took off his underwear and we sponged him over, and he had some pills in his pocket that he took. That was one of the questions his father asked, did he have his pills with him."[83] The collapse was unknown to the crowds and did not keep the parade from giving the primary contest an inspiring climax.

While Jack spent that final campaign evening recuperating, eight Kennedy workers produced a last-minute radio program, an effort designed to secure victory by the largest margin possible. That success was forthcoming seemed evident. The Ambassador's pollsters had shown that Jack would have little trouble winning and might even outpoll all nine rivals. Clem Norton, who considered Jack "the most impressive man I ever met," was somewhat less secure. His personal surveys had revealed that, for all the color and orchestrated hoopla, mass interest had not been aroused. With one out of every three voters not planning to participate, he was reluctant to predict.[84] Whatever the outcome, Jack had campaigned arduously, making some 450 speeches. Every conceivable gimmick had been tried. He could do no more.

Jack voted with his parents and the Fitzgeralds, then disappeared into a local movie house to view the Marx Brothers in *A Night in Casablanca*. Then as the returns began to come in, he drove to the various local offices to thank his workers. When he arrived in Brighton, one of the higher-income areas and one without significant "favorite son" opposition, the favorable tide was impressive. Broderick remembered that, as Jack acknowledged the staff's efforts, "there were actually tears." The supposedly impassive, cool Kennedy "choked up with emotion with the people that were there. . . . He just choked up, and then he got down and he shook hands."[85] He took that ward with sixty-six percent of the total vote.

That was his best locality. Norton's apprehensions of a low turnout were justified, and, possibly compounded by rain that Tuesday. Only some 30 percent of the registered voters cast ballots. But Kennedy's share was 40.5 percent of the total vote. In Cambridge and Charlestown, where Neville and Cotter offered strong opposition, Jack did remarkably well. He drew 41 percent to Neville's 49 percent in Cambridge and was beaten by Cotter in Charlestown by just 5 percent. Nowhere, despite that crowded field, did Kennedy get less than 34 percent, and that was in East Boston, where votes were distributed among the two Russos, Cotter, and the others.[86]

The crew had gathered early at the Tremont Street headquarters. While the victory was the real contest in a district where the Democratic nomination ensured the November results, they were strangely subdued. "It was very, very quiet there," Mark Dalton said. "Several members of the Kennedy family were there. Mr. Kennedy was there. . . . We were happy that Jack had won, but there certainly was no tremendous victory celebration that night."[87]

In November there was only token opposition offered by a Somerville Republican, Lester W. Bowen, and Jack won handily, outpolling him by 69,093 to 26,007. Statewide, meanwhile, Republicans succeeded, as they did nationally. Governor Tobin's insecurity was well founded and Robert Fiske Bradford removed him from the State House, opening speculation about Kennedy's fate had he run for the lieutenant governorship. Another Democratic loss was Henry Cabot Lodge, Jr.'s, victory over the old stalwart incumbent, Senator David I. Walsh. As in the rest of the country, Democrats were hurt by antilabor efforts to associate the CIO and its Political Action Committee with communism, especially in heavily industrialized Roman Catholic areas.[88]

The Kennedys had passed their first test. They had analyzed what it took to penetrate the governing establishment and had applied all their power and talent. He was launched, as a very junior member of a minority party, in the new Eightieth Congress. However mixed Jack's emotions were at the value of his own achievement, the second son had finished first.

11

Portrait of a Congressman

Not having a serious opponent for the general election at least enabled Jack Kennedy to enjoy the summer. Finally he could attempt to regain his strength, spending most of the hot weather at Hyannis Port and making only token appearances before the balloting. He also watched with considerable amusement the rush by politicians to retroactively declare their loyalty to his candidacy.[1]

Over the Labor Day weekend, Jack was chairman when some thirty thousand Veterans of Foreign Wars came to Boston, and once again life was hectic. He marched in the big parade, met delegates from all over the country, participated in various large and small committee meetings, and chaired the main session.

As the commander of Post 5880, Kennedy offered a resolution from the floor. Contrary to the position of the national organization, which, like the American Legion, catered to the real-estate lobby rather than primarily to individual veterans, the motion endorsed a current congressional bill sponsored by a coalition of liberals and conservatives to provide for low-cost public housing. Among the veterans groups, the Wagner-Ellender-Taft Bill, as it was known, received early support only from the recently organized American Veterans Committee.[2]

163

Passage of the Kennedy resolution represented a victory for the bread-and-butter needs of the major group that had given him the nomination. Their defiance of the Veterans of Foreign Wars' old-guard leadership brought a vigorous denunciation from Louis Starr, the newly elected commander-in-chief. Starr challenged the legality of Kennedy's resolution. But Jack promptly denied Starr's contention that the veterans had acted unwittingly because the acoustics in the hall were so poor that they did not know what was going on. The commander-in-chief prudently retreated from his absurd position and got behind Wagner-Ellender-Taft, even calling for the President to convene a special session of the Congress to secure its passage.

Later that September, on the last Saturday of the month, Jack returned to Wallingford for a visit to Choate. As part of its fiftieth anniversary celebration, his old prep school had invited him as its featured speaker. George St. John was still headmaster but about to retire and turn the job over to his son. For Jack, the old "Mucker," the homecoming was a delightful occasion, as it was for the excited students and faculty. Choate alumni, meanwhile, found another reason for having pride in the onetime troublesome adolescent.

Jack went to Chicago on January 22 to accept a gold key in honor of having been included among the "ten most outstanding young men of the year" by the United States Junior Chamber of Commerce. Chosen along with the young Pulitizer prize-winning historian Arthur M. Schlesinger, Jr., labor leader Joseph A. Beirne, cartoonist Bill Mauldin, and Charles G. Bolte of the American Veterans Committee, Kennedy was cited "for his example that all young men owe their land a civic responsibility, and for his interest in veterans housing."[3]

The award, after much competition, had been decided by a screening committee of key industrialists. As in his election campaign, Jack had prominent assistance. But unlike that victory, this one required nothing on his part, just acceptance of the honor. Once again, from behind the scenes, the Ambassador had engineered the process, operating through a New York press agent named Steve Hannagan. Through Joseph Kennedy's friend and Hyannis Port neighbor, singer Morton Downey, William M. Jeffers, president of the Union Pacific Railroad, was brought into the campaign. Jeffers was also one of the panel of judges empowered to choose the finalists. On January 13, six days before the public announcement, Jeffers wired Hannagan with the message OUR MAN WON.[4] The latest accolade, coming less than three weeks after his swearing-in as a member of the Eightieth Congress, enhanced his standing.

When he arrived in Washington to take his seat, he was the glamorous young bachelor, the most enticing new figure on Capitol Hill in many years. In a column syndicated in New England, Clem Norton hailed Jack as one with "moral courage" and independence. "Here is wealth standing up for what is right."[5]

Jack began his Washington house-hunting in November. He found an attractive three-story row house at 1528 Thirty-first Street in Georgetown. For three hundred dollars a month, it housed not only Kennedy but his sister Eunice, who, thanks to her father, had a job as an executive secretary of the Juvenile Delinquency Committee of the Justice Department. There was also a cook imported from Rose's household, a domestic, and Billy Sutton, who lived there for free. Sutton remembered the place as virtually "a Hollywood hotel," with guests likely to pop in unpredictably at any moment—the Ambassador, Rose Kennedy, Lem Billings, Torby Macdonald, whoever.[6]

Jack arrived from Palm Beach to take his seat in the new Congress on January 3. That body, later made famous by Truman's shrewd 1948 campaign, resulted from the very conservative coloration of the November elections. The so-called "class of 1946" was antilabor, anticommunist, and pro-business. Kennedy, however, had been elected from a working-class big-city district and, as his position on the housing bill had already demonstrated, accepted the New Deal heritage of governmental responsibility. Geography, economics, and sociology set him apart from the ideological shifts that governed so many colleagues.

While unable to claim the distinction of being the youngest man in the Congress, very likely Kennedy was the sickest newcomer. One colleague thought he looked "decrepit." Richard Bolling, who entered the legislature from Missouri two years later, said that "he was a frail, sick, hollow man when I saw him in 1947."[7] Pain constantly impeded his performance, contributing to divert his interests and forcing extended absences. Freshman John Blatnik of Minnesota, who also came in with Jack, remembered that he would never complain. But still, Blatnik said, "You could see it bothered him, and someone with him is very much aware of it, day in and day out."[8] For most of the time, Kennedy was restricted to a regimen of bland food. Nor did he drink very much. An occasional daiquiri was about his greatest indulgence. Lunch usually came from Kennedy's Georgetown kitchen. Margaret Ambrose, his cook, prepared it to suit the congressman's diet, and then George Thomas, his domestic, drove it to the Hill, where Kennedy occupied Room 322 in the Old House Office Building.

There can be little doubt that Jack suddenly found the situation anticlimactic. Much about his behavior suggested impatience, sometimes discomfort. The preceding years had been very exhilarating, supporting expectations of achievement from a son of Joseph P. Kennedy. The publication of *Why England Slept* had brought attention, almost all favorable, and the *PT 109* episode brought more publicity and actual fame. He was no longer simply Joe Junior's obscure younger brother. The campaign and subsequent victory in Boston resulted in more praise, adulation and flattery, with crowds treating the young man as a godsend. Just as such individuals as Arthur Krock, Frank Morrissey, and countless others catered to his father, the younger Kennedy was also developing his little band of loyalists. But in the House he was adrift, isolated, away from his sources of power. He was but one of 435 congressmen, and a very junior member at that, with a long way to go before he could hope to gain the authority of key committee posts, let alone match the clout of such Democratic big guns as Minority Leader Sam Rayburn and John McCormack, the party's whip. He did get some attention because he was the Ambassador's son, and being named among the ten outstanding young men of the year was also helpful. Basically, however, he was in a role he did not relish—servicing the mundane needs of the Eleventh District of Massachusetts—when, really, he cared much more about broader international and national matters.[9]

He was only too happy to leave the running of the Washington office to Ted Reardon and his new personal secretary, Mary Davis. Davis had already worked for three congressmen and came to Kennedy after her previous employer had been defeated. Bringing considerable experience to the staff, she became the nerve center of Room 322. For a time Billy Sutton also worked there. Back in Boston, Kennedy set up a district office in Room 1702 of the Federal Building, leaving its functions to Frank Morrissey, the Ambassador's "agent," who, according to one reporter, Jack "absolutely hated."[10] Renting a three-room apartment at 122 Bowdoin Street, a ten-story building facing the gold-domed State House, Jack established an official residence within the district. The structure had seen better days but the rooms were adequate as a *pied-à-terre*. The congressman often flew there for weekends, spending as little time as possible in the Washington office. "He had a very active district," Mary Davis has said. "Besides that, people all over Massachusetts and the United States wrote to him," but he had little realization of how much work the office had to handle. Nor did he seem to care, answering her protests about his absence in spite of all that had to be done with a typical Joseph P. Kennedy response: "Mary, you'll just have to work a little harder."[11]

When he was present, he fantasized being elsewhere. He kept a golf club in a corner of his office and loved to putt an imaginary ball and follow through with a deft stroke. He talked football a lot and gave the impression that, if he could realize his dreams, he'd like nothing better than to put on a uniform and helmet and toss the ball like Otto Graham of the Cleveland Browns. "He really cherished this dream of being a great football star," Sutton told an interviewer. "That's why he admired Torby and Whizzer White and Kenny O'Donnell so much, especially Torby." Whenever he could, he went up to Harvard, where his brother Bobby was O'Donnell's teammate. Sutton speculated that he loved the sport so much because of his own poor health and chronic pain.

He was just disinterested and bored in Washington, according to Justice William O. Douglas. Time "was heavy on his hands . . . he had nothing of all-consuming interest. . . . He never seemed to get into the midstream of any tremendous political thought, or political action, or any idea of promoting this or reforming that—nothing." Then the Ambassador's good friend and former associate from SEC days added, "And he was sort of drifting. And when he started drifting, then I think he became more of a playboy."[12]

Finding women and having a good time was never hard for Jack Kennedy. He had charm, intelligence, and, of greater importance, money and power. He was a very "eligible" bachelor. He dated all kinds of women; it didn't seem to matter, as long as they were attractive. Most were dates that he would take to a movie, his favorite diversion next to football. Some were "one-night" stands, whom a good friend and loyal retainer, like Billy Sutton, would squire away the next morning. He often went to New York nightspots, enhancing his dashing reputation. Later, he double-dated with such congressional pals as George Smathers, the handsome conservative from Florida, and Frank "Topper" Thompson, Jr., the New Jersey liberal, who won his nickname for his ability to "top" any joke Jack and the others might tell. "Jack was relatively shy," Representative Thompson said, "but he could afford to be because the girls just went crazy about him, and it was a question of sort of sorting them out."[13]

The relationships were ephemeral and numerous. The affair with Gene Tierney ended in 1947. Another woman whom he dated early that year was Durie Malcolm Desloge from the wealthy Palm Beach "cottage colony." Divorced that month for a second time and about to marry again, she had gone out with Joe Junior.[14] Although she and Jack saw each other only once—and, according to Bobby Kennedy, she may have had a closer relationship with Joe Junior—her descendence from the socially prominent Blauvelt family would later cause President Kennedy some distress—and give her much amusement—when a genealogist of the Dutch clan in America claimed that they had been married.[15] Another friendship coincided with the period of his alleged marriage to Mrs. Desloge, a relationship which led to charges of a payoff to prevent matrimony. The woman involved was Alicia Darr, born Barbara Maria Kopczynska, whose Polish-Jewish heritage reportedly led Joseph P. Kennedy to break off her engagement to Jack in 1951. Darr, who later married movie actor Edmund Purdom and then Singer sewing machine heir Alfred Corning Clark, denied ever having had an affair with Jack or taking any money from the family.[16] But despite such stories, no single romantic association emerged from that period, although Jack had what one colleague called "a smorgasbord of women" to choose from.[17]

Such superficial involvements brought inevitable comparisons with his father. Not only did the son appear to be duplicating the Ambassador's way with women, but even that part of his life was not exempt from paternal intervention. Just as with Inga Arvad earlier, Joe Kennedy kept his eye on Jack's private life. "Mr. Kennedy always called up the girls Jack was taking out and asked them to dinner," said a friend of both Eunice and her brother, remembering the night the Ambassador startled her at Hyannis Port by slipping into the guest bedroom and kissing her good night when she was in her nightgown ready for bed. That was something, she had heard, that "he did to everyone."[18]

Nor did the Ambassador keep out of Jack's personal financial affairs. Even later on, after his son had been elected to the Senate, he appealed to George Smathers for help in teaching Jack about money. Perhaps George, both as a lawyer, fellow senator, and close friend, could do something about the situation. Joe Kennedy had just visited Jack, tried to talk about it, and failed—again. He told Smathers that Jack had absolutely no understanding about his own finances. "I would like to tell you something about it," he explained, "so that you might tell him what the financial situation is and where his money comes from and things of that kind." Smathers performed his mission. But he, too, had little success because "every time I would talk about it he wasn't too much interested. His mind was just not geared to that sort of thing."[19]

Yet, there was a conflict about money in Kennedy's mind, something that wavered between close scrutiny and aristocratic indifference to the banality of the subject. When he heard that Dave Powers had worked as a newsboy, he wanted to know how a newsboy made money. He listened carefully, and asked probing questions about tips and profits from selling two-cent papers. Told that the Sunday papers brought a gain of three cents for each sale, Kennedy replied, "That's pretty good, isn't it."[20] Smathers remembered going with Jack to a fancy clothiers at the urging of the Ambassador, who told both young men to pick out suits for themselves. While Smathers selected a reasonably expensive outfit, Kennedy scrutinized the price of "every suit in the shop" and "picked one out with cloth so cheap and inferior that it was embarrassing." In Europe together, Smathers found his friend as conscious of money as he had been during his 1937 trip. When they rented a car, he complained about the high cost of gas. He also expressed annoyance at restaurant prices.[21] Nevertheless, there were occasions when he could be generous, usually in very private ways, unlike the increasingly publicized philanthropic offerings of his father. Ed Berube, a bus driver who had worked the local wards for Jack politically in Boston, became the recipient of weekly personal checks of eighty-five dollars to tide him through a long strike. "I would have lost my home," recalled Berube. "It was a personal check. It wasn't a payroll. It was his own check."[22] Like other wealthy men, Kennedy would reward loyalty.

Like them, also, he was oblivious of the need to carry money, a trait shared by his brothers and sisters. Cab drivers sometimes were paid by checks because Jack often carried no change or bills.[23] Being his companion could be costly. On dates the women might be stuck having to dip into their own purses to pay for two admissions. He would invite people to lunch or dinner and have no money, leaving his secretary to pick up the bill. Others with but a tiny fraction of Kennedy's fiscal means, such as Torby and Topper Thompson, went out with him at the risk of compiling a formidable outlay. "I got stuck for a hundred cab fares," said Thompson. "Torby Macdonald the same way, but Torby and I would get even. We'd go to Harvey's to dinner and we'd toss a coin as to who was going to sign Jack's name to the check." Once, in New York, Torby decided that he needed some suits. He and Thompson went to Brooks Brothers. Torby picked three fine suits off the rack and had them fitted. "Cash or charge?" asked the salesman, and Macdonald replied, "Charge," then signed the slip with the name of John F. Kennedy. Puzzled, the salesman looked up at the hulking, athletic frame of Torby Macdonald and said, "I've waited on Senator Kennedy and he doesn't wear this size clothes." Torby looked back at him with a straight face and replied, "I've gained weight."[24] His friends soon learned that, fortunately, they could also retrieve losses by applying to Paul Murphy in New York. Murphy handled such matters from Joseph Kennedy's Park

Avenue office and took care of issuing reimbursements in a perfectly routine manner.

Absentmindedness, or possibly little toleration for the attention required, also characterized Kennedy's attitude toward clothes, which did not exactly please his mother, who had always insisted that each of her children, especially the girls, learn the fundamentals of proper attire. Rose noted that, as children, Joe Junior tended to have "a better defined sense of neatness and order" while Jack was "offhand" about what he would wear. Despite the difference in their sizes, Jack would forgetfully help himself to Joe's clothes.[25] When he grew older, Jack did not change very much. At Harvard a tailor made his outfits to order because his frame made it difficult to buy them off the rack, which undoubtedly compounded the nuisance. It was easier not to bother at all, and photographs provide evidence of that attitude. One snapshot shows him standing with Torby on the deck of a ship while crossing the Atlantic. While Macdonald's trousers are far too long, brushing below his heels, Jack's cuffs are exactly the reverse, several inches above the tops of his shoes.[26] In Washington his unconventional dress drew stares and disapproval. He could be seen lunching in the congressional cafeteria in a sweater and sneakers.[27]

Mainly, during those early days, people with little knowledge of his physical pain regarded him as shy, even somewhat of a loner. Most freshmen began their new role with some trepidation and in that respect Jack was not very different. But to some he also seemed reticent, taking the position of an observer.[28] "He wasn't a member of the House team," said newsman Charles Bartlett. "He didn't have that sort of avuncular regard for Sam Rayburn. I think he was a young man sort of looking at the seniors. And he did it with a good deal of humor and with some very good insight. But he looked at it more or less as an outsider."[29] He was most reluctant to talk about himself, especially about his wartime experiences. But, brought into social situations, he would display his usual charm and good humor, and in conversations seemed intent on pressing his companion for information.

But single-mindedness about what he needed to know from others could also result in self-centered behavior. One colleague introduced Kennedy in the lobby of a Washington hotel to a labor leader excited over his chance to meet the congressman. Sitting down together to drink Cokes, the union official could hardly contain his pleasure. "Congressman Kennedy," he began to say, "I want to tell you something about your grandfather. You know, years back I was helping your grandfather." Then he began to relate an incident and, halfway through his story, Kennedy suddenly turned to the other congressman and said, "You know that vote on the floor today? What was that amendment? I wasn't there." The labor leader, visibly upset, paused, recovered, and struggled to continue what he was saying when Kennedy, totally oblivious of the other man's determination, interrupted again by asking his colleague another question about something that had happened on the floor. "The thing is that if you had told Kennedy he had hurt the man's feelings," explained the congressman, "he honestly wouldn't know what you were talking about, any more than you had walked and stepped on an ant. He wouldn't be aware of the fact that the man had feelings that had been stepped on. He may have been interested in hearing what the fellow had to say at the start; then maybe it got a little boring. He wasn't paying attention. His mind was back on the floor."[30]

He had few close colleagues. Smathers was about his only real friend, although he did have more than a passing acquaintance with Henry Jackson, who had been elected from the state of Washington seven years earlier. To some extent, too, he established rapport with fellow members of the Education and Labor Committee, especially Charles Kersten. Congressman John Rankin of Mississippi, the ardent segregationist, recurs among the names of Jack's favorite jokesters.[31]

He seemed to have an affinity for conservatives, or perhaps he was most comfortable with those who lacked liberal dogmatism. Joseph Rauh, Jr., the Americans for Democratic Action attorney and quintessential Washington guardian of liberalism, met Kennedy one evening shortly after he arrived in the capital. "He seemed rather overawed by the economic theories of Leon Henderson and some of the more liberal economists that were there that night," said Rauh.[32] Kennedy later told an interviewer that he was annoyed by letters that chided him for not being a "true liberal" and was quoted as saying, "I'd be very happy to tell them I'm not a liberal at all. I never joined the Americans for Democratic Action or the American Veterans Committee," he said.[33]

He especially liked two southern Democrats, Richard Russell of Georgia and Spessard Holland of Florida. Kennedy's work on a labor bill also brought him into contact with Senator Robert A. Taft of Ohio. The austere Republican, twenty-eight years older than Jack, had served in the Senate since 1939. The two men could never be regarded as friends and they differed over several points on the legislation being drafted. But Kennedy frequently expressed his admiration for Taft, considering him honorable, capable, and a good fighter.[34]

A friendship Kennedy did establish while living with Eunice in Georgetown was with Senator Joseph R. McCarthy, the Wisconsin Republican. McCarthy, like Kennedy, belonged to the "class of 1946." He, like Kennedy, had also served in the South Pacific where they apparently first met in the Solomons. McCarthy had begun his political career as a Democrat, with prewar service as a Wisconsin circuit court judge. McCarthy switched parties and took advantage of incumbent Senator Robert LaFollette, Jr.'s, political difficulties to win the Republican primary and then the election. He quickly displayed talents for shrewdness and theatrics and what Jack Kennedy, eight years younger, could also appreciate—"energy, intelligence, and political skill in abundant qualities."[35] A bachelor, McCarthy quickly became a popular newcomer on the Washington cocktail circuit. While Jack Kennedy did not share his fondness for alcohol, he could appreciate the other man's sense of fun and appetite for women.

More important were McCarthy's growing connections with various members of Jack Kennedy's family. He became one of Eunice's favorite guests at the Georgetown home. Through Eunice, he met R. Sargent Shriver—a handsome descendant of an old eastern shore Maryland family—who had made a distinguished record at Yale. Lured away from his job with *Newsweek* magazine by Joe Kennedy, who took an interest in the young man after he had met Eunice at a New York cocktail party in 1946, Shriver joined the Ambassador's New York staff before being placed in Chicago to help run the vast Merchandise Mart. For a while he also went to Washington to help Eunice in her work on problems of juvenile delinquency for the Justice Department.

"I saw Joe McCarthy there when Joe McCarthy first came to Washington," Shriver recalled, and by the time he got to Chicago, McCarthy was someone he "knew quite well." When Shriver and Eunice Kennedy were married in 1953, the senator sent them a silver cigarette box.[36] And for a while McCarthy dated Jack's younger sister, Pat, in Washington and Hyannis Port.[37] On March 15, 1947, when Jack Kennedy flew to Boston to attend the annual St. Patrick's Day Clover Club Dinner at the Statler Hotel, McCarthy sat near him at the head table along with a contingent of local politicians. The senator was the only significant out-of-stater.

McCarthy's sudden national prominence followed the establishment of his relations with the Kennedys. His Wheeling, West Virginia, speech of early February 1950, containing the allegation that 205 State Department employees were Communists, converted a routine Senate career into what epitomized the excesses of the Red-hunting era. His shrewd exploitation of a national paranoia that had been mounting for years made him the voice of those who had been looking for simple answers of why the world had not been going their way. Promptly backed by fellow Republicans desperate for a winning issue, his wild accusations pulverized potential opposition.[38] So dominant did he become that he would make many forget that the Red Scare had preceded his West Virginia speech.

For Jack Kennedy, Joe McCarthy became a personal problem that would not disappear. Their relationship was inseparable from his father's association with the Wisconsin senator, for Joe Kennedy clearly supported the anti-Communist crusade. He contributed to McCarthy's cause; he expedited assistance from such influential people as Cardinal Spellman; he phoned with endless advice, which McCarthy had no choice but to suffer patiently. On several occasions he brought him to Arthur Krock's Georgetown house as a "valued personal friend."[39] During McCarthy's first summer of prominence, he took a Northeast Airlines flight and, without publicity, landed at the Barnstable Municipal airport near Hyannis for a holiday visit to the Kennedy home. "A close friend of Eunice and her husband-to-be," noted a local historian, "McCarthy was warmly received by Joseph P. Kennedy, an unabashed admirer."[40] The Ambassador's younger son, Bobby, even became an assistant counsel on the senator's investigating committee. So involved with McCarthy's career had the Kennedys become that turning from the senator later would have been an act of disloyalty.

To assume that Jack found Joe McCarthy personally offensive misunderstands the character of young Kennedy, who, in his own way, found the Wisconsin senator congenial. Comments Kennedy made about the senator at Harvard showed that his "liking for McCarthy seemed to be on a personal basis."[41] "I think he liked McCarthy personally and sort of hated to say too much against him," one of Jack's secretaries has recalled.[42] George Smathers, who was as able as anyone else at the time to understand the relationship between the two men, tried to describe the distinctions. "In my many conversations with Jack Kennedy about Joe McCarthy, I got the idea that Jack liked McCarthy. He thought he was a pretty good guy and figured that he had made an original mistake, which was to overstate his case. . . . He was friendly to McCarthy all the way through. He apparently had known Joe some time before McCarthy became as famous as he became. . . . I always had the feeling that Jack Kennedy was very sympathetic to Joe—not with what Joe was saying—

but sympathetic with Joe as a person." Thirteen years after making these observations, Smathers backed away from the stress on the personal feelings Jack had for McCarthy and made the emphatic statement that he liked the senator principally because of involvements of the rest of his family, especially his father. The Ambassador's closeness to McCarthy, Smathers remembers Kennedy telling him, became one of considerable embarrassment.[43] Charles Bartlett also described Kennedy's attitude toward McCarthy as "such a great obligational issue."[44] The increasing attempts to create a personality gulf between Kennedy and McCarthy obscure Jack's personal character by stereotyping it with Brahmin loathing for the senator's boorish and vulgar behavior, thereby also helping to create a gap between their political views. The fact is that in their younger days there was much compatibility.

About the only aspect of their private behavior that would have kept the two men apart was McCarthy's fondness for liquor, but even that weakness became more serious later. Otherwise, Jack Kennedy, Brahmin bearing and all, had neither lost his boyish "Mucker's Club" zest nor recoiled at raw obscenity. If in the drawing rooms of the gentry he could charm the elite with a refined intellect and boyish charms, he could also engage in profanity, a talent undoubtedly advanced by his naval career. His verbal crudities easily matched McCarthy's. He could understand, respect, and relate to Kenny O'Donnell more and more as the years went by, together with the latter's almost incredible fondness for expletives. He could spend hour upon hour—indeed, be perfectly at home with—the homespun geniality of Dave Powers, whose skills as a humorist and Irish raconteur were a link to the ethnic background for one who had acquired "Brahmin ways." He could womanize and engage in sexual adventures that would have disgraced most fraternity houses. Once, Kennedy sent a prepaid airline ticket for a flight from San Francisco to Washington for a West Coast beauty who had spent nights with Jack in various California spots.[45] When she reached Washington, however, she disappeared for several days, her whereabouts a mystery. One of Jack's pranksterish friends had squired her away for himself. "You son of a bitch," the friend recalled that Jack said, "I don't mind your balling my girl friend. But at least you could pick up half the tab."[46]

Personal recollections enumerate similar incidents involving McCarthy. Yet while Kennedy and the Wisconsin senator shared such ideas of masculinity, McCarthy's flamboyant, reckless *political* style was alien to Jack's own public personality. Many others in Washington behaved irresponsibly without drawing Kennedy's disapproval. Jack was, in fact, more uncomfortable with those who moralized, who had the arrogance to assume their monopolization of the truth and were unwilling to compromise. About McCarthy, his greatest concern was that he had become excessive, had both overstated his claims and overreached himself.

In the Eightieth Congress, Jack Kennedy and Richard Nixon were the most junior members of the Education and Labor Committee. A continent apart in their origins and a world apart in their social backgrounds, they nevertheless brought compatible sentiments to the proceedings. They sat together, Nixon has written, "like a pair of unmatched bookends."[47] As was true of most of the other freshmen, they agreed that labor —organized labor—had become too powerful, almost monopolistic, since the Wagner Act. They also agreed not only in the inherent evil of communism but that it was an alien force, controlled, in fact, by a foreign power, and hence not permissible within the ranks of unionism in a free society. Labor leaders with Marxist inclinations were traitors to the interests of the very workers they sought to lead. What differentiated the two young congressmen was not so much ideology as party. Nixon's was in tune with the heartland of the Grand Old Party and consistent with the arguments that had helped win his election. Kennedy, too, could feel that labor threatened the national interest. But unlike his counterpart from California, he had had to accommodate his views to a union-oriented constituency.

The committee's ostensible purpose was to hold hearings on a bill to revise the National Labor Relations Act of 1935, known simply as the Wagner Act. Its chairman, eighteen-year veteran Republican Fred Hartley of New Jersey, had risen to the top because the committee's actual ranking Republican was, unlike his GOP colleagues, pro-labor. He was therefore persuaded to give up the Education and Labor Committee for Public Lands. The accession of the antilabor Hartley was, then, a clear signal of what was to come. Mary Norton of New Jersey, the ranking Democrat, was sufficiently upset to resign from the committee, as restrictive legislation was sure to follow.

Hartley operated on two levels. The first pertained to the legislative objective, the drafting of a bill. With the help of lawyers close to the National Association of Manufacturers, the process began early, possibly even before any hearings were held, and was completed very quickly. The committee's legislative proposal was produced before the Senate's version. A concerted effort was made to establish a close association in the public mind between militant unionism and subversive communism. Far better publicized generally, this position was also less controversial within the committee than were arguments over labor law. Operating a full three years before McCarthy's startling rise and holding its hearings a few days before President Truman issued his Loyalty Order of 1947, the committee frequently emulated the procedures of the un-American activities committee. At one point in the hearings, Representative Arthur Klein of New York interrupted to remind his colleagues that the writing of a new labor bill and not communism was their mission.[48] But the process worked for Jack Kennedy as he made hometown headlines.

His initial appointment to the committee had drawn speculation from a *Boston Herald* columnist, Bill Mullins, that the assignment had been either "a hostile act designed to destroy him" or a friendly act "to give him a chance to show his mettle right at the outset, and thus make or break him. The only question is this: is he ready for such a baptism in this big league?"[49]

The New Englander lost little time, plunging almost immediately along with his colleagues into the question of industrial communism. On Thursday, March 13, he had an especially big day. For the first time in elective office, he made headlines. Actually, his most animated parrying did not get much attention, but for Kennedy it was a satisfying experience.

The scene was the large Caucus Room in the Old House Office Building. The witness was the Washington representative of the United Electrical, Radio, and Machine Workers of America, a Californian named Russ Nixon. Nixon, who was not related to the congressman, held a doctorate in economics from Harvard, where he had also instructed Jack Kennedy. Just before the war he had left Harvard and gone to work for John L. Lewis and later the United Electrical Workers, then dominated by an organized Communist minority.

Kennedy sat by and watched Dr. Nixon, a confident, somewhat contentious, cooperative, and yet strong-minded intelligent man, tieless, and with an open shirt collar, tell the committee that the so-called labor monopoly was not the threat to the country. Nixon said, in fact, that it served to check the power of big business. His union counterbalanced the economic might of an electrical industry dominated by the Mellon and Morgan groups that held "about 45 percent of the total facilities of the industry in which we are organized." He cited General Electric and Westinghouse as corporations that were the subjects of "several indictments or even trials that are presently proceeding" under the nation's antimonopoly laws. He fended off questions designed to further the association of organized labor with the "international Communist conspiracy." He defended the right of union officials to be Communists just as he would if they were Democrats, Republicans, Socialists, or apolitical.

For days the committee had been eager to grill him, to tear him to shreds, and they predicted that each shred would be colored a dark crimson. But the witness's sophistication contrasted with the simplistic and often ludicrous statements of the congressmen. No doubt Nixon was enjoying their sophistry, and clearly, he got the better of the exchanges. Then came Jack Kennedy's turn. He began by saying that, as "a former pupil of yours I have been impressed by the dexterity with which you have answered the questions today." Nixon replied, "I had to set a model for a pupil, you know, Mr. Kennedy." But Kennedy got right to the point, stepping up the pace of his questions and demonstrating an impressive familiarity with the union. He asked whether the UE representative agreed with Congressman Klein's statement that the question of communism was out of order and irrelevant to the business of the committee. Dr. Nixon said he agreed with Klein and accused those raising the Communist issue of trying to cause dissension and evasion of other questions. Kennedy kept pressing, however, wanting to know whether communism constituted "a threat to the economic and political system of the United States?"

"I do not think it is a threat," said Nixon. "I think what is a threat is our failure to meet some of the basic economic problems of the people in a democratic way, and also what is a threat is our failure year after year to expand the basic civil rights of our people. . . . The problems of the Negro people, the limitations of suffrage in the South, the many other issues of civil rights need to be expanded. I think we have no room for fear of democracy in this country, and if we really do not have fear for it, we will expand and wipe out the limitations and that will be the best answer. . . ."

"Mr. Nixon," said Kennedy, "I agree with a great deal that you have said."

But Kennedy was not making any concessions. He wanted to get on with the question of communism, then pressing Nixon to acknowledge the presence of Communists within the union's leadership. He quoted a doctrine about the need to "resort to all sorts of artifices, evasion, subterfuges, only so as to get into the trade unions and remain in them and to carry on Communist work in them, at all costs."

"I did not teach you that at Harvard, did I?" asked Nixon.

"No, you did not," said Kennedy. "I am reading from Lenin, in which is described the procedure which should be adopted to get into trade unions and how they conduct themselves once they are in."

Kennedy's performance was impressive as he forced the witness into a defensive posture. Although not a lawyer, as were most of his colleagues, he managed to subdue Nixon's superiority and he alone pursued the witness with crisp documentary evidence free of platitudes. "A 'freshman' *House* member with the 'coral dust' of Pacific Islands still 'clinging to his heels,' stole the 'show' from his older colleagues yesterday," reporter George E. Reedy said in describing the session over radio station WOL that evening.[50] Jack's satisfaction was further enhanced a few minutes after completing his questioning of Russ Nixon. Pressed by another congressman to substantiate his contention that the committee was biased, Nixon conceded that Kennedy was one of its six pro-labor members.[51]

But Kennedy's real notoriety came from the motion he made in the even more sensational hearings involving the Allis-Chalmers manufacturing corporation of Milwaukee, the nation's third largest nonelectrical machinery manufacturer, and Local 248 of the United Auto Workers. That afternoon was the climax of attempts to demonstrate that the local's past and current presidents, Harold Christoffel and Robert Buse, had been instruments of international communism. Among committee members, Congressman Kersten's involvement was most immediate, since he also came from Milwaukee. The company had been strikebound since April 1946 and was seeking to prove that the present stoppage, like the seventy-six-day walkout in 1941, was part of a subversive plan.

The testimony presented to the committee by Allis-Chalmers management witnesses constituted a detailed damnation of Local 248 for having fallen under Communist leadership during the past ten years. They charged that the '41 strike, which had taken place before Pearl Harbor and during the period of Nazi-Soviet rapprochement, had been the product of subversion, designed to cripple the company's ability to fulfill some forty million dollars in Navy contracts. It had been, they charged, ordered, engineered, and manipulated by the Communist Party, which had achieved a strike vote by using over twenty-two hundred fraudulent ballots. Moreover, its past president, Christoffel, currently a member of the union's bargaining team, was a longtime member of the Communist Party. So were its current president, Buse, three of its other officers, eight members of the Local 248 bargaining committee, and "22 other union stewards and committeemen." Ties were also drawn to Fred Blair, the party's Wisconsin chairman.[52]

On May 1, a Saturday, the committee met with a scant quorum of fourteen of its twenty-five members in attendance. Buse led off with a statement that vigorously denied any Communist domination and charged the company with using such claims as a tactic to break both the current strike and the union. When Kennedy's turn came, he began with skeptical quizzing of Buse's denial that either he or his union had anything to do with the Communist Party. Then the twenty-nine-year-old congressman played teacher to union leader Buse:

KENNEDY: What do you think is the aim of the Communist Party?
BUSE: From what I gather, the aim of the Communist Party is to create a state of socialism.
KENNEDY: What do you mean by socialism?
BUSE: Similar to that that they have in Russia, I guess.
KENNEDY: Do you think there is any difference between the system in England and the system in Russia?
BUSE: They have a king in England.
KENNEDY: Do you think they have a socialist economy?
BUSE: To some extent they probably have.
KENNEDY: But you do not know what the difference is, besides having a king. You do not know what the difference between socialism [as] practiced in England and as it is practiced in Russia.
BUSE: What I mean, in England I do not believe they have socialism. They may have some. I think they are trying to socialize some industries but not completely. And so far as I understand, socialism in Russia is complete.
KENNEDY: Would you call Russia a democracy?
BUSE: I would not know. I do not think so.
KENNEDY: Why do you not think so?
BUSE: Well, I can only gather from what I read. I have not been to Russia and I have not observed what freedom the people have, and from everywhere you get conflicting reports. . . .
KENNEDY: I think I would like to inform you what I believe to be the main difference between socialism in England and socialism in Russia. They have a freedom of opposition which they do not have in Russia. Do you not think that is important?
BUSE: I would not know if they have any opposition or not in Russia.
KENNEDY: Well, I do not think you are equipped to tell whether a

member of your union is a Communist if you do not know any of the answers to any of the things that I have asked you.

When the committee reconvened on Monday, Kennedy, obviously well prepared, went to work on Christoffel, cross-examining him and using massive documentary evidence to show how the union's paper had changed its position during the war, from opposing intervention to calling for an all-out effort—coinciding with the German invasion of the Soviet Union. Kennedy cited the Wisconsin edition of the *CIO News,* the official publication of the Milwaukee County Industrial Union Council, and its positions during Christoffel's term as president. Through the edition of July 23, 1941, which was already in the mail at the time of the German invasion, the paper continually attacked what it called the "Roosevelt War Program." But the edition published immediately after the invasion contained the headline MILWAUKEE COUNCIL CALLS FOR ALL AID TO BRITAIN, SOVIET UNION. Jack Kennedy questioned Christoffel about the reasons for the abrupt change, and the union man replied that he had had nothing to do with the paper.

Kennedy had Christoffel in an embarrassing contradiction. The witness had contended that it was not the union that had obstructed defense considerations by striking in 1941 but Allis-Chalmers president Max Babb, who was one of the "largest contributors" to the America First Committee. Yet under intense questioning, Christoffel was forced to gradually concede that the Milwaukee County Council itself had opposed conscription as well as lend-lease shipments to aid the Allies— positions virtually identical with those of America First.

His coup against Christoffel, however, came on March 13. The man who provided the leverage was Louis F. Budenz, an assistant professor of economics at Fordham University in New York, a Jesuit institution. Budenz, on his way toward becoming one of the most celebrated turncoats of a period when ex-Communists became overnight models of veracity, integrity, and patriotism, had been managing editor of the *Daily Worker.* For six years he had also been a member of the national committee of the Communist Party. The fifty-five-year-old convert to capitalism had also returned to the Catholicism of his Indiana childhood. Taking his seat in the committee room, Budenz demolished the non-Communist claims of both Christoffel and Buse. Budenz offered testimony that the 1941 strike against Allis-Chalmers was part of a "snowballing" of strikes organized by the Communist Party to halt national defense. In the Milwaukee home of a party member Eugene Dennis, the party secretary, ordered Christoffel to commence the strike on his "representation that there could be grievances which would act at the direction of the political committee." According to Budenz, management charges that the strike vote had been made possible by "stuffed" ballots were correct. To make the importance of his testimony entirely clear, Budenz then added, under prodding from Kersten, that "strikes are hit upon as a technique when Moscow wants that sort of a policy to be carried out. You understand that the Communist Party is only a fifth column for the Soviet Union and nothing else."

Budenz completed his testimony and Kennedy offered a motion calling for perjury indictments of both Buse and Christoffel, which Kersten quickly seconded. But Congressman Gerald Landis of Indiana, chairing the session in Hartley's absence, ruled it out of order and said that the matter would be decided in a closed executive session, which then concluded that no action should be taken until Hartley returned.[53]

His motion gave Jack Kennedy headlines. To some, his move had greater significance. Congressman Kersten later described Jack's motion as "like one of the shots fired at Concord Bridge. It was the opening skirmish between Congress and the American Communist Conspiracy."[54] The perjury motion underscored Kennedy's role by giving him credit for domestic Red-hunting at a time that predated his California colleague's pursuit of Alger Hiss and McCarthy's entry into the national anti-Communist crusade.

Christoffel was later indicted and convicted of perjury in the District Court for the District of Columbia, which handed down a five-year prison sentence, confirmed by the Court of Appeals. That brought an appeal to the Supreme Court on a technicality involving the accused's rights to due process because of the lack of a quorum at the time he completed his appearance in the Caucus Room on Saturday March 13. The high court finally agreed with the defendant that the lower court's instructions to the jury on the subject of a quorum were erroneous and reversed the decision by a 5–4 vote. Kennedy quickly issued a statement deploring the latest action as one bound to hinder the operations of committees and, possibly, the entire legislative process. He argued that a quorum had been present at the start of the testimony and that nobody, including Christoffel, had raised a point of order at that time about its absence.

"What a travesty on justice," Kennedy added in remarks inserted in the *Congressional Record*, "that a Communist witness testifies untruthfully before a recognized committee of the House and then escapes the consequences of perjury by a technical claim that a specified number of Congressmen were not present at a particular moment."[55]

An early Kennedy biographer, James MacGregor Burns, later noted that "Kennedy's remark about the Supreme Court disturbed those who saw in the courts the last bulwark against violations of due process."[56]

Christoffel, who had long since lost his Allis-Chalmers job, also lost his legal fight. Tried again and convicted, he received a four-year sentence in 1950, which was later reduced to sixteen months. "Another conspicuous traitor to this country was flushed out by our own Representative John F. Kennedy," exulted Bill Mullins, the *Boston Herald*'s pro-McCarthy writer. One month after the Wisconsin senator's celebrated talk to the women's club in Wheeling, Mullins added with irony, "Kennedy was called a witch-hunter."[57]

Shortly after the hearings, *Cosmopolitan* magazine published the responses of a dozen congressmen to the question "What is the most urgent problem facing America today?" Kennedy replied that it was the lack of national unity and requested the eradication of subversives, while Joe McCarthy, answering the same question, cited the "inconsistency between our wage scales and the cost of living."[58]

Kennedy was absent from the final House approval of the Mundt-Nixon Bill, which aimed at subversion by mandating the registration of Communist and Communist-front organizations; it passed by an overwhelming 319–58 vote on May 19, 1948.[59] He did vote to continue the funding for the already controversial House Un-American Activities Committee, then chaired by J. Parnell Thomas of New Jersey.

Establishing appropriate anti-Communist credentials was assuredly most politic for the freshman from Boston in 1947, but bucking the popular sentiment behind aging, diabetic Jim Curley was quite another matter. Curley's troubles began with his conviction in 1946 for fraudulent use of the mails in connection with wartime defense contracts. By a 2–1 vote, the United States Circuit Court of Appeals rejected his appeal. Since shortly after his latest election as mayor the "Purple Shamrock" had been confined to the federal penitentiary in Danbury, Connecticut, serving a six to eighteen-month term. His confinement, especially in view of failing health at seventy-one, was hardly popular among the rank and file.

Never one to accept defeat when any other possibility existed, Curley persuaded Congressman John McCormack to draw up a petition for the commutation of his sentence by President Truman. McCormack, then the party's House minority whip, explained that "Jim Curley asked me to get signatures, so I just got the signatures, that's all. I got a little over a hundred signatures, as I remember."[60]

One of those inevitably solicited to contribute was Jack Kennedy. Kennedy, only a half year into his first term, was thereby tossed a dilemma. To decline would be a slap in the face of not only Curley but the mayor's supporters, many of whom had voted for Kennedy. And greater consequences could follow the brazen defiance of a colleague as powerful as McCormack. But signing might imply an association with the past, with the traditional ethnic machine way of doing business that his own campaign had attempted to disavow. On a more personal level, supporting Curley would be hard for Jack to explain to Grandfather Fitzgerald, the old politician's ancient rival.

"Has anyone talked with the President or anything?" Kennedy asked McCormack when presented with the document.

"No," said McCormack. "If you don't want to sign it, don't sign it."

McCormack later explained that he understood that the young congressman had his own reasons and that his rejection brought no particular animosity.[61] But the matter did not seem so easily disposable at the time, at least to Kennedy. It called for serious consultations among his closest associates, which included his father and Bart Brickley, as well as Joe Kane, Billy Sutton, and Mark Dalton.

"My strong reaction," recalls Dalton, "was that he was a young man starting his political career, just on the threshold of it, and I thought that the older people who were putting the pressure on him to sign this petition had a terrible nerve."[62] While Dalton firmly opposed giving it support, Sutton thought he had no choice but to add his name. The attitudes of both Kane and the Ambassador differed. Joe Kennedy had had McCormack's tentative support for the party's presidential nomination in early 1940. Through former Police Commissioner Joseph F. Timilty, Jack's father had also had decent relations with Curley. Nor would there have been much inclination on the part of the Ambassador to worry about Honey Fitz's sensitivities, especially since their own relationship, never very warm, had further deteriorated after his father-in-law's 1942 race against Joe Casey. Nevertheless, the Ambassador felt that Jack should disassociate himself from Curley, and Jack did precisely that.

Not signing had distinct advantages. Consistent with the tenor of Kennedy's 1946 campaign, it was a stroke for personal independence, one separating him from the old pols. That kind of stance had another bonus: attractiveness to Massachusetts's Yankee voters, both Republicans and Democrats, who could hardly fail to get the message that young Jack Kennedy was not just another Irish political hack. And, of course, his position pleased Grandfather Fitzgerald.[63]

Among Kennedy's Irish working-class supporters, however, the decision was not popular. Almost unanimously they agreed with the assessment of one who called it "a hell of a mistake politically . . . because if there was one fellow who was entitled to a pardon, it was Curley, who had done so much for the district, which was the congressional district that Jack Kennedy was then representing. They were Curleyites in that district, and it was the Curleyites who elected Jack Kennedy."[64]

In the face of that kind of sentiment, Kennedy did not simply say that Curley had been found guilty, that his appeal had been turned down, and that his treatment should not differ from that given to any other citizen. Instead, he argued on the technicality that he had not been in Congress when Curley had committed his crime. Kennedy went through considerable efforts, even asserting that he had checked with the Surgeon General to determine if Curley was really feigning his illness, a position still maintained by loyalists who have cited Curley's "sudden recovery" upon being returned to City Hall when Truman released him after five months at Danbury. Additionally, Ted Reardon has been quoted as offering another disingenuous explanation for Kennedy's decision. "We had received so many appeals from people asking us for help to free their loved ones who were in jail," he said, "and some of their reasons were pathetically sad, and we just had to say no, we couldn't help them, there was just nothing we could do."[65] Nevertheless, what remained was the fact that John Kennedy was the *only* Massachusetts Democratic congressman who refused to sign.

Hartley's sixty-seven-page majority Labor Committee draft, a step toward the Taft-Hartley Act, was totally unacceptable to most minority members. In signing a dissent, Kennedy joined five colleagues. Even that was unsatisfactory; terming the legislation a "slave labor bill" exceeded his sense of proportion and failed to express his own doubts about labor's excesses. Going along with fellow Democrats of the minority was less important than clarifying his own reaction.

Working with the aid of Joseph Healy, one of his father's Boston attorneys flown down to Washington for that purpose, Kennedy filed a supplemental statement. For a freshman, the move was considered a rather bold assertion of independence. But it did what Kennedy desired:

it took a position somewhere between the excesses of organized labor's protests and the pious claims of Republicans that their real concern was the best interests of the workers. Carefully, it contained the reminder that "the twelve years since the passage of the Wagner Act have been marked by turbulence and unrest." Then, charging that the majority draft would, at the same time, jeopardize union shops, it warned that, if passed in its present form, it would "bring not peace but labor war" by playing "into the hands of the radicals in our unions, who preach the doctrine of the class struggle."[66]

Read on the House floor one week after Hartley had reported the majority version out from the committee, the statement was impressive. Even such a pro-management paper as the *New York Herald Tribune* praised Kennedy for his "most effective opposition speech."[67] Kennedy had clearly supported the principle of the closed shop, industrywide bargaining, and opposed government injunctions to end key strikes, such as the one pending against the telephone companies. He contended that government moves to squash walkouts had little to do with the evils supposedly being legislated against: racketeering and featherbedding. On April 17, just before the final vote on the Hartley bill, Kennedy offered an amendment removing the need for management approval before workers could choose a union shop. But with ninety-three Democrats joining the Republicans, the antilabor tide carried by a decisive 308–107.[68]

Thereupon came a debate between two opposing committee freshmen. Frank Buchanan, a Pennsylvania Democrat, brought together Nixon and Kennedy, the newcomers with the brightest political futures. The debate was a poorly attended, largely ignored affair at the Penn McKee Hotel in McKeesport, Pennsylvania. Located in the Pittsburgh area, a region dominated by steelworkers, the audience was divided between vociferous labor supporters and representatives of local and rural conservatism.

Both were welcomed by McKeesport Mayor Charles A. Kincaid and introduced by moderator William Baird. The two congressmen emphasized the moderate approaches of their respective views. Nixon lauded the legislation as upholding fundamental labor rights and chided union leaders for refusing to cooperate with the committee in writing a bill. At the same time, of course, he ignored the corporate involvement in its authorship. Kennedy, as he had done before, questioned the bill's relationship to the interests of the workingmen and asserted that its provisions threatened to "strangle by restraint the American labor movement." Characteristically, he acknowledged that some of its provisions were praiseworthy and declared himself in favor of "responsibility" by both sides in contracts.[69]

En route back to Washington by train that night, the two men shared a *Capital Limited* berth, secure that each had enunciated an appropriate stance on the leading issue of the day and, as Nixon later commented, seeing themselves as "political opponents but not political rivals." Unlike the Californian, Kennedy cast a negative vote that June against the final Taft-Hartley Bill. Senate approval followed just three days later, creating the basis for President Truman's politically astute veto.

Kennedy's position brought him praise. Arthur Krock devoted his "In the Nation" column to Taft-Hartley and cited Kennedy as a "rarity" in Congress for both opposing the Hartley Bill and the conference report, while upholding the presidential veto. Unlike most others, Krock pointed out, Kennedy had something other than the status quo to offer as a substitute.[70]

Kennedy also affirmed his pro-labor position. The *CIO News* box score showed him voting "wrong" just twice out of fifty-seven opportunities during his six years in the House.[71] Labor's League for Political Education gave him a 94 percent pro-labor legislative rating.[72] While continuing to dissent from those who called it a "slave labor" bill, Kennedy nevertheless remained a persistent voice for Taft-Hartley modification, endorsing the more salutary Lesinski recommendations in 1949 and calling for outright repeal in a floor debate on April 28 with the argument that it "makes the government a vital, inept and prejudicial participant in labor-management relations throughout this country."[73] After he reached the Senate, he linked its impediments to unionization with the regional difficulties of New England versus the South.[74]

Above all, John Kennedy suppressed his own doubts about labor power for his working-class constituents. Along with other urban Democrats, especially those from the Northeast, he consistently supported federal responsibility for raising minimum wages and keeping price and rent controls. Also, as in his 1946 campaign and especially his stance before the VFW convention in Boston, he continued to identify himself with the housing problem. In common with other large cities, Boston needed more units to provide for lower-income residents. Builders, meanwhile, were finding higher profits in constructing homes and apartments for the affluent. In Congress relief was being formulated in the Wagner-Ellender-Taft Bill, which was designed to construct fifteen million new homes at a low cost during the next ten years.

While the Education and Labor Committee was holding its hearings on communism and labor unions, Kennedy flew out to Chicago to be present at the opening session of the annual National Public Housing Conference. He told them that rising building costs had increased the need for the bill and suggested two possible courses for remediation. One would use federal funds to make loans to public bodies to build rental units at prices affordable to veterans, "with the provision for the sale of that housing to private interests when the emergency is over and prices have declined." The other, Kennedy explained, would be by providing "such firm guarantees to private investment that private capital will be induced to finance rental housing, amortized over a long period of years, of a type to meet veterans' needs."[75] On the floor of Congress he warned that lifting rent controls from new construction, according to a bill proposed by Banking and Commerce Committee Chairman Jesse Wolcott of Michigan, a Republican, would not solve the problem. "This will merely mean that houses will be constructed so that the average veteran cannot buy them."[76]

In this matter, as in others before, publicist John Galvin was useful. He helped to organize and became chairman of the Massachusetts Allied Veterans' Housing Council, which then functioned in both the interests of the immediate issue and Congressman Kennedy. Organized to lobby for the WET bill, the eleven-man group formulated their strategy in Kennedy's office.[77] They also staged a rally in Boston at which Kennedy was the only Massachusetts congressman present, although John McCormack sent word that he favored the legislation. Using his forum to the fullest, Kennedy went after the American Legion. The Legion opposed the legislation that was so popular among individual veterans. Kennedy charged that the Legion's "scatter-gun shooting tactics" were chiefly responsible for keeping the veterans from presenting a solid front. That brought a rejoinder from the American Legion's state adjutant, who denounced Kennedy as an "embryo congressman" whose actions resembled those of "a fool rushing in where angels fear to tread."[78]

Kennedy then made a radio appeal in behalf of the Wagner-Ellender-Taft Bill. He hoped to go over the head of the Legion and reach the rank and file, and so solicited an "avalanche" of letters. The commander of one of the larger Boston-area posts wrote, "We want you to know that we favor this housing legislation and we back you 100 per cent regardless of the organization's national policy." Supporting resolutions flowed from virtually every other veterans organization. But the legislation, effectively blocked by Wolcott's committee, never did make it through the Eightieth Congress.[79]

That ended neither the housing struggle nor Kennedy's clash with the

Legion. In 1948 Kennedy was named chairman of the National Housing Committee of AMVETS and, the next year, introduced a housing bill closely patterned after what President Truman had included among his Fair Deal proposals. The Kennedy version provided for slum clearance, low-rent public housing, a housing research program, and farm housing. He believed that the government should build 135,000 public-housing units annually, pointing out that, in his own district, ten to fifteen families applied for each available public-housing unit. But Legion criticism continued despite earlier hopeful signs, including a recommendation by the organization's executive committee, at an Indianapolis session in 1948, that the bill be given its formal endorsement.[80] During a floor debate on the issue in early 1949, Kennedy charged the American Legion's hierarchy with being unrepresentative of its membership. "The leadership of the American Legion has not had a constructive thought for the benefit of this country since 1918!"[81]

The statement was daring. Colleagues were startled. For a young congressman, he had shown a lot of gumption. But as Kennedy had long since discovered, his position was popular with the rank and file. And when the bill passed the Democratic-controlled Eighty-first Congress during the summer of 1949, it carried the *official* support of the American Legion, along with every other veterans organization.[82] "As it turned out," Ken O'Donnell and Dave Powers have written, "Kennedy's attack against the Legion on the housing issue did him more good politically than any other single stand that he took on a legislative controversy during his six years in the House of Representatives."[83] At the next state convention of the Legion in Massachusetts, Kennedy got a fine reception.

Still, Kennedy's record did not make him a progressive New Deal Democrat. When dealing in theory, when lecturing about the nature of government, he fell back to the classical liberal doctrines held by his father that had come to seem conservative in the years since they were first formulated. Along with his Whiggish belief in the rule of the elite, he had the liberal's concern for the maximization of freedom for the individual. When considering social issues, he seemed to embrace the utilitarianism of Jeremy Bentham. At other times, when thinking about "free enterprise," he seemed to echo the words of Adam Smith. And behind it all were the ideas of John Stuart Mill, who had noted that the "struggle between liberty and authority is the most conspicuous feature in the portions of history with which we are earliest familiar. . . ." A business group, the Council of State Chambers of Commerce, issued a tabulation late in 1951 that showed Kennedy's record on "spending" versus "economizing" as more fiscally conservative than eleven other Massachusetts Democrats.[84] Even while voting as a New Deal liberal on the so-called bread-and-butter issues for his constituents, Kennedy's instinctive distaste for radical change remained visible.

Thoroughly on record over working-class issues, Kennedy appeared in South Bend, Indiana, in early 1950. There, at age thirty-two, he became the youngest man ever to receive an honorary Degree of Law from the University of Notre Dame. Speaking at the Jesuit institution, his commencement talk sounded more like Joe Kennedy's views than his own congressional persona. By telling the students that "the scarlet thread that runs throughout the world—is one of resignation of major problems into the all-absorbing hands of the great Leviathan—the state," Kennedy was lamenting the loss of will, a lack of faith in the certitude of democratic capitalism, that had too often surrendered to radicalism. He acknowledged its power was less severe in America but warned that the evil was reaching our own shores, unless "we become concerned with maintaining the authority of the people, of the individual, over the state." Kennedy warned about the "ever expanding power of the Federal government" and quoted the Irish orator and statesman Henry Grattan to reassert the conviction that "control over local affairs is the essence of liberty."[85]

Such classically liberal sentiments agreed with the highly conservative "Declaration of Principles" issued by congressional Republicans later that year. Also consistent was Jack's observation to his friend Red Fay in November that he was "glad to . . . see Nixon win by a big vote" over Helen Gahagan Douglas for the Senate seat in California.[86] Earlier, Jack had gone to Nixon's office, told him that he obviously could not give his own endorsement, but that "it isn't going to break my heart if you can turn the Senate's loss into Hollywood's gain." Before leaving, he gave him an envelope with a one-thousand-dollar contribution from his father.[87]

Along with fellow committee members Kersten and Owens, Kennedy was scheduled to visit Russia in September to "study education and labor conditions."[88] Instead, incapacitated, he was rushed back from London to New York on the *Queen Elizabeth,* then flown by chartered plane to the New England Baptist Hospital, carried the final steps on a stretcher after an ambulance trip from the airport. New York and Boston papers identified his condition as a recurrence of the old South Pacific malaria. In reality it was the start of an illness that remained hidden from the press. Not until 1960 would there be acknowledgments, after persistent rumors and charges.

Several things are now known. The first leg of his journey abroad was a sentimental visit to Ireland. A letter from his Aunt Loretta, a sister of the Ambassador, directed him to the old Kennedy home at New Ross. For three days Jack stayed in the twelfth-century Lismore Castle in southern Ireland where, finally, he was reunited with his sister Kathleen. And there, according to Pamela Churchill (who had recently divorced Winston Churchill's son Randolph and would later marry Averell Harriman) Kennedy learned that Kick was in love with yet a second Protestant nobleman, Lord Fitzwilliam.[89]

Kennedy interrupted that Lismore Castle visit by driving along the coast and then following the shore of the Barrow River to New Ross, with Pamela as his companion. The visit was unsuccessful. There were a number of Kennedys, all right, but no serious distinct relationships with his own family in America. "It sounded from their conversation as if all the Kennedys had emigrated," Kennedy said later. "I spent about an hour there surrounded by chickens and pigs, and left in a flow of nostalgia and sentiment. This was not punctured by the English lady, Pamela Churchill, turning to me as we drove off and saying, 'That was just like Tobacco Road!' She had not understood at all the magic of the afternoon."[90]

Once back in the castle, however, he became ill. He sent home for medication, then flew to London, where, progressively weaker, he was removed to the London Clinic. Placed in the care of Lord Beaverbrook's doctor, Sir Daniel Davis, he was diagnosed a victim of Addison's Disease. "That young American friend of yours," Dr. Davis told Pamela Churchill, "he hasn't got a year to live."[91]

For the transatlantic passage, he was confined to the ship's hospital. On October 25 the *Boston Post* reported that the congressman had "been ill for the past seven weeks with malaria" and had been released by the Lahey Clinic. From there he had gone to Hyannis Port for a two-week recuperation before returning to Boston.[92] By early December political writer Bill Mullins was telling readers that Kennedy was back on the job, "entirely recovered from the attack of Navy-born malaria which laid him low in England several months ago."[93] Obviously, the press merely reported family handouts. To Dr. St. John at Choate, Kennedy wrote, "I'm completely recovered from my bout with malaria," and then added, with a touch of nostalgia, "Tell Mrs. St. John she needn't worry—from here on in, I'll take good care of myself."[94]

But Jack Kennedy was a victim of Addison's Disease. Addison's has several manifestations. Mostly, the disease impairs the excretion of the adrenal glands, reducing the patient's immunity to illness. Weakness, loss of weight (which would explain the reduction Jack had experienced), loss of appetite, pigmentation of exposed skin, and most seriously of course, a mortality rate that resulted from almost inevitable infections that the body could not fight. Surgery, however minor, could easily be fatal. At the Lahey Clinic in Boston, he was treated by Dr. Elmer Bartels, a thyroid specialist.[95] Kennedy remained under the doctor's close care, visiting him on at least April 3, 1948, January 29, 1949, and August 4, 1949.[96] During this entire period he often commuted to Boston and New York for medical reasons.[97] And in May of 1955 Kennedy came under the care of Dr. Janet Travell, a New York pharmacologist with an office at 9 West Sixteenth Street.[98] But by that time the most serious implications of Addison's Disease had been largely overcome.

Nevertheless, whispers about the condition plagued Kennedy for many years, always threatening public revelation, with all the horrors of a dreaded disease that would inevitably preclude any political responsibility. When revelations about Addison's could no longer be stilled, especially after John Connally, acting in the interests of Lyndon Johnson, made the charge just before the 1960 Democratic convention prepared to select its candidates, efforts were made to counter the alarming political consequences. A typical example of the "official" explanation appears in Arthur Schlesinger, Jr.'s, *A Thousand Days*. Although published after his death, readers were told that Jack Kennedy did not have Addison's in the classic sense—that is, caused by tuberculosis of the adrenal glands—that he had not had tuberculosis in any form and that, with modern methods of treatment, his adrenal insufficiency—evidently induced by the long night of swimming during the *PT 109* episode, and the subsequent malaria—presented no serious problem.[99]

Nevertheless, a detailed medical report, published in the *Archive of Surgery*, described Kennedy as having a "marked adrenocortical insufficiency," which rendered his subsequent back operations hazardous.[100] Joseph Alsop, who saw a great deal of Kennedy at his Georgetown home, a welcome retreat from problems, remembers that some of the doctors at first suspected that he had Hodgkin's Disease, which would have been fatal. Moreover, Addison's itself, left to the treatment then available, would have severely reduced the patient's longevity. Kennedy told Alsop that he expected to die in his early forties.[101]

"The doctors say I've got a sort of slow-motion leukemia, but they tell me I'll probably last until I'm forty-five," Schlesinger quoted him telling Alsop at one point.[102] That was how Jack chose to explain his Addison's.

In such conversations, Kennedy appeared wryly fatalistic and gave the impression of little desire except to live out whatever time remained. Alsop got the feeling that he "really did not remember clearly political events between the time he came to Congress and when he found ambition. Until then, he did what his father wanted him to do without paying much attention."[103] A close family friend recalled that, at the time, Jack "was good and sick. And so sick that it was an irritation for both of them, for his father and for himself. It threatened to get in the way of everything they were trying to accomplish."[104]

Furthermore, the medical report left no doubt that Kennedy's Addison's Disease, contrary to the information given to unwary biographers, was a "classic" case, one that required the standard treatment. Namely, daily injections of desoxycorticosterone acetate pellets (DOCA). Such pellets, 150 mg strong, were then implanted in Jack Kennedy's thighs. That required, according to Joan and Clay Blair, the maintenance of "safe-deposit boxes around the country containing cortisone and DOCA so that Jack would never run out."[105]

The real godsend was the arrival of cortisone in a form that could be taken orally. Its effect was dramatic, remarkably contributing to not only the patient's stamina but to his sense of well-being—even to his sexual appetites. There were side effects for someone on so high a daily maintenance as was Kennedy (25 mg), side effects that medical authorities warn can damage other parts of the system and cause added weight and facial puffiness.[106]

With his son debilitated before the end of his first year in the House, Ambassador Kennedy reached out for help. James Landis, the chairman of the Civil Aeronautics Board, had been informed by President Truman that his appointment would not be renewed at the end of the year. Landis, just about fifty years old, had been an old Joseph Kennedy associate. Described by Justice Douglas as "an able, intense, and humorless man," he had graduated from Harvard Law, had been a protégé of Felix Frankfurter, and had clerked for Associate Justice Louis D. Brandeis. After a Washington stint, Landis succeeded Joe Kennedy as chairman of the SEC until 1937, when Harvard recalled him to become the dean of its law school. Not by any means attractive—described, rather, as sharp-beaked, with piercing eyes and a prominent forehead that helped give him a forbidding appearance—Landis was considered by

Douglas "as able as any New Dealer I knew. Some called him diabolical, but he was merely intense, withdrawn, introspective."[107] Ambassador Kennedy now snatched him to join his enterprises.

The acquisition of Jim Landis bolstered Joe Kennedy's administrative and legal staff. Through Landis, the Ambassador secured closer ties with experts from the academic world than he had ever enjoyed from the battery of lawyers and accountants who had been previously recruited. Of even greater importance was Landis's talent and personal dedication —a shrewd, first-rate aide, one totally devoted to his employer. That automatically placed him at the service of any Kennedy needing help. As one paper noted when Jack first went to Washington, "you may rest assured that his father . . . has some of the best experts look over the boy's talks in advance of their deliverance."[108] With the further complication of the congressman's physical problems, such help became especially indispensable. Those who ran Joe Kennedy's New York office, including Landis and all his associates, constituted a formidable behind-the-scenes unofficial staff in behalf of Jack Kennedy, one quite apart from any public payroll.

Nothing about it was irregular. It merely emulated other officeholders who had private means that enabled them to hire personal staffs and reach out for endless advisers. The Kennedy machinery, however, was distinctive in one vital respect: the continuing role of the Ambassador. Jack Kennedy's physical condition obviously made such assistance invaluable. It kept him dependent and impaired his ability to exert a freer and personally more satisfying role. He had to tolerate the circumstances he described soon after taking his congressional seat when he told newspaperwoman Elizabeth Oldfield that "for a long time I was Joseph P. Kennedy's son, then I was Kathleen's brother, then Eunice's brother." Then he added, "Some day I hope to be able to stand on my own feet."[109]

There were many such comments, mostly made in private asides to close friends. All were submerged behind the facade of Kennedy family unity. Additionally, the Ambassador himself, who was sufficiently astute to understand the potentially counterproductive nature of his efforts, chose to minimize his own visibility. He hired aides. He expedited. He utilized contacts, official and unofficial. Joe Kennedy understood the distinctions between the political realities within the Eleventh District of Massachusetts and ideological satisfaction. Not that the Ambassador was an ideologue, at least in the ordinary sense. But his position conveyed the visceral responses of the successful businessman, confident that the rest of the world can also profit from his genius. Yet because of his sophistication, the Ambassador was prudent enough to exchange selective restraints for the broader benefits of actual power, to make concessions to specific situations. Meanwhile, he could not always be restrained: he was, at heart, too much of an activist. Aided by the helpful promotion of Arthur Krock in the pages of *The New York Times,* he continued to be outspoken, although uneasy about his detachment from national influence. Finally, he did move back into an official role by winning appointments to the two commissions on the reorganization of the government that were established under former president Herbert Hoover, a great favorite of the Kennedy family. Otherwise father and son respected the distinctivenesses of their respective missions.

Park Avenue had long since become the headquarters of the Kennedy enterprises, first at number 270 and later at 230.[110] In that New York nerve center, Landis was ensconced with his own staff. There, in addition to servicing the complex financial and legal needs of his employer (including the preparation of the Ambassador's memoirs), Landis oversaw drafts of proposed articles for publication under the congressman's signature, ideas for legislation, the gathering of background material to assist the Washington office, and made suggestions for political responses pertaining to a wide variety of matters. The central directive was simple enough: Do whatever could help Jack's career.

When the young congressman sent the New York office a proposed article entitled "What Price Officers for the Next War?" he received a response from one of Landis's aides, James A. Fayne. The ex-broker and longtime Joe Kennedy executive wrote that "I feel that from what your Dad said you had in mind, you will have to dramatize your treatment of a subject which might be a dull one to the average reader. Therefore, I am suggesting an introduction to your material and one insertion."[111] Fayne then passed the article on to Landis, appending a notation that the Ambassador "says there is no urgent reason for haste so am leaving this with you for attention when possible."

Almost three years later, after publicity over a West Point "cribbing" scandal had brought Senator Russell's Armed Services Committee into the process of finding solutions for improving the selection of prospective cadets, *The New York Times Magazine* ran John Kennedy's by-line under an article called "How Should Cadets be Picked?"[112] Always tuned in to the Kennedy interests, Landis promptly advised the Ambassador to get out a news release summarizing the article for the Boston papers. After all, the Sunday *Times Magazine* had a relatively meager circulation in that area.[113] Similarly, young Kennedy and Landis shared a newspaper by-line for an article called "Kennedy Challenges Churchill's Version of Belgian Surrender," which defended King Leopold from the personal criticism for his role in Belgium's surrender as depicted in the account written by the British wartime leader.[114]

With the help of whatever supportive apparatus his father could muster, Jack Kennedy had become an adequate congressman, displaying flashes of talent, ingratiating himself here and there, but mainly seeming lethargic and bored. Obediently, he was going through the motions of fulfilling the role of replacing Joe Junior. Outsiders, unaware of the family mission, had little reason to predict a productive future. As the Representative from the Eleventh of Massachusetts, he duly compromised notions of classical liberalism by delivering on the so-called bread-and-butter issues. Without much concern for civil liberties, he rivaled most colleagues and appeased constituents by exploiting the national obsession over anticommunism. Yet, he remained an independent force, not showing much regard for partisan obligations within the Commonwealth or on Capitol Hill. He was a young man who failed to convince others that he had much ambition or clarity about his goals. While he hardly appeared robust, few realized the seriousness of his physical condition. Before the miracle of cortisone, the prospect of an early death kept him from trying very hard to develop either his ability or hereditary gifts for much more than having a good time. His attendance record was among the worst in the House. What was the sense if he was not going to survive his forties.

12

"America's Younger Statesman"

On May 13, 1948, Jack Kennedy received a message from the Rhine River Valley of France. Kick, on a spring holiday to the Riviera, had been killed when her plane crashed into the Cévennes Mountains in the Ardèche near the village of Privas. Immediately, Jack called his father, who was waiting to meet her in Paris. Joe Kennedy rushed to the scene, halfway between Lyons and Marseille, and waited in the rain until a cart brought Kathleen's body down the mountainside.[1]

The Boston papers headlined the news. *The New York Times* carried the story on the front page. The weather had been rough; rain and fog covered much of the Continent. That night alone, storms were responsible for the loss of some fifty-five people in various aircraft, and the turbulence had destroyed the light plane carrying Kathleen Kennedy.[2] The plane had been chartered in London by Lord Fitzwilliam, who had wanted to inspect his stable of racehorses near Cannes. Together they crashed into the mountain.

For some time the Kennedys had not liked what they had seen of that relationship. Later, when writing her memoirs, Rose would completely ignore Fitzwilliam. Now Joe Kennedy set out to protect the family interest by hiding the truth about Kick's final romance. A friend close to Kathleen and her parents recalled that "the extraordinary thing was the power of old Joe to get that story into the press about how she [Kathleen] had just happened to meet him [Fitzwilliam] at a cocktail party and accept a ride to the south of France. And they all bought it."[3]

Severe as was Jack Kennedy's personal loss, there are no accounts of his seeking seclusion. Kathleen had been the most kindred member of his family, the only one with whom he could question either God or parents. Her death had coincided with a low point of his own morale in a grief shared with Torby. But it was not a subject for discussion, and congressional associates were not tactless enough to bring it up.

Jack made periodic visits to Dr. Jordan at the Lahey Clinic, took doses of DOCA pellets, contended with his bad back, and was only incidentally troubled by malaria. To the Boston pols, however, he was valuable as a source of money and patronage. He could deliver much more of the latter if he held statewide office. So even before 1947 had ended, hardly much after his initial confinement because of Addison's, reports began to circulate that Massachusetts Democrats were trying to persuade him to run for the party's gubernatorial nomination in 1948. One source, identified as close to Maurice Tobin, said that not only did the former governor favor the idea, but that Congressman McCormack might also be interested in promoting Kennedy. Bill Mullins, closer to the family than most writers, cautioned that "this must be taken with a pinch of salt because of the assumption that they are far from being bosom companions as the result of young Kennedy's blunt refusal to sign the clemency petition in behalf of Mayor Curley."[4] Skeptics were saying that McCormack was really interested in denying the governorship to Paul Dever or trying to promote himself to become President Truman's running mate on the national ticket.

Yet Kennedy's activities away from Washington supported the speculation. His speaking calendar resembled a congressman looking for a much broader constituency; his absenteeism from the Hill increased as he toured various parts of Massachusetts. He spoke out on Taft-Hartley, on New England's competitive problems with the South, on housing, on the threat of domestic radicalism. More and more, he directed statements toward the problem of European communism.

Meanwhile, Kennedy received assurances from the Boston leaders of Henry A. Wallace's new Progressive Party that if he chose to run, they would support him for the governorship. His Cold War statements were still more tolerable to the leftists than a choice from among Governor Robert Bradford or Paul Dever. And although Progressive Party spokeswoman Marjorie Lansing criticized "some of Kennedy's political acts," she felt he would be acceptable.[5]

"Completely recovered in health," wrote Bill Mullins, with more than slight exaggeration, "Kennedy is physically fit for anything."[6] Mullins predicted he would concentrate on reelection to Congress and would forego a race for the governorship. That failed to stop a Worcester lawyer, acting on his own, from filing gubernatorial candidacy papers for Kennedy.[7] Two additional sets of nomination papers were submitted in New Bedford, but Kennedy quickly disavowed any notion that he could be drafted for the State House.[8]

Kennedy was clearly at a confused, and depressed, stage of his career. He had little taste for a new fight but little patience with the notion of serving out his days in the House of Representatives. Jack's loyal friend, Charles Spalding, looking back upon that period, thought that "the job as a congressman after he had it for a little while began to look like a Three I League job to a major-league player."[9] The starting line-up and the routes to power were denied freshmen by the seniority system. Jack felt the limitation keenly. Where the Education and Labor Committee had afforded an opportunity, he had made the most of it. But as one of 435 members, and starting from the bottom, he could easily languish for many years before obtaining a significant voice. The consensus, however, was that he should stay on, that he could benefit from more "seasoning."[10]

Overlooked in all this is the obvious point, obscured by the recognition that a Kennedy had to be ambitious, that further depressed by the loss of Kathleen and barely regaining strength after the 1946 campaign, a *sick* Jack Kennedy preferred to wait it out. A contest for the Senate, if he chose that alternative course, was also regarded as quixotic, certainly with the solid Leverett Saltonstall as the incumbent and with the anticipated strength of the Republican vote in 1948. Just standing still, he could be renominated and reelected by acclamation. Nobody, Democrat or Republican, was ready to challenge Kennedy's assumed right to another term. The easiest, and wisest, course for him was to wait for the right opportunity. Perhaps the governorship, after Paul Dever had had his try at defeating the incumbent Bradford, would place Kennedy at the historic foundation for a presidential race, or, if things broke differently, a Senate seat at a future date.

Once he entered public life, Kennedy found that his personal faith became a public matter. It was a time of mounting bitterness and suspicion between Roman Catholics and Protestants. The Roman Catholic Church in America again felt defensive and even embattled. In June 1947 Francis Cardinal Spellman of New York declared that "bigotry once again is eating its way into the vital organs of the greatest nation on the face of the earth, our own beloved America. Once again a crusade is being preached against the Catholic Church in the United States."[11] Given such an atmosphere, Kennedy could hardly safeguard his religious beliefs as a private matter.

The bitterness was sharp throughout his congressional career. Some of it came from restlessness among Catholic Democrats who reflected Joe Kennedy's reservations about Roosevelt and who, unlike the liberals within the party, were partisans of Franco's Spain and sympathized with individuals like Al Smith and later Jim Farley, who distrusted the extreme New Dealers. That was a very important part of the Kennedy household orientation. Many had also heeded the oratory of Father Charles Coughlin. During the war, challenges to Catholic power appeared in such publications as the liberal *New Republic* and the Protestant *Christian Century*. Bishop G. Bromley Oxnam, the president of the Federal Council of Churches, said that "serious tension is developing between Roman Catholics and Protestants in the United States."[12] The reality of the situation toward the close of World War II was the presence of Communist control over large and predominantly Catholic areas of the world, regions that had sent many emigrants to America. Catholic reactions naturally grew even fiercer than before. All too often, their militant anticommunism adopted the rhetoric of nativism, the very sentiment that had been so hostile to their own presence in America. Not only did they become louder and louder, but they began to be the vanguard in the battle for American values.

Kennedy recognized that sentiment when he appeared at a communal breakfast in Boston and urged American Catholics to seek political leadership to bulwark the nation against the radicalism that would follow a great depression. He noted that Catholics were the most effective force doing just that in Belgium, Holland, and Italy; and with direct references to two left-wing congressmen from New York City, he warned that "with a big bust in our economy, we will have more Marcantonios and Isacsons in Congress, and strong Catholic leadership will be essential."[13]

Once again, Catholics were betraying their insecurities about acceptance as Americans. Considering that they were a relatively newer immigrant group, such difficulties might be countered while simultaneously waging a war against communism. At the same time, while Catholics became more militant through fear, the very demonstration of their power began to unsettle traditionally secure Protestant groups.

Through columnist Drew Pearson, Dr. Daniel Poling, a prominent Protestant preacher who was also a former Republican candidate for Philadelphia's mayoralty, invited Kennedy, as a public figure who also represented the Catholic faith, to participate in a fund-raising dinner as a tribute to four chaplains who had gone down with the Army transport *Dorchester* during the war. Others with similar functions to Kennedy's at the banquet, scheduled for the Bellevue-Stratford Hotel in Philadelphia, were Senator Herbert Lehman of New York, who was billed as a special representative of President Truman to speak for the Jewish faith, and Charles P. Taft, Cincinnati's mayor and also president of the Federal Council of Churches of Christ in the United States, who represented Protestants. Kennedy himself was to be the third key speaker, with ex–Supreme Court Justice Owen J. Roberts as the toastmaster. The affair was also to commemorate a chapel on the campus of Temple University in honor of the four chaplains.

Just a few days before the dinner, Kennedy, obviously embarrassed, informed Pearson that he had to decline the invitation because he had no credentials "to attend in the capacity in which I had been asked."[14] As he himself later admitted, he had been notified cf the displeasure of William Cardinal Dougherty and the Philadelphia clergy.[15] The problem related to the presence of the chapel in the sacristy of the Baptist church. Such participation with other faiths, he was reminded, opposed the rules, customs, and procedures of the Catholic Church. Furthermore, the Philadelphia Archdiocese balked at Kennedy, a layman, appearing as a representative of the Church.

Belatedly, then, Kennedy explained to the Reverend Poling that he would be delighted to appear at any time there was a memorial but that he had no credentials for that particular type of function. As Kennedy later acknowledged in a formal statement, the "Archdiocese of Philadelphia was unable to support the drive."[16] Meanwhile, the affair's sponsors made last-minute reprints of the banquet's program that omitted Kennedy's name, and they had to proceed without a representative of the Roman Catholic faith. No public references were made to Kennedy's declension, but as Poling later wrote, "But those of us who knew were indeed heartsick. The Chapel of Four Chaplains is a symbol of a cause that is dearer to me than my physical existence."[17]

At the time, in December of 1947, it was no more than an inconvenience for the sponsors of the dinner. But for those concerned with such things later on, it provided ammunition for charging that Kennedy, although a public servant, would allow himself to bow to the "dictates" of the Catholic Church regardless of civic obligations.

The Four Chaplains incident was a minor one, and other religious issues troubled Kennedy more immediately. The Supreme Court had inadvertently added to suspicions of Catholic strength when, in the case of *Everson* v. *Board of Education* in 1947, it approved the use of public funds to reimburse private-school pupils for transportation in New Jersey. Protestants, some already angry at the Church's attitude toward birth control and censorship, feared Catholic threats to American democracy. Guardians of church-state separation found supporters from among various non-Catholic denominations. Paul Blanshard, a Unitarian critic, wrote a series of articles condemning hierarchical power, which resulted in the banning of *The Nation* from the public schools of New York City and libraries of Catholic institutions. Blanshard pointed with alarm to the power of the Church in America. He then claimed that the failure to agree on the constitutionality of religious issues had "created the longest and most acrimonious Church-state controversy in the history of congress."[18]

Father John Wright, who was close to Archbishop Cushing, reminded Kennedy, almost as soon as the congressman first took his seat in Washington, that "Catholics all over the United States are opposed to the Thomas-Hill-Taft Federal Aid to Education Bill upon which, given your committee affiliation, you may have to take a position." The cleric's opposition had nothing to do with any kind of philosophical fear of the results of federal aid to education, but rather that the proposed legislation would make it impossible for many states to use such funds for parochial schools.[19]

During the subsequent meetings of the Education and Labor Committee, Kennedy expressed his basic agreement that parochial school children should not be deprived of the services that were being proposed for children generally. He agreed that they should also be able to participate in the general welfare provisions that would cover such auxiliary areas as transportation, school lunches, health protection, and textbooks. Anything else would be discriminatory. He also thought direct support for parochial schools would violate the First Amendment but upheld direct reimbursement to the children themselves.[20]

The church-state debates were something that congressmen wanted to avoid perhaps more than any other issue. The flow of books and articles by Blanshard in the wake of the New Jersey court decision further stepped up what Roman Catholics regarded as attacks by the Protestant majority on their rights as American citizens. The issue was further complicated by acrimony between many segments of American Catholic life, especially the Church, and liberal non-Catholics over a series of international developments, including support for the Spanish Falangists, Franklin D. Roosevelt and Yalta, and, what alarmed Catholics in particular, the growth of the international Communist "conspiracy." The sentiment was typically expressed in such terms as "Communism is anti-God, anti-social, anti-human; that is, anti-Catholic."[21] For Catholics, then, communism would be, in the postwar era, the equivalent menace of what had been represented by the Third Reich during and before the war. *The Tablet,* a diocesan paper published in Brooklyn, made the statement even before the fighting in Europe had stopped that "Nazism is brown Fascism; Communism is Red Fascism. Both destroy liberty, peace and religion."[22]

To upholders of federal assistance to private schools, the most obnoxious legislation by far was the bill authored by Congressman Graham Barden of North Carolina. Barden, who was appointed by Education and Labor Committee Chairman John Lesinski as chairman of a subcommittee to deal with the question, produced a document in June that unequivocally prohibited any participation in federal expenditures for such purposes. By the summer of 1949, then, the issue reached a far greater public explosion.

Francis Cardinal Spellman sent an open letter denouncing Eleanor Roosevelt for her newspaper column that supported the principle of separation of church and state. Most intemperately, the cardinal concluded his letter: "For whatever you may say in the future, your record of anti-Catholicism stands for all to see—a record which you yourself wrote on the pages of history which cannot be recalled—documents of discrimination unworthy of an American mother!"[23]

The attack on Mrs. Roosevelt undoubtedly resulted from accumulated hostilities against Franklin D. Roosevelt's widow by those elements of the Church who had long since regarded her as suspect on the question of firm anticommunism and, hence, insufficiently strong as a friend of Catholicism. In the wake of the Roosevelt-Spellman dispute, which later received a public patching-up during a visit paid by the cardinal to Mrs. Roosevelt's home at Hyde Park (a rapprochement that carried the approval of Pope Pius XII), the Gallup Poll tested public opinion on the issue.[24]

The national survey inquired about popular attitudes concerning a potential $300 million in aid to schools in poorer states, as the Barden bill called for, and whether the respondents agreed that the money should go entirely to public schools. The results confirmed the sharp national differences. While fifty-nine percent of Protestants said that it should be exclusively for public-school use, only twelve percent of the Catholics agreed with that; and while only thirty-one percent of Protestants venturing an opinion agreed that part should go to parochial schools, Catholics were emphatic by seventy-nine percent.[25]

Anger and fear, tension and hostility—among the two major Christian groups rivalry was putting a remarkable strain on American political life by the late summer and fall of 1949. It spilled over into the special senatorial election between John Foster Dulles, who had been appointed to the seat on an interim basis, and Herbert H. Lehman. Lehman, in addition to denouncing the ban on *The Nation* because of the Blanshard articles, had been an outspoken supporter of Mrs. Roosevelt in her controversy with the cardinal. Ten years later, in looking back upon that, he wrote to a close aide that "I believe that the most courageous act of my public life was the defense which I made of Mrs. Roosevelt when she was attacked by Cardinal Spellman."[26]

The excesses of Cardinal Spellman's letter went far toward destroying any possibility for calm debate on the issue, for a recognition that both sides had valid points. Parochial schools, which educated some thirteen percent of America's children, were having financial trouble; additional assistance to public education, without recognizing private institutional needs for construction and salaries, could only further undermine that position. A very real factor in the debates was the payment of taxes for education by parents regardless of whether their children went to public schools. Parochial-school interests also argued that their use of religious institutions for educational purposes reduced the economic burdens on public instruction. Finally, in the *Everson* v. *Board of Education* decision, the Supreme Court ruled 5–4 that there was no violation of the First Amendment by the act of aiding the child rather than the school. Justice Hugo Black's majority decision made a very clear distinction between federal funding of parochial schools and assistance for taxpaying citizens. So grounds certainly did exist for rational dialogue somewhere between the Thomas bill, which would have kept assistance from private schools in states that barred such aid but which, at the same time, contained two provisions to ensure federal funds for black schools, and the much more restrictive Barden bill. The North Carolinian used his states' rights doctrine very conveniently, letting each state do what it wanted about financing black education and, at the same time, forbidding them from deciding to divert any federal money for private schools. Chairman Lesinski denounced the Barden version as both "anti-Catholic and anti-Negro." But the cardinal, in attacking Mrs. Roosevelt, ignored the fact that she had not endorsed the Barden bill. Moreover, the prelate chose to overlook her subsequent columns, which modified her position to the point of supporting the legality of nondenominational prayers in public classrooms.[27]

Along with Blanshard, Barden and Spellman then were the extremists who foreclosed progress. One notable attempt at compromise was made by two congressmen, a Catholic and a Baptist: the then House Majority Leader John W. McCormack and the Democratic whip, Percy Priest of Tennessee. But Barden and Spellman had provided the incendiary touch and positions had become, in the words of one, "more inflexible rather than more flexible."[28]

In such a climate, John Kennedy's position is not difficult to understand. During the proceedings of the Education and Labor Committee in 1947, he had been clear about general agreement with the New Jersey decision and the principle of permitting parochial schoolchildren to participate as beneficiaries of certain forms of federal assistance. Monsignor Frederick Hockwalt of the National Catholic Welfare Conference considered Kennedy "an ardent and successful spokesman in opposition to the Barden bill."[29] Kennedy attempted to make the legislation more palatable by proposing an amendment that would permit parochial schools to receive aid for noneducational services.

Kennedy's attitude requires a closer look, however, because his own presidential candidacy a decade later provoked a national controversy. A Catholic from a Catholic district, his personal attitude had to contain strong contrary convictions before he could ignore what was politically prudent. When the final vote came up in 1950, he warned a colleague from New Jersey that voting against auxiliary aid for parochial schoolchildren would have political dangers. "I told Charlie at the time," he later said about Congressman Howell, "that he was wrong on that issue, that it was going to hurt him."[30]

Kennedy's resignation from the Four Chaplains dinner had already demonstrated his own consistency with the Church's position. He had made no secret of his approval of the *Everson* decision. He could see no reason why a formula should not be devised. But his was a rational view that could not penetrate the heat.

On August 1, in the middle of the long debate of that day, Kennedy introduced a federal aid bill that would distribute $300 million annually to states to finance minimum education programs and reduce irregularities. Ten percent of the funds were to be earmarked for compensation for such auxiliary school services as bus transportation, health services, and textbooks for private and parochial schools. But the committee members failed to reconcile their differences.[31] Disgusted, midway during the stormy meeting he made a motion that sought to delay further consideration of the entire subject for the balance of that session of Congress. Perhaps passions would cool. Perhaps the Spellman-Roosevelt-Barden antagonisms would recede. Kennedy lost. He was defeated in his committee 13–12.[32]

Later the following March he joined with Lesinski in helping to kill the Senate-sponsored Thomas bill 13–12. Both men regarded it as inadequate because it did not ensure auxiliary benefits for non-public school students. Republicans, including Nixon, opposed it because of their opposition to the principle of *any* federal funding for education.[33] One week earlier, Kennedy had unsuccessfully proposed a mild school-aid program that was confined to bus transportation. For his constituents, then, he had shown where he stood. *The Pilot,* published by the Boston Archdiocese, proudly hailed him as a "white knight" who "has already proved himself to be a statesman in the best sense of the word."[34]

Through a frequent outlet for his views, James G. Colbert of the *Boston Post,* Kennedy further clarified his position. "Many people have the erroneous impression," Colbert quoted him as explaining, "that some of us on the committee who have fought various proposed bills on federal aid have done so because we insisted that non-public, including parochial schools and school systems, should receive supporting federal funds just as public schools and school systems would receive as aid." That, he emphasized, was not the case. He aligned himself with the National Catholic Welfare Conference's contention that "if federal money is to be spent for education," parochial schoolchildren should not be left out. They "should benefit at least to the extent of obtaining federal aid in meeting the expenses of their school-bus transportation. The differentiation is between aid for operation of parochial schools and aid for personal services such as bus transportation for parochial school children."[35]

However he might explain it, wherever he drew the line between constitutional protections for the separation of church and state and equal treatment for all, there were those who would always suspect such legal distinctions. As with his backing off from the Four Chaplains affair, he had created future problems for himself, problems that were, albeit, unavoidable. For the former, he would be hounded by Dr. Poling. For the latter, he acquired the additional opposition of Mrs. Roosevelt, who was quoted as saying she was "certainly opposed" to Kennedy's transportation proposal.[36] Given Eleanor Roosevelt's experience with the Kennedys, that was simply another black mark on their record. Jack's father had provided several: his attitude toward the Germans and the war, his relations with the Roosevelt White House, and, especially as far as Mrs. Roosevelt was concerned, his crude remarks about her as reported by Louis Lyons. Now she was seeing Joe Kennedy's son in action. What else could she have expected?

Mrs. Roosevelt's sentiments toward the younger Kennedy must have been further colored by a reminder of the past that made headlines less than a week before the Spellman flare-up. The State Department released the publication of German papers that quoted talks Ambassador Kennedy had had in London in 1938 with Hitler's ambassador, Dr. Herbert von Dirksen.

That correspondence, possibly somewhat embellished by von Dirksen's own needs, further damned Joe Kennedy's reputation. Kennedy was quoted as having said that President Roosevelt was not anti-German but was surrounded by trusted informants, most of whom were Jews "and did not dare say anything good about Germany." Von Dirksen also alleged that the American had been greatly impressed by a report made by Colonel Charles Lindbergh, "who had spoken very favorably of Germany . . . Lindbergh and his wife spoke to me in the same manner regarding their impressions of Germany and German aviation when I became acquainted with them recently at a court ball in Buckingham Palace."[37]

The publication of such a reminder of Joe Kennedy's reputed anti-Semitic and pro-Nazi attitudes coincided with Jack Kennedy's gradual steps toward staking out a more independent role, particularly in the area of foreign policy. While with Justice Douglas at Palm Beach during this period, Ambassador Kennedy seemed perplexed, not only about his close association with someone so politically at odds with himself but also about the drift of his son Jack. He said to Douglas, "You know, I must be nuts. I can't understand how the two men that I admire most in public life, my son Jack and your own self, stand for ideas that I so bitterly oppose."[38]

Kay Halle, an old friend of Jimmy Roosevelt's wife, recalled a conversation with the Ambassador and his son at a cocktail party given by Drew Pearson early in the congressman's Washington career.

"Kay," she remembered the father saying, "I wish you would tell Jack that he's going to vote the wrong way. . . . I think Jack is making a terrible mistake." At which the congressman turned to his father and said: "Now, look here, Dad, you have your political views and I have mine. I'm going to vote exactly the way I feel I must vote on this. I've got great respect for you but when it comes to voting, I'm voting my way."

The Ambassador then turned to Halle, smiled, and said, "Well, Kay, that's why I settled a million dollars on each one of them, so they could spit in my eye if they wished."[39]

To a journalist, Congressman Kennedy explained that the significant differences with his father were over foreign policy. "We don't even discuss it anymore," said Kennedy, "because we're just so far apart, there's no point in it. I've given up arguing with him. I make up my own mind and my own decisions."[40]

Although clearly a politic sentiment for the consumption of a newspaperman, the public differences over foreign policy between Kennedy and his ex-ambassador father reveal fundamental disagreements. One viewed America as capable of strengthening itself merely through a more aggressive assertion of unrestricted capitalism. The other subscribed to the emerging Cold War containment philosophy of both American liberals and conservatives. On the broader issue of the responsibility for Soviet and Chinese Communist hegemony, there was not an iota of difference between father and son. While the congressman went along with his fellow Democrats and supported the President on such matters as the Truman Doctrine and the Marshall Plan, as well as the other aid programs, his father proposed accepting Communist expansionism because he felt it would inevitably be checked by its own failures, which would then free Americans to make sound investments in the rehabilitation and economic future of nations that had temporarily fallen under Marxist control. Father James Cronin of the National Catholic Welfare Conference quickly objected to Joe Kennedy's position by claiming that "if this policy were adopted, it could well mean that we would have taken the first steps toward self-destruction. A new isolationism would fit perfectly into Soviet plans for world domination."[41]

The Ambassador's positions plainly dissented from the conventional wisdom of stemming Communist expansionism through the containment programs that had been accepted by 1947 and 1948. He voiced apprehensions about the possibility of another war, which were not dissimilar to the fears that he had stated before the Second World War. And so he wrote to Lord Beaverbrook in early 1948 that "I shudder to think what the end of the next war would be. There are so many more places now where a war would break out, as compared with the last World War, that I haven't much confidence in the situation." And then, referring to the opposition posed to the Truman policy by Progressive Party candidate Henry A. Wallace, Ambassador Kennedy added, "Wallace is surprisingly strong because he is advocating peace."[42]

The senior Kennedy took his freewheeling critique of American foreign policy to the Charlottesville campus of the University of Virginia on December 12, 1950, one-half year after the outbreak of the Korean War. He appeared under the sponsorship of the Student Legal Forum, of which law student Robert Kennedy was then president. Speaking just one month after Chinese Communist "volunteer" forces had converted the conflict into an "entirely new" war, he proposed that the United States get out of Korea and any other place in Asia where we could not hope to hold our defense. His congressman son had earlier doubted the administration's appraisal of the magnitude of the Korean situation; but unlike the view now expressed by the Ambassador, Jack Kennedy dismissed—as academic—questions about the wisdom of intervention. He told a Shriners convention his hope that "our effort there will not denude other areas of troops that have a more strategic importance," especially Germany, which had only two highly vulnerable divisions.[43] But despite disagreements with his father, John F. Kennedy's position accepted the general wisdom against repeating the lessons of pre-World War II noninterventionism, the miscalculations that he had described in *Why England Slept.* Jack parted from most Democrats by holding Roosevelt responsible for the failure of Yalta and blamed the State Department and President Truman for the "loss" of China. His position became so emphatic that after one speech critical of the administration's responses, a Haverhill, Massachusetts, paper commented editorially that "the political point of the Kennedy speech is that the Republicans should try to sign him up for a job with their speaking bureau."[44]

The point had some merit. Apart from his early endorsement of the Truman Doctrine, which was stated eloquently in a foreign-policy address at the University of North Carolina and his basic acceptance of the

Marshall Plan, the young congressman showed that he was no dependable ally of the Democratic administration nor of the one that had preceded it, again in keeping with his nonpartisan course.

His positions combined acceptance of Cold War containment with a substantial dosage of the kind of blame for Communist gains that appeared in not only some of the more strident elements of the Catholic press but also that marked the early postwar rebellion against Democratic foreign policy particularly common to Irish-American voters. That kind of sentiment made it very easy to blame Roosevelt, Truman, the State Department, Dean Acheson, and the "China hands" for what had gone wrong.

Further building his political base, he struck out for a broader field. Hence, he took a prominent role in supporting Italy's Christian Democrats under Prime Minister DeGasperi as the government in Rome faced a challenge from a unified "Front" that threatened to give the Communists a key voice in the Italian government. Here, Kennedy paralleled the State Department's own efforts to counter left-wing gains. He appealed to Massachusetts's Italian-Americans to write letters to their kinsmen abroad telling them about American democracy and the contributions that their new homeland had been making since the end of the war toward Italian rehabilitation, and later lauded the letter-writing campaign for having been instrumental in helping to turn the tide.[45] Before Polish groups, he explained the continuation of Communist control as the direct result of Yalta and the Teheran Conference, where Roosevelt "failed" to recognize that he had been misled by Stalin.[46] But where he moved closest to what had become the right-wing critique of the failures of American foreign policy was his castigation of the government for the situation in Asia.

The Far East had become the special concern of anti-administration conservatives who had backed Chiang Kai-shek and simultaneously denounced the Yalta Agreements. During the period between Chiang's abandonment of the mainland and Truman's firing of General Douglas MacArthur in April of 1951, Kennedy's positions were almost indistinguishable from some of the more excessive critics of Truman and Secretary of State Dean Acheson. He initially reacted with disapproval of news that the general had been relieved of his Far Eastern command but tempered such dissent a few days later by opposing MacArthur's proposal to bomb Manchuria with the warning that the Soviet Union would go to war to prevent the collapse of the People's Republic of China.[47]

In a House of Representatives floor speech on January 25, 1949,

Kennedy placed the failure of Far Eastern policy "squarely with the White House and the Department of State." The great blunder, he held, was making continued aid contingent upon the formation by the Kuomintang of a coalition with the Communists. And then in a sentence that foreshadowed the claims of Joe McCarthy and revealed his own misgivings about establishing democracy as a form of government, Kennedy charged that "so concerned were our diplomats and their advisers, the Lattimores and the Fairbanks, with the imperfection of the democratic system of China after 20 years of war and the tales of corruption in high places that they lost sight of our tremendous stake in a non-Communist China." He urged his colleagues to "assume the responsibility of preventing the onrushing tide of communism from engulfing all of Asia."[48] Five days later, in Salem, Massachusetts, Kennedy repeated the same theme, reminding his audience that, at Yalta, "a sick Roosevelt with the advice of General Marshall and other Chiefs of Staff, gave the Kurile Islands as well as the control of various strategic Chinese ports, such as Port Arthur and Darien, to the Soviet Union." And he again blamed "the Lattimores and the Fairbanks" and declared that our Chinese policy "has reaped the whirlwind." In a portentous conclusion, he added, "This is the tragic story of China, whose freedom we once fought to preserve. What our young men have saved, our diplomats and our President have frittered away."[49]

In the wake of the Chinese collapse, Kennedy attempted to convert into an issue what he regarded as another administration blunder: inadequate spending for defense, especially for the protection of civilians on the home front. A letter to President Truman expressed shock that only one government official was working full time on such plans despite the President's announcement that Russia had achieved an atomic explosion. Pointing out that it would take months, "and even years," to prepare adequate plans for atomic defenses of American cities, he urged the President to speed up the program. In a separate statement to the press, Kennedy favored not having the program for civilian defense continued under the responsibility of the National Security Resources Board but placed under the control of a permanent civilian defense agency.[50] His emphasis foreshadowed his presidential response to the Berlin crisis of 1961.

On October 31, Jack made public an account of the warm support inspired by his position among a variety of groups and individuals, including Bernard Baruch, the financier who savored his entrée to leading public figures. Still, the only specific references to supporters that he could name, besides Baruch, were the directors of civilian defense for the states of Louisiana and New Jersey, the chairman of the Civilian Protection Group in New York, and the Chamber of Commerce of Honolulu. So Kennedy followed through with what he had. On November 17 he dispatched letters to the editors of forty-five Massachusetts newspapers citing the great recent public interest in the subject and noting the stepping-up of stronger federal activities in this field. His letters endorsed the report of Civil Defense for National Security known as the Hopley Report.[51] He later told reporters, "If an atomic bomb were dropped on one of our cities tomorrow, nobody would know what to do, where to go or even whom to see or what to do. All would be panic and confusion."[52] And as he came closer to making a statewide race for the Senate in 1952, he became a greater advocate of a more powerful strike force as well, sharply supporting stronger ground and air power. "Sooner or later the policy of speaking boldly and carrying a small stick," he told a meeting of Shriners in Boston, "must inevitably be challenged as much as the Communist-chosen area concerning which our policy is confused and unsettled." His voice also became louder in behalf of preventing reduced Air Force appropriations and he introduced an amendment calling for an early buildup of plane construction. A news release in April 1952 reminded constituents that "in 1947 and 1948 he stood almost alone in voting against tax cuts, saying the money should be used to build a strong Air Force."[53]

The so-called Mallan affair, however, involved Jack in far greater controversy. A dispute that became an issue in the 1952 campaign and was never quite resolved, it plagued him until the eve of his presidential campaign. The Mallan reportage did not appear until almost two years after the event took place; but when it did, in the pages of *The New Republic,* it became an embarrassment that Kennedy's friends attempted to counter because of its significance among a broader Democratic constituency than just the Eleventh District of Massachusetts. Kennedy himself tried to charge that John P. Mallan, the author of the piece, had misquoted him and as late as 1959, when examining the draft manuscript of Burns's account of what had taken place, Kennedy wrote in the margin that Burns's version was inaccurate because Mallan was not present at the event.[54]

Unfortunately for Kennedy, Mallan was indeed present, as a student in a seminar offered by Professor Arthur Holcombe in the Harvard Graduate School of Public Administration on November 10, 1950. Mallan, in fact, was more than just present: he was directly involved in questioning Kennedy about some of the views that were later reported. His reportage made several points, some of which attributed direct quotes to the congressmen's reactions.

According to Mallan, Kennedy told the students that he could see no reason why we were fighting in Korea. Responding to a question about European assistance that had been raised by Mallan himself, Kennedy said that sooner or later we would "have to get all these foreigners off our backs." Asked about the McCarran Act, which had been passed over Truman's veto earlier that fall, with its provisions for the registration of Communists and Communist-front organizations and for their internment during national emergencies in addition to the restriction of entry into the United States of those who had belonged to totalitarian organizations, Kennedy endorsed the measure and added that not enough had been done about Communists in government. The discussion moved to Joe McCarthy.

In response to a question about his regard for the senator from Wisconsin, he replied that he rather respected McCarthy and thought he "knew Joe pretty well, and he may have something." He also told them that he had no great respect for Dean Acheson or indeed for almost any member of the Fair Deal administration of Truman's. Mallan reported that the seminar heard him say that he was very happy that Richard Nixon had just won the senatorial election in California by defeating Helen Gahagan Douglas. Mallan then added a personal observation: "Their feelings were not exactly assuaged when it was brought out in later conversation with the disarmingly frank and charming Mr. Kennedy that his reasons for these views were in many cases not so much ideological as a matter of casual intuitive feeling. His liking for McCarthy seemed to be on a personal basis, as was his feeling that Mrs. Douglas was 'not the sort of person I'd like working with on committees.' While he opposed what he supposed to be Communist influence at home, he refused to become emotionally aroused even on this issue."[55]

Coming to light, as it did, in the midst of his 1952 campaign, Kennedy's comments suddenly brought concerted efforts to undermine Mallan's credibility. As soon as the magazine appeared, the student was confronted by Gardner "Pat" Jackson of the campaign staff, in addition to Professor Holcombe, and he immediately agreed that the title of the article "Massachusetts: Liberal and Corrupt," had been unfortunate. That had not been his choice. The publication had altered the original title and thereby distorted its presentation, as Mallan then complained to *The New Republic.* Explaining to Kennedy about the accuracy of his statements, however, Mallan said he had compared his notes with those of several members of the seminar and they had agreed with his version. He added, "I can assure you that there was a general reaction to your comments among both students and at least some faculty along the lines I described."[56]

Most interesting was Holcombe's letter to *The New Republic*. Holcombe's greatest displeasure lit upon the "serious factual error" that the meeting was an informal gathering of Harvard students and professors. It was a formal meeting, offered by the graduate school, of Holcombe's seminar on legislative process. He explained that Kennedy appeared at his invitation in the belief that he was facing a strictly academic audience and with the reasonable expectation that anything he might say in reply to questions by students would be off the record and not be used against him in a subsequent political campaign. Holcombe also pointed out that there was no official transcript of the proceedings and he denied that others present could corroborate the *precise* words.[57] Mallan's response, contained in the same issue, acknowledged that the meeting actually was a seminar class of Holcombe's but stood by the accuracy of the remarks, adding that one of Kennedy's responses came in reply to a question he himself had asked. The Mallan article was essentially accurate. As Mallan himself readily admitted, some of the wording, perhaps some of the phraseology, may have been imprecise, but they reflected Kennedy's sentiments. The fact is that Kennedy, in a 1959 letter to Holcombe, wanted vindication on the basis of his record as a representative and a senator. In 1950, however, Mallan was dealing with the congressman and his views as of that date. And it was indeed the representative of the Eleventh District of Massachusetts who, as in his father's Charlottesville address of the following month, had castigated the administration for not knowing what it was doing in Korea; it was Kennedy who had complained to his constituents that Europeans were not carrying their fair burden of responsibilities for Western defense; it was Kennedy who had repeatedly, from his early days in Congress—when he went after Russ Nixon and Harold Christoffel—continued to concern himself with Communists or radicals; it was Kennedy, along with his family, who had developed a rapport with Joe McCarthy, and by saying that he "knew Joe pretty well, and he may have something," was being strikingly honest and in no way inconsistent with his personal regard for the senator. Criticism of Dean Acheson and the Truman administration was perfectly in line with the position he had taken on several occasions, especially with regard to Far Eastern policy. And his satisfaction with the

Nixon defeat of Mrs. Douglas has been confirmed by not only Kennedy's statement to Red Fay but by Joe Kennedy's financial contribution to that campaign, which Nixon himself has more recently described in his memoirs.

Although the Mallan affair did not become public until the midst of the 1952 campaign, there is little reason to doubt the essential faithfulness with which it described Congressman Kennedy in 1950. His position on foreign policy relative to his father's resembled two roads diverging from time to time and merging again every now and then, but essentially going in the same direction.

Jack Kennedy had been an effective spokesman for the opposition. Not much separated him from the "Asia firsters" or the "China Lobby" element that chastized the Democratic administration for Communist successes in the Far East. Still, he carefully sidestepped association with his father's position. Asked for his reaction to the Ambassador's Charlottesville comments about getting out of Korea, he told Senator Walter George of Georgia, the ranking Democrat on the Foreign Relations Committee, that "I do believe for myself, and I do not like to speak for my father" and suggested that his father's position could be obtained by questioning him directly.[58] The new year, however, would see the young congressman discover more about the world, first about Europe and then Asia, enhancing his own candidacy for a statewide race and broadening his education, a process that had a significant modifying effect on his thinking.

Meanwhile, his family situation was also undergoing changes. On October 2, little more than a month before Jack faced Professor Holcombe's seminar, Grandfather Fitzgerald, a contributor to the creation of urban ethnic political machines, died at the age of eighty-seven. For Jack, that severed one more link with the past, a connection about which he had always been ambivalent: respecting Honey Fitz for his political acumen and at the same time regarding him as somewhat of the sort of anachronism from which his own generation had to escape.

On bread-and-butter issues Jack also differed superficially from his father. Jack's labor and housing record appealed to a liberal urban constituency with low family incomes. His response to related domestic issues formed a composite between his own views and the essential economic needs of the Eleventh. Consequently, he championed liberalizing immigration laws, becoming through the years one of the more persistent critics of the quota-system relic of the 1920's that discriminated against the admission of immigrants from Southern and Eastern Europe, of whom the overwhelming number were either Roman Catholic or Jewish. Accordingly, Kennedy supported legislation to make special provisions for increasing the quotas to permit the entry of "displaced persons" from Communist-dominated areas of Europe. Only some forty-two thousand such individuals had been admitted under President Truman's directive of 1945. With the obstacle posed by the reluctance on Capitol Hill to facilitate any enlargement of Jewish migration, in particular, through fallacious fears that that group would become a significant beneficiary of a liberalized Displaced Persons Bill, Kennedy was among those who pressed for increasing the overall total eligible for admission. He told the Greater Boston branch of the Hebrew Immigrant Aid Society about his optimism that the House would pass such legislation once yanked out of committee.[59] He also opposed what ultimately became the McCarran-Walter Act, first voting for a motion to have it sent back to committee with the complaint that it contained provisions restricting rather than liberalizing the immigration system. (He passed over the McCarran-Walter provisions for screening out "subversives" and deporting immigrants for "Communist and Communist-front" affiliations even if they were American citizens.) Kennedy argued against basing quota allotments on the highly prejudicial 1920 census data and suggested that as long as such a system was necessary, at least the 1950 census should be reflected, which had already been provided for in bills introduced in the Senate by Hubert Humphrey and Herbert Lehman.[60]

Concurrently, Kennedy's early actions seemed sympathetic with rectifying existing racial inequities. His attitudes emerged most clearly through his membership in the House District of Columbia Committee, an association that notoriously contained little appeal "for the folks back home." In evaluating Kennedy's record with the committee, nothing suggests indifference. He opposed a sales tax for the District, pointing out the burdens placed by such levies on those in the lowest income groups, and offered alternate means of solving the city's financial problems.[61] He was also regarded as one of the members of the committee spearheading the drive to gain home rule for the District. An enabling bill was tied up through the efforts of the four top-ranking members of the House District Committee, then headed by John L. McMillan of South Carolina. All four were from the South and had little sympathy with enfranchising the sizable black vote in the capital. Kennedy was reported leading the drive to get that home-rule bill out of the committee. On March 3, 1950, he inserted in the *Congressional Record* a long memorandum called "The Case for Home Rule for Washington," which supported a bill sponsored by Republican Congressman James Auchincloss of New Jersey and Senator Estes Kefauver of Tennessee.[62] With the further aid of Senator Taft, it passed the Senate by a voice vote in July 1949 but remained bottled up in the House committee by the Dixie delegation. Kennedy rounded up 170 signatures for a discharge petition to extricate the bill but fell short of the required 218. "The trouble, of course, is the large potential Negro vote in Washington. A handful of Southern bourbons just can't swallow democracy even in the nation's capital," editorialized the *Boston Herald*.[63] Two years later, during the Democratic Party's presidential nominating convention, Kennedy urged the National Committee to pledge itself to a revision of the Senate's rules to limit filibusters, the traditional bane of civil-rights legislation. He favored amending the rule making closure possible with the simple majority of senators present in the chamber.[64]

There is no reason to believe that Kennedy's civil-rights positions did much, at the time, to enhance his credentials as a liberal. Mostly, as in the rest of the country, such issues were then generally ignored. In his own district the black population was limited and their voting even scarcer. Not many working-class blacks were then exercised over such issues. The leadership in the effort to obtain justice was still largely in the hands of an elite few, both black and white and both Republicans and Democrats. Political motivations to explain Kennedy's interest, then, are not very compelling. Much more important was his instinctive feeling of noblesse oblige—protecting the peasants from the bourgeoisie and, to Jack, the operation of simple justice.

Other actions were more in tune with representing the Eleventh District. During his later congressional years especially, the closer he moved toward a statewide candidacy, the more he stressed the Commonwealth's deteriorating economy. Competition with cheap southern labor and high rates for electricity in New England were pushing textile and shoe manufacturers out of the region. Kennedy consequently used his membership on the Education and Labor Committee to press inquiries into the loss of jobs. On May 17, 1950, he was able to announce that the rivers and harbors authorization bill just signed by the President would provide for the modification of the Mystic River project in Boston and have economic significance to the bordering industrial cities of Somerville, Medford, Chelsea, and Everett. He urged that the federal government use money from off-shore oil for the construction of schools and hospitals, a position generally led in the Senate by Lister Hill of Alabama.[65]

Kennedy also argued that Massachusetts taxpayers could not be expected to support the Tennessee Valley Authority because of the loss to the South of basic New England industries, which was accelerated by the cheap power supplied by such government programs. And he was among those who helped achieve a fourteen-million-dollar cut in TVA appropriations. That kind of position later led to the suggestion by Senator Richard Russell of Georgia that a Kennedy senatorial campaign could attract substantial Republican support in addition to workers worried about job security. Russell advised Jim Landis that Kennedy ought to meet with the Independent Union of United Shoe Machinery Companies. That could, he pointed out, lead to a gathering of shop foremen who could ultimately deliver some three or four thousand votes.[66]

Despite his involvement in several domestic issues, Jack's basic bent had always been toward foreign affairs. Being able to exert a significant influence over diplomacy could more nearly fulfill his self-image. On January 8, 1951, he left on a five-week trip to Europe, which took him to England, France, and Italy, nations that belonged to the newly established North Atlantic Treaty Organization. He also went to West Germany, Yugoslavia, and Spain, whose capacities and loyalties "are obviously tied up in the question of the defense of the west," he told the Senate Foreign Relations Committee upon his return.[67]

He first stopped at London, arriving on the night of January 9, and after a three-day "investigation of the progress of Britain's rearmament," he left by air for a tour of the Continent. In Yugoslavia he met with Marshall Tito. The Communist leader's independence from Soviet control was then almost three years old and he told the visiting congressman that he did not expect a Cominform attack on his country that spring. Since he was not a prophet, he added, he was nevertheless obliged to prepare for any eventuality. Tito expressed to Kennedy the view that the United States and the other Western powers were strong enough to at least attempt to negotiate some of the outstanding problems with the Soviets. He owed his faith in Western strength to the prompt response in Korea and the progress of rearmament programs.

The continuing, quiet influence of the Ambassador persisted during Jack's absence from the country, helping to generate friendly coverage for his son's overseas activities. Aside from Joe Kennedy's connections with Henry Luce, Krock, and the Hearst organization, so helpful in providing national coverage, the Ambassador exerted influence most directly over the local New England region that was so important for

Jack's immediate political career. In Boston such writers as Jim Colbert and Bill Mullins could be relied upon to be helpful. They and their colleagues contributed substantial promotional material, often accompanied by photographs, to the many papers the city had in that day, the *Post,* the *Globe,* the *Herald American,* the *Sunday Advertiser,* the *Traveler.* Much of their copy was also picked up by various local papers throughout the state. *The Berkshire Eagle* of Pittsfield, an independent paper in the western part of Massachusetts, was virtually alone in carrying dispassionate, critical commentary. The Ambassador's intervention also affected the airwaves in New England. Yankee Network outlets, for example, lauded Jack's audience with Tito. Its radio listeners were also told that the "tour is one of the first of its kind ever made in recent years and may have a bearing upon the final vote in Congress in connection with the army to be placed under General Eisenhower." Moreover, under the guise of news, Yankee Network stations declared that Kennedy was one of the "ablest and younger members of the national house" and was "very highly regarded and his findings may have tremendous influence upon the future course of this country in the arming of Western Europe." The network's news service editor was Leland Bickford, who had pledged the Ambassador his efforts to "do everything possible to help John." Bickford flatteringly told Joe that the congressman could become the first Catholic president "if he is handled properly and he has been up to this time."[68]

On the morning of January 30, Jack Kennedy was received by Pope Pius XII, whom he had met earlier as Cardinal Pacelli. The news of the papal audience was immediately relayed by Kennedy in a telegram to Mary Davis in Washington with instructions that the information be released to the people of Boston through Frank Morrissey's office.[69]

Soon after his return to the States, he testified before the Senate Foreign Relations Committee. To an interested audience, he made some cogent points about what he considered proper American contributions to mutual security. He urged the establishment of a ratio to make sure that the other nations contribute to defense in proportion to the American obligation. "I am not advocating a ratio system in order to limit our contribution to Western Europe," he told Senator Wayne Morse of Oregon. "It is not a backhanded way of trying to pull out of Western Europe. I am in favor of the ratio system in order to make the Europeans do more, and I think that, if we do not do that, my conviction from this trip is that this thing is not going to be done quickly enough. . . ." As he had done in speeches before groups of voters, he supported the American contribution of four additional divisions to augment the two already there. And so what the ratio system was designed to do, he explained, was to establish a device that would actuate an automatic limitation of the American commitment because, as he told Senator Alexander Wiley, the committee's chairman, it was obvious to him that "in not one of these countries does their effort in relation to the amount of money spent for defense in proportion to their national income, bear any comparison to what we are going to spend. . . . None of the other nations of the North Atlantic Pact are going to devote percentages of its income in any relationship to ours or even to Great Britain's."

Furthermore, Kennedy was beginning to learn something to balance the views that he had been expressing so stridently before his trip. His travels revealed more clearly the improbabilities of a Russian invasion of Western Europe. And finally Kennedy learned that, contrary to the fear and hysteria that the Truman administration and its critics had helped to promote in America since March 1947 about a possible invasion, there were obvious deterrents that would keep the Iron Curtain from advancing toward the Atlantic. So Kennedy told Senator Wiley that the feeding of Western Europe would in itself be a tremendous job and it would be highly improbable for the Russians to risk the start of a war when the very best they could get out of it would be a stalemate. And out of that stalemate might very well come atomic bombing. "Why should they throw everything into the game, why should they take risks they don't have to—especially when things are going well in the Far East? In addition, Stalin is an old man, and old men are traditionally cautious," Kennedy said. Yet he told the committee that we had no choice but to build strength for self-defense. When Wiley wanted to know whether that would not simply provoke the Russians, Kennedy said, "If that stimulates attack, then that will come. But to refuse to do it because of that reason would seem to me to be the height of foolishness." In direct contrast with his father's position, Kennedy told them that "Europe is our first line of defense."[70]

Four days before his committee appearance, Kennedy spoke over a 540-station Mutual Broadcasting Company national radio hookup on "Issues in the Defense of the West." And in that talk, which gave him a coast-to-coast audience, he warned about the importance of saving Western Europe. But he felt we ought not endanger our own survival in the process. There, too, he pressed the theme of European contributions to the mutual sacrifice.[71]

Appropriately enough, *Boston's Political Times* ran a large and suita-

bly flattering front-page portrait under the heading KENNEDY ACQUIR-
ING TITLE, "AMERICA'S YOUNGER STATESMAN."[72] Promoting him, it
made the point that while Bernard Baruch had been regarded as Amer-
ica's elder statesman, no one had yet been given the honor of being called
America's younger statesman. After listening to Congressman
Kennedy's national hookup of his observations of the situation in
Europe: "We are convinced that Mr. Kennedy is fast approaching the
title—if it is possible for anyone to acquire it."[73] The hand of the local
Kennedy operatives was indeed visible.

The Kennedy European trip gave him the reputation of expertise in
foreign affairs. On the House floor on April 8, he denounced the harsh-
ness of the 1947 Italian peace treaty, explaining that the terms had been
negotiated during the days when America was still "appeasing Russia"
in the hope that peace between the two nations could be realized.[74]
Meanwhile, a Massachusetts paper called *The Jewish Advocate* told its
readers that young Kennedy has been growing up independently, not
unduly influenced by his father, and had moved forward into the realm
of modern foreign politics with keen insight and liberal views. Most of
all, the *Advocate* stressed his renunciation of isolationism toward the
problem of establishing a defensive containment policy around the aggressive Soviets.[75] In Washington, Kennedy introduced a bill that would
ban the shipment of strategic materials to the port of Hong Kong, thus
denying American companies the right to commerce with Communist
China by way of that British colony.[76] Following so soon after Truman's
dismissal of General MacArthur, Kennedy's stroke reflected the public
outrage over the People's Republic's involvement in the Korean War.

Jack Kennedy had only recently returned from Europe when he met
Jacqueline Bouvier. The daughter of Janet Norton Lee and John Vernou
Bouvier III, Jackie was born in Southampton, Long Island, on July 28,
1929, twelve years after Kennedy. Appropriately, for the child of a Social
Register family, she attended Miss Porter's School for Girls at Farming-
ton, Connecticut, where she made somewhat of a mark by winning
attention for her intelligence, appreciation of the arts, and a keen sense
of history.[77] She then studied at Vassar College and at the Sorbonne in
Paris before getting her B.A. from George Washington University.

Her exposure to high society included life at the immense Hammersmith Farm home of her stepfather, Hugh D. Auchincloss, in Newport,
Rhode Island; the estate at Merrywood, in McLean, Virginia, overlooking the Potomac; and the Bouvier homes at East Hampton on Long

Island and on Park Avenue. She rode horses, went fox-hunting, and had a flair for style, which as she matured enabled her to project an elegant, glamorous presence. Photographs betray the transition from an ordinary, even awkward adolescent to a comely young women. Even when her physical maturity had been reached, however, she had yet to become the self-possessed, highly confident, and competent woman of later years.

During the spring of 1951, while Jackie was still a student at George Washington University, she was invited to a dinner party at the home of Charles Bartlett. The gifted Washington correspondent of *The Chattanooga Times* had taken special care to also ensure the presence of Congressman Kennedy. For about two years the journalist had been trying to get them together.[78] Since his own family owned a winter home at Hobe Sound, Florida, only some thirty miles from Palm Beach, it was not extraordinary that he had already gotten to know the Kennedys, having first met Jack before the 1946 campaign. He met Miss Bouvier shortly after his own arrival in Washington in 1948. His determination to match the young couple followed soon afterward. Asked why he had that sort of compulsion, Bartlett recalls having a "gut feeling," a "feeling that these two were very special. Jackie had a sort of quiet glamour about her and Jack was a young, gangling fellow with unusual charm, and I just thought it might be good. I felt they would compensate each other in ways that were exciting enough to hold the other's interest."[79]

Bartlett's first attempt occurred at his brother's wedding in East Hampton on Long Island. He tried to steer Jackie through a crowded room of guests to where the congressman was standing. But en route, he made a mistake. He first stopped to introduce her to ex-heavyweight boxing champion Gene Tunney. By the time that conversation ended, Kennedy was gone. Not until the dinner at their home that spring evening in 1951 were Bartlett and his wife Martha able to bring them together.

It may not have been their first meeting. Jacqueline's mother recalls that "Hugh-die and I knew him when Jackie was in France at the Sorbonne." Thus, the young lady might have had at least a superficial knowledge of the congressman at that time. However trivial that Parisian encounter may have been, Jack Kennedy nevertheless impressed both Hugh D. Auchincloss and Janet as "one of the most attractive young men we had ever met in our lives."[80]

The immediate outcome of the Bartlett dinner was also unproductive, for no special rapport developed. Kennedy walked out after her, however, and muttered somewhat diffidently, "Shall we go someplace and have a drink?" But she had to reject the invitation. A young man was waiting in her car.[81]

Most likely the stranger was John G. W. Husted, Jr. A Yale graduate and Manhattan stockbroker from a proper northern Westchester County family, he had been courting Jackie for some time. At one point they had even announced their engagement.[82] The Husted connection, however, did not last very long; it dissolved, with the engagement formally broken "by mutual consent" a few months later. She thought Husted was immature and he and his work dull.[83]

Neither were there any early consequences of her meeting with Kennedy. His absences from Washington were more frequent. Long weekends were filled with crowded speaking schedules throughout Massachusetts. Later that year he went to Asia, spending seven weeks abroad. Miss Bouvier, meanwhile, found a job as an "inquiring photographer" with the *Washington Times-Herald.*

She knew little about photography. Nor did she need to. That she wound up with Frank Waldrop's paper, the one that had hired Kathleen Kennedy, was no surprise considering that she, like Jack's late sister, also knew Krock. Still, had Jackie merely walked into Waldrop's office as a stranger, ignorant about the mysteries of photographic technicalities, she would have been an enticing prospect. Once hired, she took a "crash" course that taught her all that was necessary for taking quick snapshots.

Jacqueline Bouvier came from a family that, like the Kennedys, had made it "big" in America. The crucial difference was the timing. Their fortune had come earlier. The clan was so successful that Jackie's grandfather invented an aristocratic pedigree to establish blood ties with European nobility. John Vernou Bouvier, Jr., published a book in 1890 that fabricated the lineage. He had discovered Bouvier nobility in the province of Dauphine—the Bouviers de la Fontaine—and adopted them as his own, even taking their motto and coat of arms. His genealogy was dedicated to his grandchildren "and to those who may later add to their joyous company." Thus, he had established a foundation for Bouvier aristocratic pretenses, one that survived unquestioned until their association with an American president developed sufficient scholarly interest to inspire scrutiny of Jacqueline Bouvier's grandfather's claims.[84] Ever since their arrival, the French Catholic Bouviers had tried to breach the dominant Anglo-Saxon Protestant establishment. Success came within one generation, helped by financial acumen on Wall Street and expeditious marriages of the three daughters of the family's American founder, Michel Bouvier, to the Drexel, Patterson, and Dixon families, moving them rapidly from mundane origins in southern France to American high society.[85]

Jacqueline's father was John Vernou Bouvier III, the second son of John V. Bouvier, Jr. He may very well have been the most significant influence in his daughter's life, possibly a model for every man she met. With a seat on the New York Stock Exchange, Bouvier began a career as one of the more colorful operators on Wall Street. Although his ancestry was as much British as French, he nevertheless retained a dark Latin complexion with romantic good looks that led to such nicknames as "The Sheik" and "The Black Prince." He liked to identify himself with Rhett Butler of *Gone with the Wind,* but, mostly, he was known as "Black Jack" Bouvier, a name given by other stockbrokers inspired by the popular sobriquet for General John Pershing.

Bouvier's career combined chasing women and making money through rapid turnovers on the stock exchange. During the Roaring Twenties, the parties at his elegant apartment at 375 Park Avenue were focal points for New York socialites. He appeared especially dashing with his figure enhanced by custom-made continental clothes that emphasized his chest, sharply indented his waist, and flattened his hips. By the late 1920's he had accumulated a fortune of $750,000 and a wife, Janet Norton Lee. For Janet, despite the rise of her own father from a modest Irish family, marriage into the Bouviers in 1928 was a big advance. The Lees were *nouveau* while the Bouviers had had money and position for several generations. And, as the family's biographer points out, while the Lees lacked style, "the Bouviers were among the most elegant, and fashion-conscious families of New York."

Other than women and liquor, the big undoing of Jack Bouvier's life was the great Wall Street crash. He did well at first, playing the same game that Joe Kennedy had mastered—selling short. But soon the continued fall of stock prices destroyed his profits. That threw the gallant "Black Jack" at the mercy of his father-in-law. He had never had good relations with James T. Lee, the self-made realtor and banker. Now, however, Lee agreed to help his son-in-law. But there was an important condition. Jack had to scale down his life-style, which meant giving up several club memberships and leading an existence largely dictated by Lee. Humiliated, Bouvier nevertheless had little choice, ultimately even having to accept his father-in-law's offer to live with Janet and daughter Jacqueline rent free in an apartment building Lee owned and managed at 740 Park Avenue. And so, very rapidly, Jack Bouvier descended from bold independence to subdued subservience.

He later made a bit of a comeback, including a two-million-dollar profit by speculating in liquor, but he then lost out by gambling on bad stocks, high living—including the maintenance of a Park Avenue duplex and East Hampton cottage—a wife and two daughters, two servants and a chauffeur, and a stable of seven horses. So, as John Davis has pointed out, by January of 1935 his net worth had dropped to another new low of $106,444.94. The blame, placed by Jack Bouvier, was directed straight at Joseph P. Kennedy.

As director of the Securities and Exchange Commission, one of Kennedy's first steps was to end the practice of operators like Jack Bouvier, who bought the stocks in which they specialized, thereby jacking them up, enabling them to participate in a racket that facilitated profit-taking before the stocks would come back down. Kennedy required that a specialist be limited to buying his own stocks only on the downswing. So "Black Jack," along with several other brokers, learned to hate Roosevelt and his New Deal and everything that went along with it, including the SEC and Joseph P. Kennedy. The latter was especially galling because he himself had been an operator "who had drawn all the honey he could from the hive when no holds were barred and was now stopping the very practices from which he had earned his fortune."

A timely inheritance, in 1935, enabled the Bouviers to recover and they formed a new brokerage firm. But at just that point Black Jack's troubles with Janet became serious. They tried a six-month separation, leaving her with the custody of two daughters, Jacqueline and her sister Lee. Janet and her children remained in James Lee's luxurious duplex at 730 Park Avenue, later moving to 1 Gracie Square, while Bouvier went to live in one room at the Westbury Hotel. An attempted reunion failed, and that was followed by a divorce, after which he rededicated himself to the pursuit of women.

Jacqueline and her sister became pawns of the estrangement. From a distance their father became increasingly jealous of their involvement with Janet and the Lees. The girls were prizes in a contest for affections, a situation that intensified when their mother remarried—this time to another stockbroker but one wealthier than Bouvier and with impeccable social credentials, Hugh D. Auchincloss. A general partner in the Washington brokerage house of Auchincloss, Parker and Redpath, he had been married twice before, first to the daughter of a Russian naval officer and then to Nina Gore Vidal, the daughter of T. B. Gore, the blind Oklahoma senator, and the mother of writer Gore Vidal. With her second marriage in 1942, Jack Bouvier watched Janet move into a far more enviable financial and social position. She could offer Jacqueline far more than could he, including a life in the heart of fashionable Newport summer society, where Janet became mistress of Hammersmith Farm, which overlooked Narragansett Bay from a hill above Ocean Drive.

Jacqueline and her sister were further removed from their father, away from East Hampton and New York, to Hammersmith Farm and to Merrywood, the Auchincloss estate overlooking the Potomac River. Increasingly competitive, Bouvier vied for their affections and became almost irrationally jealous of their closeness to Janet and Auchincloss. He was quite sure they were taking the girls away from him. In addition to paying for their education, Bouvier then countered by lavishing them with money. He kept their horses. He gave them monthly allowances, maintained charge accounts for them at the finest stores, and, wrote Davis, "since the staid Auchinclosses were, in Jack's opinion, a much duller family than the Bouviers, lacking the Bouvier's originality and style, he was reasonably confident that he could keep his daughters from identifying wholly with his rivals."[86]

Getting caught in that situation gave Jackie and her sister an insecurity that made them all the more determined to prove their own worth and, in some way, to compensate for their parents' separation. Jacqueline learned that she had to provide for her own emotional fortifications. "In a sense," a biographer has written, "both parents had let her down. She would not let herself down. If she was running her own show, it would be quite a show."[87]

Jack Kennedy continued to keep in touch with Dr. Sara Jordan at the Lahey Clinic. When he returned from Europe, she received a copy of his congressional testimony, which had been privately reprinted. He also assured the doctor of his physical progress and she responded somewhat skeptically with the hope that he really meant it. Her doubts were understandable. Travel had certainly not eased the pressure on his back. He was in pain most of the time and getting around required crutches. Walking on the marble floors of the House Office Building and the Capitol exacerbated the hardship. Finally, for the "first time in seven weeks," said a published report in September, "the young Congressman was able to throw away his crutches and make the trip to Boston to cast his ballot for Mayor and other offices in the preliminary city election."[88] At just about that time, Kennedy sent Dr. Jordan a biography of Disraeli. "You were very kind to think of me," she wrote back. "I was hoping to hear from you last Monday by phone, as to how you were; but in talking with your mother one night, I found that you had flown off to Washington on Monday, so I presume you weren't able to call me before leaving." Then, with professional concern, she added, "Do let me know as soon as you get this letter, how your back is. I hope it is doing well."[89]

By October, Kennedy was ready to leave on his second overseas trip of the year; this time he was joining Bobby and sister Pat on a tour of the Far East. Carefully, he continued to keep Dr. Jordan informed about his plans, which brought her reassurance that, during her own absence from the clinic, she could be reached at the Mountain View House in Whitefield, New Hampshire. "I am delighted you are feeling better," she added.[90]

His precautions could not prevent what followed. In Japan, Jack again became ill, not simply an aggravation of the back trouble but an acute condition that seemed to threaten his life. Removed for emergency treatment to a military hospital on Okinawa, his condition was critical as his fever rose to over 106. With a history of malaria having already served to cover up for Addison's, and with Kennedy's medical records guarded by the family, precise statements are difficult to make. Theodore Sorensen has gone so far as to write, when commenting on that particular ordeal, that "it is impossible to say which of these bouts was due to his adrenals, which was jaundice, hepatitis or malaria, or which of these may have helped bring on the other," which, given the circumstances, is about the only judgment possible.[91] Further evidence of his debilitation was the cancellation of a planned visit to Formosa. When he returned to the States, he spent time recuperating in a fairly isolated and remote spot in Virginia. By then it was mid-November. A few days later he had sufficient stamina, evidently enforced by determination, to face a large audience at the Boston Chamber of Commerce.[92]

He returned highly critical of what he had seen of British and French colonialism, and he expressed such findings to the businessmen. After having obtained a close-up view of both the Middle and Far East, his education had been advanced. It enabled him to understand the potency of nationalism as a force more significant than communism and as something utilized by Communists to gain their own ends.

As he then reported in a national radio address, the trip had given him a chance to speak with all types of leaders, including Eisenhower, General Matthew Ridgeway, General Jean Marie de Lattre de Tassigny, the commander in chief of the French troops in Indochina, as well as such prime ministers as Ben Gurion of Israel and Nehru of India. Throughout, he reported, he had seen more than just simple American blunders. He had seen "the fires of nationalism so long dormant [which] have been kindled and are now ablaze. . . . Colonialism is not a topic for tea-talk discussion; it is the daily fare of millions of men." In paying his first visit to Indochina and Korea, he found a "spirit of revolution," a clash between "civilizations striving to be born and those struggling desperately to retain what they had held so long." The concern of communism, he found, was relegated largely to an exploitative capitalization of such grievances. The basic problem in Asia was what Kennedy termed "the inevitable birth-pangs of Asia's rising nationalism," to which he added: "It is tragic to report that not only have we made no new friends, but we have lost old ones." Near the end of his broadcast, he reminded listeners of Clemenceau's warning that foreign policy "is too important to all of us to leave it to the experts and the diplomats." He included criticism of the attitude of many American ambassadors, a point he later stressed while campaigning throughout Massachusetts. Such diplomats, Kennedy reported, too frequently sided with the powerful rather than the powerless, even regarding the latter as "sinister and subversive."[93] With the convening of the new Congress in January, he introduced a bill calling for the creation of a commission to study the administration and operation of the government's overseas activities.[94]

Mostly, the trip proved instructive about the often complex relationships between nationalism and indigenous communism. The somewhat brash congressman who on the House floor, in his Salem speech of January 1949, and in his "off-the-record" comments in Professor Holcombe's seminar had repeated the anti-administration criticism of Far Eastern policy, now began to modify his tone. He talked about the complexities of nationalism and pointed out the futility of employing military power against anticolonialist native forces. He condemned the French for struggling to hold on to the "the remnants of Empire" in Vietnam and charged that the Associated States of Indochina were "as typical examples of empire and of colonialism as can be found anywhere." That visit aroused his recognition of the area's importance and demonstrated that "the Communists would be able to capture the Indo-Chinese Nationalist movement" as long as the West failed to recognize "that every country is entitled to its independence."[95] He warned an audience in Everett, Massachusetts, in March of 1952, against sending American troops to help bail the French out of Indochina; and, speaking in Lynn the following month, told a Knights of Columbus chapter that "we should not commit our ground troops to fight in French Indo-

China." The Everett speech also suggested the employment of non-Europeans to represent us in this theatre, and "especially some people of colored origin, for the Communist propaganda machine has pictured us in a terrible light" and pointed out that only the Soviet representatives "have come down to the level of the people there."[96]

At a time of containment as the sine qua non of meeting the spread of the "international Communist conspiracy," Jack Kennedy was evolving into a spokesman for a more sophisticated view. He was beginning to call attention to the soft spots of the Western cause, to the frustration of a region that had long contended with colonial domination. He told the Boston Chamber of Commerce that he opposed unlimited economic assistance to foreign nations and attacked British and French colonialism. That brought criticism by the *Traveler,* which charged that Kennedy was jeopardizing "a close alliance with these two largest democracies." The congressman retorted by pointing to the dangers of allying ourselves too closely with their imperialist policies and cited American support of British oil rights in Iran as an example of needless alienation of the Arab world, which made the *Traveler* backtrack somewhat by conceding that "Mr. Kennedy is doing a service in prodding our conscience."[97] Much later, referring to their Far Eastern trip, Bobby Kennedy recalled that Jack had returned with an impression that had indeed been "very very major." He was especially concerned about what the United States was "going to do in our relationship" with all those other countries.[98]

The expedition to the Far East enabled Jack to make another important discovery. By all accounts, it marked the first substantial creation of a bond with his brother Robert. Bobby had followed his post-Harvard journalistic stint with a legal education at the University of Virginia. While still a student, he married the sixth child of a self-made millionaire, one whose fortune came from the Great Lakes Carbon Corporation. Independently endowed, Ethel Skakel lived with her parents in a lavish Greenwich, Connecticut, mansion. With all the athletic attributes expected from one of her class with its appropriate preparation for society, she also had energy and zest for fun. Her marriage to Bobby was among the more successful unions made by the children of Joe Kennedy; clearly, the happiest enjoyed by any of his sons.

It also emphasized Jack's bachelorhood, a status of freedom that the congressman continued to find among the most rewarding aspects of Washington life. When the two brothers and Pat took that Far Eastern trip, then, Bobby already had a child named Kathleen Hartington and had graduated from law school, thereby becoming the first Kennedy to enter the legal profession. Nevertheless, those closest to him saw little evidence that his brother's marriage, which took place in June 1950, created much incentive for Jack to become a family man. But he had already reached the age of thirty-four and given the realities of American politics, having a wife was a necessary prerequisite for anyone bold enough to aim for the White House.

13

To the Senate

The only unresolved question about Jack's House career was exactly how he would escape. In retrospect, there was some regret that he had not chosen to take on Saltonstall in 1948. An unknown had run a relatively strong race against the incumbent and, in that year of Democratic surprises, Paul Dever had actually won the governorship. A statewide attempt may have succeeded, after all. In 1950, with the gubernatorial term still only two years in the Commonwealth, Dever was a shoo-in for another term, so the job was his. Kennedy, meanwhile, had a nominal opponent, an obscure Republican lawyer named Vincent J. Celeste, who was defeated without much effort. In the Eleventh, Jack ran ahead of the statewide ticket, outpolling the governor. As the 1952 election became more imminent, much depended on whether Dever would decide for a third term or would risk taking on Senator Henry Cabot Lodge, Jr. Jack would have to wait and see.

In his mind the preference was clear. Nobody around him had any doubt that he was aiming for the Senate.[1] Sister Eunice has agreed that as early as 1951 her father kept urging Jack to run, assuring him he would "knock Lodge's block off," and she wrote that "Jack made that decision with Dad's help, after Dad had thought and questioned and planned for two years."[2]

Arthur Krock's *Memoirs* claim that young Kennedy's move "to the Senate was inevitable in the pursuit of the ambition that Kennedy's father conceived before the future President had."[3] One iconoclastic account stressed Jack's cynical expediencies, lack of intellectual convictions, ruthless drives toward power, and, most prominently, the political manipulations and ambitions of Joe Kennedy.[4] While much of this contains ample factual support, the effort to depict Jack Kennedy as a sort of "Manchurian candidate" fails to understand the inner aspirations of the second son, and such portraits remain unabashed polemics.

In reality, as with the initial decision to enter politics, ambitions coincided. For one, Jack was stultified in the House. At the same time, health continued to figure in any long-range vision of the future. Talk about reaching the presidency was part pride, part bravado, and part an unwillingness to accept the truth about his physical condition. As a Kennedy, of course, another compelling factor was an ingrained self-expectation. Together, all the forces exceeded whatever satisfaction was possible by indefinite relegation to lower echelons of Washington power caused by the restrictions of a rigid seniority system. Neither was there much joy in catering to the constituents of the Eleventh. Therefore, not for a moment did he doubt the destiny preordaincd for the son of Joseph P. Kennedy. Nor is there much evidence that Addison's Disease stymied his drive. It may have exacerbated his streak of fatalism, but rather than sap expectations, such impediments posed additional challenges—to defeat the pain, defy the odds, and, with it all, survive to fulfill expectations. As Jacqueline discovered early in their relationship, only reaching the top would make for satisfaction.

Obtaining a Senate seat was, therefore, a logical stepping-stone. It would give him more of a national platform, better credentials for dealing with foreign affairs. While relocating would not obviate the frustrations of the seniority system, it would open a possible route to the presidency, historically an uncertain path, one largely reserved for those like Truman who had become vice-presidents and gone ahead by accident. In the twentieth century only one other man had advanced via the Senate and he had emerged from the peculiar circumstances within the Republican Party that produced a Harding. Such precedents favored going after the governorship.

But that course had its own pitfalls. For one, Dever, another Irish Catholic, was in his second term, had been reelected comfortably in

1950, and was still popular. Although Kennedy advance men calculated that Jack could easily defeat the governor in a primary while his odds were only fifty-fifty in a fight to defeat Lodge, risking an internecine bloodbath simply made no sense. Even more decisive was Kennedy's own lack of zeal for the State House, and not a shred of evidence suggests that Kennedy wanted Dever to step down. More weight must be given to Jack's desire to have the governor run for a third two-year term and leave open the Senate nomination. If Dever did opt to go to Washington, Kennedy might not have much choice: either confront the governor head to head or settle for the State House atop Beacon Hill. For a Kennedy, however, the most intolerable circumstance would be to leave the future to the mercy of another politician's decision.

The pending expiration of Henry Cabot Lodge's Senate term offered the most attractive opportunity. Kennedy had already seen Nixon make the climb in California, and his good friend George Smathers now sat in the Senate after a nasty campaign against Florida's ultra-liberal Claude Pepper. Not unreasonably, Smathers felt that his own success gave Jack additional incentives.[5] Only one thing was certain: Kennedy would make some kind of statewide race, a contingency for which the Kennedy forces had begun to prepare at least a year and a half in advance.[6]

Kennedy had already mastered the fundamental lesson handed down via Joe Kane, Honey Fitz, Morrissey, and the whole retinue of pols, both old and young. The effective development of a loyal cadre required granting at least the appearance of power, the identification with the decision-making process, the flattering impression that they were helping plot the candidate's course. Several meetings helped sound out the inner circle about the wisest choice of office. Ed Berube recalled a session in Mark Dalton's law office that included Ken O'Donnell and Larry O'Brien. Each was asked whether Kennedy should run for the Senate or the governorship. Berube placed himself in the minority by suggesting the Senate. "Being new in politics," he said, "I had no idea what was behind their mind because, evidently, some thought because of the patronage."[7] At a Ritz-Carlton Hotel meeting, remembered Frank Dobie, "Quite a few of us wanted him to run for governor figuring that . . . Governor Dever . . . was going to step down. But no, he had made up his mind."[8]

First, though, there was the Dever problem. The governor was either sincerely tempted to tackle Lodge or was playing his own shrewd game. No matter what, Kennedy was not going to permit him to stand in his way. The *Political Times,* running its usual handouts from the various camps, carried the assurance there "will be no conflict of objectives" between Kennedy and Dever.[9] At the start of April the *Globe* reported that Dever was planning to run for another term but would withhold any announcement until he conferred with Kennedy.[10] Meanwhile, Kennedy aides Mark Dalton and Joe Healy worked on a statement announcing Jack's candidacy. Their draft was checked out with the Ambassador and, by telephone, with Jim Landis and Arthur Krock, who offered minor suggestions. "There was some discussion with them back and forth, but by and large they thought that the statement was a fair one," recalled Dalton.[11] They were ready to go with it pending the confirmation of Dever's decision. First, the governor had to meet with Kennedy.

Richard J. Whalen, the Ambassador's skillful biographer, has explained that Dever was discouraged by the prospects of competing against Lodge. The senator's "aura of aristocracy" could be better matched by someone like Kennedy, who could confront him as a "self-confident equal."[12] While Whalen's judgment has merit, the governor did not suddenly wake up to that realization. The details of the Kennedy-Dever meeting are unknown but the substance may be surmised. Mark Dalton, then managing Jack's incipient campaign, has simply said that the session was "extremely important."[13]

Dever undoubtedly let Kennedy know that running for the Senate remained one of his options. That would force the younger man toward the State House. His other choice had to be the equally undesirable one of competing with Dever for the Senate nomination, which, in addition to the potential political ramifications, would be a costly preliminary to a difficult campaign against Lodge. Kennedy must have explained that Dever could simplify matters by going for a third term in the State House and, if he made that choice, he would have the advantages of Kennedy financial and organizational assistance.

Subsequently, both the Kennedy and Dever fund-raising functions were placed in the hands of State Senator John E. Powers. Powers had filled that function for Kennedy in 1946 and later managed Paul Dever's 1948 and 1950 campaigns in Suffolk County. He also chaired a joint Dever-Kennedy registration committee designed to produce a greater turnout in the all-important city of Boston for the November election.[14] The truth about direct Kennedy financial contributions to the Dever campaign will probably never be known. What is clear is the acceptance of a pooling of certain expenses, staff, and headquarters, all of which must have been considered during that "extremely important" meeting.[15]

With considerable resources behind him, Kennedy had negotiated his way through some of the labyrinth of the state's Democratic politics. Only Lodge remained as an obstacle.

On the afternoon of Sunday, April 6, the telephone rang in Larry O'Brien's Springfield home. O'Brien had worked for Massachusetts Representative Foster Furcolo. Now, at Jack's request, O'Brien had joined the Kennedy camp. At the other end of the line was the voice of an excited Jack Kennedy saying, "I've just talked to Dever. He's running for governor again. Here we go, Larry—we've got the race we want!"[16] That evening Kennedy made the formal announcement challenging Lodge. "Other states have vigorous leaders in the United States Senate," he read from the prepared statement, "to defend the interests and principles of their citizens—men who have definite goals based on constructive principles and who move toward these goals unswervingly. Massachusetts has need for such leadership."[17]

The distant *Miami Herald* warned that "Lodge would do well not to underestimate Kennedy's vote-getting powers."[18]

Temptations have prompted some to pronounce the 1952 campaign a replay of Jack Kennedy's primary election in 1946. Such comparisons are understandable: the fortitude of a candidate pushing himself despite severe physical limitations and pain; the character of a "lace curtain" Irishman contending for office as one very different in style and tone from the Gaelic pols more familiar to Massachusetts politics; the perfection of the tea receptions sponsored by the Kennedy women and inundated by hundreds and sometimes thousands of females of all ages eager to shake hands with the candidate; the smooth-functioning Kennedy machinery, supplied with ample financing, flooding the scene with billboards, posters, reprints of the much-circulated "Survival" article with its reminder of South Pacific heroics; and the almost surreptitious role of Ambassador Kennedy and his agents, the public relations men—the influence over important segments of the press, calling every move and directing the fulfilling of the commandment to fight for victory.

With much justification it can be said that the 1946 primary was really a warm-up for 1952, a gathering of experience and perfecting of expertise. But there were differences. Instead of merely contending against factionalized Democrats for the right to represent the Eleventh District, he was competing in the entire Commonwealth. Instead of the Mike Nevilles, John Cotters, and two fellows named Russo, he was up against an incumbent senator, also a war veteran, also the grandson of a Massachusetts politician—Henry Cabot Lodge, the chief opponent of Woodrow Wilson's plan for America's participation in the League of Nations. Instead of trying to rival fellow Irish Catholics for constituents who were mostly coreligionists, Kennedy was taking on one who epitomized old Yankee society, the last best hope of preserving the Commonwealth from the domination of the "newcomers" or "papists," as that nineteenth-century New England historian Francis Parkman and other proper Brahmins so freely called them.

Much of the country watched. *The New York Times Magazine* ran a feature story by Cabell Phillips called "Case History of a Senate Race." Lodge was almost archetypical of the cultured, well-born, and well-to-do New Englander, Phillips told his readers, while Kennedy's Irish Catholicism was strictly of the "lace curtain" variety.[19] The second campaign, then, was merely the logical fruition of the promise exhibited by the first, the "golden boy" qualities of Joe Junior now personified by John F. Kennedy.

The analogy works, but with limitations. Jack was also six years older. Much of his time was still spent on crutches. Addison's was being treated and, thanks to cortisone, reasonably contained. He had seen more of the world, read more widely, and was beginning to question quite seriously the fundamentalism of his father's domestic and international outlook.

As he began to prepare for the battle with Lodge, the old team brought in by Joe Kennedy was still largely intact. Jim Landis was a key figure. "Mother" Galvin was still getting out publicity, and Mark Dalton was the designated manager. Frank Morrissey, the Ambassador's "eyes and ears" during that first campaign, was also still around. The stocky Kennedy loyalist and manager of the congressman's Boston office filled another function. Whenever Jack arrived at Logan airport on Thursday evenings, Morrissey awaited him so they could begin another hectic weekend of driving from point to point throughout the state. Another worker, Bob Morey, did most of the driving. In the backseat with Morrissey and a pair of crutches also sat Dave Powers, the handy all-purpose aide and friend invaluable for keeping the mood high with bright Irish stories. The presence of such Kennedy veterans justified attempting to compare the two campaigns. They also continued to provide evidence of Joe Kennedy's hand.

If anything, the father's involvement in the second fight was greater than in the first. The stakes were higher. The odds against winning were much longer. Never far from his consciousness was the symbolic meaning of a Kennedy-Lodge fight. Although he had made a financial contribution to Lodge's campaign against Joe Casey in 1942, after the pathetic attempt to revive Honey Fitz's political career, that had been a last-ditch effort to stop Roosevelt's man. Now his son was up against the Massachusetts Yankee establishment, the power structure that had "forced" Joe Kennedy to leave Brookline for New York in 1926. As much as he plotted and directed and manipulated for Jack, his own pride was at stake. "For the Kennedys," the Ambassador once said to Krock, "it's the castle or the outhouse. Nothing in between."[20] Two months before the election he wrote to Lord Beaverbrook, "You know me well enough to know that we wouldn't be in it if we weren't going to win."[21] Whether the subsequent victory was twenty-five or seventy-five percent attributable to the Ambassador's activities and power cannot ever be demonstrated. But Joe Kennedy never threw more of himself into any fight. First, as Mrs. Kennedy later acknowledged, he "took a comfortable apartment located conveniently in central Boston at 81 Beacon Street, and from there he kept a close supervisory eye on everything and did many things to smooth the way for Jack."[22]

Then, in terms of money, talent, manpower, and personal devotion, the Ambassador made a full commitment. The battlefield comprised considerable mileage and regional differences—from the sand dunes of Cape Cod to Berkshire hills and valleys; from the scattering of small industrial cities such as Springfield, Adams, North Adams, Pittsfield, Chicopee, Holyoke, and Worcester in the interior highlands, to the blue-collar centers of Brockton, Taunton, Fall River, and New Bedford that lay between the coast and the Rhode Island border. Throughout the Commonwealth, French-Canadians, Portuguese, Poles, Irish, and Italian workers labored in the textile mills and foundries, producing cotton goods, shoes, machinery, and tools or found employment in the maritime industry. As Joe Kennedy well knew, his son's campaign had to exploit their precarious economic condition together with his party and religious identification while, at the same time, reaching into the more comfortable Protestant and Jewish suburban communities and the predominantly Republican hinterland, the region of prime Lodge strength. So, into that effort, Joe threw managerial manpower and talent.

He mobilized his New York office and whatever other recruits he could get. Jim Landis put aside (never to complete) work on the Ambassador's memoirs and became a strategist and speech-writer, specializing both on the increasingly desperate economic conditions and the opportunities to attract wavering Republican voters. From Park Avenue the

Ambassador also brought in Lynn Johnston, a Kennedy attorney also involved with operating the Merchandise Mart in Chicago. Jack also followed his father's suggestions for contacting people like Tim McInerny, the publisher of a newsletter called *Independent Editorial Services, Ltd.,* which went to editors and executives. McInerny, who had earlier suggested that the congressman promote his attractions among ethnic groups with ties to Eastern Europe by offering the sort of resolution that the national Republican convention later incorporated as its "captive peoples" resolution, discussed other possible talent. The Ambassador was personally high on Ralph Coghlan. Coghlan had been with the *St. Louis Post-Dispatch* and was present with Louis Lyons at that famous "off-the-record" interview, but, unlike his Boston colleague, had not disseminated Joe Kennedy's tactless comments, thus earning his everlasting gratitude. Coghlan had since become the head of Harvard's new Nieman Foundation for journalism. Jack, however, came away from his session with McInerny with less enthusiasm for Coghlan. "I am not completely sure he is exactly what I want," he wrote a few days before his formal entry into the campaign. "I think Shriver would be ideal," Jack added, "if the Mart can spare him, since I am sure he could be most helpful on research, writing speeches, etc., and I think his judgment would be useful. If possible, it would be good to get him as soon as possible. Can the Mart spare him?"[23] Shriver came in; but so did Coghlan, under the Ambassador's personal instructions to work on the formulation of issues and to expedite the promotion of publicity for Jack by using Joe's contacts to make sure that Jack's presence at the party's national convention in Chicago that year not be ignored by the television crews. The Ambassador also enrolled *Boston Globe* financial writer John Harriman and the fiscal management skills of John J. Ford, who ran the Kennedy chain of New England movie theaters. From Beacon Street, the father orchestrated the complex matters to be handled by the writers and contacted others throughout the country for additional advice and assistance. Mornings were often devoted to conferences in the apartment. When father and son were not together, the telephone became their link. "He'd have something on his mind and if he really wasn't sure of himself, Jack would call his father," said Tom Broderick. "His father was very, very helpful in many of his decisions. . . . His father was always available, and he could always get to him."[24]

Capable of easily exploiting any weakness, Joe Kennedy could also, as usual, be hard to take. He publicly humiliated Mark Dalton, denouncing the competence of someone who had worked for Jack since the 1946 campaign, forcing him to leave the staff. Ken O'Donnell viewed the Ambassador as a destructive curmudgeon. "The campaign began as an absolute disaster," O'Donnell recalled, and he argued with Jack that matters could only be straightened out by somebody who could talk up to his father. O'Donnell, a Harvard football teammate and friend of Bobby's, felt he lacked the qualifications to do the job himself. Nor did anyone else have the moxie. Jack, perturbed, finally relented but with anger, because, as O'Donnell pointed out, "nobody likes the bad news of politics," so Bobby was reached by phone in New York and persuaded to take a leave from his Justice Department job so he could try to help organize things in Massachusetts.[25] Joe Kennedy's contribution was clearly not without its price. But Jack Kennedy had little choice. He had to operate within his father's machinery. Furthermore, remembered Larry O'Brien, he was not yet a "natural politician; he was too reserved, too private. To stand at a factory gate and shake hands with the workers was never easy, nor was he ever fully at ease with the old-style political leaders of Massachusetts."[26] "I didn't think he was going to live through the campaign," said an observer who was close to Jack's brother Ted. But the candidate "absolutely had to; he had to show his father."[27] Irwin Ross later wrote that "only a fierce competitiveness allowed him to overcome the psychological handicap of his father's vast success."[28] Nevertheless, there were moments of near collapse. He was usually in pain and feverish.

The strain was evident at the start of the most arduous period, the commencement of the "official," announced portion of the candidacy, after both he and Lodge had declared themselves and it was all out in the open. On the morning of the twentieth, he opened his formal state-wide campaign in western Massachusetts, an area already intensively canvassed during the previous months of preparation with Morrissey. Then he had to move on, to more appearances, to scheduled meetings farther north in the Hoosac Valley factory town of Adams. Watching him that day led a friend from *The Berkshire Eagle* to voice dismay over his obvious weariness. "Good Lord," he told Kennedy, "the election isn't until November and if you don't slow down, you will be foggy and dull as hell."[29] "The only time in my life that I can ever remember having conferences with a man in a bathtub was during that campaign," said Phil Fine, a leading Kennedy contact with the Jewish community. "He would take a bath and sit and soak in the bath. The quietest place in the apartment [at 122 Bowdoin Street] to talk was in the bathtub, while you'd sit down on the closed toilet seat and you'd be able to discuss business there in an effectual manner as opposed to going out in a room and having six people yelling at him."[30] On the road he seldom got a full night's sleep, often depending on the rest he could get from throwing his head back on a backseat pillow, while subsisting on cheeseburgers and malteds. At a Springfield fire station he succumbed to the impulse to demonstrate his agility by sliding down a fire pole from the third floor to the first. When he hit the bottom, he doubled up with pain. The reaggravation of his back made crutches indispensable. But still he tried to keep his agony private, while the managers feared the potency of Kennedy's physical condition as a campaign issue. To explain his absence from his campaign office at 44 Kilby Street, callers were informed he had "suffered a recurrence of an old war injury to his back a few weeks ago," a not-so-subtle re-evocation of sympathy for the war hero.[31] Before entering a hall for a speech, Powers would take his crutches and place them outside the auditorium, unseen by the crowd. He often stood for several hours on receiving lines while in severe pain. Yet there was no other way. He wanted to win. Any reduced effort could have destroyed his political career on the spot.

Sargent Shriver, himself very much involved as a strategist and speechwriter,* caught some of Jack's efforts to reconcile his own individuality with the massive programming. Shriver, looking over what he considered a superb speech prepared by Landis, remembered the following dialogue with Kennedy:

"Well, look, Jack," said Shriver, "but this is a fantastic speech. Look at the way it's structured. The language is excellent. Just give that speech."

But it was one of those instances when the congressman rebelled. "I just can't give that speech," he insisted. "Look, Sarge," he explained, "—we're stuck with my personality. And we have to give the speeches that conform to my personality. That speech would have been great for Franklin Roosevelt. But it's no good for me."[32]

Long before the campaign even began, Joe Kennedy had Landis start gathering data about New England's economic plight. There were the charges to be developed during the campaign that the loss of industries to the South through competition from cheap labor and lower energy costs had been permitted to continue despite the incumbency of two Republican senators, one of whom was now standing for reelection. A

*Eunice Kennedy was also active but not yet married to Shriver.

secondary factor was one the Ambassador could exploit more easily than most. His own connections with New England financial interests, heavily Republican, made it easier for Jack to capitalize on their conclusion that, as Landis later pointed out, Henry Cabot Lodge, Jr., had been unable to do much about the situation or even had little inclination to act.[33]

To such Republicans, as well as to others simply more conservative than their senator, Lodge had another weakness. His opposition to a GOP nomination for Robert A. Taft, motivated partly by a fear of the Ohio conservative's lack of appeal, risked the disaffection of Commonwealth admirers of "Mr. Republican." They watched with dismay as Lodge joined the vanguard of those who worked to convince General Eisenhower to leave the Army so that the party's nomination could go to a staunch internationalist, one whose great personal popularity could also draw a large bipartisan vote. While the general was still at his NATO command outside Paris, Joe Kennedy monitored the situation. From Krock, the Ambassador learned that the general would be amenable, if the circumstances were right. He relayed his information to Jack with the explanation that Ike "would not take the Democratic one [nomination] and Krock therefore feels that nothing can stop him from getting it and that Eisenhower wants a clean sweep all the way down and could not get it on the Democratic side."[34]

When the general, who had appeared to be playing coy, yielded to the importunities of Lodge, together with those from New York Governor Thomas E. Dewey, General Lucius Clay, and several well-placed industrialists and financiers, and finally resigned from the Army and returned to the United States to stop Taft, the Kennedys were in a position to exploit the opportunity. And the die-hard Taftites were ready to display their own loyalty by retaliating against Lodge. One Boston banker and disappointed Republican, T. Walter Taylor, was asked by the Ambassador to form an "Independents for Kennedy" group. Communicating with Taft delegates, he informed them that "something is being done to assure Senator Lodge's defeat. . . . Ambassador Kennedy . . . a very close friend of Senator Taft's, has supported the Senator during the campaign and has spent a large amount of time with the Senator during his campaign, requested me to open and direct a headquarters for his son whom you know is seeking election to the Senate." The operation then opened its headquarters at Boston's Sheraton Plaza Hotel.

Better publicized was the apostasy of newspaper publisher Basil Brewer. Brewer's paper was the New Bedford *Standard-Times*. Circulated widely throughout the populous southeastern quarter of Massachusetts, its viewpoint was distinctively conservative and Republican.

Like so many other businessmen, Brewer was also close to the Ambassador, a relationship that expedited his proximity to the congressman himself.[35] He had also been a precampaign manager for Taft. Inevitably, that brought him into conflict with Lodge's efforts for Eisenhower, so much so that his paper denounced the senator as "a Truman socialistic New Dealer."[36] Even before the Eisenhower forces had succeeded in stopping the Taftites at the party's national convention in Chicago, Brewer's potential value was not overlooked by the Kennedys, father and son. Sending Jack a clipping of the *Boston Herald* of May 7 that reported Brewer's position, Francis X. McCann reminded him that it bore "out the previous thought that he might possibly be a leader of an anti-Lodge Republican group in this state."[37]

Once the Republicans had chosen the general over Taft, Brewer confirmed Kennedy's hopes. At first he publicly denied any involvement or even knowledge of any move to enlist the former Taft clubs behind Kennedy, but soon thereafter his paper, "by special permission of the *Reader's Digest,*" reprinted the Hersey article, creating, in the words of a local historian, an "immediate, if unpublicized, furor centering on editorial motives."[38]

On the twenty-fifth of September, Brewer dispelled all doubts. He called a press conference at the Sheraton Plaza. And there the short, well-dressed, and pleasant-looking Brewer, embellished with a rosette in the lapel of his dark-gray suit and bearing what some thought was a resemblance to Joe Kennedy, adjusted his black-rimmed spectacles as he faced the newsmen with a thick folder of notes and memoranda. He made his major point quickly by denouncing the alliance of Taft and Eisenhower forces occurring in the Commonwealth and throughout the nation. He, for one, would certainly not capitulate to the overtures being made by the presidential candidate to their former intraparty opponents. "Therefore," said the publisher to the assembled reporters, "there need be no further delay in announcing our wholehearted support of Congressman John Kennedy and opposition to Henry Cabot Lodge." Adopting what had become a standard Kennedy campaign response, he took the offensive against the senator's absenteeism while explaining the congressman's as due to "war service-connected illnesses."[39] When the Lodge forces placed a three-column advertisement denigrating Kennedy's voting and absentee record in comparison with the senator's, only the New Bedford *Standard-Times* refused to publish it. Brewer explained that rejection as a publisher's responsibility for the truthfulness of advertising.[40]

If the Brewer move was a coup for the Kennedys, one regarded as "a shattering blow to Lodge's already wobbling campaign," the Ambassador's hand was much more visible in the conversion of another newspaper publisher. The only missing link was direct proof that Joe Kennedy deliberately extended a $500,000 loan to John Fox for the conversion of the *Boston Post* from a pro-Lodge to a pro-Kennedy paper. The entire episode came to light six years later during hearings in Washington on special favors granted by Sherman Adams, the assistant to President Eisenhower, to New England textile manufacturer Bernard Goldfine. Fox admitted that he had "borrowed" the money and said that he had favored Kennedy merely because of opposition to the administration's candidate and a desire to "get the Communists out of the White House." Brewer himself stepped in to minimize embarrassment to the Kennedys by claiming that he had used his own influence to sway the *Post* because of aversion to Lodge politically.[41]

The question was whether the Ambassador had initiated a quid pro quo or whether Fox, desperately short of cash, had made his move as a bait for a loan. Revealing the affair in 1958, when Kennedy power was increasing, certainly inhibited Fox's candor. Besides, after that testimony before Senator Oren Harris's committee, the Ambassador issued a statement that the matter was "a purely commercial transaction—for sixty days only with full collateral at full interest and was fully repaid on time —and was simply one of many commercial transactions in which this office has participated."[42]

The circumstances behind the endorsement encouraged suspicion. Under Fox, who had made a fortune in real estate, oil, and gas, the *Post* became conservative and Republican and, moreover, vehemently anti-Communist. Fox himself, as with many segments of Boston's populace and press, was also a strong backer of Senator Joe McCarthy and a supporter of Taft for the party's presidential nomination. Unlike Brewer, however, he became reconciled to the Eisenhower leadership and also backed Lodge, which he had intended to do when he bought the paper.[43] Unfortunately for Fox, who had prematurely sold bullish Western Union stock to buy the *Post,* the paper was in deep financial trouble.

Robert L. Lee recalled the circumstances of Fox's abrupt switch from Lodge to the congressman. Lee and Maurice Tobin were with the Ambassador when "a telephone call came through, and [the Ambassador] had to leave the apartment to make a visit with Mr. Fox. . . . About an hour afterwards, when Mr. Kennedy returned, he stated that the *Post* within two days would openly endorse Congressman Kennedy for

United States Senator."[44] Jack Kennedy got the dramatic major endorsement and John Fox obtained his half-million-dollar loan.

The Kennedys, of course, continued to deny any connection between the money and the *Post*'s switch. So did Fox. The publisher maintained that, just three weeks before the election, Brewer urged him to abandon Lodge. Fox later explained to Richard Whalen that he planned to stick with Lodge only if Taft or McCarthy asked him to do so within a week. But no such word came, even after a personal telephone call in a vain attempt to reach McCarthy in Seattle. Fox, after preparing an editorial for the paper's morning edition announcing the Kennedy endorsement, then tried to call Jack to break the good news. Failing to reach the candidate himself, he called Joe Kennedy. When the Ambassador suddenly left Lee and Tobin behind in his apartment, it was to meet with the publisher for "a drink and a chat" in the 99 Club, which Fox owned. There, the publisher simply told the father that the paper was about to back his son, which reportedly brought tears to the Ambassador's eyes. "He told me then," Fox said, "that if I needed anything in the world, all I had to do was ask him." Explaining his fiscal straits, the publisher got his money.[45] Many years later, Jack Kennedy privately acknowledged the political motives behind the transaction.[46]

Whether the *Post* or the *Standard-Times,* or any such sources or combination of sources, determined the final election outcome cannot be demonstrated. No doubt the Boston paper's last-minute conversion gained some votes, possibly from unhappy, wavering Republicans. Whatever the reasons, as with the campaign itself, Joe Kennedy's proximity to the center of action was certain—a factor in the delicate matter involving Senator Joe McCarthy.

In 1952 Dwight D. Eisenhower succumbed to McCarthy's tyranny. Campaigning in Wisconsin, Ike caved in to the politic advice that the dairy state, of all places, was not an appropriate spot to deliver a speech praising General George C. Marshall. The Republican presidential candidate's admiration for his military colleague simply had to await a less incendiary locale, one that would not automatically stake out a challenge to the senator who had lumped the former general of the Army and secretary of state with the other American "traitors" who had been the handmaidens of international Communist success. Eisenhower choked on that concession; some members of his entourage almost quit the campaign right then and there; Republicans hoping for a new voice of sanity, wanting to disassociate themselves from the wild junior senator, were disappointed, if not disillusioned. Others took a calmer view, arguing that honoring the very man cited by McCarthy would be a pointed and unnecessary affront if done in the senator's own territory. Opportunities would occur in noncontroversial places. An election had to be won. Eisenhower was convinced. He hadn't resigned from the Army to lose.

Kennedy also had to face the McCarthy dilemma. Ordinarily there would have been no question of such an intrusion into Massachusetts politics. McCarthy had nothing to do with the economy of the Commonwealth and had, in fact, taken no stand one way or another. He was a Republican and Kennedy was a Democrat, and the Republican incumbent had little use for the Wisconsin senator. *Abhorrence* would be a more appropriate word.

Kenneth P. O'Donnell, interviewed shortly before his death, argued that McCarthy was irrelevant as an issue to the vast majority of Massachusetts voters. Even support among the Irish Catholics was less than it seemed.[47] Earlier, O'Donnell had told interviewers that the ties between Joe Kennedy and Joe McCarthy were "exaggerated." Although conceding the probability that the Ambassador had contributed some three thousand dollars to the senator's reelection, O'Donnell, who personally detested McCarthy and did not have much more use for Joe Kennedy, took a charitable view of Jack's father. He thought it understandable that "Joe Kennedy, who had been so assaulted by the press itself—and who had the kind of personality that would react—would think Joe McCarthy was being unduly put upon and come to his assistance." Of Bobby Kennedy's sympathy for the senator, he was quite direct, not thinking that the son's loyalty for his father's views was in the least strange. O'Donnell explained that he "used to tell Bobby what I thought of Joe McCarthy on the telephone, and on the other end there'd be silence. . . . After a while he'd say, 'He isn't that bad, but I agree, you know, but . . .' And he kept defending his pasha."[48]

O'Donnell was not alone among the Kennedyites with an aversion toward McCarthy. Jim Landis, Joe Kennedy's right-hand man, shared the distaste. So did Gardner "Pat" Jackson, but he was an obvious foe. His experience against rightists dated back to the Sacco-Vanzetti case and the New Deal. He had even gone along for a while with Henry Wallace's 1948 Progressive Party campaign, until he, too, became disillusioned with both the candidate and his Communist supporters. He then associated with the anti-Communist liberal ADA. Pat Jackson had been recruited by Jack, not the Ambassador, as a link with Massachusetts liberals; his current association with the CIO made him even more valuable.[49]

But most Kennedyites, with the exception of Gardner, agreed that McCarthy was one issue Jack should avoid. There were simply too many votes to be lost, especially in South Boston.[50] Despite O'Donnell's *ex post facto* attempt to minimize the issue, Father Donald Crosby, who has placed in better perspective the alleged solidarity of American Catholics for McCarthy, has nevertheless made clear that not only were the Commonwealth's 750,000 Irish among the senator's most ardent followers but their numbers included the highest concentration of McCarthyites in the land.[51]

At the same time, Jack had begun to have qualms about his old friend's anti-Communist crusade. Along with discovering other realities about the world through his Far Eastern trip, Kennedy displayed a marked tendency to tone down his former willingness to accept the dubious notion that Communist gains somehow derived from the incompetence or duplicity of Americans. Appearing on a *Meet the Press* broadcast in late 1951, after returning from Asia, he acknowledged that "the stories of communism within the executive branch of the government have more or less died out and I think that determined efforts have been made to rid the executive branch of the government of the communists, and I think it's been done on the whole," which appeared to concede that there was not much left for McCarthy to police.[52]

However, Jack still retained loyalty to his old friend along with sensitivity toward his father's position. At least one occasion evoked Jack's feeling with considerable emotion. On February 9, 1952, he attended a dinner on the Harvard campus commemorating the one hundredth anniversary of the founding of the Spee Club. One of the after-dinner speakers exulted about the spirit of Harvard and lauded the old alma mater for never having produced an Alger Hiss, even though the law school had. But he was even happier, he said, that neither the college nor the law school had turned out a Joe McCarthy. At that point, Jack Kennedy, angered, stood up, interrupted the speaker with force and said, "How dare you couple the name of a great American patriot with that of a traitor!" The room, hitherto noisy, suddenly silenced. A number of people tried to calm things down; but Kennedy's anger was very visible, his demeanor abrupt. He did not leave the dinner right then and there but departed at the end of the dessert rather than waiting for the other speeches. The incident was hushed up but was recalled by one of those present at the occasion—Robert Amory, the brother of writer Cleveland

Amory and a longtime deputy director of the Central Intelligence Agency. To Amory, the incident illustrated Kennedy's ambivalence vis-à-vis McCarthy during that period.[53]

In short, by 1952, whatever his personal regard, Jack Kennedy was among those Americans who felt that assumptions of even rampant, officially tolerated subversion might no longer justify McCarthy's methods. Still, he retained sufficient loyalties that merged with political realities and helped make his political situation almost untenable. When campaigning, he encountered the potent abhorrence of the senator that existed in the Commonwealth's extensive and influential academic community; not only was there widespread Ivy League horror at what had come to be called "McCarthyism," but any man who was at the same time a son of Joseph P. Kennedy and unwilling to denounce a Republican like McCarthy was doubly suspect. In an effort to deal with the problem and placate that group, Kennedy had Pat Jackson and his friends send letters to the professors with assurances that he would be "unremitting in his fight against Communism," but, at the same time, would not tolerate methods that would undermine "the very civil liberties our nation is taking leadership to preserve."[54] Otherwise, he himself would say nothing directly about the senator, also rejecting a request from the Democratic National Committee to oppose McCarthy in a pre-election radio broadcast.

Jack's reluctance to criticize McCarthy exacerbated his problems with the Jewish community. The old ethnic tensions were very much alive, a factor that may account in part for McCarthy's strong attractions in Massachusetts. Jack Kennedy, however, had to contend with the burden of his father's record and his own silence about Joe McCarthy, all of which was as suspect to a still insecure minority as the dominant Yankees had always been to his fellow Irish-Americans. The problem was worsened by his need to oppose Lodge, whose own pro-Israel record was unquestioned and who had the assistance of a Jewish administrative assistant, Maxwell Rabb. Not to have done their best to stoke anti-Kennedy suspicions along such lines would have been expecting too much of the Lodge campaign staff.

Kennedy simply had troubles with the Jewish voters. Once the State Department had released its papers delineating his father's discussions with the Nazis, an enormous amount of suspicion affected the son's candidacy. Not only had the original release been covered by the press, but the ethnic publications took care that the story would not go unnoticed. The *Jewish Weekly Times* of July 21, 1949, placed the Ambassa-

dor's diplomatic relations under the headline GERMAN DOCUMENTS AL-
LEGE KENNEDY HELD ANTI-SEMITIC VIEWS. Word also circulated
through the Jewish communities within such centers as Brookline, Chelsea, Roxbury, and Dorchester that the Ambassador was also Senator
McCarthy's leading financial benefactor.[55]

Compounding candidate Kennedy's problems with that small but potentially influential group of voters was a dispatch from Washington by
Eddie Michelson reporting that Jack Kennedy had introduced a resolution in Congress to reduce appropriations for the new state of Israel.
Michelson, the son of an old Jewish family in Pittsfield, whose brother
was also a newspaperman, had worked for the *St. Louis Post-Dispatch*
and had been a legman for Robert S. Allen after the latter had dissolved
his partnership with Drew Pearson on the "Washington Merry Go-
Round" columns. Now Eddie Michelson's story about Kennedy and
Israel appeared in *The Berkshire Eagle*. While the presentation implied
an anti-Israel position by the congressman, his resolution had actually
involved reducing an overall $175 million from allocations from the Near
and Middle East with Kennedy's subsequent explanation that he was
hesitant about placing money that would never reach the masses in the
hands of despotic rulers. Israel, a democracy, was specifically not a target
for the cut. The *Eagle* subsequently ran a clarification, but the suspicion
had been created.[56]

Jack, therefore, had to be immunized from his father, Joe McCarthy,
and allegations of anti-Israel hostility. The process of winning over the
potential Democratic vote forced a series of meetings, including an off-
the-record session at the Parker House in downtown Boston as early as
February 27, when a breakfast was attended by Kennedy and about
twenty or thirty people, mostly Jewish lawyers and judges. There he
explained the Middle Eastern "misunderstanding" to their satisfaction;
and, as Hirsh Freed remembered, they "went away satisfied of the brilliance and his leadership and of his true devotion to any cause he espoused."[57] More meetings were held with community leaders, including
such prominent local figures as Freed, Phil Fine, and Dewey Stone. Some
met with the Ambassador himself and heard his critique of the accuracy
of what the German ambassador to Great Britain had actually informed
Berlin and how his own diplomatic role, given the sensitivity of the
situation, could easily have been distorted. The corps of Jewish leaders
behind Kennedy established a Friends Committee that enrolled a statewide list of contributors. They inundated Jewish committees showing a
propaganda film from Israel, employing sound trucks with recordings

urging pedestrians to "hear John Kennedy on Israel," and introducing every conceivable Jewish member of Congress, in addition to Franklin D. Roosevelt, Jr. Especially effective was their own local pol, Minority Leader John McCormack, so widely trusted by that community that he was known as "Rabbi John," partly because he supposedly secured the first West Point admission for a Jewish candidate.[58] Acting at the Ambassador's request, McCormack gathered several hundred Jewish civic leaders. Facing the dinner guests, the veteran politician was at his best. Foster Furcolo, who was also present, remembered that McCormack, despite having been spurned by Kennedy earlier over the Curley petition, told them, "I want to tell you why you should all be for Jack Kennedy. He put his life right on the line for Israel and the Jewish people. I'll tell you about it. There was a bill to give Israel a hundred-million-dollar cut. They were going to eliminate the hundred million dollars. I went to Jack Kennedy."

Then, with his audience listening intently to their trusted Washington representative, he continued. " 'Jack,' " McCormack quoted himself, " 'we've got to save Israel.' He said, 'Are you willing to put your political life on the line for Israel?' I said, 'Yes, John, I am.' 'Then I want you to offer an amendment,' " he said Kennedy told him. " 'If you cut this by fifty million dollars then you can get the fifty million dollars for Israel.' " Jack Kennedy, McCormack declared emphatically, "put his political life on the line for Israel."

When it was over, McCormack asked Furcolo: "Well, what do you think?"

"I'm a little sick to my stomach," said the other congressman.

"Well, I know," said McCormack. "But you've got to go through for a Democrat."[59] McCormack's nephew, Edward, explained that "there was always the question of accuracy of the Speaker [sic] reporting of what happened, but in any event this was considered by the leaders of the Jewish community to be adequate."[60]

When the Friends Committee sponsored a midsummer dinner for Kennedy at the Boston Club, Kennedy faced the state's most ardent enemies of McCarthy and, mentioning him by name for the first and only time during the campaign, limited his criticism of the senator to economic issues. Perceiving their continued skepticism about his credentials as a Democrat seeking votes from those worried about the status of civil liberties and McCarthyism, he finally asked: "What more do you want? Remember, I'm running for the Senate, not my father," which evoked a spontaneous and warm round of applause.[61] Phil Fine, who along with

Dewey Stone had helped to introduce the candidate, recalled, "Before the meeting was over that night, every person in that hall had voluntarily come over and said they wanted to work for him. And they did work for him." Fine also pointed out that "what John Kennedy had to do in the Jewish community during this time was to prove that he was an entity and an individual with a mind and a character of his own as opposed to that which might have been attributed to him by his father or by other people."[62]

The candidate's declarations of independence paralleled the Ambassador's efforts to insulate him from the controversies posed by the McCarthy question. A possible visit to Massachusetts by the Wisconsin senator, probably at the behest of national committee concern for the survival of an embattled Republican incumbent, could potentially sway significant numbers of Democrats behind Lodge. At least that was the contemporary wisdom, carrying the assumption of McCarthy's potency. That would have had the effect of forcing Kennedy either to openly compete for that vote and upsetting his liberal supporters or suffer the consequences of Lodge's windfall. Defenders of Kennedy's desire to remain aloof would long be convinced of the wisdom of such strategy, holding that despite the contrary experience of Brien McMahon and Bill Benton of Connecticut, such boldness could have killed Jack's career on the spot.[63] Westbrook Pegler, the conservative newspaper columnist and friend of both the Ambassador and McCarthy, later wrote that "Joe Kennedy asked me to persuade McCarthy to keep out of Massachusetts." That, Pegler declared, was the logical "payoff" for the Kennedy beneficence and he then added, "I told McCarthy to let Lodge croak and foolishly ventured that Jack Kennedy, though a Democrat, was at heart a fine American."[64]

McCarthy did not involve himself in the campaign. Two years before Pegler's revelations in the Hearst papers, Jack Kennedy wrote to him denying that his father had "diligently sought" assistance from McCarthy for his election and that there had been cooperation. "My father at no time asked Senator McCarthy for any assistance," Jack Kennedy asserted to Pegler, nor was anyone else authorized to render it for him. On the contrary, Lodge had made his own decision that a McCarthy visit and endorsement "might cost him more votes than it would gain him. Whether Senator McCarthy would have accepted such an invitation, had it been offered, is, of course, not known to any of us."[65]

Whatever may have been conveyed to McCarthy, he *did* offer to campaign. He contacted Lodge saying he was ready to address Massachusetts voters. That was late in the campaign, during the final two weeks; in other words, long after any request had been transmitted from the Ambassador. But McCarthy made one stipulation: he would not attack Kennedy directly. Lodge pondered the offer for a while. Then, as he later recalled, "I sent back word that if he wanted to come in and attack my opponent that would be one thing, but I knew he didn't want to do that and I certainly didn't want him coming in just on the basis of defending me."[66] The only certainty was that Kennedy was one of the rare Democrats immune from a McCarthy attack.

Before Stevenson's planned visit to canvass Massachusetts, the Ambassador warned the presidential candidate against attacking McCarthy while in the Commonwealth.[67] Joe Kennedy was surprisingly close to the Stevenson cause, having already generated considerable enthusiasm over his chances of beating Eisenhower. Stevenson's appointee as national chairman, Steve Mitchell, said that Kennedy Senior contributed at least twenty-five thousand dollars.[68]

There was, however, something more important than McCarthy, more durable, less controversial, and much safer politically: the fear of communism itself. Just before Stevenson's first swing through the state, Sargent Shriver forwarded a four-page memorandum advising of some potent ammunition that could help Jack's chances. Shriver urged Stevenson to remind voters that Kennedy and not Nixon had been first in exposing Communists in the labor movement, that although Nixon sat on the committee with Kennedy, Jack "was the man . . . that got Christoffel—it was not Nixon. It set a pattern." Shriver explained to Stevenson that "up there this anti-Communist business is a good thing to emphasize."[69]

Stevenson visited Springfield two days after Shriver's memorandum. He began to speak on a platform before some eight thousand gathered in the street in front of the City Hall and had just begun to mention Kennedy with the statement that "John Kennedy is my type of guy," adding, "I wonder how many of you know that it was Congressman Kennedy and not Senator Nixon who got the first citation of a Communist for perjury," when a sudden torrential downpour and windstorm broke up the rally. Once they reassembled indoors, Stevenson immediately resumed his point. "I'm afraid that Congressman Kennedy was almost washed out of my speech out there." They laughed and Stevenson glowed. "I just wanted to add to what I had to say about him that I wonder how many of you know that it was Congressman Kennedy who got the first citation of a Communist for perjury. And that was Christoffel, the labor leader, who held up the Allis-Chalmers plant for so long in Milwaukee. What is more, he was convicted."[70]

When Pat Jackson attempted to get the Kennedy people to criticize McCarthy, he collided directly with the Ambassador's iron will. Jackson had prepared a newspaper ad containing statements by ninety-nine Notre Dame faculty members under the following heading: COMMUNISM AND MCCARTHY: BOTH WRONG. There it was, the prototype of the kind of approach anyone would dare to use when attacking McCarthy, a defensive statement asserting the critic's own vehement anticommunism. Showing it to Kennedy, Jackson found the candidate hardly ebullient over the idea. Finally, he agreed to sign it but on one condition: if Congressman McCormack would also add his name. McCormack agreed. Encouraged, Jackson rushed it over to the Bowdoin Street apartment for final clearance.

He found the small quarters jammed. The candidate himself was in his overcoat about to leave. Around a card table at the center of the room, were Joe Kennedy, making a rare appearance at the apartment, together with Jim Landis, John Harriman, and Joe Healy. Before rushing out, Jack asked Jackson to read the statement aloud. He hardly got very far before the Ambassador jumped up so vehemently that he virtually upended the table. "You're trying to ruin Jack," he shouted and, red-faced, raged on that he liked McCarthy and that Jackson's liberal friends, labor unionists, and Jews were out to destroy his son. So intemperate was the Ambassador that Jackson momentarily feared a physical attack. "I can't estimate how long he poured it on me," Jackson said later. "It was just a stream of stuff—always referring to 'you and your sheeny friends'."[71]

The next morning, Jackson met Jack Kennedy in the same apartment. "I hear you really had it yesterday, didn't you?" said Kennedy.

That provoked a discussion about the Ambassador, with Pat Jackson finally asking, "How do you explain your father?"

"My father's one motive that you can understand, Pat, is love of his family," he replied, and then after further reflection added softly, "although sometimes I think it's really pride."[72]

The Jackson incident neither ended the campaign's problems with McCarthy nor McCarthyism. By mid-October, Mallan's article in *The New Republic* with its account of Jack's appearance before Holcombe's seminar was tantalizing and outraging Boston's intellectual community. Meanwhile, Ted Reardon prepared a forty-page exposé demonstrating Lodge's "softness" on communism, his "straddling on the big issue of the guilt or innocence of Owen Lattimore, John Service and Philip Jessup." Another compilation paralleled the Kennedy and Lodge positions and cited Jack's accusatory speeches that blamed the State Department for "failure of our foreign policy in the Far East" and contrasted his record with Lodge, "a 100%" supporter of the administration's foreign policy who "never raised his voice about the conciliatory and appeasing Administration policy in China and the Far East." At the end of October came a Kennedy press release charging Lodge with muffing his chance to do something about communism because of his absences after assignment to the Tydings Committee investigation of McCarthy's charges.[73]

Theodore C. Sorensen, who joined the staff after Kennedy reached the Senate, later quoted Jack Kennedy as having said about McCarthy, "Perhaps we were not as sensitive as some and should have acted earlier."[74] Kennedy, of course, was referring to more than merely the 1952 campaign. The matter would continue to plague him. While his own responsibility could never be absolved, as he climbed politically, he began to discover the price of some of his greatest sources of strength.

The outcome was a great Kennedy triumph, accomplished despite the lack of substantive differences with the incumbent and negating Lodge's own polls that showed he would have a better chance with Eisenhower rather than with Taft heading the party's Massachusetts slate.[75] The senatorial candidates fought over each other's extensive records of absenteeism from Washington. They argued over who could do more for the Commonwealth, which translated into which man could best do something to attract industry and federal money into the state. And they played the ethnic game, with Lodge's own fluent French giving him an edge over Kennedy with the considerable population of Canadian extraction, and his Italian sister-in-law appealing for Italo-American votes. Charles Bartlett remembered Frank Morrissey "telling about how the Italians were going to decorate Henry Cabot Lodge with some kind of special thing, so they decided that they'd better have one for Jack. The man bringing Cabot Lodge's decoration went down on a train from Montreal and they hijacked him off the train so Jack would get his decoration first."[76]

To the voters at large in the general election, despite the apostasy of the Taftites, Lodge's identification with the "above-politics" and "nonpartisan" Eisenhower was another advantage. But when the candidates met head-on in a debate at the South Junior High School in

Waltham before an overflow crowd estimated at three thousand in a 640-seat auditorium, with many forced to depend on loudspeakers so they could listen from the lawn, Kennedy astutely cornered Lodge with an array of assaults. They charged the Republican with being his party's "number one . . . supporter of the Democratic foreign policy" and with responsibility for the GOP's position on price controls, labor, Eisenhower's states' rights attitude toward civil rights and offshore oil, as well as with being the candidate of a divided party that had a midwestern hard core clinging fondly to the belief that there was no anticolonialist revolution in Asia and that our lines of defense still began on the two great oceans. "To claim our successes were bipartisan, our failures Democratic is good politics perhaps but not good sense," said Kennedy in an appeal for crossover votes. Both loud boos and cheers followed his statement that he would work toward repeal of the Taft-Hartley Act.[77] Meanwhile, as the contenders debated, the Ambassador sat in the balcony scribbling notes for two runners to deliver to his son on the platform.[78]

There were also the "teas" made familiar during the earlier campaigns, appearances by Rose Kennedy, then sixty, thin, still vivacious, immaculately dressed, inviting the ladies up to the platform for personal meetings with her son and daughters. "For approximately two hours," reported Cabell Phillips after watching the Commander Hotel reception in Cambridge, "an unbroken line of women filed slowly across the stage, shaking hands with each of the Kennedys, mumbling confused introductions and pleasantries, and pushed on through a side-door into the lobby, still packed with those waiting their turn to go through the receiving line."[79] At one big tea at Fall River, Dave Powers stood at the door with a clicker, counting the women while Jack leaned on his crutches and shook their hands. When his counter reached two thousand, he quit, but the line went on. Some sixty thousand women were estimated to have met the Kennedy women, which included door-to-door visits by the mother and her three daughters. For Jack, they were exploiting the fact that the thirty-five-year-old bachelor's sex appeal had become the talk of the campaign. As powerful as that appeal may have been, the Kennedy charm transcended mere sex. His unsuccessful opponent recalled that he "had a tremendous and well-deserved popularity and he was an extraordinarily likable man. In fact, I liked him. So often in a campaign, you look for a man's faults and then campaign on them. Well, in his case, you didn't do that."[80]

The windup showed Kennedy clearly emerging from his underdog

role. John Fox's *Boston Post,* observing that the Lodge-John F. Kennedy
fight resembled the reversal of their grandfathers' battle for the Senate
thirty-six years ago, also reported a straw poll of Greater Boston showing
both Eisenhower and Jack leading their respective tickets. Kennedy, it
added, seemed especially popular with women voters.[81]

Meanwhile, with the Dever gubernatorial candidacy in trouble, the
Kennedy campaign quietly jettisoned the alliance. "We wished Dever
well," O'Brien has written, "but he was falling behind while we were
pulling ahead; and we didn't want to blow a year of work in the last two
weeks of the campaign."[82] The Kennedy staff, distributing photocopies
of the ballot in preparation for election day, omitted the governor's name
from those given out in places where Dever was weak. "Now, every
candidate is interested primarily in himself," Foster Furcolo said when
discussing the tactic, "but normally what they do is they also take a
position for the Democratic candidates."[83] From the Lodge camp a
desperate, last-minute anti-Kennedy stroke was the flooding of Jewish
districts with a flier that announced: GERMAN DOCUMENTS ALLEGE
KENNEDY HELD ANTI-SEMITIC VIEWS, together with a *Washington Star*
story about the Nazi papers, which brought a successful Kennedy
counterattack that, ironically, denounced the stroke as a "McCarthy"
tactic.[84] Kennedy's campaign ended with a round of appearances
throughout the Greater Boston area, the heartland of the Democratic
vote. There were last-minute rallies in Pemberton Square and he was
cheered on by three thousand others who jammed Symphony Hall that
final night.[85]

Kennedy's confidence that the votes would go his way was only qualified optimism. His comment to Torby Macdonald about "what kind of
a job Eisenhower will give Lodge" probably revealed more whimsy than
arrogance, and his restlessness in the Beacon Street apartment accurately
gauged the uncertainty of the final decision.[86] Not until seven the next
morning did Lodge concede defeat. While Eisenhower's popularity combined with the anti-Truman, anti-Democratic tide to crush Stevenson
statewide, with Christian Herter also edging out Dever, Kennedy won
a narrow seventy thousand plurality over Lodge, or 51.5 percent of the
senatorial ballots. The Lodge camp, acknowledging Jack's personal popularity, explained that their man had been sabotaged by disgruntled
Taftites.[87] But, like the far less formidable Vincent Celeste in 1950, Lodge
lost to a candidate running as a Democrat who had once more defied the
party's national fortunes. As in his election to Congress, Kennedy as a
political force managed to make his party association hardly more than
incidental.

Bobby Kennedy, in an interview with Joan Simpson Burns, surmised that Jack would have lost that fight without the advantage of an independent statewide organization. That was, in fact, one of the prime pieces of Kennedy strategy. In a state with a chaotic conglomeration of factions loosely gathered under the Democratic umbrella, Jack's people established their own machine. Headed by directors known as Kennedy "secretaries" to avoid offending local party chairmen, they numbered some three hundred units. Their strength came from emphasizing the candidate rather than the party and by playing a deft combination of anticommunism and social welfare issues, while at the same time detaching themselves from the controversy over McCarthy.

There were, of course, the enormous advantages made possible by the Ambassador, his influences, contacts, and ability to ladle out pure cash. No actual figures for 1952 would be accurate or very meaningful, but spending was lavish on both sides. The Massachusetts Republican state organization invested over one million on its entire ticket while the Kennedy committees, not counting party fund-raising efforts, reported expenses of just under $350,000. Through additional donations, the Kennedy family gave over seventy thousand dollars. Others suspected that the Kennedy investment came closer to several million dollars, with more conservative estimates favoring a still impressive four or five hundred thousand. Probably the most valid point was made by David Koskoff, who has pointed to the pricelessness of the "organizational talents of Joseph Kennedy, Landis, and the staff from the Joseph P. Kennedy offices."[88]

Equally significant was another development, far more subtle but, in the long run, more germane to John F. Kennedy's very existence as an individual and political figure. The 1952 campaign marked somewhat of a watershed, a transition between the Ambassador's domain, so essential heretofore despite the relatively modest price paid by the son for such services, to Jack's gradual insertion of his own people into the staff. The relatively significant roles of Kane, Morrissey, Landis, Krock, Galvin, and Reardon would begin to fade. Not only such temporary aides as Pat Jackson but other newcomers would essentially be Jack's people. They, like Jackson, had joined at the candidate's behest, wholly free of either the Ambassador's sponsorship or approval. Larry O'Brien's organizational abilities, including the establishment of the suprapartisan system of "Kennedy secretaries," was a key contribution. Ken O'Donnell, having been introduced via Bobby and certainly no sycophant of the Ambassador, helped keep the staff viable at a critical moment and gained considerable experience for future Kennedy plans. But perhaps the most significant personality to arise in 1952 was indeed a member of the family, one who could work with both Jack and Joe Kennedy: young Bobby, whose energy, organizational ability, toughness, and loyalty constituted a major discovery. Finally, only months after the victory, when entering the Senate as a new independent political personality, Jack's entourage was joined by another one of his major choices, Ted Sorensen.

Equally important, Kennedy had successfully manipulated elements of national disenchantment with the administration in Washington: frustration over an increasingly less secure world and apprehensions that setbacks came from internal laxity. A new postwar brand of political leadership was beginning to emerge, with Kennedy in the vanguard. A new-generation Democrat, he was burdened neither by strong partisanship nor identifications with past policies, nor responsibility for having made the world so imperfect.

14

The Senator from New England

The new senator was sworn in on January 3, 1953. Adhering to custom, he was escorted down the aisle by the senior senator from his state, a solidly Yankee Republican with the well-established name of Leverett Saltonstall. Kennedy, amidst his gray-haired seniors, seemed slightly uneasy, somewhat self-conscious. Surreptitiously, he buttoned his coat to tuck away a protruding necktie.

Defeating Lodge had transformed him into a figure of national interest. He was no longer just the Ambassador's son who had used his family's finances to acquire a congressional seat. No—winning this one was something more notable. At a time when Republicans swept into the presidency and took control of Congress, acquiring a majority for only the second time since before the New Deal, his achievement was not easy to dismiss, despite all the prattle about teas, the role of the Kennedy women, and the winner being a rich glamour boy.

Little wonder, then, that his bachelor status became more noticeable on Capitol Hill. In his mid-thirties and still unmarried, he had an obvious attraction for Washington's unattached females. He dated a great many young women, often instructing his personal secretary to line up some beauty to accompany him to the movies, his favorite diversion. That spring *The Saturday Evening Post* helped further his man-about-Washington reputation with an article by Paul F. Healy called "The Senate's Gay Young Bachelor." In Healy's much publicized piece, he was the youthful senator with the "bumper crop of lightly combed brown hair that shoots over his right eyebrow and always makes him look as though he had just stepped out of a shower." He was an informal, casual millionaire who caused women in the galleries to swoon. "Just about the most eligible bachelor in the United States," went dashing around Washington in "his long convertible, hatless and with the car's top down" and was "photographed with a glamour girl in a night club."[1] But the article did not convey the sort of image he wanted. It did not, as Healy himself indicated below the magazine's romantic title, explain his diffidence, the serious, sober, and even withdrawn and intellectual side, which, among his senatorial colleagues, made him somewhat of a loner, an outsider to the established cliques. The piece was irritating, and he resented the playboy connotation.[2]

True, marriage was something Jack Kennedy had carefully avoided. His younger brother Bobby had already taken that step; and, on May 23, just a few months after Jack entered the Senate, Eunice married Sargent Shriver after a prolonged romance. If Jacqueline Bouvier had not entered his life, and if political requisites had been perceived differently, he could have gone on indefinitely as the "Senate's Confirmed Bachelor," sampling as he went along, behaving every bit as much as Harriet Beecher Stowe commented about Aaron Burr: "He never saw a beautiful face and form without a sort of restless desire to experiment upon it and try his power over the inferior inhabitant."[3]

However, on September 12 of the same year he entered the Senate, at St. Mary's Roman Catholic church in Newport, Rhode Island, the Kennedy-Bouvier (or Kennedy-Auchincloss) wedding took place. Gore Vidal has described the marriage as "an 18th century affair: a practical union on both sides."[4] But Vidal was being too acerbic. Although it received lavish attention and the match was later trumpeted as the American equivalent of a royal wedding, the Kennedy-Bouvier courtship had no unusual family sponsorship.

Nor were there significant interfamily frictions. Jacqueline ultimately developed a strong bond with the Ambassador, coming to regard him somewhat as a surrogate father, as a resolution of the conflict precipitated by her own parents' divorce. And the Auchinclosses, as most people, were won over by Jack's personal qualities. "I loved him dearly,"

Janet Auchincloss recalled, "and I think he was terribly fond of my husband and myself." She also denied having opposed Jack in any way.[5] A smooth relationship, and even compatibility, developed between Kennedy and Janet's ex-husband, Jack Bouvier. "They were very much alike," Jacqueline said. "We three had dinner before we were engaged, and they talked about politics and sports and girls—what all red-blooded men like to talk about."[6]

But Kennedy had trepidations during the courtship, doubting that the Auchinclosses were exactly eager to accept him into their estates overlooking Narragansett Bay and the Potomac. Writing to Red Fay, Jack advised that his friend's "special project" would be her mother, "one fine girl—but who has a tendency to think I am not good enough for her daughter."[7] One night, with Ed Berube at the wheel as Jack rode with several close friends toward the Hammersmith Farm estate at Newport, he relaxed by resting his feet atop the dashboard. As the car rushed across the dark and empty roads, he joined in a boisterous rendition of "My Wild Irish Rose," totally indifferent about his inability to carry a tune. Upon entering Newport itself at close to 3 A.M. and nearing the Auchincloss estate, Kennedy thought better about their joviality, suddenly fearing that their voices would filter through open windows. "Let's cut it down," he urged his companions. "I'm not too solid with the family, and they might throw me out."[8]

He was not entirely kidding. Jackie's people were staunch Republicans for whom voting for any Democrat, even Jack Kennedy, would have been heresy.[9] Also his mother-in-law, having married into the social world of Hugh D. Auchincloss, did not necessarily regard the nouveau riche Kennedys as a find. Jack once again, as in his political rise, was conscious of the price as well as the benefits of being the son of Joseph P. Kennedy.

Of more enduring consequence was Jackie's introduction into his close-knit world of noisy politics and masculine horseplay, which involved a band of hangers-on who encouraged the frivolous side of his personality. She found them distasteful, déclassé, corruptive of Jack. She forever suspected that Jack longed to relive his bachelorhood. While dancing with George Smathers one night, Jacqueline whispered into his ear, "I bet you and Jack wish you were back in Italy by yourselves."[10] When Jack went off to France, she suspected he was accompanying his friends to a Parisian rendezvous with a certain "Belgian princess." Conscious of Jack's attraction to women, she questioned the nefarious influence of his old buddies. Nor did she care at all for their political focus, for the inherent obligations, and their perpetual presence. They never seemed to not be around. Politics and promiscuity were all part of the price of being married to John Kennedy.

"I think the best thing I can do is to be a distraction," she told Irwin Ross. "A politician, after all, lives and breathes politics all day long. If he comes home to more table-thumping how can the poor fellow ever relax?"[11] But when compounded by their conflicting attitude toward spending money and emotional stress, Jackie's disdain for the political world made for future problems.

Once Kennedy's campaigning ended, their courtship proceeded swiftly. They were together as the senator escorted Miss Bouvier to President Eisenhower's inaugural ball. She, in turn, helped to stimulate his interest by finding excuses for visits to his office as the *Times-Herald*'s inquiring photographer. She even managed to include him as the subject of an interview when, on April 21, 1953, her column quoted his whimsical observation that "I've often thought that the country might be better off if we Senators and Pages traded jobs." Her secretary suspected that Lee Bouvier's marriage to Michael Canfield that spring helped inspire Jackie's desire for a domestic life.[12] Kennedy's own attentions were captured and their relationship assumed far more than a casual interest. They began to exchange gifts; he by giving her books. "He's not the candy-and-flowers type," she explained. So, while she received such works as Marquis James's *The Raven* and John Buchan's *Pilgrim's Way*, she reciprocated by presenting him with two books she had written for him and illustrated with her own sketches.[13] Clearly, the young woman who had confided to a cousin her disinterest in Kennedy because he seemed too quixotic by telling her that he "intended to become President" was beginning to overcome her hesitations.

Much of the subsequent wooing took place across the transatlantic telephone cables. In May, assigned by her newspaper to cover the coronation of Queen Elizabeth II, she went to London. Communications, however, continued between the British capital, Washington, and Hyannis Port. One of them contained Kennedy's marriage proposal, which Jackie accepted when she returned. Friends were then told about their engagement but only under a promise of secrecy to safeguard the veracity of Paul Healy's pending *Saturday Evening Post* article. The official announcement came on June 25. Jackie meanwhile quit her job to prepare for the coming event. After the adjournment of the first session of the Eighty-third Congress, Kennedy left in August for a sailing vacation with Torby off the French coast, returning to Hyannis Port near the end of the month. That brought him back in time for a mammoth bachelor dinner at Boston's Parker House. Red Fay subsequently recalled the gathering of some 350 who honored Jack that evening, noting his surprise at discovering that the guests included a wide assortment of the local social structure. Among those Jack personally dropped off at their homes when the evening was over were a factory worker, a man who ran a laundry, and Ed Berube, the bus driver.[14]

The wedding itself had the aura of a royal affair, one differentiated from routine Newport social events by the presence, both actually and vicariously, of privileged commoners. While mass attention is not unusual for elaborate weddings at the established summer resort, that element was magnified by the festivities for the freshman senator and the stepdaughter of the master of Hammersmith Farm. For the two to three thousand who crowded around St. Mary's under bright sunshine, it was as though they had been included among the guests to occupy one of the 550 seats.

Inside, it was another matter. Heralded by *The Boston Globe* as "one of the most notable weddings in this old and fashionable resort," all traditional formalities of class, faith, and tradition were observed. Archbishop Cushing performed the ceremony and read to the couple a blessing that had been sent from Pope Pius XII himself. The fifteen ushers included Kennedy's old friends, both in and out of Congress, such as George Smathers, Red Fay, Torby Macdonald, and Lem Billings. Bobby Kennedy was the best man, while Jacqueline's sister, Lee Bouvier Canfield, served as matron of honor. Seated before them was a wide array of financial and social luminaries, industrialists and business tycoons such as Robert Young, the Gimbels, the Vanderbilts, ambassadors, and such other notables as Marion Davies, as well as Jack's political friends from New England. There was also a large congressional delegation, ranging all the way from Speaker Joe Martin to Kennedy's successor from the Eleventh District, Thomas P. "Tip" O'Neill. When Jack and Bobby came down the aisle to take their places at the altar, they appeared, in words of one observer, "too tanned and handsome to be believed." Those who looked more closely noticed a number of long red scratches on the groom's face, the result of a headlong plunge into a briar patch during the previous day's touch-football game.

For most guests however, the bridal procession was the high point. Tall and elegant, Jacqueline wore cream taffeta with a tight-fitting bodice and full skirt. Her grandmother's yellow lace veil fell away from a tiara of orange blossoms. Jackie walked down the aisle, not on the arm of her father, who had rehearsed the ritual the day before, but with stepfather Hugh-die. The papers later explained that John Bouvier had become "ill" and so Janet's second husband had taken over. For Bouvier, however, the event had created a crescendo borne from his personal crises and the humiliation of enduring an Auchincloss-staged wedding for his daughter. In his misery, he had passed out drunk at the Viking Hotel.[15]

The reception afterward followed Newport's best traditions. The twelve hundred Social Registerites, politicos, and other friends spent three hours being entertained by the Meyer Davis society band on the lawn of the Hammersmith Farm. Just below Jacqueline's third-floor bedroom, a great striped tent sheltered the tables set up for the luncheon. For two hours the bride and groom stood in the receiving line greeting the guests. Within easy view, Black Angus cattle grazed on the slopes. Most of the dancing was done by the socialites, while the spectators represented the political world.

That was not the only division. In preparing toasts for the event, Joe Kennedy, asked whether he viewed the occasion as a contest between the two families, replied firmly, "We don't want the Auchincloss side in any way to outshine our boy."[16] An aunt of Jackie's vouched for Bouvier dignity versus the other side's gaucheries. "The whole Kennedy clan is unperturbed by publicity. We feel differently about it. Their clan is totally united; ours is not."[17] Meanwhile, the most undignified scene was being resolved in the privacy of the Viking, as the loser quietly packed his suitcase and checked out to return to Park Avenue.

Then, not wasting any time themselves, Mr. and Mrs. John F. Kennedy left Hammersmith Farm for the flight to New York, where they spent the night at the Waldorf-Astoria. Another plane flew them to Acapulco, Mexico. One of Jacqueline's first acts at the honeymoon villa above the Pacific was to send a letter of forgiveness to her father.[18]

By that time, Jack Kennedy had completed another sort of marriage. Two weeks after his swearing-in in January, he took on a new legislative assistant, Theodore C. Sorensen. At twenty-four the tall, intense intellectual with horn-rimmed glasses, looking like an eager but insecure graduate student ready to serve his sponsor, had few illusions. Contemplating joining the staff of the new senator from Massachusetts brought the warning from a fellow lawyer that Kennedy would not hire anyone without the Ambassador's approval, "and, with the exception of Jim Landis, Joe Kennedy hasn't hired a non-Catholic in fifty years!"[19] Furthermore, Sorensen ventured into a world far from his liberal and progressive background. The Jack Kennedy who had referred to a Wisconsin delegate at the party's 1952 national convention as one of "you northern liberals" was still known for his father, his success over Lodge, and for little else.[20] Sorensen recalled that Kennedy's "political philosophy was unformed" and he thought the freshman Senator "needed an education." A far more experienced Washington observer, columnist Drew Pearson, lunched with Kennedy at just about the time Sorensen first met him, and came away perplexed. And commenting on what he regarded as Jack's arrogance, Pearson recorded in his diary that he "has the makings of a first-class Senator or a first-class fascist—probably depending on whether the right kind of people take the trouble to surround him. There was a time when I didn't quite understand why F.D.R. broke with Joe Kennedy. But the more I see of Jack, the more I can understand it."[21]

Ted Sorensen had much of that same haughtiness and zeal for action. Efforts at additional comparisons run dry. He was not born to the ruling class. He was from a different universe, connected with neither the world of Ambassador Kennedy nor the parochialism of Massachusetts politics. He regarded politics as a means of accomplishing ideological goals and his remark about being "personally convinced that the liberal who is rationally committed is more reliable than the liberal who is emotionally committed" stated his position perfectly.[22] It also made possible a career with Jack Kennedy.

But the two could never become companions. The wide age gap was significant at that stage of their lives, of course. Also, Sorensen had no power or inherent potential for obtaining much on his own. He lacked the money and the personal flair that Kennedy had worked so hard to master. He had a better sense of humor than people suspected, but, unlike the senator, kept it in reserve and struck most associates as dour and austere. Evelyn Lincoln, Kennedy's personal secretary, has written that Sorensen was "a quiet, reserved, quizzical intellectual," a Rock of Gibraltar who was "devoted, loyal, and dedicated to the Senator in every way possible. Time meant nothing to him—he gave it all to the Senator."[23] As Dwight Eisenhower learned about Sherman Adams, Wilson about Colonel House, and FDR about Harry Hopkins, Kennedy needed Sorensen. Sorensen did not have to be liked to be used and appreciated.

Unlike Kennedy, his background was rooted in western progressivism. His mother, Annis Chaikin, descended from a Russian Jewish family. A suffragette and League of Women Voters activist, she studied at the University of Nebraska. Sorensen's father was a progressive Republican with close ties to Senator George Norris. Young Theodore, who, like his brothers, retained his mother's maiden name, went on to the University of Nebraska, where he made Phi Beta Kappa. At the university's law school Sorensen became editor of the law review and was first in his class.[24]

From there he went to Washington, where he became a lawyer with the Federal Security Agency and then worked for eight months on Capitol Hill. The young man Kennedy then interviewed on two separate occasions that January of 1953 was, in addition to having been active in the civil-rights movement to the extent of having helped to found a chapter of CORE in Nebraska, a member of the Americans for Democratic Action and a subscriber to such publications on the left as the New York City paper *PM* and *The New Republic.* Also in his background was a decision that would later plague him when President Jimmy Carter attempted to appoint him as director of the Central Intelligence Agency: he had registered for the draft in 1945 as a noncombatant. Like his mother, he was a pacifist.[25]

The Sorensen who met with the newly elected Senator John F. Kennedy in January of 1953, then, was a committed progressive, a civil-rights activist before such reform became fashionable, and a critic of militarism. He had also published articles on academic freedom in *The Progressive,* and in *The New Republic* a piece called "School Doors Swing Open," a review of the relative ease with which universities in southern and border states had integrated. Sorensen's literary talents constituted major assets for the senator.[26]

Such credentials were quite impressive, especially for one of Sorensen's age. He would also bring to the staff a political dimension hitherto lacking: exposure to and identification with points of view not usually associated with either the Ambassador or his son. From the outset, then, after their first meeting, Kennedy appears to have been more receptive than was the young man, whose progressive qualms continued to nag at him. At the second interview Sorensen asked about Kennedy's positions about his father, Senator McCarthy, and the Catholic Church. "He must have thought I was an odd duck," Sorensen later recalled, "and I don't remember exactly what I asked or exactly what he said." There was, however, mutual satisfaction, although Sorensen heard Kennedy say that he thought "Owen Lattimore* was guilty of indiscretion."[27] Almost

---

*Professor Lattimore of Johns Hopkins University was a State Department consultant who was accused by Senator Joe McCarthy of being "the top Russian espionage agent in this country."

immediately afterward, Kennedy's office informed an American Federation of Labor official in Boston that his new legislative assistant's "chief function . . . will be to work on the legislative program for Massachusetts."[28]

Any questions Sorensen may have had about long-range plans being concocted for the new senator were dispelled by the night of Friday, January 16, the end of his first week on the job. As a legislative assistant, he occupied just one corner of a triad. Room 362 of the Old Senate Office Building was but the Capitol Hill branch of the Kennedy enterprise. Space in the Federal Office Building in Boston took care of the need to provide ready access to constituents. Less well known than those two offices, and normally not placed before the public's view, was the continuing operation at his father's headquarters on Park Avenue in New York City, where such devoted legal talents as Dean James Landis, Lynn Johnston, and Jim Fayne continued to give substantial time to the interests of the Ambassador's son. That first Friday Sorensen found himself in what must have been a somewhat intimidating situation for a novice, and one which simultaneously brought together Senator John Kennedy's three outlets.

For several long hours, Sorensen conferred in Boston with four older and more experienced men; mainly, they had acquired some expertise concerning the economic plight not only of Massachusetts but of New England. One of them, Landis, had gathered data about the unemployment situation, the departure of textile mills and shoe companies, the disadvantageous wages and electrical costs that burdened the region's manufacturers. With them was John Harriman, who had contributed his talents to Kennedy's senatorial campaign, together with Harvard professor Seymour Harris and an economist who worked for the Federal Reserve Bank. Through the long afternoon and evening, Sorensen listened carefully and took notes, and also made certain to record the names of additional people to see.

As Kennedy himself had informed the AFL man only two days earlier, Sorensen's first task involved the formulation of an economic legislative program for Masachusetts. The four men present with Sorensen talked about the economy of the Commonwealth: the high unemployment, which had actually reached one quarter of the labor force in the city of Lawrence during the preceding summer; the disadvantages of local in-

Almost three years before Kennedy's comment to Sorensen, Senate hearings had cleared him of such charges.

dustry trying to compete with low-wage, cheap-energy regions; the problem caused by the Fulbright Amendment to the Walsh-Healy Act of 1936, which enabled southern manufacturers to bring court suits to challenge wage-setting for companies that had government contracts; the need for a retrained labor force capable of attracting new kinds of business to the Commonwealth; the disadvantageous railroad, trucking, and shipping rates, all serving as further depressants to the economy; the plight of the fishing industry, although "no longer one of the prime industries of Massachusetts," one that "still has a great deal of popular and political appeal."[29] But within the circle of Kennedy planners, the vision was ambitious.

It soon became obvious that claiming that the new senator would do more for Massachusetts, as the campaign against Lodge had promised, was an understatement. The Commonwealth's economy could not be separated from the rest of New England. Water resources, labor costs, shipping problems, were all interwoven as the Northeast searched for new ways to supplant recent losses to competing parts of the country, especially the South. Those at that Friday meeting pointed out that efforts should be made to win the support of selective southern states, by showing, for example, that North Carolina was itself being subjected to a similar kind of low-wage and low-cost competition from Alabama and Mississippi. A state like North Carolina, while causing problems for the New England economy, might thereby be weaned away from regional loyalties and induced by common interests to join an alliance with the North. New England itself could be aided by the harnessing of water-power resources to lower the region's energy costs, albeit such efforts had previously been defeated by private power interests that killed a regional plan in the Vermont legislature.

Reporting back to Ambassador Kennedy about the meeting, Landis pointed out that, last "but not least," the discussion visualized "the organization of a New England delegation so that it would become an effective bloc in Congress." To achieve that, added the former dean of Harvard's Law School, required the formulation of "a program of some kind in which both Massachusetts and the New England delegates would have a common interest and they can then be united to form a bloc."[30]

Quite clearly, if Kennedy hoped to move on to higher office, whenever the opportunity might arise, even the first month of his Senate term was not too soon to plan. The most obvious way of expanding from the inherent limitations in representing Massachusetts, then, was to become a specialist in promoting first the economic interests of New England

and, simultaneously, the virtues of interstate cooperation based on recognition of mutual self-interests. The discussion that Friday left no doubt about the importance of Jack Kennedy's achieving a reputation as a senator "who has the entire national interest at heart."[31] Limiting his arguments to the subsidized migration of labor and capital and against cheap, nonunion wage competition, without incorporating the broader appeal, would undoubtedly antagonize the South. As the States Rights Democrats had shown in 1948 and Eisenhower's candidacy had reaffirmed in 1952, the region was no longer "solid" for any Democrat.

Therefore, John Kennedy's first hundred days in the Senate was largely devoted to the preparation of his major move. Sorensen worked with him to coordinate suggestions and to formulate a series of papers for both personal delivery on the Senate floor and transmission to appropriate agencies. The first result was the submission of a statement on February 19 to the Federal Power Commission supporting the development of hydroelectric power on the International Rapids section of the St. Lawrence River.[32]

By mid-March, Sorenson had completed his draft memorandum on proposed legislation to have the federal government clear the way for a Regional Industrial Development Corporation, "presumably," he wrote to Kennedy, "for New England as part of your 'New England Program.'" Their new plan for a Regional Industrial Development Corporation, by providing loans and technical assistance and promoting and retraining of labor and worker mobility, as well as liaison with appropriate federal agencies and attractions for capital investment, "could make an invaluable contribution to the battle for the expansion and diversification of the economies of New England," Sorensen concluded.[33] The work of the young legislative assistant was then scrutinized in New York by Landis, Johnston, and Fayne, and further consultations were suggested.[34]

Finally, all the proposals were in place. On April 23, Kennedy appeared before the Senate Public Works Committee to testify in support of a flood-control plan for the Connecticut River Valley, of which he was one of the co-sponsors. All the usual conditions were present for major Senate speeches, including a nearly empty floor and considerably more attentive spectators in the galleries. As always before such pronouncements, Kennedy's office provided the press, especially New England papers, with advance copies, which constituted a 159-page book that called the message *The Economic Problems of New England: A Program for Congressional Action.* Read during three separate daily sessions, interrupted only occasionally by remarks from colleagues, it synthesized all the work that had been going on in the various Kennedy offices since long before the election. Together, they comprised a detailed analysis of the economic difficulties that had been plaguing New England. The Kennedy message assumed the close involvement of the federal government in the region's recovery. It also dismissed the reservation that such support for regional industrial development corporations would dilute special advantages for New England by providing parity for other areas.

The three messages advanced a program of federal supports that combined regional interests with national considerations. Carefully, Kennedy denied that the circumstances were peculiar to New England. He argued that rather than penalize the South, his proposals would raise its standard of living by stimulating industrialization, improving markets, preventing "unjust discrimination and unfair competition against its industries, and in many other ways to help the economy of that region."[35]

Overall, it was an impressive, comprehensive analysis and call for action, the most significant postwar catalog of regional economic dislocations that illustrated the relationship between the federal government as a cause of such changes and as an essential partner with local action in finding remedies. For a freshman, traditionally expected to be properly passive during his senatorial nonage, the performance was bold. Moreover, whatever the number of hands that had contributed to the message —ranging from Professor Harris to Landis and the Ambassador's crew at the New York office and to Sorensen's talent at soliciting more expertise and providing the literary and thematic structures—impromptu exchanges with colleagues on the floor demonstrated Kennedy's own mastery of the complexities. He had absorbed the findings and advice of the experts and had made the final product his own. As he told Senator Paul Douglas during an exchange on the final day, "one of the basic tasks now in the areas which have gone ahead is not to turn the clock back and thus lower their standards but to attempt, through legislation and through encouragement by contributions from the Federal Government, to bring about a general raising of such standards throughout the Nation."[36] Wayne Morse, the Oregon maverick, became effusive on the opening day, breaking in with the remark that the Massachusetts senator was delivering "from the standpoint of careful analysis and penetrating content . . . one of the most able speeches I have listened to during this session of Congress."[37] And from the South came the voice of Senator Spessard Holland of Florida, who quickly observed the dependence of his own state's tourist trade on northeastern prosperity.[38] The New England papers, major and minor, fell into line with general praise, most devoting flattering editorials to the region's new spokesman. "Senator John F. Kennedy has shown one of the reasons he was able to make such an impression at the polls last year," declared the *Reading* (Mass.) *Chronicle.* "He is an intelligent and earnest young man going about his job in a workmanlike manner."[39]

Kennedy's domestic political responses were tactical, not ideological. For pragmatic economic advice he consulted more and more with Seymour Harris, visiting the professor's home and Cambridge office on several occasions. From Harris he received academic fortification for the political advantages of tariff protectionism to safeguard New England's surviving mills against Japanese and British competition.[40] On the very day John Fox's *Boston Post* ran a front-page editorial accusing Kennedy, among other heresies, of promoting the economic development of different regions while neglecting Massachusetts—under the headline JUNIOR SENATOR-AT-LARGE—he introduced a bill to cushion local industry from competing imports.[41] He argued for the need to assist those "injured by the existing tax structure." Two years later, he testified before the U.S. Tariff Commission on behalf of action to relieve the domestic fishing industry from the "crushing burden" of imports of ground fish, his comments echoing the complaints of industry spokesmen.[42]

During the fall of 1953, Sorensen labored on a manuscript for possible publication by Harvard University Press under Kennedy's by-line. It was hoped that it would embellish Kennedy's identification with New England's economic problems and their relationship to the federal government. The May speeches had comprised the heart of what there was to say on the subject, furnishing material for spin-off speeches and articles. On November 8, *The New York Times Magazine* published, also under Kennedy's name, an article called "What's the Matter in New England?" Substantially Sorensen's work, the article was then carefully scrutinized and revised by the Ambassador, who was assured by Landis that "Jack will read it in the next day or so up in Hyannis."[43] By the end of the year Sorensen confessed that work on the book project had left him "somewhat stale." He could do little to enliven the material. From Palm Beach in December, Kennedy suggested that the manuscript be sent on to Landis to see if he "could not add some sparkle and punch to it."[44]

The book project died, but other pieces dealing with minimum wages and Social Security had already appeared under Kennedy's name in *American Magazine* and *The New Republic.*[45] In February the Kennedy name reached the liberal readers of *The New Republic* with another discussion of Social Security, and *The New York Times Magazine* ran a substantial appeal for greater public involvement in foreign policy.[46] In January *The Atlantic Monthly* ran an article by John F. Kennedy called "New England and the South," a further elaboration of the basic theme. As with so much being turned out, that too resulted from a Sorensen-Landis collaboration and was barely altered by the senator. "Both he and his father liked it very much," Sorensen informed Landis.[47]

The Kennedy literary apparatus was operating with considerable momentum and, showing far more concern than most legislative offices with getting into print, was eager to follow through with more public relations successes. In August, a few days after the appearance of the latest *Times* article, Sorensen wrote a magazine editor that he was "disappointed that we have not seen your smiling face in Washington in many months," and added: "It occurs to me that Senator John Kennedy is past due for another article to boost the circulation of *American Magazine.* Several possible subjects occur to me," he wrote, and listed such ideas as "Are We Gambling with Our Security?" "Must You Retire at 65?" "A City Senator Looks at the Farm Problem," "Lobbyists—Good or Evil?" "What is Happening to Our Fishing Industry?" "What Happens When Unemployment Comes?" and "How Fair Are Our Immigration Laws?"[48] The Kennedy establishment was obviously prepared to fulfill a variety of publication needs. Sorensen was indeed becoming indispensable.

It was Sorensen, the Nebraskan, as he himself noted wryly, who also became the secretary of a formal organization called the New England Senators Conference. Kennedy, working closely with his Republican colleague, Saltonstall, moved to implement bipartisan cooperation by the region's twelve senators. The first in a long series of meetings began with a luncheon conference on March 5, 1954, with the stated aim of considering "the effect on our region's economy of particular proposals before the legislative or executive branches of the federal government, including the . . . effect of proposed unemployment compensation revisions on our region's areas of chronic labor surplus."[49] Acting both within and without the group, Kennedy continued at the forefront of the concerned senators. It was all very elaborate, carefully prepared, and, most of all, excellent promotion for Kennedy as the leader of a New England bloc.[50] To balance charges of provincialism, however, and to safeguard his efforts to be portrayed as a statesman capable of transcending parochial interests, he had already taken a bold step with a major speech to the

Senate on January 14, 1954, supporting the St. Lawrence Seaway project.

Distinguished precedents supplied an appealing setting. John Quincy Adams had outraged New England shipping interests back in 1807 by voting for Jefferson's Embargo Act. Another Massachusetts senator, aging Daniel Webster, championed the Compromise of 1850, also exposing himself to charges of regional betrayal. Voting for the Seaway, then, evidently risked the immediate sort of hostility suffered by Adams and Webster—from the local chambers of commerce, the railroad and shipping interests, the dock workers, all fearful of sacrificing Boston's port for the interests of remote places. The Commonwealth's politicians were naturally in harmony about denouncing the waterway. Kennedy, in his own election to the Senate, had gone along with their wisdom. Yet, he knew that, as with Adams and Webster, there would be ultimate vindication—the triumph of national interest politics over parochialism. One newspaperman, Jack L. Bell, has recalled that Jack "just made up his mind that if he was ever going to be bigger than Massachusetts, then he'd better go against public opinion in his state."[51]

From the moment he entered the Senate, Kennedy's advisers had contemplated that position. Warming to the idea, he asked Sorensen to help arm him with reasoning that would deny the likelihood of harmful consequences to New England. Kennedy and his aide struggled with the issue, the younger man diligently gathering data and arguments from all sides. Meanwhile, in early December, the Senator appeared at Boston's Symphony Hall to address a convocation of Northeastern University. Pointedly, he directed his theme toward the dilemma of voting one's convictions or surrendering to the self-interest demands of constituents. He quoted from Dryden's "Epilogue to the Duke de Guise" about the dangers of being "true to neither cause" and recalled Edmund Burke's warning that forsaking principles meant forfeiting "the only thing which makes you pardon so many errors and imperfections in me."[52]

He was convinced. The issue transcended mundane politics. The time had come for a heroic stand. Sorensen contributed the helpful assurance that the Seaway would actually be in the best interests of Massachusetts as well as the country, and Kennedy told him to go ahead with a draft. "Let's see how it comes out," he said.[53] Encouragement from such colleagues as George Aiken of Vermont and Congressman John Blatnik of Minnesota, with whom he worked closely on the issue, softened whatever trepidations remained. Blatnik recalls that Kennedy was certain that "economic improvements in any part of the country contribute to the total upgrading of the entire country."[54] With the final decision made,

Jack took the speech home for further study. He slept little that night.

Kennedy's fifteen-minute talk highlighted the debate. Pointing out that no member of the Massachusetts congressional delegation had voted in favor of a Seaway on six different opportunities over a period of twenty years, he rejected notions that the Port of Boston would be harmed. Most shipping through its docks was coastwise, intra-port, and local. Unable to specify any direct benefit the Seaway would assuredly offer the Commonwealth, he recalled that his defense of New England's economy had always supported federal programs that would promote national policies. Stubborn refusal to recognize legitimate needs of other regions would be shortsighted. Harmful retaliation might even follow. "We cannot continue so narrow and destructive a position," he declared, and concluded by quoting from Webster: "One country, one Constitution, one destiny."[55]

This time, however, Kennedy was one of the three Seaway supporters from Massachusetts. Two members of the Commonwealth's congressional delegation, Jack's friend Eddie Boland and John Heselton, both from hinterland districts relatively secure from Port interests, joined him when the House completed its action almost three months later. In the Senate, Saltonstall, in contrast with Kennedy, cast a negative vote. The responses of the Massachusetts legislators in both houses, despite the defections of the three men, confirmed the continued power of the anti-Seaway pressures.

The expected anger against Kennedy materialized. The *Boston Post* accused him of "ruining New England."[56] He was also warned not to march in the St. Patrick's Day parade. Possibly most damaging were suspicions, heard again in charges when he ran for reelection in 1958, that Kennedy's vote had something to do with his father's ownership of the Merchandise Mart in Chicago. For obvious reasons, the Seaway did enjoy wide support from the Great Lakes Region, which certainly was instrumental in getting the United States to join with Canada in developing the waterway to the Atlantic. The Merchandise Mart would invariably benefit from an economic boom in the area. Blatnik later recalled that that consideration never arose during his work with Jack on the subject.[57] Nor does any other evidence point in that direction. Ted Sorensen has said, quite simply, that "the design of the speech was to recognize what was right and speak up for it," and then added, with the triumphant satisfaction of a pragmatist, "but it certainly had the effect of making him a national figure."[58]

Sorensen's memoir of his life with Kennedy claims that the senator's speech marked the turning point in the Seaway debate.[59] In 1955, when James Landis was asked by Ambassador Kennedy for a compilation of situations where legislators displayed extraordinary courage by differing with their constituents in favor of the national interest, he included the following words: "Jack met the problem on the St. Lawrence Waterway."[60]

15

The Senator and the World

Foreign affairs, however, was the area of far more personal concern to John Kennedy. His experiences in Europe, assisted by his father's appointment to the Court of St. James's, had encouraged further fascination. Slowly, his perceptions uncovered conflicts between his own observations and the ideas he had learned at the dinner table. *Why England Slept* had attempted to resolve that dilemma; his unpublished piece on disarmament incorporated his father's reservations about military solutions. Yet, as a product of the Kennedy household, he was exposed to the notion that softness by liberal democracies betrayed their own weaknesses and prepared the way for Communist advances. He had entertained the possibility that the sort of totalitarian rule evident in Mussolini's Italy and Franco's Spain were plausible alternatives to popular rule, although traveling to the south of France had confronted him with impressions quite contrary to his father's views of the Falangists.

As he matured, Kennedy continued to probe, travel, and read. He had gained additional insights about the problems of the NATO nations, the nature of the American contribution, and the complexities of Western European defense. His journey to the Far East had been salutary for correcting his own earlier acceptance of the simplistic notion that the spread of communism in Asia had resulted from State Department blunders. As a young senator, now, he was far better educated about the nuances of cultural differences, nationalism, and the varieties of indigenous communism. He wanted to continue to explore and learn.

On the eighteenth of October, 1953, Jack met with Adlai Stevenson at the home of the defeated Democratic presidential candidate. Present on that occasion was Professor Walter Johnson of the University of Chicago, the veteran of the draft Stevenson movement for the presidential nomination. As was Kennedy's usual approach when meeting scholars, he suggested that Johnson send him a copy of a reading list to enhance his own background. The professor promptly forwarded a copy of the bibliography for his History 380A graduate course on eighteenth- and nineteenth-century American political history.[1] Two days after that mailing went out, Johnson received a phone call from Sargent Shriver. Shriver, then with the Merchandise Mart, called to request materials for his brother-in-law that would provide background reading to challenge his doubts about the wisdom of the forthcoming summit meeting of the Big Four in Berlin. Johnson suggested that Kennedy consult some articles in *Foreign Affairs;* he also used the opportunity of contact by advising the senator that his own trip abroad had revealed universal fear about American desires for war and concern that the United States had become militaristic and uninterested in negotiations. The hope was that American willingness to go into such a conference, even without realistic expectations of success, might dispel Communist propaganda that we were "warmongers."[2]

At the same time, Ted Sorensen sent Kennedy a long memorandum warning that his endorsement of a Big Four conference would require "a very cautious and precise statement of policy" because such a conference on the highest level may be desirable only under certain limited conditions and for certain limited purposes. It should be preceded by a preliminary meeting of the four foreign ministers and great advance expectations should be avoided. There should also be a firm display of unity among the three Western states in their meetings with the Russians. Such a conference, though, will be desirable or feasible, concluded Sorensen, because there is always the possibility of substantive results and, as had Professor Johnson, he noted its potential propaganda value.[3]

Sorensen's memo reflected his boss's skepticism, an attitude every bit as cautious about a premature summit conference as that of the administration and key members of the Western alliance. A preliminary meeting of the Big Three heads of state, including Great Britain, France, and the United States, had been scheduled for Bermuda in June but was then postponed for a variety of reasons. Not until December did they get together in Bermuda and not until 1955 did the President go to the conference in Geneva—and then only with many misgivings. Had the decision been up to Kennedy, he would have been no more eager to rush to the summit.

He was as convinced as Eisenhower and Secretary of State Dulles that Western leadership had inevitably fallen on American shoulders and that the nation's resolve was being challenged. "We are in truth the last hope on earth," he told the Boston College Varsity Club, echoing Churchill. "If we do not stand it now—if we do not stand firm amid the conflicting tides of neutralism, resignation, isolation and indifference, then all will be lost, and one by one free countries of the earth will fall until finally the direct assault will begin on the great citadel—the United States." He compared the "crisis" to the march of the Huns and Mongols "seeking the ephemeral goal of world domination. Their defeat this time is inevitable as it was then—for, in the last analysis and in truth, if we but see it, God and the right are on our side, and we cannot fail."[4]

Refusing to play the back-bencher for international problems, Kennedy did not shy away from harsh criticism of the administration's defense policies. He harped at the relationship between security and military strength. He criticized the Eisenhower concern with paring the military budget and the creation of a streamlined "new look" for a cheaper but more effective retaliatory striking force, all consistent with Secretary of State Dulles's concepts of the capability of reacting "massively" at a place and time of our choice. Already becoming popular on the lecture circuit, Kennedy's voice began to be heard both on and off the Senate floor. He took a direct swipe at the administration in a Princeton speech in May of 1954 by stressing the need to "spend enough to give a clear margin of superiority over our enemies. Any other policy is dangerous, possibly fatal. Our defense appropriations for last year and this will not give us that superiority."[5] He continued to warn that administration efforts to economize on defense would dilute the effectiveness of our foreign policy. In June of that year, he led a drive in the Senate to boost defense spending by $350 million in an effort to forestall a projected two-division cut in Army strength. He charged the administration with failure of leadership, of talking tough about "massive retaliation" while simultaneously stripping military power and alienating America's top allies. His role, commented *The Berkshire Eagle,* "on the whole is the sort of thing that one would expect from Adlai Stevenson rather than from the back-bencher. . . ."[6]

At the request of Earl Latham, Kennedy appeared at Amherst College in the spring of 1956 and warned that reduced American defense production in view of the arms race with the Soviets would have the Russians ahead of us in a few years. The outcome, he said, will be felt in "important effects in our diplomatic bargaining position."[7] These were standard positions for the Democratic opposition, no more and no less truculent than the prevalent acceptance of the East-West competition; but throughout, he continued the basic theme that military strength was related to diplomatic success, very much as he had done in his book. It differed very little from his 1948 comment that "if you're strong in national defense, you have a force for maintaining your own security because a strong national defense will result in diplomatic strength."[8]

Kennedy's sharpest dissent with Eisenhower-Dulles policies came over what he regarded as the vulnerability of increasingly unpopular regimes in the developing nations, or the "Third World," as they would later be called. He had, since that 1951 trip to Asia, begun to focus more on both the deteriorating situation in Indochina and the broader problem of colonialism. He warned that the rising countries of the Middle East may be recognizing that America may not be on their side when we do nothing to formulate solutions to their problems. He cited recent Algerian uprisings against the French as further evidence.[9] Only later would Kennedy stir a ruckus by diving headlong into the middle of the Algerian situation; but his concern with the Far East and colonialism kept him close to developments in Indochina from the moment he entered the Senate.

Jack's trip to the region had left him convinced about the ability of local Communists to exploit foreign resistance to independence. Most of all, he was skeptical about the quality and tenacity of French commitments to self-rule and suspected their claims about the adequacy of spending for South Vietnam's economic welfare. Further American aid, he felt, should be tied to the implementation of specific reforms.[10]

In April 1953 Kennedy delegated an old college friend, Langdon P. Marvin, Jr., to supervise the gathering of data about both America's European ally and the State Department's attitude. In response to Marvin's request, Priscilla Johnson, a specialist in Soviet affairs who worked for Kennedy until that spring, largely confirmed Kennedy's suspicions. Her information came from discussions with Robert Hoey, who manned the State Department's Indochina desk. She learned, first of all, that

Kennedy was right about French spending. An overwhelming proportion, some 80 percent, was for military purposes, a figure Kennedy regarded as way out of line. Most needed, Johnson reported, were fiscal reforms, land tenure, and public-health reforms.[11] A large part of her findings involved the complexities with which the State Department viewed the situation.

The Indochinese had been tied by treaty agreements since 1949 that forced them to turn to the French for technical assistance before seeking it elsewhere, except where the expenditure of another nation's funds was involved. Kennedy also found out that while the Americans might wish to send in experts on tariffs and taxation, it could not do so without French permission. Our policy, therefore, had been to try to get the French to do it themselves.

The previous fall, under the auspices of the Mutual Security Administration, a complete survey of Indochina's technical requirements was accomplished. And still, Kennedy learned, they were reluctant to move because American relations with France in Indochina could not be separated from the American efforts to induce her ally to join in the European Defense Community. There was also Hoey's belief that the question was not really so much a matter of reform, since reform implied the existence of institutions to be changed. Therefore, it should be a question of progress. Rather than the maladministration of ongoing programs, the problem was one of introducing hitherto nonexistent institutions. Furthermore, according to the State Department, immediate reforms could have a disruptive effect on the economies of the three states, so it was necessary to proceed cautiously in making changes that were complex and far-reaching. Finally, Kennedy discovered, Washington was hesitant to push the French because they might reach an accommodation with the Communist Viet Minh rebels through fear of being unable to retain the requisite political and economic controls over Indochina after the achievement of a settlement. Priscilla Johnson reported that that school of thought "maintains that the fear of a separate French accommodation with the Vietminh plus the desire not to jeopardize French cooperation with E.D.C. is what has kept us from insisting on a greater degree of independence for the Indo-Chinese states and on greater concessions from the French generally." Her long memorandum advised that the State Department's Indochina desk appeared to veer somewhere between fear that the French would either appease the Viet Minh insurgents or back out of EDC if we did demand more. Hoey, for one, thought the United States should pressure them to grant Indochina the substance as well as the form of self-government. Johnson also found out that Edward Gullion, the former chargé d'affaires in Saigon and "an unusually able exponent" of the view that fear of French accommodation and concern over EDC was keeping Washington from taking a tougher line, was reluctant to discuss his views over the telephone but would be glad to meet with the senator at his home.[12]

Gullion helped persuade Kennedy to push demands for a French grant of independence. The American chargé d'affaires, regarded as pro-Vietnamese by the French, thought a commitment should have been extracted with the signing of the 1949 treaty; subsequent problems only compounded the difficulty.[13] Kennedy's first acquaintance with Gullion had been in Washington in 1947, and the two also met during Jack's 1951 visit to Saigon. At that point Jack discovered that the young diplomat, then only thirty-eight, was a dissenter from State Department policy and that their doubts meshed. During 1953 and afterward they had many additional conversations in Washington. Gullion's position toward Indochina then became inseparable from Kennedy's, with the State Department even suspecting him of contributing to the senator's speeches on the subject.

Pressure for the French to facilitate self-rule and limitations of the American involvement in the light of Vietnamese colonialism became the key concern of Kennedy's subsequent remarks. He began to push the administration, demanding to know from the State Department what efforts had been made to move the French from their "too little and too late" concessions to the Indochinese. He pointed out the increasing American commitments that paralleled the deteriorating situation, asserting that we therefore have "the right and the obligation to insist that all steps essential to victory be taken, and certainly it is of primary importance to give to the native population of three states the feeling that they have not been given the shadow of independence but its substance."[14] A long response from the State Department came in the form of a letter from Assistant Secretary Thruston Morton. "The defeat of the Communist forces in Indochina leave the three states capable of freely negotiating their future relationship with France and all other countries," assured Morton. "Meanwhile, complete unity of feeling and determination as between France and the Associated States, and ourselves, are indispensable if Communist engulfment of Southeast Asia and beyond is to be avoided." Morton also argued that the current size of the French forces was necessary because of the lack of replacements for the foreseeable future. Therefore, the French government must maintain the willingness, along with its citizens, "to continue to endure the human and financial sacrifices of the French protective effort which has encountered serious opposition in France."[15]

A test of strength came early that summer over an amendment to the Mutual Security Act of 1951, a test that arose over the question of a new budgetary grant to France of $400 million. On July 1 Kennedy rose to express his agreement with the views of Senators Goldwater, Magnuson, Dirksen, and others who stated their apprehensions about Indochina. He saw little reason for the United States to spend much for military assistance to France in that area "if there are not present in the area conditions under which native groups can be rallied to the support of the independence movement." Referring to his statements of the day before, in which he had emphatically supported continued aid to France while urging that the funds "be administered in such way as to encourage through all means available the freedom and independence desired by the Associated States," he declared those conditions were not present. There was, further, no indication that the native armies, which the French had attempted to rally in the area, "are crusading armies." In fact, Kennedy pointed out, the majority of the population appeared to be in sympathy with the Communist movement of Ho Chi Minh, so he thought it of vital importance that the United States emphasize and use its prestige to advance the movement for independence, not only because such action would help the military operations in the area but also because, as Barry Goldwater had pointed out, the position of the United States would then be firmly understood in all of Asia. His only objection to the amendment of the senator from Arizona was that it appeared to be an ultimatum to France. Kennedy pointed out that there were many groups in NATO that would be happy to pull out of the long and bloody war. They, after all, were bearing the military burdens while American assistance had been primarily economic. Therefore, the Goldwater amendment, if accepted, could be regarded by the French as an adequate excuse for withdrawing their effort.

Kennedy then offered his own amendment, one that would place the United States in the position of stating that the money should be used for the purposes as stipulated in the act and also in such a way as to encourage aspirations of the Associated States for independence and provide for much needed training for the Vietnamese. That kind of amendment, he told his colleagues, would accomplish the objectives sought by Goldwater. He charged that the State Department had made pious declarations during the past three years, saying that it was in favor of independence for the Associated States and at the same time fearful that the French would actually pull out. He reminded his colleagues that the fact that one who had attempted to become premier of France while calling for negotiations with Ho Chi Minh failed by only thirteen votes to head the government demonstrated the strength of opinion in that country in behalf of complete withdrawal from Indochina. Furthermore, he held that while the United States had put its prestige directly behind the French in the struggle, providing large sums of money in rendering assistance, there were no conditions present in Indochina that would permit a victory for the colonial forces. Indeed, regardless of the steady increase in American assistance since 1950, indications were against such a victory. Kennedy argued that his amendment, by tying the $400 million dollars in aid to the objective of eventual independence, would stimulate self-government, thereby enhancing the support of the native population for the war effort, at present nil. He thought that the United States should not precipitate disaster by causing the French to pull out completely, which the Goldwater amendment sought. Therefore, unless the Senate stated that Americans would stop further assistance if the French failed to take such a major step, the consequences might be unfortunate. So he said that his amendment, less restrictive than Goldwater's, reduced the chance of such an unfortunate consequence. At the same time, it indicated the American commitment behind the people of the Associated States to gain their independence. The administration, of course, was opposed, and the Kennedy amendment was defeated by a lopsided 64–17, leaving the $400 million in aid money without his desired conditions.[16]

With the arrival of 1954, the Indochina situation became more critical. Kennedy used the occasion of a speech before the Cathedral Club in Brooklyn, New York, to point to the increasing desperation of the French fight against the Communist Vietnamese forces led by Ho Chi Minh. Still, he made very clear that Ho, despite his lifelong record as a Communist, "has influence penetrating all groups of society because of his years of battle against French colonialism." That situation was very different from Korea, where we were supporting a native government desirous of independence from the Communists. Indochina, because of its long experience under French colonialism, had come to regard the Europeans as the real oppressors. The rebels, Communists or not, were seen as their liberators. That led the natives, unlike the Koreans, to play only a small role in the war against the Communists. The burden had, therefore, been carried chiefly by the French, with an increasingly large

American military investment. Meanwhile, the pressures in France, the growing sentiment for cutting their investment and loss, for either withdrawing or working out a negotiated settlement with the Viet Minh, would ultimately and inevitably lead to Communist domination in Indochina. It was probably the only country in the world where many observers believed the Communists would win a free election. The Viet Minh were consistently gathering support and increasing their military strength. With the Chinese Communists potentially reaching over 150 modern divisions within two years, they would then become the third single greatest military power in the world, and that power would be under the control of a native leadership that had increasingly evidenced "aggressive and rapacious intentions toward the countries along their southern border." Then Kennedy asked: "Under these circumstances, we must ask how the new Dulles policy and its dependence upon the threat of atomic retaliation will fare in these areas of guerilla warfare. At what point would the threat of atomic weapons be used in the struggles in Southeast Asia—in French Indochina—particularly where the chief burden is carried on the one side by native communists and on the other by the troops of a Western power, which once held the country under colonial rule? Under these conditions," he asked, "at what point would our new policy come into play?"[17]

Kennedy's remarks were made more than two months before President Eisenhower mentioned the "domino" principle. The senator linked the maintenance of a non-Communist regime in Indochina to the security of all Southeast Asia. If that land should be "lost," he warned, "undoubtedly within a short time, Burma, Thailand, Malaya and Indonesia and other new independent states might fall under the control of the Communist bloc in a series of chain reactions." Indochina, therefore, "may well be the keystone to the defense of all of Asia." Where in that situation, he wanted to know, could Secretary Dulles's concept of "massive retaliatory power" be employed?

His words, then, also constituted a challenge to the administration's concepts of meeting the threat. "It seems to me that we could be placed in a most difficult position of either giving no aid at all of the kind that is necessary to bring victory to us in that area," he said, "or the wrong kind of aid which would alienate the people of great sections of the world who might feel that the remedy was worse than the disease." Sharply questioning the Eisenhower-Dulles policy, he wanted to know what would be the relationship of the approach to any attacks upon those nations "who may at that time be neutral or unfriendly in their attitudes toward a defensive alliance with the United States?" He asked, "of what value would atomic retaliation be in opposing a Communist advance which rested not upon military invasion but upon local insurrection and political deterioration?" Such words would later seem ironic and haunt him when he sat in the White House. Then he added, "In this country, one of our most fundamental rights is to petition and question the Executive and Legislative branches of the Government about the policies which they pursue." Neither foreign nor domestic policy, said Kennedy, "can be effectively maintained in a Democracy such as ours unless it is understood and supported by the great majority of the people."[18] Once again, the reconciliation of democracy with policy provoked Jack's anxiety.

Events in Southeast Asia received more attention during the second session of the Eighty-third Congress. The French remnants were becoming increasingly beseiged and depleted. The plan of General Henri Navarre to check the Viet Minh had failed. Having already succeeded in dividing Indochina into two parts by an invasion of central and southern Laos, enemy soldiers began to overrun the Red River Delta and had infiltrated the French main line of resistance. On March 20 General Paul Ely reached Washington from Paris and confirmed the ominous predicament of the French Union forces. General Ely's message about the hopelessness of being able to hold on to the garrison at Dien Bien Phu in northeastern Vietnam without additional American materiel and aviation technicians touched off increasing concern in Washington about the challenge to continued American nonintervention.

But the French, accepting the reality of inevitable defeat, hoped that American assistance could at least enable them to preserve sufficient bargaining strength by the opening of the Geneva conference on April 26. General Ely, meanwhile, found Admiral Arthur Radford, the chairman of the Joint Chiefs of Staff, most receptive to his requests for military assistance. Radford delineated the prospect of a massive striking force to destroy Viet Minh positions around Dien Bien Phu, a projected operation that became known as *Operation Vulture.* Lacking assurances that there would indeed be no massive American military entanglement, and unaware that Secretary Dulles and President Eisenhower were, in fact, constructing obstacles to the kind of suggestion advanced by Admiral Radford, congressional concern increased.[19] The assumption that a Communist victory would jeopardize "free world" security in Southeast Asia through the workings of the domino theory were accepted in statements made on the Senate floor on the thirty-first day of March by such

Democrats as Hubert Humphrey of Minnesota, John Stennis of Mississippi, and Paul Douglas of Illinois, just as Jack Kennedy himself had been endorsing that logic.

The debate came to the forefront in the Senate on Tuesday, April 6. Carefully prepared with a masterful speech, John Kennedy synthesized his critique of both the administration's possible responses and French colonialism. He appeared to support the Eisenhower-Dulles position that any intervention by the United States would have to be in conjunction with both British and French forces in forming a "united action." But Kennedy went beyond that point and, in outlining the questions and obstacles, scored his own points.

He charged that the administration spokesmen had left too much unsaid. They had been overlooking the realities within the Associated States. He argued that the popularity of Ho and his followers would turn any negotiated peace resulting from a partition of the area between Viet Minh and French Union forces, or a coalition government, into a state eventually under complete Communist domination. Another alternative, he said, would be for the United States to underwrite the French and persuade them to continue their struggle, but that would be dependent on increasing American support. But, he warned, "to pour money, materiel, and men into the jungles of Indochina without at least a remote prospect of victory would be dangerously futile and self-destructive." He proceeded to review the series of optimistic reports, citing the President, Dulles, Assistant Secretary of State for Far Eastern Affairs Walter S. Robertson, and even former Secretary of State Dean Acheson, that minimized obvious realities. Less than two weeks earlier, he pointed out, Admiral Radford himself had stated "the French are going to win." And Dulles had told the Overseas Press Club in New York that he did not expect that there would be a Communist victory in the country. Nevertheless, Kennedy argued, "such victory today appears to be desperately remote, to say the least. . . ." He then asserted "that no amount of American military assistance in Indochina can conquer an enemy which is everywhere and at the same time nowhere, 'an enemy of the people' which has the sympathy and covert support of the people."[20]

Without political independence for the Associated States, he said, it would simply be regarded by the other Asian nations as a war of colonialism and the "united action" that is so essential for victory would most likely wind up as unilateral action by the United States. And that kind of intervention, without support from the people of the region, without support of the great masses of their people, and with increasing reluctance by the French "would be virtually impossible in the type of military situation which prevails in Indochina." Borrowing from the recent experience in Korea, Kennedy pointed to what he called the "hordes of Chinese Communist troops poised just across the border in anticipation of our unilateral entry into their kind of battle ground." French economic domination, he argued, betrayed assurances given to the American people that the Associated States already had or were on the verge of complete independence. There can be no success, Kennedy warned, "without a change in the contractual relationships which presently exist between the Associated States and the French Union." In no way, he urged, should we channel American men and machines "into that hopeless internecine struggle" without having the French grant legitimate independence and freedom. He concluded by quoting Thomas Jefferson on the importance of enlightening public opinion rather than hiding the truth.[21]

The speech highlighted the day's debate, precipitating a ninety-minute discussion. The freshman senator received effusive praise from several colleagues on both sides of the aisle. Republican Majority Leader William Knowland quickly added his agreement with Kennedy's concept of a collective security arrangement that included Asians and not only Europeans. Knowland commended Kennedy for "a very well-thought out and provocative speech, which I think both the Senate and the country should read with interest."[22] Kennedy then went on to say that "what is needed far more to fight Communist aggression in Indochina is an effective native army to meet their native armies," and that native army meant an army from within Indochina, not Filipinos, or Thais, or New Zealanders, or Australians. "Guarantees of outside countries will have no appreciable effect on the struggle as it is presently being waged," he said on April 14.[23] Later, reacting to suggestions of Vice-President Nixon about the possibility of sending American ground forces into the country, Kennedy commented in Chicago that if we were to take such threats at their face value, "we are about to enter the jungle to do battle with the tiger." Addressing the Cook County Democratic Party's dinner, he reiterated that the United States "cannot save those who will not be saved," and added that free Asian nations must play their part.[24]

Continuing as a critic, he spoke in Los Angeles and charged that the American people "have been deceived for political reasons on the life and death matters of war and peace," and added that the United States has never before prepared for a major conflict by emphasizing weakness rather than strength. On television, he said he thought Indochina was lost. He warned that American intervention with combat troops would not succeed because the Chinese Communists would only widen the conflict. In speech after speech, before the Whig-Cliosophic Society of Princeton University, before the Executives Club in Chicago at the end of May, he deplored the inability to recognize the nature and significance of the independence movement.[25]

In the Senate only Everett Dirksen of Illinois dissented from any plan that might send American troops to Indochina. In an extended exchange with Dirksen, Kennedy explained that he visualized two treaties, one granting the Vietnamese people complete independence; the second would be a tie binding them to the French Union on the basis of full equality—and that should be a prerequisite to any American action.[26]

The Kennedy speech drew wide press reaction and was credited with having stirred the debate. Most papers noted his words in editorial columns, giving him far-reaching national attention and projecting him as a leader in the delicate area involving the formulation of foreign policy. His words were then put to the President at a news conference the following day. When asked if he agreed that Indochina's independence should be a condition before the acceptance of an all-out American effort, the President hedged. He said he had always tried to insist on the principle that "no outside country can come in and be really helpful unless it is doing something that the local people want." But, he added, "I can't say that the associated states want independence in the sense that the United States is independent. I do not know what they want."[27]

Kennedy's comments on Indochina touched informed observers as nothing he had said before. "Keep your eye on young Democratic Senator John Kennedy," proclaimed a columnist for the *Brooklyn Eagle*. "He's been getting a build-up for a nationwide campaign such as a Vice Presidential candidate."[28] Others pointed out that his increased visibility indicated that he was being primed as a party warhorse for the 1954 midterm elections. While he still had some way to go before developing into a truly effective speaker, he was winning points for sincerity, personal attractiveness, and for contending head-on with the issues. The *Worcester Telegram* hailed him as the nearest thing to an ideal that the Massachusetts Democratic Party had been able to produce in recent campaigns. Nevertheless, there were still the disclaimers and reluctance to grant him much credit. Added the *Telegram,* "Even he is getting by on a platform more of youthful romanticism than of—as yet—proven ability and established worth."[29]

But his speaking engagements had begun to take their toll. His back condition gradually worsened. By mid-July crutches became indispensable. His public appearances were becoming sharply curtailed. When a settlement that divided Vietnam at the 17th parallel and removed French control was reached at Geneva, it was Sorensen and not Kennedy who reacted publicly. Sorensen called it a victory for the Communists and predicted that they would achieve further gains in the area. The situation, he said, proved that America must rely on assistance from Free World allies and the United Nations. While Sorensen was making his comments in New England, Jack's pain had become unbearable. Still reluctant to admit his discomfort, he had nevertheless visited Bethesda Naval Hospital.[30]

Public activity masked Jack Kennedy's physical condition. On one level he had moved ahead, defying pain and discomfort. Using the Senate as a forum, he had combined regionalism with national interests, creating both the foundation for future favorite-son support as well as for broader political appeals. As a foreign-policy spokesman, he was evolving beyond mere condemnation of American responsibility for international realignments. The ramifications of ideology and nationalism were influencing his analyses. Formulating opposition to administration policies assumed Churchillian skepticism about agreements to mitigate international differences without prior bargaining strength, a theme that came naturally to the author of *Why England Slept.* Applauded by colleagues, they nevertheless found it hard to take him seriously. He was still young, inexperienced, ill, and, despite his marriage, a playboy with pretensions.

16

Dismal Days

There were some redeeming things about 1954: Kennedy's prominence and eloquence on the matter of French colonialism in Southeast Asia and American avoidance of a direct, Korean-type military intervention. On a more intimate level, however, he could hardly regard the year as anything but dismal. Poor health continued to threaten incapacitation, while, simultaneously, the question of what to do about Joe McCarthy became unavoidable. The long Army-McCarthy hearings televised nationally that spring helped to expose the self-proclaimed savior from internal communism as a ruthless charlatan, who, under the scrutiny of Army counsel Joseph Welch, displayed before the American public qualities that quickly destroyed his credibility. While Kennedy had to contend with the debilitating state of his back, Senator Ralph Flanders of Vermont, a spunky, outspoken Yankee Republican who had unleashed some devastating satire against McCarthy months earlier, introduced a resolution asking the Senate to censure McCarthy for behavior unbecoming a member of the Upper Chamber. Thus, Kennedy was confronted with a personal and ethical trauma; the consequences were bound to be significant no matter what he did. His own camp responded with conflicting signals about his obligations toward the family's friend from Wisconsin.

Partisan considerations added complications. However slight his commitment to partisanship, retaining valid Democratic credentials was far more vital to him now than it had been when he merely represented his Massachusetts district or even campaigned against Lodge. Any hopes of winning the party's nomination for higher office depended on maintaining loyal ties and somehow balancing them with his personal tendencies toward independence. But that was not easy to do. Despite the fact that several other Democrats were reluctant to attack McCarthy, believing that it was either politically dangerous or unnecessary, as the Wisconsin senator was destroying himself, Kennedy's party generally was becoming more critical and ready to respond to the altered political climate. Maintaining expedient party ties meant going along.

Tentative steps in that direction had already been made. Soon after entering the Senate, he became part of the nine-member Democratic Senate Campaign Committee, under Earle C. Clements of Kentucky. Joining with the party's liberals, Kennedy supported the confirmation of his old Harvard president, James Conant, as High Commissioner to West Germany despite objections, led by McCarthy and others, that the nominee's critical attitude toward parochial education and earlier advocacy of punitive treatment toward postwar Germany demonstrated a radicalism at variance with the American public. Kennedy similarly disregarded the opposition from McCarthy and the right wing in approving Charles Bohlen as ambassador to Russia. Especially irritating to McCarthy was Kennedy's vote against the appointment of a friend to the Federal Communications Commission. Within the Government Operations Committee, Jack helped to thwart McCarthy's choice for the committee's chief counsel and objected to a hasty and possibly unconstitutional contempt citation against left-wing author Corliss Lamont for refusing to answer questions about his books.[1] None of these positions, however, placed him before the public as an opponent of either McCarthy's methods or mission.

Furthermore, he balanced his considerations very carefully. Avoiding suspicions of radicalism, he announced full support for the campaign backed by both the Hearst papers and the American Legion to revise the flag salute to include the words *under God.*[2] He unequivocably opposed amending the Constitution to give eighteen-year-olds the right to vote because he had not found "sufficient" grounds for making such a serious change.[3] Meanwhile, as a spokesman for the national party and its liberal wing, he toured the country and identified himself with a series of partisan functions. He joined with the group raising funds for a memorial building and library in Missouri to honor former President Truman. With the Kennedy Foundation making its own generous contribution, Jack was at the center of the enterprise when Truman came to Boston to promote efforts for the institution, throwing a luncheon for the ex-president at the Sheraton-Plaza Hotel. The event was organized by a committee that included Torby Macdonald. Kennedy was also photographed walking with Truman on St. James Avenue.[4]

Crossing the country that spring on behalf of Democratic candidates and their fund-raising efforts, he appeared as the featured speaker at the party's Jefferson-Jackson Day dinner at Boise, Idaho, and fired a broadside at the Republican White House, branding it a "do-nothing" administration. His talk attracted five hundred people who overflowed the Crystal Ballroom of the Hotel Boise and filled the mezzanine, the lobby, and the downstairs dining room. Citing rising unemployment and sluggish economic expansion, he urged the creation of jobs for the 700,000 people annually entering the labor market to "make our standard of living the greatest in the world, not to mention the millions of the world whose markets and needs for our goods and food stuffs are barely tapped."[5] Editorialized *The Idaho Statesman,* "Senator Kennedy delivered just about the kind of address we have come to expect from touring party leaders who are being incorrectly briefed on what to say in Idaho."[6] In Chicago, praising both Senator Douglas and the Democratic Party, he claimed that the Eisenhower "crusade" had been "broken and crashed down upon the beach." He was also the featured speaker of the southern California Jefferson-Jackson Day dinner in the Biltmore Bowl in Pasadena, a hundred-dollar-a-plate affair sponsored by Democratic Party leaders to raise funds for the 1954 campaign.[7] On the evening of May 14, he was back east and spoke at Malden, Massachusetts, to promote Torby Macdonald's campaign for a congressional seat from a heavily Republican district. In late June he flew to Brainard Field, near Hartford, Connecticut, in a DC-3 with Jackie and sister Pat, who was accompanied by her husband, Peter Lawford. Kennedy then keynoted the Democratic state convention at the Bushnell Memorial Auditorium. He referred to the McCarthy issue on that occasion, but only to cite the Wisconsinian's dispute with the Army as a manifestation of the GOP's "abdication of leadership." He charged that the Free World's security was "rapidly dissolving under the heat of Communist intimidation and subversion," and blamed the Republicans for weakening the Air Force and Army "to dangerously inadequate levels."[8]

The Berkshire Eagle continued to comment perceptively and somewhat audaciously from its catbird seat in the hills of western Massachusetts and observed that Kennedy's attack against the Eisenhower regime was a new development in the freshman's career.[9] *The Middletown Press* praised his unquestioned "eloquence" and concluded that the "man who defeated former Senator Henry Cabot Lodge, Jr., is quite a fellow."[10] Two weeks later, in a Senate discussion with Mike Mansfield, Kennedy continued his anti-administration remarks, charging that Eisenhower's and Dulles's vagueness on the question of the admission of Communist China to the UN, "has contributed to our difficulties in Indochina." He also upbraided the administration's inadequate policy toward colonialism for easing the recent turn toward communism in both British Guiana and Guatemala. He wanted the United States to "adopt a policy of encouraging all the peoples of the earth, regardless of what alliances we have in other parts of the world, to move toward independence."[11] Overall, despite his studied nonalliance with traditional Democratic politics in Massachusetts, Kennedy's national ambitions were moving him toward an expediently partisan position, but even that could not make the McCarthy issue disappear.

Kennedy's new partisanship, however, did not extend to his home state. In Massachusetts, he resisted boosting State Treasurer Foster Furcolo's attempt to unseat Kennedy's Republican colleague, Saltonstall. At the Democratic state convention that endorsed Furcolo's nomination, Kennedy delivered a perfunctory speech that predicted victory for the party and said he would help to achieve it. His talk, however, was loaded with clichés and lacked much conviction, failing to match the rousing performance of ex-Governor Dever.[12] Furcolo clearly posed a dilemma for Kennedy.

The Kennedy-Furcolo relationship long remained one of those intrinsically tense affairs, somewhat forshadowing Jack's difficulties with Adlai Stevenson. Born in New Haven in 1911, the son of an Italo-American doctor and an Irish mother, Furcolo had received both undergraduate and law degrees from Yale, plus a certificate in labor legislation from the university's Labor Management Center. Before becoming state treasurer, he served as Kennedy's colleague in the Eighty-first Congress. Larry O'Brien, who worked for Furcolo at that time, noticed as early as 1948 that Kennedy was reluctant to do anything that might assist the fortunes of a potential future rival for statewide office.[13] Also bright, articulate, and well educated, Furcolo had an additional attraction for Italo-Americans, the traditional ethnic rivals among Massachusetts Democrats. James MacGregor Burns, who knew both men, recalls that Furcolo "really had a tough time with Kennedy, if only because they were both young, ambitious, competitive politicians."[14] Furcolo had accommodated himself to the sensitivities of the Commonwealth's traditionalists, mitigating his progressivism with a public statement declaring that the party could only be hurt by continuing to associate with the Americans for Democratic Action. Now Furcolo's efforts against Saltonstall, which probably could not succeed, would antagonize a key member of Kennedy's New England coalition. Assistance for Furcolo would also jeopardize Kennedy's overtures to the Commonwealth's independents and Republicans by sealing his reputation as a partisan.[15]

Consequently, it was not surprising to see the collaboration of both the Saltonstall and Kennedy offices in issuing communiqués putting forth their cooperation on behalf of the economic interests of Massachusetts, all of which clearly signaled a pronounced distaste by Kennedy toward that fellow Democrat, Furcolo. Rebutting published reports, Furcolo later denied suspecting Kennedy of "attempting to head off any Saltonstall support of a Kennedy opponent four years later." Ken O'Donnell also denied a deal was involved.[16]

The big blowup came in a Boston television studio. Kennedy was present, presumably to endorse the statewide Democratic ticket, which included Furcolo, who had won the party's preconvention primary nine weeks earlier, and Representative Robert F. Murphy of Malden, the gubernatorial contender. As early as August 8 the *Boston Herald* noted that Ambassador Kennedy had made substantial financial contributions to Murphy's campaign, which was rather pointed, because Furcolo received no such help.[17] But, together in that TV studio, the three men prepared to go on the air.

In the studio the crutch-supported Kennedy, beset with pain and prepared to enter the hospital for his back operation, was being pressed by Furcolo to criticize Saltonstall directly. That, at least, was the way Larry O'Brien recalled the incident.[18] Ken O'Donnell explained that Kennedy's illness and virtual inability to walk left him in no mood to respond to Furcolo's anti-Saltonstall importunities.[19] According to another pro-Kennedy source, Dave Powers, Kennedy went on the show after Furcolo's advisers told their man to milk a last opportunity to get a clear-cut endorsement. Kennedy merely confined his on-camera statement to looking toward Murphy, rather than at Furcolo, and limiting his endorsement to a simple statement that specified that his wishes for success were reserved for only Murphy and the Democratic Party, completely omitting Furcolo's name.[20]

Furcolo's own recollection of the imbroglio differed. He denied vigorously that he expected Kennedy to attack Saltonstall.[21] He was about to go on the program with Murphy and Kennedy and was prepared to go along with however Kennedy wanted the program done. Kennedy decided to have teleprompter cards prepared. "So they were going to have a run through it with these idiot cards, and I had someone who went down there to run through my part. What they had in this fifteen-minute broadcast was Kennedy sitting in the middle and me on one side of him and Murphy on the other. The way the broadcast would go would be Kennedy would say something and then I would bring up, say, the shoe manufacturers, and I would compliment Kennedy on what he had done as a senator as far as shoes were concerned. Then Murphy would bring up something Kennedy had done as far as the fishing industry was concerned. When I got there, Kennedy and Murphy had been there probably a half hour before me, and I said, 'Jack, you don't have anything in here endorsing the Democratic ticket. You endorse myself and Murphy but you don't have the Democratic ticket.' And Kennedy said, 'My very presence here would indicate that I'm for the whole Democratic ticket.' " Then, what Kennedy did was to simply end up his speech with the simple statement "I wish you both good luck." Furcolo turned to Kennedy and said, "The only thing I suggest is that at the end why don't you insert the words *and the Democratic ticket,* so it will be 'I wish you both and the Democratic ticket good luck.' " Furcolo reported that Kennedy's response was, "No, I don't need to do that," and, as he remembered, the senator added, "I think you've a hell of a nerve to ask me." Then, on crutches, he walked out. About five minutes later Frank Morrissey came running in and said, "What's the matter?" Furcolo heard afterward that Kennedy said to Morrissey, "That goddamn guinea . . ." or words to that effect. "So we didn't know what the story was going to be. We didn't know whether he was coming down or wasn't. Well, another half hour went by and then it was time to go on the air. So he came down about two minutes before the thing [air time] and we sat down together and went through the broadcast exactly as it was on the idiot card, with one exception. At the end, instead of him saying 'I wish you both good luck' (whether he misread it or intended to) he said, 'I wish you, Bob, good luck.' "[22]

The newspapers did not publicize Kennedy's snub. But, to remove any doubts about its meaning, Morrissey volunteered that the omission of the endorsement of Furcolo was intentional and specified that Kennedy's personal blessing would be limited to Murphy. The following week Jack entered the Hospital for Special Surgery in New York and no further attempt was made to mitigate the damage. Pointedly, Bobby Kennedy, to whom inquiries were referred by the senator, simply declared, "That's the end of it. There'll be nothing more." The younger Kennedy explained, after the break between his brother and Furcolo was revealed, that the senator had endorsed "the entire Democratic ticket" in the television program and consciously let the matter stand.[23] Bobby, attempting to gloss over the rift by resting on the statement that his brother would support the entire state ticket, failed to deny or dispute the point that the senator intended to withhold personal endorsement.

What really happened supports the contention of favoritism toward Murphy's candidacy rather than Furcolo's. Murphy had actually gone to Hyannis Port and had worked on the script with Kennedy before returning to Boston with him by plane. Some fifteen minutes before air time, Furcolo entered the studio, where Kennedy and Murphy were awaiting him. He looked over the script and showed his dissatisfaction. He wanted a stronger endorsement from Kennedy instead of devoting most of the discussion to the Commonwealth's economic situation. Kennedy retorted that they lacked the time for that kind of change; ill and irritable, he helped provoke a heated argument. For a while it seemed that Jack might not go on the air at all. Thanks to Murphy, who entered the fray as a peacemaker, the program went on as scheduled. Toward its conclusion, both Murphy and Furcolo thanked Kennedy for appearing with them at personal sacrifice to himself. A statement that had been added to the script by Murphy was read by Furcolo as planned, although it might have appeared at the time that he was speaking extemporaneously. Another dispute between Kennedy and Furcolo occurred after they were off the air. That centered principally over what should have been said in the speech, and then Kennedy, Furcolo, and Murphy went their respective ways.[24]

In the November elections, Furcolo lost to Saltonstall by some thirty thousand votes, but Murphy, who had had Kennedy's direct endorsement and the family's financial aid, missed the governorship by seventy-five thousand votes. Ironically, Murphy ran substantially behind Furcolo in every Democratic center of the state.[25] Furcolo's later explanation of Kennedy's role in that 1954 incident was that the senator was playing for the Republican vote, especially in the western part of the state, and was trying to avoid close party identification. Furcolo also disputed allegations that Kennedy was in a great deal of pain in the studio, holding that that story was a convenient one spread around afterward. Rather bitterly, Furcolo contended that the entire episode would have been unnoticed except for the Morrissey statement.[26]

Despite a carefully staged rapprochment with Kennedy, Furcolo's bitterness remains. To this day he recalls that Kennedy "didn't like people to take a position contrary to him in any way. He didn't like that at all. I don't know whether you'd call it vindictive or not. . . . He just couldn't be aware of the fact that anyone could have a position different than his."[27] Furcolo, unfortunately, was also a victim of a period in Kennedy's career when a conjuncture of the requirements of partisanship, illness, and the McCarthy dilemma were making Jack more irritable, more demanding, and less ready to make concessions. Furcolo was also too proud to tolerate being victimized by Kennedy power.

In 1957, after a carefully staged détente had been achieved with Kennedy, Furcolo published a little political satire under the pseudonym of "John Foster." In a parable viewing the process as a horse race, a political career began "because of a horse named Candidate," all skill-fully manipulated by "George." Its mythical hero, Pete Martin, soon finds himself endowed with undreamed-of personal qualities and a highly fictionalized personal background, much in contrast with the reality of one who has not the haziest notion of what a representative is supposed to do. "What kind of a candidate are you, anyway?" George asks him. "You mean you want to say something definite? That ain't no good. . . . The smart politician just talks and he don't say anything." In an obviously satiric allusion to the Kennedy promotion of his "education" at the London School of Economics, Pete Martin learns that he can claim credit for having "attended" a place called Chicago University because it gave a two-week seminar every summer in public speaking, one that could have been taken on his vacation. Inspecting a flier with that credit, Pete concludes: "Anyway, it didn't say I had graduated from there or anything—it just said I had 'attended,' and I suppose that if I had just been there even once it was 'attending.' "[28]

Jack's hectic political activities hardly added to the tranquillity of the first years of married life. Jacqueline had to cope with habitual disorderliness and attempted to improve his consciousness about his own appearance. Also annoying were his frequent absences. Most were for political reasons. But he also went on vacations without her, usually tagging along with such friends as Torby and Lem Billings. On Tuesday evenings he made regular trips to Baltimore for a speed-reading course, which ultimately enabled him to consume the written word at a rate approaching a remarkable twelve hundred words a minute. But then, the increasing back trouble forced him to give that up. The combination of political activities, personal habits, and physical limitations gradually tended to make that a very difficult period for the newly married couple. For Jackie, it was especially troublesome. At that stage she was still shy, reticent, and lacked the self-confidence that later became more characteristic. All accounts agree that the marriage failed to start smoothly.[29]

Right after they left for their Acapulco honeymoon, Jackie had a foreshadowing of what life would be like. She would have preferred to have remained at that spot, swimming, boating, fishing, and making the most of those romantic days. But Jack was impatient to move on. He insisted on driving up the Coast from Mexico to California and visiting with Red Fay on the Monterey Peninsula just below San Francisco. There, Jacqueline found herself subjected to a visit with people she did not know and with whom she was not very comfortable. At one point they also drove to Palo Alto to visit another one of Jack's naval friends, Tom Casey. On the final day of her stay on the West Coast, the new Mrs. Kennedy found herself in the sole company of Fay's wife Anita, being given a guided tour of the Bay area. Jack and Red had gone off together to see a professional football game. Red Fay has recorded that, "I'm sure this didn't seem a particularly unusual arrangement to Jack."[30] Then, once having returned east during the second week of October, she was compelled to spend much of her time with his family on the Cape.

As the wife of an ambitious senator, she soon saw clearly the character of her role. On a Sunday night in mid-October, she and her husband were the subjects of the first half of Edward R. Murrow's popular thirty-minute television program on CBS, *Person to Person*. For the "live" show, technicians and cameramen invaded the cramped Bowdoin Street apartment. Explaining to his audience that the Kennedys had been married for only a month, he said they were still house-hunting in Washington. Therefore, they had to spend a lot of time in Boston, "at what used to be the bachelor establishment of the senator." As the television screen showed the building across the street from the State House, Murrow, chain-smoking in his New York City CBS studio, explained that they were living in an apartment "on the third floor of the building you are looking at now, over a barbershop, just at the edge of Beacon Hill." He introduced Kennedy as one who, at the age of thirty-six, had already accomplished what most American boys merely dream about doing. He had even, said Murrow, been a "football star" and a "newspaper reporter." He had now fulfilled the dream of marriage to a most "attractive bride."[31]

The nationally televised program was a carefully staged and stilted affair, set in an obviously overstuffed living room. Jackie sat on a couch alongside the senator, her first public presentation as the young, elegant wife of the handsome, serious, intellectual, and, above all, dedicated public servant. Her neat and simple-looking print dress harmonized with his conventional business suit. The screen showed her nervousness. The few comments made to her by Murrow were answered softly and briefly. She could still have been at Miss Porter's, in the dean's office awaiting a verdict about the consequences of a misdeed; or at a tea coping with the need to make small talk with a group of strangers. She showed proper pride and admiration for the man she had just married while Murrow, his cigarette smoke visible on screen, asked all the right questions. The senator, his looks belying the twelve-year age difference with his wife, responded to the opportunities by rising, which revealed no sign of physical discomfort, and then, for the camera, displayed his mementos —the model of a PT boat; the famous coconut that had been inscribed with the rescue message; and a picture of the destroyer named for his brother Joe. Then Jack talked about the circumstances of Joe's heroic death.

Murrow continued to feed the cues. He elicited Kennedy's earnest concern about preventing another war through maintaining strength, which, the senator carefully pointed out, included having an "Air Force second to none." He led Kennedy into a brief but informed recitation about the Taft-Hartley Law and the state of the economy. Avoided entirely was any reference to Senator McCarthy, whose activities were currently so prominent. Nor were any judgments asked about the wisdom of the Korean armistice terms.

Murrow then asked whether he did much reading. "I used to very much and try to do as much as I can now," Kennedy replied. That gave the interviewer the opening to have Kennedy introduce his literary selection by asking whether he had found anything useful or, "if I can use the word, particularly inspirational?" Reaching for a nearby book, Jack opened it and said that it contained a favorite passage from a letter by Alan Seeger, the American poet Kennedy readily identified as the author of "I Have a Rendezvous with Death." He explained that the letter written to Seeger's mother just before his death as a World War I volunteer contained "good advice for all of us." In a monotone, with dignified sincerity, he began to read:

Whether I am on the winning or losing side is not the point with me; it is being on the side where my sympathies lie that matters, and I am ready to see it through to the end. Success in life means doing that thing that which nothing else conceivable seems more noble or satisfying or remunerative, and this enviable state I can truly say that I enjoy, for had I the choice I would be nowhere else in the world than where I am.

In the Washington area, the newlyweds used the Auchincloss estate at Merrywood until they rented a typically narrow and small Georgetown house at 3321 Dent Place, N.W., just a few blocks from the campus of Georgetown University. Jack then suggested that, since Jacqueline would inevitably be involved with politics, she take advantage of their accessibility to the university by studying American history. The Georgetown School of Foreign Service was then the only part of the university that admitted women.

So, for the spring semester of 1954, she enrolled in a large class taught by a thirty-three-year-old native of Brooklyn, Dr. Jules Davids. The course surveyed American history since 1865 and necessitated Jacqueline's reading of the standard textbook by Samuel Eliot Morison and Henry Steele Commager. Professor Davids assigned *Nationalism and Sectionalism in America* by David Potter and Thomas Manning as an additional requirement. Along with the other students, Jackie had to write essays on problems drawn from that volume. She told her professor that Kennedy enjoyed reviewing the Potter and Manning problem questions with her. Her essays were at what Davids describes as a "comfortable B level" and she passed her final exam in June of 1954 with a grade of 89.[32]

Much publicity circulated around the country about the attractive couple. In those early postwar years, when veterans commonly combined the responsibilities of raising their own young families with completing advanced education under the GI Bill, the media portrayed the Kennedys in similar circumstances. That spring, several newspapers carried feature stories about how they worked, studied, and hobbied together.

He, it was reported, stopped playing bridge and had taken up painting "as a past-time" to "share" that interest with his wife. She bought him a Christmas present that included a big easel, oil paints, brushes, and a supply of canvases for him to paint the studies of boats, houses, and landscapes that, she said, were "made up right out of his head" and without the benefit of a single art lesson. She went fox-hunting in Virginia while "he snapped her picture wistfully."[33] One photo-essay designed for Sunday rotogravure sections made a special effort to portray them as a modest, hardworking, and romantic collegiate couple. A picture showed Jackie carrying books while walking out of their Georgetown home. Behind her, the senator stood in the doorway seeing his wife off to her class at the university. Another snapshot depicted a youthful-looking Kennedy, his hair still in a careless tousle, at the desk in his home pouring over papers while his wife sat nearby reading a book. "The Massachusetts Democrat isn't sending his wife out to earn their bread and butter, however," readers were assured. "Mrs. Kennedy is a student in the Georgetown University Foreign Service School. Her schedule forces her to leave for morning classes earlier than her husband must make his Congressional appearance," thereby implying that her course load was comprised of more than just the class taught by Davids.[34] Ruth Montgomery's New York *Daily News* column explained that the youngest Senate wife, in addition to dabbling in watercolors and studying history textbooks, was also writing children's stories for the amusement of six-year-old Jamie and eight-year-old Janet Auchincloss, her half-brother and -sister.[35]

Beneath the bucolic portraits, however, was the reality. Jacqueline's adjustment to political life was uncomfortable at best. Several points of tension became prominent. Her antipathy toward his old friends, some of whom, like Lem Billings, seemed forever present, caused additional strains. Her carefree attitude toward money clashed with his frugality. His back problems exacerbated marital tensions. In Europe shortly after their marriage, while Jack was recuperating from his surgery, the Duchess of Windsor arched her eyebrows and, looking Jackie over, remarked, "Oh, my dear, it must be hard on you with no personal life at this time."[36]

Nor did recovery from physical limitations do much to improve their married life. Jack, pursuing his fondness for the company of beautiful women, mingled with New York's social set, participating in the city's nightlife at such clubs as the Stork or El Morocco. At parties among the well-born, well-to-do, and influential, he could also be seen, sometimes as a shy, somewhat introspective figure, almost resembling the brooding detachment of his younger brother Bobby, usually alone in a corner "like a wall-flower." Often, he came with some elegant woman friend. One was Lady Jean Campbell, a granddaughter of Lord Beaverbrook and the daughter of the Duke of Argyll. Linked romantically to such eminent Americans as Henry Luce, she also became Norman Mailer's third wife.[37] New Yorkers of the "silk-stocking" set, well connected with the city's liberal establishment that Jack Kennedy later tried to cultivate, had no trouble recalling how close Lady Jean and the senator were in those days. There were simultaneous other involvements.[38] Letters and telegrams in the Kennedy Library files include items containing titillating suggestions of varied and numerous intimacies. When inspected, they offer more than the mere hint of hyperactive liaisons and rendezvous. But discretion was part of the education received from his father, and so he usually had a "beard" to ensure anonymity and a good friend like Langdon Marvin or brother-in-law Peter Lawford to make advance provisions for a room at a fine hotel, often the Carlyle.[39]

Family pressures remained strong against Kennedy's tangling with McCarthy. After Jack's election to the Senate, his brother Bobby went to work for McCarthy's committee as chief counsel. And, unquestionably, Joseph P. Kennedy was wholeheartedly opposed to his son's participation in any kind of censure move. Less than two weeks before a vote on the Flanders Resolution seemed likely, Jack's father sent his son clippings from the European press. The items from the *Sunday Observer*, he pointedly informed him, refuted the notions about how the senator's activities were disgracing America's image overseas that were being circulated in derogatory stories by McCarthy's enemies. "The public isn't the slightest bit interested. Any agitation against him is caused by the same kind of groups here as in America," wrote the Ambassador from Paris. "As far as strained relations which we have heard so much about, that's a lot of bunk."[40]

Yet on this issue as on others, Jack Kennedy was showing signs of following a more independent course. McCarthy's methods were increasingly disturbing. He had not been very happy about Bobby's association with the senator's investigations subcommittee. He was undoubtedly pleased when his brother quit after a dispute over the procedures pursued by McCarthy's aides, Roy Cohn and G. David Schine.[41] Some of Kennedy's concern about McCarthy himself was expressed in a letter that he wrote to the American Civil Liberties

Union as early as October of 1952, in which he lamented the excesses that were being carried out in congressional investigations. He suggested that the committee hire counsel to cross-examine accusers on behalf of the accused. But while conceding that some legislators had made irresponsible charges, he was not ready to deny such power to his colleagues, hoping that the democratic process could cleanse the system of undesirables through the ballot box.[42] At the same time, he was not ready to deny the possibility that McCarthy might be raising significant issues and felt that they should be considered despite the pressures that were building up against him.[43]

When Senator McCarthy declared on January 15 that he would cite for contempt two uncooperative witnesses who refused to identify associates as members of the Communist Party, Kennedy sought legal advice from Harvard Law School Professor Mark De Wolfe Howe. While Howe responded with his thought that McCarthy had proposed that the Senate "should endorse his degradation of decency by adding its sanction to his violation of due process," Kennedy was not satisfied. He defended the citation as only a legal formality and was reluctant to either fault McCarthy or sympathize with the witnesses.[44] He did, however, criticize McCarthy's proposal to investigate communism in the colleges.[45] Basically, however, he was shying away from any kind of direct commitment.

In that way he was little different from others in his party, who preferred the convenient justification that McCarthy was a problem for the Republicans. Certainly, with congressional elections coming up that fall, fear was general of a loss of votes regardless of how they came out on the issue. Southern Democrats had another concern. The Flanders Resolution, as originally drafted, would have opened up precedents for future assaults on the prerogatives of committee chairmen that could ultimately be used against them when their party resumed majority power, as they hoped it would after the elections.[46] Kennedy himself, appearing on a *Meet the Press* program, which, as the newspapers reported, was telecast in color that day from New York, avoided either praise or condemnation. He simply doubted that McCarthy could do much for Republicans trying to win offices in Massachusetts. At the same time, Kennedy's own personal inclinations persisted. Asked by a reporter what he thought of McCarthy, he replied, "Not very much. But I get along with him. When I was in the House, I used to get along with Marcantonio and Rankin. As long as they don't step in my way, I don't want to get into personal fights."[47]

But just being ambivalent had gotten Kennedy into some trouble. His brother Bobby had, by then, shifted sides and gone to work for the Army against McCarthy. And, in a partisan vein, Jack expressed "shock" during that *Meet the Press* program about certain Republican statements that called the Democratic Party a "party of treason," an assertion that had been most clearly identified with McCarthy himself. Kennedy voted to apply the Hatch Act to restrict State Department Security Chief Scott McLeod, whose activities were being praised and supported by McCarthy, from traveling through the country making speeches about Reds. That brought the wrath of the *Boston Post* to inspire that front-page editorial calling Kennedy the "Junior Senator-at-Large" from Massachusetts. Fox's paper said Jack had been supported for election (neatly overlooking the half-million-dollar loan the publisher had received from the Ambassador) "only because of the two candidates he had shown no evidence of being soft on communism," and lectured him for not having discovered that "cleaning communists out of government is not a party matter. If he wants to maintain his political viability he ought to consult a few solid and loyal Democrats in Massachusetts who are every bit as determined to clean communism out of government as is Senator McCarthy."[48] But Flanders, not Fox, posed the real dilemma for all but a small band of liberals.

If Democrats from most of the country feared the consequences of political courage in getting behind Flanders, clearly Kennedy from Massachusetts had more to worry about. His colleague, Saltonstall, who was up for reelection that year, had said even less about McCarthy, despite his lack of family ties. Saltonstall was content to see which way Kennedy would go before acting on his own. After the Flanders attack, *The Berkshire Eagle* noted editorially that it was "certainly futile to expect any candidate running for Massachusetts statewide political office with any chance of winning to criticize Senator McCarthy. Adherents of both parties are evidently scared to death of offending the Boston electorate."[49] In some ways, because Saltonstall was a member of McCarthy's party, the difficulty was greater for him. Although the Eisenhower administration pressured the Republican senator to oppose McCarthy, neither he nor Furcolo broke their silence on the issue. As the Lowell *Optic* commented in October, every Massachusetts voter "has an opinion on McCarthy. If they all continue to keep quiet on McCarthy it is a question just who will benefit from the general silence. If this occurs it will be a strange campaign indeed, the candidates all ducking the main issue as far as Massachusetts is concerned."[50]

Few dissented from the conventional wisdom that the situation in Massachusetts was more sensitive than elsewhere. "If Senator Saltonstall were to make his position on McCarthy clear now," stated the Southbridge *Evening News* on October 7, "he might well be committing political suicide." Kennedy, while not a candidate that year, could easily have jeopardized the size of his future statewide majorities and placed himself in a dangerously controversial position, which is anathema for those with national ambitions requiring a wide consensus.

The fact remains that it was to Kennedy, a fellow Irish Catholic, to whom McCarthy's supporters turned as the man who would not, in their view, become a traitor. Writing at the beginning of the year, long before the Flanders attack had exacerbated the issue, Arthur Schlesinger, Jr., then at Harvard, informed Governor G. Mennen Williams of Michigan that the anti-McCarthy attacks—and especially the use of the term *McCarthyism,* which the historian thought "unfortunate"—had been counterproductive. They had provoked latent feelings of discrimination and persecution in the local Irish community, which "had produced a certain closing of the ranks behind the Senator on the grounds of racial solidarity."[51] Of the two senators from Massachusetts, Kennedy became by far the greater recipient of pro-McCarthy mail. While Saltonstall's letters showed a twenty-to-one ratio against the controversial senator, Kennedy's divided in the proportion of only seven against McCarthy to three in his favor. *The Berkshire Eagle* commented that that difference was not accidental, especially because a politician's mail is likely to correspond to his own political views.[52]

Now the question before Kennedy and his Senate colleagues was what to do about the Flanders Resolution, or, more precisely, how to avoid contending with its implications. After four years of unsubstantiated allegations and disregard for individual rights, constitutional guarantees, and indifference to the victims of his political profiteering, Joe McCarthy had finally overreached himself. He had personally excoriated General Ralph W. Zwicker for having countenanced the promotion, and then an honorable discharge, for an Army dentist who had invoked the Fifth Amendment when applying for a commission under the Doctors Draft Act. The decorated general, who had distinguished himself in the Battle of the Bulge, was told by McCarthy that he was "not fit to wear that uniform." The subsequent Army-McCarthy Hearings had inflamed that public relations disaster, especially when the senator retaliated against being placed on the defensive by publicly embarrassing a young man in Joseph Welch's law firm for having joined a left-wing legal group while in college. Flanders first introduced a stringent resolution that discomfited the leadership of both parties.

With that touchy issue before them, every effort was made to defer action until after election day. The resolution was allowed to sit on the table without action until, with the approval of the Vermont senator, it was sent on to the Rules Committee. Flanders, however, stressed that he would not condone having it lost in the rush to adjournment. But the Republican Policy Committee declared its unanimous opposition to any tampering with existing committee arrangements. When their majority leader, Senator Knowland, announced that he would move to table the motion, some Democrats, worried about precedents that could boomerang, were also relieved. But Flanders persisted. In mid-July he announced that in two weeks he would offer a new motion, one that would be merely a moral statement, which would avoid tampering with committee prerogatives. Along with other Democrats, Kennedy waited to see which way Minority Leader Lyndon B. Johnson would signal the course for the party. In turn, Saltonstall watched Kennedy.

Difficulties then broke out over the resolution, with most of the efforts moving toward postponement. Johnson held firm about not committing himself, while Hubert Humphrey lectured the minority leader "in no uncertain words" that it was the "duty and the responsibility of the Democratic Party to line up behind . . . Senator Flanders's motion." But the Democratic leadership refused to make the motion a party issue, leaving it for each member to vote his own convictions. Flanders, with the lobbying assistance of Maurice Rosenblatt's National Committee for an Effective Congress, produced a draft of thirty-three charges, introducing them on July 30 with his call for censure. Knowland promptly moved expeditiously to have the Flanders proposal and all substitutes turned over to a six-man select committee chosen by Vice-President Richard Nixon. With a 75–12 vote, the minority holding out for an immediate showdown, Knowland's motion passed. After a further series of conferences, the composition of the select committee was created on August 5. It was announced that Republican Senator Arthur Watkins, a Utah conservative, would head the panel. The move had succeeded. They had delayed any kind of action until after the elections.[53]

Kennedy was prepared to make a statement if one had been necessary when the Flanders motion came to the floor. That afternoon Kennedy met with a group of liberals in Senator Lehman's office to discuss strategy, and approved the decision to censure McCarthy on legal grounds.

The liberal efforts to bring the issue to a vote were undercut when Senator Wayne Morse of Oregon agreed that personal guilt was not a censurable matter until a committee had weighed the questions and answers. That night, Sorensen went to the floor with Kennedy. Many years later, after stressing Kennedy's readiness to support Flanders, Sorensen recalled that "Morse's speech killed the liberal strategy. And what made liberals so mad was that Morse had been at their strategy meeting and approved their action. Then Johnson and Knowland set up a resolution for the committee. Meanwhile, there was no censure vote. There was no need for Jack's speech."[54]

The question was, what about Kennedy's speech? Would he actually have upheld the censure? Sorensen remained positive about the answer. Firmly, he said that regardless of Jack's father, regardless of the involvement of his brother Bobby, regardless of the difficulties of his Massachusetts constituency, he would have gone along with the move. "And there is no doubt in my mind that he was prepared with the speech that he had in his hand on the floor that night to support censure. The Flanders Resolution was simply a resolution of censure. It did not have a bill of particulars as later came out of the Watkins Committee; so there weren't qualified yeses and qualified nos. Either you were yes or you were no, and everyone was entitled to state what his reasons for that were."[55]

The undelivered speech was relegated to the files, largely ignored. Most of the wording was drafted by Sorensen, with the collaboration of Kennedy, whose emendations appear on the pages. Upon close inspection, the speech contains a curious combination of Sorensen's craftsmanship and background as a Norris progressive, Bobby Kennedy's disdain for Roy Cohn and G. David Schine, Ambassador Kennedy's arguments in denial of alleged international damage committed by McCarthy, and, finally, John Kennedy's attitudes and political perceptions. While it agreed that censuring McCarthy was in order, its essential argument in no way took exception to his mission, his methods, and the integrity of his anti-Communist crusade.

Riding squarely down the center, avoiding condemnation but finally resting on the need to uphold the dignity of the Senate with the support of the words used by George Norris in 1929 in the case of Hiram Bingham, the speech stressed that the present action "does not involve the vindication or the condemnation of an individual Senator. It does not involve his views and objectives in years gone by. It is instead an action which serves to express our severe disapproval of particular conduct permitted, if not encouraged, by a particular Senator." As for his own attitude toward Joe McCarthy, the Kennedy statement took care to assert his own past support, including voting for full appropriations of funds for McCarthy's committee, for his amendment to reduce assistance to nations trading with the Communists, and in not having tried to end his investigations of Communist subversives. Such issues, declared the document, were not among those being considered before the Senate. He then also carefully disassociated himself from Flanders, charging the Vermont Republican with inconsistency in his own record toward McCarthy. Nor was Kennedy prepared to state that he was for censure because of any past misconduct; he recalled that he had never made any public objection to such behavior. "Nor," it stated, "do I agree with those who would override our basic concepts of due process by censuring an individual without reference to any single act deserving of censure." Reiterating Ambassador Kennedy's point, it rejected an anti-McCarthy move as a way of conciliating foreign opinion. He would not censure the senator because of an alleged divisive effect upon the American people. Then he went on to make clear his only grounds to justify an anti-McCarthy vote. Not McCarthy himself but the conduct of Cohn and Schine, largely as had been developed during the Army-McCarthy hearings and reflecting the experience and animus of Bobby Kennedy toward those two aides, became the specific targets of Jack's condemnation.

He held McCarthy culpable for only one misdeed: having supported and tolerated Roy Cohn's activities in his clash with the Army on behalf of G. David Schine. Cohn had insisted that the Army had drafted Schine to hold as a hostage to get McCarthy to call off his investigation of Fort Monmouth. The military, in turn, had charged Cohn with lobbying for special treatment for his collaborator, accusations that had led to the televised hearings. Kennedy concluded that McCarthy's responsibility for the tactics of his young aides deserved censure so the Senate could reassert its honor and dignity.[56]

Then, in mid-August, Kennedy joined with Hubert Humphrey and Wayne Morse to further sanitize themselves against "softness toward communism" charges in preparation for possibly having to cast an anti-McCarthy vote. Humphrey gathered supporters in behalf of a dubious bill to "outlaw" membership in the Communist Party. Remembering that such legislation had once been introduced by Mike Mansfield, he corralled Morse and Kennedy and suggested reviving the bill as an amendment to a piece of legislation designed to strengthen existing laws against Communist-dominated labor unions. Kennedy went along with the move, which also had the blessings of Lyndon Johnson. But the doubts of civil libertarians and those who questioned its effort to outlaw membership in the Communist Party provoked heated opposition from such liberals as Eleanor Roosevelt and the ADA. The Senate bill was also opposed as being unsound by such anti-Communists as Attorney General Herbert Brownell and FBI Director J. Edgar Hoover.

Interviewed shortly before his death in 1977, Hubert Humphrey confirmed an association between the Communist Control Act and the proceedings then being studied by the Watkins Committee. "Very definitely," he replied emphatically. "And I was so damn sick and tired with having Joe McCarthy bring up communism every fifteen minutes in the Senate that I said, 'If you really want to deal with this issue, let's deal with it across the board, come on, boys, because this fellow is a phoney and a fraud and we're going to have to deal with him,' and that's why. ... And I wanted to have it crystal clear in everybody's mind that Hubert Humphrey was a vigorous anti-Communist, non-Communist. So the Communist Control Act did that, so that when I got ready to put my vote on the line against Joe McCarthy, there was good reason for it." Humphrey then thought somewhat more and added, "I'm not very proud of the Communist Control Act, I'll be honest with you."[57]

In the climate of the day, what Jack Kennedy had done in teaming up with such liberals as Humphrey and Morse was to further immunize himself against the prevailing fear of countering McCarthy. Not a single senator dared to vote against the Humphrey-Kennedy-Morse version.

The final bill, however, that came out of the House-Senate conference committee softened its more dubious provisions, such as the one pertaining to mere membership, rendering it basically innocuous. Joe McCarthy opposed it.[58] From Jack Kennedy's home state came the following comment from the North Adams *Transcript:* "Much as we detest skunks, we think the Kennedy-type attack not only risks hurting the hunters more than the hunted but also that it smells so highly of vindictive political phonus bolonus that the hunters may find themselves hunting each other instead of the skunks they're supposed to be after. And the Katzenjammer Kids, Hubert, and John, and Wayne, they laughed, and laughed, and laughed."[59]

Cynics would always suspect the timing of Jack Kennedy's entrance to the New York Hospital for Special Surgery. With the Watkins Committee studying how to handle the McCarthy case and a vote on censure pending, it seemed a logical and prudent moment for one so sensitive to the matter to avoid having to confront the issue. Chronically skeptical

Drew Pearson made a flat statement in late September that Kennedy "will choose the particular moment of the McCarthy debate to be hospitalized because of his huge McCarthy following in Massachusetts."[60]

That assumed a delicate conspiracy between Jack, nature, and the judgment of the battery of doctors continually being consulted. It further failed to explain why he did not duck out of being prepared to make a statement, if one had been called for, on the Flanders Resolution. Already on crutches, Jack Kennedy made no effort to use his illness to avoid that expected confrontation.

The preceding year offered many instances of continuing medical attention. What was officially described as "malaria" forced his confinement to George Washington University Hospital in mid-July of 1953. After a brief stay, he got away to the Cape for the weekend and returned to his office by the following Monday.[61] Right after his Cathedral Club speech in January, he kept a weekend appointment about his back with Dr. Philip D. Wilson at the New York Hospital for Special Surgery. The indications are, then, that in early 1954, in addition to treatment for Addison's Disease, assuming that many of the reports of malaria were simply subterfuges for his problem with adrenal insufficiency, the back was beginning to complicate matters.[62] In late April he went back to the Lahey Clinic for what was described as a routine physical checkup. Coinciding with a heavy speaking schedule, with the southern California Jefferson-Jackson Day dinner appearance planned for the following day, his medical visit had to be more than simply elective. He was, fortunately, released in sufficient time to fly west.[63]

But most of that spring, starting with late May, the back necessitated constant use of crutches. Evelyn Lincoln noticed that he usually hid them before visitors entered his office. He also tried to move to a suite nearer to the Senate floor to spare himself the walk through the long corridors with their hard marble floors in order to reach the elevators when answering quorum or roll calls, but the seniority system thwarted that attempted switch. His secretary reported that he became so increasingly irritable, especially because of his efforts to hide his agony, that she found herself contemplating escaping to a different job. "But he was making such an effort to carry on, I felt it my duty to stay as long as I could stand it."[64] Finally, during the long Senate debates in July, the pain became so intense that he began to remain in the chamber rather than return to his office between quorum calls. Leverett Saltonstall asked the Senate to permit Kennedy to deliver a speech while sitting on the arm of his chair. In early July, Kennedy went to Bethesda Naval Hospital for treatment. A few days before the expected floor action on the Flanders Resolution, *The Boston Globe* reported the possibility that his doctors might decide that another operation was unavoidable.[65] So he was on crutches while ready with the prepared statement on McCarthy. Newspaper pictures showing him addressing the State Federation of Labor Convention at Worcester, Massachusetts, a few days later, reveal that he leaned on them while delivering his speech. That stopover was en route to Boston for further medical treatment.[66] In September when he visited Torby Macdonald's campaign headquarters in Malden, having made a special plane trip from Hyannis, the crutches were still evident.[67]

Most of that month was spent on the Cape. But then the decision was made that, however great the risk posed by the complications of the Addison's Disease, surgery was unavoidable. With Jackie at his side, he entered the New York Hospital for Special Surgery on October 10. Several tests and X rays were taken; the actual operation was postponed three times before his physical condition permitted major spinal work. As a postoperative report later stated, without identifying Kennedy by name but merely presenting it as a case study of a patient with adrenal insufficiency due to Addison's requiring elective surgery, "orthopedic consultation suggested that he might be helped by a lumbo-sacral fusion together with a sacroiliac fusion." But, explained the medical account, that because of Addison's, the operation was deemed dangerous. The decision to go ahead was a reluctant one. But without surgical intervention, he would become incapacitated. Therefore, it was decided "to perform the operations by doing two different procedures at different times if necessary and by having a team versed in endrocrinology and surgical physiology help in the management of this patient before, during, and after the operation."[68]

On the twenty-first of October, Kennedy was operated on by Dr. Philip D. Wilson with Dr. Ephraim Shorr of the New York Hospital serving in an advisory capacity. The following day Dr. Wilson told the press that it would be another forty-eight hours before a definite judgment of the results could be made; but a hospital spokesman reported that "the operation was successful and his condition is good."[69] But then, on the third postoperative day, complications set in. He developed a urinary tract infection that resisted antibiotics. The situation seemed grave. Kennedy slipped into a coma and was placed on the critical list. His father walked into Arthur Krock's office and, weeping in a chair opposite the journalist's desk, said that he thought Jack was dying. It was the one moment, Krock has recalled, that Joe Kennedy's emotion equaled what he had shown over the death of his oldest son.[70] The family rushed to the hospital, where Jack was given the last rites of the Church. The complication had apparently been compounded by Kennedy's rejection of the recommendation that the surgery be done in two separate operations and his insistence that both fusions be performed simultaneously. The recovery was agonizingly gradual, with his condition closely monitored.

While Kennedy was recuperating in the hospital, the Watkins Committee brought in its recommendations in the case of Senator Joe McCarthy. They advocated that the senator not be "censured" but "condemned" for his behavior toward the Privileges and Elections Subcommittee and his abuse of its members. On December 2 the condemnation was voted by 67–22. Critics of Kennedy's absence because of his hospitalization were subsequently told that he was in no condition to even register his attitude by the parliamentary device of "pairing" to go on record in favor of the majority position. Yet Theodore Sorensen was at the other end of a telephone, ready and eager to fulfill such instructions on behalf of his boss. All Sorensen needed was a call from the hospital. Reflecting back to that time, he believes that Kennedy "was sufficiently conscious in that hospital to get a message to me on how he wanted to be paired. I think he deliberately did not contact me."[71] Jack remained the only Democrat who failed to either vote or pair against McCarthy.

Had John Kennedy made that call, or had he authorized a surrogate to deliver the word for him, a great deal of future embarrassment inimical to his ambitions would have been spared. Anticipating the commotion that would be raised upon his departure from the hospital, he told his friend Charles Spalding, "You know, when I get downstairs I know exactly what's going to happen. Those reporters are going to lean over my stretcher. There's going to be about ninety-five faces bent over me with great concern, and everyone of those guys is going to say, 'Now, Senator, what about McCarthy?'" Rhetorically, he asked, "Do you know what I'm going to do? I'm going to reach for my back and I'm just going to yell, 'Oow,' and then I'm going to pull the sheet over my head and hope we can get out of there.'"[72] Kennedy later compared the situation to a jury. "If somebody is not there, why should they be allowed a judgment on it?" he asked. "There are Senators missing votes all the time, and this is being made a big issue of because they're turning it around."[73] Privately, however, he admitted his dilemma. Conscious of the incendiary nature of the issue at home, pressured by his father's position, he took advantage of his indisposition and remained silent. At least when John Fox ran a page-one editorial that blasted those New Englanders who had voted against McCarthy as having acted "in accordance with the desires of the Kremlin," John Kennedy was not one of his targets.[74]

The senator remained at the hospital until December 21. Then, placed on a stretcher, he was flown to his parents' Palm Beach home to continue his recuperation, making a Christmas family reunion possible for 1954.

17

"Profiles in Courage"

The new year began dismally as little good news came from Palm Beach. One report said the senator would be unable to return to Washington before April and might even have to quit his seat.[1] For a while, additional apprehensions were relieved by news-service accounts that quoted Ambassador Kennedy as saying that his son was recovering steadily from the October operation and was able to walk again. That optimism was quickly dashed, however, with the outlook for further delay and the discovery that Jack's lingering discomfort was caused by a silver plate that had been placed in his spine.

After his return to the hospital on February 10, the plate was removed and a bone graft performed. Then came two more weeks of hospitalization, followed once again by a return to Florida for a new period of recuperation. As he left from Teterboro airport in New Jersey on a private plane with his brother Teddy, a hospital bulletin advised that Kennedy's condition was good and he hoped to return to Washington by the end of March.[2]

At Palm Beach, however, the Ambassador was despondent. Expectations of an early recovery were again revised. He told the press that Jack had come within twenty minutes of being lost—twice.[3] That brought a new wave of speculation about the imminence of the senator's resignation. With Christian Herter as governor, a Republican successor was anticipated. But some composure was restored by William Randolph Hearst, Jr., who told of having "dropped in" to visit with the senator in Palm Beach and finding him "looking tanned and fit again," expecting to return to the Hill in about two weeks.[4]

Instead of going to Washington, however, Kennedy went to New York for a consultation with Dr. Shorr at the Hospital for Special Surgery. Entering on April 26, he remained overnight, checking out at 6:40 the next evening, smiling and telling reporters that he felt "fine." He rushed back to Newark airport for the flight back to Palm Beach.[5] On the twentieth of May he sent word that he planned to return to Washington the following week.

That report resulted from an interview that Jack gave to Minna Littmann of Basil Brewer's *Standard-Times*. He and the woman reporter sat on the terrace, separated by a low wall from the waves that washed upon the sand on the beach below. Nearby was a long table, covered by a denim mattress, that Jack used for sunbathing. Appearing golden brown from head to toe, he explained that last year's tan had not completely faded and that a new one had built up quickly. "Things went fine when I was off my crutches in April," he said. "My back would begin to ache towards the end of the day, but that was to be expected. And then I fell in my room. One of the screws of my crutch had worked loose and I swung around somehow and lost my balance." As he talked, he reached for a crutch that rested against the table and tightened a screw at the base, giving it an extra turn for safety. That, he explained, was the second setback. The first was the need to return to the hospital for the substitution of the bone graft for the silver plate that had impeded recovery. During the period without the crutches, he and Jacqueline had left the estate only a few times, once to attend mass at St. Edward's Church and, occasionally, to take in some movies. Besides that, he had not ventured much beyond the estate, which was secluded from North Ocean Boulevard by high shrubbery.[6]

He slid off the table with surprising ease and grabbed the crutches, then led her across the wide, lush lawn, past coconut palms and exotic shrubbery, to the broad Spanish-type stucco mansion that his father had bought twenty-five years before. "You might like to see where I live," he said, calling his guest into the first-floor wing, which was only a step or two above the level of the lawn. The living room of a two-room bath-suite had been converted into a bedroom study. The place was covered with books. They were piled high on cabinets, bookcases, and the mantelpiece. Around the hospital bed were worktables, filing cabinets, a dictating machine, and, at a handy distance, a telephone. He explained that he kept himself very busy in that room, starting at about 8 A.M. with breakfast in bed. Then he went through the morning newspapers, from New York, Boston, Miami, Palm Beach, and the *Congressional Record*. After that came the daily mail. "Most of my mail has gone directly to my office in Washington, but there is always some to handle here. I have dictated my replies, and send the tape-recordings and the originals by air-mail to Washington, every night, for my office staff to take care of," he explained. "Afternoons, I talk by telephone with the office. After that as long as I was confined to bed, I worked on my books. Evenings, I take time off to look at television and read for pleasure." He recalled that he had been recorded since March on seventy-three percent of all legislative votes by the process of pairing; since March 16, that level had reached one hundred percent. "We've sponsored or co-sponsored 24 bills since January 1," he told her proudly. "My average for the same period in other years was 26. We've received and answered 15,000 pieces of mail from constituents."[7]

He also told her that he was once again trying to do without crutches for a few hours; within three days, he expected to put them aside permanently. He requested that the big news of his pending return be withheld until the filing of her account because he had already had enough of premature expectations. He was looking forward to the full resumption of senatorial duties, planned to attend the fifteenth reunion of his Harvard class in June, and was inviting 280 members of the legislature and the State House press corps to be his guests at the family home at Hyannis Port on June 10. He explained that he was looking forward to his thirty-eighth birthday on May 29. "I'll certainly be glad to get out of my 37th year."[8]

He had not, observed the reporter, lost his boyishness. His brown hair, which looked golden in the sunlight, appeared as thick and bright as ever; and his enforced long inactivity did not seem to have slackened the leanness of his tall body. "If the Senate hadn't kept such long hours— I could have taken it easy—perhaps I mightn't have gone to the hospital last Fall. But I'd probably have had to go through with the operation eventually. There's so much walking to do at the Capitol, and the floors are so hard. They've found me a room near the Senate floor," he added. "That will be a help. Mrs. Kennedy is in Washington today, seeing about our new living quarters." The reporter's suggestion that he might use a wheelchair occasionally to get about the Capitol fell on deaf ears.[9]

A few days later, he was back in Washington. Accompanying him on the flight that twenty-third of May was his wife and sister Jean. A battery of television and newsreel cameras awaited him. As he stood with Jackie, his neat business suit, a polka-dotted tie, and a handkerchief in his breast pocket gave him the additional air of just having returned from a relaxing, pleasurable vacation. Yet almost as though to dispel that idea, he explained how he had kept up with developments while in Palm Beach. He had read the *Congressional Record* every day, quipping that that was "an inspiring experience." He also examined the transcripts of two important committees, the Senate Education and Labor Committee and the Senate Government Operations Committee, especially since he was also the chairman of the Subcommittee on Government Reorganization. Hearings on the recommendations of the Hoover Commission would soon be held. While in Florida he had also had to keep up with the work of that commission on the reorganization of the Executive Branch.[10] Since the lease on their rented home had expired, the Kennedys lodged temporarily in the old Congressional Hotel on Capitol Hill before buying a spacious white brick Georgian mansion, Hickory Hill, in rolling hill country overlooking the Potomac at McLean, Virginia.

On Tuesday, May 24, Jack arrived on Capitol Hill. He walked slowly, obviously a process that required great effort. Yet, to accommodate the newsmen, he climbed the front steps of the Capitol; and instead of riding over to the Senate Office Building, he walked across the Capitol grounds with Reardon and Sorensen. When he left the elevator near his third-floor office, there was another mob of newsmen and photographers. He shook hands with the secretarial staff and walked into the inner office, where strong photographic lights were trained on him. On his desk a big basket of fruit and candy from Dick Nixon contained a note that read "Welcome home."

At 4:07 P.M., he limped into the Senate. Immediately, an unofficial reception committee was formed by the Democratic whip, Senator Earle Clements; Senator Walter George, the president pro tempore; and Senators J. William Fulbright and Richard Russell. They led him into the chamber, where the majority leader, Lyndon Johnson and the Republican leader, William Knowland, both expressed appropriate courtesies to acknowledge his return.[11]

Once again, the next day's papers gave the story wide coverage. A typical editorial came from the independently Republican New York

Herald Tribune, which welcomed him back and noted that, along with his colleague Saltonstall, "he has helped give his state vigorous and intelligent representation in the Senate. He was one of the first legislators in Washington to take a clear and unequivocal stand in favor of the St. Lawrence Seaway; on this and other issues he has displayed characteristic forthrightness and understanding of national interests." Then, noting his illness and the persistent doubts that he would ever return, the editorial said, "But young Jack Kennedy comes from a bold and sturdy breed, and he's back on the job again."[12]

Even while he was returning to Washington, Dr. Shorr telephoned Dr. Janet Travell, a fifty-three-year-old pharmacologist connected with New York Hospital, and made an appointment for Kennedy to see her on Thursday, May 26. At one thirty that day, Kennedy arrived by cab at her 9 West Sixteenth Street office. Unseen by newsmen, he was again on crutches. The steps from the sidewalk down to the doctor's ground-floor office were an impediment. The pain in the left side of his back and leg discouraged shifting too much weight to that side and the stiff right knee could not carry the full burden of his body. Both the cab driver and Dr. Shorr had to help him down the steps.

Finally seated before the pharmacologist, he seemed tired and discouraged, not at all very talkative, a vast contrast from his conduct at the Capitol two days earlier. He sat quietly, mostly wanting to hear what she had to say, reluctant to repeat what had become an old and boring story. The doctor noted that he was pale and anemic, his 155 pounds barely adequate to cover his frame. She thought his movements were guarded, his body turning entirely as a single unit to face either of the two doctors in the room. The motion and rotation of his back was similarly restricted. Dr. Travell found calluses under each of his armpits, where the skin had borne the pressure of crutches. She explained the requirements of his muscles, of the consequences of pain and the stiffness of the joint after an injury. She was able to increase the range of motion of his right knee by a brief and simple treatment of the muscles that were in spasm. While she explained what should be done, the senator sat in an old-fashioned North Carolina rocker with a caned, wooden back. He was skeptical about any future course of medical treatment. He had heard it all before. He wanted to know how long he'd have to wait for improved knee motion and was reluctant to accept still another doctor and still another kind of treatment. The best thing to do, she explained, would be to admit him to the New York Hospital for intensive treatment and some additional tests.[13]

He was then taken, with the rocking chair, directly to the Cornell Medical Center at New York Hospital, where he was installed in a fifteenth-floor room of the Baker Pavilion. Dr. Travell had managed to transport the chair in her two-door sedan by dismantling it. At the hospital he remained under her care for a week. No word went out to the press. His whereabouts were not reported. The Senate had recessed at 10:30 A.M. on May 27 for the Memorial Holiday weekend. Similarly, no one noticed that on Sunday, May 29, Kennedy managed to leave the hospital on a pass to celebrate his thirty-eighth birthday.

On the first of June, the senator was back on the job. His colleagues were still totally unaware that despite his grand return on May 23 and 24, which was heralded throughout the country as evidence of recuperation, most of the time thereafter until that day had been spent in New York City under the further treatment of Dr. Travell. For the next few months, he continued to make weekend trips to New York Hospital for back-strengthening muscular therapy.[14]

His physical and political involvement continued to take up almost all of his time. On July 3 he was admitted to New England Baptist Hospital, where he spent a week with more X rays and checkups of his back and, presumably, the attention of Dr. Sara Jordan to the progress of the cortisone control of the Addison's Disease. Right after he left that hospital, he returned to New York Hospital, entering on July 13, while hospital spokesmen declined to say whether that checkup had anything to do with the spinal operations in October and February.[15] He had also fulfilled his plans to give a commencement address and be present to receive an honorary degree at Assumption College in Worcester. He had met with his father at Hyannis Port to discuss further political plans. And, as the highlight of the Massachusetts Jefferson-Jackson Day hundred-dollar-a-plate roast beef dinner at the Hotel Sheraton-Plaza in Boston, he met with Foster Furcolo. The Democrats in attendance hailed the public "renewal" of the Kennedy-Furcolo "friendship." Furcolo introduced the senator as a "national hero" and Kennedy, responding accordingly, called Furcolo's remarks "as nice an introduction as I've gotten."[16] The next day, he hosted the big outing at Hyannis Port, which was jammed with politicians and all kinds of hangers-on. By late July, after his visits to the hospitals in New York and Boston, he was back in the Senate, carrying out his duties and preparing to leave for another overseas trip.

He left on August 5. On the letterhead of the Grand Hotel de la Ville, Rome, Jacqueline wrote to Ted Sorensen, "I hope you had a nice summer. We did—thank heavens— & J is getting along so well—well [sic] be home about Oct 11 to see you then."[17] On Monday, September 19, Jack Kennedy had a private audience with Pope Pius XII at Castle Gandolfo. A photograph shows him painfully leaning on crutches while standing with the Pope. Nevertheless, he moved on to Warsaw "to make a study of conditions in Communist Poland."[18]

Jack Kennedy reached Warsaw in an old American DC-3 with a Polish crew. Driving through the city offered views of reconstruction. Streets were crowded with many pedestrians but there were few automobiles. His car passed the largest building in Eastern Europe, the Palace of Culture, which, Kennedy noted, was a "gift from the Russian people to their comrades in Poland" and a constant reminder of Soviet oppression. He learned that the current local joke told about a mythical ad in the newspapers with the following notice: "Will trade luxurious 5-room apartment with a view of the Palace of Culture for anything." He found that, while the people were reasonably well dressed, discretion inhibited much communication with Westerners about their hardships. One example, he heard, involved the maid of a couple who worked in the American embassy who had a furnished one-room apartment with another girl. A married couple was then moved in with them, although the woman was pregnant and ill. The maid could give up the room only at the risk of losing her possessions. "This all seems to be part of a Communist campaign to wreck family life; and thus the Government concentrates on building theaters, sports stadiums, and monuments rather than homes," he wrote.[19]

Kennedy observed that the most depressing sight was the old ghetto, which contained the remnants of the Warsaw Uprising. "The ghetto is now a great field near the heart of the city, with a few wooden shacks on it, bearing neat testimony to the most savage mass extermination in history. Of the 2 1/2 million Jews who lived in pre-war Poland, only 80 thousand survive." And of those survivors, the great majority, he had been told, desired permission to go to Israel.[20]

He also learned about the many measures taken to compel the Poles to conformity, the check on political reliability of Polish youths as prerequisites for being given technical training, the lighter taxation for the friends of the authorities, the government-controlled press—with the papers especially throttled by the withholding of newsprint, the refusal of distribution facilities, and direct censorship. Only the Catholic Church provided a barrier between the complete domination of the people by the state. The struggle between church and state, he reported, was "completely savage." He thought that the collectivization of the peasants represented a major challenge for the regime and observed that the process was still in its infancy. The Poles, he recalled, were continuing their historical dilemma as the victims of successive invasions and partitions, especially by the Germans and the Russians.[21]

Kennedy detailed his experiences after reaching Paris in late September, sending them on to Sorensen for placement as an article in the Boston papers. His observations provoked a much more sober evaluation of totalitarianism than what he had seen in Italy in 1937 or had heard about Franco's Spain. His view of the Soviet Union confirmed Alice-Leone Moats's *Blind Date with Mars,* the book he had read while still in the South Pacific, rather than his mother's earlier enchantment with the government's ability to impose order and efficiency. He learned that while Eastern Europe lacked the perils of democracy, the leadership had little public support or confidence. For the masses, the government provided few satisfactions, leaving the Church to fill the void; and that, Jack thought, was without much power or influence. For the potential readers, he concluded, "The barbarian may have taken the knife out of his teeth to smile [a reference to the recent summit conference at Geneva] —but the knife itself is still in his fist."[22] Kennedy's dire findings included the realization that rule by an elite could be impotent without popular endorsement.

Kennedy returned with Jackie aboard the *United States* on October 12, he and his wife smiling broadly, undoubtedly pleased to be back home. That same day he rushed over to Sixteenth Street to see Janet Travell. The doctor asked about the photographs showing him with crutches while with the Pope. He grinned and said, "I used the crutches only then because I couldn't kneel gracefully." He also admitted, however, that the discomfort had increased since he had left the country in early August. The doctor then prescribed weekly visits for continued Novocain treatment of his muscle spasms. During eight weeks that fall, he managed to leave Washington on various days, the plans always subject to last-minute revisions. One intrusion into his schedule came in mid-November when Jacqueline ended her touch-football "career" by breaking an ankle while playing with Teddy on the Hyannis Port lawn. That confined her to the New England Baptist Hospital for five days. By December both Kennedys were ready for a respite at Palm Beach.[23]

In mid-December, from Palm Beach, he telephoned his New York doctor and asked her to visit him at the North Ocean Boulevard home for the forthcoming weekend, offering to place her on a Friday afternoon flight to Florida. Foregoing a planned fifty-fourth birthday celebration with her own family, she arrived on the night of the sixteenth. Appearing for breakfast the next day, she noted that the senator had already had his morning swim in the pool and was soaking up the sun within a partially sunken enclosure that had been built near the water. Looking back over that scene, Dr. Travell wondered, "My host and his beautiful bride of two years had that health-giving world to hold forever. What forces drove him to leave it for the ravages of politics? After all *his pain* and suffering, had he not fought his share of his country's battles?"[24] Not until she knew Jack Kennedy much better did she understand why he could not stop.

On December 18, 1955, while Dr. Travell was with him at Palm Beach, *The New York Times Magazine* featured an article by John F. Kennedy called "The Challenge of Political Courage," adapted, readers were advised, from his forthcoming book, *Profiles in Courage.* Indeed, when he had returned to the Senate in May, he had revealed for the first time that a book was in progress. Newspapers explained that Jack Kennedy was working on a "history" of the United States Senate.

Published at the start of 1956, *Profiles in Courage* found a receptive audience and no shortage of reviewers. From *The New York Times* and New York *Herald Tribune* to more obscure publications, commentators fell into line, generally praising the work for its thoughtful, inspirational examples of courage within the Senate. In a major front-page discussion in *The New York Times Book Review,* which featured a large picture of a dignified, serious-looking Jack Kennedy, Cabell Phillips declared satisfaction at having a "first-rate politician write a thoughtful and persuasive book about political integrity" and went on to praise the author for being "no dilettante at his trade, but a solid journeyman full of ideals, but few illusions. His book," concluded Phillips, was "the sort to restore respect for a venerable and much abused profession."[25] In the *Herald Tribune,* Lewis Gannett pointed out that the book's clarity and dramatic qualities obviously stemmed from the author's prior experience as a newspaperman. Moreover, wrote Gannett, the book contained a message for the future, one that set high standards for Kennedy himself. Gannett added the qualm that some of his colleagues will "regard it as highly irregular for a young Senator to write such a book as this."[26] In Boston the City Council immediately passed an order requiring the School Committee to incorporate the book as an integral part of the history curriculum, while

Councilor Gabriel F. Piemonte hailed the book as a "great lesson in democracy." Kennedy's old naval friend and VFW compatriot, Ed McLaughlin, quickly agreed and said that his own personal association had shown him that his friend's whole life "epitomizes a profile in courage."[27] Once again celebrated as an author, Kennedy was a featured speaker at the annual dinner of the National Book award in New York City on February 7 and was photographed with such other eminent literary figures as W. H. Auden, John O'Hara, and Hubert Kubly.[28] The next day he was at the Book and Author Luncheon of *The Washington Post.* In the Presidential Room of the Hotel Statler, he was hailed by the paper's president and publisher Philip Graham, who introduced him to the largely feminine audience as "the handsomest male speaker present."[29] "This is a great book that every student of government—in fact every voter—should read. No one can fail to derive a great feeling of pride in these men who fate chose to play a decisive part in history, often at great cost personally and politically," wrote the reviewer for the *Oregon Journal.*[30]

The book itself was uncomplicated, written in clear, frequently dramatic language without any jargon; its style and theme made it perfectly suitable for the average reader. Its thrust was simple and its conclusion adhered to the best Whiggish concept of representative government. Those blessed with the responsibility for guiding the public's affairs must discharge their functions in the best interests of the commonwealth. Recalling that he had been advised upon entering the Congress that "the way to get along is to go along," Kennedy's theme addressed itself to the conflict inherent in a senator acting as the agent of the national need. One with better access to information and deliberation must necessarily find himself at variance with positions that are parochial and regional. The highest virtue of courage and patriotism, therefore, was the ability to resist local biases by placing expertise at the service of the national good. In each of the cases, according to the analysis presented by the book, the decision was initially unpopular. Kennedy himself pointed out that he did not necessarily agree with every particular historical stand; yet each one attested to a broader patriotism. Lucidly, the book enumerated an honor roll. The case studies constituted a judicious mixture of Republicans and Democrats. Their common denominator stressed the abandonment of "narrow" party interests for the greater good.

"In the days ahead," he wrote in the opening chapter on "Courage and Politics," "only the very courageous will be able to take the hard and unpopular decisions necessary for our survival in the struggle with a powerful enemy. . . . And only the very courageous will be able to keep alive the spirit of individualism and dissent which gave birth to this nation, nourished it as an infant and carried it through its severest test upon the attainment of its maturity."[31]

John Quincy Adams defied the interests of Massachusetts and regional and parochial needs to support, first, the Louisiana Purchase and then Jefferson's Embargo Act. Daniel Webster, also from Massachusetts, ignored most of the North by appealing to the interests of nationalism over sectionalism with his Seventh of March Speech defending the Compromise of 1850. Thomas Hart Benton kept Missouri from joining the seceding slave states. Sam Houston cast a lonely vote for the Kansas-Nebraska Bill. There was Edmund Ross of Kansas, who, along with six other "courageous Republicans," refused to go along with the impeachment move against Andrew Johnson. And in the post-Reconstruction period, Lucius Q. C. Lamar of Mississippi eulogized the late Charles Sumner—the South's most implacable enemy—because Lamar was more interested in the promotion of national unity than in the continuation of sectional strife. George Norris of Nebraska was lauded for opposing the tyrannical rule of "Uncle Joe" Cannon, helping to reduce the power that "placed party above all other considerations, a power that fed on party loyalty, patronage and political organizations." Robert Taft was similary eulogized for daring to take the unpopular stand of opposing the Nuremburg Trials because he believed that the Constitution prohibited *ex post facto* laws; therefore, he defended what he regarded "to be traditional American concepts of law and justice."[32]

Concluding with a discussion of the meaning of courage, the Kennedy book argued that the national interest "rather than private or political gain, furnished the basic motivation for the actions of those whose deeds are therein described." He recalled Prime Minister Melbourne's remark, after having been annoyed by the criticism of the historian Thomas B. Macaulay "that he would like to be as sure of anything as Macaulay seems to be of everything." "The courage of life," Kennedy concluded, "is often a less dramatic spectacle than the courage of a final moment; but it is not less a magnificent mixture of triumph and tragedy. A man does what he must—in spite of personal consequences, in spite of obstacles and dangers and pressures—and that is the basis of all human morality."[33]

The book immediately became a popular item. At a time when few Americans doubted that the expansion of communism threatened their way of life, *Profiles* renewed their faith in the ability of democracy to survive by producing freely chosen leaders concerned more with the fate of the commonweal than in parochial matters. The examples also illustrated the importance of selecting those with moral purpose and a dedication to the cause of freedom, virtues assumed to be intrinsically American. Newspapers ran abridgments and serializations that featured pictures of both the author and his heroes. Best-seller lists reflected success. On NBC-TV the *Kraft Theater* devoted one hour to a dramatization of how Edmund Ross defied intimidation to do what was "right." The author of *Why England Slept* had scored a new literary triumph—this time far more consequentially.

In many ways, *Profiles* was a remarkable achievement from one currently holding legislative office. Perhaps, some have suggested, Kennedy was driven to expiate his guilt over the McCarthy affair. Although willing to credit him with its authorship, few have assumed, as the preface more than hinted, that he lacked substantial assistance. James MacGregor Burns expressed this feeling by saying that "I think Sorensen or whoever was helping him, gave him more help on the book than you or I could hope to get if we were doing one."[34] One could properly inquire about what was unusual in modern American politics for a public figure, busily preoccupied with the demands of his office, to employ a capable staff that, using his name, could draft letters to editors for publication and even prepare correspondence, books, and articles under his by-line.

The *Profiles* case was, however, exceptional—the difference between utilizing the prerequisites of office to expedite responsibilities and the manufacturing of a talent to create the image of a young senator distinctively different from conventional politicians and who, while denying that it was principally the work of others, would accept a Pulitzer prize. Enough personal recognition came his way to make it a major political coup. But it was as deceptive as installing a Chevrolet engine in a Cadillac.

The evidence is now available, perhaps as detailed as will ever be known. Relevant handwritten drafts, typescripts, and recorded tapes have been deposited with the Kennedy Library, all designed to validate his claims to authorship, as had previously been presented to private skeptics. Such material can also be augmented by those who were intimately associated with the project, who can provide corroborating details of how it was put together. Nothing in all this rejects the truth of Jack Kennedy's involvement: from start to finish, the responsibility was clearly his.

Little had engaged Jack Kennedy's personal attention more than writing *Profiles in Courage*. Once intrigued by the idea, he oversaw its compilation and organization, whether on duty in the Senate, recuperating in the hospital, convalescing in Florida, or traveling in Europe. Personalities to be included were suggested by several people; the preface acknowledges many debts, but the choices, message, and tone of the volume are unmistakably Kennedy's. As Ted Sorensen has confirmed, long after questions about the book's authorship had ceased being a matter for public debate, "the concept of the book was Kennedy's. The responsibility for the book was Kennedy's. The decision as to which individuals, which individual stories should go in to the book were all made by Kennedy. The philosophy expressed in the opening and closing chapters resolved from and reflected against was the statement and responsibility of Kennedy."[35] That testimonial does not involve agreement that the final product represented Kennedy's labor, talents as a historian, or literary skill. What was so widely hailed in 1956 and then crowned by the Pulitzer prize advisory board resulted from three fairly distinctive phases of activity.

The first began in early 1954. Sometime that spring, the idea began to form in Jack Kennedy's head. Its origin is traceable to no other source; initially, he conceived that an article would result. Charles Bartlett has connected its genesis with the dilemma over McCarthy, which was dramatized in March by Senator Flanders's speech ridiculing the senator as one who "goes forth to battle and proudly returns with the scalp of a pink army dentist."[36] For Kennedy, the imbroglio provoked the delicate question of the individual legislator's responsibility and the true meaning of representative democracy.

Before the start of the Army-McCarthy hearings, before the Flanders Resolution, and before Kennedy feared the imminence of having to commit himself on the issue, journalists and university professors were invited to submit nominees for a list of senators who had taken courageous stands. As early as April 9, Krock suggested the inclusion of Robert Taft as "the outstanding example of independent political convictions in the United States during the 20th Century" for his opposition to the Nuremberg Trials, a choice Kennedy accepted with considerable reluctance, as it implied endorsement of a contemporary and only recently deceased conservative Republican.[37] Sorensen, meanwhile, lobbied for the inclusion of George Norris and requested his father to arrange for the Norris papers to be sent to Washington. A friend of Kennedy's aide, John Bystrom of the University of Minnesota, contributed a treatise on the progressive Republican. The list of "courageous" profiles grew. That spring and summer the growing dilemma over McCarthy, accompanied by the emergence of the censure question, heightened Kennedy's interest in the project.[38] Further stimulation came when Jack read Herbert Agar's *The Price of Union.*

Professor Davids believes that Jacqueline's studies for his course were an additional factor, with Kennedy's interest in her work helping to trigger his own contemplation of the American past.[39] In Jacqueline's presence Davids lectured "rather dramatically" about John Adams's plucky move to pull out the carpet from under Alexander Hamilton's quasi-war with France and lauded the President's decision to send a peace mission to Paris after the XYZ affair, which led to Hamilton's vindictive reaction and Adams's downfall. The Kennedys—Jackie and her husband—doubtless followed their usual pattern of discussing both the literature and lectures involved in the course. But that particular lecture on Adams led to a telephone call to Davids from Sorensen. The professor was told about the project. Sorensen and Kennedy warned Davids not to expect the book to do well commercially and pointed out that they had to proceed with a limited budget. Nevertheless, would he help put it together for a nominal fee?[40]

By early 1955 the idea of expanding the article gained momentum. Sorensen worked with several clerical assistants, who took dictation, transcribed from Dictabelts, and typed.[41] Gradually, instead of a piece suitable for the pages of the *Atlantic* or *Harper's,* a small book was visualized, possibly called "Patterns of Political Courage." Publisher Cass Canfield of Harper and Brothers, who was also the father of Lee Bouvier's husband, Michael, suggested that each case history could be developed to establish more fully the historical context in which the events occurred and strengthening the dramatic interest.[42]

The second phase began after the removal of the silver plate from Jack's back and his return to Palm Beach. By then it was confirmed that a book project was under way. Harper and Brothers came through with a contract in April that included a five-hundred-dollar advance for a work under the tentative title of "These Great Men," with Evan Thomas, the son of the leading American socialist, doing the editing for the publishing house. At about the same time, Thomas asked Kennedy to consider such alternatives as "These Brave Men" and "The Patriots."[43]

On May 3 Jim Landis submitted a thoughtful memorandum of nearly five single-spaced pages. Summarizing the project's basic theme as the conflict "between the Senator's independent thinking as to the welfare of the nation and the known desires and wishes of the constituents that he represents," he projected the concept of courage as exemplified in "substantially every case" by the senator following "his own ideas rather than the wishes of his constituents." That was the conflict: how to reconcile the popular wills inherent in a democracy with the educated knowledge of its representatives. "Then we come to those cases where the articulated aspirations of the State must be set aside," wrote Landis. "The grounds for this generally are that (a) the people of the State have been misinformed or sold a particular viewpoint by pure propaganda, or (b) that they are against the national interest." Guiding the thesis, Landis raised questions about the appropriate times for senators to assert themselves instead of the popular will. "Where does localism end and nationalism override it? And where does the little man, whose votes really elect him, fit into the picture? Surely not merely on patronage. Representative government to survive must mean more than that." There were no easy answers, Landis suggested; the "problems require thought rather than research. But well done, it will hit with the power of a hydrogen bomb."[44] Jack probably was amused by Landis's metaphor, which simply showed the enthusiasm with which the project was launched, but the memorandum nevertheless covered the essence of what materialized.

Additional guidance was solicited from such academicians as Arthur Schlesinger, Jr., Walter Johnson, James MacGregor Burns, Allan Nevins, and Arthur Holcombe, who contributed the quotation from Macaulay. Holcombe also noted that the manuscript "steered what seems to me a sound course between partisan extremes of opinion. While I, an ancestral Republican and Whig, caught my breath occasionally, I can not honestly say, after due reflection, that you, presumably an ancestral Democrat, as well as an active one, have taken liberties with history."[45] Nevins later provided additional criticism and the foreword. Davids also submitted his own detailed critique, which stressed the weakness of the organization and urged a more clearly defined approach, prompting Kennedy to ask the Georgetown professor for the draft of a chapter that might become a model for reworking the material that had already been written.[46] Working under considerable pressure, Davids drafted a twenty-two-page chapter on Webster, which was then forwarded to Schlesinger for an additional opinion.[47] On July 4, Schlesinger sent four single-spaced pages of criticism that examined the entire manuscript in great detail.[48]

Meanwhile, Sorensen had a full-time project on his hands. During the first half of 1955, just about all of his time was spent on the book; he often put in twelve-hour days. Both he and Davids were also given access to Kennedy's Library of Congress study room. Through William R. Tansill of the Legislative Research Office, they received about six hundred items. Tansill also helped compile a bibliography but, contrary to rumors that circulated within the Library of Congress, did no actual writing. "I was impressed with the volume of materials," he later remembered. "He [Kennedy] wanted one hell of a lot of stuff and I ran down every possible lead I could in regards to it; manuscript sources and all kinds of things. . . . Photoduplication (Verifax) of Congressional materials, Congressional documents of every kind, reports, etc."[49]

During the senator's hospitalization in February, Sorensen carried books and documents to his bedside in New York. Then, at Palm Beach, they worked together with the assistance of secretaries, and additional material was dictated. From his Washington office Sorensen performed multiple functions as coordinator of the structure and director of the flow of paperwork to and from the various contributors and critics. After the Webster chapter, Davids submitted twenty-six pages on Sam Houston, twenty-four on Lucius Q. C. Lamar, a twenty-six-page chapter on George W. Norris, and a thirteen-page essay on "The Meaning of Political Courage" for the closing section. Sorensen himself drafted the chapters on John Quincy Adams, Thomas Hart Benton, and Edmund Ross, plus the section on "Additional Men of Courage." Landis, other than his memorandum, wrote a chapter on Robert A. Taft and helped rework the Webster material. Kennedy then combined Davids's and Sorensen's work on "The Meaning of Courage" and completed Chapter XI by adding his own personal comments and observations.[50]

Interviewed about his role twenty-two years later, Sorensen noted that it was a "sensitive" matter and declined to be quoted taking credit for the work. Nevertheless, he acknowledged that "I prepared the materials on which the book is based." Pressed more closely to delineate the differences between his contributions and Kennedy's, he replied, "The opening and closing chapters, which are more personal and more reflections of his philosophy, probably were more heavily influenced by his literary style than those that were simply historical accounts."[51] Davids, neither a lawyer nor a Kennedy employee, has stated more directly that he and Sorensen did the major bulk of the research and drafting of chapters.[52]

From Florida, Kennedy kept in touch with the project. His closest involvement came during that second phase. It was at that point that he told Minna Littmann about the Library of Congress furnishing him with boxes of books to enable him to proceed with the work from his bed. "He was flat on his back in March, but in May he could sit up and then we even took interruptions for a swim in the ocean. The way Jack worked was to take all the material, mine and his, pencil it, dictate the fresh copy in his own words, pencil it again, dictate it again—he never used a typewriter" was the way Sorensen described the process to the authors of a book that was published in 1960.[53]

By the time Kennedy left Florida, the project was well advanced but far from complete. The chapters on Adams, Webster, Benton, and Ross were finished. The discussion of Norris needed to be reworked on the basis of a new draft by Sorensen and a memorandum provided by Davids. A revised version of the Taft chapter awaited final approval. Chapter X, which dealt with several miscellaneous minor figures, needed to be rewritten after a comparison with the original draft. The notes that had been gathered for the conclusion had yet to be put together for a final summary chapter. The foreword from Allan Nevins had to be done after the entire manuscript had been completed. Nor had a decision been reached about a title.[54]

Once back in Washington, Kennedy, following a prepared outline, worked on the first chapter, and then the final one received his close attention. He also solicited opinions on the relative merits of four possible titles—"Men of Courage," "Eight Were Courageous," "Call the Roll," and "Profiles of Courage." In August, just before sailing to Europe, he informed Evan Thomas that Sorensen "will be sending a completed manuscript to you as soon as he receives . . . the suggestions and criticisms of Allan Nevins." Kennedy also ruled out "Men of Courage" as a possible title, and Thomas soon afterward reported that the publishing office had decided to go with *Profiles in Courage.*[55]

The final phase hardly involved Kennedy at all. Sorensen's talents gave the manuscript its lucid and dramatic readability, which included the important function of providing for stylistic consistency. Nevertheless, when Joe Kennedy inspected the final draft, he complained that it lacked polish, which angered Thomas. "We do a certain amount of re-writing here," the editor wrote to Sorensen; "in fact I have done some myself—but this book reads like Jack Kennedy, and damn good, too. I'd just as soon it continued to read that way. Hell, I suppose we could get it rewritten by a poet or whatnot, but then it would be a different book. I think you will agree that the book has had a certain amount of editorial attention."[56] Joe Kennedy also involved himself in urging that the dust jacket contain a picture of his son on the entire top half of the back, which he considered more important than a biographical sketch in large type.[57] With Thomas now doing most of the touch-up editing, Sorensen's function consisted of getting after Nevins for the foreword, rounding up pictures from the Library of Congress and the firm of Harris & Ewing, checking the galleys, having his office prepare the index, and promoting serialization rights in various publications. Sorensen also wrote long, detailed letters to the senator in Europe keeping him informed of the book's evolution toward publication and the progress of subsidiary sales. Kennedy had left instructions that the publisher immediately reinvest ten percent of all subsidiary earnings for additional promotion; he would then reimburse Harper and Brothers and contribute funds from his share of royalties for further advertising. As he prepared to sail overseas, he also asked Thomas to avoid quoting laudatory comments from the letters of Holcombe and Johnson because they were not well known. Probably because Schlesinger was so closely identified as an ADA liberal, Kennedy added, "I think I would prefer not to have Schlesinger's comments on the cover."[58]

The news that reached him in Europe was uniformly good. Allan Nevins had lauded the work as one bound to add to Kennedy's stature and offered only minor corrections. By September arrangements had been made for prepublication in many large-circulation magazines: *Harper's*, the *Reader's Digest, Collier's, The New York Times Magazine, The Boston Globe.* Sorensen wrote that the prepublication treatment was unprecedented and that "more people will have heard of this book by January than any other." His only "sour" note was that the Kennedy photograph *Life* was planning to run would appear on the first page of the article, not on the cover. Then came television rights for the *Kraft Theater.* Three months before its publication, earnings for the author reached the $11,300 level, not bad for that stage in the life of an unpublished book in 1955. By April, however, revenues were sufficient to enable Kennedy to reimburse the publisher for $1,055 to cover Harper and Brothers' share of serialization fees that had gone into promotion. He had also spent another $1,618.40 of his own funds for advertising, especially for newspapers and periodicals in New England. That investment pushed total expenditures up to $4,503.75, which included $700 for Professor Davids's services.[59]

Along with continued serializations in various publications, sales reached respectable levels. Thomas reported that 124,665 copies had been sold by March of 1958. Kennedy continued to arrange for the publisher to reduce his own royalties for more extensive advertising.

Foreign-language editions also proliferated, including a Hebrew version published in Jerusalem in 1956 and Japanese and Persian reprints.

Politically, the book did all and even more than Kennedy could have wished. Appearing as it did, just months before the 1956 Democratic National Convention, it boosted his stature considerably. He became an instant spokesman for the politics of integrity in a party already enamored of its "egghead" titular leader, Adlai E. Stevenson. Inevitably, it also produced whispers, and even public charges, that Kennedy did not deserve credit for its authorship.

Nothing upset Kennedy more. In the basement of the Blackstone Hotel in Chicago during the 1956 convention, he became involved in a conversation with Joe Alsop and Blair Clark about the rumors of the book having been ghostwritten. Clark, a Kennedy classmate from Harvard days then covering the convention for the Columbia Broadcasting System, cracked a little joke. "Jack," he said, "I'm going to deny forever that I wrote *Why England Slept.*" Kennedy became furious.[60]

In early May of 1957, after Jack had further added to his prestige at the convention by narrating a film produced by Dore Schary, making a speech placing Stevenson in nomination, coming close to defeating Estes Kefauver for the vice-presidential nomination in a thrilling "horse race," and further impressing TV viewers by appearing on the podium to ask for unanimous support for his rival, *Profiles in Courage* was awarded the Pulitzer prize for biography. That led to more charges. Gilbert Seldes, writing in *The Village Voice,* claimed not only that it was a book for adolescents but was written with a collaborator.[61] Perhaps in response to Seldes, as well as other skeptics, the FBI, undoubtedly at the Ambassador's prompting, monitored the efforts of "a group of New York people" to verify that Arthur Krock had been the real author of *Profiles in Courage.* The bureau watched the sleuths, who intended, if the hunch could be proved, to file a charge of fraud on the awarding of the Pulitzer prize.[62]

Meanwhile, on Mike Wallace's ABC television show of December 7, 1957, columnist Drew Pearson also charged that Kennedy's book was "ghostwritten." The Kennedy people went to work immediately, aided by the legal services of Washington attorney Clark Clifford, whose effectiveness in the matter, Hugh Sidey wrote, was so great that "Kennedy never forgot his talent." They forced Pearson to make a public retraction —one drafted by Ted Sorensen—immediately preceding Wallace's show the following week.[63] Pearson wrote in his diary that he was not fully convinced. "He got a whale of a lot of help on his book," Pearson noted privately. "I'm still dubious as to whether he wrote too much of it in the final draft himself. He showed me the rough chapters—some of them worked out by Harvard professors. But he also showed enough knowledge of the book, made the book much a part of him, that basically it is his book."[64] But Pearson, of course, had not known the entire story. At the Century Club in New York City, John Oakes of *The New York Times* suggested to Harper editor Simon Michael Bessie the "strong rumor" that Kennedy had not really written the book. Bessie got upset and denounced Oakes for even circulating such a rumor. Oakes, on his next visit to the senator's Washington office, was immediately handed a letter by Kennedy noting that Oakes's acceptance of the rumor had been called to his attention. It vigorously restated his claim to the book's authorship and the legitimacy of having accepted the Pulitzer prize. Kennedy then did not dismiss the subject. He had an assistant display for Oakes the actual notebooks he had used in writing the draft of the book during his Florida recuperation. He also showed Oakes the letters from those who had provided help on specific matters. Oakes received an intimate view of Kennedy's sensitivity to the charges and pride of authorship. "I think he was very conscious . . . of the political implications of this kind of story as well as the literary and moral obligations," Oakes recalled.[65] At the same time, Martha MacGregor, the *New York Post* book editor, wrote to Kennedy about the rumor that Sorensen had written the book and was receiving half the royalties. Kennedy responded with a letter despairing that still another article on the subject by him could not clear it up any further. Again, he cited his acceptance of the Pulitzer prize.[66] Years later, in the White House, Kennedy lamented that the charge was hard to shake off and asked Krock whether he remembered seeing him writing the book at Palm Beach. Krock vouched that he did write it while "lying flat on his back on a board with a yellow pad on which he was writing the book, and that I read enough of those papers at the time to know that the product was his own."[67]

Nevertheless, neither the chronology of Jack Kennedy's life in 1954 and 1955 nor the materials accumulated in the preparation of the book even come close to supporting the contention that Jack could have been or was its major author. Those were years when, in addition to being in the Senate, Kennedy underwent two major spinal operations and was hospitalized for three additional brief periods. He was also frequently absent on appearances throughout the country in an effort to further his credentials and visibility as a Democratic leader. It was also the period when he made an extensive European tour, from August to October of 1955.

The files do show notes in Kennedy's handwriting. Written on letter-size canary looseleaf paper, they constitute scrawls in his familiar tiny, slanted, almost indecipherable hand, much of the work probably done while on his back. They indicate very rough passages without paragraphing, without any shape, largely ideas jotted down as possible sections, obviously necessitating editing. That portion of the handwritten material, the pages cited by a seemingly endless crew of witnesses ready to testify that they actually watched him write, almost as though he were an author on display at work in a glass booth, in no way resembles the final product. Much of the writing contains notes from secondary sources that were mixed together with the original, creative passages. Almost all of the actual manuscript material rests in eight folders of Box 35 in the Kennedy Library.

They offer some glimpses into Kennedy's personal involvement. The first has some notes on Lucius Lamar, but, mostly, on John Quincy Adams. The second has more on both men with notes in Kennedy's writing relating to both, and Adams material that appears on page 53 of the book. The third folder has more draft material and notes on Lamar. The fourth contains assorted notes and some draft material on the Alien and Sedition Acts of 1798, obviously in relation to Adams. A continuation of the Alien and Sedition Acts and the Constitution, with more on Adams, is in the fifth folder. The sixth has material on John Calhoun and his "American System." Folder seven has varied notes relating to such Supreme Court decisions as *Marbury* v. *Madison, McCullough* v. *Maryland,* the *Dartmouth College Case,* and the conflict between Thomas Jefferson and Aaron Burr. The final folder contains random notes on Adams, Clay, and Jackson.

There is no evidence of a Kennedy draft for the overwhelming bulk of the book; and there is evidence for concluding that much of what he did draft was simply not included in the final version. The inescapable impression is that Kennedy's own interest, other than the question of representing one's conscience rather than merely reflecting constituent desires, largely related to John Quincy Adams, and he bogged down in that area, completely out of proportion to the needs of the book. Those who took over the project, headed by Sorensen, rescued him and helped fill out the material.

If the handwritten evidence is scant, dictation could have justified his claim to authorship. The existing tapes, however, duplicate the pattern of the nearly illegible scrawls on those canary sheets. His speech was characteristically rapid (especially during that stage of his life), the voice clipped, producing an almost indecipherable staccato effect, which must have been quite a chore for the typists. Still, the typescripts contained in the folders faithfully record his words, so it is possible to follow the text while hearing his voice, which often sounds distorted from either the aging of the tapes, the fact that he was under sedation, or the need to rest on his back. The overall effect, as in the handwritten sections, is that of disorganized, somewhat incoherent, mélange from secondary sources, interspersed with quotes together with instructions for punctuation and style, and random observations. Many passages were read from Margaret Coit's biography of Calhoun. There was no attempt at creating a lucid narrative or structure. Obviously, it was data being transmitted for associates. The tapes also reveal that new recordings were made on top of the old, so that the existing reels do not represent the full extent of the dictation.[68] If the Kennedy Library collection is designed to prove his authorship, it fails to pass inspection. About all the material does demonstrate is Jack's close association with its conception and completion.

For all the practical reasons, however—limitations of time, health, and appropriate talent—the senator served principally as an overseer or, more charitably, as a sponsor and editor, one whose final approval was as important for its publication as for its birth. At the working level, research, tentative drafts, and organizational planning were left to committee labor, with such talents as Professor Davids making key contributions. But the burdens of time and literary craftsmanship were clearly Sorensen's, and he gave the book both the drama and flow that made for readability.

18

"Madly for Adlai"

It would be hard to imagine Adlai Stevenson, who did little reading, giving much attention to *Profiles in Courage*. Nevertheless, when he received a bound copy of the manuscript in October 1955, he sent a polite note with his usual graceful prose. "I certainly am honored and flattered by those very nice sentiments," Kennedy wrote back. He also explained that he was preparing a statement urging Stevenson's nomination. He would pledge his own support in a statement that would be released whenever Stevenson thought it would do most good.[1] The Governor suggested that Kennedy should "proceed as you think best," but that those around him "seem to think the sooner the better for all concerned."[2]

Stevenson's relationship with the Kennedy family was not new. The Ambassador bragged that he had "sort of" discovered the Governor. Owning the Merchandise Mart had naturally brought him close to the Illinois political establishment and when Stevenson won the governorship in 1948, Joe Kennedy was among the contributors. Later, he invited him to a football game, which the Governor declined, but they met in Springfield afterward. The Ambassador found the Governor's speeches appealing and recommended them to Jim Landis, who then helped Stevenson on problems relating to the economy of southern Illinois. Stevenson, however, remained skeptical about Joe Kennedy's support.[3] When the Governor became the Democratic Party's 1952 presidential nominee, the Ambassador was one of his backers. Steven Mitchell, who managed the campaign, recalled that Joe Kennedy turned over checks for about twenty-five thousand dollars from different funds and different groups to avoid violating the law, but they nevertheless constituted a Kennedy family contribution.[4] Kennedy had originally backed Taft for the Republican nomination, also giving money to that cause. But when Eisenhower became the GOP candidate, Joe considered him a "washout" and probable loser and so Stevenson loomed, in his eyes, as a likely winner, always a good reason for the Ambassador to get behind a man. Landis remembered that the possibility of a future Stevenson-Kennedy ticket was not far from Joe's mind and, at least as early as 1954, was more than idle contemplation in Jack Kennedy's. The long series of speech-making before his surgery had that as a potential goal, for a vice-presidential nomination might help surmount the religious barrier for a future presidential nomination and would help his 1958 reelection efforts.[5]

Unfortunately, such feelings were not reciprocated. Stevenson was fond of neither the father nor completely taken with his son. He knew Shriver through the in-law's management of the Merchandise Mart, but it was only toward Shriver that he felt any kind of warmth. He thought Jack too young, too inexperienced; he was uncomfortable about the way the family was attempting to throw money around, attitudes apparently encouraged through meetings with Lyndon Johnson. But it was toward the Ambassador himself that Stevenson's disapproval remained strongest. One incident, at the Libertyville farm, in the presence of Robert Kennedy, not only illustrated the Governor's attitude but made an impression not easily forgotten. Told that Joe Kennedy was on the phone and wanted to talk to him, Stevenson looked up, somewhat exasperated, and groaned. Before taking the call, he said quite audibly, "Oh, my God, this will be an hour and a half."[6]

Yet Stevenson was not oblivious to the advantages of having Jack Kennedy as his running mate. Most important for Stevenson was Kennedy's potential ability to counter Dwight Eisenhower's attractions to the Democratic Catholic electorate unhappy with Roosevelt and Truman for the spread of communism in Eastern Europe and Asia. Catholic voters were the Governor's softest area. His divorce was a burden that had to be overcome, but the trouble went deeper. Stevenson found it difficult to make effective appeals among the kind of blue-collar elector- ate that Kennedy penetrated with his mixture of social conservatism, anticommunism, and economic New Deal liberalism. Kennedy would give the ticket geographic balance, although in this case—and in what would be a departure from the typical means of Democratic ticket- building—he would be the one with appeal to the urban, Catholic work- ing classes, rather than to the party's southern wing.

Despite his problems with Catholic voters, Stevenson retained strong backing. Ever since the 1952 loss, he had been working to strengthen his position in the South. Influential moderates and liberals, especially in urban centers, remained enthusiastic supporters. He had to be the odds- on favorite for the 1956 nomination; and Jack Kennedy, having estab- lished a history of support for the Governor, along with the past assist- ance from his father and Jim Landis, seemed ready to exploit the oppor- tunity. But in retrospect, this appears more assertive than the Jack Kennedy of that period. He still had doubts about both his health and political ability. He had yet to demonstrate that he could become a national force. In his home state, too, the chaotic personality-based party organization threatened to undermine his political foundation. And he had given the matter little attention.

Some push to steer Kennedy in the direction of the 1956 ticket came from Ted Sorensen. On September 12, 1955, he wrote to the senator at the Hotel Du Cap D'Antibes, France, informing him that the *Boston Post*'s Jim Colbert had devoted a front-page story to a report that Steven- son's group was considering Kennedy as a likely choice. Sorensen embel- lished the account with information that Kennedy, along with Salton- stall, had received good press coverage for joint efforts to coordinate federal agency activities in behalf of the flood victims in the aftermath of hurricane Diane. He had also gotten what Sorensen called "tremen- dous coverage" for the story on the Hill-Kennedy Polio Vaccine Bill and assured the senator that he was "on the record" on eighty out of ninety- four roll-call votes during the last session, or more than eighty-five percent. So, wrote Sorensen, "despite the large number of pairs and announcements of positions this includes, it is large enough to offset any possible criticism." At the same time, the assistant was overseeing the efforts Kennedy was making to persuade Majority Leader Lyndon John- son to award him with more prestigious Capitol Hill committee assign- ments. Sarcastically, he wrote, "Lyndon Johnson has finally come through, making up for his failure to appoint you to the Foreign Rela- tions and Finance Committees. He has recommended that you be ap-

pointed to THE BOSTON NATIONAL HISTORIC SITES COMMIS-
SION!!"[7]

By that date, Stevenson himself had held an important strategy meeting at his Libertyville farm and had agreed to make the race for 1956.
"It was very gratifying, and I think now some realistic preliminary
organization work is going to proceed," he wrote to his friend Agnes
Meyer, the wife of *The Washington Post*'s publisher.[8] Less than two
weeks after that strategy session, there was talk in Massachusetts of the
possibility that Stevenson would be more palatable, presumably among
that state's large Catholic electorate, with Kennedy as his running mate.
Stevenson had gone ahead and hired pollster Elmo Roper to make surveys of the political situation.

The big earthquake that hit both Republican and Democratic politicos
came with the news from Denver on September 24, while Kennedy was
still in Europe, that President Dwight D. Eisenhower had had a major
heart attack. For several days his survival was in doubt; and, to the
politicians, possibly even more germane, so was his availability for the
1956 ticket. Immediately, Democrats who had hitherto reassured Stevenson that it was his duty to carry their party's banner, began to reassess
the situation. The 1956 Democratic presidential nomination suddenly
became a valuable prize. A close friend and supporter of Averell Harriman, George Backer, told Stevenson almost immediately afterward that
New York's governor would be in the race for himself.[9] In Tennessee,
Estes Kefauver was having similar thoughts. Having done so well in the
1952 primaries, his popularity among the rank and file had been demonstrated even while he had become *persona non grata* to the party chief-
tains for his role in the Crime Investigations of 1951 and to his fellow
southerners for having refused to join their protests against the Supreme
Court's school integration decision.

By the time Kennedy wrote to Stevenson, the Governor was also
aware of the great efforts being made by Kefauver. The aristocratic
Stevenson had reservations about the Tennesseean, who campaigned so
ardently with his familiar coonskin cap. At Arthur Schlesinger, Jr.'s,
Cambridge home, in mid-October, Stevenson had nice words to say
about Kefauver's well-organized campaign but noted the bitterness toward him on Capitol Hill and wondered whether he would be able
to perform any liaison with Congress, especially since both Johnson
and Rayburn regarded him as "the most hated man to serve in Congress
for many years." What Stevenson also wanted to avoid was being
placed in a position by Kefauver where the Tennesseean would attempt

to arrange a bargain with him for the vice presidential nomination.[10]

The entire country, meanwhile, watched the news from Fitzsimons Army Hospital near Denver. On October 23 the President stood unassisted for the first time since his heart attack. The implications for 1956 were obvious as pictures from Colorado buoyed GOP hopes by showing a smiling, obviously healthier Ike on the hospital balcony.

Although, as James Reston reported in *The New York Times,* while Republican politicians were still uncertain that he could run again, Stevenson's campaign was gaining early momentum, having been forced into high gear not only by Eisenhower's illness but by the additional challenge of Harriman. Reston also revealed the organization of the group headed by Thomas K. Finletter that, since 1953, had been formulating position papers to be used by Stevenson. Richard Russell of Georgia quickly suggested that a good man for 1956 would be Governor Frank Lausche of Ohio, thereby implying that neither Stevenson, Harriman, nor Kefauver would be acceptable to southerners.[11] On the twenty-ninth, Stevenson wrote to Kennedy that he had been on the verge of getting an endorsement from Rayburn but that had been withheld because of Johnson's attempt to get the nomination for himself.[12] Meanwhile, a leak reported by the *Chicago Tribune* of a planned Stevenson-Kefauver meeting to discuss the possibility of an arrangement for the 1956 ticket caused Stevenson to call it off. On November 15 Adlai Stevenson formally announced his presidential candidacy, a move that Kefauver then emulated on the seventeenth of December.

Jack Kennedy, meanwhile, was in Palm Beach with Dr. Travell and Jacqueline, who was recovering from her broken ankle. *The New York Times* appeared with its adaptation of the forthcoming *Profiles in Courage* and Jack Kennedy was still contemplating advice from Sorensen. He had conferred over breakfast with Stevenson on December 3 but still had not acted on Sorensen's memo that suggested the issuance of an endorsement at a press conference to be held in Washington. Sorensen's concern was twofold: it would give Kennedy more attention, but "more important, [it would] provide an opportunity to clear up all doubts about your health, which is the one question I still hear frequently raised around here when your name is discussed as a possibility for the ticket."[13]

Kennedy's objective was designation by Stevenson as the vice-presidential candidate rather than risking loss of prestige by entering any sort of preferential primary contest. Moreover, an open campaign for the second spot would defy tradition. Of Kennedy's vice-presidential bid, his brother Bobby later said, "I think he just wanted to . . . put his foot in the water and see how cold it was, but he hadn't made up his mind to swim."[14] Sorensen has since explained it simply by saying that the 1956 convention "was the only game in town, and the Kennedys like to try and win any game there is."[15] John Sharon, of Stevenson's Chicago office, was much more explicit, saying, "We were lobbied to death," by Jack Kennedy.[16]

Stevenson's law associate, Newton Minow, became friendly with the Shrivers. Sargent Shriver was then not only the general manager of the Merchandise Mart but president of the Chicago Board of Education, and, as some suspected, a potential candidate for the governorship of Illinois. Minow was invited to meet Jack Kennedy and hear him deliver a speech before the National Conference of Christians and Jews. Minow has since recalled that he "fell in love with Jack Kennedy immediately. I'd always admired him, but I was really taken with him. I was taken with his whole attitude, his whole appearance, his whole— He really sent me. I left there that night and I said to Jo in the car, 'You know, this would be the ideal candidate for Vice-President, with Adlai. This is a perfect match. He has what Adlai lacks. He has appeal to the Catholics. He will help on the divorce issue. He has appeal to young people, because of his youth. He has an appeal to a segment of the population that Adlai did very badly with in '52, the conservative Irish Catholic Democrats afraid of the soft-on-communism issue. He's perfect!'" From that point, Minow and William McCormick Blair, Jr., a Stevenson law associate and confidant, set on a two-man campaign to get Stevenson to accept Kennedy.[17]

For what appeared to be sound political reasons, the greatest opposition to Kennedy, ironically, came from Catholics. Jim Finnegan, Stevenson's manager, could not accept the notion of teaming up with Kennedy. Minow argued the point with Finnegan, an astute politician from Philadelphia, but could not make him budge. Finnegan, an Irishman, outlined Kennedy's liabilities. He emphasized opposition to Joe Kennedy. He didn't like Joe. He didn't like the family, he said. "I like Jack, from what I've seen about him. I don't really know him. But he's a kid!"[18] The more urgent worry, however, was that Catholics could not hold national office; and it was a feeling from Kennedy's co-religionist, shared by many, from Stevenson adviser Finnegan to Pennsylvania's David Lawrence, California's Pat Brown, and numerous other Roman Catholic delegates. They feared a Catholic on the ticket would rekindle the bitterness and bigotry that marred the Smith campaign of 1928, an abhorrent prospect. Those Catholics already running for state and local offices were, additionally, upset that one more "papist" would be too much to swallow for much of the electorate. They would have preferred a Protestant Kefauver, a Protestant Humphrey, a Protestant Gore, probably anybody to Kennedy.[19]

The timely publication of *Profiles in Courage* in early 1956 gave Kennedy new prominence, one that could not help but enhance his surreptitious candidacy. With Democrats still hopeful, he joined a crowded field. Typically, he poked fun at the situation by opening a talk at a testimonial dinner for George Smathers on January 19 with the statement that "the Chairman has asked me to make this announcement for the benefit of all the potential Democratic Presidential and Vice Presidential nominees who are here tonight." Then, after he had his audience's attention, he added: "The special meeting to be held for these candidates only at the close of this banquet has been moved from the club director's office to the main ballroom in order to accommodate all candidates expected to attend."[20]

However enhanced his reputation and recognition had become, a valid bid required more evidence of solid legislative achievement and command of the political situation. Success in those areas could counter liabilities of ill health and inexperience.

At the start of the Eighty-fourth Congress he immediately launched a new drive for more important committee assignments. Several requests had been made before, both in writing and in person, to the party's leader in the Senate, Lyndon B. Johnson. Kennedy's first choice was Foreign Relations; if not that, at least Appropriations. Now, in January, Sorensen compiled a memorandum that enumerated the appointments of Kennedy's colleagues. With some detailed evidence to support its contention, it argued that Kennedy had been left behind. Of all freshmen Democrats who had entered the Senate with him, only he "had failed to improve substantially his committee status since assignments were made at that time." He was the only member who served on both the Labor and Government Operations Committees "and every other Democratic member of both of those committees has been assigned to at least one major committee." In short, "no other member with his seniority lacked a single major committee assignment."[21] The death of Senator Alben Barkley at the end of April created a vacancy on the Foreign Relations Committee and prompted a renewed request, but Kennedy continued to be ignored as the seat went to Russell Long of Louisiana.

Several years later, remarks prepared for Kennedy to introduce Lyndon B. Johnson at a dinner for Harry Truman in Boston stated that *LBJ* stood for "Let's Block Jack."[22] Discretion triumphed, however, and the words were scratched. But they nevertheless remained as vestiges of tension between the two men, a conflict especially significant during Kennedy's early Senate years. Johnson had yet to accept the young man's independence, which included Kennedy's tardiness in committing himself to the choice of Johnson as the party's minority leader in the Eighty-third Congress. Compounding the damage was Kennedy's apparent ingratitude when, after Johnson had given him a warm welcome back to the Senate in May 1955 after his operation, the Texan's courtesy had not been repaid by greater voting loyalty on favored legislation. Kennedy was simply not as easily romanced by the Senate leader as were others, although Johnson had hoped to bring him into the inner circle. "In all honesty," recalled journalist Hugh Sidey, "the most vicious evaluation of Senator Kennedy was from Johnson and that got quite violent at times."[23]

As they headed toward the nominating convention in Chicago, however, Kennedy had repaired some of the damage by catering to the majority leader's personal sensitivities and political requirements. In early April, Kennedy drew a warm letter of appreciation. "You have done a great deal for me," Johnson wrote. "Some of the things I know and some I don't know. I do know, for instance, that when we decided not to have hearings on the extension of minimum wage legislation to retailers, that the decision was made by Lyndon Johnson, Lister Hill and Jack Kennedy. But when that decision was communicated to the labor unions, Jack Kennedy told them that it was his decision alone. That was a graceful gesture by a good man and a good Senator."[24] He had yet to get his committee, but a potent impediment had been eased.

Kennedy's Senate votes remained consistent with the regional interest of the Northeast. Before the bill to deregulate natural gas became involved with a revelation of improper financial contributions to secure its passage, which directly led to its veto by President Eisenhower, Kennedy spoke out about its potential impact. As a member of the select committee that investigated the original charges, Kennedy sided with the minority that wanted to use the case to recommend tightening the lobbying law to bring campaign contributions and expenditures under strict control.[25]

Of far more consequence than his position on natural gas was his opposition to continuing farm parity price supports at a rigid level. That placed him in opposition to the great majority of his fellow Democrats and on the side of the administration and Agriculture Secretary Ezra

Taft Benson. In explaining his stand, he denied that the ninety percent program had maintained either farm prices or income, and argued that "our farm programs have tended to help the well-to-do more than the poor." He became one of only four Democrats to vote against the Agriculture Act of 1956, which provided the ninety percent mandatory price supports on basic crops. At the same time, he voted for an amendment that would raise support prices for small farmers. His position was completely consistent with the interests of agriculture in Massachusetts, which was largely comprised of small poultry and dairy farmers. Their grain costs tended to rise under high price supports. Kennedy maintained that the ills of agriculture could not be cured by either fixed or sliding price supports. "Both old and new offer support to some farmers in some parts of the country that hurts other farmers in other parts of the country," he explained. "Both concentrate more on the farmer's price than on his net income, more on his guaranteed security than on his independence."[26]

Much more profitable was his leadership of the fight to prevent the elimination of the Electoral College. Substantial support existed for some kind of reform, especially since a large body of popular opinion could easily be led to agree that any change was fairer than the "winner-take-all" system. Within the Senate, however, Kennedy took the lead in countering that perceived truth. He argued that it contained a potential windfall to conservatives, especially since the rural areas of the country were overrepresented in both the Congress and the state legislatures. The Electoral College, at least, reflected the relative total populations of each state, those with the largest numbers containing significant urban areas, thereby counterbalancing the rural-dominated legislatures. So deceptive was the motivation behind the change that even as stalwart a liberal as Humphrey accommodated himself to the "reform." Humphrey, from an agricultural state, had proposed letting each state retain its two electoral votes and rewarding both to the candidate winning the plurality. Then the remaining electoral votes cast would be divided without regard to state lines. That dilution of federalism had also been the objective of those who introduced still another amendment, one that would decide the presidency by a direct popular vote.

Kennedy did his homework carefully. Among those he turned to in preparation of his position was Professor Holcombe. Holcombe thought a much better idea would be simply abolishing the Electoral College but casting each state's entire electoral vote automatically to the candidate favored by the greatest number of voters. That arrangement should be preserved as long as states continued to have equal representation in the Senate regardless of population.[27]

Basically, Kennedy established his argument along three points: (1) history had not shown evidence of sufficient abuse of the present system to warrant such a constitutional change; and so, he said, "I would be reluctant to take down a fence which has served us well in the past"; (2) there had been no demonstrated need for it and states that could legally have returned to a congressional system of deciding electoral votes had not chosen to do so, with the exception of Michigan, which abandoned a brief experiment with that form more than fifty years earlier; and (3) the maldistribution of congressional seats favoring rural interests would compound that influence over the legislatures to the executive branch as well, and such a change could tempt them to further multiply inequities. He did state that he would favor two minor changes: one that would have both chambers vote when no candidate received sufficient electoral votes, with members counting as individuals rather than as part of state delegations; and either abolishing the office of elector altogether or making it specifically nondiscretionary, thus preventing them from casting votes contrary to their instructions. When Senator Price Daniel of Texas expressed his agreement with Kennedy in opposition to a direct vote for president and vice-president but added that "we should get as close to it as we possibly can," Kennedy replied: "The reason why the Senator may also be against direct elections is that it would place tremendous influence, a disproportionate influence, in the major, pivotal States. So the Senator wants to go just far enough to deprive the States of their rightful influence, but not to go so far in the other direction as to give them what they really deserve."[28]

On the second day of the debate, Kennedy got to the essentials. He pointed out that the sponsors of the change had been frank enough to admit that what they really wanted to do was to reduce the influence of blacks, Jews, Catholics, and labor unions. One of the original proponents of an amendment, Congressman Ed Gossett, "was convinced it would make unnecessary any political recognition of the Negro, Jewish, and organized labor vote in New York City." So then Kennedy argued that "the fact that each such group is comparatively small in terms of the entire Nation, or that bloc voting by any one group—relatively nonexisting—might be numerically equal to the margin by which a candidate wins that State, hardly constitutes an evil of sufficient importance to revamp the constitution. . . ."[29]

Kennedy's position provided the necessary momentum for the reac-

344 JACK: THE STRUGGLES OF JOHN F. KENNEDY

tion. All suggested revisions were turned back. The outcome represented a prestigious achievement. The final vote on the last of a series of proposed changes came on April 5 and fell nine short of the minimum needed for the two-thirds vote of those present to ratify a constitutional amendment. Most astonishing and highlighting Kennedy's feat was the fact that fifty-five senators had originally gone on record for the proposed change, and nine of them finally voted in opposition. So did fifteen first-term senators who had not been previously committed. That ended the question.

At the same time, he continued to speak out on foreign affairs. Along with Humphrey, Kennedy strongly advocated pushing the administration toward a sturdier American commitment toward Israel, a position of importance to the same forces within the Democratic Party that gained by his championing of the Electoral College. He urged the State Department to accelerate the shipment of arms, especially since the Arabs appeared willing to get their supplies from the Soviet Union. He made a much more public commitment to the cause by addressing an "America Salutes Israel" rally at Yankee Stadium in New York City. He also accentuated criticism of the administration's military position vis-à-vis the Russians, contending in a radio interview that he had information that the Soviets were producing twice as many intercontinental bombers as the United States. He told a luncheon conference of the American Friends of Vietnam that that land represented the cornerstone of the Free World in Southeast Asia and was a test of American responsibility and determination. The next day he was in Kansas City, Missouri, telling Rockhurst College's graduating class that the administration was neglecting to separate America from Western colonialism, especially in Algeria and Indochina. Kennedy's critique of colonialism thus continued to combine with warnings of Russian exploitation of such Western vulnerability.[30]

At the political level the battle for preconvention positions became more intense. Although President Eisenhower's declaration of fitness for another term, supported by medical assurances, had deflated the value of their quest, Stevenson and Kefauver contended head-on in several primary elections. Nor was there a scarcity of possible Democratic vice-presidential candidates. Robert F. Wagner, Jr., of New York, Stuart Symington of Missouri, Albert Gore of Tennessee, Frank Lausche of Ohio, Robert Meyner of New Jersey, and practically everybody else who represented some political or geographic compromise or favorite-son ploy made his way onto a sometimes highly imaginative list, in addition to Humphrey and Kennedy. Right after Kefauver filed in late January to compete in the March 20 Minnesota primary, Humphrey issued a statement of support for Stevenson. Kennedy remained much more subdued, waiting for an appropriate moment to move.

In mid-February, Kennedy sent William McCormick Blair, Jr., the results of a private poll that had been taken by Professor Earl Latham and other political scientists and students of three colleges; it showed a rather startling sentiment. In Massachusetts, where both the Catholic and blue-collar electorate had been decidedly cool toward the Governor, he nevertheless placed ahead of Kefauver by a handsome 69–17 percentage. In Boston itself, Stevenson had seventy-eight percent as opposed to only eleven percent for Governor Frank Lausche, ten percent for Kefauver, and just one percent for Harriman. Kennedy also pointed out to Blair that the possibility of Congressman McCormack's designation as the state's favorite son at the convention had induced the survey to gauge their relative popularity. "73% voted for me, and only 13% for McCormack—so there should be no difficulty in preventing that threat," Kennedy explained.[31]

Kennedy called a press conference for March 8 to make his long-contemplated announcement. As Sorensen had urged much earlier, it took place in Washington. Kennedy told the newsmen that he would not have acted so early in the campaign if he were not confident that his choice would be nominated and could win in November. Asked about his own candidacy for the second spot, he replied, "I am not a candidate. I think a Southerner will be chosen," a prediction he had offered before.[32] Stevenson, pausing en route to his next campaign stop, wired his appreciation and noted that he looked forward to meeting with Kennedy in Chicago on March 17.[33]

The New Hampshire primary was only a partially significant victory for Kefauver, who retained a hold over a core of followers in the state from the 1952 campaign. In the preferential primary, however, or the so-called "beauty contest," Stevenson, without a fight, derived some satisfaction by winning more than one third of the vote.[34] Minnesota was much more meaningful. There, in a head-on battle, the senator from Tennessee won an upset, one that demolished optimistic feelings Stevenson had had before the vote.

The defeat enhanced the significance of Stevenson's meeting with Kennedy in Chicago three days before the Minnesota primary. Kennedy telegraphed him on the twenty-second that he had followed up on their

Saturday evening conversation by talking with Paul Dever "and we will get busy in attempting to develop a write-in vote in Massachusetts in April."[35] Stevenson's reply said simply: "In view of what happened in Minnesota, I feel it might be even more helpful."[36] Stevenson also notified Arthur Schlesinger, Jr., of the plan for Kennedy to work with Dever and, with the resources of the Massachusetts Young Democrats, to organize a Stevenson write-in. "I suppose for the present it must be considered highly confidential, however," he wrote.[37]

Before very long, both the Stevenson and Kennedy camps agreed to second thoughts about that strategy. Kennedy met with leaders of the Governor's forces in the Commonwealth on March 24 and was advised by Maurice Donahue, the state senator who headed the local Stevenson for President organization, that it would be a mistake to make an open campaign for write-in votes. A check of the 1952 write-in figures for Massachusetts revealed that Kefauver had outdrawn Stevenson by almost twenty-nine to one. At a subsequent meeting, also attended by several other politicians behind Kennedy, Frank Morrissey argued that an open campaign, in view of the Governor's poor track record in the state, could only jeopardize Kennedy's prestige.[38] Moreover, the more cautious approach was accepted by the directors of Stevenson's national campaign. Still, inaction was no solution. Alternate means of demonstrating Kennedy's ability to move Massachusetts behind Stevenson had to be found. "They all seem to feel," wrote Archibald Alexander, the executive director of the National Stevenson for President Committee, "[that] Senator Kennedy is in need of a push because both on regular Democratic matters and on the SPC [Stevenson for President Committee] inaction by him is the present roadblock."[39]

Kennedy's subsequent maneuver was both unavoidable and hazardous, a move that, in retrospect, has drawn mixed reviews. His strategy was to gain control of the state's Democratic Party organization. Whatever the evaluation of the consequences, the needs of the Stevenson campaign together with his own close personal identification with the importance of its success left him with no alternatives but to act.

The predicament had its origins in Kennedy's own detachment from the internal mechanism of the Massachusetts Democratic Party. The party as an organization had little actual power, even lacking full control of fund-raising and expenditures. In a state where influence gravitated around personalities, individuals rather than the state committee controlled the patronage. With an organization so weak, the chairmanship had little significance. It did, however, have one crucial source of power: the determination of the delegate selection process for representation of the state's party at the national convention.

For all these reasons, plus his personal proclivity for independence, Kennedy had long since concluded that it was best for him to remain aloof. Few things were as distasteful as intraparty squabbles. Moreover, that was one battle he thought he could not win. His attitude had the support of the Ambassador, who has been quoted as having advised, "Leave it alone and don't get into the gutter with those bums up there in Boston."[40] But after the Minnesota primary, the requirements of the Stevenson camp forced Kennedy to take command of a long neglected situation. Inevitably, his tardy entry disrupted the machinations of those already in charge and provoked resentment against Kennedy for being a "Johnny-come-lately" in statewide political problems.[41]

As early as 1954, there were efforts to draw the senator's attention to the Massachusetts situation. The battle centered around control by either former governor Dever or Congressman McCormack. Dever, who had been defeated in 1952 and subsequently suffered a heart attack, was losing influence. The state chairman, John Carr, was identified as Dever's man. With Carr under pressure to resign, while a legal battle revolved around the chairman's term of office and composition of the committee, efforts were being made to replace him with William H. Burke, Jr. Burke was a tavern owner and farmer from the Connecticut River Valley community of Hatfield, which gave him the nickname of "Onions." The rotund Burke epitomized the traditional clubhouse politician devoted to perquisites of power. Well schooled in the ways of factionalism, he had close ties to Jim Curley. His past included a conflict with Joe Kennedy, Jr., over FDR's third-term nomination.[42] More germane to the current situation was Burke's tie to John McCormack. The congressman had been instrumental in securing his appointment as collector of the Port of Boston, a patronage plum that came directly from the White House under Democratic administrations. That, of course, helped to seal their alliance. With the takeover of the chairmanship by Burke being engineered, Joe Healy, the Boston attorney and longtime Kennedy ally, warned the senator about the possible consequences of a leadership change. Writing at the time of Kennedy's postoperative hospitalization in early December, Healy observed to Ted Sorensen, "It is too bad that Jack is out of action at the present time, since the makeup of the State Committee will have a very vital effect on the type of delegation which we send to the National Convention in 1956."[43] Three months later, while Kennedy was in Palm Beach after his second operation and involved in the creation of *Profiles,* he was also warned by Congressman Philip J. Philbin about a great "hassle" ensuing within the state party. "Various learned 'savants' and 'intellectuals' who shape the upper crust of our party organization are conducting a campaign for control, or perhaps I should say a campaign to ensure our defeat at the next election," Philbin wrote.[44]

Kennedy's own staff did not neglect the situation. At the time Kennedy heard from Philbin, he was also scrutinizing what he called an "excellent" analysis by two of his own aides, O'Donnell and O'Brien. Kennedy's response to their view was to put off any definite "course of action" and to continue to "study" a possible plan.[45] But O'Donnell and O'Brien were insistent. Finally, reluctantly, Kennedy ratified their clandestine efforts to influence the state organization, explicitly instructing them to keep him out of sight of any direct involvement.[46] There is reason to believe that, in giving his approval, Kennedy was consciously circumventing his father's advice, which may have encouraged his own nonparticipation. As early as May 16, a full week before Jack Kennedy left Palm Beach to resume his senatorial duties, *The Berkshire Eagle* noted that professional aides of the Kennedy organization were meeting privately to build a stronger statewide organization in view of the strife that existed between John Carr and his opponents.[47]

A judicious reason for not acknowledging the involvement of the Kennedy people was the successful election of Onions Burke on the fourth of June, a decision that was contested by Carr's claim that he had been elected to a four-year term in 1952 and that the recent election was invalid since there was no actual vacancy. In December, however, the Commonwealth's Supreme Court legitimatized Burke's election, confirming once more who controlled the judgeships in Massachusetts. That development again betrayed the flimsiness of Kennedy's personal political power. Attempting to avoid an open break with McCormack, he moved to work out a deal. Jack maintained that he would agree to the choice of anybody other than Burke; but his offer was unacceptable. Burke was determined to fight. McCormack himself was far less eager for the clash. Only obligations to Burke kept him firm. As collector of the Port, Burke had given jobs to several of the congressman's friends.[48] Unfortunately, too, Burke had become a symbol of the Kennedy-Dever versus McCormack battle to control the state committee.

Having failed so far, Kennedy made his next move. Conferring with both men, he struck a bargain. Using the leverage of his own popularity as a potential favorite-son candidate at the convention, Kennedy got McCormack to agree to give him, along with Dever, power to approve the state committee's slate of delegates. While each Democratic congressman chose his own people, the state committee made the choices where no such representative existed. In exchange for a so-called "unity slate," McCormack would be the favorite son and Burke would continue in the chairmanship. The three men composed a mutually acceptable slate.[49] To bolster his own representation, Kennedy got Congressman Tip O'Neill to include Bobby among his own slate, saying that his brother was "the smartest politician I ever met in my life" and venturing the point that it would be handy to have him there in case "lightning should strike" and give Kennedy the vice-presidential nomination. O'Neill, whose home was, coincidentally, destroyed by fire at the time, could not attend the convention anyway and named Bobby in his place.[50]

The Kennedy-Dever-McCormack rapprochement collapsed during the post-Minnesota primary climate. Having rejected an open drive for a Stevenson write-in as part of the state's April 24 election to select the eighty committeemen, Kennedy's authority had to be asserted in other ways. Now he made his hazardous move. His power could only be exerted by emerging from that election with a stronger pro-Kennedy state committee. "So, we can't let Burke or McCormack know that we're trying to get our people on the state committee," Kennedy said. "At least, not for the time being. Keep working on it, but don't let Burke know about it, and don't mention my name to anybody."[51]

The broader significance was the opposition of the McCormack-Burke leadership to a pro-Stevenson commitment. The "harmony" in the wake of the "unity slate" broke down when efforts to oppose Stevenson became identified with the basic conflict over which presidential candidate to support.

A decisive force in helping to upset the rapprochement was John Fox. Fox had since turned bitterly against Jack Kennedy, not forgiving him for having opposed Scott McLeod and for failing to stand up in behalf of Joe McCarthy. Kennedy had also resisted Fox's efforts to withhold alumni financial gifts to Harvard pending the university's removal of "left-wingers" from its faculty.[52] Now, using his paper's influence, Fox worked with the McCormack-Burke alliance to launch an intensive, last-minute write-in-vote campaign for the favorite-son designation. The campaign aimed at blunting assertions of Kennedy power and undercutting Stevenson's standing. Meanwhile, the Stevenson-for-President groups carefully avoided appearing to oppose McCormack, emphasizing instead the effort to dump Burke, which was also an objective of the state's Americans for Democratic Action chapter.[53] But with the McCormack-Burke-Fox forces especially strong in Boston, where most of the voting was done, the congressman topped Stevenson's write-in total by twenty-nine thousand to nineteen thousand. At the same time, 845 voters named Kennedy as their preference.[54]

Nevertheless, a closer analysis questioned the magnitude of the victory. Most of McCormack's vote came from Boston. Even there, out of 350,000 enrolled Democrats, his favorite-son candidacy drew the support of only about 12,500, with all the political machinery actively pushing his name. Outside the metropolitan area the congressman's strength fell off sharply. In the western part of the state, where balloting was light, Stevenson actually commanded pluralities ranging from four to one to eight to one. All this occurred even though Kennedy and Dever, despite their earlier endorsements for Governor Stevenson, had remained fairly silent. More ominous for the Burke prospects was the defeat of more than fifteen of those who had originally supported him for the chairmanship. *The New York Times* reported strong pro-Stevenson support among the newly chosen committeemen.[55]

More significant, Burke had given Kennedy an excuse for abandoning his behind-the-scenes strategy. The chairman had declared that the Stevenson supporters "ought to be listening to Alger Hiss," a snide attempt to brand them with "softness toward communism." Burke had also given the McCormack campaign every kind of assistance the state committee could offer, including letters on official stationery supporting the preferred candidate, and access to the organization's list of Democrats all over the Commonwealth. If Burke's action had been to deliberately provoke Kennedy's emergence, he could not have done a better job. He had also made McCormack uncomfortable by provoking the wrath of the state's most potentially powerful political force.[56]

Kennedy's people grabbed the opportunity. Two days after the election, the senator went into Burke's own territory in the Berkshire region to confer with newly elected members, many of whom were prepared to depose the chairman at the meeting scheduled for Boston on May 19. Reporting his taking charge to Stevenson's national campaign manager, Jim Finnegan, Kennedy advised that Burke had spent the first day of May in a long conference with New York County Democratic leader Carmine DeSapio. The Tammany head was identified with the presidential candidacy of Governor Averell Harriman, so Kennedy's point was obvious. Kennedy assured Finnegan that, whatever Burke's alliances might be, he was hopeful of controlling the choice of a new chairman, one more favorably disposed toward Stevenson. "Although the Stevenson people in the state are of course already aware of this situation and working with us, so that no action on your part is required," Kennedy wrote, "I thought you might want to be kept informed of the situation because of the stakes involved."[57] Kennedy also telephoned Burke himself and arranged a breakfast session at a hotel in Northampton for Saturday, May 5.

Jack's move was one of his more difficult decisions. He had reached the point where the very possibility of a political future hinged on more than the power that came from his money and family. He had to play the political game and playing meant getting out in front by providing the personal leadership, however hazardous, however distasteful. His effort to replace Burke "puts the Senator into an arena which he tried to avoid," the Springfield *Daily News* pointed out.[58] The issue had not become clearly drawn. Burke's existence threatened to become a symbol of Kennedy ineptitude and local political leadership, which would have been a major liability in any attempt to impress either the Stevenson forces or the Massachusetts electorate of Kennedy's effectiveness. *The Berkshire Eagle* pointedly referred to Burke as the "cat's paw of the *Boston Post* in the anti-Stevenson right-wing Democrats."[59] At Northampton, then, at the session with the party chairman himself, Kennedy laid down an ultimatum.

The meeting sparked a tumultuous few days that preceded the May 19 convention. Kennedy informed Burke that he had power to remove him from the chairmanship and advised him to resign. Burke refused and vowed to defeat Kennedy. Kennedy continued his canvass of the western part of the state, then told the press of his plans to remove Burke. His reelection would be "a serious mistake." Working with the confidence that he could get support from the newly elected state committee members and realizing that the chairman was further weakened by not having control of party funds, which were in the hands of the Jefferson-Jackson Committee under the charge of Paul Dever, Kennedy acted on the day after their breakfast to make his major announcement of leadership in the anti-Burke movement. From that point on Kennedy immediately became the personal antagonist. "I do not relish being involved in this dispute," read a statement that had been prepared for him by his Boston office, accurately reflecting his own attitude.[60]

The opposition then struck back. McCormack reiterated his support for Burke, although the congressman, his heart not really in the fight, remained prudently in Washington. Burke himself issued a statement attributing Kennedy's actions to anti-McCormack maneuvering, especially because the congressman longed to be designated as the favorite son. Burke's charges also included the statement that Kennedy had told him that he would not stand by and permit McCormack to run the state party. If Burke would step down, he said Kennedy had told him at the breakfast, he would be assured the reward of a seat as Democratic national committeeman in replacement of Jim Curley, who readily confirmed that Kennedy wanted to force him out. Burke further embroidered his charges with the conclusion that all such efforts represented "a tentative drive by the pro-Stevenson forces in Massachusetts."[61]

Kennedy fired back from Washington, denying the accuracy of Burke's account and charging the chairman with trying to drive a wedge between himself and McCormack. *The Christian Science Monitor* observed that, although McCormack was not a contender for either the presidency or vice-presidency, "the intensive build-up for him in the local press could be a complicating factor unwelcome to the Kennedy forces" and noted the growing speculation that Kennedy might be given a place with Stevenson on the national ticket.[62] "His sudden entry into an intra-party dispute is a major change of character," said the *Worcester Telegram.* "And once having taken the plunge, it is difficult to see how he can withdraw."[63] With Paul Dever openly backing Kennedy, including the largely symbolic gesture of naming him as "leader" of the state's party, the perception of power was beginning to work wonders: prudent pros and labor leaders began to resolve doubts in Kennedy's favor.

But, first, stopping Burke required an alternative. Even before the start of Kennedy's open attack, there were reports that the newly elected state committeemen hostile to the incumbent were forwarding the names of several possible replacements. Kennedy had additional support from Torby Macdonald. With Kennedy assistance, Macdonald had won his 1954 battle to represent the Seventh Congressional District of Massachusetts. Now, Jack's old friend called for Burke's replacement for the good of the party and for an appointee who would finally bring some "peace and dignity" to a highly divisive organization that had sometimes verged on the ludicrous. Clearly, the intensity of the battle had only increased the importance of finding a successor. Burke's charge that Kennedy had attempted to use bribery to vacate Curley's seat gave the fight additional publicity and Kennedy the sympathy of many Democratic senatorial colleagues.

Still, no replacement emerged, while several names were mentioned as possible favorites of the new committeemen. Kennedy tried to persuade Tip O'Neill, but McCormack had little choice but to talk his protégé out of it because of his commitment to Burke. Years later, McCormack told O'Neill that he had asked Burke to get out of the fight but Burke would not let him off the hook.[64] Finally, they settled on a former mayor of the suburban city of Somerville, John "Pat" Lynch, not because he represented a credible alternative to the sort of pols common in state politics or had been identified with the Stevensonians, but because it was assumed that Lynch would be acceptable to a broad range of the party.

But when Lynch was brought in to meet Kennedy, the senator was obviously dismayed. "All of the Kennedys, and especially Jack, judged people by their appearance," O'Donnell and Powers have noted, describing the shock on Jack's face when he saw the small, bald-headed, Irish politician, the kind "that Jack always frowned upon."[65] Kennedy tried to duck out of a commitment to Lynch in favor of a more attractive figure but judiciously resigned himself to the choice.

Saturday afternoon, May 19, the date set for the showdown fight at Boston's Hotel Bradford, was hardly a convenient day for Jack Kennedy personally. At St. Patrick's Cathedral in New York that morning, he, along with brothers Bob and Ted, was scheduled to be an usher at the wedding of sister Jean and Steve Smith. A reception was then planned for the couple at the Baroque Suite and Crystal Room of the Plaza Hotel. Ken O'Donnell, however, warned the senator that he could not risk ignoring events in Boston. He had to play a personal role; he had to be on the scene; he had to meet each delegate, turn on his charm, make his own partisanship clear, leave no doubt about the power behind the "tool" called Pat Lynch. Not convinced that his presence could be that effective, especially among veteran pols, Kennedy had to be persuaded.[66]

The day developed into a commuting nightmare. First he flew from Boston to New York to be on hand while Francis Cardinal Spellman performed the ceremony. Then he made a return flight. Well before the 3 P.M. starting time for the meeting, Kennedy positioned himself in the Bradford's lobby. As all sides watched in astonishment, he became an extrovert par excellence, overwhelming the delegates with his personal radiance and authority. McCormack, meanwhile, remained in Washington, out of direct involvement. The process continued until some twenty-five minutes before the start of the meeting, enabling Kennedy to fly back to New York and join Jacqueline at the Plaza Hotel reception.

What he had left behind was a tumultuous affair, one described by virtually every observer as a scene right out of the pages of Edwin

O'Connor's accounts of traditional Boston politics. It went on for three hours, with the Burke and Lynch factions so vehement that fistfights were a constant threat. Burke himself came close to personal involvement in a bit of violence when he found a policeman stationed at the entrance to bar him from the meeting hall. Since the chairman was not a member of the committee, the officer had been assigned to keep him out. But his presence would probably not have mattered at all. The final vote defeated the incumbent by a comfortable 47–31 margin. Burke promptly charged, without offering any evidence, that Kennedy had been on hand with personal offers of cash to sway the committeemen. More important, the choice of Pat Lynch was immediately interpreted by Massachusetts Democrats as an endorsement of Stevenson.[67]

The Kennedy and Stevenson camps were delighted. Early Monday morning the senator personally telephoned the Governor to glow about the victory.[68] Sorensen then followed with his own call. The next day, in Washington, Stan Karson of the Stevenson for President Committee headquarters in Chicago met with Kennedy and found him "obviously exultant over his victory." Kennedy told Karson that the outcome had made it certain that the Governor would receive the great majority of the Massachusetts convention votes. He said that while McCormack would get the first-ballot favorite-son designation, Stevenson would get the bulk of the second ballot. But, Kennedy underlined, if those first-ballot votes should turn out to be vital for the Governor, they would not then go to McCormack. "Kennedy will see to it that this is done." Karson concluded his report of the meeting with the following observation: "I must say that my strongest feeling upon leaving Kennedy was that for the first time since I have known him over the past years, he appears to be in control over a political situation, knows it, and likes it."[69] Stevenson's finance man, Archibald Alexander, confirmed Karson's view of the senator's position, reporting that Kennedy was "not only wholeheartedly for Stevenson but disposed to be aggressive as never before."[70]

By that point a considerable vice-presidential boomlet had developed. On the first of June came a significant endorsement. Albert Gore, the Tennessee colleague of Estes Kefauver, declared his open support of a place on the ticket for Jack Kennedy.[71] At the Governors Conference in Atlantic City, Kennedy got a strong push from the New England contingent led by Governor Dennis Roberts of Rhode Island, who had begun to spearhead the senator's campaign in the region. Additional support came in a speech by Governor Abe Ribicoff of Connecticut, and the governor of North Carolina, Luther Hodges.[72] At the preprimary convention of Massachusetts Democrats at Worcester, it was obvious to the 1,440 delegates at the two-day affair that the problems of the rift were in Kennedy's hands. He promptly responded by personally endorsing their choice for governor, Foster Furcolo. Concern continued, however, about lingering personal friction. When Kennedy made a brief appearance at the convention, scattered boos could be clearly heard within the Worcester Memorial Auditorium, perhaps the first derisive reception of Jack's career.[73] He could hardly have expected the losers to enjoy their defeat.

On the fourteenth, Kennedy was the commencement speaker at Harvard University, where he also received an honorary degree. His talk on that day provided a sharp contrast to the type of political activity he had just practiced. He lamented the gap between intellectuals and professional politicians in American life, a dichotomy that he saw motivated by largely unfounded feelings of distrust. He pointed to the common ancestry of American intellectuals and politicians and cited Jefferson, Madison, and Hamilton, whose works influenced the literature of the world as well as its geography. "Books were their tools, not their enemies. . . . Our political leaders traded in the free commerce of ideas with lasting results both here and abroad." He argued that the American intellectual and scholar together must decide whether he is to be an anvil or a hammer. He cited an English mother who urged the provost of Harrow not to teach her boy poetry because he was going to stand for Parliament. "Well," concluded Kennedy, "perhaps she was right—but if more politicians knew poetry, and more poets knew politics, I am convinced that the world would be a little better place to live on this commencement day of 1956."[74] The speech was soon inserted into the *Congressional Record* by none other than Majority Leader Lyndon Johnson, who called it "the most eloquent defense of politics and politicians that has ever been my pleasure to read."

19

Preparing for Chicago

With the Massachusetts victory achieved, the push was on in behalf of both the Stevenson candidacy and to influence his choice for the second place on the ticket. That summer, Kennedy went to California to work on a project that helped give him a significant convention role. At the advice of Party Chairman Paul Butler, Hollywood producer and delegate Dore Schary had made a film to serve as an introduction to the keynote address. Kennedy was selected as the "perfect man" to do the narration. The choice was inevitable because *Profiles in Courage,* with such currency as a best-seller, had made him better known nationally than the other possibilities. His fame as a literary figure had also been enhanced by favorable impressions made during television appearances. Both factors were persuasive.[1]

Largely designed to counter the Republican campaign themes of peace and prosperity, the film imbued Democrats with the additional virtues of "responsibility" and "sincerity." Starting with the party's origins from Jefferson and Jackson, and then pausing to recall that Republican Lincoln had been succeeded by "smaller men—hotheads and fanatics, bound for vengeance against the South," it went on to laud such twentieth-century party heroes as Wilson, FDR, and Truman. Heavy stress was placed on the Democratic leadership in pulling the nation out of the Great Depression, winning World War II, and meeting "the threat of Communism" in Greece, Turkey, Berlin, and Western Europe. The narrative concluded with the vow that "the unchanging destinations of the Democratic Party, remain as always . . . free enterprise . . . prosperity, not for the few but for the many . . . freedom of thought and conscience . . . freedom from fear . . . social progress . . . security . . . peace . . . and the pursuit of happiness."[2]

Put together by writers Norman Corwin, Allen Rivkin, and Bill Gordon, the movie was called *The Pursuit of Happiness.* Schary met with Kennedy in July at the Santa Monica home of the Lawfords, where they held a screening. Aside from making some minor corrections, the senator gave his approval and the arrangements were made to add his voice. Kennedy himself contributed additional lines, as did Arthur Schlesinger, Jr., and Leonard Spiegelglass.

Since the film was regarded as a part of the keynote address, it was important to offer an advance showing to the man chosen by the convention to deliver the opening-night partisan call to action. On July 9 the identification of the keynoter was revealed. Hubert Humphrey, despite reports of his tentative early selection, was bypassed in favor of a compromise choice, a process obviously filled with much bickering. The voting had undergone several delays before the Arrangements Committee finally met in Chicago's Conrad Hilton Hotel. Scheduled to be accomplished within one hour, the secret session lasted almost triple that time. When Party Chairman Paul Butler finally came out to announce the result, he did nothing to discourage speculation that Governor Frank Clement had been a compromise choice. While he was regarded as Truman's man, it was also rumored that he had the backing of Lyndon Johnson. A Tennesseean also acceptable to the party's urban progressives, the thirty-six-year-old handsome, ruddy-faced governor was regarded as more likely than Humphrey to bridge the party's North-South division.[3]

Kennedy went to work at the studio. Technicians ran the footage, tested his voice, and they went through several rehearsals. Then the senator's voice reading the narration was added to the sound track, a process that went smoothly. "All of us who were in contact with him immediately fell in love with him because he was so quick and so charming and so cooperative, and obviously so bright and so skilled," said Schary.[4]

Kennedy also prepared for the convention by grabbing at the religious issue and attempting to allay fears that a Catholic on the ticket would create a replay of 1928.⁵ The Catholic sensitivity was very strong within the Stevenson camp, and voiced most passionately by Jim Finnegan. There was, however, some difference of opinion. Several noted that Catholic resistance to Stevenson might be tempered or somewhat neutralized if the governor had a Roman Catholic running mate.

As early as May 4 the managing editor of a magazine called *Jubilee* informed Sorensen that Kennedy had told him about material being compiled to present data on the Catholic vote, together with projections of how that was likely to relate to the rise of American Catholics to the middle class, the effect of the Communist issue, the Al Smith election of 1928, and Catholic political bosses.⁶ Meanwhile, too, Sorensen and Kennedy were doing their utmost to promote popular consideration of the issue. The June 12, 1956, issue of *Look* came out with an article by Fletcher Knebel called "Can A Catholic Become Vice President?" It led off by citing Kennedy along with Mayor Robert Wagner, Jr., of New York City, and Governor Frank Lausche of Ohio as three Catholics receiving substantial mention as possible vice-presidential candidates. Behind them, also possibilities, were such others as John McCormack, Governor Edmund Muskie of Maine, and Senator Mike Mansfield of Montana. After pointing out that Catholicism was but a minor factor in Al Smith's defeat, labeling that misconception as the "Al Smith myth," it alluded to a Sorensen memorandum, without identifying either him or Kennedy, as having been prepared by the staff of a "Democratic leader who believes the party has failed to recognize the importance of Catholic voters in past Democratic triumphs. In effect, it answers the . . . question with a thumping 'Yes.' "⁷ "The idea for that one did come from them," Knebel has since explained, "from Sorensen and Kennedy himself, while we were chewing the fat on a possible *Look* story." Sorensen helped to supply the statistical data, "ran it off in an afternoon or a day or so, and gave it to me."⁸

Even outside the Roman Catholic community, apprehension continued about the likelihood that Kennedy's name on the ticket would revive the ugliness of the Smith campaign. In New York City a prominent Protestant clergyman, the Reverend Dr. Hampton Adams, told his congregation at the Park Avenue Christian Church that he would like to vote for a Roman Catholic for either one of the two highest offices on the ticket but could not do so "because of the authority the Roman Catholic Church holds over its members."⁹ Stevenson's friend Agnes

Meyer immediately forwarded Dr. Adams's comments to the Governor's Chicago office and added her own caveat that having a Catholic on the ticket would unleash a more sophisticated but more powerfully organized opposition than in 1928 because the Protestant clergy was more formidable than in Smith's day. She added her worry that a Catholic vice-president would use his influence to get federal aid for parochial schools. Meyer, a Lutheran married to the Jewish publisher of *The Washington Post,* added that such Catholics were even more passionate about the symbolic value of sending an American ambassador to the Vatican.[10]

Other than the effort to allay the qualms of Catholic politicians, it was the fear among the non-Catholics that was one of the targets of the "Bailey Memorandum." The memorandum was misnamed, intentionally. John Bailey, the party state chairman from Connecticut and also a Roman Catholic, was, in Sorensen's words, "just a draftee" to sponsor it "because we did not want it to be the 'Kennedy Memorandum.' That was too self-serving."[11] Bailey was available—a party member of the proper faith and with the appropriate credentials to expedite its proper circulation as his own. Approached with the idea, Bailey consented to have it attributed to him, but its actual circulation was largely taken care of by the Kennedy camp and, in particular, its author, Ted Sorensen.[12]

Called "The Catholic Vote in 1952 and 1956," the memo tried to correct the misconception that Smith's loss could be blamed on his religion. It pointed out some obvious factors not sufficiently appreciated by laymen, such as the fact that 1928 was a "Republican year," that Hoover was a sure winner regardless of his Democratic opponent; further, branding the misconception as one of the great myths in politics, it also recalled the strong zeal of the Prohibition forces against such "wets" as Smith. Most important, in trying to draw comparisons with 1928, was the increasing prominence of the political role played by American Catholics in the intervening three decades, in addition to a greater national toleration of religious matters.

But the heart of the paper was more practical. Its central theme was that the Democratic ticket now needed a Catholic. Isolating fourteen states where the proportion of Catholics in the adult population ranged from twenty percent in Ohio upward to Rhode Island's sixty percent, it pointed out that they comprised 261 electoral votes, five short of the total required to win the election. Elections had been won or lost for the Democrats as a result of their ability to win those fourteen pivotal "Catholic" states. There had been a marked decline in the party's ability to do so. Having won thirteen of them in 1940, twelve in 1944, and only eight in 1948, the Eisenhower victory of 1952 was possible because *all* of those 261 electoral votes went to the Republican candidate. Therefore, the concentration of new Republican voters in those industrial states with a large number of electoral votes had been crucial. Sorensen cited a Gallup survey that said that while only thirty-four percent of all Catholics considered themselves Republicans in 1950, at least forty-four percent of them voted for Eisenhower, and about 30 percent of those Catholics were shifters to the Eisenhower column. Calling them "normally Democratic Catholics," Sorensen estimated that they constituted approximately seven percent of Eisenhower's total national vote. If, in 1952, Stevenson could have held only those Catholics who voted for Truman in 1948 but for Ike in 1952, or if he could recapture them in 1956, that would add 132 electoral votes to the Democratic column. Combined with the "solid South," he would have a majority of the electoral votes.[13]

Under Bailey's sponsorship, the memorandum received wide circulation. Not only was it handed out to the inner circle of Stevenson advisers and others of influence, but it was given additional publicity by *Time, U.S. News & World Report,* and Arthur Krock in *The New York Times.* Seemingly supporting one of its contentions, the Gallup Poll published on June 23 told of a marked decline in voter prejudice during the last sixteen years against having a Catholic for president. The Institute for Public Opinion found that whereas 62 percent had said in 1940 that they would have no objection, 73 percent were now ready to go along.[14]

At the heart of their differences was the controversy over the shift of Catholic voters toward the Republican Party, a movement discernible during the latter Roosevelt years and affecting some local voting patterns even while World War II was being fought. Arguments in refutation, such as Louis Bean's, countered the general belief among politicians that Catholic defections were significant not only in 1950, as the analyst conceded, but had been responsible for the rightward shift in 1946. Moreover, the Truman upset victory in 1948 succeeded in part because it momentarily stemmed that flow. Like other voters, Catholics were subjected to cross-pressures, conflicting economic, religious, and ethnic factors, with blue-collar workers more likely to remain loyal to the traditional party despite such factors. The essential assumption of the Sorensen argument was correct, however. Catholics were slipping toward the GOP. A majority of such voters, in fact, voted Republican in the 1956 sample conducted by the Survey Research Center of the University of Michigan, while other surveys confirmed a significant dip but a continued willingness to *identify* themselves as Democrats.[15] In that climate, the Sorensen-Bailey memorandum addressed itself to the decade-long decline and presented Kennedy as a Democrat who, by appealing to co-religionists concentrated in the large states, could become the Lochinvar of the Democratic Party.

The Sorensen-Bailey memorandum was not the only campaign tactic employed by Kennedy. Bailey went to see Stevenson and gave him both his and Governor Ribicoff's thinking about having Kennedy. As Ribicoff reported back to Kennedy, "Bailey found Adlai giving considerable thought to you for the second spot. I am sure that Stevenson holds you in the highest regard."[16] Stevenson himself, observing Kennedy carefully, noted the plan in the works to elect Jack chairman of the Massachusetts delegation. At the same time, it called for replacing Curley as national committeeman and substituting Paul Dever. "It is hoped that McCormack will go along with the above program," Schlesinger wrote to Finnegan. "If so, and if there is no objection from Chicago, Kennedy and Dever are willing to give McCormack the first ballot vote with the intention of shifting to Stevenson on the second ballot."[17] Also working for Kennedy were his friends George Smathers, who was busily conferring with southern governors in trying to line up that region, and Torby Macdonald, who was making the rounds of legislators advancing the plan by trying to influence them to urge Stevenson to select Kennedy.[18]

At the same time, *Newsweek* listed Kennedy along with Kefauver, Humphrey, and Governor Robert B. Meyner of New Jersey among the four possible Democratic vice-presidential candidates.[19] Kennedy appeared on the CBS-TV show *Face the Nation* and listed his religion, his vote on the farm bill for flexible price supports, his tender age of thirty-nine, and the geographical location of his state as reasons for doubting that he would win second place—all prudently in keeping with noncandidacy traditions, which were especially strong against overt campaigning for the vice-presidency.[20] *Newsweek* then devoted a brief feature piece on Kennedy as a young man "going places," and Foster Furcolo offered his endorsement. In mid-July, Washington columnist John O'Donnell reported that Stevenson was ready to choose Kennedy.[21]

On the twenty-sixth of July, two days after he had denied that Humphrey and Kennedy were his two likeliest choices, Stevenson met with some of his inner circle in Chicago. Part of the conversation related to the vice-presidency. The Governor said he thought Humphrey was "too radical" and indicated he had no use for Kefauver. At the same time, he dismissed Kennedy as a Catholic and cited the fact that Jim Farley had told him "America is not ready for a Catholic yet." Sam Rayburn said, "Well, if we have to have a Catholic, I hope we don't have to take that little piss-ant Kennedy. How about John McCormack?"[22]

On July 30 Hubert Humphrey made a formal announcement of his vice-presidential candidacy. Humphrey and his aides were confident that they had Stevenson's support. The Governor's assurance, they felt, had been given when Stevenson presented as a precondition Humphrey's ability to win the approval of the party's southern leadership, including Lyndon Johnson, Richard Russell, Sam Rayburn, and Lister Hill. Once having obtained that, with the assistance of Jim Finnegan and Max Kampelman, as Humphrey later claimed, he had reason for confidence that, despite Kennedy's efforts, he would be named.[23] Then Kefauver, having lost badly to Stevenson in the California primary, announced his withdrawal. Now he could "join the Stevenson bandwagon" and work "with the consensus of the party against the threat to unity from Harriman on the left." Kefauver lost little time in making it clear that like Humphrey, the announced candidate, and like Kennedy, the unannounced candidate, he would also accept second place.[24]

As the decision grew closer, the distance between Senator Kennedy and his father began to widen. Jack's age, maturity, and greater prominence were serving to relegate the Ambassador more and more to the background. After all, as Sorensen has observed, the publication of *Profiles in Courage* and heavy speech-making "had made him more widely known than most Democratic office-holders."[25] Of equal consideration was the greater liability of the Ambassador's reputation when his son sought national acceptance. During the meeting in Chicago, for example, while the Stevenson people were evaluating the potential vice-presidential candidacies of both Kennedy and Humphrey, with Finnegan, Wirtz, and Stevenson favoring the Minnesota senator, and with Blair, Schlesinger, and Newton Minow advocating Kennedy, Stevenson himself put a distinct damper on the young senator's prospects by saying, "I like Jack Kennedy, admire him, but he's too young; his father, his religion."[26] Although the Ambassador had been a Stevenson supporter and contributor in the 1952 campaign, his reputation still continued to trouble and embarrass substantial groups within the party's echelons. His personal behavior, his reputation as a charming but ruthless operator, somewhat unsavory and rakish, was hardly regarded as a welcome asset. Being his son had had its advantages, to be sure, but the burdens were also significant. As Jack Kennedy advanced on the national scene, the father became more and more of a liability, and the son, as much as he continued to admire, respect, and seek his counsel, nevertheless was compelled to strike out on his own. The Ambassador, for example, had now turned sour on his son's vice-presidential ambitions. Unrealistically, in 1952, he had thought Stevenson could defeat Eisenhower; more accurately now, he appraised the incumbent President's chances as excellent. That meant he considered it bad strategy for Jack to associate himself with the ticket, so he made efforts to dissuade his son. In May, en route to his villa on the French Riviera, he dictated a letter telling Jack about a talk he had had with Clare Boothe Luce. He informed his son that Mrs. Luce was in complete agreement that his candidacy would be foolish, arguing "that if you are chosen, it will be because you are a Catholic and not because you are big enough to do the job. She feels that a defeat would be a devastating blow to your prestige which at the moment is great, and non-partisan."[27]

The older Kennedy went on to the Riviera even as his son moved toward the Chicago convention, scheduled to begin on August 13. Jack continued to send messages overseas, keeping his father in touch with the progress of his ambition. He notified him about the activities in his behalf by Governors Ribicoff, Roberts, and Hodges, and John Bailey. He informed him that Schlesinger was in complete agreement and planned to spend a month in Stevenson's headquarters doing everything possible to help the cause. "Competition is mostly from Hubert Humphrey, who had his Governor make a statement that I would not be acceptable because of my vote on the farm bill; Senator Symington, Senator Gore, Mayor Wagner (he doesn't seem to have much support) and myself." To his father he minimized his personal role, implying that he would not do much more unless the prospects appeared worthwhile, but admitted he was planning to have Smathers consult with some of the southern senators. The prospects, he told the Ambassador, were rather limited, but to have the whole thing churning up was very useful for his future political career. "If I don't get it I can always tell them in the State that it was because of my vote on the farm bill," he wrote, thereby supplying an explanation Joe Kennedy could understand.[28] While in France, the Ambassador received a letter from Sargent Shriver saying that Stevenson had been assured that "you were 100% behind Jack, that you gave him and his campaign everything you had even if perchance you might disagree with the basic wisdom of a decision Jack might make."[29] Shriver's confidence was well founded. Included in Kennedy's entourage when he went to Chicago was Jim Landis, who was very much a part of the Kennedy for vice-president effort. By chance, Landis met Mrs. Roosevelt and tried to convince her that Jack belonged on the ticket. He found that she was not especially negative toward him personally but continued to be bothered by the McCarthy affair. Her attitude, however, made Landis suspect that her feelings were a carry-over from FDR's difficulties with Ambassador Joseph P. Kennedy.[30]

20

The Showdown
at Chicago

The Democrats arrived in Chicago with several big questions; among them, party unity was the most crucial. The ability to produce a civil-rights plank acceptable to both North and South was a factor. Governor Harriman of New York well understood that relationship to his own candidacy. His strategy involved forcing a fight for an advanced liberal statement of principles that would tear apart the North-South coalition so carefully nurtured by Stevenson. The disposition of that issue, the ability to reach a compromise, would in turn point a very strong finger at the identity of the nominee—and that, as had been traditional, would determine the choice of a running mate.

When the Stevenson backers reached Chicago the week before the convention opened, they claimed enough votes for a first-ballot victory, even though the Harriman forces challenged that arithmethic. At the same time, the vice-presidential nomination also received attention. In an interview with James Reston of *The New York Times,* Stevenson deplored the emphasis on having to nominate a Roman Catholic to regain defectors from the 1952 election. He said he wanted someone who would fill the office effectively; at the same time, he carefully named

Humphrey, Kennedy, or Wagner as among those best capable of that function. Doing that on the basis of ability rather than on religious grounds would avoid charges of opportunism. On civil rights he favored having the platform reiterate the party's dedication to the Court decisions, but argued that racial segregation was a national problem, that blacks were being discriminated against in housing and transportation in the North just as they faced public-school and voting obstacles in some parts of the South.[1]

On the Saturday before the convention opened, Paul Dever began to operate a Kennedy headquarters at the Palmer House and said that his people planned to talk to delegates from every state in the nation.[2] Although the vice-presidential talk was centering on Kefauver, Humphrey, and Kennedy, others continued to be mentioned. The speculation about Kennedy included his opposition to ninety percent farm price supports as a big obstacle, one more formidable than his religion. Catholicism, in fact, tended to be viewed mainly in positive terms as potentially recouping Democratic voters.[3] But, on that day, the real headline was made by the announcement of former president Truman's support for the presidential candidacy of New York Governor Averell Harriman, an obvious move to stop Stevenson.

If the Truman move was intended as a bombshell, it fell far short, setting off only a slight flurry. As Jonathan Daniels, a onetime press secretary of the ex-president, noted a few days later, "The Democrats here do not dislike Truman. They simply are sorry for him. He made the blunder of confusing popularity with power. He now understands that we don't necessarily vote as we cheer."[4]

On Sunday, Kennedy, assured of the solid support of all New England delegates, vigorously made the round of receptions, meeting with politicians and behaving like a candidate. Ostensibly, though, he was inactive. Nevertheless, he heard from governors Ribicoff and Roberts that progress was being made and didn't hide his pleasure.[5] That evening a hardcore group of about fifty delegates followed up an organizational meeting by launching a more concerted effort. Joined by Kennedy, they met at the Conrad Hilton Hotel, although Jack first shared a room with Torby at the Drake. His supporters were headed by Macdonald, who, along with Bob Kennedy, was named as floor manager for the convention. The *Boston Herald* reported that the movement was spurred by widespread fear among political leaders of their area that they would be badly hurt at the polls in November with a Humphrey vice-presidential nomination. Humphrey's close identification with the left-wing ADA might make him unacceptable to the bulk of New England voters. That kind of repudiation could then carry over to other elective offices, jeopardizing seats in Congress, state legislatures, and several governorships.[6] Visible evidence of pro-Kennedy movement outside New England also came in the form of the active work being done by Smathers, Hodges, and representatives Jack Flynt of Georgia, John F. Shelley of California, and Edith Green of Oregon.[7] There was still the assumption, however, that the entire effort would be pointless, because Stevenson would merely go ahead and pick his own man, so that a campaign was a waste of time, a consideration with little impact on Kennedy himself.

All such efforts were dwarfed by Kennedy's "secret weapon," which was unleashed before the eleven thousand delegates on the first night. The lights were dimmed and the Dore Schary film came on the screen. "Kennedy came before the convention tonight as a movie star," reported *The New York Times*.[8] His cultivated New England voice filled the hall. Schary, who sat with his California delegation, later recalled that "the personality of the senator just came right out. It jumped at you on the screen. The narration was good, and the film was emotional. He was immediately a candidate. There was simply no doubt about that because he racked up the whole convention."[9] And then the crowd broke into cheers at the sight and sounds of such heroes as Franklin D. Roosevelt and Truman. After the film and Clements's hell-fire keynote speech, Kennedy became the beneficiary of the first favorite-son demonstration as a band of Massachusetts delegates staged a brief but noisy parade. They waved "Kennedy for President" placards as he came to the platform to take a bow. That provoked a bigger roar than the governor of Tennessee had received for his highly emotional performance. Colonel McCormick's *Chicago Tribune* reported that Kennedy refused to appear for the ovation and that his demonstrating supporters were forced to retire in some embarrassment.[10] The Kennedy narration unquestionably raised his standing with the delegates, but most important was its national impact when viewed by millions of Americans over two television networks. An unmistakable contrast was made between his urbane manner and the excessive rhetoric of the keynoter.

On Tuesday morning, right after his exhilarating success with the Schary film, Jack Kennedy had a sharp letdown. Eleanor Roosevelt was in Chicago and vigorously behind her nominee for the presidency, Adlai Stevenson. Right after her arrival at the airport, in fact, largely to offset Harry Truman's prior endorsement of Averell Harriman, she told the press that she wanted Adlai.[11] Kennedy, of course, rightfully believed that winning Mrs. Roosevelt's acceptance for second place on the ticket could influence Stevenson's ultimate choice. One of Jack's intimates, Washington lawyer Abba Schwartz, was also a longtime personal friend of the former First Lady. Schwartz, acting as an intermediary, had arranged for Mrs. Roosevelt to meet the senator during her visit to Chicago.[12] What actually took place has been somewhat obscured by conflicting memories about precise details. But all accounts agree about the failure of Jack's mission.

During that session others came and went, causing some confusion. The actual meeting lasted less than a half hour. Nobody, however, disputes that Mrs. Roosevelt, in explaining her reluctance to back Kennedy, placed him on the defensive about Joe McCarthy. Earlier, when responding to a letter in Jack's behalf from Jim Landis, she had written, "I am troubled about Sen. K's evasive attitude on McCarthy."[13] Now, facing Kennedy himself, she repeated her concern. Her precise recollection was that he replied that that had happened "so long ago" it was no longer relevant.[14] Ralph Martin and Ed Plaut later reported that Mrs. Roosevelt explained that Kennedy's reply "just wasn't enough of an answer for me, that's all," while Kennedy maintained that she must have misunderstood him "because what I meant was that the bill of particulars against McCarthy was long before the censure movement. My position was that we couldn't indict a man for what happened before he was seated.* If he was guilty of those things, the time to stop him was before he was seated."[15] Later, as an afterthought to the *Saturday Evening Post* publication of her account, Mrs. Roosevelt appended to the description that appears in her memoir the concession that "in this case I may well have misunderstood the Senator. He has recently said that he had made statements upholding the vote of the Senate but this is not exactly what I think is called for." At the same time, she repeated her conviction that "a public servant must clearly indicate that he understands the harm that McCarthyism did to our country and that he opposes it actively, so that one would feel sure that he would always do so in the future."[16] But on the morning of their meeting, a dejected Kennedy came away feeling that "the room was so noisy and it was such a short interview, and it was hardly a place or a basis for judgment."[17] The disappointment among Kennedy loyalists that lingered long afterward is reflected in Ken O'Donnell and Dave Powers's recent charge

---

*Kennedy was referring to the fact that McCarthy was reelected in 1952 and took his seat for a new term in January 1953.

that the First Lady "berated him before a room of people. . . ."[18]

Kennedy then met with Truman in the Blackstone Hotel. Although the senator later told reporters they had not discussed the subject of his vice-presidency, insiders reported that Truman was not enthusiastic about Kennedy. He was wary about having a Roman Catholic complicate the party's already pressing problems.[19]

But the main news that came out of Chicago on that day was in the form of a report that Senator Albert Gore, who had earlier announced his support of Kennedy, was Stevenson's first choice for the vice-presidency. *The New York Times* reported that Gore had been informed of Stevenson's views but that he was reluctant to accept. His hesitancy was based on the fact that his colleague, Kefauver, would attract more widespread voter support for Stevenson than any other Democrat, although Kefauver also had strong opposition in certain vital areas. Gore, said the report, urged Stevenson to find another running mate; at the same time, he lauded Kennedy as the second strongest candidate on a Stevenson ticket, adding that religion would not be a strong handicap in the South.[20] Stevenson headquarters promptly issued a denial of a deal with Kefauver for second place.

Meanwhile, Kennedy had become an overnight hero in Chicago. He was mobbed wherever he went, on the streets, on the convention floor; the pack of curious and worshipful visitors created an obstruction and disturbance to those seated behind the Massachusetts delegation. Without having to leave his chair, Kennedy was able to meet with Democrats from all parts of the country. He thanked each visitor who wished him luck and asked them to vote for Stevenson. One of the Massachusetts delegates, John M. Shea, pushed the Kennedy cause by definitely refusing to be bound to vote for McCormack for president, saying, "I have a vote in this convention and I intend to cast it as I desire. He [McCormack] is not a genuine candidate and I shall not vote him on any subsequent ballot."[21]

On Wednesday, more apparent confirmation increased the suspicion that the Kennedy drive was ephemeral, that any effort lacked the necessary support already achieved by competitors. Kennedy, having moved to the Stockyards Inn, near the Amphitheater, left for a personal visit with Stevenson. Seeking a commitment, or at least an indication that the Governor was giving serious consideration to having him on the ticket, he got mere evasion. More devastating was Stevenson's suggestion that if the bargaining over the civil-rights plank would not require having to compensate for wounded southern feelings by a politic gesture, he might like to call upon Kennedy to make the speech to place his name in nomination. That all but convinced Jack that Stevenson had decided to go with Kefauver and was merely mollifying Kennedy. As one of the Kennedy aides later told an interviewer, "The decision wasn't made until the last minute, and this business of keeping Kennedy on the griddle for all that time, I am sure, contributed to an attitude of coolness and irritation with Stevenson that persisted far beyond 1956."[22] Irritated, Kennedy told a meeting of about a hundred New England delegates that he thought his chances were slim.[23] Other reports out of Chicago indicated that Kennedy's failure to add Massachusetts to the Stevenson bandwagon had been lethal with the Governor's camp. A key Stevenson supporter, who requested anonymity, told a reporter, "Jack has really been roughed up and his chance for the vice presidency has gone now."[24]

Even as he spoke, the haggling over the civil-rights plank continued. The bulk of the party's northern moderates, including both Stevenson as well as some Harriman people, were eager to aid Steve Mitchell's efforts to find a compromise. Just as Paul Dever was involved in that process, so was Harriman-backer John McCormack. Despite his support for Harriman, McCormack's position on the platform was not surprising. Of all northern Democrats, the Massachusetts congressman had perhaps the closest ties with colleagues from below the Mason-Dixon line. He was also chairman of the Party Platform Committee, thus giving him a key role. On this issue there was no difference with Stevenson, who stressed the importance of holding the party together at all costs and avoiding estranging the South on civil rights. "Fundamentally," recalled Paul Douglas, "the Stevenson policy was not to do anything to offend the South seriously."[25] With the exception of such outstanding advocates as Douglas and Lehman, most party stalwarts were in agreement and Stevenson got his compromise rather than the strong statement of principles being demanded by the Harriman forces. That achievement and the failure of the Truman last-minute endorsement to sweep the delegates from their prior attachments effectively killed whatever chances were left for the New York governor.

That also led to the green light for Kennedy to deliver the nominating speech. Bill Blair called from Stevenson's office and told him that the issue had been settled, the compromise had been reached, and there was no need to select a southerner. They also had a speech prepared for Kennedy's delivery, one written by Schlesinger and John Bartlow Martin. With the "canned" reading copy in their hands, Kennedy and Ted Sorensen made an important decision.

Realistically, there was nothing left to do but satisfy Stevenson's need. The Governor's choice of Kennedy for the assignment obviously aimed at exploiting the fine impression left from his narration of the film on Monday night. Such qualities escaped neither the Governor nor his advisers. At the same time, their resentment against the single-mindedness of the Kennedy operation at Chicago underlined the warnings Stevenson was certainly hearing from Eleanor Roosevelt. But neither could they dismiss the benefits of Kennedy money, as Shriver had implied by his reassurance. It was also a way to neutralize possible resentment among Catholics over bypassing Kennedy. Finally, the opportunity to have Kennedy deliver the speech before tens of millions via national TV would give the senator much desired exposure and publicity of incalculable future value. Yet, as Kennedy and Sorensen pondered the situation, they were not ready to conclude the battle on Stevenson's terms.

One last possibility remained: going before the convention with a performance sufficiently impressive to stimulate simultaneous favorable reactions across the country so effectively that even Stevenson and the other skeptics would have no choice but to recognize Kennedy's attractions as a running mate. The first step, then, was to discard the Schlesinger-Martin version, which, after all, was designed primarily to promote the Governor's cause, and to substitute their own. While serving its primary purpose, it would also be Kennedy's play.[26] But before going ahead, Kennedy also had to do something about another touchy situation. How could he place Stevenson's name in nomination and then have his delegation promptly vote for McCormack? He telephoned the congressman, explaining his situation. The matter was resolved by a simple understanding: McCormack, recognizing power realities, agreed that after his desire to be placed before the convention as a favorite son had been satisfied, he would withdraw. That would release Massachusetts from any first-ballot obligation.[27] Once they cleared that hurdle, Kennedy and Sorensen worked through the night. By 6:00 A.M., having employed the talents of the man whose lofty and facile prose had already served him so well, Jack was prepared with a Stevenson nominating speech that was a Kennedy product.

Thursday, August 16, was a day of mild confusion, a prelude for the coming frenzy. Kennedy began it with his second success of the convention. He received a great cheer when going on to the platform to make his speech in behalf of "the man from Libertyville . . . and the next

President, Adlai Stevenson," which unleashed an uninhibited march around the hall by Stevenson supporters waving banners with such slogans as "We're Madly for Adlai." Kennedy's speech was strong, adding to his credentials and providing one of the more usable lines for the subsequent Democratic campaign. He told the delegates that their strength would be up against "two tough candidates, one who takes the high road and one who takes the low road." Cognizant of his own weakness in the Midwest, Kennedy also noted that "the problems of the nation's distressed farmers, the problems of our declining small business, the problems of our maldistribution of economic gain, the problems of our hopelessly inadequate schools, the problems of our nation's health —these are the problems that cry for solution. They cry for leadership and they cry for a man equal to our times."[28] One of his rooters was Jacqueline, then in the sixth week of pregnancy. The entire Chicago scene, with its long days and nights, made physical demands that taxed her stamina. Nevertheless, she played her part gracefully. One photographer caught her looking exuberant and radiant waving a Stevenson placard while standing atop her seat on the convention floor.

After Kennedy's well-received placement of Stevenson's name in nomination, seconding speeches followed from Luther Hodges, Herbert Lehman, Governor George Leader of Pennsylvania, Congressman William Dawson of Illinois, and Congresswoman Edith Green of Oregon. The total collapse of the Truman bid for Harriman was made official when Stevenson was nominated on the first ballot by a vote of 905 1/2 to 210. The Massachusetts delegation, after fulfilling the prearranged procedure between Kennedy and McCormack, gave Stevenson 32 of its votes, Harriman 7 1/2, and 1/2 for Lyndon Johnson. Although no McCormack favorite-son vote was recorded, it nevertheless revealed Kennedy's inability to control the entire delegation. To those familiar with Massachusetts politics, that was hardly unexpected; to those looking for liabilities in Kennedy, it served as a handy sign of weakness and inexperience.

The real confusion came later that night. Stevenson had a dilemma on his hands. The identity of Stevenson's preferred running mate at that point may perhaps be never known, although a memorandum in Stevenson's possession as early as August of 1955, "put together by Blair from the two Schlesinger memos and one by Walter Johnson drawing heavily on a letter of June 24 from Schlesinger" suggested Kefauver as the best vice-presidential possibility.[29] It may not, however, by August 16, 1956, have been clear in the nominee's mind. He weighed the alternatives. He had appreciated neither Kefauver nor his style. The man always made him uncomfortable, but so did many people; and besides, Kefauver had fought hard; his primary victories had given him many committed delegates. He had a good base of support. Furthermore, the Tennessee progressive could possibly aid the ticket in the Midwest farming regions, an area of Stevenson's weakness, and he was the prime alternative to Harriman among such industrial unionists as Walter Reuther of the United Auto Workers. But there were serious problems, too. Kefauver, because of his support for civil rights, his refusal to join regional colleagues in their protest against the *Brown* v. *Topeka* decision, his independent position against political leaders, assured enormous opposition among the professionals. Stevenson may have also been swayed by talk about Kefauver's alcoholism. The nominee knew that by selecting Kefauver as his running mate, he would, at one stroke, alienate the southerners he had worked so hard to cultivate. But Humphrey was also anathema to the South. His close association with the liberal ADA made him unpopular with conservative Democrats, especially Catholics cool toward Stevenson and with a demonstrated inclination toward the Republican ticket. And yet, Stevenson had a problem. He had made a pretty fair commitment to Humphrey, who had come through with the requisite support from southern leaders.

Then there was Jack Kennedy. Choosing anyone else would make Stevenson, a divorced man, vulnerable to further defections from Catholics. At the same time, Stevenson was supersensitive about appearing to back Kennedy only because of his faith and was reluctant to have the designation go to the son of Joseph Kennedy. The Governor was also inundated by several anti-Kennedy influences, other than Mrs. Roosevelt. The Eisenhower heart attack had also emphasized anew the importance of the vice-presidency. With the Republican convention in San Francisco yet to be held, leaving the choice of a running mate to the delegates would be a remarkable stroke, not only enlivening the Democratic affair but a great contrast to the inevitable Republican ratification of a second term for Nixon's vice-presidency.

At five o'clock that afternoon, a number of Stevenson advisers gathered in his downtown Chicago law office. They included Jim Finnegan, Bill Blair, Wilson Wyatt, George Ball, Newton Minow, and Willard Wirtz. Finnegan told them that Stevenson had made a bold decision, a decision that could be interpreted as either indecisive or courageous. He had decided to leave the choice of a running mate to the delegates. He indicated that at least three men were satisfactory possibilities: Humphrey, Kennedy, and Kefauver. "I'll say one thing," Finnegan said. "If we have to have a Catholic on the ticket, at least our shirts are clean. We didn't pick one."[30] Several years later Stevenson told a friend that he fully expected Kennedy to win the nomination on the floor. He said he had wanted Kennedy all along, which was why he had asked Kennedy to nominate him.[31] In view of subsequent history, that explanation seems self-serving and begs for a closer examination of what happened in 1956 and not what the Stevenson of four years later found more convenient to record. John Sharon pointed to the heated internal battle that went on between the Kennedy, the Humphrey, and the "throw it open" forces, which was waged so furiously that Stevenson did not decide until the last minute. Sharon also recalled that while Stevenson preferred Humphrey, if he had had the choice between Kefauver and Kennedy, he would have chosen Kennedy.[32]

After his nomination, Stevenson went to the Stockyards Inn. There he was met by Finnegan, Rayburn, Johnson, Butler, Ribicoff, Battle, Arvey, Lawrence, and others. Rayburn, who had his own lingering fantasy about getting the vice-presidential nomination for himself, became heatedly angry at the nominee's decision. Johnson was only slightly less passionate. Not implausibly, both Texans feared that Kefauver was bound to win. They also argued that the move would only confirm Stevenson as indecisive. Abe Ribicoff, present to boost Kennedy, found himself in an anomalous situation. "When the name of Kennedy came up," he later recalled, "almost unanimously, they were against Kennedy because of Catholicism, and, especially, the Catholics who . . . thought he would drag them down. Then, after everybody got through talking, I said this was very ironical. I didn't think that the time would ever come when a Jew would have to stand up in a roomful of Catholics to urge the acceptability of a Catholic. . . . But none of the other Catholics spoke up for him."[33]

An open fight on the floor was precisely what the Kennedy forces did not want. To influence Stevenson's choice, yes; to stir up popular and delegate pressure, certainly; but in no way did they figure they could compete with Kefauver and his solid base of already committed delegates. Moreover, an embarrassing defeat could deflate the aura of Kennedy glamour and success achieved earlier in the week. According to a Stevenson associate, Sorensen reacted to the pending announcement of the Governor's decision by warning that the Kennedyites would not be "part of a line" and that "the whole Catholic thing will be just a bloody mess on the floor of the convention." Advised that if the religious issue could not survive a convention floor fight, it could certainly stand no chance in a national campaign, a visibly irritated Sorensen left to warn Kennedy that there was a real chance it would be left to the delegates. Kennedy, Sorensen then reported back, would not allow his name to be put in nomination. "I think that's a mistake" was the response.[34]

But by the time Stevenson made his announcement, Kennedy had already decided that, given a choice between having Stevenson designate Kefauver and waging a floor fight, the latter was the lesser evil. The obvious hostility toward the Tennesseean within many delegations combined with the legwork already done by the Kennedy people and the success of both the film narration and the speech placing Stevenson in nomination gave them a fighting chance.

"The choice will be yours," Stevenson told the delegates shortly after 11:00 P.M., Central Standard Time. "The profit will be the nation's." He emphasized that seven of the thirty-four presidents in American history had reached the White House as the result of the death of the president and that placed a heavy obligation on the convention to choose with great care. There were, he said, several men who could do the job. The four who seemed at the top of the list were Humphrey, Kefauver, Gore, and Kennedy. Within Stevenson's headquarters staff, Humphrey appeared to have the edge over the field, but there was that Kefauver delegate strength.

After Stevenson made his late-night move, Sargent Shriver walked into Kennedy's Stockyards Inn room and found Jack, Bobby, Eunice, Jean, Pat, and Teddy in what looked like a midnight family conference instead of a political meeting, except that Sorensen, John Bailey, and a few others were also present. Bobby Kennedy, with a yellow pad in his hand, was writing down the states and the delegates and Jack was figuring out which of the delegates he could get. One report said that after Stevenson threw the vice-presidential race open, Kennedy rushed up to Minow and said, "It's a fixed convention. You've set it against me." The only problem with that was that Kefauver and Humphrey felt the same way.[35] Sharon later said they were all angry at Stevenson, all the vice-presidential candidates. "It was a fantastic couple of hours juggling, keeping everybody's feelings soothed and happy, and they all left not hating him—disturbed, disappointed, but he persuaded them that what he had done was right."[36] Each hopeful left determined to fight for the nomination.

But the Ambassador thought his son should stay out of it. O'Donnell, the only person present when Bobby placed a call to his father in France, observed that Joe Kennedy's "blue language flashed all over the room."

The connection was broken before he was finished denouncing Jack as an idiot who was ruining his political career. Bobby got off the line as soon as possible. "Whew!" he said. "Is he mad!"[37]

The next twelve hours featured an entirely new battle, one that vanquished the predicted pallor of a drab Democratic affair. In effect, the clock stopped for the bevy of vice-presidential contenders. For them and their cohorts, there was no night; adrenaline had killed the need for sleep. Irrational, disorganized groping for support, almost as sophomoric as the inanities of a fraternity contest, characterized the desperation to line up delegates. At 2:30 A.M., Humphrey workers circulated literature in lakefront saloons along Michigan Avenue. An awkward-looking but beaming Kefauver enjoyed being propelled through curious onlookers by a band of loyalists and then held a news conference at 4:00 A.M. As chaotically as the others, Jack Kennedy's crew, including his sisters and brother Bobby as well as Torby Macdonald and Eddie Boland, joined the hunt for delegates.

In the Blackstone Hotel after midnight, Kennedy found a private moment in the men's room with Mayor Wagner. He told him that John McCormack had suggested that the two contenders, both eastern big-city Roman Catholics, should help each other. The one with fewer first-ballot votes should persuade his delegates to vote for the other, a bargain that McCormack later recalled could only have helped Kennedy. Wagner, glad for the inevitable recognition about to befall a nonserious candidate who was up for reelection the following year, readily agreed. He would work to persuade his delegates to provide the necessary margin to put across the Kennedy candidacy.[38] At 2:00 A.M. Kennedy telephoned George Smathers to line him up for a seconding speech or to place him in nomination, if necessary; but Abe Ribicoff readily took on that task. By sunrise that morning, overnight button factories had produced Kennedy-for-Vice-President stickpins, which went on sale outside the International Amphitheater.

The Kennedy people moved into the battle with a realistic sense of futility. Suddenly, they had to wage a last-minute campaign to corner delegates instead of merely influencing Stevenson for their man. "We were hoping to give Kefauver a good run, but we thought the prearranged deal between Stevenson and the leaders who favored Kefauver was too well set to allow an upset," O'Donnell and Powers have written. Another nagging realization was that many would agree that the party would suffer for denying second place on the ticket to a man who had come to the convention with so many delegates, one who had also worked so hard in both 1952 and 1956.

Irritation at the Kennedy push had also become evident. Ribicoff, looking back from the vantage point of many years, pointed out that "everybody tried to block Kennedy. I think that all his political life there was deep resentment. He wasn't a great senator. They looked on him as a whippersnapper. I know I remember the remarks of Lyndon Johnson, Sam Rayburn, and Harry Truman—all these men—that just looked on him as a young rich upstart who didn't have the intellectual qualifications to be president. They underestimated Kennedy's intelligence because Kennedy was generally an introverted man who never disclosed himself to other people."[39] Ribicoff's recollection represented more than just Kennedy paranoia. Steve Mitchell complained that "the Kennedys were trying to grab off everything in sight," and he was particularly bitter that Sargent Shriver's ambitions for the Illinois governorship were conflicting with his own. "There were just an awful lot of Kennedys around," said the resentful Mitchell.[40]

At noon the convention was called to order. The Amphitheater was rife with speculation. No one was certain about the outcome; all parties were eager for a clue, a word, indicative of Stevenson's personal preference. After the routine rituals had been completed, Sam Rayburn, as the convention's chairman, banged the gavel and called for order. That was at 1:05 P.M. Then began the roll call of states for the vice-presidential nominations. Kennedy, along with Sorensen, remained in the Stockyards Inn, a TV set keeping him in touch. Because the electronic tote board had been malfunctioning since the night before, those watching on small screens had an advantage over the delegates because they were able to receive the up-to-the minute tallies that were unavailable within the hall itself. Kennedy spent most of that time either soaking his back in the tub or stretched out on the bed in his shorts watching the screen, maintaining his composure. He had obvious familiarity with the mechanism that could determine the way various delegates would go. After the roll call had placed the names of Gore and Kefauver into nomination, Governor Ribicoff did his part for Kennedy. George Smathers delivered a seconding speech under the dual burden of chest pains that frightened him about the possibility of a heart attack and annoying prodding from Rayburn to wind up his remarks to comply with the two-minute limitation. On the floor, meanwhile, Robert Kennedy virtually drafted McCormack and herded an obviously reluctant recruit up to the rostrum for a seconding speech that was both tepid and unenthusiastic, offering the

Kennedy nomination for the sake of "going East" to select a candidate. McCormack barely managed to identify his man as John F. Kennedy. Finally, by the time the roll call ended at 2:30 P.M., a total of thirteen names were in nomination.

Kefauver had a clear first-ballot lead. Still his 483 1/2 votes were far short of the necessary majority. The number needed to clinch was 686 1/2; but Kennedy's strength was the big news on that first ballot. With 304 votes, he was Kefauver's strongest rival, as Gore trailed behind with 178, Wagner with 162 1/2, and Humphrey 134 1/2. Kennedy's strength came mainly from New England, which gave him 89 1/2 of its 104 votes, with only New Hampshire reserving its locked-up ballots that Kefauver had won in the March primary. Kennedy also got 46 of the 64 from Stevenson's home state of Illinois. But Jack Kennedy's real breakthrough came from the South. There he outpolled Kefauver 105 to 20 1/2 and came in second only to Gore's 136 1/2. But Gore was clearly a regional candidate, one with no real chance to win. Southern anti-Kefauver forces had clearly calculated that they could best achieve their objective by voting for Kennedy. Others, especially within the Virginia delegation, were swayed by the identification of the Massachusetts senator with Dever as well as by McCormack's efforts to work out a civil-rights compromise.

Kennedy has been described as dispassionate as he watched from the Stockyards Inn. He had good reason to have high hopes for the second ballot. Wagner did deliver, not all his delegates, but the bulk, which included 96 1/2 of New York's 98. Actress Grace Kelly's father, John, came through with 8 1/2 from Pennsylvania. Governor Robert Meyner of New Jersey managed 30 of Wagner's 31 1/2 first-ballot votes, and all 10 of Delaware's shifted to Kennedy. Robert Wagner's friends in the Puerto Rican delegation were not swayed that easily, however, having their own objections to Kennedy and retaining their 6 for the mayor.[41] Elsewhere, Kennedy profited from defections of Gore delegates.

Texas furnished the big break. Johnson and Rayburn had been trying to sell Humphrey to their delegation. But memories of the civil-rights fight of 1948 were still too vivid to make the Minnesotan acceptable. Still, the one person both congressional leaders from Texas wanted to stop was Kefauver, who was hated with "a passion" by Johnson.[42] Rayburn, as practical a politician who ever lived, was also impressed by Kennedy's first-ballot showing. As the convention's chairman and unable to work directly with the Texas delegates, he dispatched a friend to sound them out about Kennedy. Johnson worked within the caucus to argue the case for the New Englander but found his job surprisingly easy: the Texas delegation *wanted* Kennedy. Enthusiastically, then, with a powerful card for stopping Kefauver in his hands, Johnson grabbed the microphone to respond for his delegation and shouted, "Texas proudly casts its fifty-six votes for the fighting sailor who wears the scars of battle."[43] Just as Texas had moved from Gore to Kennedy, so did other states.

In the Stockyards Inn, Jack Kennedy's TV screen showed him with a second ballot total of 618 to Kefauver's 551 1/2. A cordon of Chicago police arrived, ready to provide an escort to the platform for the prospective nominee. Kennedy began to dress, selecting a blue suit and white shirt with a red-dotted light gray tie. Within the Amphitheater itself, a stampede had materialized; in the confusion, nobody knew the exact count. But without the second ballot having been closed, a number of delegations were shouting toward Rayburn for recognition. The chairman called on Kentucky, which promptly switched its 30 Gore votes to Kennedy. That brought Kennedy to within 38 1/2 of an absolute majority, a remarkably close figure, one that could normally create a steamroller strong enough to put a nominee over the top. One of Adlai Stevenson's sons, John Fell, arrived at Kennedy's room to offer his congratulations, which the senator politely waved off as a bit premature.

Considerable agitation developed within several delegations; but probably none as acute as in Tennessee's. On the floor, Gore was warned by the state's national committeewoman, Martha Ragland, that failure to deliver his votes to Kefauver would incite the vehement opposition of publisher Silliman Evans, Jr., of the Nashville *Tennessean,* and could destroy his political career.[44] Gore relayed the advice to Frank Clement. Astonished and angry over having to back Kefauver, the governor nevertheless felt that he had as few options as Gore. With the Tennessee delegation seated up front, even Rayburn, weakening eyesight and all, had no trouble seeing the state's standard being waved for recognition. At the same time, a Kefauver man and Washington lawyer, William Roberts, sent runners up to the rostrum yelling toward Rayburn, "Tennessee is going for Kennedy!"[45] Whether, in the tumult of the moment, Rayburn ever heard that will never be known. But if he thought about it at all, he had every reason to believe Kennedy would benefit, especially because of Gore's earlier endorsement of the Massachusetts senator. The startled Rayburn then heard Gore shout into the microphone, "With gratitude for the consideration and support of this great Democratic National Convention, I respectfully withdraw my name, and support my distinguished colleague, Estes Kefauver."[46]

That unleashed the turnabout. Only a few minor gains stemmed a rapid deterioration. Oklahoma's governor, Raymond Gary, holding 28 key Gore votes and reacting largely against Kennedy's farm bill position, shifted to Kefauver. Kennedy slid. Hubert Humphrey, holding 16 1/2 from his own state, acknowledged both Kefauver's primary election success in Minnesota and "our political position" by transferring them to the Tennesseean.[47] Missouri, with a handful of Catholic delegates fearful of backing Kennedy, also went to Kefauver. In the flurry of changes, an accurate running tabulation was impossible; some states switched more than once. Michigan had previously committed itself to Kefauver to place the considerable core of delegates, especially blacks, who were opposed to Stevenson, and so shifted its entire 44 votes to the Tennesseean. When the shifting stopped, Kefauver had 755 1/2 to Kennedy's 589.[48]

At the Stockyards Inn, the police cordon disappeared. "Let's go," Kennedy told Sorensen. They rushed down the back stairs, entering the Amphitheater through a rear door. At 4:22, Rayburn recognized the senator, who came up to the rostrum. The crowd roared. He spoke without notes. "I hope you'll make it unanimous," he said, even as his face betrayed deep disappointment. Then he moved away. "Go back and make a motion," whispered Rayburn. "Make a motion." He returned, made his motion, and the convention unanimously supported Kefauver. Kennedy, disappearing from the rostrum, was obviously in deep distress. "I felt like the Indian who had a lot of arrows stuck in him and, when he was asked how it felt, said, 'It only hurts when I laugh,'" he told someone. But at that despondent moment, his nationally televised concession conveyed subdued, controlled tones that contained the passion of a magnanimous loser—an impromptu appearance that captivated the nation. That afternoon, Jim Finnegan told everyone he had thought all along it would be Kefauver.[49]

"Did Stevenson keep his hands off?" asked Bill Mullins of the *Boston Herald*. "His chief manager is Jim Finnegan of Pennsylvania," he added, pointing out that on the second ballot, even before the big shift, Kennedy was only able to get 8 1/2 of Pennsylvania's 74 votes, all of which then shifted to Kefauver after the switch.[50] Possibly the most stinging analysis came from Krock's pen. Any such observation by so close a friend of the Kennedys could hardly have differed substantially from their own perceptions. Krock pointed out that the so-called "word" from Stevenson, the signal to the delegation, could have made the difference when Kennedy came some thirty-odd votes from the top. Had Stevenson hoped the convention would choose Kennedy, Krock wrote, he did not express it when and where it could have been effective.[51] Eight years later Robert Kennedy said that Stevenson's behavior perturbed Jack.[52] Others suspected that McCormack had betrayed Kennedy by whispering into Rayburn's ear to recognize Missouri, knowing that state would strengthen the Kefauver trend, a suspicion later denied by all sides, including Boland, Macdonald, and Kennedy himself. Despite the bitterness over controlling the convention, despite his reluctance to make a seconding speech, McCormack recognized Kennedy strength. He was more astute than desiring to perpetuate lingering bitterness in Massachusetts; it took little wisdom to recognize the new source of power. He had actually worked pretty closely with Rayburn when they thought Kefauver could be stopped. Asked about the episode twenty-two years later, McCormack's recollection remained vivid. "That was one of the rawest deals a man ever got, goddamn," he replied. "I didn't even know where Missouri was seated in that convention." He insisted he merely wanted Rayburn to recognize Kentucky.[53]

Jack Kennedy was bitterly disappointed, much more so than associates had expected. A wide combination of circumstances had kept him from accomplishing what would have been, in effect, a political coup. Many of the larger state delegations looked to Kefauver rather than Kennedy to be helpful for local candidates. That was especially true in the case of Catholic office-seekers fearful of the presence of another co-religionist on the ticket. The Minnesota delegation, furthermore, supported Kefauver not because of any opposition on religious grounds or Kennedy's farm record, but for other, more populist reasons, as John Blatnik recalled. "Kennedy was mainly identified with that Eastern crowd, . . . the big money crowd, whereas Kefauver, on the other hand, with his coonskin cap approach, his sidewalk campaigning, shaking every hand he could reach, typified what the Midwest liked, the rugged man of the soil, the grass roots man coming out and meeting people on a person to person basis."[54] Generally, Jack Kennedy's vote on the Benson farm bill still served him very badly. Nevertheless, he had done as well as he had in the South because he was the best bet to block first Humphrey and then Kefauver. "I think that if Mr. Rayburn had recognized South Carolina before Tennessee, Kennedy would have got the nomination. There's no doubt of it," said Georgia's Governor Marvin Griffin. "But the Tennessee delegation was right down front and was raising so much cain, he recognized them first."[55]

Kennedy's bitter disappointment was gradually tempered by another realization. Shortly after the loss, he made a transatlantic phone call to France and told his father, "We did our best. I had fun and I didn't make a fool of myself."[56] To Arthur Krock, in recognition of the surprising southern support, Jack said, "I'll be singing 'Dixie' the rest of my life."[57] "Don't feel sorry for young Jack Kennedy," advised Bill Cunningham in the *Boston Herald*. "Despite his second ballot defeat . . . he probably rates as the one real victor of the entire convention. His was the one new face that actually shone. His charisma, his dignity, his intellectuality, and, in the end, his gracious sportsmanship—contrast, for example, with Averell Harriman last night and the sour politics of former President Truman—are undoubtedly what those delegates will remember. So will those who watched it and heard it via TV and radio."[58]

The Ambassador was correct in warning Kennedy against running with Stevenson. A loss would undoubtedly have been attributed, at least in part, to the presence of a Roman Catholic on the ticket, thereby perpetuating the myths about the Al Smith defeat. In that sense and in the rise of his own national prominence prompted by the convention, Jack Kennedy, ironically, emerged as the real winner. Only in that sense, but a very important one, was Kennedy right and his father wrong. Throughout the country, including the South, editorials praised him. *The Southwest Times* of Pulaski, Virginia, was typical in calling him "one of the ablest and most promising young men on the American political scene today."[59] "As for Jack Kennedy," observed the party's presidential nominee, "I have a feeling that he was the real hero of the hour and that we shall hear a great deal more from this promising young man."[60]

When Kennedy and his wife reached Massachusetts, he explained to reporters that he had not slept in three nights. Jacqueline had also exerted herself too much, especially considering her pregnancy. When newsmen persisted with questions, Kennedy waved them off. "I have nothing to say," he said. "I've been in the news enough."[61] Less than two hours later, he flew with brother Teddy toward Paris and on to a two-week yachting vacation in the Mediterranean, the sort of August trip that had become customary after congressional adjournments. Jackie, meanwhile, went for a much needed rest at the Auchincloss estate in Newport.

There, on the twenty-third of August, complications developed. Rushed to the Newport Hospital with an internal hemorrhage, she lost the baby. A hospital spokesman attributed the miscarriage to a possible connection with the exhaustion and nervous tension of the convention.[62] Her condition was also announced as satisfactory.

The timing further strained the marriage. Jack, out of touch and completely unaware of what had happened, was cruising off the Italian coast. Only when he telephoned home from Genoa, Italy, on Sunday, August 26, did he learn what had happened. On the twenty-eighth he arrived at Boston's Logan airport on a TWA flight from Paris and transferred to a Piper Cub for the flight to Jackie's bedside. From Adlai Stevenson came the following message: "I wish there was something I could say that would help either you or her—aside from the fact that I was honored beyond measure to have you nominate me, and so beautifully, and to have had your support and encouragement in this trying task."[63]

21

The Pulitzer Prize-
Winning Senator

The mandatory layover at Hammersmith Farm was salutary for both Kennedys. Jackie, of course, needed to recover from the miscarriage; and Jack, although his physical condition had improved, got some rest and caught up with the postconvention mail that reached him from Washington.

The gains were readily obvious. In Arkansas organizers had already begun a drive to draft him for the vice-presidency in 1960.[1] Virginia's Harry Byrd assured Kennedy that his nomination would "have strengthened the ticket to a marked degree, while the nomination of Kefauver will have the opposite result."[2] Flattering editorials were commonplace among southern papers. They, along with the rest of the country, had suddenly "found" an ingratiating personality.

Stevenson, meanwhile, was in an impossible situation. His second try against Eisenhower had no more promise than the first; if anything, it was more hopeless. His new struggle was against an incumbent, an even more popular figure than in 1952, one who, despite the setback of a heart attack, had the confidence of the nation for having ended the Korean War and become a new "high priest" of prosperity. History overshadowed whatever Stevenson could say, rendering pathetic his arguments for unilateral nuclear test bans, a moratorium on the draft, and warnings that Richard Nixon could reach the presidency because he was "one heartbeat away." He seemed less the cultivated, highly literate opponent of 1952 and more the product of conventional political expediency. Finally, toward the end of the campaign, the anti-Soviet uprising in Poland and the revolt of the Hungarian "freedom fighters," together with the Anglo-French and Israeli desperate attack on Egypt, increased the President's margin of support. And yet, Stevenson's difficulties were Kennedy's opportunities.

The national campaign became both a laboratory and a chance to broaden contacts. Jack made arrangements for his brother Bobby to join Stevenson as an observer, which the Governor accepted. After all, that might somehow placate disgruntled Catholics. Bobby gained more insights about what to avoid than constructive information. He later acknowledged having begun his tutelage with admiration for Stevenson. "Then I spent six weeks with him on the campaign," Bobby explained, "and he destroyed it all."[3] Robert's conclusion was not unlike the analysis of Jim Finnegan himself, who said that "the trouble with our campaign . . . was that the professors all tried to act like politicians, and the politicians all tried to act like professors."[4] Then, after his rest at Newport, Jack Kennedy was ready to campaign for the presidential candidate.

Whether Jack helped himself with Stevenson is doubtful. The Governor's people suspected that Kennedy was working to cultivate his own political future, that his mission was indistinguishable from Bobby's. To really help Stevenson, they thought, he should concentrate on delivering the votes of his own state with its large working-class Catholic electorate. Then, perhaps, he might do some talking in a few swing states. Therefore, they were irked to find that Kennedy was mapping out his own itinerary. "When you see a senator doing much speaking outside his own state," admitted one of Jack's colleagues, "it means one of two things. He needs the money or he's got his eye on higher office. And Jack doesn't need the money."[5] During one five-week period he made at least 150 speeches or appearances in twenty-four states and logged some thirty thousand miles.[6] By the third week of September he was in California speaking in the Los Angeles area to both the United Steel Workers convention and the Committee for the Arts of the Democratic National Committee. Then he moved on to Santa Ana and San Diego, followed by a Los Angeles Town Hall address, and finally a San Francisco visit. Apprised of the complaints coming from the Stevenson camp, Kennedy then offered to cancel a series of engagements that had been planned for Indianapolis, Philadelphia, and Cleveland. As they desired, he would concentrate on his own state. "Should Governor Stevenson fail to carry Massachusetts—which is going to be an extremely difficult state to carry for a variety of economic, political and ideological reasons—I would not want it said that I was too busy campaigning in other parts of the country at the expense of my own state," he wrote to Finnegan.[7] But it was Stevenson himself who requested that Kennedy speak before the party's annual fund-raising dinner in Philadelphia on October 25.[8]

In other ways, Kennedy advanced both his own cause and the appearance of being an industrious, loyal spokesman for Stevenson. Together with the presidential candidate, he made a campaign film and then boosted him on a *Meet the Press* program as well as in a nationally televised show from Boston. Before a preelection rally from Boston, Stevenson speech-writers John Bartlow Martin and Arthur Schlesinger, Jr., made a last-minute attempt to convince Sorensen that Kennedy's speech should also attack Joe McCarthy. Sorensen was unmoved.[9]

Eisenhower's national landslide ended any doubts that Kennedy's Chicago defeat had really been a blessing. He had missed the smashup and been spared the debris. His southern support, surprising for the Catholic Kennedy, continued to grow during the campaign. So staunch a regional segregationist as columnist John Temple Graves, who was widely syndicated in the Old Confederacy, grandly noted that Kennedy was a "young man who will never forget that amazing vote of the South for him against Kefauver in 1956. It will influence his life through all its long remainder." More hopefully, Graves added: "He is too honest and New England-bred—and political—to take the Southern position on the race question, but he will never, never be a fanatic against us as Reuther and Nixon. . . . His forays into the South these days prove how deeply his thinking, choosing and belonging may have been effected [sic] by the biggest moment of his life, to wit, the one when the Solid South nearly nominated him for Vice President. . . ."[10] Kennedy assured Governor James Coleman of Mississippi that his concern over the loss of New England's textile industry did not mean that he had been " 'anti-Southern' in any sense of the word. I have," he added, "lived a good share of my life in the South, where my parents have voted for 25 years; and own a house in Virginia at the present time."[11]

Even as Kennedy was proclaiming his Virginia residence, he was preparing to abandon McLean and Hickory Hill, which, with the nursery outfitted for the baby that never came, had unhappy associations for Jacqueline. After election day Kennedy took her on a vacation trip to Europe and the Caribbean, and then they moved into a rented Georgetown home at 2808 P Street. The McLean property was sold to brother Bobby, who paid the same $125,000 that it had cost Jack less than three years earlier.

Interrupting his vacation in November and in the early part of the new year, he spoke out on developments in the Middle East. The preelection Anglo-French and Israeli drive toward the Suez Canal had been blunted by American and Russian pressure. Kennedy, when facing the B'nai B'rith in Baltimore and the National Conference of Christians and Jews in Cleveland, upheld the importance of preserving Israel and urged both Arab and American negotiators to accept the fact of that nation's existence. To the United Nations, he assigned a peacekeeping role that would preserve regional stability.[12] It seemed self-evident to Kennedy, as to most Americans, that conflict there would leave the area vulnerable to Soviet influences.

While Kennedy got around to as many groups as possible, working to develop a reputation as a spokesman on major issues, Sorensen filled a vital backup role. He compiled lists of potentially valuable contacts and made telephone calls to a wide array of political, journalistic, and academic figures. An astonishing outpouring of Christmas cards left the office that year, many with some touch of personal greeting from Kennedy himself. For the early months of 1957, the Sorensen appointment calendar reveals the cultivation of academic contacts. On January 30, for example, a key figure among those in New England colleges, Earl Latham, came to Washington and met with both Sorensen and Kennedy. Latham would subsequently be useful in assisting with issues and articles and serving as a liaison to other academicians in the region. The Kennedy office, in turn, opened its doors for Latham's political science class from Amherst.[13] Once the contact was established on a quid pro quo basis, the relationship continued. For the professor, access to the senator was indeed a coup. For the senator, Latham offered academic expertise and a fresh link with the vast New England academic community. Marjorie and Belford V. Lawson, black attorneys from Washington, were also enlisted for future assistance, the couple becoming the first tie to a hitherto ignored constituency. During that period, too, Kennedy told Dave Powers quite bluntly that "you know, if we work like hell the next four years, we will pick up all the marbles."[14]

Changes then became evident during the early months of the newly organized Eighty-fifth Congress. One involved John Kennedy's evolution toward party acceptance, if not quite regularity. His public positions more frequently corresponded with Democratic liberals, muting the old independent conservatism. He quickly joined supporters of rules to simplify ending filibusters, a reform especially dear to civil-rights advocates long since frustrated by the potent use of that parliamentary device. He also joined the liberal minority opposed to the nomination of Scott McLeod as ambassador to Ireland, a move that brought vituperation from old friends of Joe McCarthy. Even his decision to spurn an invitation to join the newly formed Democratic Advisory Council, which had been created by a group of Stevensonian liberals unhappy with their congressional leadership, was, as Kennedy informed Party Chairman Paul Butler, a step in tune with "the great majority of House and Senate members" who had refused to follow the examples of Hubert Humphrey and Estes Kefauver. Unlike them, Kennedy explained, he had to stand for reelection in 1958.[15]

Two issues, labor and immigration, became especially important for promoting his popularity with eastern liberals. Consequently, to help formulate positions on such matters, he acquired lawyers Ralph Dungan and Meyer Feldman as staff assistants. But if Kennedy had little passion for the intricacies of labor law, he had less fire for the problems of immigration. As a Roman Catholic from Massachusetts, however, a state with the ethnic mixtures similar to so many other industrial areas, escape from the topic was hardly possible. Kennedy, then, championed reforming the laws governing immigration, especially the inequities of the quota system. Since the 1920's that ceiling had made immigration to America far harder for southern and eastern Europeans—Italians, Poles, Jews, Greeks, Portuguese, all prominent not only in Massachusetts but in various sectors of New England. As one of his close associates has acknowledged in a confidential oral history interview, "Kennedy spotted immigration as an important thing and I suppose it was for Massachusetts politicians for a long while." He also disagreed with Republicans by advocating health care for older citizens, labor democracy, and federal protection against substandard wages.

Right after the Soviets launched *Sputnik I* on October 4, 1957, Kennedy used the achievement to renew previous calls for aid to education. Portentously, he related the technological advance to questions of national survival. He told a meeting of schoolteachers in Fall River that a shortage of classrooms, money, and a "consequent lack of high quality education" could, in the long run, prove to be "the undoing of our nation."[16]

In other parts of the country, he worked to repair his previous advocacy of flexible farm price supports and, as did most other Democrats, excoriated Ezra Taft Benson for agricultural policies that had led the country "down the primrose path." Jack also charged the administration with making possible "more monopolistic business mergers, more small business failures, more children going to school part-time, more farms being foreclosed, and more national resources being given away than ever before."[17]

His increased activity coincided with the recognition of his being a top contender for the 1960 Democratic nomination. A poll of Washington correspondents at the beginning of January rated him first. Although the mid-February Gallup survey reported that Kennedy, when matched against Kefauver, still trailed among Democrats 38–49, the deficit was destined to be temporary.[18] Especially helpful was the positive reaction to the renewal of efforts for a significant committee assignment. A closed session of the Senate Democratic Steering Committee awarded Kennedy Walter George's vacated seat on the Foreign Relations Committee.

The choice provoked immediate speculation. Writer Doris Fleeson was certain Lyndon Johnson had had a significant hand in the move: the majority leader was preparing a Johnson-Kennedy ticket for the next convention.[19] Others concluded that Johnson had simply blocked Kefauver, just as he had tried to do at Chicago. Less conspiratorial-minded analysts pointed out that Kennedy had been long overdue for a significant committee assignment. Kennedy's elevation to Foreign Relations, plus his chairmanship of the subcommittee of the Senate Labor and Public Welfare Committee, helped increase his exposure.

The Labor Subcommittee convened at ten on February 25, 1957, in the Old Supreme Court Chamber of the United States Capitol. Earlier, under Paul Douglas's chairmanship, twenty days of public hearings had been held and three volumes of testimony and supporting documents related to extending the coverage of minimum-wage protections under the Wages and Hours Law of 1938 had been produced. Altogether, oral testimony during 1955 and 1956 by 221 spokesmen from government, business, labor, and public-interest organizations, plus statements from nearly two hundred others, filled four volumes with more than twenty-seven hundred pages. Under Kennedy that February and March, eleven open sessions took place.

Labor Secretary James P. Mitchell appeared to open the series and returned one month later. His confrontation with Kennedy was only the first of several. More than a clash of opposing views, their positions represented the administration versus the Democratic Party's emerging challenger for 1960. As the Kennedy candidacy became more likely, so too did some gossip about Mitchell as the Republican presidential candidate. A New Jersey Republican with firm Irish-American ethnic credentials could possibly neutralize the Catholic vote.

While Kennedy backed labor's desires for higher minimum wages, Mitchell, from a working-class background and without the benefit of a college education, carried the administration's case for management. Brought up in Elizabeth, New Jersey, with his Uncle Thomas, who became a well-known movie actor, Mitchell went through successive careers as a grocer, lumberyard worker, truck driver, salesman, and finally got on-the-job training in labor-management relations. He worked in New York with the WPA during the Depression and then as director of the Industrial Personnel Division of the War Department. Before joining the Eisenhower administration, he managed personnel relations for such department stores as R. H. Macy and Bloomingdale's, where he was vice-president in charge of labor relations and operations. Within the Republican government in Washington, he was known as a moderating force, certainly a more effective advocate than his short-lived and frustrated predecessor, Martin Durkin. Blatant protectors of business interests in the cabinet like Sinclair Weeks and George Humphrey could easily snipe at Durkin as caring more about union welfare than for "the best interests of the country," but Mitchell enjoyed the leverage of a moderate Republican with a management past. Nevertheless, support of collective bargaining and sympathy with labor opposition to undermining unions by the passage of so-called "right to work" laws made him relatively acceptable to labor. Within the Eisenhower circle, Mitchell even developed somewhat of a reputation as the "social conscience of the conservatives."[20]

Neither man was a lawyer. Each, however, was fortified by specialists from their personal staffs and committee aides. Kennedy, as subcommittee chairman, had the assistance of the thirty-four-year-old Ralph Dungan. Trained in public affairs at Princeton, and having been hired as a legislative assistant, Dungan was happy to leave the senatorial office and join the subcommittee. Dungan's major function became advising Kennedy on labor law at a time when, as one colleague recalled, the senator was still learning, "very upset and nervous."[21] Also watching from nearby, Samuel V. Merrick, a counsel for Senator Wayne Morse, agreed that "Kennedy reflected the fact that he did not have very much exposure to what I would talk about as the rough 'n' tumble of economic life in the United States." Merrick thought he assumed that civilization had somehow advanced to where people were more gentlemanly than they were. Although he had few illusions about the low level of competition common in the political world, things like strikes were, "if not a medieval absurdity," at least something of the past. Organizational picketing was especially anachronistic when election machinery could determine bargaining representatives. "He really didn't understand why a union insisted upon having the right to picket for organizational purposes," said Merrick. "I doubt if he ever realized how tough and nasty most of these economic decisions in the private sector often are."[22]

Another problem was the presence of Wayne Morse. Fiercely independent, with the kind of certitude sustained by arrogance, he ranked high among senators classed as mercurial and maverick. Almost seventeen years older than Kennedy, and a Republican until Eisenhower's policies ignited one of his rebellions, finally compelling him to abandon the GOP for the Democrats, Morse treasured his expertise in labor law. In the early 1930's he had been dean of the University of Oregon Law School. As an arbitrator in labor disputes and later a public member of the National War Labor Board, he won regard as one of the nation's most prominent labor-relations experts. Now he felt that he, not Kennedy, was entitled to be chairman of the labor subcommittee. That his knowledge of labor relations was outdated was hardly easy for his pride to accept, especially as he watched the novice in the chair. He had also had to acquiesce to Kennedy's selection since the Democrats had ignored his years as a Republican and independent when calculating his seniority. But, as Merrick has noted, at that point Wayne Morse was a "good soldier. He was the adjutant, and he did what Senator Kennedy wanted him to do and was very helpful and cooperative."

Kennedy, facing those witnesses during the eleven days of hearings on minimum wages, also displayed personal qualities that won friends and loyalists. He was patient, treated with courtesy those who came before the committee, and seemed receptive to contrary opinions. Merrick thought it the supreme compliment by regarding him as the kind of person one can be confined with on a small boat for three or four days.[23]

In the witness chair, Secretary Mitchell stated the administration's viewpoint by opposing various alternative proposals to extend minimum-wage coverage. They would obliterate "meaningful" distinctions between intrastate and interstate commerce. They would be too extensive, covering virtually "all enterprises and employees everywhere."[24]

That began the first duel between Kennedy and Mitchell. Kennedy quickly challenged the legitimacy of the administration's proposals, which, he contended, would be far different from what appeared on paper. He placed Mitchell on the defensive about how many workers, especially those in retail establishments supposedly to be covered by the administration, were already earning more than the required minimum. By defining interstate commerce narrowly, the bill would exclude certain categories, especially farm laborers in addition to store workers and some fifteen thousand telephone-company employees. When he asked the secretary what percentage of those included in the administration's proposals were already actually getting the one dollar minimum, Mitchell admitted that he had no such figures.

"How can you decide that you are going to stop at 2 1/2 million, if you don't have any figures on how many of those 2 1/2 million are getting less than a dollar?" Kennedy wanted to know.

When Mitchell replied that the administration was relying on figures from Bureau of Labor Statistics surveys since 1955, Kennedy retorted that cost-of-living increases had rendered much of that information out of date. "I think it is not unreasonable," he told the cabinet officer, "when you are making these suggestions that you should give the committee at least some indication of how many people would be affected by this."

Mitchell said, "We will try to."

Kennedy also told Mitchell quite firmly that by leaving so much of minimum-wage coverage to the states, which would result from a limited interpretation of which businesses were operating according to definitions of interstate commerce, actual minimum rates would remain low. Only New York State law, as Mitchell himself pointed out, had already moved to impose a one dollar minimum.[25]

The New York Times reported that the size of the minimum, which had gone to a dollar from seventy-five cents the preceding March 1, was being soft-pedaled by labor in favor of the coverage issue.[26] That became very clear on March 4, when George Meany came in to testify. Arguing that the great majority of firms could well afford to pay a higher minimum, Meany stated labor's belief that it should be raised to at least $1.25. "The whole trend in industry and the urgent need of the future is for a shorter work week," said Meany, "yet the Secretary of Labor would permit these exempted firms to maintain working hours in excess of 40 a week without penalty."[27] Referring to a letter from Mitchell to Kennedy admitting that in the neighborhood of 400,000 of the two and a half million workers who would be covered by the proposals were actually getting less than the statutory minimum, Meany accused Mitchell of resorting to "a new and tricky" definition of what constitutes interstate commerce. Mitchell, expressing the administration's attitude, said it should not include businesses grossing less than one million dollars yearly or employing fewer than a hundred people. That, argued Meany, would effectively keep seven and a half million "outside the pale" of the dollar minimum hourly wage law. Kennedy joined the AFL-CIO president in the subsequent discussion and pointed out that only "a couple of hundred thousand" would be helped by Mitchell's proposal and that would hinder efforts to stimulate purchasing power.[28]

The entire minimum-wage controversy was obviously headed nowhere. The administration felt the political need to make some sort of conciliatory gesture in that direction, while organized labor regarded both the coverage and the one dollar minimum as inadequate. But the Chamber of Commerce opposed even a modest increase and organized labor could do little to overcome the prevailing popular indifference. With various proposals already in the hopper, each was destined to fail. Kennedy followed the hearings that spring by introducing his own bill to extend minimum-wage coverage to five million additional workers. That got out of the subcommittee but, after languishing there for two months, died in the Labor and Public Welfare Committee. In the House the chances were even less that any legislation could result and Kennedy told reporters on July 7 that he was "getting increasingly discouraged."[29]

They had gone through their motions, the administration appearing moderate and preserving "modern Republicanism," virtues proclaimed by President Eisenhower; the Democratic opposition critical but hardly inspired to offer more than perfunctory proposals in the absence of strong popular support behind the needs of low-income workers; and the major unions not making the kind of fight capable of overcoming influential pro-management interests. The posturing completed, attention turned toward the writing of a new law.

While labor issues had yet to generate much public interest, Kennedy was the personal recipient of a deluge of invitations for appearances and articles in magazines and newspapers. He served as a narrator on the popular and prestigious television show, *Omnibus,* and was featured on two programs in connection with the Middle East crisis. He joined former President Herbert Hoover at a Hoover Commission conference in Washington, which had its proceedings carried on a national radio hookup. With *Profiles in Courage* still selling well, as total sales neared ninety thousand that March in the hardcover edition and with the paperback version just coming out, Kennedy's reputation as a man of letters and scholarship was gaining him special distinctions in the Upper Chamber.

One by-product was recognition as the Senate's unofficial "historian." As a direct result of the book, Kennedy became chairman of the Special Committee on the Senate Reception Room, which had been established two years earlier to identify five outstanding senators of the past. To facilitate the selection process, he appointed a nine-member advisory committee under Allan Nevins. Among those who served with Nevins was Kennedy's former teacher, Arthur Holcombe.

For the senator it was good, nonpartisan, noncontroversial publicity. It countered no vested interests, brought no recriminations, and could be applauded by patriotic groups and the nation's schoolteachers for its devotion to the American heritage. Not only did it give him favorable publicity at home, but it also provided an opportunity for a *New York Times Magazine* article under his by-line, which explained that 150 historians and political scientists were being polled to come up with the names of the five worthies.

The winners were announced on April 30. The front page of *The New York Times* carried the pictures of Henry Clay, John Calhoun, Daniel Webster, Robert LaFollette, and Robert A. Taft as the "five greatest senators." Their portraits would be permanently hung in the Senate Reception Room, which was a nice tribute for the departed statesmen but a much more valuable step for the current senator from Massachusetts. The following Sunday another Kennedy article ran in the *New York Herald Tribune,* again explaining the process used to arrive at the distinction. Throughout the country, the award received wide publicity, closely linked with Kennedy as the committee's chairman.[30]

The day after the *Tribune* story, the Pulitzer Prize Committee announced its list of winners for achievement in the field of letters for 1957. Along with such distinguished works as Eugene O'Neill's *Long Day's Journey into Night,* George Kennan's *Russia Leaves the War: Soviet-American Relations 1917–1920,* and a volume of verse by Richard Wilbur, *Things of this World,* went a prize to John F. Kennedy for *Profiles in Courage.* The publicity was splendid, prestigious, and devoid of any hint that the reward had ignored the recommendations of the biography jury. It also helped further the stature of a political leader whose appeal was to intelligence and quality without self-interested partisanship.

The authenticity of the book's authorship raises questions about the Pulitzer prize. Reviewing the matter in 1977, Evan Thomas offered his own skepticism about *Profiles* having been worthy of the biography award. He suspected the involvement of the ubiquitous Arthur Krock.[31] Therefore, the granting of the award, including a possible Krock connection as a lobbyist for the Ambassador, was investigated by the present author.

The judges for biography were two distinguished historians, Julian Boyd, the editor of the Jefferson papers at Princeton University, and Professor Bernard Mayo, the biographer of Henry Clay and an associate with Boyd on the Jefferson project. On February 28, 1957, Boyd forwarded to Professor John Hohenberg, the secretary of the Advisory Board on Pulitzer Prizes, a list of recommendations from the judges. Boyd and Mayo specified five works, listing them in the order of preference, and pointed out that while they had worked independently, they had "achieved a very high degree of unanimity in our recommendations for the top candidates." The first choice was Alpheus T. Mason's *Harlan Fiske Stone: Pillar of the Law,* followed by the runner-up, James MacGregor Burns's *Roosevelt; The Lion and the Fox,* and Irving Brant's *James Madison: The President, 1809–1812,* Samuel Flagg Bemis's *John Quincy Adams and the Union,* and William N. Chambers's *Old Bullion Benton.* The report stated that Mason's biography of Chief Justice Stone was a distinguished work by a leading authority on American jurisprudence, "the product of a searching mind that is also capable of clear analysis." It also noted that Burns's biography of Franklin D. Roosevelt "is a brilliant performance, and its literary quality is in our opinion superior to that of Mason's *Stone. . . .* "; but the nature of the subject kept it from having the definitive quality of Mason's work. The historians also suggested other books they had contemplated in addition to the first five: Raymond B. Fosdick's *John D. Rockefeller, Jr.,* Margaret Thorp's *Neilson of Smith,* and the second volume of the memoirs of Harry S Truman. Nowhere was John Kennedy's *Profiles in Courage* mentioned. Nor in scholarship, maturity of thought, or importance can Kennedy's book compare.[32] Yet the Advisory Board chose to ignore the recommendations and awarded the $500 prize (which Kennedy turned over to the United Negro College Fund) for what they termed "a distinguished American biography or autobiography teaching patriotic and unselfish service to the people illustrated by an eminent example."

To suggest that the Advisory Board was improperly influenced or "bought off" would be making a very bold assumption. In addition to Hohenberg, who served as the secretary and was a professor of journalism at Columbia University, the board was made up of thirteen prominent men, many but not all from the world of journalism. Those who comprised the board that year included Grayson Kirk, the president of Columbia University; Barry Bingham, president and editor of the Louisville *Courier-Journal;* Hodding Carter, the publisher and editor of the *Delta Democrat-Times* of Greenville, Mississippi; Turner Catledge, the managing editor of *The New York Times;* Norman Chandler, publisher of the *Los Angeles Times;* Robert Choate, publisher of the *Boston Herald;* Gardiner Cowles, the president of Cowles Magazines, Inc.; J. D. (Don) Ferguson, the president of *The Milwaukee Journal;* John S. Knight, the president of Knight Newspapers; Benjamin M. McKelway, the editor of *The Washington Evening Star;* Paul Miller, the executive vice-president of the Gannett Newspapers of Rochester, New York; Louis Seltzer, the editor of the *Cleveland Press;* and Joseph P. Pulitzer, Jr., the publisher of the *St. Louis Post-Dispatch.*

As John Hohenberg has written in his own book, *The Pulitzer Prizes: A History,* Krock did lobby for Kennedy. But Hohenberg later emphasized that Krock's advocacy was not at all instrumental. In fact, Krock was such a "drumbeater" that, if anything, his efforts could have been counterproductive. Nor was there evidence of visible activities by Ambassador Kennedy.[33] Joseph Pulitzer, Jr., similarly confirmed Joe Kennedy's absence from the scene, saying that there is "not a chance in a million" that the Ambassador could have had any kind of influence. He vehemently denied that the board had ever had "the slightest respect for outside influence."[34] Neither man, while stressing the board's freedom to overrule the jury, recalled that Joe Kennedy tried to promote his son's cause through personal telephone calls. Their explanation of what happened is quite simple and only a much more cynical age encourages suspicions of disingenuous innocence.

Don Ferguson had become enchanted with *Profiles,* charmed by its inspirational tone. Leaning across the big table in Columbia's Trustees Room, where the Advisory Board had gathered to make their decision, Ferguson told the others of having read the book aloud to his twelve-year-old grandson, "and the boy was absolutely fascinated. I think we should give the prize to *Profiles in Courage.*" The other members who were familiar with the book (although how many had actually read it is another matter) were impressed and decided at that point to override the weightier works recommended by the historians and give the prize to Kennedy. The decisive factor that made the Ferguson sentiment move the others was, as Hohenberg now recalls, quite simply that "at that particular point, Kennedy was so much in the news, and his book was

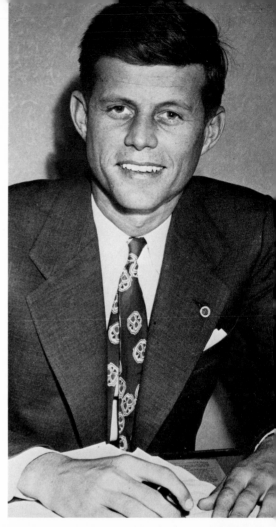

24. *Preceding page:* Jack Kennedy in Hyannis in 1946.

25. *Above:* Jack Kennedy's health begins to deteriorate. Malaria and his back injuries will be given as the causes for his several hospitalizations.

26. *Right:* Jack in 1946.

27. *Below:* On February 10, 1948, Congressman John Kennedy appears with a group of young candidates for U.S. military academies. Three months earlier he had fallen gravely ill while visiting his ancestral home in Ireland. Rushed by Pamela Churchill to Lord Beaverbrook's physician, Sir Daniel Davis, Jack's illness was diagnosed as terminal.

28. *Right:* Diagnosed as having an incurable disease that would cut short his life, Jack nonetheless pressed forward toward new political goals to fulfill his father's ambitions.

29. *Below:* Ambassador Kennedy's emergence as a substantial philanthropist coincided with the start of his second son's political career. Here, Catholic Auxiliary Bishop John J. Wright, later to become prominent in the Vatican, accepts from Congressman Kennedy a $150,000 check for a parochial school for retarded children and the Christopher Columbus Catholic Center to be located in Boston's heavily Italian North End. The money was donated by the ambassador as a memorial to Joe Junior.

30. *Facing page:* Boston's port facilities are inspected by a wan Congressman Kennedy.

31. *Right:* The introduction of cortisone for treatment of his disease gave Kennedy hope of controlling his condition. 1950.

32. *Below:* Receiving an honorary Doctorate of Law from Notre Dame University, January 29, 1950.

33. *Facing page, top:* With Bishop Christopher J. Weldon of the Diocese of Springfield in 1950.

34. *Facing page, bottom:* Kennedy's recurring back ailment has him on crutches. Another two operations would fail to rectify the problem.

35. *Above:* Jean, Pat, Bobby, and Eunice rally round their oldest brother, the new candidate for the U.S. Senate.

36. *Right:* Jack Kennedy with his father and Francis Cardinal Spellman at the dedication of the Joseph P. Kennedy Hospital for Rehabilitation of Handicapped Children in Brighton, Massachusetts. 1952.

37. Jack Kennedy and 1952 Democratic Presidential candidate Adlai Stevenson, when their relationship was still fresh and friendly and Joe Senior was a staunch campaign contributor.

38. *Facing page:* This photo adorned Jack's Senate office wall, a souvenir of the '52 Democratic campaigns in which Kennedy's victory was one of the party's few bright moments. Convinced that the young man's father had virtually bought the son's success, Harry Truman advised friends not to drink Scotch so as to deny liquor magnate Joe Kennedy additional funds.

Best of Luck to John Kennedy
Oct. 17, 1952
Harry Truman

39. *Facing page:* Jacqueline Bouvier before her parents' separation.

40. Teen-aged Jacqueline in jodhpurs, with her father *(left)*, "Black Jack," and Grandfather Bouvier at their East Hampton, Long Island, home. It was her grandfather who fabricated the family's claim to an aristocratic lineage.

41. *Facing page:* September 12, 1953. The bride, 24, and the groom, 36, in St. Mary's Church, Newport, Rhode Island.

42. *Right:* Jack and Torbert Macdonald aboard ship crossing the Atlantic on one of their several trips together. Jacqueline's despair at the two friends' casual attitude toward their attire obviously had some basis, judging from the mismatched lengths of their trouser cuffs.

43. *Below:* Jack's narration of a film at the 1956 Democratic Convention was followed by a major political turning point—the first appearance of KENNEDY FOR PRESIDENT signs paraded by adoring supporters from New England.

44. *Right:* The 1957 Pulitzer prize for *Profiles in Courage* provided an additional boost for Jack's growing reputation. However, the research, tentative drafts, and organization were left to the collective labors of others, and the literary craftsmanship was clearly the work of Ted Sorensen, who gave the book its drama and flow.

45. *Below:* The Senator and Eleanor Roosevelt, who shared her late husband's disdain for Joseph Senior and was for Jack Kennedy a stumbling block and constant reminder of the liability his father was to his political career.

46. *Facing page:* The Senator in a rare photo showing his reading glasses. By this time, April 21, 1959, he was well on his way toward an open declaration for the presidency.

47. *Left:* Other assistants may have had more influence over decision-making but few have contributed more profoundly to the characteristic tone of a political leader than did Ted Sorensen, shown here at the age of thirty-one with his boss in June 1959, less than a year before they launched their most significant venture—the run for the White House.

48. *Below:* A capacity crowd in the Senate Caucus Room on January 2, 1960, hears Kennedy's official announcement of his presidential candidacy. Having promised his senate seat to Torbert Macdonald, his close friend and ally, Jack—even now—had to relent when his father objected on the grounds that they could not rely on Torby to step aside for "baby brother" Ted when the moment came for his investiture.

so much admired by the editors around the table, most of whom had read it, that they overruled the biography jury."[35] Pulitzer agrees, admitting that "it wasn't great distinguished history in that sense. It was a book that showed a great understanding of the American political figure and how these people operated, and I think it just appealed to the board." And then, confirming that a very unliterary, unscholarly criterion had been decisive, Pulitzer added: "The appeal of this young man writing a very lively book about political figures and his— It's a funny thing, they picked this fellow. Nobody had any idea of what would happen in later history. . . . It was not history as much as it was a journalistic achievement at that time—and a political achievement. I think that's the point."[36]

Such witnesses, among the few still around to testify, probably cannot be faulted for lack of candor. Still, assurances are hard to accept. Keeping his hands off would have been out of character for the Ambassador. Allowing the Pulitzer prize to be decided by chance would have been especially unique for a man who placed so much importance on having his son gain literary respectability en route to power, and Hohenberg has admitted to Krock's visibility in the situation. Furthermore, the *Times* correspondent had been "instrumental" in deciding "several" other Pulitzer prizes.[37] His credentials as a lobbyist within that journalism fraternity were first-rate. The other certainty about his role in the *Profiles* affair was the avoidance of clumsiness and overkill. In that situation, unlike those he had influenced in the past, his intervention could indeed have been counterproductive. Krock's closeness to Joe Kennedy was too well known and the thirteen-member Advisory Board was too imposing a body to approach indiscreetly. Through at least one of his contacts, then, Krock had probably been assured that the group was amenable and that it would be prudent of him to stay in the background.

When Kennedy's award was announced, Torby Macdonald immediately sent his friend a telegram that read: "Congratulations. Understand the committee in charge of running the Irish Sweepstakes has named you winner. And recently discovered land grant deeds to the states of Texas and California show you to be the rightful owner. More coming." He signed it, "10,000 Men of Massachusetts."[38]

"Kennedy Moves Out Front," proclaimed *The Wall Street Journal* on May 24. Speculation about his future inevitably dominated every movement. Over a Pittsburgh radio station a few days later, he disclaimed any interest in the presidency. As he did whenever he disavowed such ambitions, he coupled his statement with the declaration that Catholicism would no longer be a liability. Jake Arvey, the Stevensonian leader of Illinois's vital Cook County, then made the possibility even more prominent by announcing that Kennedy was his personal favorite.

In mid-June, Kennedy gained a distinction that had eluded his father. Harvard University's Board of Governors announced that the senator had been elected to a seat on the Board of Overseers, a victory achieved by a plurality of some three thousand votes over his nearest rival. Only once before had the honor gone to a Catholic. Kennedy was present for the announcement and the award of an honorary degree of law.

Before the month had ended, new Gallup figures showed a sharp reversal. Kennedy was ahead of Kefauver 50–39. His leadership won the acknowledgment not only of the major publications but—significant for a Roman Catholic from a large eastern city—from a wide variety of small papers throughout the country. North and South, from the Woodstock (Ill.) *Daily Sentinel* (July 18), the Zanesville (Ohio) *Signal* (July 18), the Owosso (Mich.) *Argus-Press* (July 17), the *Three Rivers* (Mich.) *Commercial* (July 17), the Dunn (N.C.) *Daily Record* (July 17), and the Rockingham (N.C.) *Journal* (July 17), the verdict was consistent. That July his Senate speech on Algerian independence provided another powerful boost.

22

Human Rights– At Home and Abroad

Jack Kennedy had already seen a good portion of the world, had thought and read extensively about international affairs, and had a fine reservoir of talent available. Further, his views had continuity. If, ultimately, they should prove wise both politically and operationally, there could be real benefits. At the very least, however, unless he should make a fool of himself, he would escape from his nonage. Most of all, he could afford neither to parrot better established luminaries with devoted followers, such as Stevenson or Humphrey, nor to remain silent. In John Kennedy's case, mere availability without identification could have been disastrous. The force of his personal leadership had to overwhelm all the reasons for saying that nominating him would be too risky.

In 1957, for the first time, Kennedy's views on foreign affairs brought him international attention and, at home, more publicity than his comments on Indochina. Following the Suez War with the Anglo-French and Israeli attack upon Egypt and subsequent pullback, President Eisenhower requested congressional support for assistance to those nations of the region wanting American aid from what they feared was overt Communist aggression. Kennedy's reaction was both critical and supportive.

In the Senate on March 1, he pointed out that the resolution had been unsatisfactorily worded because it contained grave constitutional questions relating to the constitutional separation of powers, "leaving any future occupant of the White House in doubt as to whether his office has been strengthened by this broad grant of authority, weakened by a percent that requires congressional approval of inherent Executive powers, or left untouched." Mostly, he felt it was not really necessary. It offered no solutions to the immediate crisis—crises, in particular, of Communist subversion, the traffic of arms, the Suez Canal, the problem of refugees, boundaries, and questions of nationalism. The whole undertaking, in Kennedy's view, "was an unnecessary error from the time it was first conceived and submitted." The Soviet Union had already been on adequate notice that the United States was determined to resist attack. But the overriding reality was that once the resolution had been presented to the Congress and before the entire world, it could no longer be considered merely on its merits. He argued that the President had effectively preempted the Senate's freedom to act by giving them no choice but to go on record behind efforts to deter aggression. He ended his talk by quoting from Lincoln that "there are few things wholly evil or wholly good." He announced that he would vote for it because of his belief "that the evil flowing from its defeat would be preponderately greater than the good."[1]

At the same time, Kennedy continued to show consistent attention to the plight of both the people in Poland behind the Iron Curtain and the surge of nationalism in various parts of the world. He sent a letter to Secretary of State Dulles with the assurance of support for economic assistance to the Poles. Acknowledging that it would provide fuel for those who felt that withholding such aid would make things more difficult for the Communist government in Warsaw, he nevertheless added that "hunger has never been a weapon of American foreign policy—and if we can score these 'cold-war' advantages only by turning a deaf ear to Polish hunger and misery, then we will have won only a dubious 'victory' at best." He recalled his own visit to Poland less than two years earlier and his observation that the people in that country were very far from enamored with the Communist philosophy; so that while Poland may still be a satellite government, the people themselves could not properly be called satellites. To reject assistance for them because they had been unable to discard such domination would "be a brutal and dangerous policy," one that would only make them more dependent on the Russians.[2] At the Southern Hotel in Baltimore, eight hundred St.

Patrick's Day celebrants cheered him warmly while he told them that it was "equally shocking that millions of Africans and Asians look with suspicion upon the United States as a sympathizer with colonialism and continued Western domination." He reminded them of the Irish thousand-year struggle for freedom and bade them recognize that the events of the past year in Hungary, Poland, Ghana, and Algeria, where a full-fledged revolt for independence already taking place, had demonstrated that "there may be satellite governments but there are never satellite people." And then he added: "Nations may be colonized but never men. Whether a man be Hungarian or Irish, Catholic or Moslem, white or black, there forever burns within his breast the unquenchable desire to be free."[3]

Kennedy had very little reason to believe that his stands in support of nationalistic impulses and for assistance for such Communist-dominated nations as Poland would bring much popular acclaim. One Vermont paper editorialized: "Well, of course, Kennedy has never had to make a living, having been born with three or four silver spoons in his mouth, so you can't expect a man of his sheltered economic upbringing to be aware of what the Communists are up to, or to understand the realities and danger of aiding the Poles."[4]

Meanwhile, he kept in close touch with individuals intimately connected with the situation in Algeria. One was Habib Bourguiba, Jr., the son of the Tunisian president. Another was Mongi Slim, the Tunisian ambassador in Washington. Perhaps more important was Abdelkader Chanderli, a propagandist for the FLN, or the Front de Liberation Nationale, the arm of the rebellion. Through Harvard economist John Kenneth Galbraith, Chanderli and his associate, M'hammed Yazid, came into contact with Kennedy.[5] They found a receptive audience.

On July 2 Kennedy delivered before the Senate the first of a two-part address "examining America's role in the continuing struggle for independence." The first, drafted with the assistance of staff member Fred Holborn, who researched and prepared the outline, and with additional help from Harvard professor George Holman, easily gave Jack Kennedy more attention than any previous statement.

The speech evolved logically from his Indochina position. From the outset Kennedy emphasized that he would first deal with Algeria and, in a subsequent address, with Poland. His concern with both, he made clear, was with imperialism. Algeria could not be considered simply a French matter. The implications were far more extensive, especially for the United States. Like Indochina, Algeria was a perfect example of

Turgot's dictum: "Colonies are like fruit which cling to the tree only till they ripen."[6] The problem was no longer purely French because American interests inevitably had become involved. Deployment of forces there had reduced the French capacity to contribute to NATO. American military equipment had been used against the rebels, provoking hostility toward this country. The United States had also repeatedly voted in the UN with the French and against the anticolonial states of Asia and Africa. All this, Kennedy said, was despite our experience in Indochina. In the face of similar warnings, an American reaction was delayed and, in retrospect, "we might have served both the French and our own causes infinitely better, had we taken a more firm stand much earlier than we did." Therefore, despite the French regard for Algeria as an internal matter, their failure to recognize the realities of the situation there would help to induce greater hostility toward the Western nations blocking independence.[7]

Kennedy chastised the government in Paris and the policies of Robert Lacoste, the minister for Algeria. He accused them of hypocrisy for claiming Algeria as an integral part of Metropolitan France. In reality, he charged, "the French have never truly recognized Algerians as French citizens. If they permitted all Algerians to vote as French citizens, over one-sixth of all the representatives in the French Assembly would be from Algeria." And yet no more than thirty of the approximately 625 representatives were in the Assembly. The French had also denied Algerians the social, political, economic benefits held by French citizens. In handling the problem, Kennedy criticized them for misplaced faith in three areas: military conquest or pacification; social and economic reform; and political union with France. While M. Lacoste's pacification policy consisted of more imaginative measures than simple military repression, Kennedy conceded, the rebellion was too contagious to be treated by such methods. Echoing the words he himself had used about Indochina in 1954, Kennedy pointed to the futility of such a policy even if the French "could afford to increase substantially the manpower already poured into the area. . . ."[8] Nowhere within Algeria was there any "consistent progress" toward political equality and opportunity so that the people in that North African state could aspire to a common standard of French citizenship.

He concluded the speech with a plea for the United States to recognize "that the time has passed, where a series of piecemeal adjustments, or even a last attempt to incorporate Algeria fully within France, can succeed." The United States should finally face the "harsh realities of the situation" by fulfilling its responsibilities as a Free World leader within the United Nations, in the councils of the North Atlantic Treaty Organization, in the formulation of aid programs, and in diplomacy, "in shaping a course for political independence for Algeria."[9] He announced that he was submitting a resolution encouraging the President and the secretary of state to use the influence of the United States to achieve a solution toward recognizing the independent personality of Algeria and establishing a basis for a settlement interdependent with France and the neighboring nations. That might be worked either through NATO or the good offices of the prime minister of Tunisia and the Sultan of Morocco.[10]

Reactions went along mostly predictable lines. The Eisenhower administration had already labored to bring France within a Western European Union, a move made after frustrating efforts to achieve an integration within the European Defense Community. Whatever the merits or dangers the Algerian revolt held for that alliance, the sensitivity of Franco-American relationships was of paramount concern. Even before Kennedy delivered the speech, Secretary Dulles met with reporters and stated his view. Herve Alphand, the French ambassador to Washington, had called on the secretary the previous day to emphasize the damage the speech might cause unless the American government issued a quick disavowal.

The prearranged rebuttal was inadvertently made possible by a backfiring of Kennedy's office's publicity strategy. Instead of resorting to routine press gallery distribution of advance copies of the text, they had acted earlier. With the speech due on Tuesday, copies had been provided at the homes of Washington correspondents days earlier, hopefully to stimulate the desired attention. Invariably, a copy reached M. Alphand, who then rushed to take up the matter with Dulles. The secretary's comment was therefore ready and his response clear. Algeria, he said in reiterating the administration's view, was primarily a French problem and, "I would be very sorry to see it made ours." French correspondents present were also able to get a jump on the big news; in cables back home, they helped to soften the reaction. As a public-relations device, the early distribution had fizzled.[11]

As a public stand by Senator Kennedy, it gave him the ultimate attention he wanted. The reaction was swift. Virtually every paper of consequence stated an editorial position. Whatever consensus emerged indicated that Kennedy was basically correct but that it was not really our business to get involved, that the situation was much too complex and that France should be treated more diplomatically as an ally. At his routine news conference the next day, the President was asked whether he saw a stronger opposition to Western colonialism as a basis for building a more constructive expression of present American policies. Obviously reluctant to elaborate on Dulles's statement, he spoke in circles about the many complications involved in the whole standing of America in the world, the efforts to avoid taking sides in either the domestic or international quarrels. That meant we were better off working quietly, behind the scenes, instead of impairing our effectiveness by getting up and shouting. As a general principle, the President concluded, he agreed with Mr. Dulles's reaction. Toward the end of the conference, responding to another question about Algeria, the President endorsed the argument that it was an internal problem primarily because it was part of Metropolitan France, "at least legally, and you try to be just as fair and square and helpful as you can."[12]

Within the United States itself, most agreed with the President. Most felt that Kennedy's critique, however well intentioned, should not inspire overt American interference. Jack's father disapproved more fundamentally, but kept his reaction prudently restrained, confiding to James Landis that the position represented both unsound policy and bad politics. When Jack called to get the Ambassador's response, he reportedly told him, "You lucky mush. You don't know it and neither does anyone else, but within a few months everyone is going to know just how right you are on Algeria."[13]

Whatever the long-term evaluations, the immediate debate was worldwide. The French tried to play down its importance. A Foreign Ministry spokesman followed the tactic of dismissing Kennedy's statement as a purely American political matter, just as the Algerian problem was a French concern. Lacoste himself expressed his own shock at Kennedy's demand for American intervention and indicated he might extend "a solemn invitation" to the senator to visit Algeria.[14] Alistair Cooke, writing in *The Manchester Guardian Weekly,* was perhaps the most personally devastating in impugning Kennedy's motives. He considered the speech as having "brilliantly served its purpose of pitching him into centre-stage from where this week he will deliver a lament for the barbarities of the Russians in Poland. This is as safe a mode of indignation as any man from Massachusetts could express." Cooke reasoned that Algeria was a country that, knowing "neither friend nor enemy in Massachusetts," was "no liability to his own constituents."[15] Three days after his initial reaction, Robert Lacoste still toyed with the idea of inviting Kennedy and said he was ready to accommodate him with whatever planes, Jeeps, helicopters, and guarantees for his safety that would be needed. He would also be given an opportunity to inspect the prisons and internment camps; he could check out for himself the allegations from Moslems and French sympathizers that the government security forces had been torturing prisoners. Lacoste said a Red Cross mission had just completed a fifty-day inspection of the prisons and camps and had told them that conditions were much improved from those of a year ago.

Domestic criticism of Kennedy came more than from merely the Republican opposition. While much of the Senate debate split along party lines, Kennedy had to withstand the qualms of what normally might have been regarded as friendly sources. There was nothing surprising about the sort of vitriolic attacks that came from publisher William Loeb's Manchester (N.H.) *Union Leader,* which declared, "If Senator Kennedy is really interested in doing something about colonialism, why doesn't he take on our enemies instead of our allies? We can think of any number of Red satellites whose cause Kennedy can make his own," a statement that the paper followed up three days later by saying that the whole attack showed that Kennedy "is still somewhat wet behind the ears when it comes to recognizing a communist conspiracy."[16] Much more temperate, much more considered of the complex issues involved, *The New York Times,* very far removed politically from Loeb or his paper, worried that Kennedy's efforts, however sincere his desire to be helpful, might have risked exacerbating the situation.

Meanwhile, in Paris, Arthur Schlesinger, Jr., met with Adlai Stevenson, who had reached the French capital after a visit to Africa. He found Stevenson upset that Kennedy was criticizing an ally and thereby jeopardizing the unity of NATO. "Stevenson thought that Kennedy's speech was terrible and defended the policy of the French government at the time," Schlesinger later told John Bartlow Martin.[17] Both Schlesinger and Stevenson agreed on at least one thing: that the call for "independence" was ill advised, an attitude that the historian then relayed to Kennedy. The senator responded by saying he had "tried to take account of the complex issues which you raise though I did not try to spell out in detail the exact protections which an Algerian settlement might provide for the *colons.* I quite agree with you, too, that independence provides no quick cure for the Algerian economy and that the lack of an administrative and technical elite in North Africa is a serious problem." He concluded by observing to the professor that, despite extensive editorial criticism, he was gratified by letters of approval coming from the public and, he added, "essentially from academics and Arabs!"[18] He was certainly more disturbed, however, to read that Stevenson later spoke in Bonn, West Germany, and charged that immediate independence for Algeria would be "an invitation for chaos."[19]

Among Kennedy's severest critics were Jews worried that Algerian terrorism was being promoted by President Gamal Abdel Nasser of Egypt. In the backwash of the Suez War, it was easy for those alarmed about the ability of the state of Israel to survive to exaggerate Nasser's role in fomenting the revolution and in supplying arms to the FLN. Thus Algerian independence could be feared as strengthening Israel's enemies. One prominent American friend of the Jewish state, Herbert Lehman, in St. Moritz, Switzerland, at the time of the speech, found himself "surprised, confused, and somewhat disturbed" to read what Kennedy had said.[20] Congressman Emanuel Celler of Brooklyn, like Lehman a liberal Democrat and supporter of the Jewish homeland, called Kennedy's suggestion "as immature as it is unfair." He feared it had created a bad situation that could only "encourage the insurgents to inaugurate more brutalities against the French and other Europeans."[21] After *The New York Times* carried a letter from Roger Baldwin, Donald Harrington, George M. Hauser, Reinhold Niebuhr, and Norman Thomas endorsing the Kennedy resolution, Celler argued that the situation was too complex to be painted either all black or all white and wondered whether Kennedy realized that eliminating the French from Algeria would create a vacuum that would be quickly filled by Communist influences and that the rebellion was being fomented and supplied with arms by the Communist-backed Nasser.[22]

Also from within the Democratic Party came perhaps the most damaging attack against Kennedy's statement. In Medford, Massachusetts, on the night of October 25, former secretary of state Dean Acheson, speaking at the Fletcher School of Law and Diplomacy of Tufts University, delivered the last of a series of three lectures. He avoided Kennedy's name but left no doubt about the identification of his target. He said the proposal for American backing of Algerian independence failed to understand the "humiliating agony of the loss of power," and as Stevenson had done, Acheson said that a French pullout could only be followed by chaos.[23] Kennedy, of course, had many defenders. Mike Mansfield, Joseph Clark, Henry Jackson, Richard Neuberger, among others, took the Senate floor in favor of the resolution. "It looks as if the Democratic party was beginning to show some real signs of life on foreign policy," wrote Chester Bowles.[24] In France itself, Kennedy got warm support from such diverse opponents of the government's policy as Jean-Jacques

Servan-Schreiber, whose *L'Express* carried the full text of the speech, Professor Raymond Aron of the Sorbonne, and the conservative editor of *Le Figaro.* "Many Frenchmen of all parties have privately shared these views for some time," wrote Dorothy Thompson from Paris.[25]

On the Senate floor, Kennedy responded to his critics. He said he had fully expected attacks from both the French government and the State Department and stood by his initial statement that the revolt had "great international implications." He also defended the speech in an article that appeared in *America* under the title "The Algerian Crisis: A New Phase?"[26] Although Kennedy continued to champion the Algerian revolution, his comments gradually became more muted and less frequent. He, too, began to develop reservations about the call for independence and told aides that he was "wary of being known as the Senator from Algeria."[27] David Halberstam later recalled that kind of retreat in a popular book called *The Best and the Brightest,* and chided Kennedy by writing that the Algerian speech "gave him an identification with the independence movement throughout the world" and caused him to "immediately search for another country to give a speech on, choosing Poland this time, a reasonably safe and secure topic, since he could be for freedom without offending his constituents."[28] That overlooks the fact that the major statement on Poland was coupled with the Algerian speech. Rather than a backing off toward a safer topic, it was the second part of the series called "The Struggle Against Imperialism." The United States, in Kennedy's view, could not condemn Western colonialism while ignoring Soviet violations of self-rule. He saw it as consistent with his advocacy of economic aid to Poland and, at the time of that speech on August 21, introduced a bill to clear the way for financial aid and commercial relations with nations behind the Iron Curtain. He also suggested the opening of cultural, scientific, and educational exchanges, pointing out that some progress had already been made in unofficial student exchanges through the Ford and Rockefeller foundations. He advocated a program of technical assistance to the government, as well as humanitarian relief to repatriates returning from Russia. The complex problems of Eastern Europe, he warned, "will never be solved with an excess of caution or an avoidance of risk."[29]

Having been invited three months before the Algeria speech by Hamilton Fish Armstrong to contribute to *Foreign Affairs* "on the evolution and execution of our foreign policy," Kennedy's article appeared on the pages of that publication's October 1957 issue. Largely the product of Sorensen's prose skills, with additional contributions from Earl Latham, it charged the administration with failing to appreciate "how the forces of nationalism are rewriting the geopolitical map of the world" and urged the reshaping of "the old conceptions of war and peace" to meet the requirements in "the light of new realities."[30]

And although such enlightenment tended to simplify complex global relationships, Kennedy's position was basically sound. Each alternative had inherent risks. However indelicate for Franco-American relations, Kennedy's appraisal confronted the situation more perceptively than the prevailing rejection of the reality of nationalism for conventional Cold War assumptions. Some of Kennedy's most telling points came in the pages of *America*, where he warned that the "longer legitimate Algerian aspirations are suppressed, the greater becomes the danger of a reactionary or Communist takeover in all of Africa" and that neither France nor her allies "could afford another Indo-China."[31]

For all the outrage at Kennedy's audacity, the status quo in Algeria was not tenable. The Fourth Republic collapsed. Within one year after the speech came the formation of the Fifth Republic. In the United Nations the Eisenhower administration began to abstain on the Algerian question. While that "is hardly a policy," Kennedy wrote privately, it did "at least reveal increasing skepticism, even in official quarters, that France was willing to take the steps necessary to achieve a negotiated solution in Algeria."[32] The Eisenhower administration had long since had a report, written months before Kennedy's speech, detailing Richard Nixon's highly critical analysis of French policy.[33]

To charge Kennedy with political opportunism invalidates neither the legitimacy of his convictions nor his responsibility to speak out. The closest student of the civil war has since observed that "no speech on foreign affairs by Senator Kennedy attracted more attention, both at home and abroad, and under such pressure United States official policy on Algeria now began to shift."[34]

Even as John Kennedy spoke out on Algerian independence, pointing the way, as he later acknowledged by oversimplifying the matter, he was in the middle of the political, legal, and social complexities posed by the emerging Civil Rights Act of 1957. Unlike the Algerian formula toward self-determination, responding to the first federal legislation toward racial equality since Reconstruction forced Kennedy into a close evaluation of the implications. While the North African controversy raged over an issue largely academic for the American electorate, the question of race relations at home, so soon after the Supreme Court's desegregation decision, encouraged caution and expediency. For Lyndon Johnson it became a prudent way of reaching out to a national constituency while preserving regional ties. For Hubert Humphrey it helped reaffirm his credentials as a civil-rights fighter. For John Kennedy the question could not have been more ill-timed: increasing identification with the party's liberals, if it included civil rights, could readily sacrifice southern support. Any move by the Congress to strengthen the Justice Department's enforcement powers risked revolt.

Southerners accepted Kennedy as one who understood the complexities of the issue. They knew he was no fire-eater. He had defended the Supreme Court against liberal criticism that the order to effectuate integration of schools "with all deliberate speed" was, as Michigan's Governor G. Mennen Williams charged, "weasel words." The Court, Kennedy said, did not need "assistance from any of us."[35] Clearly, Kennedy and blacks had not yet gotten to know each other, the senator had not advanced beyond inchoate opposition to discrimination, and, to Ted Sorensen's distress, was still "shaped primarily by political expediency instead of basic human principles."[36]

That spring, following his showing at the Democratic convention, Kennedy went on to cultivate the South and found large and enthusiastic audiences everywhere. Appearing at the Arkansas Bar Association meeting, he received two standing ovations, also drawing a laugh by remarking that "if Governor Faubus and the Arkansas delegation had been able to secure me 22 more votes, my political career would now be over."[37] He spoke at the University of South Carolina, delivered a strong argument for farm price protection before the Southeastern Peanut Association in Atlanta, and went on to the University of Georgia at Athens. He joined with the state's senators, Richard Russell and Herman Talmadge, on a local television program. The *Boston Herald* promptly announced that his two-day visit to Georgia left him the favorite for the party's nomination in a region normally hostile to northern Democrats.[38]

When the key votes on the civil-rights bill came up that spring, Kennedy twice joined the minority, first pleasing the southerners, then the northern liberals. He voted with a small group of nonsouthern Democrats, including Wayne Morse, to oppose efforts designed to prevent the measure from consignment to the Judiciary Committee, where segregationists hoped it could be defeated.

Southern praise for Kennedy came quickly. Mississippi's ardent segregationist Senator James Eastland, the chairman of the Judiciary Committee, said he would strongly support Kennedy for the presidency.

Dixie columnist John Temple Graves hailed him as a "novel personality" capable of becoming the "living antithesis of Earl Warren."[39] Kennedy thanked Graves with the hope that a "moderate philosophy on behalf of the *national* interest" would enable him to "feel a common bond with many Southerners."[40] At the same time, Doris Fleeson, writing a nationally syndicated column, explained that Kennedy's civil-rights vote suggested that he would "like to keep his friends in the South and is aware that the Southerners very often exercise a veto power over Democratic national nominees."[41]

Liberals and pro-civil-rights moderates saw betrayal. Like Wayne Morse, Kennedy had to defend himself from charges that he had sold out civil rights to log-roll for southern support for the Hells Canyon power project. Explaining that he had backed the dam because the natural resources "would be lost forever to the Northwest if we failed to build the dam with the maximum potential," he justified his vote through concern for setting a dangerous precedent, one in which bypassing committees "can be used against our causes and other liberal issues in the future."[42] At best, the argument was disingenuous, but it was the only explanation he could offer. "Even veteran Democratic 'wheelhorses' are disturbed," noted the *Providence Chronicle,* after noting his lame response had failed to satisfy black supporters.[43] *The New Republic*'s TRB felt "a little uncomfortable over Presidential aspirant John Kennedy's flirtation with Southern politicians."[44] The Boston branch of the NAACP quickly organized an emergency civil-rights conference at the Sheraton Plaza Hotel. Now their immediate concern was how both Massachusetts senators would vote on Title III of the bill, which sought to give the attorney general broad enforcement powers against individuals accused of violating another's civil rights.

Saltonstall attended. Kennedy sent a telegram promising that a bill will be passed "regardless of how long we have to stay in Washington" and was personally represented by Congressman Torbert Macdonald. Clarence Mitchell, the director of the NAACP's Washington Bureau, addressed the meeting, but left the Sheraton Plaza still uncertain how either of the two senators would vote on Title III if one "were taken tomorrow." By Tuesday, however, two days after the Boston gathering, Kennedy, unlike Saltonstall, announced that he would vote for Title III because its rejection would imply that Congress was opposed to the Court's desegregation decision.[45] Kennedy thus lined up with the liberals in the most significant attempt to give the bill actual strength, but their effort was futile. It never had a decent chance of passing.

Another controversy, however, revolved around an amendment empowering judges to require that criminal contempt cases be tried by juries, altering the usual procedure in the case of such suits brought by the federal government. Offered by Senators Joseph O'Mahoney and Kefauver, it attempted to write into the Senate bill what had, under administration pressure, been defeated in the House five times before. The provision placed liberals and civil libertarians in a quandary. Attacking it could easily make them appear reckless about maintaining fundamental constitutional guarantees of trial by jury. With it, however, enforcement of the bill could well become impossible. Most of the party's liberals, including the Massachusetts ADA leadership, were ready to view its inclusion as a serious dilution of the bill.[46] "Feelings on this are mixed," Lyndon Johnson was advised by aide George Reedy. *"Practically all of them are convinced that Southern juries will not convict a white man accused of violating a Negro's civil rights. But they are uneasy about the idea of abandoning jury trial* [sic]."[47]

Much more than on the first two items, which involved precedent and symbolism, Kennedy's response was both legalistic and expedient. The pressure was heavy from all sides. "In this civil rights battle," declared the Orlando *Sentinel,* "Sen. Kennedy has a real chance to repay his true friends," and called for a "display of his usual courage" by voting for the jury-trial amendment.[48] Since the Eisenhower administration itself opposed the jury-trial amendment, undoubtedly enjoying the discomfort of divided Democrats, James Reston reported that they were counting on Kennedy's support.[49] Kennedy, meanwhile, consulted with Jim Landis as well as Arthur E. Sutherland, Mark DeWolfe Howe, and Paul A. Freund of the Harvard Law School.

Their views were decidedly mixed. Nobody was completely encouraging, except possibly for Howe. And even he, in a telephone conversation on July 31, backed the O'Mahoney amendment largely as a means of getting the bill accepted by the South, while conceding only that "there is some merit in the jury trial position." Sutherland definitely thought the bill would be weakened with it but, like Howe, felt it would be better than nothing. Freund's letter was most ambivalent, so much so that Rauh thought it left either option open. "I think Senator Kennedy misused that letter a little bit," the ADA leader subsequently recalled. "I think he wanted to be on both sides at that time." Freund indicated that he himself would have voted against it but that inclusion of the jury trial would "not in my view constitute a betrayal of principle." Whatever the course, he advised, it was "a matter of judgment on which your own wisdom will yield a better answer than any I might venture."[50]

There is every reason to believe that the dilemma delayed Kennedy's decision until the last moment. Not until Tuesday, July 30, when Senators Henry Jackson and Frank Church added a section to the jury-trial amendment to wipe out all state discriminations against black jurors in federal courts, did Kennedy make up his mind. On August 1 he announced his decision, coupling it with the satisfaction that his legal consultations had not produced "a serious legal or constitutional problem raised by requiring a jury trial in criminal contempt cases."[51]

The following day, after a long debate, Kennedy joined the majority in a 51–42 vote to include the jury-trial amendment. The preceding debate had been tense, and the galleries were jammed. Kennedy's choice maintained for him, as William S. White noted in the *Times,* a "stout" bridge to the South and Border States, quite unlike the status of Humphrey and others who "have been hard civil rights men all the way."[52] Invariably, the price could not be dodged. A black paper in Massachusetts angrily charged Kennedy with joining fifty other senators in voting "to continue to let White Americans deny Black Americans their constitutional right to vote if they so desire. . . . Does Senator Kennedy propose, for example, that a public official in Massachusetts accused of not issuing a qualified motorist a driver's license should be tried by a jury?" Another, in Salem, declared that Kennedy's "balloon for the Democratic nomination for President received a terrific shock by the integration question" and added that the contest was still "worth watching as candidates remove the hoods from their heads."[53] In Boston, after addressing eight hundred members of the Jewish Labor Committee, Kennedy was attacked by the organization's regional director for opening himself up to "suspicion as to whether he considers it more important to his career to vote in line with the principles and wishes of his home state voters or to compromise and curry favor with Southern interests."[54] Warnings came from others that his increased identification with the South would not necessarily bring the nomination. Most cutting of all, and most quotable, was an item reporting that a colleague had wondered, "Why not show a little less profile and a little more courage?"[55]

But attention was soon diverted toward Arkansas, where Governor Faubus made the most of the race issue by blocking court-ordered integration of Little Rock's Central High School. Compliance came only after days of violence and under the guns of National Guardsmen federalized by President Eisenhower and ordered to secure the admission of the nine black students. Not since Reconstruction had southerners been so infuriated. When Jack Kennedy arrived for a speaking engagement in Jackson, Mississippi, on October 17, nobody could be certain how any northern politician would be greeted.

Kennedy had political friends in the state. Its delegation had shifted to him during the second-ballot roll call at the Chicago convention. Most recently, he had been praised by such stalwarts as Senator Eastland and Representative William Colmer. Governor Coleman was also with him. Although his original attraction had been as a means of stopping Kefauver, many now regarded Kennedy as the best the South could get in 1960. As John Temple Graves told his readers, "He is too intelligent to be making the advances without some sort of marriage in mind."[56] Since the convention, Congressman Frank Smith, a rotund southern liberal from Greenwood, had considered himself a Kennedy partisan. Smith, who was made a delegate through the intervention of the governor, had actively worked to round up vice-presidential votes for the senator. Smith had also arranged the Jackson appearance before a five-dollar-a-plate banquet of Mississippi Young Democrats.

The congressman acted as host for the occasion, greeting Kennedy at the airport and escorting him to the Heidelberg Hotel, where an overflow crowd of nearly two thousand awaited him in the Victory Room. Kennedy's prepared speech recalled one of his "profiles in courage," the state's post-Reconstruction leader, Lucius Q. C. Lamar, and his plea for national unity. It also championed the cause of moderation, warning that party disunity could jeopardize congressional control and the prized committee chairmanships.[57]

When he stepped off the plane, however, he learned of a challenge from the state Republican chairman, Wirt Yerger, Jr., designed to embarrass him on the race issue. "Is it not a fact," Yerger had said, "that he voted for the infamous section three of the so-called Civil Rights Bill?"[58] The chairman's remarks were already in the press.

Kennedy made his usual number of emendations on the text of the speech, scrawling the changes in an almost illegible hand. He deleted whole sections, including a lecture against bolting the party, a reference to "David Copperfield's friend Mr. Micawber," as well as advice about the benefits possible for the South when "prosperity is distributed to the poor as well as the rich," but what he had to say at the end was an extemporaneous response to Yerger. He acknowledged that, as he had said in his own city of Boston, he upheld the Supreme Court's desegration decision as the "supreme law of the land," words that he had deleted from the first half of the text, and remarked that "I think most of us agree on the necessity to uphold law and order in every part of the land." Shifted to the end of his speech, the words enabled him to deliver the final punch line: "Now I invite the Republican chairman to tell us his views and those of President Eisenhower and Vice President Nixon."[59]

The ovation was powerful. The Young Democrats stood and applauded. Kennedy had moved them; whether for his views or his counterchallenge nobody knew. Most suspected the latter. One Mississippi paper, after quoting his endorsement of the Court's decision, concluded its editorial caustically by saying, "Thank you, Mr. Kennedy. You have told us all we need to know."[60]

He spent that night as a guest in the Governor's Mansion, with the additional company of Senators Stennis and Eastland, and then left for a speaking engagement at the University of Florida in Gainesville. Returning north to New York City, he addressed the Hungarian Freedom Fighters and received the Charter Day Award of Yeshiva University at a Waldorf-Astoria dinner. His bronze plaque hailed him as "a torchbearer of the liberal tradition" and carried the additional inscription that "through his integrity and loyalty to the Democratic heritage, popular writings and public utterances, he has contributed nobly to the advancement of democracy." In Washington on the thirty-first, he faced the AFL-CIO Industrial Union Convention and, the next day, delivered the Howard Crawley Memorial Lecture at the University of Pennsylvania. During the next three weeks of November, Kennedy visited Peabody, Massachusetts; Topeka, Kansas; Oklahoma City; Lawrence, Kansas; Reno, Nevada; Salt Lake City, Utah; Toronto, Canada; New York City; and Daytona Beach, Florida.

Jack Kennedy was thus strengthening his position as a national political figure. He had established himself as an important voice, not only as an independent spokesman, but as a prominent new light within the Democratic Party. Yet, as contending with the growing divisions over civil rights was making very obvious, he was also inheriting the traps of the party's sectional divisions.

Improved health had made such political activity much less painful and far more successful. Cortisone, despite its potential long-run dangers, was helpful in bolstering his stamina; and while it made his face noticeably puffy, the filling-out had its photogenic benefits. Additionally, removing the metal plate enabled his back wound to heal and the detested crutches were finally discarded. And yet there continued to be a significant threat of re-injury, of carelessness that could damage and even cripple his fragile back.

One especially painful incident occurred at a Sulgrave Club party in Washington while chatting with Kay Halle. Absorbed in their conversation, Kennedy talked while propped against the back of a nearby chair. "Suddenly," Halle remembered, "the girl who was sitting in the chair got up, which meant that Jack went down, slid, and fell straight on the floor on the bottom of his spine. He turned white as a sheet."

Aware of the potential spinal dangers Kennedy could receive from attempting to lift himself by an unequal distribution of his weight, Halle cautioned him to rest on the floor and not try to move precipitously. But the flattened Kennedy refused to stay down.

"Take my two hands, and if you're going to get up, I'll pull you up evenly," she advised.

He rose with her assistance, then regained his seat. "I knew that he must have been in desperate pain, but he just went straight on with the conversation. The understandable pallor was finally replaced by his normal ruddiness. I was absolutely staggered, because when he landed, I could hear his spine hit the floor," she told an interviewer. "I thought that was the most remarkable demonstration of his iron courage and power to dominate the physical with his will."[61]

Jack also remained vulnerable to debilitating infections. During that fall of 1957, the Asian flu epidemic that swept the country also caught him, although the attending physician, Dr. Louis E. Burns, who was called in to see the senator at Hammersmith Farm, firmly declared that he had come down with "virus influenza" unrelated to the outbreak. Stricken during his fourth wedding anniversary, he was described as up and about and planning to visit Cape Cod for the weekend. But the illness was more persistent and when the weekend came, Kennedy was still in Newport, and described by Dr. Burns as "tired, with a touch of the grippe." By the following week, instead of going to Hyannis Port, he was removed to New York Hospital for treatment of a "grippe infection," the result of a secondary complication. Meanwhile, his speech-making commitments were covered when Bobby substituted for him at the final session of the United States Conference of Mayors in New York City, Governor Furcolo covered an engagement at Manchester, New Hampshire, and George Smathers took his place at a Small Business Conference dinner in Boston's Hotel Statler.[62] Released from the hospital in late September, he resumed his work as though nothing had happened. In and out of physical disorders, he had long since learned to minimize their impact.

After the endorsement of the Supreme Court's civil-rights position that he had made in Jackson, Mississippi, in mid-October and the extensive national speech-making tour that consumed most of November, Jack returned to Boston by Sunday, November 24. Interviewed on NBC-TV that day, he told his questioners that he saw no reason why a Roman Catholic could not fulfill the oath to defend the Constitution and still adhere to his religion.[63]

On Wednesday, Kennedy was in New York City, where, at eight fifteen that morning, Jacqueline gave birth at New York Hospital to a seven-pound, two-ounce baby girl. This time, unlike the miscarriage the year before, Jack was present while the infant arrived by a cesarean section. Named Caroline after her mother's sister, she was christened in the Bouvier Chapel of St. Patrick's Cathedral, which had been donated by Jacqueline's granduncle, Michael Bouvier; and Robert Kennedy became the godfather. Three weeks after her birth, Jack and Jackie moved with their child into a new home, a Federal-style building at 3307 N Street in Georgetown. Caroline's birth, of course, assisted the family image so vital for a national political career; but the baby was a godsend to both parents, especially, after the disappointment of 1956. To Jack, she was a delightful addition. At forty, older than average to have a first child, he welcomed the tiny newcomer and she lifted his mood considerably. As a father, at least, he could never be accused of being remote and uninvolved. He showed emotions that some thought were most uncharacteristic.

23

Labor "Reform"

To Joseph P. Kennedy, Bobby's plan to pursue an investigation of racketeering within the Teamster Union that involved the current president, David Beck, as well as Jimmy Hoffa—about to become his successor—was madness. Nothing could more effectively provoke labor animosity toward the Kennedys. At Hyannis Port during the 1956 Christmas holidays, the Ambassador argued that point with his younger son; but Bobby was determined. The groundwork had already been laid. With resumption of Democratic control over the Senate, he had an opportunity to develop evidence showing, as he later wrote in *The Enemy Within,* that "Dave Beck, the president of America's largest and most powerful union, the Teamsters, was a crook."[1] Even when his father enlisted Justice William O. Douglas to talk him out of it, Bobby remained firm.[2]

Thus was born the "rackets committee," really the Senate Select Committee on Improper Activities in the Labor or Management Field; or, as commonly called, the McClellan Committee. A compromise body, the product of a hasty arrangement, it had been necessitated by the intransigence of the Teamsters about cooperating with the Permanent Subcommittee. For the senators, getting a chance to delve into labor corruption was too alluring to dismiss. Both the Labor Committee and the Permanent Subcommittee vied for the plum. Aside from the latter's difficulties in getting cooperation from the Teamster attorneys, placing the hearing under the Select Committee's jurisdiction also negated the possibility that a change of party control in the middle of the congressional session could install Joe McCarthy as its chairman. Out of consideration both for avoiding that hazard and to establish a sound legal basis came the eight-member bipartisan group drawn from the membership of both contending bodies.

Its senior Democrat, John McClellan, a lean and somewhat crusty sixty-one-year-old conservative Arkansan replete with credits for his performance in the Army-McCarthy hearings, became the chairman. Republican representation included such foes of organized labor as Barry Goldwater of Arizona, Karl Mundt of South Dakota, and, in its early days, the increasingly pathetic and alcoholic McCarthy, soon to succumb to the lethal combination of liquor and hepatitis. The only Republican not considered blatantly antilabor was Irving Ives of New York, a former dean of the Cornell University School of Industrial and Labor Relations. But Ives was preparing to leave the committee.

The risks for Democrats needing organized-labor support were assumed to be great. Henry Jackson of Washington and Stuart Symington both had to face reelection in 1958 and declined to serve. As his father would clearly have preferred, Jack Kennedy could have followed their lead instead of joining his brother. After all, fighting for survival at the polls was an easily understood objective on Capitol Hill. Senator Kennedy explained that he "stuck" his "neck out" but that Bobby, who was retained by McClellan as the chief counsel for the Select Committee, wanted him there "in order to keep it more balanced."[3]

Yet, as much as partisans maintain that the brothers took great risks by serving on the McClellan Committee, with Bobby quoted as pointing to the potential hazards for Jack in 1958 and 1960, it is unlikely that they approached the assignment expecting to sacrifice their careers. Nor is it likely that anyone as tough as the younger brother—tougher than Jack, by all accounts—would have gone into that affair with such innocence. After William O. Douglas tried to dissuade him, the justice reported back to Mrs. Douglas Bobby's feeling that it was "too great an opportunity."[4]

But labor had every right to be apprehensive. After McClellan and Kennedy, the other Democrats were Sam Ervin of North Carolina and Pat McNamara of Michigan. McNamara, with close ties to Walter

Reuther and the United Auto Workers, was a passionate defender of unions, while Ervin was a southern conservative. Labor itself regarded Kennedy as the only other friendly Democrat. Hence, the reality was of a potential five-to-three bias in favor of management, at best, with most of the press and electronic media happy to disseminate choice tales of labor malfeasance. While pretending righteous protection of the "public interest," the McClellan Committee was a potential propaganda device for compelling unions, whether honest or dishonest, to swallow more restrictive legislation, a reality not overlooked within the administration.

Therefore, although the Kennedys approached the McClellan Committee with confidence, it always held the potential of being a mixed blessing. A slight tilt in the "wrong" direction could easily outrage the sachems of organized labor, especially such powers as Reuther and George Meany. A Kennedy reputation as "too soft" could kill his standing with the large number of conservatives, especially southern, who were ready to view him as a new-generation Democrat—untainted by Roosevelt's "socialistic" New Deal and the Yalta "sell-out" and never accused of domestic or international "softness" toward communism. Nevertheless, when compared with Jackson and Symington, Jack Kennedy had a greater burden. He had to establish a reputation for legislative and political competence.

Pursuing Teamster venality, delving into the financial and labor abuses of the nation's largest union, was mainly Bobby's work together with his staff of forty-two investigators. Aiding him were his old Harvard roommate and administrative assistant Ken O'Donnell, over forty General Accounting Office personnel, FBI agents, policemen, professional investigators, and such newspapermen as Clark Mollenhoff, John Seigenthaler, Ed Guthman, and Pierre Salinger, who were valuable at various stages.[5] Looking into the activities of Dave Beck and associations with such racketeers as Johnny Dioguardi (better known as Johnny Dio) of New York, they ultimately compiled documentation that included income-tax returns, photocopies of checks, affidavits, copious files, and some 150,000 letters from citizens. In Robert Kennedy's suite in the Old Senate Office Building, boxes on top of boxes reached to the ceiling, almost hiding walls decorated with a picture of the destroyer *Joseph P. Kennedy, Jr.,* and a framed quotation from Winston Churchill with the words: "We shall not flag or fail . . . we shall never surrender."[6]

The committee's extensive pursuit of Hoffa was fine theater and lively copy. Hoffa's own personality and skillfully defiant appearances, in which he shrewdly left "taking the Fifth" to associates, gave the hearing the drama that grabbed popular attention. By offering the personification of a corrupt union leader and thereby highlighting the failures of "union democracy," the hearings also served the interests of management. Alan McAdams's careful study of the legislative history of this period recognizes that the committee helped to create public awareness of the need to correct wrongdoing in unions and, thus, "in ways which were sometimes direct and sometimes indirect," decided the outcome.[7] Handy leverage was furnished to a broad array of anti-union groups throughout the nation behind a campaign to exploit the publicity.

Bobby ultimately became principally identified with his Churchillian pursuit of the Teamster president. Clearly, that was Bobby's show. Jack's preoccupation was elsewhere, largely for several other reasons. Much time was taken up with the Labor Subcommittee and by extensive efforts for reelection in 1958 and promotion of national ambitions. Still, as Robert Kennedy had anticipated, the senator's presence and influence encouraged assumptions that he was operating in tandem with his brother.

He and Bob did work together during the weeks in 1958 devoted by the committee to the United Auto Workers troubles with the Kohler Company and a concluded strike against four plants of the Perfect Circle Company in Indiana. Partisan Kennedy accounts stress their lack of associations with Walter Reuther and his union. The labor leader had backed Kefauver during the convention.[8] Moreover, the action of the McClellan Committee was suspected by UAW leaders as the start of a plan to discredit the entire American labor movement. There can be little doubt, however, that before things went too far, neither Kennedy was going to alienate the potential political assets of Reuther and his important union. Months before the UAW phase of the hearings began, Senator Kennedy joined with Reuther and other labor leaders at a convention of the Industrial Union Department of the AFL-CIO in Washington. The Massachusetts *CIO News* of November 1957 featured a picture showing them together.

Initially, the conservative members were eager to get their hands on the Kohler situation. Four years of strife and violence against nonstrikers promised good headlines to condemn union hooliganism. The pro-labor minority resisted an inquiry by arguing that the proper place to settle such disputes was the bargaining room. Inevitably, suspicions associated the Kennedys with the UAW's cause. Holmes Alexander, a syndicated columnist, reported that Senator Kennedy was trying to help "Reuther

build his United Auto Workers from the ruins of the Teamsters' Brother-
hood" and charged "an accommodation in the making between the
Senator and Reuther."[9] The Republican members suspected Bobby
Kennedy of resisting getting Reuther on the stand to preserve his support
in 1960.[10] Tensions became public in late December when Senator
McNamara charged that some of the Republican members—who had
already been identified by the AFL-CIO as Goldwater, Carl Curtis, and
Karl Mundt—were out to "get" the UAW and its president. Reuther
himself complained to a TV audience that the "rackets committee" was
more concerned with "partisan politics," especially with the Republicans
trying "to differentiate between what the Democrats are doing and what
they think they ought to do." In the early spring, McNamara declared
that he was wasting his time with a "rigged" committee and resigned his
membership.[11]

Both Kennedys now worked to dispel strong impressions that the
minority friendly to labor was trying to protect Reuther and the
UAW from exposure in the Kohler affair. Jack suspected the majority with doing everything possible to exploit that sentiment by stall-
ing. Finally, on January 8, he challenged their antilabor bluff. He expressed mock surprise that the very members of the committee who
were advancing the Reuther cover-up thesis were reluctant to expedite matters by moving ahead with the Kohler investigation, placing
the onus for delay on them and arguing that the Perfect Circle Company hearings they were eager to air could follow afterward. To head
the Kohler on-site investigation, Bobby shrewdly encouraged McClellan to select a Republican, Jack McGovern, a protégé of Styles
Bridges of New Hampshire and a staff acquisition who had been
recommended by Goldwater. As columnist Paul Healy pointed out,
"That puts the responsibility squarely on Republican shoulders."[12]
The outmaneuvered Republicans had little choice. Meeting the Phoenix Press Club in Goldwater's home state in late February, Kennedy
needled his colleague. He asserted the committee's right to investigate
Reuther on violence in the Kohler strike but, he added, unless laws
were breached, they had no right to question the labor leader's political influence in Michigan "just because some of the committee members don't like Reuther."[13]

Kennedy's comment about Reuther was a direct barb at Goldwater,
who was getting known as the chamber's most outspoken foe of organized labor and of the UAW chief. Yet, as different as their political
positions were, the two senators frequently traded good-natured jabs as

they shared a sense of humor frequently not far above fraternity-level fun.

At one point during the floor proceedings on labor legislation, Kennedy was annoyed at the Arizonian. As Kennedy sat in the presiding officer's chair, having voluntarily accepted the obligation on the promise that he would be relieved at six o'clock so he could keep a dinner engagement, Goldwater rambled on with a long prepared talk. Only one other senator was in the chamber, and that man was reluctant to relieve Kennedy. Finally, with the clock nearing seven and Goldwater still orating, Kennedy picked up a piece of paper and wrote a note to his Republican friend.

"Do you always have to be such a shit?" it asked.

Goldwater paused, looked at it, and laughed. "Well," he later recalled, "I decided then I'd let him off. After all, he was in bad shape. So I finally sat down."[14]

Nothing, of course, could get Goldwater and Kennedy to agree over Walter Reuther. Through the mid and late 1950's, the Arizonan gained increasing renown as among the Senate's most vehement antilaborites, while Reuther symbolized liberal unionism. On March 4 Goldwater made a clumsy attempt to link the Kohler UAW strikers with Communist plotters. After questioning a witness about his Trotskyite activities from 1944 to 1947, Goldwater suggested that the old affiliation was significant to the investigation because it showed he once belonged to a group "solely devoted to violence and revolution." That made him conclude that the violent methods of Communists were "the cornerstone" of UAW activity. Jack Kennedy responded: "My brother's name was Joe, and Stalin's name was Joe, but this should scarcely support an argument that they had anything in common."[15]

Reuther, fiery, redheaded, articulate, and well versed in both the politics and economics of his field, finally faced the committee. For three days Reuther dissected the company's labor record, pointing out that the forty-five-month-old strike had been fully reviewed by the National Labor Relations Board in more than two years of previous hearings, which contradicted much of what Herbert Kohler had said to the panel on the day before Reuther's opening testimony. Reuther enumerated the Kohler collection of weapons and detailed the company's network of spies; acknowledging that crimes had been committed by physical attacks on the two nonstrikers, he refused Goldwater's efforts to link him with personal responsibility.[16] Reuther denounced Goldwater's recent statement that it was Kohler's right "not to have a union if he can win a strike" and asked whether the senator thought that "under the Taft-Hartley law a company can decide not to have a union and destroy the union? I maintain they can't."

The usually affable Goldwater was visibly angry. Confronted with the labor leader considered by the Arizonan as the personification of the antibusiness, socialist trend in America, he said: "I will tell you what; someday you and I are going to get together and lock horns."

Reuther retorted, "We are together now and I would like to ask you right now—"

But Goldwater cut him short. "You save that," he admonished the labor leader.

"I am asking a fundamental question," Reuther insisted.

Kennedy remained studiously detached from Reuther. He wandered in and out of the Caucus Room during the exchange, as did other members of the committee. His own cross-examining role was perfunctory, and that was largely to make the point that NLRB failure to adjudicate the situation "has contributed a good deal to many of the difficulties we have seen in the last five weeks before this committee in regard to the Kohler matter."[17] On the second day of the testimony, he again left the room periodically and hardly participated at all. Finally, when Reuther concluded his role on March 29, Kennedy was gone. Nevertheless, his covert role was significant. Jack, in fact, had been instrumental in expediting Reuther's chance to testify. Although Reuther felt more rapport with Robert, sensing that the younger brother was less detached, more committed, and more of an activist, he considered the senator "a real saint towards the UAW."[18] If their mutual experience corrected Reuther's earlier reluctance to take Kennedy seriously, it also educated Jack about Reuther. He was not simply a utopian, "knee-jerk" liberal theorist. As Ted Sorensen later wrote, "Some were great talkers and some were great 'doers'—and some, like Walter Reuther, were both."[19]

Although some dozen unions came before it, McClellan's group gave by far the greatest attention to the Teamsters. "It has been the biggest, most spectacular congressional investigation in recent years," wrote John Bartlow Martin, in a series of *Saturday Evening Post* articles.[20] They heard a total of 1,366 witnesses; the transcripts and documentation filled 21 United States Government Printing Office volumes and 20,432 pages. In contrast, the UAW portion began on February 26, 1958, and continued intermittently until September 1959, with 32 days of testimony from 102 witnesses and a printed record of 2,572 pages.

While Jack's active association with the committee's major inquiry into Hoffa and the Teamsters was only peripheral, the McClellan Committee preserved his delicate balance between opposing labor corruption and upholding the "legitimate rights" of workers. He had also managed to establish a potentially productive association with Walter Reuther. Essentially, however, the McClellan Committee provided the backdrop for Kennedy's most significant Senate role—as head of the Labor Subcommittee that wrote major legislation attempting to reform practices publicized by the rackets hearings.

The advantage of attaching Kennedy's name to a major piece of labor legislation was self-evident. Taking the leadership against irresponsible union officials could provide a broader base for a senator from the industrial northeast. In one of the more candid comments made on the floor during the endless debates, Jacob Javits expressed the simple but telling point that underscored all the deliberations. "Labor leaders," said the New York Republican, "are not popular in this country."[21]

Ted Sorensen has written that, for the first time in his congressional career, Jack "concentrated intensively and almost exclusively for a period of years on a single piece of legislation."[22] While the McClellan Committee was largely Bobby's show, the Labor Subcommittee was Jack's. Most of his colleagues, especially those on the Democratic side, appeared willing to cooperate and let him take the initiative, a measure of how they regarded the sensitivities involved. In the fall of 1957 Kennedy directed the enlistment of a Labor Advisory Committee of scholars and labor relations experts led by Archibald Cox of Harvard Law School to offer expertise on the design of possible legislation. Until the closing days of their work, there remained a strong probability that any new law would bear the Kennedy name.

From the start, Kennedy tried to call attention to other evidence developed by the McClellan Committee that most of the other politicians preferred to ignore. Kennedy argued that the activities of Beck and Hoffa clearly demonstrated the dependence of corruption on cooperation from businessmen and unethical lawyers. He hammered away at them frequently, rarely speaking out about labor malfeasance without citing its handmaidens. If Beck had made large windfalls, credit "an alliance of big business with big labor with apparently little regard being paid to the rights of union members whose funds were involved." He cited the officials of several companies, including Montgomery Ward. He argued that there was a "peculiar and abnormal" relationship between Beck's family and the Anheuser-Busch brewery when Beck obtained a Budweiser beer distributorship for his son. In a complex series of loans, Kennedy pointed out, the Fruehauf Trailer Company also enjoyed "peculiar" dealings with Beck. Associated Transport, perhaps the nation's biggest truck line, had also figured in the Fruehauf-Beck loans. Sewell Avery, the head of Montgomery Ward, "showed very little regard" for his employees in a purported deal, denied by Beck, to swap support of Teamster-voted stock in a proxy fight for a collective-bargaining contract with the union. He pointed to the purchase of Montgomery Ward's stock by the Teamsters. The stock was then voted to support Avery's successful proxy battle, which was followed immediately afterward by Teamsters moving in with a free hand to organize the company. "The employees were either put in the union involuntarily or they had been kept out by Avery until the proxy fight," Kennedy charged.[23]

At the McClellan Committee hearing in August, Kennedy cited evidence that some of the lawyers who had testified had been "advising clients of more than their rights." In his role as director of Fruehauf, one lawyer had endorsed a $1.5 million loan from the Teamsters to the Fruehauf Foundation for the purchase of the corporation's stock. Other attorneys were also involved, said Kennedy. He named Herman E. Cooper of New York, Joseph Jacobs of Atlanta, Sam Bassett of Seattle, and Alfons Landa of Washington, all of whom, Kennedy suggested, were working hand in hand with corrupt union leaders and businessmen. Two lawyers, Leon Reich and Alexander Eltman of New York, who counseled six associates of Johnny Dio, were questioned closely by committee members and one was put under oath. All took the Fifth Amendment. Joseph Loftus, the labor reporter who followed the hearings for the *Times,* noted that it was a rough day for lawyers.[24]

Then Kennedy aimed at the businessmen themselves. Merrill Hermanson of Scarsdale, New York, who owned a plant with one hundred employees, told of being introduced to Johnny Dio after Dio had helped him clear up "some labor trouble" within his company that had interfered with deliveries for the nonunion firm. The businessman was introduced to Dio by Irving Bitz, who was identified to Bobby Kennedy as "a notorious hoodlum." Hermanson then signed a contract with Equitable Research, a Dio front that listed Dio as its vice-president, and paid him $150 per month. When questioned by McClellan, Hermanson acknowledged that he had paid out "protection" money for protection that he didn't get.

Kennedy then spoke up. "You were using one of the worst hoodlums in New York to prevent your plant from being unionized, and you didn't decide until last week to drop his services."

Hermanson then admitted that he had known of Dio's indictment in connection with the acid blinding of labor writer Victor Riesel.[25]

At a University of Florida homecoming law breakfast on October 19, Kennedy called on lawyers to police their own profession against the kind of unethical practices that were uncovered in the Senate investigation of labor leaders. Lawyers as a group, Kennedy said, cannot prevent every incident of wrongdoing but that "professional opinion can prevent individual incidents of impropriety from turning into an epidemic."[26]

As the Labor Advisory Committee, or "blue ribbon panel"—as it came to be known—began the drafting of a bill that fall, Kennedy anticipated the consternation that would arise within the AFL-CIO. Facing them at a convention in Washington in late October, he warned that they must expect legislation "some of which you will not welcome."[27] Actually, George Meany, as president of the union, had already anticipated legislative action at the inception of the McClellan hearings and had directed the writing of a code of democratic procedure, which had been drafted or prepared by Arthur Goldberg, the AFL-CIO's special counsel. It represented a self-policing measure to prevent malpractices of the type disclosed before the rackets committee.[28]

In early 1958 Kennedy introduced two bills. Joining with seventeen other senators in early February, his proposal called for improving and strengthening the federal-state unemployment insurance program to establish national standards for benefit amounts and other necessary improvements. The bill would enable every worker to draw benefits for a uniform period of thirty-nine weeks instead of being cut off at the end of five, ten, fifteen, or, in many cases, twenty-six weeks, as was then the practice.[29] On March 11 he placed before the Senate a bill that he described as one designed to "safeguard union finances and to curb certain improper and undemocratic practices—including the abuse of trusteeships." Tied closely to rackets committee findings, the proposed legislation required unions to make full disclosure of their financial records and prohibited them from lending more than twenty-five hundred dollars to anyone. It further provided for strict management of locals under trusteeships.[30]

Two weeks later, Kennedy's subcommittee began the first of fifteen days of open hearings on legislation to implement the findings and recommendations of the McClellan Committee. The first interim report from the rackets hearings called for the regulation and control of pension, health, and welfare funds; legislation to place a tighter rein on union funds; the insurance of union democracy; curbing the activities of middlemen in labor-management disputes; and legislation to clarify the "no man's land," pertaining to disputes preempted by state courts from federal jurisdiction but left without jurisdiction by the National Labor Relations Board.

The leadoff witness, Secretary of Labor Mitchell, spoke in support of the President's special message to Congress of January 23, which included a call for amendments to the Taft-Hartley Act. Among them was a provision to cope with the "no man's land" problem. The administration, along with most management spokesmen, called for specifying the transference to the states of matters over which the NLRB declined to assert jurisdiction. Kennedy, however, reminded Mitchell that his own original statement had expressed the hope of the subcommittee "that these hearings would be confined" to the McClellan Committee recommendations and that including such provisions to reform the Taft-Hartley Act "would result in no act at all."[31] Supporters of organized labor, he was warning, would block anything that exploited the situation to toughen Taft-Hartley.

Labor's turn came the next day, coinciding with Walter Reuther's initial testimony before the McClellan Committee on the Kohler strike. AFL-CIO President Meany appeared before Kennedy's group and read a scathing ten-thousand-word statement criticizing most of the provisions of the proposed legislation. He regarded as unprecedented and discriminatory against labor a proposal to require every officer and employee of a union to file personal financial reports that would be open to the public. He wanted to know why similar reports should not be required from members of Congress and important government officials. Meany reminded them that the AFL-CIO had urged both major parties to call for corrective legislation to be written into their platforms in 1956. "There will be testimony here from men whose sole desire is to destroy the labor movement," said the union president, "not clean up any sort of corruption. Such testimony, we submit, does not deserve your serious attention." As Meany faced Kennedy, there was a sudden adversary relationship with the senator who had been described as carrying "the hopes of the labor movement." "You are starting from the personal assumption that legislation is necessary—I don't," said Meany, slapping the table.

Then Kennedy interjected, "Mr. Meany, you have devoted a good deal of your statement to criticizing my suggested legislation, and I am now going to place in the record in a little more detail than I did when I read them off to you, the names of the advisory committee who gave unanimous endorsement to the two bills that I have introduced." Kennedy read the roster of the "blue ribbon panel," together with each member's credentials. All nine were from Harvard, MIT, Brown, Princeton, and Yale, and all had impressive backgrounds in the fields of labor relations, economics, and law.

"My only comment is," Meany erupted, " 'God save us from our friends.' "

Softly, Kennedy responded, "I say that, too, Mr. Meany."[32]

Outraged, Meany then met privately with Kennedy. "And actually, when I got to discussing it with Senator Kennedy," the labor leader later said, "he readily saw that the way the bill was drawn that it would have been really unjust, and we had no problem on that."[33]

The Kennedy-Meany relationship then turned around, with Meany discovering "that if you had a good case, if you had an argument he would go along with you."[34] After his private sessions with the union president, Kennedy introduced a bill covering four "additional problems in the labor field," all designed to modify provisions in the existing Taft-Hartley Act, and all designed as concessions or "sweeteners" to mollify organized labor. Written, in part, to eliminate "special problems which unions in the building and construction industries have encountered under the Taft-Hartley Act," they eased the requirements for certification of unions in the industry, eliminated a "union-busting" provision prohibiting voting by economic strikers who had been replaced during the course of the strike, and made it "unlawful for an employer directly or indirectly to bribe or attempt to influence by surreptitious means the course of his labor relations."[35]

When Kennedy faced the biennial convention of the Amalgamated Clothing Workers of America at Atlantic City, his references to labor's efforts to clean its own house were more complimentary than even those made by the top labor officials. Kennedy carried the assurances of Jacob Potofsky, the Amalgamated's president, that his union would support the proposed reforms if they emerged from the committee in a manner that would wipe out malpractices without undermining the ability of funds to fulfill their legitimate functions. Pointing out that fewer than one-hundredth of one percent of union officials had been accused of wrongdoing, Kennedy stressed his determination to outlaw "right-to-work" laws along with other matters detrimental to unions. As he had done many times before, he cited the involvement of employers and businessmen in the rackets that had been disclosed.[36] Three days later in Milwaukee, before Wisconsin Democratic leaders, he heard himself praised as a friend of labor and listened with obvious satisfaction as a United Auto Workers official rejected any attempt to label him as antilabor. The lunchers applauded enthusiastically and Kennedy grinned happily.[37]

Meany's return before the subcommittee on May 22 accentuated the new climate. Having obtained concessions in the form of the Taft-Hartley revisions, he was much more conciliatory. He cited the AFL-CIO's General Board statement admitting the existence of a problem and asked congressional assistance to clean labor's house without wrecking it. Warning about the danger of excessive government regulation, he said he preferred self-policing wherever possible, a position also taken by John L. Lewis of the United Mine Workers. In marked contrast to their previous exchange in March, Kennedy responded with satisfaction, saying, "I think that's an excellent and very positive statement." Kennedy then predicted that the reform bill to be reported out by his subcommittee, while fulfilling the McClellan recommendations, would steer a middle course, somewhere between the supporters of restrictive legislation and the opponents of any new federal regulations of unions. The bill that resulted carried the bipartisan Kennedy-Ives label and bore the expertise of George Meany's chief counsel, Arthur Goldberg, as well as Archibald Cox.[38]

Introduced on June 2, the Kennedy-Ives Bill had everything in its favor: labor got its Taft-Hartley "sweeteners," incorporated in the last of the six titles, and that won it the approval of the AFL-CIO. McClellan, the rackets committee chairman, also endorsed it as consistent with the group's recommendations. Support was bipartisan and ostensibly faithful to the administration's own position, especially as expressed by Jim Mitchell. With only minor changes, the subcommittee sent it to the full committee on June 4. Only two days later, with just Goldwater objecting, it went to the floor.

Suddenly an unexpected attack changed its prospects. With Secretary Mitchell in Geneva, Switzerland, attending a labor conference, hopes increased that the administration would acquiesce and accept the bill. Instead, his Washington office issued a statement charging that Kennedy-Ives contained "imperfections, omissions or loop-holes," which diluted whatever protection existed for the public and union members. The secretary was quoted as saying that it would provide "only illusory protection, and that it would be almost impossible to administer." In short, without providing adequate remedies, it would delude Americans into believing "they had protection they did not in fact have." Most startling to the press and on Capitol Hill generally was the contrast created by the message with Mitchell's own testimony before the sub-committee on May 22.

Irving Ives speculated that the administration had chosen to "make a Republican thing" out of the reforms, leading to the conclusion that it was best seen as a 1958 congressional campaign issue. Doris Fleeson noted that "Mitchell clearly thinks of himself as the answer to Kennedy and as such has his eye on second place on a Nixon GOP ticket."[39] Mitchell quickly followed his original message with a more detailed attack, which coincided with the Kennedy and Ives response at a joint news conference. The secretary's objections were denounced as "un-called for—utterly uncalled for." Kennedy termed "completely inaccu-rate" Mitchell's charge that certain instances of labor corruption would not have been uncovered had the provisions of Kennedy-Ives been in effect, and pointed out that some of the secretary's objections were to sections of the legislation not offered by friends of labor but by Goldwa-ter. Using Mitchell's reasoning, Kennedy stated, the Goldwater provi-sions would rescue from the reporting requirement not sixty percent but seventy-five percent of the unions.[40]

Administration supporters rushed to introduce amendments. Some were accepted, winning the acquiescence of Kennedy and Ives. All told, they did nothing to alter either the spirit or intent of the measure. The most significant changes were turned back on the third day of the fight, discouraging further attempts to incorporate administration proposals. Still, despite Kennedy's vociferous opposition, the Senate voted 66–20 in favor of including a non-Communist affidavit requirement for union officers. Kennedy argued that they were unnecessary because existing laws already offered such "protection" and, moreover, they would "have no effect on the conduct of employers." Finally, at 7:20 P.M. on the fifth day, the amended Kennedy-Ives Bill sailed through by a vote of 88–1, with Nevada's George "Molly" Malone the lone dissenter.[41]

Jack Kennedy's bill, enmeshed in a quagmire of political complications, never had a chance to advance. Plagued by a serious economic downturn since 1957, embarrassed by revelations that the President's special assist-ant, Sherman Adams, had indebted himself to manufacturer Bernard Goldfine, the administration needed some issue capable of sustaining that fall's election campaign. An Eisenhower acceptance of Kennedy-

Ives risked a Republican revolt, especially from among those most sensitive to the lobbying of the National Association of Manufacturers and the U.S. Chamber of Commerce. Stepping up their lobbying after the Senate had cleared Kennedy-Ives, the NAM called the reform bill "a fraud and a delusion."[42] The Chamber of Commerce, joining in a demand for more stringent regulations of unions, felt that the bill had "little reform" value and claimed that some of its provisions would actually favor labor and might thereby "do irreparable harm."[43] The main targets of business, of course, were the Taft-Hartley "sweeteners" of Title VI, especially the one permitting strikers to vote on a choice of whether or not to have a union instead of, as under the prevailing law, limiting such power to those who replaced strikers. Exerting a squeeze from the other direction was the predictable opposition from the Teamsters, seconded by the United Mine Workers. UMW leader John L. Lewis hated the entire principle of federal regulations. Both worked from labor's side of the issue to defeat Kennedy-Ives.[44]

About the only strong support came from Walter Reuther. However, he represented a minority faction of the AFL-CIO, while George Meany, with stronger potential backing, failed to muster his forces. The AFL-CIO leadership, despite having given Kennedy-Ives its endorsement, obviously preferred to let it die in the Eighty-sixth Congress with the hope that the fall elections would provide a friendlier lineup on Capitol Hill. Key congressmen in a position to do something about expediting the legislation once it reached the House noted the absence of AFL-CIO lobbyists, whose abstention made the point even more emphatic. "They know what they are doing," said one House Democrat. "They are enjoying this."[45]

For more than a month Kennedy-Ives languished in the House. Speaker Sam Rayburn held the Senate-passed measure on his desk. Finally, however, when Rayburn did act during the last week in July, he referred it to the Education and Labor Committee, thus seeming to bury it forever.

Why had it been shelved? Everyone had an effective answer. The NAM and the Chamber of Commerce said that labor did not really want reform. Mitchell accused the Democratic congressional leaders of surrendering, and, at the same time, criticized the major management groups for their "unwarranted" opposition. Kennedy simply said, "Unlike Mr. Mitchell, who never lifted a finger to help Senator Ives and me to pass this legislation, I cannot take any partisan satisfaction out of our failure to obtain passage of a strong labor reform bill in this Congress."[46]

Rayburn's move turned out to be more inflammatory than he had anticipated. Having held it "40 days and 40 nights," as Mitchell charged, he was both surprised and embarrassed. His action clearly threatened to validate Republican campaign claims that a Democratic Congress had been irresponsible for failing to produce labor reforms. And so Rayburn came under increasing pressure from House Democrats who were also arguing that sending it to the committee had encouraged rumors that the business lobby was responsible for having it pigeonholed.

A group of Democrats gathered to force Rayburn's hand. Congressmen George McGovern of South Dakota, Stewart Udall of Arizona, and Frank Thompson of New Jersey, Kennedy's personal friend, plotted to bring Kennedy-Ives to a vote. Kennedy himself joined them in several conferences to plan the course. Warned by Thompson of the possibility of a House adjournment without taking any action, Kennedy joined a meeting of about a dozen congressmen in the New Jerseyan's office. "We discussed the need for the House to act on the legislation—to vote on it, whether or not it passed," Thompson later recalled. "And we discussed at some length that need and the possibilities . . . of the House adjourning without acting. At this meeting Senator Kennedy impressed enormously the members of the House who were in my office." They discussed the dangers of bringing the bill up through suspension of the rules, which required a two-thirds vote to pass. Kennedy impressed them with his clear knowledge not only of the rule for bringing bills up under suspension but of the pitfalls involved, and they talked at length about the wisdom of taking that course. Kennedy then convinced "anyone in that room who wasn't up till then convinced, of the need for bringing it up, even if it lost, in order to demonstrate the determination that there should be a labor reform," Thompson told an interviewer in 1965. Kennedy was "acutely aware" of the adverse impact on public sentiment if the bill did not even come to a vote.[47] Finally, in an attempt to regain the initiative by placing the Republicans on the defensive, the bill was brought to the floor using the procedure permitting committees to be bypassed by a two-thirds vote of the House.[48]

That route permitted little debate and no amendments. Strongly opposed by a combination of Republicans and southern Democrats, it fell far short of the required margin, even failing by eight votes to get a simple majority. Kennedy, hardly shocked at the outcome, declared that "Jimmy Hoffa can rejoice at his continued good luck. Honest union members and the general public can only regard it as a tragedy that politics has prevented the recommendations of the McClellan committee from being carried out this year."[49] When Kennedy called Mitchell "the chief stumbling block," the secretary challenged the senator to debate the reasons for the impasse. Kennedy refused, saying he was "more interested in labor legislation than in a debate and if Mr. Mitchell had been equally interested I think we would have had a reform bill in this session, especially after it passed the Senate 88–1." He was delighted to learn that Hoffa would find it difficult to give him political support and promised that the bill would be reintroduced at the next session, "and as far as I am concerned will receive top priority."[50]

24

"The Perfect Politician"

Nobody who watched Jack Kennedy's work with the Labor Subcommittee needed to be convinced about his ambition. Still, before explicitly seeking national office, he had to overcome the reelection hurdle in Massachusetts; not that his victory was ever in doubt, but the politicians and the country had to be shown an emphatic sweep in his home state. They also had to be convinced that he was not merely the second son of Joe Kennedy fulfilling his dad's ambitions but was of sufficient stature on his own. And yet there was no denying that, however independent and capable Jack had become, surreptitious assistance from his father was invaluable. As in the past, that was true in the months before Jack had to stand for reelection.

How fully the Ambassador used his well-placed friends for promotional purposes can never be known. Richard Whalen's comment that he was determined to "sell Jack like soap flakes" probably conveys the general sense of activity with substantial accuracy. Whalen also describes a scene with the Ambassador and a journalist in Palm Beach as early as 1957 when, with a map of the United States spread out before them, potentially valuable contacts were pinpointed for mobilization in various parts of the country.[1]

In one way or another, the Kennedy network hardly ever rested, often working through such friends as Henry Luce, William Randolph Hearst, Jr., and Arthur Krock. In Massachusetts, the Ambassador made good use of the Washington correspondents of the *Globe* and the *Herald,* in addition to Basil Brewer's accommodating New Bedford *Standard-Times.* All together, along with the older Kennedy's Hollywood and business contacts, they were invaluable openings to the powerful and influential. A thousand mutual-assistance relationships maintained Joe Kennedy's proximity to the center of action.

Gossip about the Ambassador's role followed every new step that boosted Jack. One small Vermont paper, for example, noting the senator's picture on the cover of national magazines, along with other publicity, speculated that "Papa Kennedy intends to use the Kennedy millions to give young John a crack at the Democratic nomination for president next time."[2] In the Massachusetts State House, the Ambassador's name came up during a debate on the sales tax between John E. Powers, the Kennedyite and state senator, and Senator Philip Graham. Graham argued that the Commonwealth's residents were so heavily taxed that many of them were moving to Florida and other states to find more favorable tax advantages. To clinch his point, he waved his finger at Powers and shouted, "Take Joseph P. Kennedy. Has he ever invested any of his wealth in Massachusetts? Of course not. He has invested in Chicago and elsewhere, but never in Massachusetts." Then, delivering his coup de grâce, he challenged Powers to name "one investment in Massachusetts that Joseph P. Kennedy has ever made." A grinning Powers retorted, "United States Senator John F. Kennedy." The chamber erupted with appreciative laughter and applause, which abruptly ended Graham's complaint.[3]

Through Jim Fayne in the Park Avenue office, the Ambassador fed material to syndicated columnist Marquis Childs to promote an article boosting the impression of a strong Kennedy tide. Childs, after noting that it was rare for anyone to rise as rapidly and steadily as Kennedy had in ten years since coming to the House, added that he was fighting against such probable liabilites for a presidential contender as his youth and religion. He portrayed the senator as one with a liberal record now under attack from "the thunderers on the isolated right." For his efforts, Childs immediately received an offer from the Ambassador to do a book about his son. The overture was just as promptly rejected; Childs feared it would compromise his journalistic position.[4]

When Tom Gerber wrote an article in the *Boston Herald* on New Year's Day under the headline "Sen. Kennedy Plans to 'Run Scared' in

1958 Race," Frank Morrissey forwarded a clipping to the Ambassador and noted that Gerber had "followed through on every specific suggestion that you gave me this morning." Morrissey also informed him that another paper, the *Boston Traveler,* planned to use a story supplied about Bobby. "The line that you gave me—when the lady in the audience asked Bobby during the question period about Senator McClellan for President, Bobby paused and smiled and said that McClellan would be his second choice—gave them something to hang the story on. This, I know, if you weren't the world's greatest financier and economist, you certainly would have made a terrific managing editor of the newspaper."⁵ It was Tom Gerber who, in May, published a *Boston Herald* article discussing how Kennedy was being mentioned universally for one of the two spots on the 1960 ticket. Gerber noted that more and more Kennedy was finding his name mentioned as *the* leading candidate.⁶

The Ambassador also had associations dating back to the 1940 efforts against Roosevelt, with Virginia's senior Senator Byrd. *The Winchester Evening Star* was published and edited by the senator's son, Harry F. Byrd, Jr. An editorial in his paper on February 15 called attention to an *American Mercury* article that referred to Senator Kennedy as "the perfect politician." The article assured conservatives by recalling that his father left government service because of the leftward trend of the New Deal. It went on to compare Jack Kennedy with Nixon and concluded that "Kennedy has been regarded by many as the Democratic counterpart for the GOP's Richard Nixon. Nixon probably is basically a moderate conservative though with some liberal tendencies. Kennedy is basically a moderate liberal, but with many conservative leanings. Neither is an extremist in any sense." The younger Byrd, commenting on *The American Mercury* article on his editorial page, concluded that "there are political observers who say these two young men likely will meet someday in a showdown battle for the presidency. The tides of political fortunes being what they are, this prediction might be questionable. But no one around Washington seems to doubt the current statement that Jack Kennedy at 39 is a 'young man on his way.' "⁷ A few days later Jack sent Byrd a letter of appreciation.

The Ambassador also gave interviews in Palm Beach to *Boston Herald* newsman Bill Cunningham. The father emphasized that it was up to Jack to decide his future. "I guess it's not a secret that Jack and I don't see eye-to-eye on certain things—the agricultural problem, just to name one —and I think it would be unfair to him to have some smart reporter smell out some difference between my views and his on some public matters and write a story about 'the dissension in the Kennedy family.' For there is no dissension and there isn't going to be. I respect his views as to his own opinion. I know he reaches them after reasoning things out in his own way. I've never tried to influence his thinking and never shall. That's the truth and he'll tell you. For that reason, I have withdrawn completely from public life."[8]

Other newsmen, such as Fletcher Knebel, wrote with the benefit of inside information about the rising Kennedy popularity. Knebel, reporting that Kennedy was Washington's "hottest tourist attraction," recorded the number of speaking-engagement invitations since January 1 as 950. "This June, at graduation time, degrees will patter about his shoulders with the persistence of spring rains," Knebel wrote, and then he also noted the phenomenon of *Profiles in Courage* remaining on the best-seller list after sixty-six weeks.[9]

The Hearst and Scripps-Howard press also did their share to promote the senator to conservative readers.

The image-making was well under way. A new type of Democrat, well informed, dynamic, moderate, and, above all, with prudent fiscal ideas, one who could speak for a broad American consensus, could hardly escape the attention of even less sophisticated citizens. Without specifically saying so, especially in deference to the President occupying the White House, he contrasted with the passive, aging general, still enormously popular but lacking vibrant qualities of leadership. Harold Martin wrote an article in *The Saturday Evening Post* under the title "The Amazing Kennedys" and tried to spell out the qualities possessed by the senator. He decided that Kennedy was a clean-cut, smiling American boy, one who appeared "trustworthy, loyal, brave, clean and reverent, boldly facing up to the challenges of the Atomic Age."[10] The strategy could hardly have worked much better.

The latest Gallup Poll was only one piece of evidence attesting to his rise. His strength as a possible presidential candidate dominated the gossip at the Governors Conference in Williamsburg, Virginia, at the end of June. A staff writer for the Lynn (Mass.) *Sunday Telegram-News* reported Washington observers figured that Kennedy had already been virtually nominated. He was the hottest thing in the country. He was being buried under invitations to speak in every state in the Union. Photographers from national magazines were following him around wherever he went, in the Senate, at speaking engagements, in his home, where some three hundred to four hundred pictures were taken.[11] In July he and his brother Bobby were the subject of an eight-page illustrated feature in *Look.* The article, called "The Rise of the Brothers Kennedy," included sixteen photographs of the two in their Washington jobs, with their families, and with the public. Appearing on a *Meet the Press* interview, Hubert Humphrey volunteered the opinion that Kennedy was running "way out front" for the 1960 nomination. In August, Kennedy went with Torby Macdonald to San Diego, where, at the naval base, an ABC-TV crew was preparing a television film about his South Pacific wartime adventures for a program called *Navy Log.* When the program appeared that October 17, the segment was named "PT 109," firmly reestablishing Kennedy's wartime record. Kennedy both introduced the program on film and served as a consultant during its production. While they were in California, a photograph in a San Diego paper showed Jack and Torby as two exceedingly handsome, youthful-looking men, contentedly relaxing under palm trees on the beach. And several months later, *Time* made Kennedy the subject of its cover story and subsequently reported receiving more letters and favorable comment than such features had ever drawn before.[12]

The Kennedy drive, of course, was aimed first at reelection in Massachusetts in 1958, not merely to win but to crush his opponent so overwhelmingly that it would erase all doubts about his own popularity. Still, success in Massachusetts would not assure national office. Despite the fanfare, especially evident in the pages of friendly newspapers in his own state, Kennedy was competing in a party where liberal intellectuals were looking for substantive alternatives. And despite his stands on Algeria and labor reform, the frequent Kennedy publicity made many perceive him as more of a celebrity than a national leader. Consequently, they had not entirely abandoned their devotion to Stevenson; if not Stevenson, there were other acceptable alternatives, such as Hubert Humphrey. There were, as William V. Shannon noted, those far more experienced, far more tested, and without a father as controversial as Joseph P. Kennedy. "There is a growing tendency on the part of Americans to 'consume' political figures in much the same sense we consume entertainment personalities and in the movies," wrote Shannon. "Month after month, from the glossy pages of *Life* to the multicolored cover of *Redbook,* Jack and Jackie Kennedy smile out at millions of readers; he with his tousled hair and winning smile, she with her dark eyes and beautiful face. We hear of her pregnancy, of his wartime heroism, of their fondness for sailing. But what has all this to do with statesmanship?"[13]

The night Jack Kennedy stopped at Tucson to participate in a forum on "America's Leadership Reappraised," somebody asked, "Do you think a 42-year-old can meet the demands made on the president?" The senator's face turned its most ingratiatingly Irish, as it usually did when he smiled, and he replied, "I don't know about a 42-year-old man, but I think a 43-year-old can."[14]

Three weeks later he spoke at the Gridiron Club dinner in Washington, the annual affair usually devoted to an evening of fun for the journalistic fraternity. One skit, based on the song "My Heart Belongs to Daddy," opened with: "We send all the bills to Daddy 'cause Daddy pays them so well." When Kennedy's turn came to speak, he began by making an announcement, "I have just received the following wire from my generous daddy: 'Dear Jack—Don't buy a single vote more than is necessary—I'll be damned if I'm going to pay for a landslide.' "

He went on to express his "appreciation" to Sam Rayburn. His devotion to "Mr. Sam," he explained, was even greater than the one to his father. "At the last Democratic Convention," he pointed out, "if he had not recognized the Tennessee and Oklahoma delegations when he did, I might have won that race with Kefauver—and my political career would now be over." Noting the abundance of potential candidates for 1960, he said that a "recent A.P. survey asked each Senator about his preference for the Presidency—and 96 Senators each received one vote." Then he told of having "dreamed about 1960 myself the other night, and I told Stuart Symington and Lyndon Johnson about it in the cloakroom yesterday. I told them how the Lord came into my bedroom, anointed my head, and said: 'John Kennedy, I appoint you President of the United States.' Stu Symington said: 'That's strange, Jack, because I, too, had a similar dream last night, in which the Lord anointed me and declared Stuart Symington, President of the United States *and* outer space.' And Lyndon Johnson said: 'That's very interesting, gentlemen: because I, too, had a similar dream last night—and I don't remember anointing either one of you.' "[15]

During the month before the Gridiron Dinner, Gallup polls confirmed the potency of Kennedy's candidacy. Among Democrats with a preference, Kennedy led Kefauver 61–39, a gain of eleven points since June of 1957. Of possibly greater interest to the party itself, was his 56–44 lead against the most likely Republican opponent, Vice-President Nixon. Kennedy's greatest margin was in the South, where he was ahead by a two-to-one ratio. The Gallup organization, however, reported on June 11 that when Stevenson's name was included, the Governor still led the list among Democrats, with twenty-three percent compared to nineteen for Kennedy, sixteen for Kefauver, and twelve for Johnson.[16] Against

Nixon, not counting the "undecideds," Stevenson trailed by six points. That reflected part of the higher esteem for the Vice-President after his South American trip to Caracas and Lima, where he had been the target of angry anti-American mobs. As a direct consequence of the sympathetic publicity that portrayed how he and his wife, Pat, had braved the violence, his surge placed him just two points behind Kennedy by mid-June.

Meanwhile, Jack's relations with Stevenson grew more strained. Lingering antipathies from the Chicago convention deepened with the approach of the 1960 campaign. Stevenson had already drawn some pique from Kennedy with his criticism of the Algeria speech. In the summer of 1958 he annoyed Jack once more when he was quoted in the "Washington Whispers" section of *U.S. News & World Report* as having told reporters in London that Kennedy "has three strikes against him: religion, too young, too rich."[17] Bill Blair, who was with Stevenson at the time, then attempted to clarify what had happened. The Governor, Blair explained, had been cornered at a cocktail party given by reporter Joe Fromm and was asked, "Doesn't Jack Kennedy have two strikes against him, such as his religion?" According to Blair, what Stevenson had really said was that he supposed some people would hold those things against him but "that he didn't think these were important considerations and that after all people could always think of reasons for being against someone if they want to."[18] However much that may have mollified Kennedy, and it is not likely that it did, he was additionally miffed when Stevenson, upon arriving in Helsinki, Finland, was asked by reporters for a further clarification. He praised Kennedy as presidential material but withheld outright support. "Mr. Kennedy is a capable, competent man," Stevenson told them. "There are lots of capable, competent men in the Democratic party. As I am not a candidate, I cannot comment on those who are."[19] Jack Kennedy could only have read that "clarification" as a backhanded compliment.

More than that, though, it stung. To Kennedy such comments were petulant and ungenerous, especially coming from the two-time loser who was disclaiming any interest in another try. They also hurt with the very people he had to win over, the Stevensonians—disproportionately upper-middle-class, professionals and intellectuals, ideological and committed. They were opinion-makers and active contributors, both financially and inspirationally, with enough loyalty to the Governor that inhibited defections to someone lacking his blessing.

At the bottom of such attitudes was the persistent feeling that

Kennedy was reaching too high, too fast, and too soon. Money and telegenic attributes had perhaps placed him where he did not belong. William S. White, assessing Jack's rise to the top, agreed that wealth had certainly helped put Kennedy in the Senate to begin with and thought that he "would be better off just now if he did not have a large and well-advertised bank account—and if his father . . . did not have an even bigger and better one."[20]

Too many rivals were eager to shoot him down. With Eisenhower finally eliminated and the controversial and distrusted Nixon looking more and more like the GOP's candidate, the Democratic prize might well go to someone without the liabilities Stevenson's comments had helped advertise. Prudently, Kennedy began to moderate his drive. Devoting himself to legislation, especially the labor bills, might convince skeptics when they read assessments like the one provided by Cabell Phillips in *The New York Times Magazine* that said Kennedy "does not intend to sacrifice his Senate career on the altar of his presidential ambition."[21] In mid-August, James Reston told his readers that the senator "is swinging for the fences now, and, by general agreement, his batting average in this session has been pretty good."[22]

Having been created, the momentum had sufficient force of its own. Sentiment among the southern governors who met in Lexington, Kentucky, that September seemed to rule out any possibility of a third-party movement and showed a strong inclination toward Kennedy. A North Carolina paper explained Kennedy's popularity in the region as having to do more with his personal qualities than voting record. "To put it simply, he has sought the support of the South. In a time when most national politicians seek favor by condemning the South, this can be effective flattery. . . . But his record shows it to be somewhat of a new-found love, and it may involve him in a serious triangle with his liberal constituents and associates in the Northern wing of the party."[23]

With less than a month to go before reelection, Kennedy and Jacqueline visited Parkersburg, West Virginia, in support of the local Democratic ticket. Somewhat self-consciously, he rode down the main street in a scarlet Cadillac convertible furnished by his hosts. In the hoopla of the parade, with music provided by the Parkersburg High School band, was a "Democratic" donkey. Once out of the car and liberated from the carnivallike atmosphere, he had his turn on the platform, where he spoke with the self-assurance that had been developing only recently. His speech was sprinkled with quotations from Shakespeare, Justice Holmes,

Woodrow Wilson, and the Founding Fathers. "His clothes and hair-do are a masterpiece of contrived casualness," observed James Reston. "Even with Mrs. Kennedy on the platform, his influence with lady politicians is almost naughty. In short, the effect is one of a serious and personable young man with a fresh personality."

In late October, Harry Truman arrived in Boston for a testimonial dinner in honor of Edward J. McCormack, the congressman's nephew then serving an interim appointment as the Commonwealth's attorney general. Newsmen around the former president were told that Kennedy was "a very good man and he has just as good a chance as anyone" for the 1960 nomination. But he declined to "nominate" any Democrat.[24]

The much-heralded Eisenhower "luck" had begun to run dry. Beginning with the summer of 1957, the economy entered into a serious recession also accompanied by the disturbing phenomenon known as "stagflation," the stubborn holding of high price levels, even inflationary, that defied the laws of supply and demand. For a Republican administration returned to office on a "peace and prosperity" slogan, the condition was especially embarrassing. It was also damaging for the aura of antiseptic morality that Eisenhower promised for Washington when headlines told the story of Sherman Adams, the President's special chief assistant on the White House staff. Adams, a stereotype character of New Hampshire granite, the epitome of Yankee rectitude, whose frugal ways and austere personality ostensibly immunized him from the material temptations of power, had succumbed to enticements. In exchange for giving Bernard Goldfine, a New England textile manufacturer, privileged entrée to government, Adams had accepted hotel accommodations and a much publicized vicuña coat. Unknown at the time was his additional acceptance of some $150,000 or more in direct cash payments.[25] After an initial public display of dependence upon the assistant to the President, Eisenhower finally forced his resignation. Simultaneously, the prompt dispatch of Marines to Lebanon at the request of President Camille Chamoun, who refused to abide by his country's constitutional limitation of his tenure, brought momentary apprehensions of military involvement. Fortunately, not a shot was fired and the tensions evaporated. Once again, despite an overthrow of the Iraqi government that had given Chamoun his pretext, the Middle East seemed stable and the "boys" came home. Nevertheless, the combination of recession, corruption within 1600 Pennsylvania Avenue, and the specter of American troops dashing to extinguish fires in remote places diluted the confident security felt by most Americans under the Eisenhower leadership. For Kennedy and the Democrats, the congressional elections of 1958 could well be anticipated with optimism.

Other shocks had weakened the administration since the fall of 1957. The most dramatic was the Soviet coup in launching a space satellite, *Sputnik I,* which upset American complacency all the more because of earlier publicity from Washington that the United States was ready to preempt that field. The Russians, meanwhile, not terribly cooperative, said nothing but got there first. National pride, suddenly deflated by advanced technology from a society better known for Cossacks, Siberian labor camps, and tundra, demanded explanations. Some suggested a Red hoax. The overwhelming majority of Americans, however, turned to self-searching, trying to understand the failure of American "know-how." The Eisenhower administration showed its concern by enlisting Dr. James Killian, the president of the Massachusetts Institute of Technology, as a special science adviser to the White House.

The second shock came from a "leak" to the press about the contents of the classified Gaither Report. Under the leadership of H. Rowan Gaither, Jr., chairman of the board of the Ford Foundation, a presidential panel looking into civilian defense as a means of minimizing potential nuclear-attack destruction, provided additional evidence of Soviet progress. For the first time, there was the warning of a dangerous "missile gap." Russian rate of military advances, reported the Gaither panel, was soon expected to give them the capacity to deliver a knockout nuclear blow to the American continent. The findings, which were submitted before *Sputnik,* included a call for increased military spending. Although it endorsed similar recommendations already made by the Rockefeller Brothers report, Eisenhower refused to panic and clung to the administration's "new look" defense program with its emphasis on massive striking deterrence.

Jack Kennedy's response was decidedly moderate, mostly emphasizing educational and economic indications. Only five days after *Sputnik,* he told the Economic Club of Chicago that the "great challenge to the status and security of the world in the next several years may be neither military nor political, but economic—and the most critical problem in this economic sphere is the problem of the underdeveloped nations."[26] His observations discreetly avoided condemning Eisenhower shortcomings in favor of generalized comments about the inadequacy of American competitive initiatives.

The new preoccupation with defense policies coincided with

Kennedy's need to bolster the interests of Massachusetts. New England's distressed economy, set back even further by the recession, begged for fresh federal funds. Throughout the Commonwealth, industrial centers from Taunton in the south and east to Pittsfield and North Adams in the Berkshire highlands were debilitated by chronic high unemployment, which by early 1958 exceeded 12 percent in some "labor-surplus" areas. As Kennedy told the Peabody Chamber of Commerce, exactly one month after the launching of *Sputnik,* "the problems of New England are national problems" not soluble by already burdened localities.[27] Kennedy, accordingly, pressed the Defense Department to channel contracts toward places that most needed assistance. Notwithstanding his previous warnings that relying on defense spending was no long-term solution for the economy, he now called for invoking the Employment Act of 1946 for stimulating "useful employment opportunities" by the federal government. The cause was pushed within the New England Conference, which listed the fight to obtain more military construction as the number-one item in its summary of actions "successfully" urged during 1957–1958.[28] In the summer of 1958 Kennedy's office issued a statement asking for more defense contracts for New England and complained that a mere $249,000 in preference awards had been given to Massachusetts labor-surplus areas during the month of May.[29]

Nationally, Jack Kennedy appealed with mixed voices to different audiences. At a Democratic rally in Topeka, Kansas, he claimed that the American people were "no longer willing to be lulled by paternalistic assurances, spoonfed scientific fictitious predictions, or pious platitudes of faith and hope" and warned that penny-pinching and mismanagement were helping to lose the satellite race. At the same time, he cautioned against a "crash" missile-building program, such as the one that had created the atomic bomb during World War II.[30]

On the evening of November 7, when the President addressed the nation on the role of science in national security, Kennedy was in Oklahoma City about to address a Jefferson-Jackson Day twenty-five-dollar box luncheon. The President surveyed the defense program, and acknowledged that "in the years ahead we could fall behind—unless we now face up to certain pressing requirements and set out to meet them at once." Eisenhower concluded with the announcement that he had created the office of Special Assistant to the President for Science and Technology to be headed by Dr. Killian.[31] As the President spoke, Kennedy left the stage and went to the back room where, with Senator

Robert Kerr, he listened to the talk over a transistor radio. While eating, he revised his prepared text.

Kennedy, then, facing the Oklahoma Democrats, delivered an instant rebuttal. He called the President's move "belated" and charged that Eisenhower had failed to tell the people "that we may be as much as several years behind in rocket motors, new fuels, jet engines, radar and nuclear-powered plants," and added that the country's position was "far more grim than the President indicated." His forty-eight hundred listeners at the fried-chicken-and-beans outing applauded frequently.[32]

On December 8 *The New York Times* appeared with a much more careful elaboration of his position in the form of an article under Kennedy's by-line. Headlined KENNEDY WANTS U.S. TO SACRIFICE, it declared that neither a "Fortress America" nor a "go-it-alone-policy" were viable alternatives and called for a reappraisal of strength and strategy with a view toward modernizing the total defense system. "Sputnik has implications for conventional weapons and armies as well as modern," he wrote. "If we are prepared only to fight total wars of massive retaliation . . . we shall witness further Soviet advances through the 'sputnik diplomacy' of intimidation and peripheral wars." He also urged attention to the needs of the uncommitted states, not only for military and defense but for economic recovery and growth. "Especially must we reformulate aid programs to meet the urgent need of under-developed countries suffering from over-population and capital starvation." He further urged that the political and diplomatic tasks were as great as those of the military and economic. Having called attention to the military and economic requirements, he concluded his article in a manner reminiscent of the unpublished piece Lieutenant Kennedy had written in early 1945. "We must critically evaluate our entire position on disarmament, now that all the trump cards are not in our hand, to see if we cannot halt the race for destruction."[33]

Kennedy's call to decelerate the arms race was not an inconsistency. He viewed military strength as a prerequisite for that achievement, regarding arms as but one response to the international situation. Lessening the arms race was one of the objectives of responsible leadership. In subsequent speeches, he continued to urge the primacy of economic assistance.[34]

Kennedy also proposed an amendment that would end the prohibition on giving economic aid to countries behind the Iron Curtain, especially Poland, excluding only the Soviet Union, the People's Republic of China, and North Korea. With surreptitious aid from the State Department, he took the lead in drafting enabling legislation that harmonized with positions previously taken by the administration. Subsequent protests by Republican senators, especially Minority Leader Knowland and Styles Bridges of New Hampshire, induced the President to back away for fear of antagonizing the party's right wing. Knowland had argued that the provision would have permitted the use of American tax dollars to make Iron Curtain "slaves" comply with their masters. Without the President's support, Kennedy's amendment was turned back in the Senate by a one-vote margin.[35]

That defeat did not stop Kennedy from arguing in behalf of the effectiveness of nonmilitary responses. Viewing its rejection as a missed opportunity, he thought it could still be salvaged. How to engage in the international competition with the Soviets by means other than clearly delineated military assumptions, especially those inherent in the administration's "new look" policy of massive retaliation, was at the heart of the major speech Jack Kennedy delivered in the Senate on August 14, 1958. As it became a significant part of his presidential campaign, charges about a missile gap were identified with Kennedy, as though he had invented the concept. The popular perception that its stress was military misses Kennedy's intellectual objectives while emphasizing what undoubtedly became the politic thing to argue.[36]

Kennedy was engaging in a dialogue that had had the attention of weapons and strategic experts both in and out of the administration. Thomas K. Finletter had raised the issue for Stevenson in 1956. The missile gap had been defined by General James Gavin as that period "in which our own offensive and defensive missile capabilities will lag so far behind those of the Soviets as to place us in a position of great peril."[37]

Kennedy was most directly influenced by General Gavin, whose ideas appeared in a book called *War and Peace in the Space Age,* and Joseph Alsop. Alsop became an especially vigorous advocate of the missile-gap theory. Estimates that appeared during the summer of 1958 enumerating expected Russian ICBM strength in comparison with that of the United States and showing the increased Soviet potential for first-strike power had actually been supplied by him.[38]

A Senate debate was provoked by the publication in the *St. Louis Post-Dispatch* of an article by Brigadier General Thomas R. Phillips. Phillips claimed that the Rand Corporation, examining the period of expected Russian nuclear striking-power superiority, had been led to make a "study of the circumstances in which the United States ought to surrender." Angered, Russell of Georgia promptly introduced an amendment to a military appropriations bill designed to forbid the Defense Department to spend any of its funds "on plans for the surrender of the United States." Nobody on the floor questioned the basis for the Rand scientists' conclusions, and Stuart Symington vouched for their accuracy.[39]

Late that day, Kennedy delivered his August 14 speech. Again, he reached into English history and that nation's experiences with survival. He began by recalling the demise of British continental power with the loss of Calais in 1558, which Kennedy used to illustrate that, instead of destroying England's standing, it ultimately promoted the utilization of different resources with different policies that "brought a new power and new security." Therefore, Kennedy said, as we are "about to lose the power foundation that has long stood behind our basic military and diplomatic strategy" we, too, must learn to utilize other resources. Then he merely reiterated the previous assumptions for believing that a gap would occur, drawing very largely on Gavin's estimates, and that the loss of America's superior nuclear striking power would constitute the equivalent of the British ouster from Calais. While he called for providing greater security until the appearance of American solid-fuel missiles and deplored the administration for giving priority to budgetary limitations "without regard to our military position," he argued that "the years of the gap demand something more than a purely military answer."[40]

The nonmilitary offensive was at the heart of Kennedy's argument. Most welcome would be our ability to work toward "a reduction of armaments, a reduction of tensions, and a reduction of areas of dispute. The goal of universal disarmament—at least in the area of nuclear weapons and long-range ballistic missiles—takes on an urgency not heretofore demonstrated by American negotiators who felt they held most of the trump cards." Recognizing, however, the improbability of being able to negotiate arms limitations as long as the Soviets were "in the driver's seat," he called for taking advantage of the remaining opportunities to make the most of the enemy's weaknesses. We should, therefore, exploit our economic and industrial advantage, which could be achieved in part by exporting capital through the Development Loan Fund. America could also "export the revolutionary ideas of the Declaration of Independence, and thus lead, not frustrate, the nationalistic movement against imperialism of any variety, East and West." We should also take advantage of the geographic factors and encourage local resistance to "the Red tide." Citing the one-vote margin by which his proposal to legalize aid to satellite countries was defeated, he asked for a reversal of the policies that hamstring such efforts and for a policy by which we can "wean the satellites from the Soviets, and . . . drive new wedges into each new crack in the Iron Curtain." Far from a militaristic formulation to the suspected appearance of a missile gap, Kennedy concluded that "we should certainly use all elements of national policy—economic, diplomatic, and military—in order to prepare us for the most serious test in our nation's history, which will be impending in the next five years."[41]

Thereafter, the moderation inherent in his own analysis yielded to portentous Cold War alarms, the temptations of trying to win an election in a nation frightened by an enemy that seemed unremitting and omnipotent. As Sorensen later explained to an interviewer, "he found that he could use to political advantage . . . [the] theme that this country was not doing all that it was capable of doing."[42] Kennedy told a gathering of midwestern Democrats that lagging American power might enable the Russians to find "a new short cut to world domination" and charged the Republican administration with six years of "steady deterioration in our capacity to fight brush-fire wars."[43] When he and Jackie arrived at the Wood County airport near Parkersburg for that colorful reception in October, he continued to hit hard on foreign policy and attacked the administration for emphasizing "budgets over security."[44] He spoke that day with far more self-assurance, but the high-minded approach of the Senate speech had been exhausted, had yielded to the passion for mass approval. Jack Kennedy was also beginning to hit his stride.

25

Emphatic Reelection

Kennedy's 1958 reelection has been described as "probably as nearly perfect in planning an operation as an election campaign in any off-year could be."[1] Its perfection minimized the need for the candidate's personal participation, freeing him for national matters. Massachusetts was canvassed in just seventeen days of intensive speech-making and hand-shaking. "But," Ted Kennedy told Burton Hersh some years later, "people *felt* he was there, it made it appear he was there most of the *tie*-um, but of course there were enormous demands on him in other parts of the country."[2]

Only one thing mattered: an overwhelming victory. The weaker his rival, the greater the need for a crushing margin—one sufficient to "send a message" capable of convincing the most durable skeptics. Once he had passed that milestone, he could launch the real fight.

Only momentarily did Republicans even contemplate offering substantial competition. The Eisenhower administration, fearing what an easy victory could do to strengthen Kennedy as an opponent for the Republican nominee in 1960, toyed with trying to get a "name" candidate. Failure followed efforts to entice Henry Cabot Lodge, Jr., to enter a

rematch. Elliot Richardson, then a thirty-seven-year-old assistant secretary in the Department of Health, Education, and Welfare, was another
possibility. Richardson, however, was still relatively unknown and unim-
pressed with the prospect of making the sacrifice. Others thought
Kennedy could be given some stiff competition by Representative Edith
Nourse Rogers, who as representative of Massachusetts Fifth District
since 1925, had a local reputation as the "grand old lady of American
politics," and enjoyed strong ties to veterans groups, a position she
furthered as chairman of the Veterans Affairs Committee. But the prospect of countering Kennedy with a seventy-seven-year-old hardly excited
Bay State Republicans. One strong but lesser-known possibility, Charles
Gibbons, a former Republican state chairman, withdrew after hopefuls
thought he could mount a decent challenge. That left John S. Ames, a
traditional Republican Yankee from the "right side of the tracks." Ames
went into the GOP state convention in Worcester with the blessings of
the party stalwarts, but when that affair concluded, the nominee was
Vincent J. Celeste, who had swayed the delegates with an impassioned
speech vowing a fighting campaign.[3]

Celeste differed from both Ames and Kennedy in just about every way.
A thirty-four-year-old lawyer who had been defeated by Kennedy in the
Eleventh District in 1950, he was an Italo-American from the North End
and lived on the top floor of a three-decker in East Boston's tough
waterfront district. His immigrant background was far more visible than
Kennedy's. A graduate of the Maritime Academy at King's Point, New
York, his law degree came from Suffolk Law School, the opposite pole
from Harvard in the region's status-conscious educational hierarchy.
The son of a candy-maker, Celeste had sold clothing, worked in a boiler
shop, and found other means of menial employment to make his way
through school. He—and not Kennedy—became, in effect, the ethnic
Catholic in that race.

Not for a minute did anyone regard him as a credible threat, but
Celeste nevertheless posed the same kind of problem that a weak chal-
lenger does to the prestige of a champion prizefighter. Any decent show-
ing could seriously undermine the value of Kennedy's victory. And
Celeste went with all his strength. He made a populist appeal in an effort
to draw working-class votes to the Republican ticket. He charged
Kennedy with heading a "financial steamroller" capable of buying off all
Republicans. He accused the senator of softness, because of his political
ambitions, toward labor leaders like Walter Reuther. He condemned
Kennedy for damaging the local economy by voting for the St. Lawrence

Seaway and of hurting the Civil Rights Bill by teaming up with the southern Democrats behind the jury-trial amendment. The short but sturdy and compactly built competitor met voters by thrusting out his hand and introducing himself with "I'm Vinny Celeste, running for United States Senator against that millionaire, Jack Kennedy."[4]

While Celeste was a nuisance, potentially embarrassing to the image of invincibility, real trouble came from within the Commonwealth's Democratic organization. Kennedy's personal coterie and independence had defied them. Haunting him now was his tenuous relationship with John McCormack. Tip O'Neill remembers that when he first entered Congress as Kennedy's successor from the Eleventh District, Jack acknowledged to him that he regretted the "shabby" treatment given McCormack.[5] To exacerbate matters, Onions Burke vowed to enter the fight as a candidate. "How would it look to the nation if a leading candidate for the presidential nomination in 1960 were seriously challenged in a preprimary convention?" Burke asked, in a statement more rhetorical than substantive.[6] Still another old wound was his relationship with Foster Furcolo. Having been elected as governor in 1956, he was now seeking reelection.

Larry O'Brien had long been anticipating such difficulties, warning Jack as early as May of 1957 to prepare for the dangers within the state. "We have developed a massive program which in my opinion will be tremendously effective," O'Brien had also advised. "It will require great effort on our part but it is geared to limit your direct and personal participation to an absolute minimum. Without question, maximum achievement will depend greatly on political diplomacy and to assure this, effort must be expended by a small group of people over a long period of time."[7] They staged a "Kennedy-McCormack unity dinner" with some six thousand Democrats in attendance, "the biggest dinner ever held in Massachusetts," O'Brien later wrote. "The dinner didn't solve all our problems, but it gave the political columnists something positive to write about, instead of constant stories of a Kennedy-McCormack feud."[8] Then at a luncheon on April 19 for ward chairmen of the regular machine and about four hundred "secretaries" of the Kennedy organization, speeches were made by all three Kennedy brothers, with the senator announcing that his youngest brother, only twenty-six and a University of Virginia law student, would be campaign manager.

There was only one striking similarity with the 1952 campaign—the role of Ambassador Kennedy. Once again he was behind the scenes, supervising, manipulating, running the show, and spending an estimated

$1.5 million. Again he removed himself to Beacon Street, subletting an apartment in the building of an old Harvard classmate, Massachusetts Chief Justice Raymond S. Wilkins. "It was the old man who really ran those goddamned campaigns, you know," one insider told Burton Hersh. Still, Jack Kennedy himself has been depicted as mediating between his father's desires and those of his staff.[9] "My father is a wonderful business-man, but as a politician he's well—that's something else," Jack was saying at the time.[10] When the Ambassador objected with some vehemence to Larry O'Brien's concentrated schedule of personal appearances for his son, arguing that television could be better utilized to reduce the physical strain, Jack interceded and O'Brien got his way.[11]

Sensitive to the charges of excessive wealth made by Celeste, the Kennedys tried to spend their money for the statewide campaign without giving the impression that the financing was lavish. Instead of local headquarters throughout the city of Boston, they opened a single down-town location at 170 Tremont Street. Gone, too, was the practice of papering everything in sight with Kennedy posters. Also slashed was the TV budget, sacrificed in favor of Jack's personal campaigning. Teddy manned the Tremont Street office and worked tirelessly, taking advantage of every chance to huckster additional votes. He was also, as *The Boston Globe* noted, "customarily surrounded by a flock of young beauties," despite the fact that he was already engaged to marry Joan Bennett, a Bronxville, New York, debutante he had met while at Manhattanville College for a dedication speech.[12] With Ted on Tremont Street was his brother-in-law, Steve Smith, who had become "comptroller of the currency," a post closely tied to the Park Avenue headquarters.

The Kennedy women and teas were largely superceded by personal visits throughout the state by Jacqueline. Appearing both with her husband as well as alone, she was thereby introduced to campaign politics, her French especially helpful with the large number of Massachusetts voters of Canadian origin. Her fluency with Italian was an additional asset to Kennedy among an ethnic group somewhat cooler to his appeal. "I always felt that Jackie was amused and somewhat intrigued by politics, by the people, and by the sheer spectacle of it," Larry O'Brien recalled. He also remembered how he had to hold the lighted cigarettes so Jackie could take furtive puffs while in public.[13]

Absent for most of the campaign was brother Bobby, whose work on the McClellan Committee received priority. But backing up the candidate with speech-writing functions was the ubiquitous Sorensen, by now a seasoned political hand, while Ralph Dungan and Fred Holborn assisted from the Washington office with research and final drafts. Many of Kennedy's speeches were composed by him from the memos they supplied and then dictated for final typing. In the Boston office, Frank Morrissey continued to tend to administrative details.

Their efforts against Celeste created fewer tensions than the rivalry between Jack Kennedy and Foster Furcolo, the consensus Irish Catholic and the ethnic half-Irish Italo-American. After the highly publicized television station incident during the 1954 campaign, the two men had staged a public rapprochement in time for Furcolo to win his governorship. Superficial handshaking, however, failed to conceal basic differences, both in temperament, party regularity, and appeal to different sectors of the electorate, with Furcolo retaining greater loyalty among the sizable numbers of those of Italian descent. Their 1954 blowup was almost duplicated two years later when harmony was supposedly in order. At radio station WBZ in Boston, Furcolo was present with the senator and Congressman McCormack for a campaign broadcast. As Furcolo remembers it, "McCormack's nephew Eddie, who was like a son, was running against Chris Herter, the son of the ex-Republican governor. John McCormack wanted to say a plug of some kind or other for his nephew. Kennedy said that if some words were said against Herter, he would get off and walk out in the middle of the program. Someone came to me to speak to Kennedy, and I said I wasn't going to interfere. But that was the position he took that time." Moreover, before that 1958 campaign began, Kennedy sought to convince Torby Macdonald to make a fight for the gubernatorial nomination, preferring to have his close friend instead of Furcolo join him on the statewide ticket. Macdonald at first agreed. He began to speak outside his district and did some statewide canvassing, before finally deciding he preferred Capitol Hill over the hazards of life in the labyrinth of Massachusetts politics. Nevertheless, the effort again demonstrated, as during those tense moments at the radio station, that any attempt at collaboration between the governor and the senator inevitably skirted a second falling-out.[14]

Repairing another weak area required intense interest in the Commonwealth's black vote. Wards Four, Nine and Twelve, within the city of Boston, were especially scrutinized through the efforts of Marjorie Lawson. Not only was there the simple numerical objective in getting out the strongest possible showing for the senator among blacks but, as Lawson reported back to Kennedy, "political analysts would look at the returns in these areas, whenever the Senator's candidacy for national office might become imminent."[15] Mounting a concerted effort, direct mailings were sent to registered voters in the predominantly black precincts. Most important, it included reprints of brochures and letters assuring those voters of Kennedy's position on civil rights as reported by black newspapers. Marjorie Lawson also worked with Ruth M. Batson, the president of the New England Region of the NAACP and the only black on the Democratic State Committee, in a get-out-the-vote campaign.[16]

This part of the civil-rights effort became all the more urgent when Kennedy found himself criticized, both pointedly and unfairly, by Roy Wilkins. The executive secretary of the NAACP appeared in Pittsfield, the leading center of the Berkshire section of Massachusetts, and condemned Kennedy's performance during the passage of the Civil Rights Act of 1957 and his chumminess with southern political leaders. Wilkins trod not too carefully between the accurate and the inaccurate, between the symbolic and the hyperbolic. Speaking on a Saturday night in April, he castigated Kennedy for his jury-trial amendment vote, which was fair enough. Kennedy had voted for it in cases of criminal contempt. But Wilkins went on to criticize Kennedy for his closeness to such segregationists as Senator Talmadge and Governor Marvin Griffin of Georgia; and Wilkins told the gathering of the New England NAACP that newspapers had carried pictures of Jack Kennedy smiling and embracing Griffin. "No pal of Griffin's can possibly be a pal of mine," said Wilkins. "Griffin thinks I'm an animal."[17]

The Kennedy staff, especially Lawson and Sorensen, worked at blunting the attack. A letter was drafted for Kennedy expressing his resentment at Wilkins's statements in the senator's home state, especially before the election, and, at least according to the newspaper reports, his failure to mention that Kennedy had supported the important Title III provision, which would have given implementive powers to the attorney general. Wilkins had referred to the Title III support, all right, but had simply done so within the context of saying that the Massachusetts senators had divided on that issue. He had, clearly, used the Pittsfield occasion not to praise Kennedy for Title III but to condemn him for the jury trial and his southern associations. Kennedy also denied that he had ever been photographed with Governor Griffin. He had seen him just twice, once at the 1956 convention and then when his old college classmate, Robert Troutman, Jr., of Atlanta, had invited the senator to deliver the University of Georgia commencement address.[18] Wilkins responded rather lamely with the acknowledgment that there had indeed been no Kennedy-Griffin photograph and what he had said had simply been "a figure of speech and was not intended to be a report of an actual photograph. . . . Your friendly reception by Deep Southerners easily conjures in the minds of Negro citizens a picture of you arm in arm with them," he wrote, and then noted that Kennedy was being "hailed by the Dixiecrat leaders of South Carolina, Georgia, and Mississippi, which, with Alabama, are the 'worst' states on the Negro question."[19]

Marjorie Lawson then became a significant figure in moving to repair the damage. She and the staff resented not only the attack from Wilkins but also from such NAACP leaders as Clarence Mitchell of the Washington office. They were zeroing in on Kennedy from among the nearly three dozen nonsouthern senators who had backed the jury trial, which, Kennedy let Wilkins know, raised a suspicion "among many liberal Senators that I have been singled out for political reasons," especially since Mitchell's close association with Vice-President Nixon was well known in Washington.[20] Kennedy also suggested that he and Wilkins meet at an early date.

Meanwhile, both Lawsons, Marjorie and her husband Belford, went to work with Boston's black leadership. In June the local NAACP was reorganized and Belford Lawson persuaded Herbert E. Tucker, Jr., the president of the Boston branch, to move toward healing matters by accepting the chairmanship of a dinner and tea designed to close the gap between the senator and the black community. Among their ranks substantial resistance continued—largely, however, confined to the NAACP officials. Remembering Nixon's tie-breaking vote on Rule XII in the Senate, they had little reason for less faith in the Vice-President's civil-rights commitment than Kennedy's. It was, in fact, a period when Nixon became an honorary member of the NAACP. Nevertheless, the anti-Kennedy sentiment was considerably diluted with the help of a clarifying letter sent by Wilkins to reduce the sting of his Pittsfield remarks. The letter, Lawson later reported, "followed efforts undertaken by Ted Sorensen in Washington and by me in New York." Both Lawsons also lobbied effectively with NAACP board members and managed to create considerable pressure on Wilkins to soften his position. Wilkins's letter was also read at the Boston dinner on October 18 and at an NAACP tea.[21] Their efforts ensured that there would be no substantial black defections to Celeste. To further help matters, Senator Douglas, while suppressing his own qualms about Jack's voting record and courting of southern politicians, came to Boston to vouch for Kennedy's civil-rights record. Lou Harris reported that seventy-four percent of the state's blacks planned to vote for the Democratic candidate against Celeste.

While Kennedy and the efforts of such people as the Lawsons and Sorensen effectively moved to repair much of the damage of the Wilkins statement, there is no real evidence of pending rank-and-file deterioration; as the Democratic candidate in that Massachusetts election, his share of the vote would have been substantial in any case. Its major influence was undoubtedly in encouraging a greater turnout. But, as Carl Brauer has pointed out, Kennedy's hold over that minority vote did not render them, at that point, among his most faithful supporters.[22]

In June, Furcolo's entry in the September primary for a second nomination was coupled with an endorsement of Kennedy's reelection. Within the next few weeks, local papers, carrying copy obviously produced in the candidate's headquarters, reported that both men had brought together "in active and enthusiastic collaboration thousands of party leaders and workers on every level to participate under inspired guidance," a collaboration, readers were told, that reached "a new high mark in effective party harmony in the state."[23] Two weeks later they were reported engaged in a joint voter-registration drive, one that foresaw the possibility of registering 300,000 new party members able to vote in November. "The cooperative registration drive of Kennedy and Gov. Furcolo," said the stories, "has produced the most effective and public-spirited demonstration of citizen participation in government ever recorded in the history of either party," with a pronounced shift away from the Republicans because of the "progressive stand by Furcolo and Kennedy in areas of unemployment and anti-recession measures."[24] Meanwhile, before the primary voting on September 9, Kennedy sailed to Europe with Jackie on a tour in connection with the Foreign Relations Committee, and Furcolo was left without a formidable Republican challenger with the death, just nine days before the primary, of state Attorney General George Fingold. Returning from Europe on the tenth, Kennedy learned the results of the primary.

Victory, of course, was never in doubt. Neither man had significant opposition. What rankled Kennedy were the figures showing him with 6,733 less statewide than Furcolo. More galling was the comparative count of blank ballots recorded for each man. In that category Kennedy received 7,293 more than Furcolo; or, to put it another way, the gubernatorial candidate outdid the senator by getting the support of seventy-nine percent. Kennedy's figure was seventy-eight percent.[25]

Immediate consternation arose. Some theorized that Kennedy had lost votes because, after having gotten the state legislature to arrange the primary ticket so that the Senate contest would head the paper ballots, his name appeared by itself in the first column on the left side, where voters could easily overlook it if they failed to unfold the sheet completely. And it was true that Kennedy did better with machines than with paper ballots. But in some heavily Democratic wards within the city of Boston, Furcolo ran ahead. In the largely Italian community of East Boston, Furcolo outdrew him 8,591 to 6,734, which was not surprising. More unsettling was Furcolo's 3,996 to 3,601 advantage in largely Irish Charlestown and 3,996 to 3,638 margin in South Boston, all wards with voting machines, leading to the inevitable suspicion that a combination of opponents had sabotaged the Kennedy vote. Followers of Curley and Burke were suspected, as well as unionists upset by Bobby's crusade against the Teamsters. Larry O'Brien reports another suspicion. "It was assumed," he wrote, "although there was no actual evidence, that Furcolo, because of the continuing Kennedy-Furcolo feud, had passed the word to his Italian-American followers to vote for Furcolo but not for Kennedy and, thus, to embarrass Kennedy." Accordingly, the senator exploded. "Damn it, Larry," he said, "I didn't go into politics to run behind Foster Furcolo. We've got to do better in the general election."[26]

The night after the primary, a strategy session took place in the home of Judge John F. Fox. In attendance were Furcolo and his campaign manager, Congressman O'Neill, a protégé of John McCormack. O'Neill's appointment to head the Furcolo campaign had been made with the approval of Ambassador Kennedy, thereby satisfying the congressman's conditional acceptance of the designation. The group in Judge Fox's home decided on a joint television appearance by both Kennedy and Furcolo, although the governor doubted that Jack would be agreeable. When Tip O'Neill informed Kennedy, who was in Palm Beach, that a joint program had been set for the following Tuesday evening, Kennedy exploded about his having acted without his knowledge or prior approval and warned of the need for advance consultation before any further sessions were scheduled.[27]

Coordinating campaign activities with Furcolo had distinct limitations. The governor's greatest strength came from his appeal to party loyalty. Kennedy's style and flair for independence transcended ethnic attractions and appealed to the broad range of Massachusetts voters. The Kennedy camp also refused to go along with the Furcolo request for conjoint bumper stickers and suffered in silence when the governor's campaign committee acted unilaterally by displaying both candidates side by side on billboards throughout the Commonwealth. Nor did the

Kennedy campaign welcome the inherently partisan support of Harry S Truman.[28]

As election day neared, Kennedy's anxieties grew. Especially because of Celeste, only a solid majority of at least 500,000 votes could constitute a victory. Kennedy and the Ambassador agreed that that would clear the way to the presidency.[29] During those final seventy-two hours, radio and TV promotion increased sharply. On the night of Sunday, November 3, Kennedy appeared with Furcolo, John McCormack, and the congressman's nephew Edward McCormack (whom the governor had appointed to fill the attorney general's vacancy created by the death of Fingold) for a joint television appearance. When the big day came, the senator awaited the returns in his father's Beacon Street apartment.

He didn't remain long. From the earliest count the trend was unmistakable. A great and emphatic victory was being recorded with heavy margins over Celeste coming from every part of the state. Even the tiny Berkshire County town of Mt. Washington, in the extreme southwestern corner of Massachusetts, abandoned its traditional Republicanism and went for Kennedy. When he joined the crowd at Tremont Street, it was with Jackie, Bobby's wife Ethel, his sister Jean and brother Ted. They all walked through the throng of well-wishers. Some were hailing "our next President." Kennedy kept shaking hands freely and smiling, then led his entourage to a visit of the city's newspaper offices and radio and television stations.[30]

He had accomplished his mission against Celeste. A record turnout for an off-year election had given Kennedy 73.6 percent of the total senatorial vote, even greater than the previous high achieved by Leverett Saltonstall in 1944. But that was a presidential election year, with heavier voting. The final returns showed Kennedy's at 874,608. He was doubtless also pleased to learn that Furcolo had won with just 56.2 percent.[31]

Throughout the country, Democrats did well. In California, Senator William Knowland, having staked his political future on support of a right-to-work referendum, was solidly defeated by Edmund "Pat" Brown. Unions, spurred into action by the deepening recession, accomplished their goal in seventy percent of the congressional elections. Kennedy's Labor and Public Welfare Committee gained two additional Democrats and his subcommittee remained in liberal hands—all apparently a discouraging portent for those seeking to achieve more restrictive labor legislation.

In the entire nation, only Mike Mansfield of Montana, with 76.2 percent, had won a Senate seat with a greater margin than Kennedy.

New York State's gubernatorial election, in defiance of the Democratic trend, produced a decisive loss by the incumbent, Averell Harriman, to Nelson Rockefeller. Writing from Washington, D.C., on November 9, James Reston noted that the nation's newspapers and television screens were preoccupied with the two new personality champions of American politics, Rockefeller and Kennedy. "The emphasis," he wrote, "has been on how to win the Presidency rather than on how to run it."[32] That same day, Reston was also one of Kennedy's interviewers on the nationally televised *Meet the Press* program.

"Senator Kennedy," asked *The New York Times*'s Washington correspondent, "are you now seeking delegates to the 1960 Presidential Nominating Convention?"

"I am not."

Reston, persisting: "Have you established or will you establish headquarters looking to 1960?"

"No."

"Do you have any plans to go into the preferential primaries of 1960?" Reston tried again.

"I don't."

Now Reston wanted to know "what is it about the mythology of American politics that makes candidates for the presidency not admit that they are candidates?"

"Well," replied the senator, "I think mythology and the Bible has told us that there is a time and place for everything. We have just finished a campaign for the Senate. Nineteen sixty is two years away. It seems to me for those men who might be candidates, that the appropriate time for them to make a final decision is in 1960 and when they have made a final decision, to announce it."

In response to further questioning, Kennedy said it was "unfortunate" that so many Republicans had chosen to wage their campaigns against Walter Reuther instead of Jimmy Hoffa, "who was surrounded by racketeers and crooks and who himself shouldn't hold the position of responsibility that he does." He also voiced confidence that the new Congress would pass the Kennedy-Ives Bill.[33]

After that Sunday program, Kennedy flew west, pausing to speak to local Democrats in Seattle before changing planes and going on to Ketchikan, Alaska, an eight-thousand-mile flight to promote Democratic fortunes in the newly admitted state's November 25 elections. Returning well before Teddy's wedding on the twenty-ninth, Jack Kennedy was best man when his youngest brother married Joan Bennett.

The ceremony, officiated by Francis Cardinal Spellman, took place at St. Joseph's Church, in Bronxville, which the Kennedys had attended during their years on Pondfield Road.

Ken O'Donnell and Dave Powers, describing their mood once Kennedy had been reelected, have written that "we were already thinking about the next ball game."[34] Cocky or not, the arithmetic bolstered their ability to look forward to the coming tests with considerable optimism. The Massachusetts outcome received national attention. Democratic state chairmen, polled by the Associated Press, agreed that Kennedy was the most likely nominee for 1960.[35] Henry Luce's flagship publication, *Time,* agreed, even while expressing the common caveat that Kennedy could still become "one of the flowers that bloom in the spring," wilting in the end under such crushing liabilities as his age, religion, farmer opposition, and the general belief that Daddy Kennedy would spend endlessly to ensure success.[36]

The postelection Gallup surveys added confirmation but also, like *Time,* suggested the need for caution. The Democratic rank and file still preferred Stevenson over all other possibilities, and Kennedy was the only one even close. Among independents, however, Stevenson faded and Kennedy led the field by ten percentage points. Dropping all other names, as the Gallup poll showed a few days later, gave Kennedy a "trial heat" tie with Stevenson among all voters and a seventeen-point lead with independents. Within the following week, subsequent figures showed Kennedy with a comfortable edge over two of the leading Republican rivals, Nixon and Rockefeller.[37] The Rockefeller prominence made for uneasiness, as some suggested that the Democrats would be reluctant to nominate Kennedy against New York's Republican governor because they would thereby throw away the rich-man argument.[38]

Simultaneously, Ted Sorensen had begun implementing the apparatus long since prepared for utilizing the academic clusters in New England. He had in mind their expertise in such fields as defense, foreign policy, public health and medical research, education, agriculture, fiscal affairs, outer-space science, etc. Sorensen's initial meeting with the area's professors took place at the Hotel Commander in Cambridge on Wednesday, December 3. Under the nominal chairmanship of Latham, who was then in Cambridge only temporarily and unable to perform leadership or organizational functions, the professors were brought together as an Academic Advisory Committee. Thus began the Kennedy "brain trust," with such academics as Paul Samuelson, Arthur Schlesinger, Jr., Archibald Cox, John Kenneth Galbraith, Abe Chayes, Seymour Harris,

Jerome Wiesner, Walt Whitman Rostow, and Henry Kissinger.[39] Daniel Ellsberg, then a fellow at Harvard and associated with the Rand Corporation, contributed analyses of defense matters.

Kissinger, it was clear even then, owed his first loyalty to Governor Rockefeller, whom he was serving as a foreign-policy adviser. Then at the head of Harvard's Defense Studies Program, Kissinger denigrated Kennedy's chances of making it all the way to the top. But he hedged his bets, directing his administrative assistant, Deirdre Henderson, a young Wells College graduate, to respond positively to requests for assistance from both men. Kissinger's avowed Republicanism had little to do with determining his ultimate allegiance. When Henderson met Kennedy and expressed her concern about Kissinger's dual role, the senator laughed it off with the comment, "They're all the same—don't worry about it." Kennedy appeared not to care whether Kissinger "worked for ten people, I'm sure."[40]

Nor did Jack Kennedy have many illusions about the rest of the intellectual community. They were sources to be tapped, advisers for rumination, and an influential body to woo, especially since their loyalties were still principally with such possible rivals as Stevenson and Senator Hubert H. Humphrey. He also, as Chayes recalled, had "a good perception of the relation between the scholarly community and the governmental community." He remained skeptical and, as his father had drummed into him, knew the value of contradictory opinions and the hazards of modish academic theories. Meeting with them several times that year, he demonstrated "what was his beautifully subtle and discriminatory mastery of both the fact of any problem and the considerations bearing on a solution to it."[41] In their informal sessions, Kennedy gathered comments from each expert. Once, Chayes remembered, he went around the table of some thirty professors, "all of them quite distinguished, and asked each of them to say what it was in his particular field that people should be working at in Washington and . . . I just remember a terrible sense of inadequacy in the response of this collection of brains; nobody really was able to come up with anything terribly important."[42] Clearly, they were more impressed with him than he was with them. His few off-the-cuff remarks were usually highly effective. Henderson remembers that each time the professors met the senator "they became more impressed with his brain power, that there was substance as well as charm." Overall, "he had more perspective than some of them did on the balance between conservative policy and liberal policy."[43]

They were mainly "liberal liberals" who had tended to view Kennedy "as much more in the middle, as a pragmatist, as the good-looking Washington Senator." He was not a typical intellectual, so they failed to perceive him as one of their own. His credentials defied their prejudices. They tended to be suspicious of Boston's Irish Catholic leadership, and any son of Joseph P. Kennedy could not be wholly immune from such influences. His failure to develop the "proper" position vis-à-vis Joe McCarthy seemed consistent with his background. He was flirting with the South and having it both ways over civil rights. Academicians were especially mindful of his earlier foreign-policy statements that seemed to reflect "China Lobby" positions. Still, as Paul Samuelson has observed, for all their reservations, the Massachusetts academics had less resistance to Kennedy because, unlike colleagues in other parts of the country, they had been subjected to a much more formidable "softening-up process." Even later, colleagues Samuelson met in California could not understand how anybody could be for him.

Such views were most distressing when uttered by one so influential among Democratic liberals as Eleanor Roosevelt. She had long since become the "grand old lady" of the party, the most visible link between the New Deal past, now considerably embellished by romantic memories of the old idealism, and the progressive minority of the decade that resisted the "man in the gray flannel suit" mentality of Sloane Wilson's "hero" and William Whyte's "organization man." To one with her frame of references, Kennedy epitomized the new managerial elite that had neither principles nor character, that had neither heart nor a keen understanding of government in modern American society.

Mostly, an accumulation of experiences had sharpened her bias. She had backed Kennedy over Lodge in 1952, numbering him among "these young courageous representatives," but the distaste of the past still lingered. There had been the matter of his father that especially aroused her hostility. That the son was merely a carbon copy of the father was doubtless reinforced when Congressman Kennedy, in the midst of her dispute with Cardinal Spellman, supported federal aid for parochial-school students. Although consciousness of a national constituency led Kennedy to reverse himself on aid for parochial schools, Mrs. Roosevelt's continuing fear of the Church fortified suspicions.[44] All doubts were reaffirmed when, after her support for his senatorial seat, he failed to react positively against McCarthy. Despite vigorous efforts to woo her, she remained adamant.

Her mind appeared set. In early 1957 she pointedly excluded Jack Kennedy from a list of potential presidential candidates that included

Wayne Morse, Joseph Clark, Mennen Williams, Edmund Muskie, and Chester Bowles.[45] When *The Saturday Evening Post* serialized her memoirs, she attributed the McCarthy issue to her attitude during the convention and then told an interviewer that she remained opposed to Kennedy. Jim Landis, acting on the direction of the Ambassador, played peacemaker and returned empty-handed. Dismissing her as hopelessly anti-Catholic, Joe Kennedy washed his hands of the matter; but Jack cited her backing for Al Smith in 1928 and was less convinced the cause was lost.[46] There matters rested but briefly, until she appeared on the *College News Conference* TV program on December 7, 1958, one month after Kennedy's reelection, and made her most acerbic attack yet.

Of all the Democratic candidates, she said, Humphrey came closest to having the "spark of greatness." Kennedy, while obviously a young man with much charm, was not someone with whom she would feel comfortable placing future difficult decisions. While the senator understood and admired courage, he "has not quite the independence to have it." Making her meaning unmistakable, she added that the Ambassador had been spending "oodles of money all over the country" for his son and "probably has paid representatives in every state by now," an effort that would be "perfectly permissible" if the senator had done it for himself.[47]

Thus began a direct exchange between Jack Kennedy and the venerable "Mrs. R." Kennedy challenged her to name "one such representative or one such example of any spending by my father around the country on my behalf."[48] She hedged. Lacking specific information, she rested her case on having been "told that your father said openly he would spend any money to make his son the first Catholic President of this country, and many people, as I travel about, tell me of money spent by him in your behalf. This seems commonly accepted as a fact."[49] Had she known Kennedy better, she would have thought twice before issuing that sort of explanation. Predictably, but politely, he expressed "disappointment" that she had been open to "rumor or allegation" and assumed her argument could produce nothing more than "gossip and speculation." If nothing more solid turned up, he suggested, her "reputation for fairness" could be preserved by correcting "the record in a fair and gracious manner."[50] In her newspaper column of January 6, she acceded to his request for "fairness" by printing an extended portion of his letter, which still failed to satisfy Kennedy's desire for a direct statement that she had "been unable to find evidence to justify the rumors." But, he indicated, he was ready to let the matter drop if *she* felt the column had done the job. She persisted, however, offering to write another column on the controversy and lamely stated that she had never claimed that her opposition to him was based on such rumors. "Maybe," she wrote, "like in the case of my family, you suffer from the mere fact that many people know your father and also know that there is money in your family. We have always found somewhat similar things occur, and except for a few names I could not name the people in the case of my family."[51]

Kennedy had had enough. He withdrew, merely thanking her for her letter and the offer of another column, saying "I believe we can let it stand for the present." One week later, on January 29, Mrs. Roosevelt used Western Union to fire off the following communication: MY DEAR BOY I ONLY SAY THESE THINGS FOR YOUR OWN GOOD I HAVE FOUND IN LIFETIME OF ADVERSITY THAT WHEN BLOWS ARE RAINED ON ONE, IT IS ADVISABLE TO TURN THE OTHER PROFILE.[52]

26

Courting the Liberals

Mrs. Roosevelt's bilious telegram reached Kennedy precisely as he attempted to improve his civil-liberties reputation. Together with a liberal colleague from Pennsylvania, Joseph S. Clark, Jr., Philadelphia's former "good government" mayor and an ADA stalwart, Kennedy introduced a bill aimed at striking from the National Defense Education Act of 1958 requirements for affidavits of loyalty and statements of allegiance as prerequisites for both students and teachers seeking education loans. Previously, the Kennedy-Ives Bill had sought to relieve labor leaders from what many considered one of the more demeaning and ineffectual vestiges of the domestic Cold War. Now, supported by a wide array of the nation's leading university and college presidents, he questioned both the logic and value of such tests in academia.

Two years after the death of Joe McCarthy, inhibitions remained; "softness" toward communism was still perceived as potentially lethal. Kennedy managed to maneuver the bill through the Labor Committee and then, as Joe Clark recalled, "We took about an equal part in the floor debate."[1] Opposition was vigorous, especially from such "dedicated" anti-Communists as Karl Mundt of South Dakota. Finally, to make it palatable for conservatives and timid liberals, Winston Prouty, a Vermont Republican, successfully obtained an amendment that would have repealed only the affidavit. Loyalty-oath requirements were kept, while perjury penalties were added for false swearing. Kennedy, hesitant about accepting the change, was finally convinced by Leverett Saltonstall to go along; but, withal, the bill was recommitted and killed for that session.[2]

Why the Kennedy effort? Abe Chayes later said he had "reasons" for believing that Kennedy had acted to offset his taint on the McCarthy question. It also served as a good talking point for promoting his candidacy among other academics.[3] Meyer Feldman, however, interviewed much earlier, while the campaign preliminaries were under way, said it had all been Kennedy's own idea, without any prior discussion. He explained that the senator telephoned from Florida one midnight and simply said, "I've been thinking about that loyalty oath for teachers and I think it ought to be thrown out." Feldman and Sorensen then worked on it; Kennedy added polish; then the recommendations were made. Unlike Chayes, who recalled selling the change to Kennedy via Sorensen, Feldman remains convinced that his actions on the matter were not governed by political expediency.[4]

Despite Feldman's testimony, Kennedy's motivations were clearly less than one hundred percent pure. The pressures exerted by the liberal intellectuals he was trying to cultivate, let alone the skepticism of an Eleanor Roosevelt, argued for opposing the loyalty oath as a cleansing ploy, a timely trim. Kennedy often made private comments about the ethics of an *ex post facto* denunciation of the dead McCarthy. Opposing loyalty oaths placed him on the side of championing civil liberties without the need to make what he considered a retroactive "cheap shot" against the late senator. Undoubtedly, too, such oaths offended his classical liberal concern with individual freedom. Appearing before the Philadelphia chapter of the Americans for Democratic Action, Joe Clark's group, the day after the bill was introduced in the Senate, Kennedy found a receptive audience. He associated himself with the purest New Deal liberalism. He called the Eisenhower administration "tired and timid" and outlined the "malign effects" of "poverty, discrimination, illness and injustice." Referring to civil liberties, he warned that the nation faced "new inroads on the public's right to know" with "new expansion instead of limitations on wiretapping."[5]

Nor did he confine himself to just that band of liberals at the Roosevelt Day Dinner. For the benefit of William Evjue, the editor of the vigorously anti-McCarthy Madison *Capital Times* in Wisconsin, he reported that he had found similar concern over loyalty oaths among "many educators" in the Philadelphia area.[6]

Adlai Stevenson's associate, Bill Blair, undertook the task of mailing to Mrs. Roosevelt an updated accounting of Kennedy's civil-liberties record "sent to me by a friend in Washington." Needless to say, Blair also informed her, "I am not supporting anyone for the Democratic nomination in 1960, but I do think Jack Kennedy's record on civil liberties is better than he is sometimes given credit for."[7] Chester Bowles, then serving a term in the House, assured Kennedy he could be counted on to get to "Mrs. R." wherever and whenever possible.[8] After Kennedy faced liberal Democratic leaders at a Jefferson-Jackson Day dinner in Detroit on May 23, Michigan's party chairman, Neil Staebler, wrote Sorensen that Kennedy had "greatly strengthened the hopes of many of us who want to regard him as a practicing, outspoken liberal. He made an indelible impression of a man of great spirit and good will."[9] Kennedy followed through in July, just before the bottling-up of the amended version, by directing Staebler's attention to the legislation "in the hope that you may see fit to exert your leadership in the Party on behalf of this measure."[10]

The bill was lost, but the point was made. At precisely that moment, however, a new embarrassment threatened. Word reached Kennedy that the Madison *Capital Times,* whether at Evjue's initiative or through some other staff members, might resurrect from oblivion John Mallan's version of Kennedy's 1950 Harvard talk—at this point a potentially devastating ghost. Anxiously, Kennedy appealed to Arthur Holcombe. "This is part of the same old idea that I was somehow 'soft' on McCarthyism," he explained, and requested a "letter indicating the falsehoods in this article."[11] Holcombe's papers lack authorship of any further defense. Very likely, the professor preferred to rest on his explanation that had been published in *The New Republic* shortly after the article appeared, which mainly charged that Mallan had violated the seminar's off-the-record ground rules.

Spending an evening with Governor Gaylord Nelson of Wisconsin, in whose state's presidential preference primary Kennedy hoped to enter, Arthur Schlesinger, Jr., found the chief executive familiar with the Mallan story. The governor was eager to know about any possible disavowal beyond Holcombe's concern with confidentiality. Schlesinger knew of none. Their session also convinced the Harvard historian that attempted refutations should be done by passing the word around privately to certain "strategic individuals" and, at the same time, avoiding public statements that would simply give the incident more publicity.[12] Shortly afterward, when, as the author of a proposed biography of Kennedy, James MacGregor Burns showed the senator a draft of the manuscript with a description of Mallan's account, Kennedy penciled in the margin the comment that the reportage was inaccurate. Although Mallan had long since published the revelation that he had personally asked one of the provocative questions at the seminar, Kennedy's notation denied that the author had been present. Sorensen added the objection that the "Mallan article is dignified by your book instead of being exposed for what it is." Burns, however, rejected the misinformation about Mallan's absence and, while keeping the account substantially intact, balanced his rendition by citing others who recalled Kennedy's talk as "not philosophical but mainly practical" and "more personal and political than ideological."[13] How close *The Capital Times* came to reviving *The New Republic* article or whether Evjue was dissuaded either directly or through a Kennedy partisan, such as Madison's mayor, Ivan Nestigen, may never be known. None of the principals remain to testify. One can reasonably surmise that, for John F. Kennedy, at that moment in his preparations for formal candidacy, it was a close call.

Only an appreciation of Kennedy's difficulties in convincing liberals of his attractiveness can fully enable one to gauge how destructive it would have been for the Mallan matter to have been resurrected at that moment. The aura of opportunism and ideological coquettishness persisted, it seemed, no matter what he said or did. Pat McNamara, who served with him on the McClellan Committee, told Drew Pearson, "As between Kennedy and Nixon if they both were running for President, I would have a hard time making up my mind who to vote for."[14] Pearson personally accepted that evaluation, as did Eric Sevareid, who was writing a book about potential candidates for 1960. Schlesinger has written that at Cambridge he and Galbraith "resolved to do what we could to combat the growing mistrust."[15]

There were times when it seemed all too much. Just what did he have to do to prove that he could win? What would satisfy the party's doctrinaire liberals? He felt that they would have liked to have seen him make what he regarded as a gratuitous and even undignified postmortem attack on McCarthy in the vilest of language, thereby denouncing, in effect, not only his own past but his family's associations and values. They would have liked to have seen him, in equally harsh terms, denounce southern resistance to integration and speak with the moral fervor of a Martin Luther King. Satisfying them also meant embracing massive social programs. They were not interested in new ideas, independent thought; they were eager to replace Eisenhower conservativism with a social welfare type of democracy. They were, in short, ready to have Kennedy burdened with the kind of positions that would have made him totally unacceptable to all but the liberal-labor-intellectual wing of the party, thereby making his nomination impossible, a dilemma that already plagued Hubert Humphrey, who faced continuing southern opposition because of his advanced views on civil rights and unions. And even if Kennedy became the candidate, that position would have made him incompatible with the electorate. He was already having enough trouble with the issues of youth and Catholicism. How absurd he would be to go before the nation as a brash youth and radical Catholic. Besides, that would not be Jack Kennedy.

Nor would it have suited Stevenson's character. But the Stevenson partisans overlooked such limitations in their hero. He did not need such purity. *His* disdain for the masses and moderation in civil rights and economic issues were the virtues of a cultivated, cultured, doyen, one who, despite his prejudices, was trusted as an instinctive progressive. He was, however, seventeen years older, not a Catholic, and not the son of Joseph P. Kennedy.

Nothing Stevenson said seemed to convince them that the party's titular leader was out of the picture. Stevenson then acted with apparent firmness. One month after his defeat in 1956, the Governor declared that he was withdrawing from presidential politics and indicated his preference for devoting himself to the newly established Democratic Advisory Council. Appearing on *Meet the Press* in May of 1957, he disclaimed another try for the White House. Later he told a New York City press conference that he could "conceive of no circumstance" that would make him do so. "I will not be the nominee," he said in June of 1959, and stated over a *College Press Conference* TV broadcast in December his preference "to maintain an attitude of vertical neutrality" in the coming campaign. That same month, Stevenson told Schlesinger that he had considered issuing what he mistakenly called a "Grant statement," thereby substituting the name of the Civil War general who had become a president, for the general who had actually made that statement, William T. Sherman. Schlesinger noted in his diary that Stevenson had made a "interesting Freudian slip."[16] Stevenson's longtime law associate, J. Edward Day, later recalled a conversation he had with the Governor shortly afterward. "Oh no," Stevenson told him that day. "I'm not going to be a candidate. I want you to talk to a lot of these friends of ours. They're talking about me running, and tell them to stop talking about me running." Day told him that if Stevenson was not going to become a candidate, he was going to come out for Kennedy. Stevenson replied to that with, "Well, I think the Catholic issue is going to be badly against him, and, after all, Nixon must be beaten." Day thought that what Stevenson really meant was, "I want to be urged to run, and I want to be nominated."[17]

To his friends, Stevenson's most frequently repeated theme was the importance of keeping Nixon from the presidency, which was why Bill Blair wanted him to support Kennedy, who, Blair thought, was the only sure one who could realize that goal.[18] To another associate, John Sharon, Stevenson expressed reservations, not about Jack Kennedy himself, whom he called "first rate," but about Joe Kennedy and about the Ambassador's prewar position. "If the Governor had liked Jack Kennedy more, he might have had a different attitude, but he thought Jack Kennedy was a kid and inexperienced, and he thought the family was throwing their money around and this and that. So that was a big part of the problem," Newton Minow has said.[19] As early as 1957, Kennedy conveyed his determination to Stevenson through Minow. As Minow remembered the conversation, they were together at a dinner when he said to Kennedy, "You know, Jack, if you are interested in politics in 1960 and if you are alive, you can be the Democratic nominee for vice-president." Kennedy looked at Minow and said, "Vice-president? I'm not interested in running for vice-president. I'm interested in running for president." Minow thought he was being wildly optimistic, absurd. "You're only thirty-nine years old, you haven't got a chance to run for president," he told him. And Kennedy said, "No, Newt, if I'm ever going to make it I'm going to make it in 1960. I'm going to go for president."[20]

Stevenson had also promised both Lyndon Johnson and Stuart Symington that he would remain neutral. It was Johnson, however, to whom the Governor had moved especially close. In a talk with Stevenson, Johnson delivered a venemous anti-Kennedy tirade and expressed his own determination to fight for the nomination to the end, promising that if he could not get it, he would throw all his support to Stevenson. He kept taking from his pocket reports of voter surveys that he said supported his point that Kennedy could not win an election. As Sharon heard it, Johnson said to Stevenson, "It's either going to be you or it's going to be me, and if it isn't going to be me it's going to be you, and

I'll see to it you get it. Whoever you want on the ticket, that's your decision."[21]

Throughout this period, Stevenson and Kennedy played coy with each other, their contacts mostly going through such intermediaries as Bill Blair and Schlesinger. Sharon thought that Kennedy made a great mistake by not phoning the Governor personally more often. Instead, Jack's usual route went through Blair, a course that left Stevenson considerably annoyed. At the same time, both men watched each other with intense interest. Kennedy discounted the potency of Humphrey's candidacy, feeling that hostility to the liberal among southerners would finally kill his chances. He also doubted that Johnson could surmount the northern liberal opposition. Therefore, only Stevenson was a formidable obstruction. No matter what Kennedy said to the contrary, he had always had it in the back of his mind that, in the end, he might have to settle and accept second place on a Stevenson ticket.[22] When, in April of 1959, a friendly journalist told Stevenson about his travels with Kennedy, Stevenson expressed personal doubts about him. Nevertheless, he tried to follow the senator's progress closely. Meeting with the Governor again in Libertyville that spring, the journalist, John Steele of *Time,* found Stevenson not very sympathetic to Kennedy's problem of overcoming his youthful appearance and the public image of "that nice young man from back east." Stevenson, on that occasion, wondered if Kennedy had the balance and judgment to lead the nation, and, reminiscent of an attitude he had expressed before toward Estes Kefauver, speculated aloud about Jack appearing too eager and seeking the presidency with too much passion. While his private preference was clearly for Humphrey, he was concerned that Symington might emerge as the nominee, thereby bringing in the "old Truman crowd." Should that become a real possibility, Stevenson talked about acting to bring together Humphrey and Kennedy, or perhaps endorsing one or the other in order to stop Symington.[23] Jim Rowe, who was working and traveling with Humphrey, told Stevenson about his confidence that the Governor's partisans, the "issue" people, were largely behind Humphrey. "In some states he is second to you. In others it is Stevenson or Humphrey," Rowe explained.[24] When a Rowland Evans, Jr., story appeared stating that Stevenson preferred Johnson, the Governor issued a statement dismissing it as a "total fabrication" and promptly notified Kennedy, along with Johnson, Humphrey, and Symington, of his disavowal.[25] Schlesinger, meeting with Kennedy at Hyannis Port in July, found the senator inclined toward either Humphrey or Governor Orville Freeman of Minnesota as his running mate, but fearful that Stevenson's "sleeping candidacy" was his greatest threat.[26]

According to information received by Rowe, George Meany considered any one of three possible candidates, Humphrey, Symington, or Kennedy, as friendly to labor, "but not Adlai."[27] That meant both Reuther and Meany were finding Kennedy acceptable. Even to the Stevensonian doubters, more and more toward late 1959 they were coming around to the view that Kennedy would be the best number-two man behind the Governor. When Chester Bowles informed Stevenson that Governor Nelson was strongly in favor of a Stevenson-Kennedy ticket and that other Democrats were hopeful that Stevenson "could somehow be induced to run," the party's titular leader expressed his interest in the report and shared the view that "for Kennedy to enter the primary there is only going to embarrass and aggravate Gaylord Nelson and probably lead to an unspectacular victory which will not help him very much. If he challenges Brown or DiSalle, he will earn a lot of ill will in their states. Thank God, I don't have to worry about these things any more!"[28]

The resistance of few groups was as painful or frustrating to John Kennedy as was that of the reform Democrats of Manhattan County in New York City. Few matched the intense hostility toward his entire milieu: his faith, his father, his McCarthy taint, his "Boston hack" associates, his dubious liberalism—more than anything else, perhaps, his pretense to the throne rightfully Stevenson's. He had had an old Princeton association, however brief, with Jack Baltzell, now in 1959 the reform leader of the Ninth Assembly District; a South Pacific PT boat friendship with Anthony Akers, a three-time anti-Tammany Hall congressional candidate and now the chairman of the New York City Community Mental Health Board; and socialized with the congenial aristocratic group that included such young, bright, and industrious "good government," "silk stocking district" campaigners as Catherine and Russell D. Hemenway. There also was the outstanding attorney and former law professor, Lloyd K. Garrison, certainly of impeccable lineage, and the well-to-do and well-connected Thomas K. Finletter, who had served Truman as secretary of the Air Force.

It had been Finletter who had taken his suggestion in 1953 and gone on to organize an informal group of brain-trusters to formulate liberal positions on the vital issues of the day. The ex-Air Force secretary also helped raise funds for the Democratic Advisory Council, a sort of shadow government of Stevensonians that operated out of an apartment on Constitution Avenue, removed from Capitol Hill and the Johnson-Rayburn leadership. The most fateful turning point, however, had come at the party's state convention in Buffalo, when Finletter's senatorial nomination was quashed by the power of the New York State Chairman, Michael Prendergast, and Tammany Hall leader Carmine DeSapio. At DeSapio's direction, the nomination had gone to District Attorney Frank Hogan, a poor candidate in any event—but, more important, the symbolic triumph of the "bosses." After Hogan lost the general election to Kenneth Keating, while Nelson Rockefeller completed the Republican success by winning the governorship, Finletter, Lehman, and Mrs. Roosevelt formed what they called the Committee for Democratic Voters.

The New York reform movement dated from shortly after Truman's surprise victory of 1948 with the formation by Upper East Side "silk-stocking" Manhattanites in the Ninth Assembly District of the Lexington Democratic Club. Independently well off, they sought to replace traditional clubhouse leaders with a new political breed—more idealistic, more concerned with issues and principles. With Mrs. Roosevelt, they fumed when DeSapio delivered the state's delegation to Harriman rather than Stevenson in 1956.[29]

While DeSapio and the organization appeared to favor Johnson for 1960, the Roosevelt-Lehman-Finletter group pushed for Stevenson. Those behind Kennedy were such county leaders as Charlie Buckley in the Bronx, Peter Crotty in Erie, and John English, a youthful, crew-cut lawyer in suburban Nassau, who looked not at all like the stereotyped Irish politicians who made second homes out of neighborhood clubhouses. Ethnic and cultural rivalries further strained the competition. Liberal upper-middle-class Catholics were in short supply, and the reformers were predominantly Jewish, or white Anglo-Saxon Protestants, and mostly Ivy League. A pronounced suspicion of Catholic politicians and the Church colored their views. Those who counted themselves among Kennedy's grass-roots supporters were predominantly Catholic. In certain places, especially upstate New York, they swapped Italian identities for Irish surnames. Moreover, to Stevensonians, the Kennedy pluggers were déclassé hacks, recalling the cigar-chomping, beer-guzzling, ethnic politics of clubhouse lore. Richard Wade, then a professor of history at the University of Rochester, recalls how identification as a Kennedy supporter was then tantamount to being categorized among the lower orders.[30]

Early in Kennedy's senatorial career, when Tony Akers ran with

Lexington Club blessing to unseat Republican Congressman Frederick Coudert, Jack Kennedy was persuaded to appear at a well-publicized and well-attended rally for his old PT boat friend in the Yorkville part of the district. Reformers remembered how, at that occasion, when their hope had been to attract some Irish Catholic support, he "lit no fires at all." After a heroic introduction, embellished with tales of the South Pacific and the glories of his magnificent family, he appeared jocular, told one lame joke, and "bombed out," raising doubts about being of any future value.[31] A more updated effort to win over some Irish Catholics to the Committee for Democratic Voters was the enrolling of Police Commissioner Francis Adams. Adams was ethnic window dressing.[32] And he was for Jack, declaring quietly and, conscious of his reform surroundings, with a letter to the senator acknowledging that "this may well be a lethal embrace and I want you to feel entirely free to disregard it."[33]

Weaning away Stevenson's affluent Protestant and Jewish supporters was one matter, but despite a continued feeling that Humphrey was too "leftish" to win, he was somewhat of a greater threat than the Governor because of his appeal to party regulars, many of whom were ready to support a Humphrey-Kennedy ticket.[34] Their reluctance to believe that Kennedy could actually be nominated also encouraged toying around with a Stevenson-Kennedy combination. Some, in fact, appeared to be "commuting" between the two candidates. People like John Sharon and Bill Blair were "friendly" to Kennedy but loyal Stevensonians when dealing with the reformers, while Minow remained responsive to getting behind the senator if the Governor remained coy. Schlesinger, close to all three principles—Humphrey, Stevenson, and Kennedy—tried to keep his friends, Tom Finletter and Marietta Tree, the latter a Lexington Club stalwart related to the Massachusetts Peabodys, open-minded about Kennedy. Following an unproductive Kennedy-Finletter talk that spring, Schlesinger arranged to bring them together again at Locke-Ober's in Boston after the Harvard commencement in early June. Finletter first went on the *Let's Find Out* radio interview program and defended his committee against Prendergast's charges that they were pushing their own candidate. Nor was it true, he added, that they were "particularly and specifically" against Kennedy and, at the same time, tried to quash notions that religion had anything to do with it.[35]

Their Locke-Ober conference seems to have gone well. Kennedy said most of the right things, including opposition to Lewis Strauss as Eisenhower's secretary of commerce, a cause that had become the bête noire of the liberals. Schlesinger, who was also present, later wrote that "Finletter thereafter succeeded to some degree in tempering the anti-Kennedy reflexes of the New York reformers."[36]

With good reason, close associates doubt Finletter's fidelity to the Stevenson cause. Their own preference for the Governor—or Humphrey, as an alternative—rendered Jack unacceptable, his utility shaping up mainly as a vice-presidential choice on a Stevenson ticket, a balance that could soften some Roman Catholic resistance. As receptive to Kennedy as Finletter was getting, his ambiance was permeated with those far more liberal, far more resistant toward a Roman Catholic, and much more reflective of Eleanor Roosevelt's hostility toward a son of Joseph P. Kennedy. From Finletter's position, it was much easier to be swept along than to buck the tide. If he could reverse things, however, the potential importance to Kennedy could be great. Kennedy's ability to win over the New York reformers, like their Massachusetts counterparts, was viewed as an essential step in attracting other clusters of the party's intellectual left wing, the Stevenson loyalists.[37]

That August, while Kennedy's Washington activities were devoted to salvaging the remnants of the labor-reform legislation, jarring news came from New York. It had not been unexpected. Prendergast announced that the county chairman had decided that the delegation would attend the national convention without its usual support for a favorite-son candidate. Worse than that was the decision to back Mayor Robert Wagner as the favorite son for the vice-presidency, under the assumption that despite his popularity at the polls, Kennedy would fail to get the nomination. That would produce a presidential candidate from the Midwest or Far West. A horse trade for New York's large delegation could conceivably elevate Wagner. That would effectively kill any substantial New York support for Kennedy. The mayor was also a Roman Catholic and it could hardly be expected that they could be running mates.[38]

Kennedy was furious. DeSapio's hand was obvious, but Kennedy thought he saw Truman's. The former president had boosted New York's advocacy of Harriman at the 1956 convention. More recently, a Truman meeting with Sam Rayburn in Washington had brought agreement that Symington and Johnson were the only possible choices. Kennedy suspected that, combined with the efforts to shut him out of New York, the delegation might well succumb to Truman's pressures for Symington, who had already been wooing people like Finletter.[39] "There is no doubt that the action was instigated by the powers that be at the top," Kennedy suggested privately. Rejecting the idea of trying to penetrate New York by putting up independent slates of candidates to counter the organization, Kennedy just about wrote off trying to win over the state directly. He hoped that entry in the primaries elsewhere "would produce sufficient ground swell in New York that the New York delegates would then find it difficult to move in the direction of Symington, which looks like it is moving at this time. The road to Paris is through Peiping."[40]

Kennedy was correct about the New York reformers. There was no percentage in trying to woo them head-on. They had their heroes and would not let go. For one accustomed to fierce loyalists, their commitment for Stevenson was incomprehensible. But then again, a lot of things about Stevenson were hard for Jack Kennedy to understand; the reformers, "eggheads," and even the Governor's extraordinary appeal to women. Stevenson's sensitivity did not fit the Kennedy concept of masculinity. To one congressional friend a bemused Kennedy said, commenting on Adlai's sex appeal, "He must be a switcher."[41] Their talents, strengths, and frames of reference, unfortunately, would forever manufacture animosities rather than the sort of intelligent mutual leadership in such short supply. Stevenson, from Libertyville, Illinois, was the guru of the New York reformers. Kennedy, a cultural WASP that American ethnicity refused to release from the world of his fathers, was approached from a different and, alas, suspect direction.

Meanwhile, Kennedy's public expressions on the issues were winning some converts. A significant inroad came on the first of October, when he spoke at the University of Rochester in upstate New York at the invitation of Professor Wade and the History Society. Nikita Khrushchev had just completed his flamboyant tour of the United States and had recently returned to the Soviet Union, leaving behind hints of better future East-West relations, and cultural and economic ties, but no resolution of substantive issues. At Rochester, Kennedy chose to respond to the significance of the chairman's visit and delivered a measured appraisal of the international situation, one neither bellicose nor optimistic, but a statement that warned both about the complexities and the dangers of believing all differences could be swept away pell-mell. He viewed the visit as a "cause for redoubled efforts, not relaxation," one justifying more and not less "sacrifice to protect and extend the world's frontiers of freedom," and warned that the "real roots of the Soviet-American conflict cannot be easily settled by negotiations." And yet, he advised, it was "far better that we meet on the summit than at the brink" and urged "a new approach to the Russians—one that is just as hard-headed and just as realistic as Mr. Khrushchev's, but one that might well end the current phase—the frozen, belligerent, brink-of-war phase—of the long Cold War."[42] Wade recalled the speech as most impressive to such people as Finletter, whose warmth toward Kennedy's position subsequently became more pronounced.[43]

In any event, Kennedy had to avoid offending whatever support he did have. Feeling that the committed liberals were too closely wedded to Stevenson to warrant any efforts that might antagonize his friends, Kennedy made a tentative decision not to appear at a Democratic Advisory Council dinner planned for Mrs. Roosevelt at the Waldorf Astoria in December and also rejected an invitation to address the Lexington Club.

Schlesinger considered both decisions unwise. "Tom Finletter and I and a few others have been trying to combat this situation and get you a fair hearing," he wrote. "It has been an uphill job, but some progress has been made. Now much of the ground has been lost." He lamented Kennedy's failure to appreciate the symbolic value that the Lexington Club had for the party's liberals and, at the same time, their importance as financial contributors and opinion-makers, especially through the media, which made them "influential out of all proportion to their numbers." Moreover, Kennedy was advised, being identified with county leaders Buckley and Crotty might very well undercut his efforts to go before the electorate in a general election as an independent, good-government kind of candidate. "I would urge you not to underestimate the disadvantages of alienating the New York liberal Democrats—this advantage is even more serious perhaps for the election than for the convention—and I would think that this is a problem requiring effective counteraction before it drifts beyond the point of no return." One little way in which the damage could still be somewhat salvaged would be by reconsidering his reluctance to attend the Roosevelt dinner.[44]

One week after the Schlesinger letter, Paul Butler announced that Kennedy had reversed himself and had joined the Democratic Advisory Council.[45] Kennedy, then, was present when the council staged its fund-raising affair in Mrs. Roosevelt's honor. Harry Truman, whose Diamond Jubilee celebration Kennedy had attended in Boston on May 8, was also there, along with the party's current crop of potential candidates. Only Lyndon Johnson was absent, a direct result of his continuing opposition to the council. Kennedy spoke, as did his rivals, and was received politely. The gathering clearly preferred to think of Stevenson as the potential nominee and gave him the most enthusiastic applause.

Schlesinger met with Stevenson on December 29. The Governor told him he still preferred Humphrey but was worried about the senator's "impetuosity of judgment." He said he liked Jack Kennedy personally but was concerned about an alleged "profound anti-European prejudice reported to him by Elmo Roper and Barry Bingham." Stevenson also remained, as usual, passionate about the urgency of stopping Nixon.[46] The next day, Hubert Humphrey, the heir-apparent of Democratic liberals, formally announced his candidacy. Any firm declination by the Governor would surely precipitate a rush by the party's left wing not to Kennedy but to the senator from Minnesota.

27

The Literary Campaign

Under Sorensen's diligent direction, the Kennedy public-relations apparatus accelerated its tempo. Unprecedented in its scope, Kennedy's staff spearheaded the groundwork for capturing the party's nomination by exploiting his reputation as a writer and historian, as an intelligent, devoted, and sincere student of the American past and present—now also a Pulitzer prize winner. The final Senate years, therefore, brought a remarkable outpouring of publications that found their way into numerous accommodating periodicals.

Sorensen took care of most literary functions, serving as an editor, expediter, and artistic craftsman. The products included a gracefully written, somewhat filiopietistic summary of the Atlantic migration to America designed to convince readers about the inherent bias of the quota system. Published in 1958 by the Anti-Defamation League of B'nai B'rith as *A Nation of Immigrants,* it became a handy supplement for high school social studies courses as well as a contributor to the argument for reform. Concurrently, there was a constant flow of other material—articles, book reviews, guest editorials—all in addition to the numerous speeches made during this period, many of which were also published.

Their sheer quantity, considering also their diversity and research requirements, would have overwhelmed any full-time writer working around the clock.

Kennedy's campaign was remarkable; in the age of television, it emphasized the printed word. Probably never again will a politician with national ambitions spearhead a comparable drive. In Kennedy's case, the literary campaign jibed with his own instincts and political perceptions. Outside his office, nobody could have been aware of the total volume of the output. While only the most unsophisticated might expect someone in his position to have authored all that appeared under his name, what emerged was a considerable achievement. In one unguarded moment, Kennedy admitted to interviewer Richard Neuberger that his crowded schedule made even most of his reading superficial.[1]

For the general public, there was no way to distinguish between Kennedy and his ghostwriters. Once one realizes the latters' involvement, the danger exists of ignoring Kennedy's personal role, thereby depriving him of credit for at least spiritual and intellectual inspiration. Nevertheless, the Sorensen papers offer considerable insights into the "backstage" operation. When, for example, Sorensen forwarded to Kennedy the draft of an article that ultimately appeared in the October 1957 issue of *Foreign Affairs* as "A Democrat Looks at Foreign Policy," there was little doubt about how it had been put together. As Professor Latham had written to Sorensen the previous month, "I hope that it is not too late to send you the delayed word on foreign affairs for the article that you, the Senator, and who knows who else are writing for *Foreign Affairs.*"[2] Finally sending it on to Kennedy, Sorensen added the hope that it was "reasonably satisfactory, and won't interfere too much with your enjoying your trip to California." When *Foreign Affairs* editor Hamilton Fish Armstrong received it, the article came with a cover letter over Kennedy's signature stating that "it has been a pleasure for me to write it and to ponder some of the issues which it treats."[3] Such illusions were furthered before the public by the kind of statement that appeared in the Boston *Guardian* marveling that "somewhere in this crammed schedule, Kennedy has managed to produce a lengthy article for *Life* Magazine . . . and a humorous article for *Look.* . . ."[4] While that undoubtedly provoked admiration, the bulk of the output was yet to come.

The articles ranged from the prestigious analysis of the role of nationalism in the Cold War that appeared in *Foreign Affairs* to contributions for popular picture magazines and even specialized professional and company publications. One called "Putting the Labor Investigators in Their Proper Perspective" came out in the *Plant Council News* of the Standard Oil Company's unit in Baton Rouge, Louisiana. The February 1958 *McCall's* carried a discussion of "three American women of courage"—Anne Hutchinson, Jeanette Rankin, and Prudence Crandell. The *Kiwanis Magazine* appeared simultaneously with a Kennedy "guest editorial" on "Citizenship and Politics." He reached elementary-school teachers through *Instructor* magazine, urging the teaching of public affairs and upholding the value of "idealism in our public life." The organ of the Delta Zeta Sorority, called *The Chatterbox,* had a Kennedy by-line for a discussion of "Education and the Cold War." The *General Electric Defense Quarterly* came out in early 1959 with "Congress: How it Works Toward a More Organized Defense Effort," while the *Georgetown Law Review* ran "Congressional Lobbies: A Chronic Problem Re-Examined." Correspondents learned how easy it was to get an article out of Kennedy's office, properly revised, if needed—made to order—to suit almost any need. *Look* was offered a light story, together with delightful Grandma Moses-style drawings by Jacqueline Kennedy, about experiences of campaigning with Stevenson in a losing cause.[5]

Several articles appeared in *The New York Times Magazine* and *The Reporter.* Others reached audiences through the *Reader's Digest, Coronet, Life, Look,* the *Foreign Policy Bulletin,* the *NEA Journal, The Progressive,* and a biographical sketch of Founding Father Oliver Ellsworth of Connecticut went to the *Encyclopaedia Britannica.* At the same time, all between 1957 and 1959, there were book reviews: William S. White's *Citadel* in *The New Leader; Massachusetts People and Politics 1919–1933* by J. Joseph Huthmacher and *What Are We For* by Arthur Larson, in *The New York Times Book Review;* B. H. Liddell Hart's *Deterrent on Defense* in the *Saturday Review.*[6]

Notable was a Kennedy review of Oscar Handlin's *Al Smith and His America* for *The Washington Post.* The Kennedy treatment of Professor Handlin's biography reflected the senator's own current efforts. The review completely omitted any reference to Smith's Catholicism or its relationship to the 1928 campaign. It also praised the Democratic leader for possessing "above all else a practical intelligence which responded naturally to the stress of events and the felt needs of his environment . . . [while] distrusting idealists." Judging Smith's ability, it noted that he "was able to make progress without sacrificing his conviction that partisanship and political compromise are both essential ingredients of American politics." And then it praised a trait that would most often be associated with Kennedy himself: "Moreover, he had an unusual capacity to face and absorb facts and to mobilize talents from the professions."[7]

The self-consciousness that colored the review of Handlin's book was overshadowed by a Kennedy discussion of Richard Rovere's *Senator Joe McCarthy* in *The Washington Post.* Rovere was highly critical. He tried to neither mitigate nor excuse. To him, McCarthy was a rogue, a demagogue poisonous to the national well-being. Not unexpectedly, the biography brought denunciations from the Wisconsin senator's faithful admirers, and its author was, among many groups, condemned for having disgraced McCarthy's memory. Kennedy's review shrewdly guessed that McCarthy himself would have welcomed renewing the controversy, and, more charitably than loyalists were willing to grant, praised it for mixing "sympathy with condemnation." Still, it failed to become a forum for any *ex post facto* Kennedy attack. He was contented to accept Rovere's basic point that "McCarthy owed both his success and his fall to his own qualities." The review, written in 1959, however, saved its most acerbic criticism for the late Senator Taft and the Republican Party for having lent encouragement and assistance.[8]

There should be little wonder, then, why Drew Pearson's charge about the authorship of *Profiles,* coming when it did—in the middle of the literary campaign—should have caused so much consternation. That great blast on the Mike Wallace show threatened to demolish with one stroke all that Kennedy and his staff had been laboring to promote about their man's talents and credibility. Another interested party, of course, was the publisher, Harper & Brothers, which had done so well with the book. Both Cass Canfield and Evan Thomas were, however, intrigued by something else—getting somebody to do an authorized biography of the senator.

The Kennedy office agreed to cooperate. But they made one stipulation: the writer had to be acceptable to them. That began an unexpectedly difficult search. Thomas had his eye on magazine writer Harold Martin, who had contributed the skillfully written, highly laudatory *Saturday Evening Post* article called "The Amazing Kennedys." Martin seemed to have all the requirements: talent, access to sources, the popular touch, and a feeling for Kennedy. Suddenly, however, the Ambassador emerged to complicate matters. Through John Harriman, he was trying to arrange with another publisher, Doubleday, for an entirely different biography of Jack. But Joe Kennedy was clearly having his own troubles. Asked why he became involved independently, when he could hardly not have known that his son's aides had already agreed to cooperate with Harper & Brothers, Thomas recalled that the Ambassador was trying to show that he was in charge. "He was a tough nut. It was in his nature to go off unilaterally. He was not going to tie himself down with any one editor."[9]

Thomas, too, was finding the process more difficult than he had assumed. The preferred biographers were already busily involved in other matters or committed elsewhere. "Now, damn it," Thomas wrote with exasperation one year after having attempted to launch the project, "it seems that Cass and I have been turned down by every writer acceptable to your office, largely I think because they aren't *quite* convinced that the subject is hot."[10] Martin pleaded that he had other priorities and asked for guarantees of complete independence so he could write his own kind of book. John Gunther said he already had too many hectic assignments. Both John Hersey and Theodore H. White were involved with novels and unwilling to suspend their work. Robert J. Donovan was reluctant; he also had other things to do, as did Harrison Salisbury. Stewart Alsop argued that while he liked Kennedy, he did not want to tie himself down to a single subject. Walter Lord, while a good writer and acceptable, was already under contract with Harper for two books. Meanwhile, Sorensen, after examining a list of seventeen possible authors suggested by Thomas, vetoed "even approaching" Eric Sevareid, John Brooks, Rowland Evans, and Jim Bishop, "for a variety of reasons, most of which you can surmise." While Thomas and Sorensen opposed as too "amateurish," and possibly hostile to Kennedy, writers Ed Plaut and Ralph Martin, the two men had expressed a desire to do the project. Rejected by Harper, they went on to Doubleday.[11]

Thomas held out some hope that he could enlist Marquis Childs, or perhaps Bob Considine, but he still wanted Harold Martin. By September of 1958, no solution had been found, and Thomas, as well as Canfield, was getting impatient. Thomas sent Kennedy a copy of his telegram to Childs explaining that a sense of urgency "stems from desire to head off a couple of amateurs," a reference to the two writers being signed up by Doubleday.[12] In late October the frustrated editor called Harold Martin at his Atlanta home. He told him that both the senator and Sorensen were willing to give him the requested freedom. Martin made no definite commitment during that conversation but Evans was sufficiently encouraged to feel free to announce that a professional had been enrolled to do the job. In addition to getting his desired freedom spelled out in writing, however, Martin also had to complete other work before being able to take several months off for the project. Until Martin could be firmly nailed down, Thomas continued to sound out Stewart Alsop and Joe McCarthy, a magazine writer who already had a contract with *Look* for a three-part article on the Kennedys.[13]

At that point, in mid-November 1958, right after Jack Kennedy had won reelection, he and Sorensen decided that Thomas would have to clear it with the Ambassador. After all, he and Rose Kennedy would inevitably be asked to cooperate with any writer given a contract. Less than three weeks after Thomas called Harold Martin with the assurance of "no-strings-attached" cooperation, he had to inform the writer that, to his own "considerable dismay and embarrassment, the Ambassador has put his foot down with a thud, at least as far as his wife and himself are concerned. He has also said in no uncertain terms that he can't see how we can publish an authoritative book without coming to them for background information." Evan Thomas believed that Joe Kennedy was piqued because he was not "controlling the show." With that, Harper & Brothers canceled all plans for a Kennedy biography. Thomas then suggested that Jack persuade his family to at least cooperate with McCarthy for his magazine articles, which they did.[14]

Ralph Martin and Ed Plaut went ahead and signed with Doubleday to write what was issued in 1960 as *Front Runner, Dark Horse.* That same year, Dial brought out McCarthy's *The Remarkable Kennedys.* Ironically, totally unrelated to all of this, a skillful and relatively candid biography did appear in time for the 1960 campaign. After Professor James MacGregor Burns lost a congressional race in 1958, Sorensen suggested the possibility of joining the Kennedy staff. Burns declined for personal reasons, however, and countered with the idea of doing a Kennedy biography.

Finally, unofficially, and without any Harper connection, an ideal biographer filled the need. As a prestigious scholar, well respected by the liberal academic community, the value of his contribution was immediately recognized, a selling point that Jack must have used with his father. Consequently, Burns received full cooperation, even being permitted to go through the files of the senator's office while working nights in the building. The book was produced after obligatory submission of the manuscript to Sorensen and Kennedy, who then did their best to cajole the author into making concessions to their feeling that, at several points, the portrait was insufficiently flattering. They objected to the discussion of the McCarthy issue, the account of Kennedy's relations with his father, and to the depiction of the senator as without much depth of commitment to specific issues. As Sorensen advised Burns, "the impression should never be given that he does not believe deeply in what he says or will not fight fiercely for the causes in which he believes."[15] Burns understood their reaction as the natural belief in their man's superiority, which, by definition, should have yielded a more flattering portrait.[16] But the book succeeded far beyond the kind of job that had originally been conceived by Harper and Sorensen. For all its balance and gentle reservations about the senator's detachment, it portrayed him as an intelligent, articulate rising leader, who, if lacking a credible anti-McCarthy record, had nevertheless upheld civil liberties and, in other ways, opposed "McCarthyism." Mindful of Adlai Stevenson's liberal constituency, Burns's book introduced Kennedy as another "egghead," albeit one more decisive and dynamic.

Even while Jim Burns was researching his biography, the Kennedy literary apparatus moved ahead with a new project, designed to attract the liberal followers of Stevenson and Humphrey. Thomas had lunch with Jack Kennedy in late November 1958, shortly after the plan to have Harold Martin go ahead with a biography had been scotched by the Ambassador's putting "his foot down." Kennedy explained his father's position while the Harper editor countered with a proposal for an alternate project, a book largely comprised of the senator's foreign-policy statements. Kennedy failed to buy the idea right away and Thomas pursued the matter. "Can't say how much I hope you'll give serious consideration to an annotated group of your public articles and speeches showing how solid your mature judgment has been through the years— especially in foreign policy," Thomas wrote the day before Christmas.[17] Kennedy himself pondered the suggestion for much of the winter, at one point seemingly dismissing the whole idea, until finally agreeing in February. Thomas also succeeded in selling the project to John Fischer, the editor of *Harper's* magazine, suggesting that the project could serve three interests: the magazine, Harper books, and the senator. The book was designed to comprise some four to six chapters, with an interview conducted by Fischer to enable Kennedy to wrap up his view in a final chapter. By the spring the project was under way. Conceived by Thomas under the title of *The Image of Peace,* because, as he wrote to Sorensen, "I think that all foreign and defense policy relates to peace as the ultimate objective, though not of course peace without honor, etc.," it eventually became a significant preconvention publication called *The Strategy of Peace.*[18]

The evidence shows that, once Kennedy accepted the idea, the compilation had his close attention. Deirdre Henderson, with a letter of introduction from her brother-in-law, Paul Pennoyer, Jr., left Kissinger and joined Kennedy's Washington office to coordinate the contributions of the Academic Advisory Committee. Through Earl Latham, she solicited ideas for the new book from academicians. Historian Allan Nevins, recently retired from Columbia University, agreed to serve as its editor. Nevins, who later told Adlai Stevenson that he hoped the Democratic Convention would come up with a Stevenson-Kennedy ticket, adhered to his policy of refusing any advance for his work and assigned all royalties to the Columbia University Oral History Research Office, which he had founded.[19] Besides writing an introduction, Nevins's function was to do the final editing.

Aside from the work by Sorensen and Kennedy, the preliminary manuscript was prepared by Harris Wofford, Jr. Wofford was a thirty-three-year-old civil-rights lawyer with degrees from the University of Chicago and the Yale Law School. He had worked for Chester Bowles and in Dean Acheson's Washington law firm before becoming a legal assistant to Father Theodore Hesburgh and the Civil Rights Commission. When recruited for *The Strategy of Peace,* he was at South Bend, Indiana, as an associate professor at the Notre Dame Law School. Wofford did further editing and arranging of the speeches selected before passing the entire work on to Nevins for the final editing and writing of background material. Pleased with the project's progress, Nevins wrote to Sorensen in mid-November that he expected that the volume would "contribute as much to public enlightenment as Stevenson's collection of speeches did four years ago, and think it will be more widely read."[20] Through the fall, Sorensen, Wofford, and Nevins worked closely on the compilation, organization, and editing. The anthology constituted a comprehensive selection of Kennedy's major foreign-policy statements.

Finally, everything was ready for John Fischer to interview the senator. But, although the subject was to be foreign affairs, Thomas hoped something more newsworthy could come out of the session. "I'm hoping that he will be able to cover McCarthy and birth control," he wrote to Nevins six days before the scheduled interview, "but my fingers are crossed."[21] The question of birth control was, of course, one of the more ticklish ones for Kennedy. The day after his appearance before the Philadelphia Americans for Democratic Action, Joe Clark, whose wife was active in the Planned Parenthood Association, asked Kennedy how he, as a Roman Catholic, felt about the problem. Clark had suggested the importance of having family-planning information available, "not only in domestic matters, particularly in terms of poor and under-privileged people in the great cities—but also abroad." As Clark remembered Kennedy's reply, he said, "It's bound to come. It's just a question of time. The Church will come around. I intend to be as brave as I dare."[22] Later, to a private inquiry that expressed skepticism about how he would stand on the question, Kennedy responded by saying that "consideration of legislation is essentially a political issue" and added his belief that "those who have no religious or moral scruples concerning the use of contraceptives should not be hampered in their freedom of choice." He followed that up with a letter requesting that his comments remain confidential.[23] Interviewed by James Reston in late November, Kennedy said he opposed having the American government advocate birth control in other countries. Individual nations, he explained, should make their own decision. "I think it would be the greatest psychological mistake for us to appear to advocate limitation of the black, or brown, or yellow peoples whose population is increasing no faster than in the United States."[24] Fortunately, President Eisenhower's own acceptance of that position removed much of the potential controversy from Kennedy's. Asked again by Fischer, he repeated that it should be left up to the individual nations. But those who advocated birth control as well as those in opposition, Kennedy suggested, should help to meet the problem by supporting greater American economic assistance to such countries. Those opposed to birth control, he told Fischer, were morally committed "to sustain a real American effort of assistance in those areas." They could not be both against birth control and against economic assistance.[25]

The McCarthy matter was even touchier. Fischer broached the question by pointing to the possible harm to America's reputation abroad, which Kennedy readily conceded. As he had done so often before, Jack preferred not to discuss McCarthy as a personality. He agreed that "McCarthy was a symbol" and "a force himself," and immediately recalled his own devotion to civil liberties by recounting his efforts to repeal the loyalty oath. Fischer, however, pressed on. He wanted to know how the senator felt about the damage done to democratic rights and where he stood at the time. Without hinting at what arguments he had been ready to use, Kennedy cited his own willingness to vote for censure had that come up during the summer of 1954. When the issue did arise, he reminded Fischer, he had been in the hospital for about a month, and then concluded his remarks by emphasizing that not only he but the entire Senate "could have done better here in that period in the United

488 JACK: THE STRUGGLES OF JOHN F. KENNEDY

States." His words left no doubt about his lack of sympathy for McCarthy's methods, but neither did he say anything about the crusader's veracity or value to the cause of internal security. Afterward, however, Sorensen notified Evan Thomas that the senator had decided, in accordance with the original understanding, to eliminate the McCarthy section entirely as a matter that would strike "a rather jarring note on which to end the entire work." Three days later Sorensen added that both he and Kennedy had developed strong feelings that the McCarthy question was "wholly inappropriate" and that Fischer had been correct for not including it in his original list.[26]

When *The Strategy of Peace* came off the presses early that spring, some 250 complimentary copies went to such individuals as professors, journalists, lawyers, union chiefs, clergymen, business executives, and financiers. Notably absent were political leaders. Ted Sorensen has recalled that the mass mailing was their "largest single effort to woo the intellectuals" in the different primary states.[27] But the volume's substantive intellectual context encountered the problem of finding a broader audience. At Harpers, those responsible for handling more popular books refused to carry it. To get any kind of trade reception with a simultaneous paperback version, the price had to be kept below one dollar, so it reached the stalls with a ninety-five-cent list price. Nor did the book get much attention from reviewers. "So the hell with them," Thomas wrote. "We'll advertise outside of the book review sections . . . We'll be in dailies all over and a week from Sunday we'll have an ad in the section that has the News of the Week in Review in the *Times.* I have a theory that that's the serious audience for the book anyhow."[28]

28

The Labor Trap

The summer of 1959 brought the twin misfortune of a brilliant performance hidden from public view in the privacy of a conference committee and, despite his skillful work, the frustration of Kennedy's two-year effort to write a labor-reform bill. The final product reported out of the committee in September and signed into law by the President represented considerably more supervision of organized labor with provisions sufficiently severe for Kennedy to discreetly withdraw his name from co-sponsorship. The resultant Landrum-Griffin Act, or the Labor-Management Reporting and Disclosure Act of 1959, contradicted the expectations justified by labor's gains during the 1958 off-year elections. "A somewhat groggy labor movement took stock this week of the acid fruits of its political 'victory' last November and wondered whether it could survive another such triumph," wrote labor reporter A. H. Raskin.[1] The outcome reflected the antilabor lobbying of many different business groups but also left evidence of attempts to sidetrack Jack Kennedy's presidential drive.

With most of the work having been done by Archie Cox and Arthur Goldberg, Kennedy's new bill, co-sponsored by Sam Ervin of North

Carolina, had been introduced as a replacement for Kennedy-Ives. Kennedy brought it to the floor by pointing to modifications designed to defuse business opposition. Some were balking at provisions monitoring employer reporting practices that could interfere with the normal process of relations with personnel, including the possibility that wages and bonuses could come under the category of prohibited bribes. It was not, Kennedy stressed, a bill in industrial relations. It was primarily a labor-management reform bill dealing with racketeering. "The two areas of legislation should not be confused or combined," he told the chamber. He also hoped that he would not be criticized by labor or management for what it failed to do by way of introducing Taft-Hartley amendments and new collective-bargaining rules. "Let us first stop racketeering without becoming bogged down in the heated and complex issues raised by the entire Taft-Hartley Act. Then let us consider revising that law ..."[2] Nevertheless, the bill contained the Title VI "sweeteners" and had the approval of labor leaders. Walter Reuther praised it for taking "a real step in the right direction . . . to equip the labor movement and the Government in dealing effectively with corruption and racketeering both in labor and in management. And I think we need to understand there is corruption in both places."[3] Other bills were, of course, introduced quickly thereafter, including the administration's version. Offered by Barry Goldwater, but pushed chiefly by McClellan so that the Arizonan's antilabor reputation would not hurt the bill, it followed the general lines of Kennedy-Ives but contained Taft-Hartley revisions desired by management as well as labor. Kennedy objected to the Goldwater bill by claiming that it sought not only to tighten secondary boycott provisions of Taft-Hartley but to expand them "drastically." He suggested awaiting completion of the McClellan Committee report and the recommendations of the Advisory Panel before moving off into that direction, which could then be taken care of in a second bill.[4]

When the hearings began on January 28 in Room 4232 of the New Senate Office Building, Kennedy presided and labor's representative, Andrew Biemiller, a former congressman from Milwaukee, spoke for George Meany. Biemiller was very firm about accepting the Kennedy-Ervin Bill with the Title VI Taft-Hartley sweeteners. He told Goldwater that labor would not support the bill without Title VI. Kennedy then pointed out that the Taft-Hartley changes in the Kennedy-Ervin Bill, S. 505, had originally been inserted with the assistance of the administration.[5] Now, of course, strategy had shifted. A presidential election was nearing. The opposing party's potential nominee was closely identified with the subcommittee's bill. Management groups were pressuring for McClellan Committee revelations as a rationale for further labor restrictions. Moreover, Democrats, as the majority party, could be sorely embarrassed by failure to produce the kind of bill ostensibly warranted by their 1958 election victories. Obviously, then, the administration was in no mood to be cooperative.

Archie Cox then testified. Explaining that he was more familiar with the legislation than any other person in the country, he emphasized the need for changes in two essentially different areas: internal union reforms and labor-management relations. They should be handled separately, he urged, because mixing them would simply cause confusion. He argued that internal reforms should not become an excuse for repressive measures; weakening union bargaining power was no way to protect union members against financial dishonesty or provide guarantees of internal democracy. Legislation directed at reform should not be concerned with weakening the unions.[6]

The conflict between the administration and the Labor Subcommittee was then joined on the political level. Personal differences between Kennedy and the secretary had been building since the previous summer, when James Mitchell had attacked the Kennedy-Ives Bill from Geneva. Their new meeting on February 4, 1959, encouraged speculation that a Kennedy nomination by the Democrats could well promote Mitchell's candidacy for the Republican vice-presidential nomination, thereby neutralizing, in part, the appeal to Roman Catholics. Mitchell now appeared as the principal architect of the administration's bill. He had, earlier in the week, rejected an overture by Kennedy, who had sent Arthur Goldberg to him as an emissary, to try to work out a bipartisan labor bill. Mitchell said that his ideas and the senator's were too far apart.[7] Mitchell's direct purpose in appearing before the committee was to discuss the legislation and recommendations that the President had made in his labor message.

Neither man was a lawyer, but Mitchell was an expert in labor relations. Kennedy parried and outmaneuvered him at every turn, finally forcing the secretary to turn to his counsel, Stuart Rothman. Nor did Rothman prove to be much of a match for the senator, who persisted in picking at the flaws in the administration's bill.

Kennedy had to persevere by treading carefully. The Kennedy brothers' own efforts had shown the need to police the Becks and Hoffas. But that had, at the same time, given labor's opponents a powerful bludgeon against unions. For organized labor, some changes were inevitable—

politically, if for no other justification. Most of all, however, it was John Kennedy representing labor.

On February 19 Senator McClellan, now coordinated with the administration, introduced S. 1137, which he later described as "designed to provide effective remedies for some of the perversion of decent unionism and flagrant exploitations and abuses that have been exposed by more than 1,200 witnesses who have appeared and testified before the Senate select committee. . . ."[8] He also advocated dropping from the Kennedy-Ervin Bill all provisions dealing with the Taft-Hartley amendments, especially those embodied in Title VI, and preferred separate legislation later to revise Taft-Hartley. Meanwhile, the original Kennedy-Ervin Bill had been altered with the addition of fifty-six amendments without changing the overall substance of the original legislation, except instead of S. 505, it was now designated as S. 155. The revised Kennedy-Ervin Bill was reported out favorably to the Senate on the fourteenth of April.

Then began the effort to wound Kennedy and dilute his legislation. Ervin, breaking with his co-sponsor, introduced an amendment to strike Title VI. He proposed an additional bill to restrict jurisdictional picketing as well as secondary boycotts. Utilizing the McClellan Committee findings, he argued for the need of a law to "protect" rank-and-file members "who have the misfortune to belong to unions controlled by officers who are dictatorial or corrupt [but] have no protection whatever."[9]

Kennedy then went through an exposition of the legislation. Paul Douglas later told an interviewer, "As I listened to Senator Kennedy expound the provisions in the bill which he recommended, I thought it was the most masterly performance that I had ever heard on labor law and particularly the secondary boycott. It established him in my mind as a man with a truly first-rate intellect."[10] But then, Goldwater continued to argue, a ban on secondary boycotts and "blackmail picketing" should be a part of the Taft-Hartley amendments, finally making what he thought was the offer to agree to limit the field only to boycotts and picketing, if Kennedy were to permit the striking of Title VI. Kennedy retorted: "I do not see how the Senator from Arizona can be a successful businessman. That is one of the worst deals I have ever heard of. When I say something is noncontroversial, I always exempt the Senator from Arizona." On the following day, Title VI was retained by a substantial vote.

On the night of the twenty-second, however, John McClellan turned the entire debate into a crusade for righteousness. The man who had become most identified with the question of labor corruption through his chairmanship of the committee, offered an amendment, shrewdly called a "bill of rights" for the workingman. As McClellan warmed to his subject, his evangelical fervor increased. He argued that it protected workers by enabling the secretary of labor, through the attorney general, to obtain injunctions on behalf of fifteen million union members. Samuel Merrick, who sat next to Kennedy while McClellan went on, recalled that they were being bathed "in verbal fireworks . . . the vibrations and the fulminations. . . . McClellan looked like he was having a stroke on the spot. And I think Kennedy reacted as though 'This is out of control, this situation.' It was. It is not often that oratorical power changes much in congressional debate. But this was one of those occasions."[11] McClellan made points that were difficult to deny to the voters back home and reinforced the power of the conservative coalition. As McClellan continued with his oratory, senators murmured that the southern Democrat was handing them their "chance to vote against Kennedy."[12]

Kennedy then took up the fight. He argued that union members were already provided those rights more satisfactorily under state law and by provisions of the Taft-Hartley Act. Enactment of the McClellan "bill of rights" proposal would merely wipe out "the present exhaustive remedies provided under the common law of the various States . . . and only the rights suggested by the Senator from Arkansas would then be available to union members."[13]

On the twenty-fourth Kennedy got into a sharp exchange with McClellan on the Senate floor. "The difference between the Senator from Arkansas and me is that every time he sees a union, he sees racketeering," charged Kennedy. "Every time I see a union—except in a few cases, relatively speaking—I do not see racketeers; I see men and women who are attempting to advance their economic interests. The Senator from Arkansas proposes to apply a universal standard because some racketeers have been exposed. This, in my opinion, would prevent any further union organization in this country."

McClellan insisted that he only wanted to "prevent racketeering in unionism."

But Kennedy went on, saying that "two evenings ago, the Senate . . . adopted the amendment, and did so on the basis of taking action to stop racketeering. But surely the Senate must realize the effect of that amendment, not only on racketeers but also on all unions."[14]

The vote on the "bill of rights" was an opportunity to gang up on

Kennedy from all sides, and it was adopted 47–46, with Vice-President Nixon presiding and casting the tie-breaking vote. The one-vote difference could easily have been overcome with the presence of either Senators Douglas or Humphrey, but both were off on official business, encouraged to leave by the complacency of both labor lobbyists and Johnson, all equally unprepared for McClellan's move. Comments reported among senators were to the effect: "Well, you can't call it the Kennedy bill now," and "No, and he doesn't want it called that either."[15] Meanwhile, Lyndon Johnson also had it both ways. Several members of the so-called "Johnson network," Dennis Chavez of New Mexico, Margaret Chase Smith of Maine, and Tom Dodd of Connecticut, inexplicably sided with McClellan. Johnson himself opposed the amendment; but, as Evans and Novak have pointed out, he did not "seem to exhibit the same agitation and involvement he usually did when a close vote was at stake." To play the other side of the road, when explaining to his conservative constituents why his personal vote had been against the "bill of rights," he used an argument drawn up by a member of his staff that said he had acted because the amendment could have been an opening wedge for "a broad federal FEPC program" by providing tools "much broader than any ever proposed under civil rights bills." Johnson promptly termed the McClellan measure as an "equal rights amendment," which caused a furor and, thanks to an amendment to a compromise introduced by Tom Kuchel of California, led to the final acceptance of a watered-down version. When the Kennedy bill finally moved to the House after being reported out on the twenty-fourth, it also had the compromise marks of Kuchel and Jacob Javits of New York as well as the original Kennedy-Ervin sponsorship. Archie Cox and the labor representatives had also worked to draft revisions to modify the McClellan amendment.[16]

The original action on the "bill of rights" had been seen as serving Johnson's purpose and also damaging to the presidential prospects of Richard Nixon, who had cast the decisive anti-union vote. For Kennedy, especially, the political loss was regarded as substantial. The final compromise fashioned by Kuchel was at Kennedy's urging. The Californian worked it out with a bipartisan group on a Friday, introducing it that evening, and got it passed, much to the consternation of those who had hoped that the "bill of rights" had damaged Kennedy's hopes. Some of his fellow Republicans promptly charged Kuchel with "bailing the Democrats out of a disastrous dilemma." He had, rather, accomplished something more important, more partisan, than such colleagues admitted; he had rescued the bill from sole Democratic authorship and modified the "bill of rights" to make it more acceptable to labor. On the twenty-fifth the Kennedy-Ervin Bill, having incorporated the Kuchel amendment by a wide margin, passed the Senate with but a single dissent before going on to the House.

To Adlai Stevenson, Kennedy wrote on May 8 that the "action of the Senate—in the Democratic 86th Congress—in passing by a vote of 90 to 1 the Kennedy-Ervin Labor-Management Reform Bill ought to make final one fact: That the Republicans will never again be able to denounce our party as the protector of labor bosses and racketeers. . . ."[17] His words echoed justifications for the Communist Control Act of 1954.

Kennedy was trying to put a good face on a rapidly deteriorating situation. When his bill went to the House, it came under the twin onslaught of the Teamsters lobby and business organizations, all of which were more than a match for the efforts of the AFL-CIO, which lacked a program and action. From the start the situation in the House looked grim. In June, Kennedy sent a memorandum to Representative Stuart Udall of Arizona discussing the problem of having to engineer through a bill that would be sufficiently attractive to win over southern votes. He pointed out "that if the House goes wild, the result might be no bill at all."[18]

The bill that came out of the House was influenced by the combined forces of management and the Teamsters. Kennedy warned that the adoption of the Landrum-Griffin Bill would endanger final passage of any reform legislation by complicating chances for a conciliation of the Senate and House versions. He called for its rejection, arguing that Landrum-Griffin really substituted punitive measures for responsible legislation aimed at the Hoffas, the Dios, and Nathan Sheffermans.[19]

Three days later, the President made his move in the form of a timely, vital address to the nation, which gave a big boost for the more conservative House version, the Landrum-Griffin Bill. His endorsement brought a great response, encouraging a rash of mail from citizens in behalf of legislation far more restrictive than anything visualized by the Senate. That sent Landrum-Griffin to the conference to be worked out by the members from each chamber.

Indeed, for some of the conservatives, Landrum-Griffin did not go far enough in supervising organized labor. A secondary objective was to place Kennedy at the center of controversy over the final bill. Graham Barden, who chaired the House conference committee, slyly arranged to give Kennedy the "honor" of presiding over the conferees. Kennedy sat on one side of the table, faced by Barden, who as Merrick remembered, had an "enormous amount of shrewdness and a kind of rural cunning and a lot of back-country flavor in his talk—a kind of elemental, coarse type of human being. He gave the impression he had played poker since he was two. He was enjoying himself every minute of it, facing what undoubtedly must have seemed to him like a young man in need of being cut down."[20] "Barden attempted to dominate it on the first day or two," said Frank Thompson, Jr., "and Jack showed remarkable skill, strength, and toughness in saying, 'Look, I'm chairman of this conference and I'm going to run this conference,' and he ran it. Oddly enough—I don't know why—I didn't realize for some reason or other that Jack wasn't a lawyer. I am one. I was convinced that he was a lawyer until halfway through the conference. . . . And then I suddenly realized, first, that he wasn't a lawyer; secondly, what a brilliant and quick mind he had. He had Archie Cox from Harvard there. Archie helped all of us. But Archie would just give Jack a clue, a few words, and Jack would pick it up, read the Senate version and the House version, and showed a remarkable ability to pick up and run with great skill. I've seen only a handful of senators in the many conferences I've been in who were in that class."[21]

For Kennedy, then, being in that chairmanship placed him in a leadership position but at the same time served the purposes of the conservative coalition, thereby making him vulnerable for a final bill for which he would be blamed by those elements of the labor movement skeptical about his role. Richard Bolling cited Kennedy's performance as the first indication he had of how much Kennedy had changed since 1947. "He started out, I take it, very upset and nervous, and he saw that he had, I guess, the crisis of his political life on his hands, and he came through brilliantly. They tell me he was just as tough as a boot and just as effective as he could be. . . . he had to carry the ball, and I'm told that he did a brilliant job in that conference."[22] George Meany praised Kennedy, saying he was convinced that if not for his knowledge of matters and his standing up at the time of need, the Landrum-Griffin Bill would have been much harsher.[23] Yet at the same time, a split occurred, one that had been inevitable for some time, between Kennedy and his older colleague, Wayne Morse.

Morse, midway through the conference committee's work, began to finally do what he had been aching to do since the two began their service together on the Labor Subcommittee. He broke with Kennedy, going his own way and, finally, voted against the committee's report. Morse rebelled from a simple slight to his pride; and Kennedy provided that opening by not waiting for the Oregonian before explaining to the committee the essence of the conference's progress, concluding his exposition without Morse's presence, which did not give the senior senator an opportunity to make his own views known. Morse "announced in a grand sort of way that he was not going to sign the conference report."[24]

"Hey, Sam," Kennedy asked Merrick, who was sitting next to him on a leather sofa, "what happened to Wayne?" As Merrick reconstructed the conversation, he said, "Well, Senator, I think the real trouble was that you didn't give him enough notice. You didn't consider him at that afternoon session. He wasn't there, and you didn't wait for him."

Merrick, however, like Meany and Thompson, believed that Kennedy, as conference chairman, salvaged the best bill possible from the situation. Kennedy had labored without success to eliminate the Taft-Hartley amendments opposed by unions and had no choice but to yield to what was essentially the House's version of the bill, including restrictions on picketing, secondary boycotts, and state jurisdiction over so-called "no man's land cases." He also had to yield on common situs picketing, which would have permitted building-trade unions to picket a joint construction site. But his efforts were directly responsible for keeping the bill from being a total disaster for labor. With the aid of other pro-labor conferees, he won exemptions from some of the new Taft-Hartley provisions for garment and construction unions. When the AFL-CIO issued an official statement on September 2 that called the conference bill "worse" for labor than the original Taft-Hartley Act, it nevertheless also praised Kennedy for softening the blow.[25]

Without Kennedy's name on the final bill, it was signed into law by President Eisenhower on September 14, 1959, representing a further antilabor drift. Kennedy, of course, had only too gladly disassociated his name from the legislation, but individual union members and certain militant labor leaders lumped him together with the anti-union members of the committee. Some dismissed him as a Pontius Pilate. The battling and often fiery leader of New York City's Transit Workers, Mike Quill, promptly denounced the Kennedy brothers as among the "fakers who tried to cut our throats."[26] Jack reached Atlantic City on October 12 to face the convention of the United Auto Workers amid obvious hostility. The unionists had received Hubert Humphrey the day before with affection. But Kennedy had to enter discreetly by being ushered down an aisle removed from a concentration of derisive delegates. He spoke well, drawing only a polite response. Leonard Woodcock of the UAW recalled, "There were those inside the labor movement and inside our union who were dubbing it the Landrum-Griffin-Kennedy bill and really doing a job on him." During a moment alone with the senator, Woodcock asked whether he really thought a Catholic could be elected president. Kennedy told him that the answer to that question would be somewhat clarified by March, an allusion to the very safe New Hampshire primary. Then the senator gave the impression of being fatalistic about it all, as though to shrug his shoulders and explain that, well, if unsuccessful, "there are other ways in which I can serve my country."[27]

Of course, as chairman of the conference committee, he was able to take advantage of his prominence by utilizing the news media to make points with the public, conveying the fact that he was taking the initiative and carrying the battle against great odds. More than anything else, those legislators who watched Kennedy closely gained their most impressive view of his abilities as a member of the Senate, one that was particularly striking as he moved toward formal announcement of his candidacy.

29

Taking the Step

Only with difficulty could Jack imagine himself taking second place. Since 1956, his ambition had grown; his stature had increased, as had his self-confidence. What could have been a coup four years earlier now appeared as an unacceptable alternative. Remaining in the Senate or doing something else seemed more attractive than the traditional anonymity of the vice-presidency. Still, he was realistic enough to know the options. He had gambled—unavoidably, in retrospect—by having been such a visible candidate for so long. While it helped raise him from a minor figure to one who had to be taken seriously, it inevitably exposed him to the hazards posed by ambitious rivals and the prominence of his own liabilities. Either could easily be fatal.

In a question-and-answer session following a Columbia University School of Journalism lecture on March 5, 1959, James Reston discussed the growth of a "stop Kennedy" movement. Reston believed that, given the expected strength of Humphrey and Symington in the Middle West and Border States, and of Johnson in Dixie, the holding ability of favorite sons, especially Governor Brown of California, could easily tie up enough delegates to deadlock the convention. The need to go through several ballots might be prevented by a "smoky room" deal.[1]

Two days after the Reston talk, Democrats gathered in Milwaukee for a Midwest conference of the party found Bobby and Sorensen representing Jack Kennedy. Sorensen applied strong pressure to line up votes; one participant described him as a high-pressure salesman looking for a deal. Bobby addressed the group and arranged a press conference. "The papers had billed this meeting as a stop Kennedy move," reported a Michigan delegate, who suspected that the younger Kennedy was trying to take headlines from Humphrey.[2] Another observer, Violet Gunther of the ADA, filed a personal memorandum noting that "Kennedy's name was kept afloat in what was otherwise a pretty strongly Humphrey gathering." She was told by Jim Doyle, the Wisconsin chairman, that he had not given up on Stevenson and was looking for a deadlock that would favor the Governor for a third nomination.[3] Quite obviously, arrows could come from all directions.

Ben Bradlee of *Newsweek* magazine reported that after watching Lyndon Johnson at Harrisburg, Pennsylvania, he had no doubt that he was seeing a man who was "looking hopefully beyond the confines of the Senate majority leadership." Bradlee thought that Johnson was too unpolished, even too uncouth, to make much personal headway. "His personal mannerisms are destructive of the dignified image. He's somebody's gabby Texas cousin from Fort Worth. Friendly, relishing a good yarn, socially conspiratorial with a hand on the shoulder and a whispered pleasantry. None of it adds up to President," Bradlee advised Kennedy. But there was a real threat that Johnson would reach the convention with a bloc of three hundred or more delegates, which he might keep for himself for three or four ballots before allowing them to go off in different directions. "He's to be feared not as a potential winner but as a gameplayer who might try to maneuver you right out of the contest in Los Angeles."[4]

By June the situation acquired an additional complication. Kennedy learned that Wisconsin's Governor Nelson had urged Senator William Proxmire to run in the primary as the state's favorite son to avoid a contest between Humphrey and Kennedy. Kennedy immediately let Proxmire know, in a personal and confidential note, that he intended to enter a slate of delegates in the Wisconsin primary. His own workers, Kennedy pointed out, had been operating under Mayor Nestingen and had already prepared the way for a pro-Kennedy slate. He left no doubt about wanting Proxmire out of the way so he could confront Humphrey head-on. Proxmire stepped aside, and, to Humphrey's distress, did nothing to impede Kennedy. In 1979 Proxmire explained that he never intended to compete. He told Nelson that "if he insisted on running as a favorite son I'd run against him, and we're going to have a contest between the two of us. And I did exactly that. I told Gaylord that if he ran as a favorite son, I'd run as a favorite son; and Gaylord immediately got out of it."[5] Clearly, in no state were the Kennedy forces making such intense precampaign preparations as in Wisconsin.

Hard as it may seem to believe in retrospect, in early 1959 public consciousness of Jack's religion was still relatively limited. Southern support for his candidacy, still considered strong at that time, was doubtless linked in some part to such ignorance. A Gallup poll that spring confirmed that while fifty-seven percent preferred Kennedy to Nixon, fewer than half seemed aware of the religious factor.[6] At *Look* magazine, Knebel and editor Dan Mich, who had long since discovered the Kennedy value to their circulation, decided to pursue the religious angle. Knebel, who had contributed the pre-1956 convention article on Catholicism and the vice-presidency, interviewed Kennedy in late 1958. Knebel reported that Kennedy had been prompted to clarify his position on church-state issues and his views of the relationship of a Roman Catholic officeholder to the Constitution. After a conversation with Dr. Henry Knox Sherrill, Kennedy realized that if such an eminent Protestant as Sherrill, who had been the presiding bishop of the Episcopal Church, was uncertain about his views, others might be similarly troubled. Prepared for the need to offer some clarification, then, when he met with Knebel, Kennedy explained that "whatever one's religion in his private life may be, for the officeholder nothing takes precedence over his oath to uphold the Constitution and all its parts—including the first amendment and the strict separation of church and state. Without reference to the presidency," he went on, "I believe as a senator that the separation of church and state is fundamental to our American concept and heritage and should remain so." Kennedy was also reported to be "flatly opposed" to the appointment of an ambassador to the Vatican as well as to the use of federal funds to support parochial or private schools. He allowed for the possibility, however, of support for such "fringe" items as buses, lunches, or other services, where the issue was mostly social or economic rather than religious. Individual cases, he suggested, should be judged on their merits within the law as interpreted by the states.[7]

A variety of reactions came from Protestants. They ranged from approval to unalloyed suspicion. Perhaps the most militant of the "respectable" groups critical of the Catholic Church, "Protestants and Other Americans United for Separation of Church and State," ultimately saw fit to grant its "top citation" for 1959 to Kennedy for his "forthright statement . . . in which he characterized as unconstitutional the appropriation of public funds for parochial schools" and praised his words for their "refreshing candor."[8] Other Protestants, less concerned with Kennedy as an ecclesiastical threat, expressed uneasiness about the temporal character of his words. Martin Marty, the associate editor of *The Christian Century,* wrote that Kennedy was "spiritually rootless and politically almost disturbingly secular," while Robert McAfee Brown wrote in *Christianity and Crisis* that Kennedy had demonstrated "that he is a regular irregular Christian."[9]

Between the early months of 1959 and the year's end, awareness of Kennedy's religion increased significantly. The issue became much more of a topic for open discussion. As it did, Protestant groups passed resolutions questioning Kennedy's fitness for the presidency and, consequently, they stimulated popular consciousness of his Catholicism. In midsummer a correspondent for *The Wall Street Journal* noted that "whatever the outcome of Mr. Kennedy's candidacy, the main impression the cross-country traveler gets is that most people are not indifferent to the matter of Roman Catholicism and the Presidency."[10] Although Kennedy was heretofore regarded by southerners as far more acceptable, largely because of his greater moderation on civil rights than Hubert Humphrey, growing awareness of his religion began to erode Kennedy's support within that region. Exactly how damaging Kennedy's religion would be in the South was hard to calculate. Virginia's junior senator, A. Willis Robertson, writing to the editor of the *Richmond Times-Dispatch* in late 1958, acknowledged that "certain leaders" were contending that there was "no prejudice in the South against a Catholic for the presidency" but suspected that whatever toleration existed would evaporate "in the secrecy of the ballot box."[11]

Kennedy's problem was further compounded because of the identification of Roman Catholic churches in the South with leading efforts to achieve greater compliance with the Supreme Court's desegregation decisions.[12] When Governor Patterson of Alabama endorsed Kennedy in the late spring of 1959, criticism was strong, surprisingly strong when compared with the way his statement would have been received a year earlier. Eugene "Bull" Connor, the commissioner of public safety of Birmingham, reacted to the governor's declaration by writing to Kennedy to inquire about his stand on school integration. "As far as I am concerned," Connor stated, "this is the number one problem, not only in the South, but all over the nation today."[13] The increasing consciousness made southern opposition, which mounted through the year, more obvious because it was also more vocal.

Northern resistance to a Roman Catholic, always a strong undercurrent among liberals, especially among the very groups of intellectuals Kennedy was attempting to cultivate, was also pronounced. There were those in Massachusetts, for example, who had helped elect him to the Senate but had qualms about sending a Catholic to the White House. The outpourings began to come from less sophisticated, and traditionally anti-Catholic sources. A Findlay, Ohio, pamphlet contained ominous warnings. Headlines throughout the world, it declared, would herald the Church's great triumph upon Kennedy's election as president. "To those whose eyes are open to the history, practice, and teachings of Romanism, the . . . headlines . . . would lucidly sound a warning of the 'beginning of the end' to a hundred and one liberties which are enjoyed in Protestant countries. Witness the conditions of Spain's 20,000 Protestants."[14]

On the other end of the spectrum, Kennedy had to contend with substantial numbers of Catholics. A Jesuit priest, identified only as "one of the Catholic Church's outstanding intellectuals," was quoted as saying, "A Catholic is fine as a member of the board, but not as chairman."[15] When James Reston telephoned Kennedy in November to get his position on birth control, his call was in response to a statement that had been issued by Catholic bishops criticizing what they called "population alarmists" who support public programs promoting birth-control methods. Kennedy suspected the timing of their declaration and did not hide his feeling that they had acted out of hostility toward his candidacy. Kennedy told Kate Louchheim, the vice-chairman of the Democratic National Committee, that the opposition of high Catholic clerics to his candidacy should be sufficient proof that the Church as such was not an issue.[16] Finding a story in a Chicago paper about the head of Notre Dame's sociology department warning that the nomination of a Catholic for president would inevitably arouse anti-Catholicism, Kennedy muttered, half under his breath, "Why don't they mind their own business?"[17] John Cogley, who later helped Kennedy handle religious matters, recalled the senator's feeling that "some members of the hierarchy were not averse to embarrassing him. Yes, I think that's true; I think he did feel that. I don't say all the Catholic bishops, but I think there were, here and there, bishops he felt were out to get him, to embarrass him—not to get him but to embarrass him—mainly because they were Republicans or because they didn't like what they thought was the liberal tenor of his thinking."[18]

Like the Protestant commentaries, they were upset that he had gone so far in expunging spirituality from his public responsibilities. While they did not like opposition to federal support for parochial schools, they expressed greater concern that he had allowed himself to be the subject of an inquisition about such matters as separation of church and state and the distinction between religion and private life, areas that they certainly did not see as incompatible. *America* was impatient "at the earnest Massachusetts Senator's efforts to appease bigots, rather than of disagreement with the positive points he made. A Catholic political candidate, if he must make a profession of his faith, should not seem to give quarter to religious bigotry, even at the risk of having his words distorted."[19] When Arthur Krock responded that it was hard for him to understand how Kennedy could be charged with "appeasing the bigots," *America* explained that it was "humiliating for Catholics that even a man with the brilliant war record of Senator Kennedy thought himself obliged to answer questions that everyone knows are the remnants of the bad old days of Know-Nothingism. . . . We are sorry that the Senator did not put his foot down. We hope that from now on he will refuse to entertain any such notion."[20] An exception to this view was taken by John Cogley, who, writing in *Commonweal,* sympathized with Kennedy's having permitted himself to be questioned and acknowledged that "many Americans of good will have special concerns about having a Catholic for President." He pointed out that it "would be foolhardy for a Catholic Presidential candidate not to make his position on Church-State questions clear."[21]

On April 9 Kennedy told reporters in Washington that "all questions that interest or disturb people should be answered."[22] One report indicated that the Council of Bishops of the Methodist Church asked Kennedy to meet with them on the fifteenth, but it was unlikely that Kennedy or his associates would have agreed that he should go into their lair at that particular point and there is no record of the encounter ever having taken place. In August he did attend a meeting—but with a select corps of Washington newsmen at the Statler-Hilton Hotel at Sixteenth and K Streets, the site of the Gridiron Club gatherings. That session was initiated by Sorensen, who pointed out to Fletcher Knebel that Kennedy would like to become better acquainted with some of the Washington reporters who were Gridiron friends of Knebel's. "Can you get some of them together and have one of those off-the-record things?" suggested Sorensen.[23]

The journalist and Sorensen went over the lists of reporters with an emphasis on names that the senator knew only casually or not at all. Those selected were invited to dine with him at the hotel. Kennedy reminded them that the session was off the record. If they wanted to report the story, it would have to be without quoting him directly or indirectly. One reporter told Kennedy that he looked like a shoo-in to get a lot of delegates from a number of states, especially some of the leading states that had Catholic governors. Kennedy then explained that the reality was quite different. In such states the religious factor was actually working against him. The reluctance of those governors to make Catholicism an issue tended to make them lean the other way. Mike DiSalle of Ohio seemed prepared to support him; such other Catholic governors as Edmund Brown of California, David Lawrence of Pennsylvania, and Steve McNichols of Colorado were far more wary of the risks.

The session had not only been arranged to suit the Kennedy purpose but, insofar as the press was concerned, to get a story about the man who had clearly become the hottest political figure in Washington. Accordingly, to make that possible, they followed the usual campaign practice of paying all expenses for the dinner, including Kennedy and Sorensen's share. Not surprisingly, the newsworthy part of the conference soon "leaked." Edward Folliard of *The Washington Post,* one of those who had been present, filed a story that respected the no-attribution rule but nevertheless sounded unmistakably as though he had drawn from Kennedy himself. Drew Pearson was then inspired to do a little of his own investigative work and got one of the participants to tell him what went on. Pearson's story was carried in the *Post* on August 25 with revelations about the secret meeting. The exposé said that Kennedy had cited DiSalle along with Lawrence, Brown, and McNichols as governors "who did not think that the Catholic Church should become an issue in the coming campaign."[24]

Kennedy blew up. As Knebel later remembered the incident, Kennedy called him as soon as Pearson's account appeared. He acknowledged that the story was basically correct but feared the consequences of its circulation. "I did say it, but—" Knebel has quoted him. The senator then requested the newsman to send telegrams to all Catholic governors mentioned to deny its accuracy. Knebel balked; the relationship with his source was verging on the unethical. But, as he later recalled, "You know, that's the way the Kennedys were. They were rough. And he was putting the pressure on me; without saying so, the clear impression was that if I didn't do that, our relationship wasn't going to be as hot in the future as it had been." So Knebel sent the telegrams and Kennedy paid the bills.[25] Kennedy then dispatched a round of telegrams under his own signature. One, a vigorous denial to the *Post,* said that the governors were only concerned with selecting "the one who provides the greatest leadership in the development of the West and in strengthening of the security of the United States." To Drew Pearson, he claimed that "the only reference made to this matter at the dinner was that a Catholic being a candidate did raise problems for other Catholic politicians, but I did not—I repeat, did not—state that these men opposed me at this time, or that there was any concern that the Catholic Church would become quote too close unquote to the Democratic Party if I ran."[26]

For the party itself, Kennedy might succeed in proving his point that a Catholic could get elected. But even if he did not, they were left with the inescapable dilemma of the "Catholic issue." Having experienced growing defections among Catholic Democrats, they were in no position to simply ignore the fact that not opening the ticket—someplace on the ticket—to a Roman Catholic could become especially disastrous if the Republicans were to go along with someone like James Mitchell.

A late-summer *Congressional Quarterly* survey showed that Lyndon Johnson led among congressional Democrats. The majority leader was the preferred presidential candidate of twenty-three percent while Stevenson and Symington were tied with eighteen percent each. Kennedy trailed with seventeen percent. As Kennedy prepared to announce his formal candidacy and readiness to compete in primaries that could demonstrate his strength among Protestants as well as Catholics, the best betting was that he would emerge with the vice-presidential nomination.[27]

In late October Jack Kennedy gathered with fifteen key aides at Bobby's Hyannis Port home. They devoted themselves to specific plans. Unless the senator really wanted to adjust himself to some other job, he knew very well, as did those around him in the room that day, about the essential role to be played by the primaries. Only by entering and impressing the country could he achieve the psychological gains to further the process of acquiring a sufficient number of committed delegates, and only by winning the convention on the first ballot, a process that could best be achieved by taking the party by storm, could he be sure of winning the nomination. Subsequent ballots could well encourage defections and evaporate any chance of victory. Kennedy spoke about the forthcoming problems. Having been campaigning since the close of the 1956 convention and having worked with phenomenal energy through 1959, even while occupied with the formulation of the labor bill, he had become intimately acquainted with all future battlegrounds. His recitation enumerated state after state; speaking without notes he recalled names, dates, and places and analyzed the operative political factors. He reeled off the personalities, the obstacles, the various pertinent data. "No one at the meeting could match his knowledge of detail," wrote one of the participants.[28]

An unpublicized, unofficial campaign office had been operating since January. The nine-room suite in the Esso Building on Constitution Avenue, just below Capitol Hill, had only the name of Stephen E. Smith on the door. There, work progressed on analyzing, gathering data, and collecting some forty thousand to fifty thousand file cards. Under Smith's supervision and working with Ken O'Donnell, Larry O'Brien, and Bob Wallace from Kennedy's Senate staff, they divided the country, region by region. Bobby was still tied up with the McClellan Committee and the preparation of his book, *The Enemy Within* (for which Krock wrote the foreword), and could not devote himself full time until the fall, but he induced his old friend, Dave Hackett, to take a leave from his editing job in Montreal to lend a hand.

Making the state-by-state examination of delegate-election procedures and rating the key individuals according to a one-to-ten numbering system to indicate their loyalty to the Kennedy cause, the staff gradually narrowed down the card files to those with the basic elements of vital information. That provided a careful survey of each delegate and alternate, complete with everything relevant about the person and with notations showing when and how each had been contacted—in effect, a massive lobbying job, with each member of the staff concentrating on certain states. O'Brien took charge of field operations, his responsibilities overlapping somewhat with O'Donnell, and they zeroed in on the states of Wisconsin and West Virginia, where the key primaries were to be held. Wallace concentrated on the Midwest. Later, at the start of September, Pierre Salinger, who had worked with Bobby for over thirty-one months as a rackets committee investigator, arrived to join the staff and went to work setting up a press operation. Hiring two secretaries, he began accumulating lists of key newsmen who would be covering the presidential campaign.[29] In December, the senator's office staff was augmented by the arrival of Richard Goodwin.

Meanwhile, Kennedy himself crisscrossed the continent, appearing at political meetings from Puerto Rico to Los Angeles and Honolulu. At the seventy-fourth annual Washington Gridiron Club dinner at the Hotel Statler-Hilton, he was introduced as the first candidate to run for president on the "family plan." With lyrics written by Fletcher Knebel to the tune of "All of Me," the enterprise was explained by "Papa Joseph P. Kennedy" with such words as:

All of us
Why not take all of us
Fabulous
You can't live without us
My son Jack
Heads the procession
Then comes Bob
Groomed for succession.

We're the most
We stretch from coast to coast
Kennedys
Just go on forever
I've got the dough
You might as well know
With one—
You get all of us.[30]

Despite Jack's greater independence, Joe worked hard behind the scenes and usually, as was his metier, on the telephone. One indication that Joe Kennedy was in there still exerting influence was the receipt of a phone call by John Harriman, *The Boston Globe* financial writer who had been hired by the Ambassador to do some speech-writing for Jack in 1952. During this period, Harriman was called and asked, "Do you think that easy money is going to be an important issue in this campaign? Does Jack have to take an unsound view, namely to be in favor of easy money, for political reasons or would it be unnecessary for him to do so?"[31]

A Joe Kennedy phone call was also placed to popular playwright Moss Hart. Speaking from Palm Beach to Hart in New York, he asked if the distinguished writer would devote some time to contribute speeches to his son's campaign. When told that the work would involve traveling with the senator, Hart, who had already suffered from cardiac problems, responded by explaining that, while he was flattered by the request, his physical condition would make it inadvisable. Had he read *Profiles in Courage*? the Ambassador wanted to know. When Hart said he had not, Joe Kennedy promised that he would soon receive a copy. The playwright and his wife, actress Kitty Carlisle, expected that the book would arrive within two or three days, probably from Florida. But, as Kitty Carlisle Hart remembers the incident, "The doorbell rang about fifteen minutes later and there was the book. Moss was so impressed with this efficiency and the extraordinary speed with which he followed through!"[32] Of course, the Ambassador had merely called the Park Avenue office, which then promptly dispatched a copy to the Hart residence.

The senior Kennedy also requested John McCormack to personally get in touch with Billy Green in Philadelphia, Charlie Buckley in The Bronx, and Pat Brown in California and help to round up some of the congressional and state powers behind his son, which the speaker then did. Ken O'Donnell recalled that the Ambassador was somewhat "overanxious," making so many personal calls to such political figures as Mayor Richard Daley of Chicago and Governor Lawrence that Jack would have been upset had he realized how many there were.[33] At the elevation of the old Kennedy friend, Bishop John Wright, to Archbishop of Pittsburgh, with Lawrence due to be present, the Ambassador asked Frank Morrissey to broach the subject of Jack's presidential nomination. Cardinal Cushing, who was also there, warned Lawrence that Catholic pessimism about the ability of a member of their church to become president could only end up by hurting the party. But Lawrence repeatedly asserted that a Catholic was not electable.[34] Joe Kennedy also got Tip O'Neill to work on Sam Rayburn. O'Neill learned that the real boss in Pennsylvania was a fellow named Joe Clark (no relation to the senator), who was the state's party treasurer and the power behind Billy

Green. When O'Neill reported this information to Jack Kennedy, who had never heard of Clark, the senator telephoned his father. "Within forty-eight hours the father had Clark as his guest at the Waldorf," O'Neill reported.[35]

But one of the best examples of Joe Kennedy's behind-the-scenes power was yet to come. *U.S. News & World Report,* in its issue dated December 21, published extensive excerpts from the John Hersey "Survival" article that had originally appeared in *The New Yorker.* Hersey was stunned; he had had no word of its impending usage. The writer promptly phoned *The New Yorker*'s lawyers and they relayed their inquiry to the other magazine, where editor David Lawrence (no relation to the governor of Pennsylvania) explained that the material had been supplied by the Kennedy office without a copyright and that he had a perfect right to print it. Hersey turned to Senator Kennedy, who offered as compensation the paperback rights to a new edition of *Why England Slept.* The novelist recalls that was "a joke at the time, because *Why England Slept* was a total bomb from the publication point of view." Even though the current Dolphin paperback ultimately did respectably, Hersey never heard anything further about such rights. In recalling the situation, he reflected that what he got from Kennedy was "the back of his hand."[36]

Shortly after that, the Ambassador went to Albany to solicit the support of the county Democratic chairman, Daniel P. O'Connell, who had reservations about Jack being a little too young for the presidency. "He is," Joe Kennedy conceded. "But I'm seventy-two and I want to be around to enjoy it." Ambassador Kennedy left Albany with O'Connell's promise of two and a half votes from his district, "a modest but satisfactory start on New York's one hundred and fourteen convention votes."[37]

At the same time, the Ambassador was aiding his son's campaign by maintaining a close and cordial relationship with FBI Director J. Edgar Hoover. Traditional greetings were sent on appropriate occasions, together with effusive exchanges of goodwill. All complimentary references about the bureau or its director were duly passed on to satisfy Hoover's vanity, and their correspondence shows a "Dear Joe" and "Edgar" relationship. The FBI's special agent based at Hyannis attended Jack's wedding and faithfully reported back the senator's remarks about a "splendid job done" and his willingness at all times to "support Mr. Hoover and the FBI."[38] When Special Agent J. J. Kelly visited at Hyannis Port with Jack and his father, Hoover was quickly informed that the senator "expressed himself as believing the FBI to be the only real Governmental agency worthy of its salt and expressed his admiration for your accomplishments."[39] Furthermore, a memorandum written during the Democratic presidential nominating convention of 1960 shows that Ambassador Kennedy was a Special Area Contact for the FBI in Boston, a designation, in the agency's words, used for "anyone whom the Bureau believes may be of assistance to and cooperative with its investigations."[40] Flattery and assistance to the director was essential to protect Jack's career, especially considering the potentially damning material in his FBI file. Nor had it hurt to have friends at the bureau when the authorship of *Profiles in Courage* was being questioned.

When, on the Monterey Peninsula in California in May of 1960, journalist Hugh Sidey, in Kennedy's presence, asked Red Fay about the Ambassador's influence on Kennedy's career, "Jack's look of real concern indicated that he wanted me to think very carefully before answering the question." Fay remembered how "highly sensitive" Kennedy was on the subject.[41] Fletcher Knebel, while preparing a chapter in Eric Sevareid's book about the potential candidates, picked up another insight about Kennedy's sensitivity toward his father's role. Hoping for a confirmation that the son's monetary inheritance was at least as high as the draft of his chapter indicated, Knebel left the manuscript for Kennedy's inspection. Soon afterward the senator asked to see the writer. In his office, he expressed his disturbance about the inclusion of the story linking the loan to John Fox of the *Boston Post* with Joseph P. Kennedy and the 1952 senatorial campaign. "Now," Kennedy told Knebel, "you know nothing like that happened. It was a straight commercial loan." He then phoned the New York office and spoke to Steve Smith, who read to Knebel the official explanation that had been made public earlier. Kennedy then turned to Knebel and asked whether that would be acceptable for the article. Knebel agreed. It sounded like the fair thing to do. Lacking any firm evidence that the Ambassador had held out the money as the price for the publisher's endorsement of his son's election, the inclusion of the Kennedy explanation would give the story better balance. The senator was obviously pleased. As they walked toward the door together, he placed his hand on the journalist's shoulder and said softly, "You know, we had to buy that fucking paper or I'd have been licked."[42]

Just reviewing Kennedy's schedule before that October 28, 1959, meeting confirms a majestic display of energy. On April 9 he opened a seven-city swing in three days through Wisconsin, delivering six speeches, with a first stop in Milwaukee at the annual Gridiron Club dinner of the Milwaukee press club in the Schroeder Hotel. At that appearance he began by saying, "I have chosen this forum and this time to make a very important announcement—I will not under any conditions or any circumstances be a candidate in 1960 for President—of the Milwaukee Press Club."[43] On July 9 a widely syndicated column by Marquis Childs appeared alleging that at least one million dollars had been spent on the campaign so far and that it was being masterminded by Joe Kennedy, which the Kennedy managers denied, even to the extent that the father had any connection with the campaign at all.[44]

On the seventeenth the Kennedy office announced that the family had formed Ken-Air Corporation, which bought a Convair plane for $385,000. The aircraft was then leased to the senator at the rate of $1.75 a mile. Named the *Caroline* and with a pilot retained by the corporation, the plane logged 110,000 miles in 1959 and 1960, which would bring the cost for leasing alone to $192,500, not including fuel, maintenance, and insurance. The plane, of course, gave Kennedy an enormous advantage. In September, accompanied by Jackie, he made a three-day preprimary tour through Wisconsin, delivering eighteen speeches in fourteen towns. He held a half-dozen press conferences and interviews and appeared on television three times, all accomplished with the assistance of the Convair. Jackie, commenting on the Wisconsin speaking trip, said that that was the first time her husband had ever told her to go ahead and campaign with him. "I usually try to stay out of the office and out of the arrangement. But it's just wrong for him to try to do too much."[45]

As a speaker, he had still needed to improve. A common observation of those who saw him up close during that period was that he seemed slightly dull, slightly professorial, sincere, and too serious, but, there again, when he answered questions from his audience he was sharp, sparkling, and supremely sure of himself.

On October 22 Kennedy appeared at the Waldorf-Astoria for the annual Al Smith Dinner. Twenty-five hundred were present, including Governor Rockefeller, Mayor Wagner, and Cardinal Spellman. Kennedy swept the great share of attention. He cracked off-the-cuff jests, evoking applause and laughter ten times in nine minutes. Although he was the final speaker of the long evening, not beginning to talk until eleven o'clock, he immediately threw out a series of politically pointed jests that took up more than half of his time, which necessitated dropping a large part of his prepared text. He told of one presidential candidate who carried fewer states than any other in his party, losing even his own. "You all know his name and his religion." Kennedy went on, "Alfred M. Landon, Protestant." He recalled that the late Governor Smith had jokingly stated that any governor of New York kept a spyglass on Washington. "But the last time I was in Washington, I noticed a worried figure on the steps of the Capitol with his spyglass turned toward Albany." The implication, of course, was that Nixon was watching Rockefeller as a rival, which produced a great deal of laughter.[46]

Before the October 28, 1959, Hyannis Port meeting, he received a field report suggesting that there were widespread doubts about his depth and maturity and whether he had either Stevenson's intellect or Eisenhower's experience. It contained a suggestion that he circulate a photograph in which he looked less youthful than the ones currently going around the country. It advised that "there is a prevailing doubt in some circles that Kennedy is a bonafide liberal . . . he must identify as a 1960 liberal in clear and unmistakable terms."[47]

When the Hyannis Port meeting reconvened that afternoon, no final decisions were made about entering the sixteen primaries scheduled for 1960, except New Hampshire, which was viewed as obligatory. The decision about Wisconsin was foremost in everybody's mind. After having lunch at Joe Kennedy's house across the lawn from Bobby's, they reassembled under the chairmanship of the younger Kennedy brother. Before completing their work at four thirty, assignments were distributed with the regional divisions under responsibility of different individuals. One point made was that Chester Bowles should be invited to join the campaign and utilized in some way; probably not directly connected with it, but he should be some sort of an adviser with a title such as "Chairman of Committee on Foreign Policy." John Bailey accepted the task of handling the Bowles situation. Ted Sorensen was given the job of creating an appropriate title for the former New Deal OPA administrator, Connecticut governor, and congressman still regarded by liberals as a venerable symbol of the Roosevelt era.[48] Bowles, of course, was close to both Humphrey and Stevenson; and, as was clear at the meeting, his greatest importance was not his expertise, not his ideas, but his appeal to the Democratic left. He found himself courted by Sorensen, twice at his Washington home and later by Kennedy personally at the Park Plaza Hotel in New York City. Kennedy explained that he wanted Bowles as his foreign-policy adviser because of their similar views and did nothing to dispel implications that Bowles might be appointed to head the State Department. For his part, Bowles was both impressed and flattered. He later told an interviewer that Kennedy had "read every book, article, and speech I had written on the subject of foreign policy and thought that I was closer to his own line of thinking than anyone else." Bowles took the matter up with Stevenson and found continued noncommitment, so he went along with Kennedy. He himself was realistic and candid about his function, acknowledging later that he did not really work closely with Kennedy as a foreign-policy adviser and saying that it "was pretty apparent that I was window-dressing, and Kennedy didn't really feel he needed this assistance. . . . In the last analysis I had very little to do with speech-writing or the general development of Kennedy's campaign."[49]

Attention at the Hyannis Port meeting was also focused upon the South, where there was always the possibility of another rebellion in the face of stiffening civil-rights demands. Such fears were not totally unwarranted. Charles Bloch, the Macon, Georgia, attorney and close friend of Richard Russell, advocated a plan to get as many southern states as possible to provide for independent electors "and try to procure the balance of power in that way. . . . I'm now convinced more than ever that we have to fight this thing with renewed vigor and energy, and that any hope of educating New York and Massachusetts people in the mass to appreciate and understand our position is a false one. Some judges, some lawyers understand it, but they can't do anything about it."[50] Bobby Kennedy, watching the Georgia situation, felt that the key man there undoubtedly was Herman Talmadge. He had some strength, and Bobby did not feel that Russell would have a great deal to say in 1960. The governor and Talmadge would go for Johnson at least on the first ballot, but without much enthusiasm. After that, if handled correctly, they might very well be persuaded to go with Kennedy, as they were claiming that the Catholic question was no longer a major problem. Then, cynically, Bobby noted that the labor criticism of Kennedy could be used to advantage in the South, adding that "anything we could get into that area about Wayne Morse's speeches against Jack on the labor situation would be extremely valuable."[51] There, as with Kennedy's letter to Adlai Stevenson on the labor bill as having exculpated the Democrats from being too close to the unions, Bobby was also trying to turn the fact of the Landrum-Griffin Bill to Kennedy's advantage.

But that was late in the year and Kennedy was moving toward his official announcement. He flew into Denver in November for a reception of businessmen set up by his old friend Byron White and toured the area, meeting with additional groups. Meanwhile, his office received a poll taken by Lou Harris that showed he could beat Humphrey in Wisconsin, so moving into that state's primary certainly became less debatable. On December 17, a UPI reporter in the robotype room of the Senate Office Building discovered a mailing being prepared by the Kennedy office with the message "I am announcing on January 2 my candidacy for the Democratic Presidential nomination."[52] With all that set up, Kennedy and Jackie and baby Caroline left in late December to spend the Christmas season at Montego Bay, Jamaica.

That was a happy, relaxed period for Jack and his family. Caroline was two years old, and her father welcomed the opportunity to frolic with her in the water and take the child sailing. Jacqueline, too—long since resigned to the requirements of political life—valued a vacation break that could only become less frequent if her husband made any headway with his immediate plans. She was also caught up in the excitement of the situation. Along with her father-in-law, with whom she had become close, Jacqueline had become a part of her husband's career. She had mastered the art of being the wife of an important politician. Her beauty combined with delicate, well-cultivated social mannerisms contributed an additional touch of glamour to the handsome, still youthful senator about to display the audacity of declaring his candidacy for the presidency of the United States. The venture, with the prospects it offered, along with their mutual interest in Caroline, helped soften the tensions that had strained the marriage earlier.

Of course, there was certainly no way of escaping the political excitement, even in Jamaica. Everything was geared toward the main goal. Cleveland Amory was with Kennedy on the beach at John Pringle's place, Round Hill. With them were also Oscar Hammerstein and William Paley. There, for the first time, they heard Kennedy's precise determination to run for the presidency. Asked by Hammerstein about the obstacles caused by anti-Catholicism, Kennedy replied, as Amory recalls, "I'm going to make it so that the prejudice is if you vote for me *for that reason.* "[53] From that Caribbean island that New Year's Eve, Kennedy spent more than a half hour on the telephone with Pierre Salinger, getting a last-minute rundown on the logistics.[54]

On January 2, a Saturday, well timed for the Sunday papers, Jack Kennedy made his announcement. Using the Senate Caucus Room and facing an audience of about three hundred friends and supporters, who constituted his cheering section, he explained that he would enter the March 8 New Hampshire primary but was reserving any decision about Wisconsin. The entire session, according to *The New York Times* reporter, had the flavor of a political rally. He confronted the religious question head-on by saying that the real issue was whether or not the candidate believes in the First Amendment provisions for the separation of church and state. The major issues that he ticked off were ending the burdensome arms race, maintaining freedom and order in the newly emerging nations, rebuilding the stature of American science and education, achieving employment without further inflation, expanding economic growth, preventing the collapse of the farm economy and the decay of our cities, and giving direction to our traditional moral purpose. Most significantly, especially as a potential successor to Eisenhower, was his emphasis on the vitality of presidential leadership, which he expressed as a force capable of generating "the most crucial decisions of this century."[55]

A significant outcome was the attention given to his firm rejection of the vice-presidential nomination, which came amid the persistent belief that he could not possibly achieve any more than that. Under no circumstance, he declared, would he accept second place on the ticket. Ironically, his advance toward formal candidacy had, by calling attention to his obstacles, brought increased doubts that he could actually capture the top spot, which led his potential rivals to underestimate his progress. To James Reston, his rejection of the vice-presidency again raised the question of the firm political support among rank-and-file Catholics. Reston saw it as a warning to Democratic leaders not to think they could reject Kennedy's candidacy and still retain the support of his backers by giving him the second spot. As a direct consequence of this dilemma, Kennedy challenged his rivals to fight it out in the primaries, saying that anyone who avoided them did not deserve to be taken seriously by the convention. He specifically mentioned Symington and Johnson.[56]

Then came the loaded questions. Bishop G. Bromley Oxnam of the Methodist Church wondered whether Kennedy would be free of "Roman Catholic hierarchical control" if he were elected. Bishop Oxnam, an influential Protestant spokesman, conceded that Kennedy was a "sincere, able person with a very fine mind." But recalling the Four Chaplains incident made him doubt that Kennedy could remain independent.[57] Interviewed on television that January 3, Kennedy again had to field the question of birth control. More than a matter of his view of the subject was whether his attitude was dominated by the Church, and he reiterated his position that it would be a political mistake to put such a request to Congress in a foreign aid bill because by combining two such controversial matters, "you'd get neither birth control nor foreign aid."[58]

Having no illusions about what was ahead, he worked at controlling as much as he could. He moved to dissuade Stevenson from taking seriously the stories, apparently circulated by Latham, that Kennedy had complained about having been treated unfairly by the Governor at the Chicago convention. He explained that he had neither spoken to Latham for at least six months nor had he ever talked to him about that episode. Stevenson was gracious. "Thanks for your letter," he wrote back. "But please don't worry; I was sure the Professor was confused."[59] Then Kennedy arranged for a meeting with Truman, which took place at the Mayflower Hotel in Washington on January 10. He got out of that session as much as he could realistically have desired. The former president, more and more, it seemed, enjoying his elder-statesman role— despite his failure at being kingmaker in 1956—was not about to make a public endorsement of anyone; and certainly not Jack Kennedy. But Kennedy was pleased to at least hear that Truman would do nothing to hurt him. Kennedy then agreed to stay out of the Ohio primary in exchange for assurances from Governor DiSalle, the state's favorite son, that he would get their seventy-four convention votes on the first ballot. Moreover, he told the press he was "delighted" that Mike DiSalle was with him, a coup that secured the first major state delegation and political leadership—and also a Catholic governor![60]

With the filing date for the April 5 Wisconsin primary approaching, entering that contest in a state where Humphrey was regarded by many as its "third senator," had to be the next major move. Gaylord Nelson, of course, was for Humphrey, with Stevenson his second choice. Dependent, however, on the backing of the state chairman, Pat Lucey, a Kennedy man, and trying to hold the support of the Roman Catholic districts for his own reelection that year, he avoided an open endorsement. At the same time, Lou Harris turned in a poll that showed Kennedy ahead of Humphrey in the state by a comfortable 60–40 margin, with his strength heavily concentrated in the industrial districts of Milwaukee and the Fox River valley, the centers of Wisconsin's Roman Catholic population. In the heavily pro-Stevenson university city of Madison, Kennedy's interests were being promoted by Mayor Nestingen and Jerry Bruno, a former campaign organizer for William Proxmire, whose efforts had been essential in securing the senator's election to Joe

McCarthy's vacated seat in 1957. On January 7 Jim Rowe informed Bill Blair that the Humphrey people were "battening down the hatches for Wisconsin," waiting for Kennedy to enter "on the bland assumption he would have to come. I believe that assumption is soon to become a reality."[61] Finally, on January 21, in Milwaukee, Kennedy announced his decision to enter both the Nebraska and Wisconsin primaries, promising that he would campaign on peace, farm problems, education, and inflation. Notably absent from his list were either civil rights or the Landrum-Griffin Bill, two items singled out by Humphrey to launch his own campaign.[62]

Epilogue:

"I Never Could Have Done It"

Jack had made his moves, had announced specific goals and placed the Kennedy name in contention. All disciplines acquired by necessity had to be mobilized: the tenacity of the junior varsity end; the backstroker who utilized Torby's assistance to fortify his body for the swimming meet; the devourer of books who developed his mind while coping with physical distress; the curious young man, fortunately immune from the economic depression that hit almost everybody else, who had had the advantages of seeing the world, finally returning and maturing suffi- ciently to cap his formal education with *Why England Slept;* the second son, diffident, groping for identification, then stepping in to replace his fallen older brother; the congressional candidate repressing pain, exhaus- tion, and the incipient stages of a serious adrenal gland disorder to nonetheless encourage expectations that he had been sent to provide new leadership; the congressman, the senator, who had upset a symbol of Massachusetts's Yankee establishment and masked his own debilita- tions, even while facing possible death, or at best, reduced longevity, to produce *Profiles in Courage,* a politic creation dictated by his concept of what it took to educate the masses for their own survival; the reserved, often shy young man, an indifferent speaker at best, who had ducked overt identification as a vice-presidential contender and then, contrary to his father's logical advice, had nevertheless plunged ahead to suffer the disappointment of defeat.

On the surface, he was cool; detached, said the critics, even as calculating as Nixon, the American Mephistopheles who became the embodiment of political evil. To such critics, John Kennedy was a pragmatic, unprincipled politician, an Irish Catholic Boston pol with refinement, whose motley buddies were links with a culture no longer his. For he was not an ethnic; he was Brahmin, and Harvard. While he had insatiable appetites for women, fun, coming out ahead, the good life, so too did he desire pleasures of the mind; only, unlike most true intellectuals, he scorned knowledge without application.

To his credit, Joe Kennedy had made certain that the world would be within his son's view, even that which he himself found distasteful, risking the possibility that, one day—as he himself put it—his children might spit in his eye. Jack's new friends were, to the Ambassador, a somewhat upsetting reminder of the bright, well-trained, gifted specialists he had seen, and loathed, around Franklin D. Roosevelt. Now, they were trying to move Jack into their world, to their values. And they, fully aware of young Kennedy's background, his traditional biases and conditioning, sensed that the pragmatic facade covered passion that sometimes broke through the exterior, not unlike the capacity they found in Adlai Stevenson: the ability to learn, to care, and to feel deeply.

Like Stevenson, Kennedy could and did cry, but his tears were like his reading glasses, imperfections that had to be hidden from the public. The inability of Kennedy and Stevenson, each with aristocratic misgivings about the public weal, to reconcile their psyches and come to terms with each other, would ultimately prove a great tragedy of American political life. During those first two post-World War II decades, only with Stevenson did Kennedy share the ability to fire the young and idealistic to desire a constructive role in American government.

Jack's inner resources would ultimately inspire not only the American people but a global audience. Having come so far, he first had to survive the enormous odds that, as late as early 1960, made it hard for the "experts" to believe he could go all the way. Joe Kennedy, taking it all in from the sidelines while doing what he did best, manipulating and accumulating, had initiated the process. But the son was not the father. "My father would be for me," Jack once told Dorothy Schiff of the *New York Post,* "if I were running as head of the Communist Party," a statement only slightly hyperbolic.[1] "I don't understand it," his father told Charles Spalding. "He's not like me at all. I never could have done it."[2]

And, as well as anybody else, the Ambassador understood that he had to remain far offstage. This was no time for reminders about Joseph P. Kennedy's association with isolationism, British defeatism, and toleration of triumphant Nazism; nor for hints that a ruthless tycoon was holding the candidate on a string. There were enough potential snags that could scuttle his son. Fortunately, from the wings, he had the power to prevent disasters.

He was, after all, still the head of the family, the man who had built the fortune that could now embrace political leadership and power. In his own mind, Joe Kennedy could never forget the blackballing at Cohasset, or the same anti-Catholicism—as he was convinced—that kept him from Harvard's Board of Overseers. Now Jack, in Joe Junior's place, was at the edge of power, real power. With some deft guidance, he could actually confound them all and make it to the top. Bobby, too, would then get his chance, with Jack's help. Joe would see to that. So another plan was intolerable, giving up the Senate seat to Torby, the way Jack and Macdonald understood the vacancy would be filled if the presidency was achieved. In the Ambassador's mind, Macdonald's independence would disregard the interests of the Kennedy succession. Torby was too assertive, irreverent—a great friend of Jack's but, alas, a free spirit. He would consider the seat his own, not an assignment to keep secure until Teddy would win it in 1964. When marriage to Kathleen had implied subservience to the Kennedys, Torby had gone running the other way. His and Jack's Damon and Pythias relationship threatened to contravene the Kennedy interest. Macdonald, in fact, would later boast to his own family, "There was a prince and there was a court, and I was not part of it, by choice." No, Jack was not considering all the elements. As much as he and Torby had assumed there would be a Senator Macdonald from Massachusetts, that was one of the mistakes Joe Kennedy could not permit.[3]

It was still only 1960 and a time of relative innocence in American life. Herbert Marcuse had yet to sway a new generation of radicals. Tom Hayden and the Port Huron Statement of the Students for a Democratic Society still belonged to the future. At the University of Wisconsin, Professor William Appleman Williams's students were preparing their historical studies questioning whether conflict rather than consensus had governed American civilization. Researchers were only beginning to upset the portrait of post-Civil War Radical Reconstruction still being taught to virtually every schoolchild and described in *Profiles in Courage* as "a black nightmare the South never could forget."[4] The civil-rights movement had yet to peak, had yet to become the "black pcwer" revolt under a new and more militant leadership. Television sets were still to show police dogs, fire hoses, and cattle prods being used against citizens demonstrating for the right to be citizens. Cities had not begun to burn and, to most Americans, Indochina was indistinguishable from China, which at least everyone knew was Red. When the President spoke, people listened and believed, even if they weren't inspired. Meanwhile, the Washington press corps happily subsisted on authorized handouts and confined knowledge of naughty behavior to whispers in fraternal gossip sessions. Few looked for a Deep Throat. Investigative journalism was still being monopolized by Drew Pearson and his protégés, most notably Jack Anderson. Only rare "lefties" bothered with I. F. Stone.

In that America, instinctively sensing that something was lacking because, elsewhere, things were palpably askew, Jack Kennedy could step forward to regenerate the spirit. As a patriotic, young, articulate leader, he, like other aristocrats before him, had educated answers for his countrymen. With the invisible "founding father" watching with a mixture of pride and bewilderment over how far his son had come, the blemishes could be kept out of sight. The country's best lawyers were available to rebut allegations, especially the one that, in claiming authorship of *Profiles in Courage* and accepting the Pulitzer prize, Jack had transgressed the bounds of normal ghostwriting services provided for public officials. Medical records were sealed and vague rumors about Addison's could be satisfied with casual, assuring explanations that there really was not much to it. Photographers recorded the hatless and often coatless vigorous-looking senator, accompanied by a wife who obviously enhanced his portrait as a man of accomplishments, and the writers did not look much beyond the pictures.

Had the story of his prolonged and intimate relationship with Inga Arvad been revealed, for example, it could easily have reignited doubts about the Ambassador and the Nazis and, by extension, Jack and Joe McCarthy. As he looked forward to the battle for the nomination and surmounting the religious question, a scandalous exposé was about the last thing he needed. Although no evidence of her spying had actually been uncovered, her close associations with leaders of the Third Reich could have provided first-rate ammunition for Jack's enemies; for the liberals, it would have confirmed the doubts they had had all along. And the evidence was there, right in the files of the FBI, easily capable of being surreptitiously "leaked" by one well experienced in such matters, J. Edgar Hoover.[5] But Jack was safe. The cultivation of the director had removed the problem. The Kennedys had not neglected that center of power.

Trained to govern, he had come a long way, physically and intellectually. He had long since replaced his fallen brother and had overcome every impediment, largely within his own disposition, to prove his worthiness. As the oldest son, he now had to carry the responsibility. On the verge of his biggest gambit, Jack Kennedy had little in mind besides how to win within the rules mandated for political success in a democracy. He knew that the country was ripe for an infusion of energy and could be excited by inspirations toward a national purpose, a new challenge. More than two decades earlier, Professor Payson Wild had talked about a new frontier. In tune with the Kennedy sense of destiny, he was ready. Even Joe Junior could not have done better.

Notes

ABBREVIATIONS USED IN NOTES

JFKL   John F. Kennedy Library

OH   Oral History Transcript

NYT   New York Times

Prologue

1. Bruce Miroff, *Pragmatic Illusions: The Presidential Politics of John F. Kennedy* (New York: McKay, 1976), p. 295.
2. Cf., Richard J. Walton, *Cold War and Counterrevolution* (New York: Viking Press, 1972); Henry Fairlie, *The Kennedy Promise* (Garden City, N. Y.: Doubleday, 1973); Louise FitzSimons, *The Kennedy Doctrine* (New York: Random House, 1972); Richard J. Barnet, *The Roots of War* (New York: Atheneum, 1972); David Halberstam, *The Best and the Brightest* (New York: Random House, 1972).
3. Tom Wicker, *Kennedy Without Tears* (New York: William Morrow and Co., 1964), p. 16.

4. Laura Berquist, interview, May 15, 1979.
5. Henry Brandon, JFKL–OH.
6. Nikita Khrushchev, *Khrushchev Remembers: The Last Testament* (Boston: Little, Brown, 1974), p. 514.
7. Donald E. Schulz, "Kennedy and the Cuban Connection," *Foreign Policy,* 26 (Spring 1977), pp. 64, 121.
8. James Wine, JFKL–OH.
9. Frank O'Ferrall, JFKL–OH.
10. Richard M. Nixon, *RN: The Memoirs of Richard Nixon* (New York: Grosset & Dunlap, 1978), p. 252.
11. Earl T. Leonard, Jr., Richard Russell Library, University of Georgia–OH.
12. Kay Halle, interview, March 9, 1979.
13. Fletcher Knebel, interview, May 15, 1979.
14. James MacGregor Burns, "Remembrances of John F. Kennedy," unpublished typescript, December 19, 1964, Burns Papers, JFKL.
15. Cf., Carol Ann Berthold, "The Image and Character of President John F. Kennedy: A Rhetorical-Critical Approach," Ph.D. dissertation, Northwestern University, 1975, pp. 149, 156; Fletcher Knebel, interview, May 8, 1979.
16. William Safire, *Before the Fall* (Garden City, N.Y.: Doubleday, 1975), p. 438.

Chapter 1: "A Happy Family"

1. Richard J. Whalen, *The Founding Father: The Story of Joseph P. Kennedy* (New York: New American Library, 1964), p. 392.
2. Ibid.
3. Arthur Krock, JFKL–OH.
4. Paul B. Fay, Jr., *The Pleasure of His Company* (New York: Harper & Row, 1966), p. 141.
5. Charles Bartlett, JFKL–OH.
6. R. Sargent Shriver, Jr., interview, November 19, 1976.
7. Stephen E. Smith, interview, April 5, 1977.
8. Joseph Alsop, interview, July 26, 1977.
9. Tim Coogan, "Sure and It's County Kennedy Now," *New York Times Magazine,* June 23, 1963, p. 32.
10. Whalen, *Founding Father,* p. 15.
11. Joseph Dinneen, *The Kennedy Family* (Boston: Little, Brown, 1959), p. 9.
12. David E. Koskoff, *Joseph P. Kennedy: A Life and Times* (Englewood Cliffs, N.J.: Prentice-Hall, 1974), p. 19; Joseph W. McCarthy, *The Remarkable Kennedys* (New York: Dial Press, 1960), p. 33.
13. Leslie G. Ainley, *Boston Mahatma: A Biography of Martin Lomasney* (Boston: Bruce Humphries, Inc., 1949), p. 67.
14. Gail Cameron, *Rose: A Biography of Rose Fitzgerald Kennedy* (New York: Putnam, 1971), p. 187.
15. Koskoff, *Joseph P. Kennedy,* p. 27.
16. Ibid., p. 40.
17. Michael R. Beschloss, "Joseph Kennedy and Franklin Roosevelt: A Study in Power and Leadership," honors thesis, Williams College, 1977, p. 35.
18. Koskoff, *Joseph P. Kennedy,* p. 35.
19. Roy Howard to Newton D. Baker, July 12, 1932, as quoted in C. H. Cramer to JFK, April 17, 1959, President's Office File, Box 136, JFKL.
20. Koskoff, *Joseph P. Kennedy,* p. 53.

21. Whalen, *Founding Father,* p. 74.
22. Harold H. Martin, "The Amazing Kennedys," *Saturday Evening Post,* September 7, 1957, p. 48.

Chapter 2: *The Kennedy Children and Their World*

1. Rose Kennedy, recorded remarks at JFK National Historical Site, Brookline, Massachusetts.
2. James Rousmaniere, interview, March 10, 1977.
3. Cameron, *Rose,* p. 20.
4. Kitty Kelley, *Jackie Oh!* (New York: Lyle Stuart, 1978), p. 71; Rose Kennedy, *Times to Remember* (Garden City, N.Y.: Doubleday, 1974), p. 286.
5. Stephen E. Smith, interview, June 5, 1979.
6. James MacGregor Burns, *John Kennedy, A Political Profile* (New York: Harcourt, Brace, 1960), p. 129.
7. Joan Meyers, ed., *John Fitzgerald Kennedy: As We Remember Him* (New York: Atheneum, 1965), p. vi.
8. William O. Douglas, JFKL–OH.
9. McCarthy, *The Remarkable Kennedys,* p. 143.
10. John Hersey, interview, December 8, 1976.
11. Meyers, ed., *JFK,* p. vi.
12. Dr. Elmer C. Bartels, interview, December 2, 1977.
13. Rose Kennedy, in *Joseph P. Kennedy: A Life and Times,* p. 85. Joseph P. Kennedy later contributed $3,700 to the Guild of St. Apollonia, an amount that undoubtedly represented his "liquid" assets at the time.
14. JFK to Rose Kennedy, n.d., JFK Papers, Box 2, JFKL.
15. Nathan Pusey, JFKL–OH.
16. Theo Lippman, Jr., *Senator Ted Kennedy: The Career Behind the Image* (New York: W. W. Norton, 1976), p. 3.
17. Charles Bartlett to JFK, n.d., President's Office File, JFKL.
18. Kay Halle, JFKL–OH.
19. Priscilla Johnson McMillan, *Marina and Lee* (New York: Harper & Row, 1977), p. 4.
20. Jacob Potofsky, Columbia–OH.
21. John Bartlow Martin, *Adlai Stevenson of Illinois* (Garden City, N.Y.: Doubleday, 1976), p. 473.
22. McCarthy, *Kennedys,* p. 55.
23. John Henry Cutler, *'Honey Fitz': Three Steps to the White House* (Indianapolis, Indiana: Bobbs-Merrill, 1962), p. 243.
24. Paul G. Pennoyer, Jr., interview, September 16, 1977.
25. James J. Storrow, Jr., interview, March 18, 1977.
26. Theodore C. Sorensen, *The Kennedy Legacy* (New York: Macmillan, 1969), p. 34.
27. William O. Douglas, JFKL–OH.
28. William V. Shannon, *The American Irish* (New York: Macmillan, 1963), p. 396.
29. John Johansen, interview, November 24, 1976; Fletcher Knebel, May 15, 1979.
30. Koskoff, *Joseph P. Kennedy,* p. 371.
31. John F. Kennedy, ed., *As We Remember Joe* (Cambridge, Mass.: privately printed at the University Press, 1945), p. 36.
32. Kay Halle, JFKL–OH.
33. George Plimpton and Jean Stein, eds., *American Journey: The Times of Robert Kennedy* (New York: Signet, 1970), p. 50.
34. JFK, *As We Remember Joe,* p. 13.

35. William O. Douglas, JFKL–OH.
36. Leo Damore, *The Cape Cod Years of John Fitzgerald Kennedy* (Englewood Cliffs, N.J.: Prentice-Hall, 1967), p. 27.
37. Robert E. Thompson and Hortense Meyers, *Robert F. Kennedy: The Brother Within* (New York: Macmillan, 1962), p. 64.
38. Arthur Krock, JFKL–OH.
39. Rose Kennedy, *Times,* p. 21.
40. JFK to Joseph P. Kennedy, December 9, 1931, JFK Personal Papers, Box 2, JFKL.
41. Hank Searls, *The Lost Prince: Young Joe, the Forgotten Kennedy* (New York: World Publishing Co., 1969), p. 40.
42. Blair Clark, interview, March 18, 1977.
43. John Hersey, interview, December 8, 1976.
44. James Rousmaniere, interview, March 10, 1977.
45. Tazewell Shepard, Jr., *John F. Kennedy: Man of the Sea* (New York: Morrow, 1965), p. 28.
46. William O. Douglas, JFKL–OH.
47. Foster Furcolo, interview, February 21, 1977; Edward Teller, Columbia–OH; William McCormick Blair, Jr., to Theodore C. Sorensen, April 2, 1957, Stevenson Papers, Box 729, Princeton.
48. Garry Wills, *Nixon Agonistes* (Boston: Houghton Mifflin, 1970), p. 32.

Chapter 3: Period of Adjustment

1. Arthur Krock, JFKL–OH.
2. John Corry, *Golden Clan* (Boston: Houghton Mifflin, 1977), pp. 169–70.
3. Blair Clark, interview, March 18, 1977.
4. Peter Hoguet, interview, December 1, 1976.
5. James J. Storrow, Jr., interview, March 18, 1977.
6. Rose Kennedy, *Times,* p. 174.
7. Ibid.
8. Hugh Packard, interview, January 11, 1978.
9. R. Sargent Shriver, interview, November 19, 1976.
10. JFK to Rose Kennedy, n.d., JFK Personal Papers, Box 30, JFKL.
11. JFK to Joseph P. Kennedy, n.d., JFK Personal Papers, Box 30, JFKL.
12. Whalen, *Founding Father,* p. 112.
13. Meyers, ed., *JFK,* p. 11.
14. Information sheet dated 1931–1932, Choate File of JFK letters, folder 5, Choate Rosemary School.
15. Interviews, Hugh Packard and Owen Morgan, January 11, 1978; Seymour St. John, interview, June 22, 1978.
16. George St. John to Joseph P. Kennedy, October 6, 1936, JFK File, Choate Rosemary Hall.
17. Ibid., November 4, 1931.
18. Seymour St. John, interview, June 22, 1978.
19. John Johansen, interview, November 24, 1976.
20. Wardell St. John to Rose Kennedy, June 10, 1930, and information sheet dated 1931–1932, JFK File, Choate Rosemary Hall.
21. Interviews, Hugh Packard and Owen Morgan, January 11, 1978.
22. Rose Kennedy, *Times,* p. 177.
23. George St. John, "Principal's Report on Applicant," April 30, 1935, Harvard Records, MS 65-185, JFKL.
24. Ralph Horton, JFKL–OH.

25. Owen Morgan, interview, January 11, 1978.
26. Meyers, ed., *JFK,* p. 15.
27. Ralph Horton, JFKL–OH.
28. Meyers, ed., *JFK,* p. 13.
29. Earl G. Leinbach, "Football Juniors Report," October 1933, JFK File, Choate Rosemary Hall.
30. Seymour St. John, interview, June 22, 1978.
31. Joan and Clay Blair, Jr., *The Search for JFK* (New York: Berkley Publishing, 1976), p. 32.
32. Hugh Packard, interview, January 11, 1978; Blair, *Search,* pp. 31–32.
33. John Johansen, interview, November 24, 1976.
34. George St. John to Joseph P. Kennedy, December 19, 1934, JFK File, Choate Rosemary Hall.
35. Blair, *Search,* p. 37.
36. Ralph Horton, JFKL–OH.
37. Rose Kennedy, *Times,* p. 181.
38. George St. John to Joseph P. Kennedy, February 11, 1935, and Joseph P. Kennedy to George St. John, February 15, 1935, JFK File, Choate Rosemary Hall.
39. Interviews, Owen Morgan and Hugh Packard, January 11, 1978.
40. George St. John to Joseph P. Kennedy, October 20, 1931, Joseph P. Kennedy, Jr., File, Choate Rosemary School.
41. Meyers, ed., *JFK,* p. 15.
42. Ibid., p. 17.
43. Ibid.
44. Seymour St. John, interview, June 22, 1978.
45. Meyers, ed., *JFK,* pp. 17–18.
46. Felix Frankfurter, JFKL–OH.
47. George St. John, "Principal's Report on Applicant," April 30, 1935, Harvard Records, MS 65-185, JFKL.
48. Clara St. John to Rose Kennedy, February 8, 1932, and to Mr. Massie, February 8, 1932, Choate Folio 4, Nos. 54 and 55, JFKL.
49. Clara St. John to Rose Kennedy, January 18, 1932, JFK File, Choate Rosemary Hall.
50. Rose Kennedy to Clara St. John, n.d., JFK File, Choate Rosemary Hall.
51. Rose Kennedy to George St. John, January 17, 1933, JFK File, Choate Rosemary Hall.
52. Clara St. John to Rose Kennedy, February 6, 1934, JFK File, Choate Rosemary Hall.
53. Joseph P. Kennedy to George St. John, September 15, 1934, JFK File, Choate Rosemary Hall.
54. John Johansen, interview, November 24, 1976; Blair, *Search,* p. 37.
55. Seymour St. John, interview, June 22, 1978.
56. Joseph P. Kennedy to George St. John, September 1, 1934, JFK File, Choate Rosemary Hall.

Chapter 4: A Harvard Man

1. JFK to Richard M. Gummere, August 30, 1935, Harvard Records, MS 65-185, JFKL.
2. George St. John to JFK, November 8, 1935, JFK File, Choate Rosemary Hall.
3. JFK to Harvard College, July 6, 1936, Harvard Records, MS 65-185, JFKL.
4. Joseph P. Kennedy to James M. Landis, August 6, 1940, Box 24, Landis Papers, Library of Congress.
5. E. J. Kahn, Jr., *The World of Swope* (New York: Simon and Schuster, 1965), pp. 380–81.
6. Rose Kennedy, *Times,* p. 202.

7. Meyers, ed., *JFK,* p. 20.
8. Rose Kennedy, *Times,* p. 203.
9. JFK to Harvard College, July 6, 1936, and Joseph P. Kennedy to Delmar Leighton, August 28, 1936, Harvard Records, MS 65-185, JFKL.
10. Searls, *Lost Prince,* pp. 90–91.
11. JFK to Harvard College, July 6, 1936, Harvard Records, MS 65-185, JFKL.
12. Joseph P. Kennedy to Delmar Leighton, August 28, 1936, Harvard Records, MS 65-185, JFKL.
13. Shepard, *JFK,* p. 29.
14. Harvard Records, MS 65-185, JFKL.
15. James Rousmaniere, interview, March 10, 1977.
16. Payson Wild, JFKL–OH.
17. Burns, *Kennedy,* p. 30.
18. Cleveland Amory, interview, May 6, 1977.
19. James Rousmaniere, interview, March 10, 1977.
20. JFK Harvard Records, MS 65-185, JFKL.
21. Gerald Walker and Donald A. Allan, "Jack Kennedy at Harvard," *Coronet,* May 1961, p. 90.
22. Blair Clark, interview, March 18, 1977.
23. JFK to William Bullitt, n.d., in Orville Bullitt, ed., *For the President, Personal and Secret* (Boston: Houghton Mifflin, 1972), p. 274; Walker and Allan, "Jack Kennedy at Harvard," p. 90.
24. James Rousmaniere, interview, March 10, 1977.
25. Cutler, *'Honey Fitz,'* pp. 292–93.
26. Cf., Burns, *Kennedy,* p. 30; McCarthy, *Kennedys,* p. 75; Rose Kennedy, *Times,* p. 215.
27. Interviews, Laurie Macdonald and Torbert Macdonald, Jr., August 6, 1979.
28. James Rousmaniere, interview, March 10, 1977; Interviews, Laurie Macdonald and Torbert Macdonald, Jr., August 6, 1979.
29. *NYT,* May 22, 1976; Interviews, Blair Clark, March 18, 1977, and Phyllis Macdonald, August 9, 1979.
30. Laurie Macdonald, interview, August 6, 1979.
31. Ibid.
32. Walker and Allan, "Kennedy at Harvard," pp. 85–86.
33. Phyllis Macdonald, interview, August 9, 1979; Tutorial Record, 1937–1938, Harvard Records, MS 65-185, JFKL.
34. Phyllis Macdonald, interview, August 9, 1979.
35. Ibid.
36. Torbert Macdonald, Jr., interview, August 6, 1969.
37. Malden (Mass.) *Evening News,* May 28, 1976; Interviews, Torbert Macdonald, Jr., and Laurie Macdonald, August 6, 1979.
38. JFK Harvard Records, MS 65-185, JFKL.
39. Tutorial Record, 1937–1938, JFK Harvard Records, MS 65-185, JFKL.
40. Ibid.
41. Payson Wild, JFKL–OH.
42. Arthur Holcombe, in Meyers, ed., *JFK,* p. 23.
43. James Rousmaniere, interview, March 10, 1977.
44. JFK, Diary of European Trip, ms., Box 1, JFK Personal Papers, JFKL.
45. Burns, *Kennedy,* p. 32.
46. JFK, Diary of European Trip.
47. Burns, *Kennedy,* p. 32.
48. JFK, Diary of European Trip.
49. Beschloss, "Joseph Kennedy and Franklin Roosevelt," pp. 95–96, 100–01.
50. James A. Farley, *Jim Farley's Story* (New York: McGraw-Hill, 1948), p. 115.

51. Sheldon Marcus, *Father Coughlin* (Boston: Little, Brown, 1973), pp. 98–100.
52. Whalen, *Founding Father,* p. 113.
53. Beschloss, "Joseph Kennedy and Franklin Roosevelt," p. 133.
54. *Boston Globe,* December 8, 1937.
55. Charles Spalding, JFKL–OH.
56. *Boston Globe,* December 10, 1937.
57. Beschloss, "Joseph Kennedy and Franklin Roosevelt," p. 159.
58. Koskoff, *Kennedy,* p. 117.
59. Lord Longford, *Kennedy* (London: Weidenfeld and Nicolson, 1976), p. 21.
60. Harold Ickes, *The Inside Struggle* (New York: Simon and Schuster, 1954), pp. 685, 370, 377.
61. William Stevenson, *A Man Called Intrepid* (New York: Harcourt, Brace, 1976), p. 83.
62. Beschloss, "Joseph Kennedy and Franklin Roosevelt," pp. 176–77.
63. Stevenson, *Intrepid,* p. 82.
64. Walter Millis, ed., *The Forrestal Diaries* (New York: Viking Press, 1951), pp. 121–22.
65. Joseph P. Lash, *Roosevelt and Churchill, 1939–1941* (New York: W. W. Norton, 1976), p. 75.
66. Ickes, *Inside Struggle,* p. 712.
67. Stevenson, *Intrepid,* pp. 83–84.
68. Beschloss, "Joseph Kennedy and Franklin Roosevelt," p. 150.
69. Koskoff, *Kennedy,* pp. 140–41; Victor Lasky, *J.F.K.: The Man and the Myth* (New York: Macmillan, 1963), pp. 52–53; Whalen, *Founding Father,* p. 217; C. L. Sulzberger, *A Long Row of Candles* (New York: Macmillan, 1969), pp. 21–23.
70. Koskoff, *Kennedy,* p. 286.
71. Cordell Hull, *Memoirs of Cordell Hull* (New York: Macmillan, 1948), Vol. 1, p. 763.
72. James Leutze, ed., *The London Journal of General Raymond E. Lee* (Boston: Little, Brown, 1971), p. 4.
73. Stevenson, *Intrepid,* p. 82.
74. Hugh Fraser, JFKL–OH.
75. Beschloss, "Joseph Kennedy and Franklin Roosevelt," p. 22.

Chapter 5: The First Book

1. Ickes, *Inside Struggle,* p. 273.
2. Searls, *Lost Prince,* p. 108.
3. Bullitt, ed., *For the President,* p. 273.
4. Payson Wild, JFKL–OH.
5. A. C. Hanford to JFK, March 17, 1939, Harvard Records, MS 65-185, JFKL.
6. Tutorial Record, 1938–1939, signed by Bruce C. Hopper, May 15, 1939, Harvard Records, MS 65-185, JFKL; Payson Wild, JFKL–OH.
7. Herbert Feis to Arthur Schlesinger, Jr., May 23, 1966, Feis Collection, Library of Congress; Joseph P. Kennedy to Arthur Bliss Lane, June 16, 1939, Arthur Bliss Lane Papers, Box 17, Yale.
8. Burns, *Kennedy,* p. 38.
9. Howard M. Sacher, *A History of Israel* (New York: Alfred A. Knopf, 1976), pp. 222–23.
10. JFK to Joseph P. Kennedy, 1939, President's Office Files, Box 135, JFKL.
11. Ibid.
12. George F. Kennan, *Memoirs 1925–1950* (Boston: Little, Brown, 1967), pp. 91–92.
13. JFK to Bureau of Registration, September 13, 1939, JFK Harvard Records, MS 65-185, JFKL; Whalen, *Founding Father,* pp. 272–73; Cutler, *'Honey Fitz,'* p. 283; McCarthy, *Kennedys,* p. 82.

14. Walker and Allan, "Kennedy at Harvard," p. 91.
15. Blair Clark, interview, March 18, 1977.
16. Payson Wild, JFKL–OH.
17. *Harvard Crimson,* May 31, 1940.
18. Ibid., June 3, 1940.
19. Ibid., June 9, 1940.
20. Blair Clark, interview, March 18, 1977.
21. *Harvard Crimson,* June 9, 1940.
22. William Y. Elliott to Clifford K. Shipton, July 29, 1964, Harvard Records, MS 65-185, JFKL.
23. James Landis, Columbia–OH.
24. Ronald J. Nurse, "America Must Not Sleep: The Development of John F. Kennedy's Foreign Policy Attitudes, 1947–1960," unpublished Ph.D. dissertation, Michigan State University, 1971, p. 1; Payson Wild, JFKL–OH.
25. JFK to Liddell Hart, December 6, 1940, Pre-Presidential Papers, Box 73, JFKL.
26. Walker and Allan, "Kennedy at Harvard," p. 92.
27. Ibid., p. 92.
28. Carl J. Friedrich, Report on Thesis for Distinction, and Friedrich to Clifford Shipton, August 3, 1964, Harvard Records, MS 65-185, JFKL.
29. Henry A. Yeomans, Report on Thesis for Distinction, Harvard Records, MS 65-185, JFKL.
30. John F. Kennedy, "Appeasement at Munich," unpublished honors thesis, Harvard University, 1940, p. 91, Harvard Records, MS 65-185, JFKL.
31. Ibid., p. 53.
32. Walker and Allan, "Kennedy at Harvard," p. 94.
33. David Nunnerly, *President Kennedy and Britain* (London: The Bodley Head, 1972), p. 21.
34. D. W. Brogan, "Young Mr. Kennedy," *The New Leader,* December 11, 1961, p. 10.
35. Meyers, ed., *JFK,* p. 35.
36. Arthur Krock, JFKL–OH.
37. Henry Luce, JFKL–OH.
38. Joseph P. Kennedy to JFK, May 20, 1940, President's Office Files, Box 129, JFKL.
39. Felix Frankfurter, JFKL–OH.
40. Joel Satz to JFK, July 23, 1940, Boston Office Files, Pre-Presidential Papers, Box 73, JFKL.
41. *New York Times Book Review,* August 11, 1940.
42. *NYT,* August 3, 1940.
43. *Christian Science Monitor,* August 31, 1940.
44. *Boston Herald,* August 3, 1940.
45. *Washington Post,* October 6, 1940.
46. Rose Kennedy, *Times,* p. 271.
47. Joseph P. Kennedy to Winston Churchill, August 14, 1940, President's Office Files, Box 129, JFKL.
48. Max Freedman, ed., *Roosevelt & Frankfurter: Their Correspondence, 1928–1945* (Boston: Little, Brown, 1967), p. 590.
49. Freda Laski, JFKL–OH.
50. John F. Kennedy, *Why England Slept* (New York: Wilfred Funk, Inc., 1940), p. 231.
51. Ibid., pp. 215–16.
52. Frank Henry to JFK, August 21, 1940, Pre-Presidential Papers, Box 73, JFKL.
53. William L. Batt, Jr., to JFK, August 22, 1940, Pre-Presidential Papers, Box 73, JFKL.
54. Joel Satz to JFK, August 23, 1940, Boston Office Files, Pre-Presidential Papers, Box 73, JFKL.
55. Ibid., September 7, 1940.

56. Ibid., October 4, 1940.
57. Gertrude Algase to JFK, August 26, 1940, Boston Office Files, Pre-Presidential Papers, Box 73, JFKL.
58. Joel Satz to JFK, October 30, 1940, and February 20, 1941, Boston Office Files, Pre-Presidential Papers, Box 73, JFKL.
59. Charles Spalding, JFKL-OH.

Chapter 6: The War

1. William Carleton, interview, May 5, 1978.
2. Bullitt, ed., *For the President,* p. 437.
3. Lash, *Roosevelt and Churchill,* p. 130.
4. Ibid., p. 146.
5. Mary Welsh Hemingway, *How It Was* (New York: Alfred A. Knopf, 1976), p. 62.
6. Beschloss, "Joseph Kennedy and Franklin Roosevelt," pp. 177, 179.
7. Stevenson, *Intrepid,* p. 149.
8. Ibid.
9. Leutze, ed., *London Journal,* pp. 95-96.
10. Ibid., p. 242.
11. Leutze, ed., *London Journal,* p. 115; Stevenson, *Intrepid,* p. 149.
12. Ibid., p. 558.
13. Leutze, ed., *London Journal,* pp. 134-35.
14. *NYT,* January 7, 1941.
15. Leutze, ed., *London Journal,* p. 208.
16. Joseph P. Kennedy to James Landis, August 6, 1940, Landis Papers, Box 24, Library of Congress.
17. JFK to Dean Hanford, September 23, 1940, Harvard Records, MS 65-185, JFKL.
18. Assistant Dean in Charge of Records at Harvard to Stanford University Registrar, September 28, 1940, Harvard Records, MS 65-185, JFKL.
19. *Stanford University News Service,* August 1, 1960.
20. Rose Kennedy, *Times,* p. 68.
21. John Johansen, interview, November 24, 1976.
22. Harry Muheim, "When JFK was Rich, Young and Happy," *Esquire,* August 1966, pp. 65-66.
23. *Stanford Daily,* October 30, 1940.
24. Blair, *Search,* p. 109.
25. Rose Kennedy, *Times,* p. 277.
26. Joel Satz to JFK, January 7, 1941, Boston Office Files, Pre-Presidential Papers, Box 73, JFKL; Gertrude Algase to JFK, January 9, 1941, in Blair, *Search,* p. 105.
27. Searls, *Lost Prince,* p. 174.
28. Blair, *Search,* p. 113.
29. Ibid., pp. 113-14.
30. Ibid., p. 114.
31. Ibid., p. 120.
32. Frank C. Waldrop, interview, April 22, 1978; John B. White to Author, April 17, 1978.
33. Kay Halle, JFKL-OH; Charles Spalding, JFKL-OH.
34. Beschloss, "Joseph Kennedy and Franklin Roosevelt," p. 37.
35. Richard Cardinal Cushing, JFKL-OH.
36. Frank C. Waldrop, interview, April 22, 1978.
37. Blair, *Search,* pp. 132-33.
38. Ibid., p. 141.

39. H. N. Bassett to N. P. Callahan, February 13, 1975, JFK File, Federal Bureau of Investigation.
40. Interviews, John B. White, April 28, 1978, and Patsy Carter, April 28, 1978.
41. H. N. Bassett to N. P. Callahan, February 13, 1975, JFK File, FBI.
42. Frank C. Waldrop, "JFK and the Nazi Spy," *The Washingtonian,* April 1975, p. 90.
43. Blair, *Search,* p. 143.
44. Patsy Carter, interview, April 28, 1978.
45. H. N. Bassett to N. P. Callahan, February 13, 1975, JFK File, FBI.
46. Blair, *Search,* p. 143.
47. Bassett to Callahan, February 13, 1975, JFK File, FBI; William C. Sullivan, *The Bureau* (New York: Norton, 1979), p. 48.
48. Peter Hoguet, interview, December 1, 1976.
49. Blair, *Search,* pp. 149–50.
50. Ibid., pp. 497–98.
51. John B. White, interview, April 28, 1978.
52. Patsy Carter, interview, April 28, 1978.
53. Paul Pennoyer, Jr., interview, September 16, 1977.
54. Patsy Carter, interview, April 28, 1978.

Chapter 7: A Hero in the South Pacific

1. Robert Bulkeley, *At Close Quarters* (Washington, D.C.: U.S. Government Printing Office, 1962), p. 29.
2. John Harllee, JFKL–OH.
3. Ibid.
4. McCarthy, *Kennedys,* pp. 294–95; Robert J. Donovan, *PT 109: John F. Kennedy in World War II* (New York: McGraw-Hill, 1961), pp. 37–38.
5. Richard Tregaskis, *John F. Kennedy and PT 109* (New York: Random House, 1962), p. 44.
6. Anthony Akers, JFKL–OH.
7. John Harllee, JFKL–OH.
8. Blair, *Search,* pp. 160–62.
9. Confidential interview.
10. John Harllee, JFKL–OH.
11. Rose Kennedy, *Times,* p. 285.
12. Kenneth P. O'Donnell, interview, December 4, 1976.
13. Patsy Carter, interview, April 22, 1978.
14. JFK to Dad and Mother, May 14, 1943, Personal and General Correspondence, Box 579, JFKL.
15. Ibid., received May 10, 1943.
16. Rose Kennedy, *Times,* pp. 209–10.
17. Alice-Leone Moats, *Blind Date With Mars* (Garden City, N.Y.: Doubleday, 1943), pp. 175–76, 232–36, 262.
18. Logbook of the U.S.S. *PT 109,* National Archives; Tregaskis, *JFK and PT 109,* pp. 99, 101.
19. JFK to Mother and Dad, received May 10, 1943, Personal and General Correspondence, Box 579, JFKL.
20. Navy Department, Office of the Chief of Naval Operations, "History of USS PT-109," n.d., President's Office Files, Box 132, JFKL.
21. Robert J. Donovan, interview, April 11, 1977.
22. John Hersey, "Survival," *The New Yorker,* June 17, 1944, p. 37.

23. Cf. *NYT,* June 4, 1961, for discussion of correct name of island shown on maps as Nauru or Ross.
24. Donovan, *PT 109,* p. 183.
25. Ibid., p. 187.
26. JFK to Mother and Dad, received September 12, 1943, Personal and General Correspondence, Box 579, JFKL.
27. George St. John to JFK, August 23, 1943, JFK File, Choate Rosemary Hall.
28. JFK to George St. John, n.d., JFK File, Choate Rosemary Hall.
29. Donovan, *PT 109,* p. 93.
30. Cameron, *Rose,* pp. 150–51.

Chapter 8: Joe

1. Blair, *Search,* p. 305.
2. Robert J. Donovan, interview, April 11, 1977.
3. Blair, *Search,* p. 305.
4. Ibid., p. 311.
5. Ibid., p. 21.
6. Paul Pennoyer, Jr., interview, September 16, 1977.
7. Robert J. Donovan, interview, April 11, 1977.
8. Ibid.
9. JFK to Mother and Dad, received September 12, 1943, Personal and General Correspondence, Box 579, JFKL.
10. JFK to Joseph P. Kennedy, October 30, 1943, Personal and General Correspondence, Box 579, JFKL.
11. JFK to Mother and Dad, received September 12, 1943, Personal and General Correspondence, Box 579, JFKL; Rose Kennedy, *Times,* pp. 293–94.
12. JFK to Family, letter received November 1, 1943, Personal and General Correspondence, Box 579, JFKL.
13. Donovan, *PT 109,* pp. 206–14.
14. Blair, *Search,* p. 299.
15. JFK to Robert F. Kennedy, November 14, 1943, in Donovan, *PT 109,* p. 216.
16. Blair, *Search,* p. 281.
17. Patsy Carter, interview, April 28, 1978.
18. Rose Kennedy, *Times,* p. 292.
19. Blair, *Search,* p. 123.
20. Rose Kennedy, *Times,* p. 295.
21. Arthur Schlesinger, Jr., *Robert Kennedy and His Times* (Boston: Houghton Mifflin, 1978), p. 55.
22. Patsy Carter, interview, April 28, 1978.
23. Logbook of PT 109, National Archives.
24. Blair, *Search,* pp. 303–22.
25. Ibid., pp. 337, 387.
26. *Washington Times-Herald,* undated newspaper clipping on microfilm roll #1, Pre-Presidential Clippings, JFKL.
27. Interviews, Joseph Alsop, July 26, 1977, and Fletcher Knebel, May 15, 1979.
28. *NYT,* January 11, 1944.
29. JFK to Inga Arvad, September 26, 1943, in Blair, *Search,* p. 286.
30. Blair, *Search,* p. 310.
31. Joseph P. Kennedy to Al Cluster, February 7, 1944, in Blair, *Search,* p. 315.
32. Ibid., pp. 317–20.

33. *NYT,* February 10, 1944; John Hersey, interview, December 8, 1976.
34. JFK to John Hersey, n.d., in Mr. Hersey's possession.
35. Cameron, *Rose,* p. 152.
36. John F. Kennedy, ed., *As We Remember Joe,* p. 54.
37. *NYT,* May 7, 1944.
38. JFK to John Hersey, n.d., in Mr. Hersey's possession.
39. John Hersey, interview, December 8, 1976.
40. Joseph P. Kennedy to Paul Palmer, July 14, 1943; Palmer to Kennedy, August 12, 1943; and typescript of article by Joseph P. Kennedy, "What Are the Facts About Peace?" Palmer Papers, Yale.
41. Paul Palmer to Joseph P. Kennedy, August 24, 1943, Palmer Papers, Yale.
42. Joseph P. Kennedy to Paul Palmer, September 10, 1943, Palmer Papers, Yale.
43. Joseph P. Kennedy to Paul Palmer, June 20, 1944, Palmer Papers, Yale.
44. JFK to Paul Palmer, June 16, 1944, Palmer Papers, Yale; Paul Palmer to John Hersey, June 19, 1944, in Mr. Hersey's possession.
45. Navy Department, Office of the Chief of Naval Operations, "History of USS PT-109," n.d., President's Office Files, Box 132, JFKL; *NYT,* June 12, 1944.
46. Theodore C. Sorensen, *Kennedy* (New York: Harper & Row, 1965), p. 40.
47. Blair, *Search,* p. 337.
48. Ibid., p. 339.
49. McCarthy, *Kennedys,* p. 150.
50. Charles Spalding, JFKL–OH.
51. Edward M. Kennedy, ed., *The Fruitful Bough: A Tribute to Joseph P. Kennedy* (privately printed, 1965), p. 207.
52. Rose Kennedy, *Times,* p. 301.
53. Cameron, *Rose,* p. 153.
54. Arthur Krock, *Memoirs: Sixty Years on the Firing Line* (New York: Funk & Wagnalls, 1968), p. 348.
55. JFK, ed., *As We Remember Joe,* pp. 3–4.
56. Kenneth P. O'Donnell and David F. Powers, *"Johnny, We Hardly Knew Ye": Memories of John Fitzgerald Kennedy* (Boston: Little, Brown, 1972), p. 19.
57. Searls, *Lost Prince,* p. 302.
58. Mark Dalton, JFKL–OH.
59. Frank C. Waldrop to Author, May 31, 1978.

Chapter 9: The Second Son Emerges

1. James A. Reed, JFKL–OH.
2. Damore, *Cape Cod Years,* pp. 72–73.
3. *NYT,* November 9, 1945.
4. McCarthy, *Kennedys,* p. 113.
5. Ibid., p. 115.
6. Ibid., p. 114; Whalen, *Founding Father,* p. 375; Frank C. Waldrop, interview, April 22, 1978.
7. Fay, *Pleasure of His Company,* p. 160.
8. JFK to Earl Leinbach, November 9, 1944, JFK File, Choate Rosemary Hall.
9. Fay, *Pleasure of His Company,* p. 160.
10. Mary Richardson to JFK, February 7, 1945, Personal and General Correspondence, Box 579, JFKL.
11. Blair, *Search,* p. 367.
12. Joseph Kennedy to Paul Palmer, February 15, 1945, Palmer Papers, Yale.

13. Edward Weeks to John F. Kennedy, April 17, 1945, Pre-Presidential Files, Box 73, JFKL.
14. Blair, *Search,* p. 368.
15. Ibid.
16. Gene Tierney, *Self-Portrait* (New York: Wyden Books, 1979), p. 143.
17. Ibid., pp. 147, 153.
18. M. F. Riblett to JFK, September 19, 1945, Pre-Presidential Papers, Box 73, JFKL.
19. *New York Journal-American,* May 16, 1945.
20. Ibid., May 9, 1945.
21. Kenneth P. O'Donnell, interview, December 4, 1976.
22. Ben Bradlee, interview, May 13, 1977.
23. Philip Nobile and Ron Rosenbaum, "The Curious Aftermath of JFK's Best and Brightest Affair," *New Times,* July 9, 1976, pp. 24–25.
24. *New York Journal-American,* June 24, 1945.
25. Blair, *Search,* p. 385; Seymour St. John, interview, June 22, 1978.
26. James V. Forrestal to JFK, September 8, 1945, Pre-Presidential Papers, Box 73, JFKL.

Chapter 10: "A New Candidate"

1. Cabell Phillips, *The Truman Presidency* (New York: Macmillan, 1966), pp. 103–04.
2. George St. John to Rose Kennedy, August 22, 1945, JFK File, Choate Rosemary Hall.
3. Mark Dalton, JFKL–OH.
4. James Reed, JFKL–OH.
5. Arthur Krock, JFKL–OH.
6. McCarthy, *Kennedys,* p. 19.
7. Ralph G. Martin and Ed Plaut, *Front Runner, Dark Horse* (Garden City, N.Y.: Doubleday, 1960), p. 131.
8. Stephen E. Smith, interview, July 6, 1977.
9. Robert Kennedy in E. M. Kennedy, ed., *Fruitful Bough,* p. 214.
10. Kenneth P. O'Donnell, interview, December 4, 1976.
11. Charles H. Trout, *Boston: The Great Depression and the New Deal* (New York: Oxford University Press, 1977), pp. 259–60.
12. Joseph Casey, JFKL–OH.
13. Krock, *Memoirs,* p. 357.
14. Koskoff, *Kennedy,* pp. 365–66.
15. Merle Miller, *Plain Speaking* (New York: Putnam, 1974), p. 186.
16. Koskoff, *Kennedy,* p. 497.
17. Trout, *Boston,* p. 40.
18. David F. Powers, interview, January 26, 1976.
19. Thomas P. O'Neill, interview, March 8, 1979.
20. *NYT,* November 8, 1945.
21. Ibid., December 16, 1945; Blair, *Search,* p. 416.
22. Thomas Broderick, JFKL–OH.
23. Edward McLaughlin, interview, August 22, 1978.
24. John C. Dowd in E. M. Kennedy, ed., *Fruitful Bough,* pp. 99–100.
25. *NYT,* April 17, 1945.
26. *NYT,* June 28 and September 14, 1945.
27. Blair, *Search,* p. 406.
28. Ibid.
29. *Boston Post,* February 27, 1946.
30. Richard Cardinal Cushing, JFKL–OH.

31. Patrick J. Mulkern, JFKL–OH.
32. David F. Powers, interview, July 24, 1978.
33. Hirsh Freed, JFKL–OH; Thomas Broderick, JFKL–OH.
34. Hirsh Freed, JFKL–OH.
35. Whalen, *Founding Father,* p. 399.
36. Bette Turrentine, "John Kennedy: Congressman, 1946–1952," unpublished essay in JFKL.
37. *Boston Sunday Globe,* September 2, 1945.
38. Scrapbook, League of Catholic Women, JFKL; Springfield *Republican,* January 15, 1946; Lynn (Mass.) *Daily Item,* February 7, 1946; *Lawrence Eagle,* February 8, 1946; Blair, *Search,* pp. 407–08.
39. Damore, *Cape Cod Years,* p. 87.
40. Mark Dalton, JFKL–OH.
41. McCarthy, *Kennedys,* p. 120; James Reed, JFKL–OH.
42. David F. Powers, interview, January 26, 1976.
43. Ibid., interviews, April 18, 1973, January 26, 1976.
44. O'Donnell and Powers, *"Johnny,"* p. 59.
45. Patrick J. Mulkern, JFKL–OH.
46. Edward McLaughlin, interview, August 22, 1978.
47. Bobbie Smith to John C. Dowd, n.d., Boston Office File, Pre-Presidential Papers, Box 73, JFKL.
48. Koskoff, *Kennedy,* p. 407.
49. Interviews, David F. Powers, January 26, 1976, and Thomas P. O'Neill, March 7, 1979.
50. Billy Sutton, JFKL–OH.
51. William De Marco, JFKL–OH.
52. Patrick J. Mulkern, JFKL–OH.
53. Martin and Plaut, *Front Runner,* p. 136.
54. Thomas Broderick, JFKL–OH.
55. Ibid.
56. Fay, *Pleasure of His Company,* p. 59.
57. Burton Hersh, *The Education of Edward Kennedy* (New York: Morrow, 1972), p. 48.
58. Hirsh Freed, JFKL–OH; Martin and Plaut, *Front Runner,* pp. 136–37.
59. O'Donnell and Powers, *"Johnny,"* p. 61.
60. Thomas Broderick, JFKL–OH.
61. Confidential source.
62. McCarthy, *Kennedys,* p. 20.
63. David F. Powers, interview, July 24, 1978.
64. Martin and Plaut, *Front Runner,* pp. 131–32; O'Donnell and Powers, *"Johnny,"* pp. 46–47.
65. Kenneth P. O'Donnell, interview, December 4, 1976.
66. Hirsh Freed, JFKL–OH.
67. Martin and Plaut, *Front Runner,* pp. 134–35.
68. Typescript, "1946 Election Platforms," Pre-Presidential Papers, Box 98, JFKL.
69. National League of Women Voters, "Questionnaire for Congressional Candidates—1946," Pre-Presidential Papers, Box 74, JFKL.
70. Blair, *Search,* p. 412.
71. Ibid., p. 463.
72. Blair Clark, interview, March 18, 1977.
73. Elizabeth Janeway to JFK, February 20, 1946, Pre-Presidential Papers, Box 74, JFKL.
74. Mark Dalton, JFKL–OH.
75. George Taylor, JFKL–OH.
76. Mark Dalton, JFKL–OH.
77. Ibid.
78. Hersh, *Edward Kennedy,* p. 54.

79. *Look,* June 11, 1946, pp. 32–36; Henry Ehrlich to JFK, May 9, 1946, Pre-Presidential Papers, Box 73, JFKL.
80. O'Donnell and Powers, *"Johnny,"* p. 65; Martin and Plaut, *Front Runner,* pp. 133–34; Blair, *Search,* p. 475; Mark Dalton and Joseph Casey, JFKL–OH; James Landis, Columbia University–OH; East Boston *Times,* March 1, 1946.
81. James Reed, JFKL–OH.
82. Ibid.
83. Robert L. Lee, JFKL–OH.
84. Clem Norton, Memorandum, Box 98, JFKL.
85. Thomas Broderick, JFKL–OH.
86. *NYT,* June 19, 1946; Blair, *Search,* pp. 478–79.
87. Mark Dalton, JFKL–OH.
88. *NYT,* November 6, 1946.

Chapter 11: Portrait of a Congressman

1. Hirsh Freed to JFK, June 21, 1946, Pre-Presidential Papers, Box 73, JFKL.
2. Joseph C. Goulden, *The Best Years, 1945–1950* (New York: Atheneum, 1976), pp. 58–59, 62–63.
3. *Future,* February 1947, p. 3.
4. Blair, *Search,* p. 514.
5. Lynn (Mass.) *Telegram-News,* May 25, 1947.
6. Blair, *Search,* p. 515.
7. George Smathers, interview, April 13, 1977; Richard Bolling, JFKL–OH.
8. John Blatnik, JFKL–OH.
9. Robert L. Lee, JFKL–OH.
10. Hersh, *Edward Kennedy,* p. 76.
11. Blair, *Search,* p. 512.
12. William O. Douglas, JFKL–OH.
13. Interviews, George Smathers, April 13, 1977, and Frank Thompson, Jr., May 13, 1977.
14. Clyde Tolson to J. Edgar Hoover, March 30, 1962, JFK File, FBI.
15. J. Edgar Hoover, Memorandum for the Files, November 22, 1961, JFK File, FBI.
16. J. Edgar Hoover to Robert Kennedy, June 4, 1963, JFK File, FBI; *NYT,* December 15, 1977; *Washington Post,* December 16, 1977; Schlesinger, *Robert Kennedy,* p. 259.
17. Frank Thompson, Jr., interview, March 13, 1977.
18. Blair, *Search,* p. 521.
19. George Smathers, JFKL–OH.
20. David F. Powers, interview, January 26, 1976.
21. George Smathers, interview, April 13, 1977.
22. Edward C. Berube, JFKL–OH.
23. James Rousmaniere, interview, March 10, 1977.
24. Frank Thompson, Jr., interview, March 13, 1977.
25. Rose Kennedy, *Times,* p. 119.
26. Meyers, ed., *JFK,* p. 28.
27. Robert L. Lee, JFKL–OH.
28. John Blatnik and Carl Albert, JFKL–OH.
29. Charles Bartlett, JFKL–OH.
30. Confidential interview.
31. George Smathers, JFKL–OH.
32. Joseph Rauh, Jr., JFKL–OH.

33. Paul Healy, "The Senate's Gay Young Bachelor," *Saturday Evening Post,* June 13, 1953, p. 127.

34. George Smathers and James Reed, JFKL–OH.

35. Jim Watts, "Dress Rehearsal for Wheeling: Joseph R. McCarthy in the Senate, 1947–1950," paper read before the Organization of American Historians, New York City, April 14, 1978.

36. R. Sargent Shriver, interview, November 19, 1976.

37. Roy Cohn, *McCarthy* (New York: New American Library, 1968), p. 66.

38. Richard M. Fried, *Men Against McCarthy* (New York: Columbia University Press, 1976), p. 57.

39. Koskoff, *Kennedy,* p. 364; Krock, *Memoirs,* p. 343.

40. Damore, *Cape Cod Years,* p. 103.

41. John P. Mallan, "Massachusetts: Liberal and Corrupt," *New Republic,* October 13, 1952, pp. 10–11.

42. Jean Mannix, JFKL–OH.

43. George Smathers, interview, April 13, 1977.

44. Charles Bartlett, JFKL–OH.

45. Kelley, *Jackie Oh!,* p. 122.

46. Confidential interview.

47. Nixon, *RN,* pp. 42–43.

48. U.S., Congress, House, *Hearings Before the Committee on Education and Labor,* 80th Cong., 1st sess., 1947, Vol. 1, p. 3577.

49. *Boston Herald,* January 17, 1947.

50. Transcript, Radio Station WOL, March 14, 1947, Pre-Presidential Papers, Box 98, JFKL.

51. U.S., Congress, House, *Hearings,* 80th Cong., 1st sess., Vol. 1, p. 3585.

52. U.S., Congress, House, *Hearings Before the Committee on Education and Labor,* 80th Cong., 1st sess., 1947, Vol. 2, pp. 1335–1487; U.S., Congress, House, Committee on Education and Labor, 80th Cong., 2d sess., House Rep. 1508, p. 3.

53. U.S., Congress, House *Hearings,* 80th Cong., 1st sess., Vol. 2, p. 2008, 2011–14, 2073, 2079–96, 2135–36, 3610–16.

54. Typescript, "The Christoffel Case—Factual Background," Pre-Presidential Papers, Box 98, JFKL.

55. *Congressional Record,* 81st Cong., 1st sess., p. A-4366.

56. Burns, *Kennedy,* p. 133; cf., David Caute, *The Great Fear* (New York: Simon and Schuster, 1978), pp. 358–59.

57. *Boston Herald,* March 3, 1950.

58. *New York Post,* July 7, 1947.

59. Congressional Quarterly Service, *Congress and the Nation, 1945–1964* (Washington, D.C.: Congressional Quarterly, 1965), Vol. 1, p. 48a.

60. John W. McCormack, interview, September 14, 1978.

61. Ibid.

62. Mark Dalton, JFKL–OH.

63. Blair, *Search,* p. 551; Sorensen, *Kennedy Legacy,* p. 43; James MacGregor Burns, JFKL–OH; Lawrence O'Brien, interview, October 19, 1976.

64. Daniel O'Brien, JFKL–OH.

65. McCarthy, *Kennedys,* p. 129; O'Donnell and Powers, *"Johnny,"* p. 74; Martin and Plaut, *Front Runner,* p. 153.

66. T. J. Reardon to Francis Morrissey, April 16, 1947, Pre-Presidential Papers, Box 98, JFKL.

67. *New York Herald Tribune,* April 17, 1947.

68. John F. Kennedy, *John Fitzgerald Kennedy: A Compilation of Statements and Speeches Made During His Service in the United States Senate and House of Representatives* (Washington, D.C.: U.S. Government Printing Office, 1964, pp. 6–7; R. Alton Lee,

Truman and the Taft-Hartley Act (Lexington: University of Kentucky Press, 1966), p. 67.

69. McKeesport *Daily News,* April 22, 1947; Nixon, *RN,* p. 43.
70. *NYT,* June 6, 1947.
71. Healy, "Senate's Gay Young Bachelor," p. 127.
72. Labor's League for Political Education, 1947–1951, Pre-Presidential Papers, Box 98, JFKL.
73. Speech Transcript, Pre-Presidential Papers, Box 96, JFKL.
74. The American Forum of the Air, June 14, 1953, "Amend the Taft-Hartley Law— Which Way?" (Washington, D.C.: Ransdell, Inc., 1953), p. 3.
75. *NYT,* March 11, 1947.
76. JFK, *Statements and Speeches,* p. 7.
77. *Boston Globe,* June 25, 1947.
78. Burns, *Kennedy,* p. 74.
79. *Army Times,* June 14, 1947.
80. JFK, *Statements and Speeches,* p. 21.
81. Burns, *Kennedy,* p. 75; O'Donnell and Powers, *"Johnny,"* p. 74.
82. Congressional Quarterly Service, *Congress and the Nation,* pp. 478–79.
83. O'Donnell and Powers, *"Johnny,"* p. 75.
84. Council of State Chambers of Commerce, News Release, November 20, 1951, Pre-Presidential Papers, Box 98, JFKL.
85. Speech transcript, Pre-Presidential Papers, Box 98, JFKL; *Boston Sunday Post,* January 29, 1950; *Boston Herald,* January 30, 1950.
86. Fay, *Pleasure of His Company,* p. 57.
87. Nixon, *RN,* p. 75.
88. *Washington Post,* July 25, 1947.
89. Blair, *Search,* p. 559.
90. Burns, *Kennedy,* p. 4.
91. Blair, *Search,* pp. 560–61.
92. *Boston Post,* October 25, 1947.
93. *Boston Herald,* December 3, 1947.
94. JFK to George St. John, December 18, 1947, JFK File, Choate Rosemary Hall.
95. Dr. Elmer Bartels, interview, December 2, 1977.
96. Blair, *Search,* pp. 564ff.; L. M. Strand to JFK, March 22, 1948; Dr. E. C. Bartels to JFK, January 25, 1949, and JFK to E. C. Bartels, August 3, 1949, Personal and General Correspondence, Box 579, JFKL.
97. Dr. Thomas Francis Cloney to JFK, February 1, 1949, Personal and General Correspondence, Box 579, JFKL.
98. Janet Travell, *Office Hours: Day and Night* (New York: World Publishing Company, 1968), p. 5.
99. Arthur M. Schlesinger, Jr., *A Thousand Days* (Boston: Houghton Mifflin, 1965), p. 96.
100. James A. Nicholas, Charles L. Busstein, et al., "Management of Adrenocortical Insufficiency During Surgery," *Archive of Surgery,* November 1955, p. 739.
101. Joseph Alsop, interview, July 26, 1977.
102. Schlesinger, *Thousand Days,* p. 96.
103. Joseph Alsop, interview, July 26, 1977.
104. Charles Spalding, JFKL–OH.
105. Blair, *Search,* p. 567.
106. Nicholas, Burstein, et al., "Management . . .," p. 739.
107. *NYT,* January 1, 1948; William O. Douglas, *Go East, Young Man* (New York: Random House, 1974), pp. 258–66.
108. Lynn (Mass.) *Sunday Telegram-News,* March 2, 1947.

109. *Washington Times-Herald,* undated newspaper clipping on microfilm roll #1, Pre-Presidential Clippings, JFKL.

110. The office still operates, now from the Pan American Building at 200 Park Avenue, New York City.

111. James A. Fayne to JFK, November 16, 1948, Landis Papers, Box 50, Library of Congress.

112. *New York Times Magazine,* August 19, 1951, pp. 16ff.

113. James Landis to Joseph P. Kennedy, August 15, 1951, Landis Papers, Box 51, Library of Congress.

114. Unidentified newspaper clipping, March 7, 1950, on microfilm roll #1, Pre-Presidential Clippings, JFKL.

Chapter 12: "America's Younger Statesman"

1. Rose Kennedy, *Times,* p. 332; Whalen, *Founding Father,* p. 375.

2. *NYT,* May 14, 1948.

3. Confidential interview.

4. *Boston Sunday Herald,* November 23, 1947.

5. *Boston Herald,* May 9, 1948.

6. Ibid.

7. *NYT,* July 21, 1948.

8. *Boston Post,* July 21, 1948.

9. Charles Spalding, JFKL–OH.

10. Cutler, *'Honey Fitz,'* p. 317.

11. John J. Kane, *Catholic-Protestant Conflicts in America* (Chicago: Regnery, 1955), p. 7.

12. Herbert S. Parmet, *The Democrats: The Years After FDR* (New York: Macmillan, 1976), pp. 51–55.

13. *Boston Post,* March 22, 1948.

14. Sorensen, *Kennedy,* p. 192.

15. Tyler Abell, ed., *Drew Pearson: Diaries, 1949–1959* (New York: Holt, Rinehart and Winston, 1974), p. 30.

16. *NYT,* January 15, 1960.

17. Daniel Poling, *Mine Eyes Have Seen* (New York: McGraw-Hill, 1959), pp. 256–58; Deane Alwyn Kemper, "John F. Kennedy Before the Greater Houston Ministerial Association, September 12, 1960: The Religious Issue," unpublished Ph. D. dissertation, Michigan State University, 1968, pp. 104–05.

18. Paul Blanshard, *God and Man in Washington* (Boston: Beacon Press, 1960), p. 140.

19. Father John Wright to JFK, January 18, 1947, Personal and General Correspondence, Box 579, JFKL.

20. Burns, *Kennedy,* p. 85; Kemper, "Houston Ministerial Association," pp. 124–26.

21. *Catholic Mirror,* April 1945, in Kenneth Wilson Underwood, *Protestant and Catholic* (Boston: Beacon Press, 1957), p. 330.

22. *The Tablet,* October 21, 1944.

23. *NYT,* July 23, 1949.

24. Joseph P. Lash, *Eleanor: The Years Alone* (New York: W. W. Norton, 1972), pp. 157–67.

25. George H. Gallup, ed., *The Gallup Poll: Public Opinion, 1935–1971,* 4 Vols., (New York: Random House, 1972), Vol. 2, p. 841.

26. Herbert Lehman to Julius C. C. Edelstein, May 21, 1959, Lehman Papers, Columbia University.

27. Seymour P. Lachman, "The Cardinal, the Congressman, and the First Lady," *Journal of Church and State* (Winter 1965) p. 45.

28. Ibid., p. 47.
29. Monsignor Frederick Hockwalt, Columbia University–OH.
30. John Sharon, JFKL–OH.
31. *Boston Globe*, August 3, 1949; Kemper, "Houston Ministerial Association," p. 123.
32. Lachman, "The Cardinal, the Congressman, and the First Lady," p. 52; *NYT*, August 3, 1944.
33. *NYT*, March 15, 1950.
34. *The Pilot*, March 18, 1950.
35. *Boston Sunday Post*, April 2, 1950.
36. *NYT*, March 7, 1950.
37. Ibid., July 17, 1949.
38. William O. Douglas, JFKL–OH.
39. Koskoff, *Kennedy*, p. 393.
40. Martin and Plaut, *Front Runner*, p. 195.
41. *NYT*, March 24, 1947.
42. Schlesinger, *RFK*, p. 71.
43. *Boston Post*, August 15, 1950.
44. Haverhill *Gazette*, August 21, 1950.
45. JFK, *Statements and Speeches*, p. 17.
46. Nurse, "America Must Not Sleep," p. 41.
47. Ibid., p. 73.
48. *Congressional Record*, January 25, 1949. p. 549.
49. Ibid., February 21, 1949, pp. A-1027–28.
50. Raleigh (N.C.) *News and Observer*, October 10, 1949; *NYT*, October 10, 1949; JFK to Harry S Truman, October 10, 1949, Personal and General Correspondence, Box 583, JFKL.
51. Press Releases, October 31 and November 17, 1949, Personal and General Correspondence, Box 583, JFKL.
52. *NYT*, June 5, 1950.
53. *Boston Post*, August 15, 1950; JFK, *Statements and Speeches*, p. 113; News Release, April 10, 1952, Pre-Presidential Papers, Box 98, JFKL.
54. James MacGregor Burns, manuscript, Sorensen Papers, Box 6, JFKL.
55. Mallan, "Massachusetts: Liberal and Corrupt," pp. 10–11.
56. John P. Mallan to Helen Fuller, October 16, 1952, and to JFK, October 15, 1952, Arthur Holcombe File, Box 75-57, JFKL.
57. *New Republic*, November 3, 1952, p. 2.
58. JFK, Statement before the Committee on Foreign Relations of the U.S. Senate, February 22, 1951.
59. Transcript, JFK, Polish-American Radio Broadcast, June 16, 1947, Pre-Presidential Papers, Box 95, JFKL; *Boston Globe*, May 1, 1950.
60. JFK, *Statements and Speeches*, p. 114.
61. Ibid., p. 43.
62. JFK, *Statements and Speeches*, pp. 51–53.
63. *Boston Herald*, March 16, 1950.
64. News Release, July 18, 1952.
65. JFK, *Statements and Speeches*, pp. 103–05.
66. James Landis to JFK, May 13, 1952, Personal and General Correspondence, Box 583, JFKL.
67. JFK, Statement before the Committee on Foreign Relations of the U.S. Senate, February 22, 1951.
68. Transcript of Yankee Network Broadcast, January 26, 1951, Personal and General Correspondence, Box 580, JFKL; Leland Bickford to Joseph P. Kennedy, n.d., Personal and General Correspondence, Box 580, JFKL.

69. Telegram, JFK to Mary Davis, January 30, 1951, Personal and General Correspondence, Box 583, JFKL.
70. JFK, Statement before the Committee on Foreign Relations of the U.S. Senate, February 22, 1951.
71. Transcript, Mutual Broadcasting Network, February 6, 1951, Pre-Presidential Papers, Box 95, JFKL.
72. *Boston's Political Times,* March 17, 1951.
73. Ibid.
74. Nurse, "America Must Not Sleep," p. 71.
75. *Jewish Advocate,* May 1951.
76. Transcript, Mutual Broadcasting System, May 9, 1951.
77. Stephen Birmingham, *Jacqueline Bouvier Kennedy Onassis* (New York: Grosset & Dunlap, 1978), p. 47.
78. Charles Bartlett, interview, October 8, 1978.
79. Ibid.
80. Janet Lee Auchincloss, interview, November 10, 1978.
81. Charles Bartlett, JFKL–OH.
82. Birmingham, *Onassis,* p. 60.
83. Ibid., p. 61.
84. John F. Davis, *The Bouviers: Portrait of an American Family* (New York: Farrar, Straus & Giroux, 1969), pp. 121–22, 182–83.
85. Ibid., p. 121.
86. Davis, *Bouviers,* pp. 223, 234–35, 240–42, 252, 276.
87. Birmingham, *Onassis,* p. 49.
88. Sara M. Jordan to JFK, April 11, 1951, Pre-Presidential Papers, Box 68, JFKL; Unidentified newspaper clipping Reel #1, Microfilm of Pre-Presidential Clippings, JFKL.
89. Sara M. Jordan to JFK, September 24, 1951, Pre-Presidential Papers, Box 68, JFKL.
90. Ibid., October 1, 1951.
91. Sorensen, *Kennedy,* p. 41.
92. JFK to Joe Kane, November 15, 1951, Pre-Presidential Papers, Box 68, JFKL; *NYT,* November 20, 1951.
93. Transcript, JFK, "Report on his Trip to the Middle and Far East," November 14, 1951, Box 95, Pre-Presidential Papers, JFKL.
94. *Congressional Record,* January 8, 1952, p. HR 5879.
95. New Bedford *Standard-Times,* May 22, 1955.
96. *Everett* (Mass.) *Leader Herald,* March 13, 1952; Lynn (Mass.) *Daily Item,* April 7, 1952.
97. *Boston Traveler,* December 15, 1951.
98. Schlesinger, *RFK,* pp. 92–93.

Chapter 13: To the Senate

1. Charles Bartlett, JFKL–OH; Krock, *Memoirs,* p. 357.
2. E. M. Kennedy, ed., *Fruitful Bough,* pp. 219, 238.
3. Krock, *Memoirs,* p. 357.
4. Lasky, *JFK,* p. 139, and *passim.*
5. George Smathers, interview, April 13, 1977.
6. James Landis, Columbia University–OH; Mark Dalton, JFKL–OH.
7. Edward C. Berube, JFKL–OH.
8. Frank Dobie, JFKL–OH.
9. *Boston's Political Times,* March 17, 1952.

10. *Boston Evening Globe,* April 2, 1952.
11. Mark Dalton, JFKL–OH.
12. Whalen, *Founding Father,* p. 418.
13. Mark Dalton, JFKL–OH.
14. *NYT,* September 22, 1952.
15. Hersh, *Edward Kennedy,* p. 72.
16. Lawrence F. O'Brien, *No Final Victories* (Garden City, N.Y.: Doubleday, 1974), p. 26.
17. *NYT,* April 7, 1952; New Bedford *Standard-Times,* April 7, 1952.
18. *Miami Herald,* April 8, 1952.
19. Cabell Phillips, "Case History of a Senate Race," *New York Times Magazine,* October 26, 1952, p. 49.
20. Arthur Krock, JFKL–OH.
21. Koskoff, *Kennedy,* p. 413.
22. Rose Kennedy, *Times,* p. 321.
23. T. A. McInerny to Joseph Kennedy, February 18, 1952, and JFK to Joseph Kennedy, March 27, 1952, Pre-Presidential Papers, Box 68, JFKL.
24. Thomas Broderick, JFKL–OH.
25. Plimpton and Stein, eds., *American Journey,* pp. 55–56.
26. O'Brien, *No Final Victories,* p. 31; Whalen, *Founding Father,* p. 420.
27. Hersh, *Edward Kennedy,* p. 73.
28. Irwin Ross, "The Senator Women Elected," *Cosmopolitan,* December 1953, p. 84.
29. John G. W. Mahanna to JFK, April 20, 1952, Pre-Presidential Papers, Box 69, JFKL.
30. Phil Fine, JFKL–OH.
31. Unidentified secretary to John H. Callahan, June 3, 1952, Pre-Presidential Papers, Box 68, JFKL.
32. R. Sargent Shriver, interview, November 19, 1976.
33. James Landis, Columbia University–OH.
34. Joseph Kennedy to JFK, July 13, 1951, Pre-Presidential Papers, Box 68, JFKL.
35. James A. Reed, JFKL–OH.
36. McCarthy, *Kennedys,* p. 137.
37. Francis X. McCann to JFK, May 7, 1952, Pre-Presidential Papers, Box 68, JFKL; *Boston Herald,* May 7, 1952.
38. *NYT,* August 9, 1952; Damore, *Cape Cod Years,* p. 111.
39. *NYT,* September 26, 1952; Damore, *Cape Cod Years,* pp. 117–18.
40. *New York Times Magazine,* November 9, 1952. p. 4.
41. Providence *Bulletin,* June 27, 1958; *NYT,* June 28, 1958.
42. *New York Herald Tribune,* June 29, 1958.
43. Koskoff, *Kennedy,* p. 415.
44. Robert L. Lee, JFKL–OH.
45. Whalen, *Founding Father,* pp. 430–31.
46. Fletcher Knebel, interview, May 15, 1979.
47. Kenneth P. O'Donnell, interview, December 4, 1976.
48. Plimpton and Stein, eds., *American Journey,* pp. 64–65.
49. Burns, *Kennedy,* p. 109; Martin and Plaut, *Front Runner,* p. 174.
50. James Landis, Columbia–OH.
51. Donald F. Crosby, "The Angry Catholics: American Catholics and Senator Joseph R. McCarthy, 1950–1957," unpublished Ph. D. dissertation, Brandeis University, 1973.
52. Schlesinger, *Thousand Days,* p. 12.
53. Robert Amory, Jr., JFKL–OH.
54. Crosby, "Angry Catholics," p. 251.
55. Phil Fine, JFKL–OH.
56. Ibid.

57. Hirsh Freed, JFKL–OH.
58. Thomas P. O'Neill, interview, March 8, 1979.
59. Foster Furcolo, interview, February 21, 1977.
60. Edward McCormack, Jr., JFKL–OH.
61. Whalen, *Founding Father*, p. 426.
62. Phil Fine, JFKL–OH.
63. Crosby, "Angry Catholics," p. 254.
64. Whalen, *Founding Father*, p. 428.
65. JFK to Westbrook Pegler, April 22, 1958, Sorensen Papers, Box 12, JFKL.
66. Henry Cabot Lodge, Jr., interview, November 1, 1978.
67. Krock, *Memoirs*, p. 342.
68. Stephen Mitchell, Columbia University–OH.
69. Sargent Shriver to Adlai Stevenson, September 17, 1952, Stevenson Papers, Box 267, Princeton.
70. *NYT*, September 20, 1952.
71. Martin and Plaut, *Front Runner*, p. 175; Crosby, "Angry Catholics," pp. 252–53; Francis Russell, *The President Makers* (Boston: Little, Brown, 1976), pp. 374–75.
72. Martin and Plaut, *Front Runner*, p. 175.
73. Lasky, *JFK*, p. 144; Undated memorandum marked "Return to Ted Reardon," and News Release, October 30, 1952, Pre-Presidential Papers, Box 24, JFKL.
74. Sorensen, *Kennedy Legacy*, p. 42.
75. Henry Cabot Lodge, Jr., interview, November 1, 1978.
76. Charles Bartlett, JFKL–OH.
77. Waltham (Mass.) *News-Tribune*, September 17, 1952.
78. Damore, *Cape Cod Years*, p. 115.
79. Phillips, "Case History of a Senate Race," p. 49.
80. Henry Cabot Lodge, Jr., interview, November 1, 1978.
81. *Boston Post*, November 2, 1952.
82. O'Brien, *No Final Victories*, p. 36.
83. Foster Furcolo, interview, February 21, 1977.
84. Martin and Plaut, *Front Runner*, p. 173.
85. *Boston Post*, November 3 and 4, 1952.
86. McCarthy, *Kennedys*, pp. 137–38; Rose Kennedy, *Times*, p. 327; Phyllis Macdonald, interview, August 9, 1979.
87. *NYT*, November 5 and 6, 1952.
88. McCarthy, *Kennedys*, pp. 138–39; Martin and Plaut, *Front Runner*, p. 183; Burns, *Kennedy*, p. 107; Koskoff, *Kennedy*, p. 416.

Chapter 14: The Senator from New England

1. Paul Healy, "The Senate's Gay Young Bachelor," p. 26.
2. Mary Barell Gallagher, *My Life With Jacqueline Kennedy* (New York: McKay, 1969), p. 17.
3. *Newsweek*, November 20, 1978, p. 124.
4. Gore Vidal to Author, n.d., 1977.
5. Janet Auchincloss, interview, November 10, 1978.
6. Davis, *Bouviers*, p. 308.
7. Fay, *Pleasure of His Company*, p. 148.
8. Edward C. Berube, JFKL–OH.
9. Davis, *Bouviers*, p. 308; Birmingham, *Onassis*, p. 94.
10. George Smathers, interview, April 13, 1977.

11. Interviews, Frank Thompson, Jr., May 13, 1977, James Rousmiere, March 10, 1977, and Phyllis Macdonald, August 9, 1979; Cass Canfield, Columbia–OH; *New York Post*, March 25, 1957.
12. Gallagher, *My Life*, pp. 15–16.
13. Eleanor Harris, "The Senator Is in a Hurry," *McCall's*, August 1957, p. 123.
14. Fay, *Pleasure of His Company*, p. 149.
15. Davis, *Bouviers*, p. 309; Birmingham, *Onassis*, p. 73.
16. George Smathers, interview, April 13, 1977.
17. Lasky, *JFK*, p. 160.
18. Davis, *Bouviers*, p. 311.
19. Sorensen, *Kennedy*, p. 11.
20. Patrick Lucey, JFKL–OH.
21. Abell, ed., *Pearson Diaries*, p. 248.
22. Lasky, *JFK*, p. 165.
23. Evelyn Lincoln, *My Twelve Years with John F. Kennedy* (New York: McKay, 1965), p. 18.
24. Allen Otten in Lester Tanzer, ed., *The Kennedy Circle* (Washington, D.C.: Robert B. Luce, 1961), p. 10; Patrick Anderson, *The President's Men* (Garden City, N.Y.: Doubleday, 1968), pp. 277–278.
25. *NYT,* January 18, 1977.
26. Tanzer, ed., *Kennedy Circle*, p. 10.
27. Lasky, *JFK,* pp. 164–65; Anderson, *President's Men,* p. 278.
28. JFK to Kenneth Kelly, January 14, 1953, Pre-Presidential Papers, Box 481, JFKL.
29. James Landis to Joseph P. Kennedy, January 21, 1953, Landis Papers, Box 50, Library of Congress.
30. Ibid.
31. Ibid.
32. JFK, "The Economic Problems of New England: A Program for Congressional Action" (Private reprint, 1953), pp. 28–30.
33. Ted Sorensen to JFK, March 13, 1953, Landis Papers, Box 50, Library of Congress.
34. James Landis to JFK, March 23, 1953, and JFK to Landis, March 24, 1953, Landis Papers, Box 50, Library of Congress.
35. JFK, "Economic Problems of New England," p. 4.
36. Ibid., p. 69.
37. Ibid., p. 23.
38. Ibid., p. 25.
39. *Reading* (Mass.) *Chronicle,* May 21, 1953.
40. Seymour Harris and William Batt, Jr., JFKL–OH.
41. *Boston Post,* June 22, 1954; JFK, *Statements and Speeches,* p. 329.
42. New Bedford *Standard-Times,* June 7, 1956.
43. James Landis to Ted Sorensen, August 28, 1953, and Sorensen to Landis, September 1, 1953, Landis Papers, Box 50, Library of Congress.
44. Ted Sorensen to James Landis, December 18, 1953, Sorensen Papers, Box 6, JFKL.
45. JFK, "Floor Beneath Wages Is Gone," *New Republic,* July 20, 1953, pp. 14–15; JFK, "What's Wrong with Social Security?" *American Magazine,* October 1953, pp. 109–12.
46. JFK, "Social Security: Constructive if Not Bold," *New Republic,* February 8, 1954, pp. 14–15, and "Foreign Policy Is the People's Business," *New York Times Magazine,* August 8, 1954, pp. 5ff.
47. Ted Sorensen to James Landis, November 17, 1953, Landis Papers, Box 50, Library of Congress.
48. Ted Sorensen to Roul Tunley, August 11, 1954, Sorensen Papers, Box 6, JFKL.
49. *Boston Post,* March 6, 1954.
50. JFK, *Statements and Speeches,* pp. 346–354.

51. Jack L. Bell, JFKL–OH.
52. Speech transcript, December 2, 1953, Pre-Presidential Papers, Box 893.
53. Ted Sorensen, interview, April 27, 1977.
54. George Aiken and John Blatnik, JFKL–OH.
55. Speech transcript, January 14, 1954, Pre-Presidential Papers, Box 893, JFKL; William R. Willoughby, *The St. Lawrence Waterway* (Madison: University of Wisconsin Press, 1961), p. 255.
56. Sorensen, *Kennedy,* p. 59.
57. John Blatnik, JFKL–OH.
58. Ted Sorensen, interview, April 27, 1977.
59. Sorensen, *Kennedy,* p. 59.
60. Memorandum, James Landis, June 3, 1955, *Profiles in Courage* Papers, Box 31, JFKL.

Chapter 15: The Senator and the World

1. Walter Johnson to JFK, October 21, 1953, Pre-Presidential Papers, Box 481, JFKL.
2. Ibid., October 23, 1953.
3. Sorensen to JFK, October 24, 1953, Sorensen Papers, Box 15, JFKL.
4. Speech transcript, February 1, 1953, Pre-Presidential Papers, Box 893, JFKL.
5. *Christian Science Monitor,* May 12, 1954.
6. *Berkshire Eagle,* June 28, 1954.
7. Holyoke *Transcript-Telegram,* May 5, 1976.
8. *Boston Globe,* February 5, 1948.
9. Holyoke *Transcript-Telegram,* May 5, 1956.
10. Langdon P. Marvin, Jr., to Priscilla Johnson, April 17, 1953, Pre-Presidential Papers, Box 481, JFKL.
11. Priscilla Johnson to JFK, April 22, 1953, Pre-Presidential Papers, Box 481, JFKL.
12. Ibid.
13. The Senator Gravel Edition, *The Pentagon Papers,* 5 vols. (Boston: Beacon Press, 1971), Vol. 1, pp. 74 and 78.
14. JFK to John Foster Dulles, May 7, 1953, Pre-Presidential Papers, Box 481, JFKL.
15. Thruston Morton to JFK, May 13, 1953, Pre-Presidential Papers, Box 481, JFKL.
16. JFK, *Statements and Speeches,* pp. 263–64; *NYT,* July 2, 1953.
17. Speech transcript, January 21, 1954, Pre-Presidential Papers, Box 893, JFKL.
18. Ibid.
19. Herbert S. Parmet, *Eisenhower and the American Crusades* (New York: Macmillan, 1972), pp. 364–65.
20. *Congressional Record,* 83d Cong., 2d sess., pp. 4671–74.
21. Ibid.
22. Ibid., p. 4675.
23. JFK, *Statements and Speeches,* pp. 295–96.
24. *Atlanta Constitution,* April 21, 1954.
25. Speech transcripts, May 11, 1954, and May 28, 1954, Pre-Presidential Papers, Box 647, JFKL; *St. Louis Post-Dispatch,* May 28, 1954.
26. *NYT,* April 7, 1954.
27. Dwight D. Eisenhower, *Public Papers of the Presidents: Dwight D. Eisenhower 1954* (Washington, D.C.: U. S. Government Printing Office, 1960), p. 384.
28. *Brooklyn Eagle,* April 26, 1954.
29. Holyoke *Transcript-Telegram,* May 1, 1954; *Worcester Telegram,* June 10, 1954.
30. Springfield (Mass.) *Morning Union,* July 27, 1954; *Boston Evening Globe,* July 26, 1954.

Chapter 16: Dismal Days

1. Robert Griffith, *The Politics of Fear: Joseph R. McCarthy and the Senate* (Lexington: University of Kentucky Press, 1970), pp. 200–01; Fried, *McCarthy,* pp. 259, 269; Burns, *Kennedy,* pp. 142–43; Sorensen, *Kennedy,* p. 46.
2. Boston *Record,* May 6, 1954.
3. JFK, *Statements and Speeches,* p. 315.
4. East Boston *Leader,* March 12, 1954; *Boston Sunday Herald,* March 14, 1954.
5. Caldwell (Idaho) *News-Tribune,* April 5, 1954.
6. *Idaho Statesman,* April 5, 1954.
7. Pasadena *Star-News,* March 25, 1954.
8. *New Haven Register,* June 26, 1954; *Christian Science Monitor,* June 26, 1954.
9. *Berkshire Eagle,* June 28, 1954.
10. *Middletown* (Conn.) *Press,* June 26, 1954.
11. JFK, *Statements and Speeches,* pp. 332–33.
12. *Worcester Telegram,* June 5, 1954.
13. O'Brien, *No Final Victories,* p. 16.
14. James MacGregor Burns to Author, March 15, 1977.
15. Foster Furcolo, interview, February 21, 1977.
16. Theo Lippman, Jr., *Senator Ted Kennedy* (New York: W. W. Norton, 1976), p. 7; Kenneth P. O'Donnell, interview, December 4, 1976; Hersh, *Edward Kennedy,* p. 91.
17. *Boston Sunday Herald,* August 8, 1954.
18. Lawrence O'Brien, interview, October 19, 1976.
19. Kenneth P. O'Donnell, interview, December 4, 1976.
20. David F. Powers, interview, January 26, 1976.
21. Foster Furcolo, interview, February 21, 1977.
22. Ibid.
23. *Beverly Times,* October 13, 1954.
24. *Newton Graphic,* October 14, 1954.
25. *Berkshire Eagle,* November 6, 1954.
26. Foster Furcolo, interview, February 21, 1977.
27. Ibid.
28. John Foster (Foster Furcolo), *Let George Do It!* (New York: Harcourt, Brace, 1957), pp. 18–19, 52.
29. Sorensen, *Kennedy Legacy,* p. 32; Birmingham, *Onassis,* p. 78.
30. Fay, *Pleasure of His Company,* p. 15.
31. *Person to Person,* CBS-TV, October 10, 1953.
32. Jules Davids to Author, November 30, 1978; New York *Daily News,* June 26, 1954.
33. *Washington Post,* May 14, 1954.
34. *Detroit News Pictorial Magazine,* March 28, 1954.
35. New York *Daily News,* June 26, 1954.
36. Cleveland Amory, interview, May 6, 1977.
37. W. A. Swanberg, *Luce and His Empire* (New York: Scribner's, 1972), pp. 403–04.
38. Blair, *Search,* p. 317.
39. Confidential interview.
40. Joseph P. Kennedy to JFK, July 19, 1954, Pre-Presidential Papers, Box 504, JFKL.
41. Schlesinger, *RFK,* p. 100.
42. Fried, *McCarthy,* p. 246.
43. JFK to D. H. Crompton, February 2, 1953, Pre-Presidential Papers, Box 482, JFKL.
44. Mark De W. Howe to JFK, January 23, 1954, and JFK to Howe, February 10, 1954, Pre-Presidential Papers, Box 649, JFKL.
45. Fried, *McCarthy,* p. 264; *NYT,* January 24, 1954.
46. Fried, *McCarthy,* pp. 292–93.

47. Martin and Plaut, *Front Runner,* p. 204.
48. *Boston Post,* June 22, 1954.
49. *Berkshire Eagle,* June 2, 1954.
50. Lowell *Optic,* October 9, 1954.
51. Arthur Schlesinger, Jr., to G. Mennen Williams, January 4, 1954, Stevenson Papers, Box 404, Princeton.
52. *Berkshire Eagle,* undated newspaper clipping on microfilm roll #1, Pre-Presidential Clippings, JFKL.
53. Fried, *McCarthy,* pp. 279, 293–98.
54. Martin and Plaut, *Front Runner,* p. 205.
55. Ted Sorensen, interview, April 27, 1977.
56. Speech transcript, July 31, 1954, Sorensen Papers, Box 12, JFKL.
57. Hubert H. Humphrey, interview, July 26, 1977; *NYT,* August 17, 1954.
58. *Omaha Evening World-Herald,* August 20, 1954.
59. North Adams *Transcript,* August 18, 1954.
60. *Wilmington* (Cal.) *Press-Journal,* September 28, 1954.
61. *NYT,* July 16, 1953.
62. Lincoln, *My Twelve Years,* p. 50.
63. *NYT,* April 30, 1954.
64. Lincoln, *My Twelve Years,* p. 53.
65. *Boston Evening Globe,* July 26, 1954.
66. Ibid., August 5, 1954.
67. Malden (Mass.) *Evening News,* Sept. 8, 1954.
68. Nicholas, Burstein, et al., "Management . . . ," p. 739.
69. Worcester *Evening Gazette,* October 22, 1954.
70. Arthur Krock, JFKL–OH.
71. Ted Sorensen, interview, April 27, 1977.
72. Charles Spalding, JFKL–OH.
73. David F. Powers, interviews, January 26, 1976 and January 6, 1977; Arthur Schlesinger, Jr., to JFK, March 11, 1958, Sorensen Papers, Box 12, JFKL.
74. *Boston Post,* December 2, 1954.

Chapter 17: "Profiles in Courage"

1. *Worcester Sunday Telegram,* January 30, 1955.
2. *NYT,* February 26, 1955.
3. Portland (Maine) *Evening Express,* March 22, 1955.
4. Pittsburgh *Sun-Telegram,* April 24, 1955.
5. Travell, *Office Hours,* p. 5; *NYT,* April 28, 1955.
6. New Bedford *Standard-Times,* May 22, 1955.
7. Ibid.
8. Ibid.
9. Ibid.
10. *NYT,* May 24, 1955; Springfield *Daily News,* May 23, 1955; *Boston Globe,* May 23, 1955.
11. *Boston Globe,* May 24, 1955; *NYT,* May 25, 1955; Boston *Record,* May 25, 1955.
12. New York *Herald Tribune,* May 25, 1955.
13. Travell, *Office Hours,* pp. 5–6.
14. New Bedford *Standard-Times,* July 21, 1955.
15. Bangor (Maine) *Patriot,* July 20, 1955.
16. *Berkshire Eagle,* June 10, 1955; *Worcester Telegram,* June 10, 1955.

17. Jacqueline Kennedy to Ted Sorensen, August 1955, *Profiles in Courage* Papers, Box 32, JFKL.
18. *NYT,* September 22, 1955.
19. JFK to Ted Sorensen, September 29, 1955, President's Office Files, Box 135, JFKL, with attached draft of article to be sent to Reardon.
20. Ibid.
21. Ibid.
22. Ibid.
23. Travell, *Office Hours,* p. 309; Boston *American,* November 18, 1955.
24. Travell, *Office Hours,* p. 308.
25. *New York Times Book Review,* January 1, 1956, pp. 1 and 21.
26. New York *Herald Tribune,* January 6, 1956.
27. New Bedford *Standard-Times,* January 10, 1956.
28. *Boston Herald,* February 9, 1956.
29. *Washington Post,* February 9, 1956.
30. *Oregon Journal,* February 19, 1956.
31. John F. Kennedy, *Profiles in Courage,* memorial edition (New York: Harper & Row, 1964), p. 39.
32. Ibid., pp. 210, 243.
33. Ibid., pp. 262, 266.
34. James MacGregor Burns, JFKL–OH.
35. Ted Sorensen, interview, May 17, 1977.
36. Charles Bartlett, JFKL–OH; Fried, *McCarthy,* p. 292.
37. Arthur Krock to JFK, April 9, 1954, President's Office Files, Box 31, JFKL; Krock, *Memoirs,* p. 355.
38. Charles Bartlett, JFKL–OH.
39. Jules Davids to Author, November 30, 1978.
40. Ibid.
41. Jean Mannix, JFKL–OH.
42. JFK to Cass Canfield, January 28, 1955, *Profiles in Courage* Papers, Box 31, JFKL.
43. Publishers Agreement signed by Evan Thomas and Frank MacGregor, April 25, 1955, Sorensen Papers, Box 7, JFKL; Evan Thomas to JFK, April 21, 1955, *Profiles in Courage* Papers, Box 31, JFKL.
44. James Landis, Memorandum, May 3, 1955, *Profiles in Courage* Papers, Box 31, JFKL.
45. Arthur Holcombe to JFK, June 30, 1955, *Profiles in Courage* Papers, Box 31, JFKL.
46. Jules Davids to JFK, February 24, 1955, and Davids to Author, November 30, 1978, *Profiles in Courage* Papers, Box 31, JFKL.
47. Jules Davids to JFK, March 19, 1955, *Profiles in Courage* Papers, Box 29, JFKL.
48. Arthur Schlesinger, Jr., to JFK, July 4, 1955, *Profiles in Courage* Papers, Box 31, JFKL.
49. William Tansill, interview, January 24, 1979.
50. Jean Mannix, JFKL–OH; Jules Davids to Author, November 30, 1978.
51. Ted Sorensen, interview, May 17, 1977.
52. Jules Davids to Author, November 30, 1978.
53. Martin and Plaut, *Front Runner,* p. 201.
54. Memorandum, May 23, 1955, *Profiles in Courage* Papers, Box 31, JFKL.
55. JFK to Evan Thomas, June 23, 1955, and August 1, 1955, and to Eunice Shriver, July 26, 1955; Evan Thomas to JFK, August 4, 1955, *Profiles in Courage* Papers, Box 31, JFKL.
56. Evan Thomas to Ted Sorensen, August 24, 1955, *Profiles in Courage* Papers, Box 31, JFKL.
57. Ted Sorensen to JFK, October 7, 1955, *Profiles in Courage* Papers, Box 31, JFKL.
58. JFK to Evan Thomas, August 1, 1955, *Profiles in Courage* Papers, Box 31, JFKL.

59. Ted Sorensen to JFK, September 12, 1955, August 12, 1955, and October 20, 1955, Sorensen Papers, Box 7, JFKL.
60. Blair Clark, interview, March 18, 1977.
61. *Village Voice,* May 15, 1957.
62. L. B. Nichols to Clyde Tolson, May 14, 1957, JFK File, FBI.
63. Sorensen Papers, Box 7, JFKL; Hugh Sidey, *John F. Kennedy, President* (New York: Atheneum, 1964), p. 12.
64. Abell, ed., *Pearson Diaries,* p. 420.
65. JFK to John B. Oakes, January 30, 1958, in the possession of Mr. Oakes; John B. Oakes, Columbia University–OH.
66. Martha MacGregor to JFK, January 20, 1958, and JFK to MacGregor, January 30, 1958, Sorensen Papers, Box 7, JFKL.
67. Krock, *Memoirs,* p. 376.
68. *Profiles in Courage* Tapes, JFKL.

Chapter 18: "Madly for Adlai"

1. JFK to Adlai Stevenson, October 21, 1955, Stevenson Papers, Box 414, Princeton.
2. Adlai Stevenson to JFK, October 29, 1955, Stevenson Papers, Box 414, Princeton.
3. Martin, *Stevenson of Illinois,* p. 457; Koskoff, *Kennedy,* p. 589.
4. Stephen Mitchell, Columbia University–OH.
5. James M. Landis, Columbia University–OH.
6. John Bartlow Martin, *Adlai Stevenson and the World* (Garden City, N.Y.: Doubleday, 1977), p. 235; Newton P. Minow, Columbia University–OH.
7. Ted Sorensen to JFK, September 12, 1955, Sorensen Papers, Box 7, JFKL.
8. Adlai Stevenson to Agnes Meyer, August 8, 1955, Stevenson Papers, Box 416, Princeton.
9. Martin, *Stevenson and the World,* p. 210.
10. Ibid., p. 218.
11. *NYT,* October 25 and 26, 1955.
12. Walter Johnson and Carol Evans, eds., *The Papers of Adlai Stevenson,* 8 vols. (Boston: Little, Brown, 1972–1979), Vol. 4, p. 564.
13. Ted Sorensen to JFK, November 22, 1955, Sorensen Papers, Box 7, JFKL.
14. Schlesinger, *RFK,* p. 131.
15. Ted Sorensen, interview, May 17, 1977.
16. John Sharon, Columbia University–OH.
17. Newton Minow, Columbia University–OH.
18. Ibid.
19. Ibid.
20. Speech transcript, January 10, 1956, Pre-Presidential Papers, Box 894, JFKL.
21. "Memorandum on Committee Status of Senator John F. Kennedy," January 1956, Sorensen Papers, Box 9, JFKL.
22. Speech transcript, May 8, 1959, Pre-Presidential Papers, Box 903, JFKL.
23. Hugh Sidey, JFKL–OH.
24. Lyndon B. Johnson to JFK, August 3, 1956, President's Office Files, Box 30, JFKL.
25. Albert Gore, JFKL–OH; JFK, *Statements and Speeches,* pp. 382–83.
26. JFK, *Statements and Speeches,* pp. 385–86.
27. Arthur Holcombe to JFK, March 13, 1956, Pre-Presidential Papers, Box 666, JFKL.
28. JFK, *Statements and Speeches,* pp. 392–409.
29. Ibid., pp. 419–25.
30. JFK to John Foster Dulles, February 29, 1956, and Roderic O'Connor to JFK, March 7, 1956, Pre-Presidential Papers, Box 674, JFKL; *NYT,* February 20, 1956; *Boston Globe,*

June 2, 1956; Nurse, "America Must Not Sleep," p. 135; Congressional Record, 84th Cong., 2d sess., pp. 9614–9615.

31. JFK to William McCormick Blair, Jr., February 15, 1956, Stevenson Papers, Box 434, Princeton.
32. *St. Louis Post-Dispatch,* March 9, 1956; Boston *American,* March 8, 1956; *Boston Globe,* March 9, 1956; *Berkshire Eagle,* March 8, 1956; Ontario (Cal.) *Daily Report,* February 20, 1956.
33. Johnson and Evans, eds., *Stevenson Papers,* Vol. 6, p. 84.
34. Bruce Jay Gorman, *Kefauver: A Political Biography* (New York: Oxford University Press, 1971), p. 225; Martin, *Stevenson and the World,* p. 276.
35. JFK to Adlai Stevenson, March 22, 1956, Stevenson Papers, Box 434, Princeton.
36. Martin, *Stevenson and the World,* p. 282.
37. Adlai Stevenson to Arthur Schlesinger, Jr., March 26, 1956, in Johnson and Evans, eds., *Stevenson Papers,* Vol. 6, p. 95.
38. Francis X. Morrissey to JFK, March 29, 1956, President's Office Files, Box 31, JFKL.
39. Archibald Alexander to James Finnegan, March 29, 1956, Stevenson Papers, Box 505, Princeton.
40. O'Donnell and Powers, *"Johnny,"* p. 105.
41. Edward McCormack, JFKL–OH.
42. Thomas P. O'Neill, interview, March 8, 1977.
43. Joseph P. Healy to Ted Sorensen, December 2, 1954, Sorensen Papers, Box 15, JFKL.
44. Philip J. Philbin to JFK, March 3, 1955, Pre-Presidential Papers, Box 503, JFKL.
45. JFK to Kenneth P. O'Donnell, March 8, 1955, Pre-Presidential Papers, Box 504, JFKL.
46. O'Brien, *No Final Victories,* p. 47.
47. *Berkshire Eagle,* May 16, 1955.
48. John McCormack, interview, January 16, 1979, and JFKL–OH; Edward McCormack, JFKL–OH.
49. O'Donnell and Powers, *"Johnny,"* p. 106; Burns, *Kennedy,* p. 175.
50. Thomas P. O'Neill, interview, March 8, 1979.
51. O'Donnell and Powers, *"Johnny,"* p. 106.
52. Ibid., pp. 108–09.
53. *Christian Science Monitor,* May 8 and 9, 1956.
54. O'Donnell and Powers, *"Johnny,"* p. 109; *NYT,* April 25, 1956; *Berkshire Eagle,* April 30, 1956.
55. *NYT,* April 25, 1956, and May 12, 1956; *Berkshire Eagle,* April 30, 1956; Boston *Sunday Advertiser,* April 29, 1956.
56. *Berkshire Eagle,* May 12, 1956; John McCormack, interview, January 16, 1979.
57. JFK to James Finnegan, May 2, 1956, Princeton.
58. Springfield *Daily News,* May 7, 1956.
59. *Berkshire Eagle,* May 12, 1956.
60. Francis X. Morrissey to JFK, May 9, 1956, President's Office Files, Box 31, JFKL.
61. *Christian Science Monitor,* May 8 and 9, 1956.
62. Ibid., May 8, 1956.
63. *Worcester Telegram,* May 9, 1956.
64. Thomas P. O'Neill, interview, March 8, 1979.
65. Powers and O'Donnell, *"Johnny,"* pp. 111–12.
66. Kenneth P. O'Donnell, interview, December 4, 1976.
67. *Boston Sunday Herald,* May 20, 1956.
68. Newton Minow to Ted Sorensen, May 21, 1956, Stevenson Papers, Box 441, Princeton.
69. Stan Karson to James Finnegan, Minow, Alexander, et al., May 22, 1956, Stevenson Papers, Princeton.

70. Archibald Alexander to Minow, Finnegan, and Karson, June 12, 1956, Stevenson Papers, Princeton.
71. *Worcester Telegram,* June 1, 1956.
72. Lowell *Sun,* July 2, 1956.
73. *NYT,* June 10, 1956.
74. *Congressional Record,* 84th Cong., 2d sess., pp. 10800–01.

Chapter 19: *Preparing for Chicago*

1. Dore Schary, interview, January 18, 1979.
2. Transcript, *Pursuit of Happiness,* Democratic National Committee news release, August 14, 1956, Stevenson Papers, Princeton.
3. *NYT,* July 10, 1956; Hubert H. Humphrey, interview, July 26, 1977.
4. Dore Schary, JFKL–OH.
5. Ted Sorensen, interview, May 17, 1977.
6. Robert L. Reynolds to Ted Sorensen, May 4, 1956, Sorensen Papers, Box 3, JFKL.
7. Fletcher Knebel, "Can a Catholic Become Vice President?" *Look,* June 12, 1956, p. 34.
8. Fletcher Knebel, interview, May 9, 1979.
9. *NYT,* July 23, 1956.
10. Agnes Meyer to Willard Wirtz, July 23, 1956, Stevenson Papers, Box 483, Princeton.
11. Ted Sorensen, interview, May 17, 1977.
12. Ibid.
13. Ted Sorensen, "The Catholic Vote in 1952 and 1956," Sorensen Papers, Box 15, JFKL.
14. New York *Herald Tribune,* June 24, 1956.
15. Angus Campbell, Philip Converse, et al., *The American Voter* (New York: John Wiley, 1960), p. 301; Everett Carll Ladd, Jr., with Charles D. Hadley, *Transformation of the American Party System* (New York: W. W. Norton, 1975), p. 117; Richard L. Rubin, *Party Dynamics* (New York: Oxford University Press, 1976), p. 49; Parmet, *Democrats,* pp. 98–143.
16. Abraham Ribicoff to JFK, June 15, 1956, Sorensen Papers, Box 9, JFKL.
17. Arthur Schlesinger, Jr., to James Finnegan, June 15, 1956, Stevenson Papers, Box 434, Princeton.
18. *Tampa Times,* July 13, 1956; *Stoneham* (Mass.) *Independent,* August 23, 1956.
19. *Newsweek,* June 18, 1956.
20. Lowell *Sun,* July 2, 1956.
21. *Newsweek,* July 9, 1956; Springfield (Mass.) *Daily News,* August 3, 1956; *Boston Post,* July 9, 1956.
22. Martin, *Stevenson and the World,* p. 344; *NYT,* July 25, 1956.
23. Hubert H. Humphrey, *The Education of a Public Man: My Life and Politics* (Garden City, N.Y.: Doubleday, 1976), p. 188.
24. Gorman, *Kefauver,* pp. 248–49.
25. Sorensen, *Kennedy,* p. 81.
26. Martin, *Stevenson and the World,* p. 243.
27. Parmet, *Democrats,* p. 170.
28. JFK to Joseph P. Kennedy, June 29, 1956, Sorensen Papers, Box 9, JFKL.
29. Sargent Shriver to Joseph P. Kennedy, June 18, 1956, in Koskoff, *Kennedy,* p. 418.
30. James Landis, Columbia University–OH.

Chapter 20: The Showdown at Chicago

1. *NYT,* August 7, 1956.
2. *Boston Sunday Herald,* August 12, 1956.
3. *NYT,* August 12, 1956.
4. *Boston Herald,* August 18, 1956.
5. *NYT,* August 13, 1956.
6. *Boston Herald,* August 14, 1956.
7. Ibid., August 13, 1956.
8. *NYT,* August 14, 1956.
9. Dore Schary, JFKL–OH.
10. *Chicago Tribune,* August 14, 1956.
11. Eleanor Roosevelt, *On My Own* (New York: Harper, 1958), p. 162.
12. Abba Schwartz, interviews, July 24 and 26, 1979.
13. Lash, *Eleanor: Years Alone,* p. 258.
14. Roosevelt, *On My Own,* p. 164.
15. Martin and Plaut, *Front Runner,* pp. 74–75.
16. Roosevelt, *On My Own,* p. 164n.
17. Martin and Plaut, *Front Runner,* p. 75.
18. O'Donnell and Powers, *"Johnny,"* p. 120.
19. *Boston Herald,* August 15, 1956.
20. *NYT,* August 15, 1956.
21. *Boston Herald,* August 15, 1956.
22. Abram Chayes, JFKL–OH.
23. *NYT,* August 17, 1956.
24. Springfield (Mass.) *Daily News,* August 15, 1956.
25. Paul Douglas, Columbia University–OH.
26. Kenneth P. O'Donnell, interview, December 4, 1976.
27. *Boston Herald,* August 17, 1956.
28. *NYT,* August 17, 1956.
29. Martin, *Stevenson and the World,* p. 199.
30. John Sharon, Columbia University–OH.
31. Martin, *Stevenson and the World,* pp. 349–50.
32. John Sharon, Columbia University–OH.
33. Abraham Ribicoff, interview, February 5, 1973.
34. John Sharon, Columbia University–OH.
35. Martin and Plaut, *Front Runner,* p. 64.
36. John Sharon, Columbia University–OH.
37. O'Donnell and Powers, *"Johnny,"* p. 122.
38. Interviews, John McCormack, January 16, 1979, and Robert Wagner, Jr., January 17, 1979.
39. Abraham Ribicoff, interview, February 5, 1973.
40. Stephen Mitchell, Columbia University–OH.
41. Robert Wagner, Jr., interview, January 17, 1979.
42. Jim Grant Bolling, JFKL–OH.
43. Rowland Evans and Robert Novak, *Lyndon B. Johnson: The Exercise of Power* (New York: New American Library, 1966), p. 238.
44. Kenneth P. O'Donnell, in Plimpton and Stein, eds., *American Journey,* pp. 80–81; Gorman, *Kefauver,* p. 258; Albert Gore, JFKL–OH; Albert Gore, *Let the Glory Out: My South and its Politics* (New York: Viking Press, 1972), p. 95; Drew Pearson in the Lynn (Mass.) *Daily Item,* August 29, 1956.
45. Martin and Plaut, *Front Runner,* pp. 96–98; Paul Douglas, *In the Fullness of Time* (New York: Harcourt Brace Jovanovich, 1972), p. 266.

46. Gore, *Let the Glory Out,* p. 95.
47. Hubert H. Humphrey, interview, July 26, 1977; Hubert H. Humphrey to JFK, September 8, 1956, President's Office Files, Box 30, JFKL.
48. Leonard Woodcock, JFKL–OH; Charles A. H. Thomson and Frances M. Shattuck, *The 1956 Presidential Campaign* (Washington, D.C.: The Brookings Institution, 1960), p. 161.
49. *NYT,* August 18, 1956.
50. *Boston Herald,* August 18, 1956; Camille Gravel, JFKL–OH.
51. *NYT,* August 18, 1956.
52. Robert F. Kennedy, JFKL–OH (John B. Martin interview).
53. John McCormack, interviews, September 14, 1978, and January 16, 1978.
54. John Blatnik, JFKL–OH.
55. *Atlanta Constitution,* August 15, 1956.
56. Whalen, *Founding Father,* p. 444.
57. Krock, *Memoirs,* p. 359.
58. *Boston Herald,* August 18, 1956.
59. *Southwest* (Pulaski, Va.) *Times,* August 24, 1956.
60. Johnson and Evans, eds., *Stevenson Papers,* Vol. 6, p. 206.
61. *Worcester Telegram,* August 19, 1956.
62. Boston *American,* August 24, 1956.
63. Johnson and Evans, eds., *Stevenson Papers,* Vol. 6, p. 194.

Chapter 21: The Pulitzer Prize-Winning Senator

1. Boston *American,* August 29, 1956.
2. Harry F. Byrd to JFK, August 20, 1956, Byrd Papers, Box 233, University of Virginia.
3. Schlesinger, *RFK,* pp. 133–36.
4. Newton Minow, Columbia University–OH.
5. *Saturday Evening Post,* September 7, 1957, p. 48.
6. JFK to Frank L. Dennis, July 9, 1958, Sorensen Papers, Box 3, JFKL.
7. JFK to James Finnegan, October 3, 1956, Stevenson Papers, Box 434, Princeton.
8. Martin, *Stevenson and the World,* p. 356.
9. Ibid., p. 389.
10. Birmingham *Post-Herald,* October 25, 1956.
11. JFK to James P. Coleman, November 1, 1956, Stevenson Papers, Box 9, JFKL.
12. John F. Kennedy, *The Strategy of Peace* ed. Allan Nevins (New York: Harper & Row, 1960), pp. 112 and 116.
13. Ted Sorensen, appointment calendar, Sorensen Papers, Box 2, JFKL.
14. David F. Powers, interview, January 26, 1976.
15. JFK to Paul Butler, February 7, 1957, Sorensen Papers, Box 9, JFKL.
16. New Bedford *Standard-Times,* October 25, 1957.
17. Topeka *State Journal,* November 7, 1957; *Lincoln Journal,* May 18, 1957.
18. *Woburn* (Mass.) *Daily Times,* January 9, 1957; Gallup, ed., *The Gallup Poll,* Vol. 2, p. 1470.
19. Providence *Sunday Journal,* January 13, 1957.
20. *NYT,* October 20, 1964; Gerald Morgan to Jack Martin, February 4, 1955, Morgan Papers, Box 35, Dwight D. Eisenhower Library; Sinclair Weeks to Dwight D. Eisenhower, January 16, 1958, Weeks Papers (private collection), Box 26; Parmet, *Eisenhower,* pp. 329–57.
21. Richard Bolling, JFKL–OH.

22. Samuel Merrick, JFKL–OH.
23. Ibid.
24. U.S. Congress, Senate, *Hearings Before the Subcommittee on Labor* 85th Cong., 1st sess., 1957, p. 22.
25. Ibid., pp. 34, 36, 43–44.
26. *NYT,* February 26, 1957.
27. U.S., Congress, Senate, *Hearings,* 85th Cong., 1st sess., p. 237.
28. Ibid., p. 238.
29. *NYT,* July 8, 1957.
30. *NYT,* May 1, 1957; New York *Herald Tribune,* May 5, 1957.
31. Evan Thomas, interview, May 20, 1977.
32. Julian Boyd to John Hohenberg, February 28, 1957, Pulitzer Prize Papers, Pulitzer Prize Office, Columbia University.
33. John Hohenberg, interview, June 18, 1977.
34. Joseph Pulitzer, Jr., interview, August 5, 1977.
35. John Hohenberg, interview, June 18, 1977; John Hohenberg, *The Pulitzer Prizes* (New York: Columbia University Press, 1974), pp. 270–73.
36. Joseph Pulitzer, Jr., interview, August 5, 1977.
37. John Hohenberg, interview, June 18, 1977.
38. *Boston Globe,* May 22, 1957.

Chapter 22: Human Rights—At Home and Abroad

1. JFK, *Statements and Speeches,* pp. 470–72.
2. JFK to John Foster Dulles, March 12, 1957, Sorensen Papers, Box 14, JFKL.
3. JFK, *Statements and Speeches,* pp. 1052–55.
4. Burlington (Vt.) *News,* May 17, 1957.
5. Ronald J. Nurse, "Critic of Colonialism: JFK and Algerian Independence," *Historian,* February 1977, p. 311.
6. JFK, *Statements and Speeches,* p. 520.
7. JFK, *Strategy of Peace,* p. 72.
8. JFK, *Statements and Speeches,* p. 526.
9. Ibid., pp. 527–28.
10. Ibid., p. 530.
11. *NYT,* July 8, 1957.
12. Eisenhower, *Public Papers of the Presidents . . . 1957,* p. 526.
13. Koskoff, *Kennedy,* p. 399.
14. *NYT,* July 3, 1957.
15. *Manchester Guardian Weekly,* July 11, 1957.
16. Manchester (N.H.) *Union Leader,* July 15 and 18, 1957.
17. Martin, *Stevenson and the World,* p. 415; Schlesinger, *RFK,* p. 199.
18. JFK to Adlai Stevenson, July 19, 1957, Schlesinger Papers, Box 919, JFKL.
19. *NYT,* July 30, 1957.
20. Herbert Lehman to Julius C. C. Edelstein, July 4, 1957, Lehman Papers, Columbia.
21. *Boston Globe,* July 4, 1957.
22. *NYT,* August 9, 1957.
23. Dean Acheson, *Power and Diplomacy* (New York: Atheneum, 1963), p. 123; *NYT,* October 26, 1957.
24. Chester Bowles to Thomas K. Finletter, July 25, 1957, Bowles Papers, Yale.
25. *Wichita Beacon,* July 19, 1957.
26. *America,* October 5, 1957, pp. 15–17.

27. Nurse, "Critic of Colonialism," p. 320; Halberstam, *Best and Brightest,* p. 95.
28. Halberstam, *Best and Brightest,* p. 95.
29. JFK, *Statements and Speeches,* pp. 550–62.
30. Hamilton Fish Armstrong to JFK, April 9, 1957; undated memo, Sorensen to JFK; JFK to Armstrong, August 15, 1957; Earl Latham to Sorensen, July 9, 1957, Sorensen Papers, Box 3, JFKL; John F. Kennedy, "A Democrat Looks at Foreign Policy," *Foreign Affairs,* October 1957, pp. 44 and 46.
31. *America,* October 5, 1957, p. 17.
32. JFK to Felix Cayo, August 18, 1959, Pre-Presidential Papers, Box 717, JFKL.
33. Nurse, "Critic of Colonialism," p. 315.
34. Alistair Horne, *A Savage War of Peace: Algeria 1954–1962* (New York: Viking Press, 1977), p. 247.
35. Carl M. Brauer, *John F. Kennedy and the Second Reconstruction* (New York: Columbia University Press, 1977), p. 18.
36. Ted Sorensen, interview, April 27, 1977.
37. *Arkansas Gazette,* June 8, 1957.
38. *Boston Herald,* June 18, 1957; Boston *Record,* June 11, 1957.
39. Birmingham *Post-Herald,* June 27, 1957.
40. JFK to John Temple Graves, July 11, 1957, microfilm reel #2, Pre-Presidential Clippings, JFKL.
41. *Waterbury American,* July 5, 1957.
42. JFK to Clarence Mitchell, July 10, 1957, Sorensen Papers, Box 9, JFKL.
43. *Providence Chronicle,* July 13, 1957.
44. *New Republic,* July 15, 1957.
45. *Boston Globe,* July 22 and 24, 1957; Lowell *Sun,* July 22, 1957.
46. Joseph Rauh, Jr., JFKL-OH; JFK to Samuel Beer, August 3, 1957, Sorensen Papers, Box 9, JFKL.
47. George Reedy to Lyndon B. Johnson, July 12, 1957, Johnson Papers, Lyndon B. Johnson Library.
48. Orlando (Fla.) *Sentinel,* August 1, 1957.
49. *NYT,* August 3, 1957.
50. JFK, *Statements and Speeches,* pp. 540–41.
51. Ibid., p. 538; New York *Herald Tribune,* August 4, 1957.
52. *NYT,* April 4, 1957.
53. Quincy *Patriot-Ledger,* August 3, 1957; Salem (Mass.) *Evening News,* October 15, 1957.
54. *Jewish Times,* August 15, 1957.
55. *NYT,* August 19, 1957; *Washington Star,* August 7, 1957.
56. Birmingham *Post-Herald,* November 23, 1957.
57. Speech transcript, Pre-Presidential Papers, Box 898, JFKL.
58. Jackson *State Times,* October 17, 1957.
59. Ibid.
60. Eupora (Miss.) *Progress,* October 25, 1957.
61. Kay Halle, JFKL-OH.
62. Fall River *Herald-News,* September 12, 1957; Laconia (N.H.) *Citizen,* September 13, 1957; Lynn (Mass.) *Telegram-News,* September 13, 1957; New Bedford *Standard-Times,* September 13, 1957; *Christian Science Monitor,* September 14, 1957; *Boston Globe,* September 19, 1957; *Boston Herald,* September 19, 1957; New York *Daily News,* September 19, 1957; New York *Herald Tribune,* September 20, 1957; *Boston Sunday Globe,* September 29, 1957.
63. *NYT,* November 25, 1957.

Chapter 23: Labor "Reform"

1. Robert F. Kennedy, *The Enemy Within* (New York: Harper, 1960), p. 3.
2. Schlesinger, *RFK,* p. 142.
3. Meyer Feldman, JFKL–OH.
4. Schlesinger, *RFK,* p. 142; O'Donnell and Powers, *"Johnny,"* p. 132.
5. John Bartlow Martin, "The Struggle to Get Hoffa," *Saturday Evening Post,* June 27–August 8, 1959, *passim;* Robert Kennedy, *Enemy Within,* p. 237.
6. Martin, "Struggle to Get Hoffa," *Saturday Evening Post,* August 27, 1959, p. 21.
7. Alan K. McAdams, *Power and Politics in Labor Legislation* (New York: Columbia University Press, 1964), pp. vi and 11.
8. *Boston Herald,* April 30, 1957.
9. Ibid.
10. *Newsweek,* July 22, 1957.
11. *NYT,* December 29, 1957; Transcript, *Face the Nation,* February 8, 1958, Pre-Presidential Papers, Box 540, JFKL; *NYT,* April 1, 1958.
12. New York *Daily News,* January 3, 1958.
13. *Arizona Republic,* February 25, 1958.
14. Jack L. Bell, JFKL–OH.
15. *NYT,* March 5, 1958.
16. U.S., Congress, Senate, Select Committee on Improper Activities in the Labor or Management Field, *Investigation of Improper Activities in the Labor or Management Field,* 85th Cong., 2d sess., 1958, pp. 10002, 10019.
17. Ibid., p. 10037.
18. Frank Cormier and William J. Eaton, *Reuther* (Englewood Cliffs, N.J.: Prentice-Hall, 1970), p. 370; Schlesinger, *RFK,* p. 191.
19. Sorensen, *Kennedy,* p. 53.
20. Martin, "Struggle to Get Hoffa," p. 30.
21. *Congressional Record,* 86th Cong., 1st sess., p. 5825.
22. Sorensen, *Kennedy,* p. 52.
23. *Worcester Telegram,* May 22, 1957; *Denver Post,* May 17, 1957; *NYT,* May 17, 1957.
24. *NYT,* August 8, 1957.
25. Ibid.
26. Ibid., October 20, 1957.
27. Ibid., November 1, 1957.
28. Ibid., May 20, 1957.
29. JFK, *Statements and Speeches,* pp. 579 and 613.
30. Ibid., p. 585; *NYT,* March 12, 1958.
31. U.S., Congress, Senate, *Hearings of Subcommittee on Labor,* 86th Cong., 1st sess., March 26, 1958, p. 31; *NYT,* March 27, 1958; Eisenhower, *Public Papers of the Presidents . . . 1958,* p. 123.
32. U.S., Congress, Senate, *Hearings of Subcommittee on Labor,* March 27, 1958, pp. 83–85; *NYT,* March 28, 1958.
33. George Meany, JFKL–OH.
34. Joseph C. Goulden, *Meany* (New York: Atheneum, 1972), p. 294.
35. JFK, *Statements and Speeches,* pp. 628–29.
36. *NYT,* May 15, 1958.
37. *Milwaukee Sentinel,* May 18, 1958.
38. *NYT,* May 24, 1958; McAdams, *Power and Politics,* p. 45.
39. *New York Post,* June 23, 1958.
40. *NYT,* June 11 and 12, 1958.
41. Ibid., June 18, 1958; JFK, *Statements and Speeches,* p. 672.
42. *NYT,* July 9, 1958.

43. *Wall Street Journal,* July 10, 1958.
44. *NYT,* August 18, 1958.
45. Ibid., August 1, 1958.
46. *NYT,* July 31, 1958.
47. Frank Thompson, Jr., JFKL–OH.
48. *NYT,* August 24, 1958.
49. Ibid., August 19, 1958.
50. Ibid., August 23, 1958, September 25 and 29, 1958.

Chapter 24: *"The Perfect Politician"*

1. Whalen, *Founding Father,* pp. 446–47.
2. St. Albans (Vt.) *Messenger,* April 5, 1957.
3. *Gazetta del Massachusetts,* July 5, 1957.
4. Marquis Childs to Joseph P. Kennedy, May 17, 1957, Sorensen Papers, Box 7, JFKL; *Rutland* (Vt.) *Daily Herald,* May 15, 1957.
5. Francis X. Morrissey to Joseph P. Kennedy, January 2, 1957, Pre-Presidential Papers, Box 527, JFKL.
6. *Boston Sunday Herald,* May 19, 1957.
7. *Winchester Evening Star,* February 15, 1957.
8. *Boston Herald,* March 19 and April 7, 1957.
9. *Minneapolis Morning Tribune,* May 9, 1957.
10. Martin, "The Amazing Kennedys," p. 48.
11. Lynn (Mass.) *Sunday Telegram-News,* July 14, 1957; New Bedford *Standard-Times,* July 23, 1957; *Rutland* (Vt.) *Herald,* July 4, 1957; *Boston Globe,* July 29, 1957.
12. *San Diego Union,* August 13, 1957; Frank Morrissey to JFK, January 9, 1958, Pre-Presidential Papers, Box 527, JFKL.
13. *New York Post,* November 11, 1957.
14. *Tucson Daily Citizen,* February 24, 1958.
15. Speech transcript, March 15, 1958, Pre-Presidential Papers, Box 900, JFKL.
16. Gallup, ed., *Gallup Poll,* Vol. 2, pp. 1539–41, 1556–57.
17. *U.S. News & World Report,* July 11, 1958, p. 27.
18. William M. Blair, Jr., to JFK, August 7, 1958, Stevenson Papers, Box 750, Princeton.
19. *NYT,* July 13, 1958.
20. *Dothan* (Ala.) *Eagle,* May 13, 1958.
21. Cabell Phillips, "How to be a Presidential Candidate," *New York Times Magazine,* July 13, 1958, p. 54.
22. *NYT,* August 18, 1958.
23. *Greenville* (S.C.) *News,* October 1, 1958; *NYT,* September 24, 1958.
24. *NYT,* October 24, 1958.
25. Schlesinger, *RFK,* p. 385; Kenneth P. O'Donnell, interview, December 4, 1976; Joseph Alsop, interview, July 26, 1977; Jack Anderson with James Boyd, *Confessions of a Muckraker* (New York: Random House, 1979), p. 308.
26. Speech transcript, October 9, 1957, Stevenson Papers, Box 729, Princeton.
27. *Daily Peabody* (Mass.) *Times,* November 7, 1957.
28. JFK to Perkins McGuire, April 3, 1958, Pre-Presidential Papers, Box 689, JFKL; Undated memorandum, Sorensen Papers, Box 13, JFKL.
29. Sudbury (Mass.) *Enterprise,* July 10, 1958.
30. Topeka *State Journal,* November 7, 1957; *Boston Herald,* November 7, 1957; *NYT,* November 15, 1957.
31. Dwight D. Eisenhower, *Public Papers of the Presidents . . . 1947,* p. 796.

32. Muskogee *Phoenix,* November 13, 1957; *Daily Oklahoman,* November 8, 1957; Danbury *News-Times,* November 9, 1957.
33. *NYT,* December 8, 1957.
34. Joseph Dolan, JFKL–OH; *Denver Post,* February 25, 1958; Baltimore *Sun,* February 28, 1958; Springfield (Mass.) *Morning Union,* June 9, 1958.
35. Springfield (Mass.) *Morning Union,* June 6, 1958; *Atlantic Monthly,* August 1958, pp. 5–6.
36. Theodore C. Sorensen, JFKL–OH.
37. Martin, *Stevenson and the World,* p. 207; JFK, *Strategy of Peace,* p. 34.
38. Thomas R. Phillips, "The Growing Missile Gap," *The Reporter,* January 8, 1959, p. 11; Roy E. Licklider, "The Missile Gap Controversy," *Political Science Quarterly* (December 1970), p. 605.
39. Joseph Alsop in the New York *Herald Tribune,* August 17, 1958.
40. JFK, *Strategy of Peace,* pp. 33–45.
41. Ibid.
42. Theodore C. Sorensen, JFKL–OH.
43. New York *Herald Tribune,* September 13, 1958.
44. *Parkersburg* (W.Va.) *Sentinel,* October 9, 1958.

Chapter 25: Emphatic Reelection

1. O'Donnell and Powers, *"Johnny,"* p. 145.
2. Hersh, *Edward Kennedy,* p. 113.
3. Francis X. Morrissey to JFK, January 7, 1958, Pre-Presidential Papers, Box 527, JFKL; *Boston Herald,* May 14, 1957; *Boston Globe,* August 1, 1957; Lowell *Optic,* June 15, 1957; Fall River *Herald-News,* June 17, 1957; *Waterbury Sunday Republican,* July 7, 1957; *NYT,* October 19, 1958.
4. *Boston Herald,* July 16, 1958; *NYT,* October 19, 1958.
5. Thomas P. O'Neill, interview, March 8, 1979.
6. Springfield (Mass.) *Morning Union,* November 18, 1957.
7. Lawrence O'Brien to JFK, May 16, 1957, Pre-Presidential Papers, Box 7, JFKL.
8. O'Brien, *No Final Victories,* pp. 51–52.
9. Ibid., p. 54; Hersh, *Edward Kennedy,* p. 112; Whalen, *Founding Father,* p. 453.
10. Hersh, *Edward Kennedy,* p. 112.
11. O'Brien, *No Final Victories,* p. 55.
12. Hersh, *Edward Kennedy,* p. 104.
13. O'Brien, *No Final Victories,* p. 56.
14. Foster Furcolo, interview, February 21, 1977; Joe Croken, interview, August 6, 1979; *Gazetta del Massachusetts,* April 11, 1958.
15. Marjorie M. Lawson to JFK, November 26, 1958, Sorensen Papers, Box 9, JFKL.
16. Ibid.
17. *Berkshire Eagle,* April 28, 1958.
18. JFK to Roy Wilkins, May 6, 1958, Sorensen Papers, Box 9, JFKL.
19. Roy Wilkins to JFK, May 29, 1958, Sorensen Papers, Box 9, JFKL.
20. JFK to Roy Wilkins, July 18, 1958, Sorensen Papers, Box 9, JFKL.
21. Roy Wilkins, interview, August 11, 1970; Marjorie Lawson to JFK, November 26, 1958, Sorensen Papers, Box 9, JFKL.
22. Brauer, *Kennedy and Second Reconstruction,* pp. 28–29.
23. *NYT,* June 21, 1958; Lynn (Mass.) *Sunday Telegram-News,* July 13, 1958.
24. Lynn (Mass.) *Sunday Telegram-News,* July 27, 1958.
25. *Christian Science Monitor,* September 20, 1958.

26. O'Brien, *No Final Victories,* p. 53.

27. Thomas P. O'Neill, interview, March 8, 1979.

28. Edward McCormack, JFKL–OH; Hersh, *Edward Kennedy,* p. 112.

29. Whalen, *Founding Father,* p. 448.

30. Lynn (Mass.) *Daily Item,* November 4, 1958; *Boston Traveler,* November 5, 1958.

31. David F. Powers to JFK, December 9, 1958, JFK Personal Papers, Box 41, JFKL.

32. *NYT,* November 10, 1958.

33. Transcript, *Meet the Press,* CBS-TV, November 9, 1958.

34. O'Donnell and Powers, *"Johnny,"* p. 146.

35. *NYT,* November 16, 1958.

36. *Time,* November 24, 1958, p. 12.

37. Gallup, ed., *Gallup Poll,* Vol. 2, pp. 1580–81.

38. *NYT,* December 9, 1958.

39. Sorensen, *Kennedy,* pp. 117–18; Abram Chayes, JFKL–OH.

40. Deirdre Henderson, interview, August 31, 1977.

41. Abram Chayes, JFKL–OH.

42. Ibid.

43. Deirdre Henderson, interview, August 31, 1977.

44. Lash, *Eleanor: Years Alone,* p. 282.

45. *Boston Herald,* February 28, 1957.

46. Lash, *Eleanor: Years Alone,* p. 280.

47. *NYT,* December 8, 1958.

48. JFK to Eleanor Roosevelt, December 11, 1958, President's Office Files, Box 32, JFKL.

49. Eleanor Roosevelt to JFK, December 18, 1958, President's Office Files, Box 32, JFKL.

50. JFK to Eleanor Roosevelt, December 29, 1958, President's Office Files, Box 32, JFKL.

51. Eleanor Roosevelt to JFK, January 20, 1959, President's Office Files, Box 32, JFKL.

52. Ibid., January 29, 1959, and JFK to Eleanor Roosevelt, January 22, 1959, President's Office Files, Box 32, JFKL.

Chapter 26: *Courting the Liberals*

1. Joseph Clark, JFKL–OH.

2. Leverett Saltonstall, JFKL–OH.

3. Abram Chayes, JFKL–OH.

4. Martin and Plaut, *Front Runner,* p. 190; Meyer Feldman to Author, June 25, 1979.

5. *Philadelphia Inquirer,* February 1, 1959.

6. JFK to William Evjue, February 6, 1959, Sorensen Papers, Box 14, JFKL.

7. William M. Blair, Jr., to Eleanor Roosevelt, March 13, 1959, President's Office Files, Box 32, JFKL.

8. Chester Bowles to JFK, May 18, 1959, Bowles Papers, Yale.

9. Neil Staebler to Theodore C. Sorensen, May 25, 1959, Staebler Papers, Box 77, Bentley Library, University of Michigan.

10. JFK to Neil Staebler, July 17, 1959, Staebler Papers, Box 77, Bentley Library, University of Michigan.

11. JFK to Arthur Holcombe, May 29, 1959, Holcombe Papers, Box MS 75-57, JFKL.

12. Arthur Schlesinger, Jr., to JFK, July 15, 1959, President's Office Files, Box 122, JFKL.

13. T. C. Sorensen to J. M. Burns, October 27, 1959, Sorensen Papers, Box 6, JFKL; Burns, *Kennedy,* p. 134.

14. Abell, ed., *Pearson Diaries,* p. 421.

15. Schlesinger, *Thousand Days,* p. 16.

16. Kenneth S. Davis, *The Politics of Honor: A Biography of Adlai E. Stevenson* (New York: Putnam, 1967), pp. 357, 399; Martin, *Stevenson and the World*, p. 469.
17. J. Edward Day, Columbia University–OH.
18. William M. Blair, Jr., Columbia University–OH.
19. Newton Minow, Columbia University–OH.
20. Ibid.
21. John Sharon, Columbia University–OH; Martin, *Stevenson and the World*, p. 449.
22. Marietta Tree, Columbia University–OH; Russell Hemenway, interview, May 18, 1979.
23. Martin, *Stevenson and the World*, pp. 449–50.
24. James Rowe to Adlai Stevenson, May 13, 1959, Stevenson Papers, Box 773, Princeton.
25. Adlai Stevenson to JFK, June 1, 1959, Stevenson Papers, Box 768, Princeton.
26. Schlesinger, *Thousand Days*, p. 17.
27. James Rowe to Blair, Minow, and Wirtz, October 13, 1959, Stevenson Papers, Box 773, Princeton.
28. Adlai Stevenson to Chester Bowles, October 21, 1959, Bowles Papers, Yale; Martin *Stevenson and the World*, p. 461.
29. Lash, *Eleanor: Years Alone*, p. 275.
30. Interviews, Richard Wade, May 24, 1979, and Russell Hemenway, May 18, 1979.
31. Russell Hemenway, interview, May 18, 1979; Anthony Akers, JFKL–OH.
32. Herbert Lehman to Eleanor Roosevelt, February 25, 1959, Eleanor Roosevelt Papers, Box 4365, Franklin D. Roosevelt Library; Russell Hemenway, interview, May 18, 1979.
33. Francis W. H. Adams to JFK, February 4, 1960, Pre-Presidential Papers, Box 31, JFKL.
34. Marvin Rosenberg to Joe Rauh, Jr., April 13, 1959, ADA Papers, Series 2, Box 53, Historical Society of Wisconsin.
35. Transcript, *Let's Find Out*, WCBS-Radio, May 31, 1959, Sorensen Papers, Box 25, JFKL.
36. Schlesinger, *Thousand Days*, p. 16.
37. Jonathan Bingham to JFK, December 22, 1959, Sorensen Papers, Box 23, JFKL; John Saltonstall, Jr., to T. C. Sorensen, Sorensen Papers, Box 23, JFKL.
38. *The Nation*, October 31, 1959, p. 273; *NYT*, August 23, 1959; *Washington Evening Star*, August 24, 1959.
39. James Rowe to William M. Blair, Jr., Willard Wirtz, and Newton Minow, May 14, 1959, Stevenson Papers, Box 773, Princeton; Richard Wade, interview, May 24, 1979.
40. JFK to Richard Wade, August 26, 1959, President's Office Files, Box 136, JFKL.
41. Frank Thompson, Jr., interview, May 13, 1977.
42. JFK, *Strategy of Peace*, pp. 10–12.
43. Richard Wade, interview, May 24, 1979.
44. Arthur Schlesinger, Jr., to JFK, November 13, 1959, President's Office Files, Box 122, JFKL.
45. *NYT*, November 12, 1959.
46. Martin, *Stevenson and the World*, p. 469.

Chapter 27: The Literary Campaign

1. *New York Times Book Review*, July 21, 1957, p. 6.
2. Earl Latham to T. C. Sorensen, July 9, 1957, Sorensen Papers, Box 3, JFKL.
3. JFK to Hamilton Fish Armstrong, August 18, 1957, Sorensen Papers, Box 3, JFKL.
4. Boston *Guardian*, March 16, 1957.
5. Laura Berquist, interview, May 15, 1979; cf. Sorensen Papers, Box 3, JFKL.
6. Cf. Boxes 3–5, Sorensen Papers, JFKL.
7. *Washington Post*, March 30, 1958.

8. Ibid., June 28, 1959.

9. Evan Thomas, interview, May 20, 1977.

10. Evan Thomas to T. C. Sorensen, October 23, 1958, Sorensen Papers, Box 7, JFKL.

11. Evan Thomas to Sorensen, January 7, 1958, John Gunther to Cass Canfield, April 30, 1958, Thomas to Sorensen, May 1, 1958, and Sorensen to Thomas, June 9, 1958, Sorensen Papers, Box 7, JFKL.

12. Evan Thomas to JFK, September 18, 1958, and Thomas to Sorensen, October 23, 1958, Sorensen Papers, Box 7, JFKL.

13. Evan Thomas to Sorensen, October 31 and November 12, 1958, Sorensen Papers, Box 7, JFKL.

14. Evan Thomas, interview, May 20, 1977; Thomas to Harold Martin, Thomas to JFK, Thomas to Kenneth McCormick, and Thomas to Joe McCarthy, November 18, 1958, Sorensen Papers, Box 7, JFKL.

15. T. C. Sorensen to J. M. Burns, October 6, 1959, Sorensen Papers, Box 6, JFKL; James M. Burns, interview, August 4, 1979.

16. J. M. Burns, "Remembrances of John F. Kennedy," unpublished typescript, December 19, 1964, Burns Papers, JFKL; J. M. Burns, interview, February 14, 1976.

17. Evan Thomas to JFK, December 24, 1958, and November 28, 1958, Sorensen Papers, Box 7, JFKL.

18. Evan Thomas to T. C. Sorensen, March 2, 1959, Sorensen Papers, Box 8, JFKL.

19. Deirdre Henderson to Earl Latham, May 12, 1959, Henderson Papers, JFKL; JFK to Allan Nevins, July 20, 1959, Sorensen Papers, Box 7, JFKL; Martin, *Stevenson and the World*, p. 466.

20. Allan Nevins to Sorensen, November 14, 1959, Sorensen Papers, Box 8, JFKL.

21. Evan Thomas to Allan Nevins, December 3, 1959, Sorensen Papers, Box 8, JFKL.

22. Joseph Clark, JFKL-OH.

23. JFK to Ruth Proskauer Smith, July 1, 1959, and November 27, 1959, Sorensen Papers, Box 15, JFKL.

24. *NYT,* November 28, 1959.

25. JFK, *Strategy of Peace,* pp. 225–26.

26. T. C. Sorensen to Evan Thomas, January 4 and 7, 1960, Sorensen Papers, Box 8, JFKL; Transcript, JFK interview by Fischer, December 9, 1959, Columbia University–OH.

27. T. C. Sorensen to 15 aides, March 11, 1960, Sorensen Papers, Box 8, Sorensen Papers, JFKL; Sorensen, *Kennedy,* p. 118.

28. Evan Thomas to JFK, March 30, 1960, President's Office Files, Box 129, JFKL.

Chapter 28: The Labor Trap

1. *NYT,* September 20, 1959.

2. *Congressional Record,* 86th Cong., 1st sess., p. 816.

3. Transcript, *Face the Nation,* February 8, 1959, Pre-Presidential Papers, Box 540, JFKL.

4. JFK, *Statements and Speeches,* p. 767.

5. U.S., Congress, Senate, *Hearings Before the Subcommittee of Labor of the Committee of Labor and Public Welfare* 86th Cong., 1st sess., 1959, p. 87.

6. Ibid., p. 113.

7. *NYT,* February 9, 1959.

8. *Congressional Record,* 86th Cong., 1st sess., p. 5803.

9. *Congressional Record,* 86th Cong., 1st sess., April 20, 1959, pp. 5627–28.

10. Paul Douglas, JFKL-OH.

11. Samuel Merrick, JFKL-OH.

12. Ibid., p. 94.

13. *Congressional Record,* April 20, 1959, p. 5630.
14. Ibid., April 24, 1959, p. 5952.
15. McAdams, *Power and Politics,* p. 109.
16. Evans and Novak, *Lyndon B. Johnson,* pp. 217–19; McAdams, *Power and Politics,* p. 107.
17. JFK to Adlai Stevenson, May 8, 1959, Stevenson Papers, Box 768, Princeton.
18. McAdams, *Power and Politics,* p. 144.
19. JFK, *Statements and Speeches,* p. 1102.
20. Samuel Merrick, JFKL–OH
21. Frank Thompson, Jr., interview, May 11, 1977.
22. Richard Bolling, JFKL–OH.
23. George Meany, JFKL–OH.
24. Samuel Merrick, JFKL–OH.
25. Congressional Quarterly Service, *Congress and the Nation,* Vol. 1, p. 610.
26. *NYT,* September 23, 1959; Meyer Feldman, JFKL–OH.
27. Leonard Woodcock, JFKL–OH.

Chapter 29: Taking the Step

1. James Reston, speech transcript, March 5, 1959, in Columbia University–OH.
2. Helen Berthelot to Margaret Price, March 11, 1959, Price Papers, Bentley Library, University of Michigan.
3. Memorandum for the Files, Violet Gunther, March 12, 1959, ADA Papers, Series 2, Box 53, Historical Society of Wisconsin.
4. Ben Bradlee to JFK, May 9, 1959, President's Office Files, Box 128, JFKL.
5. William Proxmire, interview, May 17, 1979; JFK to Proxmire, July 1, 1959, Sorensen Papers, Box 26, JFKL.
6. Gallup, ed., *Gallup Polls,* Vol. 3, p. 1606.
7. Fletcher Knebel, interview, May 8, 1979; Fletcher Knebel, "Democratic Forecast: A Catholic in 1960," *Look,* March 3, 1959, p. 17.
8. *NYT,* January 3, 1960.
9. Lawrence H. Fuchs, *John F. Kennedy and American Catholicism* (New York: Meredith Press, 1967), p. 168.
10. *Wall Street Journal,* July 30, 1959.
11. A. Willis Robertson to Virginius Dabney, December 10, 1958, Dabney Papers, University of Virginia.
12. Knebel, "Can a Catholic Become Vice President?" p. 34.
13. Eugene Connor to JFK, June 16, 1959, Pre-Presidential Papers, Box 1, JFKL.
14. Don Hill, *If America Elects a Catholic President* (Findlay, Ohio: Dunham Publishing Company, 1959), p. 42; *Wall Street Journal,* July 30, 1959.
15. Knebel, "Democratic Forecast," p. 17.
16. Fuchs, *Kennedy and Catholicism,* p. 167; Kate Louchheim, JFKL–OH.
17. Martin and Plaut, *Front Runner,* p. 443.
18. John Cogley, JFKL–OH.
19. As quoted in *Commonweal,* March 20, 1959, p. 645.
20. *America,* March 14, 1959, p. 675.
21. *Commonweal,* March 20, 1959, p. 649.
22. *NYT,* April 10, 1959.
23. Fletcher Knebel, interview, May 8, 1979.
24. *Washington Post,* August 25, 1959.
25. Fletcher Knebel, interview, May 8, 1979.

26. JFK to Drew Pearson, August 25, 1959, President's Office Files, Box 136, JFKL.
27. *Washington Sunday Star,* August 16, 1959; *Wall Street Journal,* December 29, 1959.
28. Sorensen, *Kennedy,* p. 121.
29. Pierre Salinger, *With Kennedy* (Garden City, N.Y.: Doubleday, 1966), p. 29.
30. *Washington Post,* March 15, 1959.
31. Council of Economic Advisers, JFKL–OH.
32. Krock, *Memoirs,* pp. 338–39; Kitty Carlisle Hart, interview, January 19, 1979.
33. Hersh, *Edward Kennedy,* p. 124; Kenneth P. O'Donnell, interview, December 4, 1976.
34. Francis X. Morrissey in Edward M. Kennedy, ed., *Fruitful Bough,* pp. 127–28.
35. Thomas P. O'Neill, interview, March 7, 1979.
36. John Hersey, interview, December 8, 1976.
37. Whalen, *Founding Father,* p. 450.
38. J. J. Kelly to J. Edgar Hoover, September 23, 1953, JFK File, FBI.
39. Ibid., October 23, 1953.
40. M. S. Jones to C. D. DeLoach, July 13, 1960, JFK File, FBI; Quinlan J. Shea, Jr., to Author, October 26, 1978.
41. Fay, *Pleasure of His Company,* p. 47.
42. Fletcher Knebel, interview, May 15, 1979.
43. Speech transcript, April 9, 1959, President's Office Files, Box 136, JFKL.
44. *Pasadena Independent,* July 9, 1959.
45. Martin and Plaut, *Front Runner,* pp. 213–14; Lincoln, *My Twelve Years,* p. 125; Herbert Alexander, "Financing the 1960 Election," in *Studies in Money and Politics,* 3 vols. (Princeton, N.J.: Citizens's Research Foundation, 1965–1974), Vol. 1, p. 17.
46. *NYT,* October 23, 1959.
47. J. Miller, "Some Modest Realignments in the Kennedy Image," typescript dated October 20, 1959, Robert F. Kennedy Papers, Box 7, JFKL.
48. Typescript, Minutes of Meeting, October 28, 1959, Robert F. Kennedy Papers, Box 7, JFKL.
49. Chester Bowles, JFKL–OH.
50. Charles Bloch to Roy Harris, February 13, 1959, Russell Papers, Box 6, University of Georgia.
51. Robert F. Kennedy, "Memo for the Files," November 16, 1959, Robert F. Kennedy Papers, Box 7, JFKL.
52. Salinger, *With Kennedy,* p. 30.
53. Cleveland Amory, interview, May 6, 1977.
54. Salinger, *With Kennedy,* p. 31.
55. *Boston Sunday Herald,* January 3, 1960.
56. *Boston Herald,* January 4, 1960.
57. Ibid.
58. Ibid.
59. Martin, *Stevenson and the World,* pp. 470–71.
60. Lincoln, *My Twelve Years,* p. 122; *NYT,* January 6, 1960; *Boston Herald,* January 6, 1960.
61. *Boston Herald,* January 12, 1960; William Proxmire, interview, May 17, 1979; James Rowe to William M. Blair, Jr., January 7, 1960, Stevenson Papers, Box 797, Princeton.
62. *Boston Herald,* January 22, 1960.

Epilogue: "I Never Could Have Done It"

1. Schlesinger, *RFK,* p. 199.
2. Charles Spalding, JFKL–OH.

3. Interviews, Torbert Macdonald, Jr., Laurie Macdonald, Joe Croken, August 6, 1979; Phyllis Macdonald, August 9, 1979; Frank Thompson, Jr., May 11, 1977; Russell Hemenway, May 18, 1979.
4. JFK, *Profiles in Courage,* p. 173.
5. Ovid Demaris, *The Director* (New York: Harper's Magazine Press, 1975), pp. 160, 251, 276; Sullivan, *The Bureau*, p. 50.

Acknowledgments

The notion of undertaking a closer study of John F. Kennedy and his prepresidential years evolved from an impulse to fruition with the assistance of many people. First, there was Richard Marek, who shared my view of the project and signed it for The Dial Press. His successor, Juris Jurjevics, and my agent, Betty Anne Clarke, both bore patiently with me through some difficult moments and never lost sight of their confidence that the work could be done. My good fortune was Juris's astuteness and diligence in helping to guide the manuscript toward publication. During the final, all-consuming stages, my daughter, Wendy Ellen Parmet, devoted an entire summer to a critique of the original draft and made many valuable suggestions that helped shape the manuscript into a book. Under the pressure of a tight deadline, typing was shared by Roslyn Arnow and Florence Train. As always, Marie B. Hecht took time from her own hectic schedule to offer pertinent insights.

There would, however, have been no book without the resources and personnel of the John F. Kennedy Library, located at its temporary site in Waltham, Massachusetts. There, in addition to the endless volumes of oral history transcripts that were consulted, the manuscript collections of John F. Kennedy, Theodore C. Sorensen, Lawrence O'Brien, Arthur Schlesinger, Jr., Arthur B. Holcombe, Robert F. Kennedy, and the Democratic National Committee, among others, provided the basic sources for this volume. Of incalculable value were the microfilm reels of newspaper clippings that were expedited by James N. Cedrone. At what became my second home during research for my last two books, I had the usual gracious assistance from the director, Dan H. Fenn, Jr.; the curator, Dave Powers; and a pleasant and helpful staff that included Sylvie Turner, Mary Ellen Eagan, Joan Hoopes, and, during the final stages of my work, E. William Johnson, William Moss, Deborah Greene, Allan Goodrich, James Cedrone, and Sheldon M. Stern. However successful the new Kennedy Library will undoubtedly be, the days at Waltham will remain memorable.

At Choate Rosemary Hall, an especially pleasant visit was made possible for me by Lee Sylvester, the archivist, who brought together both people and papers in the most gracious manner possible, thereby making the hours spent at Wallingford a researcher's delight. Other manuscript collections consulted were the extensive Adlai E. Stevenson papers at Princeton University; the James M. Landis papers at the Library of Congress; the Americans for Democratic Action papers at the Historical Society of Wisconsin; the papers of Chester Bowles and Arthur Bliss Lane at Yale University; and a scattering of material was also drawn from visits to the Lyndon B. Johnson Library at Austin and the Bentley Library of the University of Michigan. At Athens, Georgia, Max Gilstrap made possible my perusal of the Richard B. Russell papers in the University of Georgia. The New York Public Library assisted by making available the facilities of the Allen Room and the Wertheim Study.

Inevitably, the proliferating collections of oral history interviews became invaluable for a work of this kind. A great deal of help and cooperation was provided by the Oral History Research Office at Columbia University through Elizabeth Mason and the late Professor Louis Starr. Countless transcripts were consulted both there and at the Kennedy Library. A special debt is owed to those who did the interviewing to enable historians to profit from their expertise and legwork. Many deserve to be cited for this contribution. I am especially grateful to such interviewers as Ronald Grele, Larry Hackman, John Luter, John Mason, Ed Edwin, John Stewart, John Bartlow Martin, Fred Holborn, Kenneth S. Davis, Charles T. Morrissey, Joseph E. O'Connor, Ed Martin, John F. Henning, Eugene Gordon, Joseph Pechman, Edward M. Kennedy, Arthur Goldberg, John Newhouse, Sheldon Stern, William M. McHugh,

James A. Oesterle, Thomas F. Hogan, Anthony Lewis, Arthur Schlesinger, Jr., Michael Monroney, William Maloney, Robert J. Donovan, Daniel Lynch, Jonathan Moore, Jack Hynes, and William Moss, in addition to the others whose transcripts of conversations are now available. I am also grateful to the many individuals, some of whom wish to remain anonymous, who gave me special permission to consult the transcripts of their interviews.

Special thanks is owed to those who took time from frequently busy schedules to respond to requests for one or more formal interviews or to help clarify specific points that arose during the course of the work. Several have preferred anonymity, but I can thank Joseph W. Alsop, Cleveland Amory, Dr. Elmer C. Bartels, Charles Bartlett, Laura Berquist, Ben Bradlee, James MacGregor Burns, William G. Carleton, Patsy Carter, Blair Clark, Joe Croken, Father John Cronin, Jules Davids, Robert J. Donovan, Foster Furcolo, Kay Halle, Kitty Carlisle Hart, Russell Hemenway, Deirdre Henderson, John Hersey, Peter Hoguet, John Hohenberg, Garfield H. Horn, Hubert H. Humphrey, John Johansen, Fletcher Knebel, Henry Cabot Lodge, Jr., Laurie Macdonald, Phyllis Macdonald, Torbert Macdonald, Jr., John McCormack, Edward McLaughlin, Own Morgan, Lawrence F. O'Brien, Kenneth P. O'Donnell, Thomas P. O'Neill, Hugh S. Packard, Paul Pennoyer, Jr., Joseph Pulitzer, Jr., James A. Rousmaniere, Dave Powers, William Proxmire, Seymour St. John, Abba Schwartz, R. Sargent Shriver, George Smathers, Stephen E. Smith, Theodore C. Sorensen, R. Douglas Stuart, Jr., James J. Storrow, Jr., William Tansill, Evan Thomas, Frank Thompson, Jr., Dore Schary, Richard Wade, Robert F. Wagner, Jr., Frank C. Waldrop, and John B. White.

Finally, no privileged and potentially compromising access was sought or granted. The members of the Kennedy family were given every opportunity to contribute before a word was written, and some were helpful. Throughout, the author had both the freedom and responsibility to make the book entirely his own. And only he is accountable.

Herbert S. Parmet
Bayside, New York

Index